WORLD AFFAIRS
National and International Viewpoints

WORLD AFFAIRS

National and International Viewpoints

The titles in this collection were selected
from the Council on Foreign Relations' publication:
The Foreign Affairs 50-Year Bibliography

Advisory Editor
RONALD STEEL

THE STORY OF THE
INTEGRATION
OF THE
INDIAN STATES

V. P. MENON

ARNO PRESS
A NEW YORK TIMES COMPANY
New York • 1972

JQ
298.8
.M45
1972

Reprint Edition 1972 by Arno Press Inc.

Reprinted from a copy in The University
of Illinois Library

World Affairs: National and International Viewpoints
ISBN for complete set: 0-405-04560-3
See last pages of this volume for titles.

Manufactured in the United States of America

Library of Congress Cataloging in Publication Data

Menon, Vapal Pangunni.
    The story of the integration of the Indian States.

    (World affairs: national and international view-
points)
    Bibliography: p.
    1. State governments--India. 2. India--Constitu-
tional history. I. Title. II. Title: Integration of
the Indian States. III. Series.
[JQ298.8.M45 1972]   342'.54   72-4282
ISBN 0-405-04575-1

THE STORY OF THE
INTEGRATION
OF THE
INDIAN STATES

To the memory of

SARDAR VALLABHBHAI PATEL

*Free India's first Deputy Prime Minister and
Minister for States*

this book is affectionately
dedicated

THE STORY OF THE
INTEGRATION
OF THE
INDIAN STATES

V. P. MENON

NEW YORK
THE MACMILLAN COMPANY
1956

Published in India by
ORIENT LONGMANS PTE LTD
17 CHITTARANJAN AVENUE CALCUTTA 13
and in Great Britain by
LONGMANS GREEN AND CO LTD
6 & 7 CLIFFORD STREET LONDON W 1

PRINTED IN INDIA
by V. N. Bhattacharya, M.A., at the Inland Printing Works
60/3 Dharamtala Street Calcutta 13

PREFACE

THIS book is in part fulfilment of a promise made to the late Sardar Vallabhbhai Patel. It was his earnest desire that I should write two books, one narrating the events leading to the transfer of power and the other dealing with the integration of the Indian States.

I have taken up the integration of the States first, because the events of the four hectic years, 1947 to 1951, are so vivid in my memory. Today we think of the integration of the States only in terms of the consolidation of the country, but few pause to consider the toils and anxieties that had to be undergone till, step by step, the edifice of a consolidated India was enshrined in the Constitution. It was a co-operative effort in which every one from Sardar — our inspiration and light — down to the rank and file played his part. The entire staff of the States Ministry, both at New Delhi as well as at the regional headquarters, threw themselves heart and soul into the task. There was a unity of purpose animating every one. They are the unsung heroes who made possible the consolidation of the country.

I have narrated the whole story as objectively as it is possible for one who was in the midst of it. The events and personalities are too near for any final assessment to be attempted. This is a task for the historian of the future. I have deliberately called this book, not the history, but 'The Story of the Integration of the Indian States'.

The first four chapters provide the background to the problem of the Indian States. There I have described how the British built up the framework of princely India. I trace the events right up to the announcement of the June 3rd plan declaring the lapse of paramountcy, whereby the Indian States comprising two-fifths of the country would return to a state of political isolation. Chapter V describes how this was circumvented by the accession of the States on three subjects. The next chapter deals with Junagadh State which had acceded to Pakistan. The ten subsequent chapters deal with the consolidation of the States on a regional basis. Hyderabad, which had remained aloof, has been dealt with at length in three chapters. Kashmir follows and the Baroda interlude comes next. Then four chapters are devoted to a survey of the administrative, financial and constitutional changes and to the cost of integration. In the last chapter, entitled 'Retrospect and Prospect', I have summed up the policy of integration and expressed my personal views on some aspects of the problem.

I am deeply grateful to the Rockefeller Foundation, Humanities Division, for the generous grant given through the Indian Council of World Affairs for the preparation not only of this book but also of the companion volume on the transfer of power. I must, however, add that no responsibility attaches to the Foundation in regard to either their contents or the views expressed.

I am thankful to the Indian Council of World Affairs under whose auspices this book has been prepared and in particular to Dr A. Appadorai, its Secretary-General.

My grateful thanks are also due to several friends, Indian and English, who went through the manuscript and made many valuable suggestions.

I am thankful to the Press Information Bureau of the Government of India for having allowed me to reproduce the pictures included in this book.

Lastly, my sincere thanks are due to E. C. Gaynor and R. P. Aiyar for the help they have given me in writing this book. Their assistance has been most invaluable. My thanks are also due to the two stenographers, S. Gopalakrishnan and K. Thankappan Nair and to the typist, M. Balakrishnan who never spared themselves and who faithfully discharged whatever duties were entrusted to them.

Bangalore,
15 September 1955.   V. P. MENON

CONTENTS

Contents

ILLUSTRATIONS

Frontispiece

Sardar Vallabhbhai Patel

Between pages 172 and 173

Between pages 244 and 245

Illustrations

CARTOONS

Illustrations
MAPS

I

SETTING THE STAGE

INDIA is one geographical entity. Yet, throughout her long and chequered history, she never achieved political homogeneity. From the earliest times, spasmodic attempts were made to bring about her consolidation. A pioneering effort in this direction was made by the Magadhan kings, Bimbisara and Ajatasatru, in the sixth century B.C. But it was not till about three centuries later that under the Mauryas, and particularly Asoka, a large portion of India came under the sway of one emperor. The Mauryan empire lasted only for about a hundred years and after its disruption the country again lapsed into numerous kingdoms. Nearly five centuries later, Chandragupta, and his more illustrious son Samudragupta, brought the major part of the country under their suzerainty; and Harsha, in the seventh century, was able to make himself the undisputed master of north India. These and later attempts at political consolidation failed again and again for one chief reason: the empires were held together almost entirely by the personality and might of the emperor. The whole edifice crumbled when a line of 'supermen' came to an end.

Even under these emperors, a diversity of autonomous states constituted the mosaic of an empire. The emperor claimed suzerainty over these rulers, who offered allegiance to him; subordinated their foreign policy to his diplomatic moves; usually served him in war, and offered him tribute; but who, in other respects, retained their sovereignty. Whenever the authority of the Emperor weakened, the subordinate rulers asserted their independence. There was a perpetual struggle for supremacy. Mutual jealousies and conflicts made the country an easy prey to any organized invasion.

The Muslims were thus able to vanquish the Hindu kingdoms in north India. The first Muslim conquest was in the eighth century, when the Arabs under Muhammad-ibn-Kasim conquered Sind. But it was the conquest of the Punjab by Mahmud of Ghazni in the eleventh century that opened the gates of India to the Muslim invaders from the north-west. Muslim rule in north India was founded in A.D. 1206, when Qutb-ud-din Aibak proclaimed himself the Sultan of Delhi. From this date to 1526, the year of the downfall of the Sultanate, Delhi had as many as five Muslim dynasties and thirty-three Sultans. These Sultans attempted, from time to time, to extend their empire; and Ala-ud-din Khalji was the first of these Muslim rulers to conquer practically the whole of India.

The Moghuls appeared on the scene in 1526, when Babur defeated the last Sultan of Delhi in the Battle of Panipat. He also defeated the powerful Rajput confederacy in the decisive battle of Khanua and so laid the foundation of the Moghul empire. During the time of his grandson, Akbar, the Moghuls reached the meridian of their glory.

Neither the Sultans nor the Moghuls did away with the system of subordinate rulers. In the very condition of things it was impossible for them to have done so. It was Akbar who laid down the basic principles governing the relationship between these rulers and the emperor. He asserted his authority over them in the matter of succession and assumed to himself the power to depose any ruler for disloyalty. The sovereignty and authority of the emperor was unquestionable, subject to which however the subordinate rulers were as much despots in their respective domains as their master.

The passing away of Akbar's great-grandson Aurangzeb in 1707 was the signal for the break-up of the Moghul empire. His protracted and costly campaigns in the Deccan for conquest of the Muslim kingdoms of Bijapur and Golconda and for the subjugation of the Mahrattas had denuded his empire of much of its resources. Moreover, his short-sighted policy of religious intolerance had alienated the allegiance of the Hindus. Once his strong hand was removed, the Moghul viceroys as well as the subordinate rulers began to assert their independence, and political and military adventurers started hacking at the crumbling facade of the empire. Within the incredibly short period of twenty years from Aurangzeb's death, Moghul power had faded into 'an insubstantial pageant' and the country had fallen into a condition of masterless disorder.

It must be emphasized that not even in the palmiest days of the Hindu and Moghul empires did the entire country come under one political umbrella. No greater achievement can be credited to the British than that they brought about India's enduring political consolidation. But for this accomplishment and the rise of national consciousness in its wake, the Government of Free India could hardly have taken the final step of bringing about the peaceful integration of the princely States. Today, for the first time in the country's history, the writ of a single central Government runs from Kailas to Kanyakumari, from Kathiawar to Kamarupa (the old name of Assam). To appreciate the full significance of this achievement, it is necessary to review in broad outline how the British established themselves and built up the framework of princely India.

After the disintegration of the Moghul empire, the only power which seemed likely to step into the breach was the Mahrattas. Shivaji had laid the foundations of a mighty kingdom; but this pioneer of a resurgent Hindu empire had left no competent successor. After Shivaji's death, the Peshwas (chief ministers to the ruler) gradually took over control. In the beginning they showed promise of becoming the rallying force of the great Mahratta Confederacy. But theirs was the story of the Hindu and Moghul empires over again. Intrigue and corruption at the Peshwa's Court and perpetual wars between the Scindia and the Holkar disrupted Mahratta unity. The Mahratta armies were tax-collectors by force and showed no discrimination between the Hindu and the Muslim. The imposition of *chauth* and *sardeshmukhi* in conquered areas and the collection of these exactions by the *Mulkgiri* forces brought upon them the sullen hatred of the people.

Into this arena of confusion and unrest entered the British and the French. Both had come to India for trade. The British had come earlier and had started factories in several coastal towns in the name of the East India Company. This Company, the greatest mercantile corporation the world has ever seen, had several advantages over its French rival and, in the bid for supremacy, finally succeeded in ousting the French from the scene.

The British empire in India presents the curious phenomenon of having been built by the agents of the Company in India, at any rate during the initial stages, notwithstanding express directions to the contrary from their principals. The only interest of the Court of Directors was in trade and commerce and they frowned upon wars which ate into their profits. Treaties entered into with Indian

States in the early stages aimed at no more than the maintenance of the Company's privileged position in trade against its rivals. It was in the process of protecting its commercial stake in the country that Clive actually laid the foundations of the British empire in India.

At first the East India Company's agents in India were responsible only to the Court of Directors who derived their power from Charters given to them by the Crown. So long as the Company was interested merely in trade, these Charters were enough; but when it became a territorial power some control by Parliament became necessary. In Lord North's Regulating Act of 1773, the Parliament for the first time asserted its authority and control over the Company's activities, both in India and in England. The Act converted the Governor in Council in Bengal into a Governor-General in Council. The Governor-General had no overriding powers over his council. The control of the Governor-General in Council over the presidencies of Bombay and Madras was confined to the making of peace and war. In the words of the Montagu-Chelmsford Report, the Act created a 'Governor-General who was powerless before his own council, and an Executive that was powerless before a Supreme Court, itself immune from all responsibility for the peace and welfare of the country — a system that was made workable only by the genius and fortitude of one great man.' That was Warren Hastings, the first Governor-General. He continued the work of Clive and, indeed, left the British possessions in India much larger and more secure than he found them.

The Regulating Act was repealed by Pitt's India Act of 1784. A body was set up, known as the Board of Control, to supervise the activities of the Court of Directors. It made the control of the Governor-General over the presidency Governments effective. Later, by a supplementary Act in 1786, the Governor-General was given powers to overrule his council in special cases; he was also permitted to hold the office of Commander-in-Chief in addition to his position as Governor-General. It was this three-fold augmentation of the powers of the Governor-General that was responsible for the success which attended the efforts of the Marquess of Wellesley, the Marquess of Hastings and Lord Dalhousie in India. As Lord Dalhousie piquantly put it: 'The Governor-General is unlike any other Minister under heaven -- he is the beginning, middle and end of all.'

Fourteen years after the passing of Pitt's India Act, Wellesley came to India as Governor-General. He was given the strictest injunctions to keep the peace, not to meddle with the Indian rulers and to husband the depleted resources of the Company. He paid scant attention to these injunctions. Wellesley was convinced, when he came to India and saw the state of affairs here, that the British must become the one paramount power in the country. Towards this end, he worked for the next seven years. Apart from his military achievements, his greatest contribution was the institution of a policy of subsidiary alliances with the Indian rulers. Under this system, the State accepting subsidiary alliance was to make no wars and to carry on no negotiations with any other State without the Company's knowledge and consent; the bigger States were to maintain armies commanded by British officers for 'the preservation of the public peace' and their rulers were to cede certain territories for the upkeep of these forces; the smaller States were to pay a tribute to the Company. In return, the Company was to protect them, one and all, against external aggression and internal rebellion. A British Resident was also installed in every State that accepted the subsidiary alliance.

The system of subsidiary alliances was Trojan Horse tactics in empire-building: it gave the Company a stabilizing authority *vis-à-vis* the States and because of this 'the Governor-General was present by proxy in every State that accepted it.' Well-trained bodies of troops were posted in strategic and key positions without any cost to the Company. The fidelity of the rulers who accepted the system was thus assured.

When Wellesley was recalled in 1805 the British dominion had expanded considerably. He had successfully overcome Tippu, whose defeat and death in 1799 removed a major threat to the British empire. He practically eliminated the French influence in India. Besides, he brought many States under subsidiary alliances, the notable ones being Hyderabad, Travancore, Mysore, Baroda and Gwalior. In successfully implementing this policy, Wellesley was fortunate to have gifted colleagues like John Malcolm, Charles Metcalfe and Mountstuart Elphinstone, besides his illustrious brother, Arthur Wellesley, later the Duke of Wellington.

For the next eight years the Company was primarily concerned with looking after its trade and replenishing its depleted resources. Then came the Marquess of Hastings as the Governor-General in

1813. The interrupted policy of Warren Hastings and Wellesley was pushed by him to its logical conclusion. The successive campaigns in which he overcame Nepal, crushed the Pindaris, and finally broke the Mahratta power carried 'the spread of the British dominion over northern and central India to a stage which it was only left for Lord Dalhousie, a quarter of a century later, to complete.' Simultaneously, he resumed Wellesley's policy by extending the Company's supremacy and protection over almost all the Indian States. By the time he left the country in 1823, the British empire in India had been formed and its map in essentials drawn. Every State in India outside the Punjab and Sind was under the Company's control. 'His official seal no longer acknowledged the Governor-General as the servant of the Moghul empire and with the "fiction of the Moghul Government" ended, the British empire of India stood in its place.'

Subsequent years saw the initiation and development of a political and administrative system hitherto unknown to Indian history. Unlike the one-man rule of the Moghul emperors, the British established, in territories under their direct control, a regular and uniform system of administration composed of a hierarchy of authorities, one subordinate to another, with powers and functions clearly demarcated. The pattern commenced at the base with the districts, and converged at the apex with provincial Governors and the Governor-General, who were in their turn subordinate to the authorities in England. Administration was impersonal, since none of the offices was hereditary. Most of the Company's officers at the senior level were imbued with a sense of their mission and brought to bear on the administration the principles and practice which obtained in their country. These are some of the factors which contributed to the building of a stable structure of government.

So far as the States were concerned, the influence of the Company over their internal administration rapidly increased during the period following the retirement of Lord Hastings. Its Residents became gradually 'transformed from diplomatic agents representing a foreign power into executive and controlling officers of a superior government.' They assumed so much authority indeed that a certain Colonel Macaulay wrote to the Rajah of Cochin: 'The Resident will be glad to learn that on his arrival near Cochin, the Rajah will find it convenient to wait on him.'

The pathetic plight of the rulers under the subsidiary system has been graphically described by Henry Mead who, as a journalist, had spent over twenty years in India before the Great Revolt of 1857:

The sovereigns of what are called independent States live in a state of abject dependence upon the will of the British agency at their various Courts. The whole functions of government are in most cases exercised by the Resident, in fact, if not in appearance; and the titular monarch sighs in vain for the personal freedom enjoyed by his subjects. To know the character of his rule and seeming tendencies of his disposition, it is sufficient to have a knowledge of the capacity and likings of the British Representative. Thus General Cullen is a savant and the Rajah of Travancore builds an observatory and maintains men of science; the Resident of Indore is a person of elegant tastes and the Maharajah surrounds himself with articles of *vertu*. The Durbar Surgeon at the Mysore Court, who fulfils the duties of a government agent, is passionately fond of the sports of the turf and the Rajah keeps a large stud of horses, gives gold cups and heavy purses at races, wears topboots and has pictures of the 'great events' of past and present days.

The concentration of power without responsibility in the Residents brought in its wake corruption and favouritism. The rulers were guaranteed their position, not only against external aggression, but also against internal revolution. Thus all incentive for good government was removed and a premium was placed on indolence. In most of the States, the revenues were dissipated between the mercenaries of the Residency and the minions of the court. Conscientious statesmen in England viewed this state of affairs with grave concern. From his detached position in the India Office, John Stuart Mill advocated the elimination of the States.

Meanwhile, there were those who, with practical experience of Indian administration, discerned dangers in this new development. As early as 1825, Sir John Malcolm avowed:

I am decidedly of the opinion that the tranquillity, not to say security, of our vast oriental possessions is involved in the preservation of native principalities which are dependent on us for protection. These are also so obviously at our mercy, so entirely within our grasp, that besides other and great benefits we derive from their alliance, their co-existence with our rule is of itself a source of political strength, the value of which will never be known till it is lost.

At an earlier date still, Elphinstone had expressed himself not dissimilarly but more brutally. He held that the princes would be useful not only as buffers but as cess-pits into which the accumulating miseries of the rest of India could seep and, like warring germs, prey on each other. 'We must have some sink to receive all the corrupt matter that abounds in India, unless we are willing to taint our own system by stopping the discharge of it.'

The Charter Act of 1833 abolished the Company's trading activities, and the Company assumed the functions of the government of India. From now onward there was a radical change in its policy towards the States, partly with a view to eliminating any future threat to its territories and partly to augmenting its revenue. In 1841 the Court of Directors issued an express directive to the Governor-General 'to persevere in the one clear and direct course of abandoning no just and honourable accession of territory or revenue.'

Coorg was annexed in 1834 on the plea of the maladministration of the ruler. Sind was conquered without any justifiable reason during the Governor-Generalship of Lord Ellenborough. By his vigorous annexationist policy, Lord Dalhousie acquired vast territories for the Company. Applying the 'Doctrine of Lapse', he annexed Satara, Nagpur, Jhansi, Sambalpur, Bhagat and other States. He conquered the Punjab and pushed the frontiers to 'the natural limits of India, the base of the mountains of Afghanistan.' With regard to Oudh, he wanted to take over only its administration, but the Court of Directors ordered its complete annexation, which was done in 1856. Dalhousie went to the extent of applying the 'Doctrine of Lapse' in order to sweep away the titles and pensions of deposed rulers who died without leaving behind any natural heir.

Later events were to prove, however, that the policy of wholesale annexations was short-sighted. The annexationists were in too great a hurry and swallowed more than they could digest. They ignored Malcolm's sage advice of *festina lente*. The accretion of vast territories without adequate experienced personnel to administer them was to result in maladministration. This was all too evident during the initial period of Lord Canning's Governor-Generalship. Further, the army was lacking in discipline and the British element was inadequate in proportion. The policy of annexation had unsettled the social life of the people, especially in north India. Rulers dispossessed of their States had to get rid of their vast retinue of servants and dependents. Disinherited heirs and cast-off retainers sighed in vain for their lost estates and pensions. The disbanded armies of the rulers had thrown out many thousands of able-bodied men who with arms but without any means of livelihood were roaming about the countryside. It is said that in Oudh alone the King's forces amounted to 60,000 and the troops employed by the nobility and *zamindars* were quite as numerous. Of these, only about 12,000 were retained in service; the rest were sent adrift— to swell the ranks of the disrupted malcontents. It was surely the despair and discontent caused by this upheaval that provided the powder magazine to the Great Revolt of 1857, whatever might have been the spark that ultimately ignited it.

The Revolt was suppressed with a heavy hand. The Indian rulers for the most part, not only remained aloof from the uprising but in certain cases extended active assistance to the British in suppressing it. Lord Canning gratefully acknowledged the role of the States as 'breakwaters in the storm which would have swept over us in one great wave.' 'Where should we have been,' enquired Elphin- stone with characteristic frankness, 'if Scindia, the Nizam and the Sikh chiefs etc. had been annexed, the subordinate presidencies abolished, the whole army thrown into one and the revenue system brought into one mould?'

The realization that the States could play a vital role as one of the bulwarks of British rule led to a radical change of policy, which found expression in Queen Victoria's proclamation of 1858:

We desire no extension of our present territorial possessions; and while we will permit no aggression upon our dominions or our rights to be attempted with impunity, we shall sanction no encroachment on those of others. We shall respect the rights, dignity, and honour of Native Princes as our own; and we desire that they as well as our own subjects should enjoy that prosperity and that social advancement which can only be secured by internal peace and good government.

The *Act for the Better Government of India*[1] passed in 1858 put the imprimatur of parliamentary authority to the Queen's assurance. The last clause of the Act provided that 'all treaties made by the Company shall be binding upon Her Majesty.' Thus the policy of

---

[1] Lord Curzon described the change thus : 'In 1858 the final act of decapitation of the Company took place : the system of dual government, after lasting, with all its incongruities and misadventures, for over 80 years, was terminated ; the two rival fictions of the Court of Directors and the Board of Control both disappeared ; and the Government was transferred from the East India Company to the Crown. The Home Government of India was reconstituted on its present basis, a Secretary of State for India, assisted by an India Council, being set up.'

For the first time the Governor-General was designated Viceroy and Governor-General. This two-fold title continued till 1947. As the statutory head of the Government of India he was designated the Governor-General and as the representative of the British Sovereign he was referred to as the Viceroy.

annexation, so vigorously pursued by Dalhousie, gave way to the perpetuation of the States as separate entities.

Lord Canning carried this new policy to its next logical step by recommending, in his despatch of 30 April 1860, that the integrity of the States should be preserved by perpetuating the rule of the Princes whose power to adopt heirs should be recognized. The Secretary of State agreed to this recommendation, and *sanads* were granted to the rulers under which, in the event of the failure of natural heirs, they were authorized to adopt their successors according to their law and custom. These *sanads* were intended to remove mistrust and suspicion and 'to reassure and knit the native sovereigns to the paramount power.' No more was heard of annexation as the only means of granting the 'blessings' of civilized government to the 'suffering millions'. The new policy was to punish the ruler for extreme misgovernment and if necessary to depose him but not to annex his State for misdeeds.

The Indian States thus became part and parcel of the British empire in India. In the words of Lord Canning:

The territories under the sovereignty of the Crown became at once as important and as integral a part of India as territories under its direct domination. Together they form one direct care and the political system which the Moghuls had not completed and the Mahrattas never contemplated is now an established fact of history.

The next five decades were occupied with the task of evolving a machinery for controlling the States. This was duly accomplished. A Political Department was set up under the direct charge of the Governor-General. It had at its disposal a service known as the Indian Political Service, manned by officers taken from the Indian Civil Service and the Army. It had a police force which was maintained partly by the revenues of the Central Government and partly by contributions made by the States. The Political Department had Residents and Political Agents in all important States and groups of States. The Secretary of State kept a close control over the activities of the Political Department, mainly because of the interest of the Crown in matters affecting the rights and privileges of the rulers.

Constitutionally the States were not part of British India nor were their inhabitants British subjects. Parliament had no power to legislate for the States or their people. The Crown's relationship with the Indian States was conducted by the Governor-General in Council. Since the Governor-General was in charge of the Political

Department, his Executive Council tended in practice to leave States' affairs to him and the Political Department; so that the Political Department came gradually to assume the position of a government within a government.

The Political officers in the various States had comprehensive, though unwritten, authority. In the case of the smaller States, these officers frankly adopted the attitude of a superior towards a subordinate. Even in the case of bigger States and the States which had well-known administrators they had much their own way. Dissensions and jealousies among the rulers were systematically sustained. The States were isolated from British India in the same manner as India as a whole was isolated from the rest of Asia. Even high-ranking Government officers were required to take permission from the Political Department before visiting the States.

Along with the building up of a strong Political Department, the Crown started asserting rights and prerogatives never claimed by the East India Company and even at times cutting across treaty rights. The most outstanding example, and at the same time one of far-reaching consequence, in the relations of the paramount power with the rulers was the prerogative assumed of recognizing succession in the case of natural heirs. The first ruling in this behalf was laid down by the Government of India in 1884 in a letter addressed to the Chief Commissioner of the Central Provinces in which it was stated that 'the succession to a native State is invalid until it receives in some form the sanction of the British authority.' As regards the connected right to settle disputed successions, ' it is admittedly the right and duty of Government,' wrote the Secretary of State on 24 July 1891, 'to settle successions in the protected States of India.' This right, it was claimed, flowed essentially from the position of the British as the supreme power responsible for maintaining law and order throughout the country. That power alone had the necessary sanctions to enforce decisions regarding disputed successions. The alternative to this arrangement was civil war.

As a natural corollary, the Government of India assumed the guardianship of minor princes and also arranged for the administration of the State during a minority.

The ruler thus did not inherit his *gaddi* as of right, but as a gift from the paramount power. This, coupled with the right of the Crown to regulate the status and salutes of the rulers and to confer titles and decorations, had the effect of binding the rulers more closely to the Crown.

The political and economic consolidation of India necessitated
further encroachments on the internal sovereignty of the rulers: for
example, in the case of railway and telegraph construction, the
limitation of armaments, coinage and currency, the opium policy
and the administration of cantonments. The rulers' consent to
these measures was not sought, partly because they were often evolved piecemeal from precedents affecting individual States and partly
because, under the policy of isolation, it would have been difficult to
secure their joint assent to them within a reasonable period. The
result was that a body of usage influencing the Government's relations with the States came into force through a process which, however benevolent in intention, was nevertheless arbitrary.

Successive viceroys laid emphasis upon the duties and responsibilities of the rulers. The classic instance was the speech of Lord Curzon
at the installation of the ruler of Bahawalpur. He exhorted the
Indian ruler to be 'the servant as well as the master of his people';
emphasized that ' his revenues are not secured to him for his own
selfish gratification but for the good of his subjects'; avowed that
'his internal administration is only exempt from correction in proportion as it is honest'; advised him that 'his *gaddi* is not intended
to be a *divan* of indulgence but the stern seat of duty'; pointed out
that 'his figure should not be merely known on the playground or
on the race course or in the European hotel' and that 'his real work,
his princely duty, lies among his own people'; and warned him lastly
that 'by this test will he, in the long run, as a political institution
perish or survive.' These were undoubtedly very laudable sentiments, but little was done to translate them into practice.

A definite pattern of the Government of India's relationship with
the States in all its details had been developed by the time the first
World War broke out in August 1914. The rulers rallied to fight
for the Empire in its hour of peril, offering both their personal services and the resources of their States. Not only did they help
Britain lavishly with men, material and money, but some of them
even served as officers in different theatres of war.

The organization of the war effort involved closer co-ordination
of administrative activity in the States as well as in the provinces.
Lord Hardinge, as well as his successor Lord Chelmsford, held periodical conferences of the leading rulers with a view to furthering the
war effort. In welcoming this new development a few of the leading
rulers stressed the essential identity of interests between the two

halves of India and expressed the hope that what had now become an annual conference would develop into a permanent Council or Assembly of Princes.

Throughout the country the tide of national aspirations was rising fast. Though the Congress was not yet the popular organization it was to be under Gandhiji's leadership and had not, for instance, resorted to any mass movements, it was slowly cutting itself loose from the leadership of the moderates. The emergence of leaders like Tilak broadened the hold of the organization upon the people at large.

Britain claimed to be fighting a war to defend freedom and democracy; but the system of government by which she continued to hold India in imperial thrall was clearly at variance with her professed aims. The British Government recognized that the situation needed new handling and that there was an imperative and urgent need for a new policy. Accordingly, Edwin Samuel Montagu, the Secretary of State for India, made the historic announcement of 20 August 1917:

> The policy of His Majesty's Government, with which the Government of India are in complete accord, is that of the increasing association of Indians in every branch of the administration and the gradual development of self-governing institutions with a view to the progressive realisation of responsible government in India as an integral part of the British Empire.

Soon after making this announcement, Montagu came to India and the Viceroy and he together toured the country. In the course of their itinerary they met not only the leaders of public opinion in British India, but also several leading rulers. The Conference of Ruling Princes appointed a committee which presented a memorandum. In the summer of 1918, Montagu and Chelmsford published a joint report on Constitutional Reforms. Though the joint inquiry did not bring about any far-reaching changes in the position of the States, it was of historical importance in so far as it was the first major investigation into the relations of the States with the rest of India and with the paramount power. That the inquiry was conducted jointly by the Viceroy and the Secretary of State gave it added significance.

The authors of the joint report paid glowing tributes to the princes for the part played by them in the war, which had demonstrated their immense value as part of the polity of India. They observed that the political stir in British India could not be a matter of indifference to the princes, since hopes and aspirations were apt to overleap frontier lines like sparks across a street. Reforms in the States could not be brought about as a direct result of constitutional changes in British India; they could come only through the permeation of ideas. It was stressed that the rulers of the States and the politicians in British India should respect each other's bounds.

Looking ahead to the future, the authors of the report pictured India as presenting only the external semblance of some form of federation. They visualized that the provinces would ultimately become self-governing units, held together by a Central Government which would deal solely with matters of common concern to all of them. But the matters common to the provinces were also to a great extent those in which the States were interested, namely, defence, tariffs, exchange, opium, salt, railways, and posts and telegraphs. The gradual concentration of the Government of India upon such matters would therefore make it easier for the States, while retaining their autonomy, to enter into closer association with the Central Government if they wished to do so.

The report next dealt with the feeling expressed by some rulers that the measure of sovereignty and independence guaranteed to them by the British Government had not been accorded in full and that in course of time their individual rights and privileges would probably be whittled away. This feeling was ascribed to two causes.

In the first place, the expression 'Native States' was being applied to a collection of about seven hundred rulerships with widely different characteristics, ranging from States with full autonomy to those in which the Government of India exercised large powers of internal control, down to the owners of a few acres of land. Uniformity of terminology tended to obscure distinctions of status and a practice appropriate in the case of lesser States might inadvertently be applied to the greater ones also. The authors were convinced that it would assist and improve relations between the Crown and the States if a definite line could be drawn separating rulers who enjoyed full powers of internal administration from others who did not. Indeed, their proposals were based on this assumption and were expressed to relate only to rulers of the former class.

In the second place, there was the fact that the provision in many of the treaties guaranteeing the internal sovereignty of the rulers did not preclude the Government of India from interfering in the administration of the States. Such interference, the authors remarked, had not been employed in wanton disregard of treaty obligations. During the early days British agents found themselves compelled, often against their will, to assume responsibility for the welfare of the people, to restore order from chaos, to prevent inhuman practices, and to guide the hands of a weak or incompetent ruler as the only alternative to the termination of his rule. So, too, had the Government of India to acknowledge, as trustee, a responsibility for the proper administration of States during a minority, and also an obligation for the prevention or correction of flagrant misgovernment. Moreover, a position had been taken up by Government that the conditions under which some of the treaties were executed had undergone material changes and the literal fulfilment of particular obligations had become impracticable. Practice was based on the theory that treaties must be read as a whole and that they must be interpreted in the light of relations established between the parties not only at the time when a particular treaty was made, but subsequently. The result was that around the treaties there had grown up a body of case-law, for a proper appreciation of which one would have to explore Government archives and relevant text-books. The position caused uneasiness to some rulers who feared that usage and precedent were exercising a levelling and corroding influence upon the treaty rights of individual States.

The authors concluded that there was some ambiguity and misunderstanding as to the exact position. They suggested that the time had come when 'it would be well to review the situation, of course only by consent of parties, not necessarily with a view to any change of policy, but in order to simplify, standardize, and codify existing practice for the future.' They felt, too, that the rulers should be assured in the fullest and freest manner that no constitutional changes that might take place would impair the rights, dignities and privileges secured to them by treaties, *sanads* and engagements, or by established practice.

Indeed, the authors of the Montagu-Chelmsford report felt that the time had come to end the isolation of the rulers and that steps should be taken for joint consultations and discussions by them for the furtherance of their common interests. Lord Lytton had at one time suggested the formation of an Imperial Privy Council which should comprise some of the great rulers, but his suggestion found no acceptance with the then Secretary of State. Lord Curzon's plan for the formation of a Council of Ruling Princes had also been brushed aside by His Majesty's Government; and Lord Minto's subsequent scheme for an Advisory Council of rulers and big land-holders to combat the political discontent prevailing at the time met with the same fate. But during the viceroyalties of Lord Hardinge and Lord Chelmsford, conferences of rulers became a regular feature. The joint authors suggested that these *ad hoc* conferences should be replaced by a permanent body known as the Council of Princes, which would give the rulers 'the opportunity of informing the Government as to their sentiments and wishes, of broadening their outlook and of conferring with one another and with the Government.'

Another recommendation was that the Council of Princes should annually appoint a small Standing Committee to advise the Political Department on matters affecting the States, particularly matters of custom and usage. It was also recommended that, in the case of disputes between States, or between a State and a provincial government or the Government of India, the Viceroy in his discretion should appoint a commission composed of a High Court Judge and one nominee of each of the parties to advise him. Further, should a question ever arise of depriving the ruler of a State of his rights, dignity or powers or of debarring from succession any member of his family, the Viceroy should appoint a commission of enquiry consisting of a High Court Judge, two ruling princes and two persons of high standing nominated by him.

A still further recommendation was that all States possessing full internal powers should be placed in direct relations with the Government of India and that 'relations with States' was a subject which should be excluded from transfer to the control of the provincial legislatures. Finally, the report recommended that arrangements should be made for joint deliberation and discussion between the Council of Princes and the Council of State (the proposed Upper House of the Central Legislature) on matters of common interest.

The Government of India consulted the rulers in regard to these recommendations. The report had, as already stated, suggested that a definite line should be drawn separating the rulers who enjoyed full powers of internal administration from the others and that the Council of Princes should consist only of rulers in the former category. The Conference of Ruling Princes and Chiefs, which met at Delhi in January 1919, recommended that the rulers of States having full and unrestricted powers of civil and criminal jurisdiction in their States and the power to make their own laws should be termed 'Sovereign Princes' as against those who lacked such powers. The Government of India thought that the application of the term 'Sovereign Princes' to a select class of rulers would be inappropriate since, on the one hand, it would suggest that they possessed complete sovereign powers which was not the case and, on the other, it would imply that the powers exercised by rulers in the lower class were *not* sovereign powers—a theory which would excite much justifiable indignation. It was finally decided that there should not be any line of demarcation between the rulers and that both classes of rulers should find representation in the proposed Chamber of Princes.

The Chamber of Princes was brought into being by a Royal Proclamation on 8 February 1921. The ceremony of inauguration was performed by the Duke of Connaught, on behalf of the King-Emperor, in the *Dewan-i-am* of the Moghul Red Fort in Delhi. The Chamber was to be a deliberative, consultative and advisory body. The Proclamation defined its limits:

My Viceroy will take its counsel freely in matters relating to the territories of Indian States generally and in matters that affect these territories jointly with British India or with the rest of my Empire. It will have no concern with the internal affairs of individual States or their Rulers or with the relations of individual States with my Government, while the existing rights of these States and their freedom of action will in no way be prejudiced or impaired.

The Viceroy was to be the President of the Chamber and the members were to elect annually a Chancellor and a Pro-Chancellor from among themselves. The Chamber[1] was to contain, in the first place, 108 rulers who were to be members in their own right. These were rulers enjoying permanent dynastic salutes of eleven guns and over, together with rulers of other States who exercised such full powers as, in the opinion of the Viceroy, qualified them for individual admission. By a system of group voting, the Chamber was to include 12 additional members elected by the rulers of 127 non-salute States.

The most important recommendation of the Montagu-Chelmsford report was that relating to the codification of political practice. This roused much controversy and discussion among the rulers. Some of them accepted the position that, in the matter of the maintenance of treaty obligations, the relations of the Government of

[1] Some important States like Hyderabad and Mysore stood aloof from the Chamber.

3

India with the rulers were necessarily subject to variation through constant development of constitutional doctrine and that the literal fulfilment of an obligation might become impossible, either through change of essential circumstances or by the mere passage of time.

But there were others who held it to be in the interests of both the British Government and the States not to swerve an inch from the provisions of the treaties unless they were modified by mutual consent. They believed that the tide of usage and political practice had already undermined the foundations of the treaties and they saw no reason why it should not eventually engulf them, unless some barrier could be interposed. The Government of India, recognizing the justice of some of these arguments, felt that they were no longer entitled to exclude the rulers from a share in the framing of any practice which might have a bearing upon their prerogatives. The policy hitherto followed was that the superintendence, direction and control of the development of constitutional doctrine must remain in the hands of the paramount power; that any rules which the paramount power might frame for the guidance of its representatives in matters not provided for by treaties or otherwise were in the nature of self-denying ordinances which, however morally binding, were not suitable for promulgation and which, if codified, would tend to restrict unduly its inherent freedom of action. But times and circumstances had altered; many of the States had made considerable progress in administration, and the establishment of the Chamber of Princes, in which the rulers could voice their collective needs and aspirations, had ended the phase of isolation. Further, it would be obviously to the advantage of the Government that the concurrence of the rulers should be secured, so far as possible, to the application of doctrines which were outside the treaty framework, since this would allay unjust suspicions and relieve the Government and their officials of charges of despotic and capricious interference. Thus, the Government of India were convinced that it was necessary, on grounds of fairness and expediency, to take the rulers into confidence unreservedly in regard to the revision and development of that portion of political doctrine which was capable of being expressed in the form of general principles, in so far as it was based on considerations other than treaty rights. Accordingly, they accepted a proposal made by some of the rulers for the appointment of a Committee, comprising six rulers, the Law Member and the Political Secretary, to investigate the matter. This Committee did some useful work.

Later, in 1921, its work was taken over by the Standing Committee of the Chamber of Princes. The Standing Committee maintained a close liaison with the Political Department and discussed various issues. The conclusions reached from time to time were published as resolutions of the Political Department.

The Government of India accepted the procedure recommended by the Montagu-Chelmsford Report for the settlement of disputes between States, or between a State and a provincial government or the Government of India; also the procedure to be followed on the question of deposing a ruler or debarring from succession members of his family. In both cases, it was decided that a commission of inquiry should be appointed by the Viceroy to advise him, unless the ruler himself desired that the case should be decided by the Viceroy personally.

The process of placing the States in direct relations with the Government of India took considerable time to complete and, indeed, was not finished until well into the 'thirties. Some of the provincial governments were against the change; Sir George Lloyd, Governor of Bombay, for instance, opposed it in language reminiscent of the minutes of Sir Philip Francis and Warren Hastings. It must be stated, however, that the isolation of States consequent on their being brought into direct relations with the Government of India militated against their administrative standards keeping pace with those of the neighbouring provinces.

But no attempt was made to have joint deliberations of the Chamber of Princes and the Council of State. The gradual bringing together of the States and British India remained a pious hope. The paramount power continued to be paramount and paramountcy remained as vague and undefined as ever.

II

SPOKES IN THE WHEEL

THE introduction of the Montagu-Chelmsford Reforms was preceded by a tremendous national upsurgence throughout the country. The severity of the martial law regime in the Punjab and the holocaust of Jallianwalla Bagh had inflamed the masses generally. The Muslims in particular were deeply agitated over the terms of the draft Treaty of Sèvres, which threatened dismemberment of the Caliphate. Gandhiji preached non-violent non-co-operation not only to redress the Punjab and Khilafat wrongs but to win *swaraj*, which by 1929 came to be defined as complete independence. The Congress accepted Gandhiji's programme. It became a revolutionary body pledged to the triple boycott of the new legislatures, the law courts and educational institutions, with a view to launching mass civil disobedience. The Government had an anxious time in the face of this campaign of direct action.

In 1923, following the suspension of the non-co-operation movement and the arrest and conviction of Gandhiji, a section of Congressmen led by Chittaranjan Das and Pandit Motilal Nehru formed within the Congress the 'Swarajist Party', with the object of wrecking the legislatures, both central and provincial, from within. This party won considerable success in the general elections of that year. It made the working of dyarchy impossible in Bengal and the Central Provinces. In the Central Legislative Assembly the Swarajists, who made their presence felt in more ways than one, put forward a demand for the immediate grant of Dominion Status. In the course of the debate, Sir Malcolm Hailey, who was Home Member at the time, enquired of the Swarajists whether they contemplated extending Dominion Status to the Indian States as well and, if so, whether the States had agreed to the proposition and on what terms. Pandit Motilal Nehru replied unequivocally that if the States wanted to come in their representatives would be welcome; otherwise not.

The Swarajist leader's pronouncement was altogether in consonance with the Congress attitude towards the States. At the Nagpur session held in December 1920, the Congress had clearly laid down its policy as being one of non-intervention in the internal affairs of the States. In January 1925, Gandhiji while presiding over the Kathiawar Political Conference, declared that 'just as the National Congress cannot have any effective voice in the relations between Indian States and the British Government, even so will its interference be ineffective as to the relations between the Indian States and their subjects.' He even went so far as to say that all would be well if British India became self-governing. The Congress did not want a fight on two fronts; and it had no organization worth mentioning in the States.

Lord Irwin was appointed as Viceroy in April 1926. He felt that the political situation in the country demanded some gesture on the part of His Majesty's Government. His Majesty's Government were in agreement with his view. Accordingly in March 1927 they announced their decision to appoint a Statutory Commission to enquire into the working of the Government of India Act of 1919 and to make recommendations regarding further constitutional advance. The personnel of the Commission under the chairmanship of Sir John (later Viscount) Simon and its terms of reference were announced in November 1927.

The States were not going to be left out of the picture. With reference to certain published correspondence which had passed between the Viceroy and the Nizam of Hyderabad with regard to Berar, the late Maharajah of Patiala, in November 1926, made a statement on behalf of the rulers that they had 'perused with deep concern certain phrases employed and doctrines enunciated' in the correspondence. This was followed by a demand, made at a conference of rulers convened by the Viceroy at Simla in May 1927, for an impartial inquiry into the whole relationship between the rulers and the paramount power. The Secretary of State, Lord Birkenhead, thought the appointment of the Simon Commission a good opportunity for acceding to the rulers' demand and on 16 December 1927 appointed a Committee of three members, headed by Sir Harcourt Butler and including Professor W. S. Holdsworth and the Hon'ble S. C. Peel, to inquire into the relationship between the States and the paramount power and to suggest means for the more satisfactory adjustment of the existing economic relations between the States and British India.

Sir Harcourt Butler and his two colleagues came to India in January 1928 and visited sixteen of the States. The Committee's proceedings were held *in camera*. On the plea that it was outside their terms of reference, they did not examine the representatives of the States' subjects. They did however accept a written statement from the All-India States People's Conference which had been formed in December 1927 with the object of attaining 'responsible government for the people in the Indian States through representative institutions under the aegis of their rulers.'

The bulk of the Committee's work in hearing the case for the rulers was done in England. The rulers had engaged eminent British constitutional lawyers headed by Sir Leslie Scott, K.C. to argue their case,[1] which they did with great skill. Sir Leslie Scott urged that in the analysis of the relationship between the States and the Crown, legal principles should both be enunciated and applied. It was contended that the States possessed all original sovereign powers except those which had been transferred with their consent to the Crown; that such transfer could be effected by the consent of the States and in no other way; and that paramountcy existed and gave to the Crown definite rights and imposed on it definite duties in respect of certain matters only — those relating to foreign affairs and external and internal security — and did not confer upon the Crown any authority outside these spheres. It was held that usage could not be alleged where agreement was absent; that there might be certain cases in which the paramount power would be clearly entitled to interfere, but that there was no general discretionary right on the part of the paramount power to interfere with the internal sovereignty of the States. The relationship between the Crown and the States involved mutual rights and obligations. Counsel avowed that 'the duties which lie upon the Crown to ensure the external and internal security of the States and to keep available whatever armed forces may be necessary for these purposes are plain.'

Sir Leslie Scott's crowning achievement lay in evolving a new theory. He argued that 'the paramount power is the British Crown and no one else; and it is to it that the States have entrusted their foreign relations and external and internal security.' He asserted therefore that 'the agency and machinery used by the Crown for

---

[1] Hyderabad, Mysore and Travancore and certain Kathiawar States declined to be represented by Sir Leslie Scott and preferred to state their case directly, in writing.

carrying out its obligations must not be of such a character as to make it politically impracticable for the Crown to carry out its obligations in a satisfactory manner.' He concluded that the obligations and duties which the States and the paramount power had undertaken required mutual faith and trust and entailed a close and constant intercourse between the parties; therefore the States could not be compelled to transfer to a third party their loyalty to the British Crown.

On the question of the limitation of paramountcy, the Butler Committee disagreed with the views propounded by Sir Leslie Scott. The Committee held that the relationship of the paramount power with the States was not merely a contractual relationship resting on treaties made more than a century ago, but that it was a living, growing relationship shaped by circumstances and policy, resting on a mixture of history, theory and modern fact. It was not historically correct to assume that when the States came into contact with the British power they were independent, each possessed of full sovereignty and of a status which a modern international lawyer would hold to be governed by the rules of international law. In fact, none of the States had ever had international status. Nearly all of them were subordinate or tributary to the Moghul Empire, the Mahratta Confederacy or the Sikh Kingdom, and were dependent on them. Some were rescued by the British and others were created by them. The Committee refused to define paramountcy but asserted that 'paramountcy must remain paramount; it must fulfil its obligations, defining or adapting itself according to the shifting necessities of the time and the progressive development of the States.'

At the same time the Butler Committee showed itself only too ready to accept the ingenious suggestion of Sir Leslie Scott that the rulers should not be handed over without their prior agreement to an Indian Government in British India responsible to an Indian legislature. The Committee stated:

If any government in the nature of a Dominion Government should be constituted in British India, such a government would clearly be a new government resting on a new and written constitution. The contingency has not arisen... We feel bound, however, to draw attention to the really grave apprehension of the princes on this score and to record our strong opinion that, in view of the fact of the historical nature of the relationship between the paramount power and the princes, the latter should not be transferred without their agreement to a relationship with a new government in British India responsible to an Indian legislature. Thus was laid the foundation of a policy whereby, in later years, a wedge was to be effectively driven between the States and British India.

The Butler Committee also proposed that the Viceroy, not the Governor-General in Council, should be the agent of the Crown in all dealings with the States. Such a change, it was argued, would gratify the rulers. The Committee showered encomiums on the work of the Political Department and suggested that 'the time has come to recruit separately from the universities in England for service in the States alone' instead of the prevailing practice of recruiting for political service from the Indian Civil Service and the Indian Army.

With regard to the financial and economic relations between British India and the States, the Committee merely expressed some pious platitudes and broke no new ground.

The rulers were certainly disappointed with the finding of the Butler Committee with regard to their main hope of being freed from the unfettered discretion of the Political Department to intervene in their internal affairs. The disappointment was all the greater because no effort or expense had been spared in preparing and presenting their case to the Committee. At the same time, they were relieved that the *status quo* was to be maintained and that there was to be no immediate danger to their position.

Nationalist opinion in the country viewed the recommendations of the Butler Committee with grave apprehension. An emphatic protest was entered in the report[1] of the Committee (presided over by Pandit Motilal Nehru) which had been appointed by the All Parties' Conference in 1928 to frame a Dominion Constitution for India. The report stressed the historical, religious, sociological and economic affinities between the people of British India and of the States and uttered the warning:

It is inconceivable that the people of the States who are fired by the same ambitions and aspirations as the people of British India will quietly submit to existing conditions for ever, or that the people of British India bound by the closest ties of family, race and religion to their brethren *on the other side of an imaginary line* will never make common cause with them.

The report stressed that the matter should have been discussed at a

---

[1] Though the Butler Committee's report was published some time after the Nehru report, Sir Leslie Scott's memorandum had already found its way to the press.

Round Table Conference of the representatives of the British Government, the rulers, their subjects and the people of British India. The Nehru Committee had no doubt that 'an attempt is being made to convert the Indian States into an Indian Ulster by pressing constitutional theories into service.'

The report declared that the Government of India as a Dominion 'will be as much the King's Government as the present Government of India is, and that there is no constitutional objection to the Dominion Government of India stepping into the shoes of the present Government of India.' The rulers were warned that if they decided to take their stand upon the position so ingeniously argued for them, British India would substantially discount their profession of sympathy with its aspiration to Dominion Status. It was pointed out that the acceptance of Sir Leslie Scott's theory would mean that Dominion Status for India was ruled out for all time. The Nehru report concluded with the words: 'The natural and legitimate aspirations of India cannot and will not be allowed to be defeated or checkmated by ingenicus arguments which have no application to facts.'

The Nehru Committee was limited under its terms of reference to the framing of a constitution embracing British India alone. In the course of its work, it realized that it was necessary that the States should also be brought into the picture. It finally accepted the idea of an all-India federation which had been suggested as a solution of the problem. It assured the States that, if they were willing to join such a federation, 'we shall heartily welcome their decision and do all that lies in our power to secure to them the full enjoyment of their rights and privileges. But it must be clearly borne in mind that it would necessitate, perhaps in varying degrees, a modification of the system of government and administration prevailing within their territories. We hope and trust that, in the light of experience gained, the Indian States may make up their mind to join formally the Federation.' The Committee accordingly provided in its draft constitution that all treaties made between the East India Company and the States, and any subsequent treaties still in force, should be binding on the new Government of British India and that the new government should exercise the same rights in relation to, and discharge the same obligations towards, the States as the Government of India had exercised and discharged hitherto.

In the meantime, the Simon Commission was carrying on its

4

enquiry. All the leading Indian political parties had decided not to
co-operate with the Commission since not a single Indian had been
included in it. The Central Legislative Assembly refused to appoint
a committee to assist it. Its proceedings were rigidly boycotted; and
the Commission encountered hostile demonstrations all over the
country. The situation in the spring of 1929 looked disturbing and
bleak. In October 1929 Sir John Simon wrote to the British Prime
Minister that the Commission had entered upon the final stages of
its work and hoped to be able to present its report early the following
year. Sir John emphasized that in considering the direction which
future development of India was likely to take, it was of immense
importance to bear in mind the relations which might develop between British India and the Indian States. He suggested a scheme of
procedure to follow the publication of the Committee's report, under
which the Indian States would be brought into consultation, along
with the British Government and representatives of different parties
and interests in British India, with a view to seeking a full solution of
the Indian problem as a whole.

The Viceroy, Lord Irwin, left for England at the close of June
1929 to confer with the British Government. There had been a general election in Britain and a Labour Government had come into
power with Ramsay MacDonald as Prime Minister. On his return,
Lord Irwin made an official pronouncement to the effect that 'the
natural issue of India's constitutional progress is the attainment of
Dominion Status.' He also announced that the British Government
had accepted the suggestion made by Sir John Simon for a Round
Table Conference.

This announcement killed whatever interest there had been in
the Simon Commission, whose report when published evoked little
or no enthusiasm. In order to complete the picture, however, a
summary of its main recommendations regarding the Indian States
is necessary. The report agreed with the recommendations of the
Butler Committee that the exercise of paramountcy should be in the
hands of the Viceroy as distinguished from the Governor-General.
It quoted profusely from the development of Federation in Canada
and stressed the need for cautious advance in India. It made three
concrete proposals. Firstly, it recommended that a serious and businesslike effort should be made to draw up a list of those 'matters of
common concern' between British India and the States so often
referred to but seldom defined. Secondly, it proposed that the

preamble to any new Government of India Act should put on record
the desire to develop closer association between the States and British
India. Thirdly, it suggested the setting up of a standing consultative
body containing representatives from both British India and the
States, to be called the Council for Greater India, with powers of discussion and of reaching and recording deliberative results on topics
falling within the list of 'matters of common concern'. The Council
was to be a beginning which might one day lead to Indian federation. 'What we are proposing,' said the Commission, 'is merely a
throwing across the gap of the first strands which may in time mark
the line of a solid and enduring bridge.'

The report of the Simon Commission was submitted in May 1930.
The Government of India's recommendations thereon were sent to
the Secretary of State in September. There was, they said, an essential unity embracing the whole of India, which they hoped would at
some future time find expression in certain joint political institutions.
But they agreed with the Commission that the federal idea was at
present distant, and that the federation of Greater India, to which
they looked forward, could not be artificially hastened. In the
Government of India's view, the time had not yet come when the
general body of the States would be prepared to take a step so far-
reaching in its character as entering into any formal federal relations
with British India. Therefore, they saw the immediate problem
as one relating to constitutional development in British India
alone.

The first Round Table Conference was held in London in the
winter of 1930. The Congress had refused the invitation to attend.
The Lahore session of the Congress in December 1929 had voted for
complete independence; and in April 1930 the Congress, under
Gandhiji's leadership, had launched a mass campaign of salt satya-
graha and civil disobedience. The maintenance of law and order was
seriously threatened, and it was against the background of an India
seething with discontent that the first Round Table Conference met
in London.

The three British political parties were represented at the Round
Table Conference by sixteen delegates; and the Prime Minister,
Ramsay MacDonald, presided. There were fifty-seven political
leaders from British India and sixteen delegates from the States,
including the rulers of Kashmir, Baroda, Patiala, Indore, Bikaner,
Bhopal, Rewa, Alwar, Nawanagar, Dholpur, Korea, Sangli and

Sarila, besides Sir Akbar Hydari (Hyderabad), Sir Mirza Ismail (Mysore) and Colonel (later Sir) Kailas Narain Haksar (Gwalior).

The delegates from India arrived in London by the end of October 1930 and the formal opening of the Round Table Conference by the King took place on 12 November. The actual work of the Conference began only on the 17th. In the interval, numerous informal discussions took place between the British Indian delegates and representatives of the States.

On the first day of the plenary session of the Conference, Sir Tej Bahadur Sapru, one of the chief spokesmen of the delegates from British India, declared himself decisively for a federal, not a unitary, system of government at the centre and invited the rulers to agree forthwith to the creation of an all-India federation. The rulers would furnish, he said, a stabilizing factor; their adherence would enable the process of national unification to begin without delay; and British India would benefit from their experience in matters of defence. Sir Muhammad Shafi for one wing of the Muslim League and M.A. Jinnah for the other were in full agreement with Sir Tej Bahadur; both welcomed an all-India federation.

The Maharajah of Bikaner, the late Sir Ganga Singh, identified himself and the princely order with the aspirations of British India and with 'that passion for an equal status in the eyes of the world, expressed in the desire for Dominion Status which is the dominant force amongst all thinking Indians today.' He agreed that India must be united on a federal basis and gave an assurance that the rulers would come in provided their rights were guaranteed. The Nawab of Bhopal, Sir Hamidullah Khan, went one step further and avowed: ' We can only federate with a self-governing and federal British India.' This virtually created a common Indian front.

There were several reasons which prompted this response from the rulers. Few States were entirely untouched by the mass awakening in British India. In some of them, disturbances had taken place and authority had been challenged. Few of the rulers had any illusion as to what would happen if a campaign of civil disobedience were launched in their States. Moreover, the rulers were convinced that it would be more difficult to drive a good bargain if they waited till they were faced with a united and self-governing British India. Some of the leading rulers who controlled the Chamber of Princes were actually under the impression that their States would derive financial benefits by joining the federation. A few were actuated by personal ambition and looked forward to exercising a great influence in the administration and possibly to holding high offices in the new government. That a Labour Government was in power was also an important factor in determining their attitude.

Not all the rulers, however, were united in welcoming the federal idea. While the federationists were led by the Maharajah of Bikaner and the Nawab of Bhopal, there was another group led by the late Maharajah of Patiala, Sir Bhupindar Singh. This group regarded a confederation of States, or 'Indian India' as it was called, as a necessary preliminary to any association with British India. This view commanded good support especially from the rulers of smaller States who saw in this scheme their only chance of avoiding federal control in their internal affairs.

A Federal Structure Sub-Committee was appointed with Lord Sankey as Chairman and representatives both from the States and British India. Its report, presented on 15 January 1931, contained a comprehensive series of provisional decisions on matters on which the members of the Sub-Committee were more or less agreed. The States and the provinces were to be united in a federation. There would be certain agreed safeguards for a transitional period. The federal legislature would include members from British India and representatives from the States nominated by the rulers. The central cabinet would be chosen from amongst the members of the federal legislature; but there would be only limited responsibility at the Centre for the transitional period. No attempt was, however, made to secure a formal acceptance of the report by the Conference.

The general tone of the speeches at the conclusion of the Conference was harmonious and optimistic. The agreement on an all-India federation was hailed as a great achievement.

A Round Table Conference to evolve a constitution for India without the participation of the Congress was like enacting *Hamlet* without the Prince of Denmark. A week after the adjournment of the first Round Table Conference, Lord Irwin ordered the unconditional release of all the members of the Congress Working Committee including those who had been acting as such since civil disobedience started. Ultimately an understanding was reached between the Congress and the Government. The Gandhi-Irwin Pact, as it was called, was signed on 5 March 1931. By this Pact the Government agreed to release all the political prisoners and the Congress to suspend the civil disobedience movement. The Congress

agreed to participate in the Round Table Conference and, at the
Karachi session of the Congress on 30 March Gandhiji was appointed to represent the Congress 'with the addition of such delegates as
the Working Committee may appoint to act under his leadership.'

The second session of the Conference opened on 7 September 1931
and included, besides Gandhiji, new-comers like Pandit Madan
Mohan Malaviya, Mrs Sarojini Naidu, Sir Ali Imam, Sir Muhammad
Iqbal and G. D. Birla. Most of the leading personalities of the first
session were back in their places and the composition of the British
delegation was much the same as before. Towards the end of October,
a general election took place in Britain and a Coalition Government
came to power, with Ramsay MacDonald continuing as Prime
Minister but with the Conservatives as the dominant party. Sir
Samuel Hoare replaced Wedgwood Benn as Secretary of State for
India.

The session was almost entirely dominated by Gandhiji, who was
not opposed to the federal idea. He was, however, against dyarchy at
the Centre even for a transitional period. He claimed complete control over defence and external affairs. He insisted that responsible
government at the Centre must be established in full and at once.
The British Government did not accept Gandhiji's demand. At the
end of the Conference, the Prime Minister announced His Majesty's
Government's policy in the following words:

The great idea of an all-India federation still holds the field. The
principle of a responsible federal government, subject to certain reservations
and safeguards through a transition period, remains unchanged. And
we are all agreed that the Governors' provinces of the future are to be
responsibly governed units, enjoying the greatest possible measure of
freedom from outside interference and dictation in carrying out their
own policies in their own sphere.

This session was overshadowed by the communal problem, for
which Gandhiji tried hard to find a solution. In the end 'with deep
sorrow and deeper humiliation' he had to admit 'utter failure to
secure an agreed solution of the communal question.'

There were divisions in the princely ranks too. The main lines of
cleavage were in regard to representation of the States in the federal
legislature and the financial liabilities of the federating States. As
regards representation, there were three main divisions. The major
States, notably Hyderabad, Mysore and Baroda, demanded representation in proportion to their importance and population. The

Maharajah of Bikaner favoured an upper house of two hundred and fifty, with a fifty per cent representation for the States, so that all the members of the Chamber of Princes might have a seat; he was ready to offer one or two additional seats to the major States as a sop. The Maharajah of Patiala continued to sponsor a scheme for a confederation of the States as a first step towards federation.

As regards finance, the Federal Structure Sub-Committee's findings killed any hope that rulers could gain any financial profit by joining the federation. The apprehension that the States might probably have to contribute more, and not less, towards all-India expenditure, that federal agencies might function in the States, and that the Federal Supreme Court might gradually extend its jurisdiction over States' subjects disillusioned the rulers of any fancy that they would be gainers by joining the federation. Sir Mirza Ismail informed the Conference that Mysore would not join the federation unless relieved of its tribute; Sir Akbar Hydari suggested that unless the Nizam's wishes in regard to Berar were satisfied, Hyderabad would stand out; Baroda demanded satisfaction on the Port Okha and Salt questions before business could be done, and so on. The rulers gradually started turning their backs on federation and the outlook at the conclusion of the second Round Table Conference was far from roseate. Some of the rulers now began to hope that nothing would come out of the Conference and that they would be able to continue their sheltered existence while Hindus and Muslims pursued their differences in British India.

The third and last session of the Round Table Conference assembled on 17 November 1932. It was smaller than its predecessors; only forty-six delegates attended. Sir Akbar Hydari and Sir Mirza Ismail were there, as were most of the British Indian delegates, but none of the important rulers was present. Moreover the Opposition Labour Party refused to take part in the Conference. The serious gap at this session, as at the first, was the absence of the Congress, for the Congress had in the meantime launched another campaign of civil disobedience. The important question considered at this short session was the composition of the federal legislature. The form of the States' instrument of accession to federation was also discussed. Anxiety was expressed by the British Indian delegates at the delay in deciding the terms on which the States would join the federation. It seemed, said Sir Tej Bahadur Sapru, as if no progress had been made since the rulers' very generous and patriotic response to their invitation in

1930. Was it certain, he asked, that the rulers were still willing to come in if their rights were protected? Sir Akbar Hydari replied that the greater the difficulties appeared, the greater also was the States' determination to overcome them and attain the goal. But the Conference could not rid itself of the uneasy impression that the enthusiasm of 1930 had waned and that, in fact, the rulers were now marking time.

The Third Round Table Conference could not settle the size of the federal chambers, the proportion of British Indian and States' representation and the allocation of States' seats. The Viceroy was therefore requested by the Secretary of State to bring about an agreement on these matters. He was asked to give adequate explanation of the federal scheme to individual rulers well in advance and to secure some indication of their views in order to prepare a favourable atmosphere for the reception of the contemplated White Paper containing His Majesty's Government's proposals for constitutional advance.

After consulting some of the leading rulers and leaders of non-Congress parties, the Viceroy suggested to the Secretary of State that the States should have 90 seats in an upper house of 225 and 125 seats in a lower house of 375. This was subsequently modified by His Majesty's Government. The allocation of the seats reserved for the States was further discussed with the rulers. The Viceroy finally suggested that all States with a salute of not less than seventeen guns (there were 24 such States) should have the right of separate representation in both the houses of the federal legislature. Such separate representation might also be given to a few populous fifteen-gun and thirteen-gun States. The others were to be grouped regionally for the purpose of representation in the federal legislature.

A conference of Political Officers was held in Delhi on 7 March 1933, when they were briefed on the proposed constitutional changes, particularly with regard to the federal provisions. These officers were to explain the implications and the advantages of an all-India federation to individual rulers and to ascertain their attitude. The Chamber of Princes met at about the same time and asked for a number of safeguards, the grant of which, so they maintained, was essential before they could join the federation. They demanded that the constitution should respect their treaty rights; that there should be no interference in their internal affairs, and that a provision should be made for the States joining the federation collectively through a confederation.

In March 1933, the proposals of His Majesty's Government, in the light of the three sessions of the Round Table Conference and subsequent negotiations, were published in a White Paper; and in April a Joint Select Committee of both Houses of Parliament was appointed, with the Marquess of Linlithgow as Chairman, to consider the future government of India with special reference to the White Paper proposals. The Committee was authorized to call into consultation delegates from British India and the States. The Congress was still in the wilderness and did not participate in these discussions. The Joint Select Committee submitted its report in October 1934 after an almost unbroken session of eighteen months.

On 12 December 1934, a motion that a Bill based on the Committee's Report should be submitted to Parliament was carried in the House of Commons; and on 19 December the Government of India Bill was introduced. The Chamber of Princes appointed a Committee of fifteen States' ministers under the chairmanship of Sir Akbar Hydari to examine the Bill. The Committee observed that 'in some important respects the Bill departs from the agreed position arrived at during the meetings of the States' representatives with His Majesty's Government.' It suggested a number of amendments and alterations and declared that 'without satisfactory amendments on the lines indicated, it would not be possible for them to recommend to their rulers and to the States generally the acceptance of the proposed scheme.'

A further conference of rulers and States' representatives was held in Bombay in February 1935 when it was resolved that 'the Bill and the instrument of accession do not secure those vital interests and fundamental requisites of the States on which they have throughout laid great emphasis.' The resolution added that 'in their present form and without satisfactory modification of, and alteration to, the fundamental points, the Bill and the instrument of accession cannot be regarded as acceptable to the Indian States.' The rulers of Patiala, Bhopal and Bikaner addressed a note to the Viceroy detailing certain amendments. They pointed out that the success of further negotiations in relation to the scheme of federation would depend entirely upon the extent to which the British Government were prepared to accept those modifications.

The Secretary of State gave careful consideration to the views

5

of the rulers and circularized, through the Viceroy, a memorandum examining in detail the specific points raised. It was made clear that it was not the intention of His Majesty's Government at that stage to seek from the rulers an undertaking to enter federation or to discuss new matters which had no bearing on the form of the Bill. It was agreed, however, that the legal advisers of the rulers could meet the parliamentary draftsmen and discuss any points at issue.

The debate on the Bill lasted for forty-three days in the House of Commons and for thirteen days in the House of Lords. Its passage was resisted at every stage by diehard Conservatives like Winston Churchill in the House of Commons and Lord Salisbury in the House of Lords. The second and third readings were, however, carried by big majorities. On 4 August 1935, the Bill received the Royal assent.

The Government of India Act of 1935 provided for a constitutional relationship between the Indian States and British India on a federal basis. A special feature of the scheme was that, whereas in the case of the provinces accession to the federation was to be automatic, in the case of the States it was to be voluntary. The reasons for treating the provinces and the States differently are explained in the following extract from the Joint Select Committee's report:

The main difficulties are two: that the Indian States are wholly different in status and character from the Provinces of British India, and that they are not prepared to federate on the same terms as it is proposed to apply to the Provinces. On the first point the Indian States, unlike the British Indian Provinces, possess sovereignty in various degrees and they are, broadly speaking, under a system of personal government. Their accession to a Federation cannot therefore take place otherwise than by the voluntary act of the Ruler of each State, and after accession the representatives of the acceding State in the Federal Legislature will be nominated by the Ruler and its subjects will continue to owe allegiance to him. On the second point the Rulers have made it clear that while they are willing to consider Federation now with the Provinces of British India on certain terms, they could not, as sovereign States, agree to the exercise by a Federal Government in relation to them of a range of powers identical in all respects with those which that Government will exercise in relation to the Provinces on whom autonomy has yet to be conferred.

A State was considered to have acceded when its ruler executed an instrument of accession and after it was accepted by His Majesty. This instrument would empower the federal government, the federal legislature, the federal court and any other federal authority to exercise in relation to the State such functions as might be vested in them by or under the Act; but the authority to perform such functions was to be exercised only in respect of those matters accepted by the ruler as federal in his instrument of accession and subject to such limitations as might be specified in it. Though accession was to be voluntary, rulers were expected to accede on the first forty-seven items of the federal legislative list, including the item relating to fees in respect of matters so accepted, and the content of accession was to be as uniform as possible for all States. An instrument of accession would become operative only when His Majesty had signified his acceptance of it.

The States' representatives in the upper and lower houses of the federal legislature were to be appointed by the rulers and not elected. The Council of State, or the upper chamber, was to consist of 156 members from British India and not more than 104 from the federating States. The lower chamber, or the House of Assembly, was to consist of 250 representatives of British India and not more than 125 of the States.

It was only when a sufficient number of States had acceded (1) to occupy 52 out of the 104 seats allotted to the States in the upper house of the federal legislature and (2) to make up half the total population of all the States, that His Majesty's Government would approach Parliament with a resolution to present an address to His Majesty to declare by Proclamation that, as from the day therein appointed, there should be united in a federation under the Crown, by the name of the Federation of India, the Governors' provinces and the States which had already acceded or which might accede later.

The relationship of the rulers with the paramount power was safeguarded by creating a Crown Representative in addition to the Governor-General. In the conduct of their affairs as members of the federation, the States were to deal with the Governor-General as head of the federal government; but in their relations with the paramount power, they were to deal with the Crown Representative. The Act permitted the same individual to hold both offices; and, in fact, the same person was so appointed — with the style and title of 'Viceroy'; but he had different secretarial and other agencies for his dual functions.

The Government of India Act of 1935, other than the part relating to federation, came into force on 1 April 1937. From that date, the functions of the Crown in its relations with the States were entrusted to the Crown Representative; those functions included negotiations with the rulers for their accession to the federation.

The Viceroy who succeeded Lord Willingdon in 1936 was the Marquess of Linlithgow, who had been the Chairman of the Joint Select Committee on the Government of India Bill. He came to India fired with the ambition to inaugurate the federation during his tenure of office and the first thing to which he directed his attention was how best to accomplish this expeditiously. He thought that a direct personal approach to the rulers would induce many of them to accept it. His plan was to send his own personal emissaries to the various States to clear the rulers' doubts so that they could take a final decision without delay. The emissaries he chose were Sir Courtenay Latimer, Sir Francis Wylie and Sir Arthur Lothian, all of whom belonged to the Political Service.

The Secretary of State viewed this procedure with a certain amount of misgiving. In the end, however, he agreed to the Viceroy's proposal.

The emissaries were provided with draft copies of the instrument of accession, which had already been sent to the rulers, as well as with written instructions from the Viceroy. The draft instrument, it was stated, represented the result of lengthy discussions in the Government of India, in the India Office and between representatives of the rulers and of His Majesty's Government. The emissaries were told that the draft constituted a balanced whole and, having regard to the Government of India Act and to the history of the federal scheme, the Viceroy hoped that any difficulties which the rulers might experience in connexion with it would prove to be of such a nature that, with the assistance and advice of the emissaries, they could be dissipated without delay.

The three emissaries toured the various States in the winter of 1936-37 and met the rulers and their advisers. It became apparent in the course of these discussions that the picture which the rulers and their advisers had drawn in their own minds was of a considerably less organic federation than that which was embodied in the Government of India Act. The rulers made it clear that in their case the urge to unity was not dominant, nor were they suppliants asking to come in. The question that agitated them was not whether federation would enable them to contribute to the benefit of India as a whole, but whether their own position would be better and safer inside the federation than outside it. In effect, their attitude could be briefly summed up thus: 'We are being given the opportunity of entering a federation from which, when once we are in, there is no escape. Nor, since the ultimate interpreter of the federal constitution is the Federal Court, can the Government of India or anyone else predict the course of future events or anticipate the use which federation will make of its powers. We owe it therefore to ourselves and to our successors to safeguard to the utmost our own position inside the federation. That is the light in which you must regard the limitations which we have proposed, and if they seem unduly numerous and too widely drawn, remember that we have good reason for making them so.'

The limitations proposed by the rulers could, in the main, be traced to a desire to safeguard two things: firstly, their sovereignty and secondly, their financial position; and although the relative importance assigned to one or the other varied from State to State, both were regarded as vital by the States as a whole.

Early in 1937, the emissaries submitted their reports to the Viceroy. They indicated that the rulers were in a bargaining mood and suggested many far-reaching concessions to induce them to join the federation. The rulers also sent their replies to the Viceroy stating the terms on which alone they were prepared to come in. The next few months were spent in an exhaustive examination of the points raised in the reports of the emissaries and in the replies of the rulers.

In May 1937 the Secretary of State (the Marquess of Zetland) had informal talks with a number of rulers and Indian politicians who happened to be in England. It was his impression that the rulers generally were unwilling to enter the federation; that the Viceroy was dealing with unwilling sellers and in consequence was tempted to put his offers high; that the position would be different if the rulers were able to see that they would be safer inside the federation than out of it. Moreover, there was a risk in negotiating with individual States on particular items. A concession on an individual item to a particular State might have comparatively small importance, but the cumulative effect of granting it all round might be highly prejudicial to the interests of federation. The Secretary of State suggested therefore that it would be better first to decide provisionally under each item the maximum concessions which could be offered consistently with a real federation and then to settle (in the case of major States whose accession would be necessary for the federation) *all* the concessions under the main heads which could be offered to each of them. The right time for making such an aggregate offer would, he thought, require careful consideration.

Lord Linlithgow, on the other hand, was most keen that no slackness in the negotiations should be allowed to creep in or any disturbance made in the plan for securing federation at the earliest possible moment. The feeling among the general run of the States was one of more or less reluctant acceptance of the inevitable, whilst, among the 'diehard' minority, opposition to the federation scheme and a desire to infect waverers with their intransigent attitude was as strong as ever. It was therefore most essential that negotiations should not be held up. He considered that the best course would be, as soon as agreement was reached with the India Office on any particular issue, to communicate the substance of the conclusions reached to each State through the local political officer.

Apart from details of procedure, the most difficult issue which presented itself for consideration related to certain fiscal rights enjoyed by States which would be lost to them if they joined the federation. Certain States were deriving considerable revenue from items of taxation included in the Federal List; e.g. the Kathiawar States and Kashmir[1] in regard to customs and States like Mysore and Ranpur in regard to sugar excise, while almost all States to some extent shared in the match excise pool. Other items of revenue derived by States were in respect of corporation tax and salt.

In the course of the tour of the emissaries, the rulers (including those of all the major States) demanded recognition of their right to retain their existing revenues from these sources. This demand led the emissaries to enunciate the principle of *status quo*, which meant that, in return for full accession on these subjects, the rulers would be assured permanently of the revenue they obtained from those sources. Lord Linlithgow felt that, if federation meant an immediate sacrifice of revenue, it would have no attraction for the States; that the principle of *status quo* in regard to such fiscal items should therefore be conceded even if an amendment of the Government of India Act of 1935 was found necessary for the purpose.

The Secretary of State, on the other hand, was opposed to the proposal as it would involve a permanent and material alteration in the interests of the States to the prejudice of British India. Such concessions were incompatible with the general scheme of federation

[1] The State of Jammu and Kashmir was entitled to a rebate on all goods transmitted in bond from seaports in British India to that State.

and would arouse most damaging controversy both in Britain and in India. Though the Secretary of State was alive to the difficulty of persuading the rulers to come in under the Act as it stood and was prepared for a temporary alleviation of the conditions designed to bridge the States in the transition from their present position to the scheme of federation, he was emphatic that any such amendment must leave the scheme of the Act inviolate. Nor was he prepared to move such amendments unless he could be assured that, if made, they would bring in the rulers. Indeed, he was certain that no amendment of the Act, or of the instrument of accession, could maintain the States in an unduly preferential position in the federation indefinitely or indeed for very long.

When they found that the Secretary of State was not prepared to go to the extent of amending the Act to maintain the principle of *status quo*, the Political Department proceeded to examine how best the rulers' demands could be met within the four corners of the Act. There were further discussions and consultations, the course of which it would be tedious to follow in detail. Most of the States continued to put forward extravagant demands. Hyderabad wanted satisfaction on the question of Berar and, while refusing to accede on several important items, was prepared to accede on others subject only to severe limitations. Mysore and Indore, which were levying corporation tax, were anxious to continue to do so permanently, and not for ten years only as provided in the Act. States having agreements on salt refused to accede on that subject. One of the limitations suggested, with particular reference to the match excise, went so far as to propose an amendment of Section 140 of the Government of India Act (which empowered the Federal Legislature in the imposition of excise duties, to determine the amount and to lay down the principles of distribution of such duties) so as to guarantee the States the *status quo* position, under which all States got a share of the proceeds of match excise whether matches were produced in the State or not and, even where matches were produced, the payment made bore no relation to the quantity of matches produced in the State. There were some rulers who even suggested that the Federal Government should not directly exercise any administrative functions in their States, but that all such functions should devolve on State governments or authorities as agents of the Government of India.

Instead of putting a brake on the never-ceasing demands of the rulers and stressing the advantages to be gained by their entering the federation, the Political Department seemed to spend its time more in emphasizing the loss the rulers would suffer if they were to federate and in instituting a search for expedients wherewith to make good or mitigate that loss. The result was a tendency to give in to the rulers all along the line.

Little or no progress could be achieved in the negotiations with the rulers and the position threatened to become stagnant. The Secretary of State was naturally anxious. He suggested to the Viceroy that progress could only be made by confronting the rulers with the full terms of the offer in a published form so as to leave them in no doubt that it was in fact a final offer in respect of essentials. Sir Hawthorne Lewis, then Reforms Commissioner, welcomed this suggestion. He held that the publication of the offer and the public comment that was likely to follow might convince the rulers, as private negotiations could hardly do, that the terms offered were not to be despised; and the result might well be to make them hasten to accept where otherwise they might hesitate. The Political Department, however, was opposed to the proposal and it was finally dropped.

The rulers and their ministers met in conference at Bombay in November 1938. While reiterating their faith in the idea of an all-India federation, they stressed the need for specific and effective safeguards without which 'the rulers and their successors would find themselves unable, in the fast changing circumstances of the country, to duly discharge their duties to the Crown, to their dynasties and to their peoples.'

The Viceroy at last decided to confront the rulers with the final offer. Accordingly, in January 1939, he addressed a circular letter to the rulers of all the salute States, enclosing the revised drafts of the general clauses of the instrument of accession, the three schedules to the instrument and the draft acceptance of His Majesty. The letter emphasized that there was no prospect of any substantial variation of the terms indicated in the direction of allowing a lesser measure of accession than that which was shown therein, or of modifying or adding to the limitations specified. The rulers were asked to inform the Viceroy within six months whether they would be prepared to execute instruments of accession within those terms.

The reply came sooner than was expected. At a second conference of rulers and States' ministers held in Bombay, the following resolution was passed:

The Conference of Princes and Ministers assembled at Bombay, having considered the revised draft of the instrument of accession and connected papers, resolves that the terms on the basis of which accession is offered are fundamentally unsatisfactory in the directions indicated in the report of the Hydari Committee of Ministers and confirmed by the recommendations of the Gwalior Conference and are therefore unacceptable. At the same time, the Conference records its belief that it could not be the intention of His Majesty's Government to close the door on all-India federation.

The attitude of the rulers at the Bombay Conference did not come as a surprise. The methods adopted by some of the States' representatives are worthy of note. In the formal meetings of the rulers and States' representatives, they would not take a definite stand one way or the other; but subsequently, they would run up to the Political Department and plead for further concessions so that they could 'bring round the reasonable section of the rulers.' The Political Department would then get busy to convert the Viceroy to these demands; and there was thus a merry-go-round of demands and concessions.

After the Bombay Conference, the States' representatives followed their usual tactics. The Dewan of a prominent State went to the Political Adviser and told him that, if a guarantee could be given in respect of the customs rights of Baroda and the maritime States of Kathiawar, as well as Kashmir, there was every likelihood that those States would agree to join the federation. It was suggested that, if they came in, others would follow suit. This new proposal was seized on with alacrity and Lord Linlithgow suggested to the Secretary of State that it was essential that some major States should be encouraged to give a definite lead in the matter of accession; that Hyderabad and Mysore had more or less turned their backs on federation, but that he had good reason to believe that both Kashmir and Baroda would be ready to accede if only they were allowed to safeguard in their instruments of accession their rights in respect of customs and other financial matters. With Kashmir and Baroda and the maritime States of Kathiawar reassured on this particular issue, his firm opinion was that the tide would turn strongly in favour of federation.

The Secretary of State found much to object to in these proposals. He wanted to know whether it was the Viceroy's intention to protect by limitation certain selected treaty rights of only certain selected States and otherwise to maintain refusal to this method of protecting

6

States' rights in general. And how precisely was this to be done? Apart from practical and tactical difficulties the task of redrafting many of the treaty rights of the rulers in such a manner as to make them justiciable by the Federal Court would be almost impossible. One had to consider the effect on the attitude of British India of embedding permanently in the constitution provisions which would be regarded as distinctly anti-federal. Moreover, legal protection of that kind could not in the end withstand the play of political forces, and the maximum of friction would be generated if those forces could establish equilibrium only by breaches of the constitution. Finally he enquired whether, assuming the feasibility of the plan, the Viceroy was satisfied that the result would be to ensure a sufficient proportion of States to enable federation to be established.

No such assurance was forthcoming. Federation was still as distant as ever. Such was the position towards the beginning of August 1939.

In the meantime, the provincial part of the Government of India Act of 1935 had been put into operation and elections to the provincial legislatures had been held in 1937. The Congress had swept the polls in six provinces and in July of that year had formed ministries. A little later, with the support of a few independent members, Congress ministries were also formed in two other provinces, viz. Assam and the North-West Frontier Province.

The overwhelming success of the Congress encouraged States' subjects to agitate for civil liberties and responsible government. There was unrest in Mysore, Travancore, Kashmir, Hyderabad, Jaipur, Rajkot and the Orissa States, to name only a few. In the Orissa States, there was an outbreak of lawlessness, and in Ranpur the Political Agent, Major Bazalgette, was murdered. In Mysore, the agitation reached a high pitch. In October 1937 the All-India Congress Committee, meeting at Calcutta, censured the Mysore Government in the sharpest terms for its policy of repression and appealed to the people of Indian States and British India 'to give all support and encouragement to the people of Mysore in the struggle against the State for the right of self-determination.'

Gandhiji was not happy over this resolution and criticized it in the columns of the *Harijan* as going against the Congress creed of non-interference with States. Gandhiji's view was welcomed by Government circles; but in January 1938, he threatened to make Jaipur an all-India issue when Jamnalal Bajaj, one of his close associates, was arrested. Gandhiji declared that the Congress would be neglecting its duty if it allowed the spirit of the people of Jaipur to be crushed for want of support from the Congress. In February 1938, at the Haripura session of the Congress, a fuller though more moderately worded resolution was passed. The Congress reiterated its objective of standing for the same political, social and economic freedom in the States as in the case of the rest of India, and of considering the States as integral parts of India. The Congress, the resolution continued, was not yet able to obtain the liberation of the States' subjects by itself operating within their borders. In the existing conditions, 'the burden of carrying on the struggle for freedom must fall on the people of the States.' Only false hopes would be raised if they relied on extraneous help or assistance or on the prestige of the Congress name. The Congress as an organization could only offer moral support and sympathy. Individual Congressmen would be free to render further assistance in their individual capacities, but the Congress committees which had come into existence in the States 'must submit to the control of the Working Committee and must not engage in politics under the Congress name.'

This resolution was intended to soft-pedal the agitation in the States. But it was not easy even for Gandhiji to draw a *khadi* curtain screening the States from the general mass awakening. A radical left-wing had by this time developed within the Congress; and it pleaded for a revolutionary policy in regard to the States. Meanwhile individual Congressmen started leading the agitation in the States themselves. The All-India Congress Committee meeting in Delhi in September 1938 condemned repression in Travancore, Hyderabad, Kashmir and the Orissa States. The Congress ministries of provinces adjoining States declined to use their statutory powers to prevent agitation being organized within their provinces and launched beyond them. The situation was compared to the form of 'non-intervention' practised in the civil war in Spain. On 3 December 1938, Gandhiji acclaimed the simultaneous awakening in the States as due to the 'time spirit' and declared that there was no half-way house between total extinction of the States and full responsible government. Referring to a rumour that the British Government would go back on a statement made by Lord Winterton in Parliament about the right of rulers to grant responsible government to their people, he announced that any such recantation would 'precipitate a first-class crisis whose magnitude it is difficult to foretell.'

Alluding to the excesses committed by the States' police in suppressing agitation, he claimed that ministers in the provinces had the moral right and duty to take notice of gross misrule in the States, and to advise the paramount power on what should be done. He then gave warning that the Congress policy of non-interference might be abandoned; and he advised the rulers to cultivate friendly relations 'with an organization which bids fair in the future, not very distant, to replace the paramount power — let me hope, by friendly arrangement.'

Lord Linlithgow realized that unless some radical reforms were brought about in the States, it would only be a question of time before they succumbed to the Congress agitation. The bigger States were capable of looking after themselves; it was the future of the middle-sized and small States about which he was anxious. He felt that, with regard to the latter, the policy of abstention from interference which the British Government had for some years pursued could no longer be defended and should be abandoned; that active pressure should be brought to bear on these States to effect administrative reform, such as improving the quality of the officials; removing obsolete and vexatious imposts; limiting the privy purse to ten per cent of the total revenue of the States; ensuring that the finances were maintained on a sound basis, and the publishing of an annual budget and administration report. On the constitutional level, Lord Linlithgow wanted to bring stronger pressure to bear on the rulers than had hitherto been the case in the matter of sponsoring representative institutions and establishing some form of constitutional government within the States. But these proposals were not to the taste of the Political Department. They were doubtful about the case for representative forms of government in the States and felt that something on the lines of the *panchayat* system devised in Jodhpur and elsewhere would adequately meet the case. They were against the rulers being hustled in the matter of constitutional advance; and were of the opinion that the question should be left to the Chamber of Princes.

The Secretary of State was in agreement with Lord Linlithgow's proposals as regards administrative reforms. But on the vital issue of constitutional advance he considered that, on both political and practical grounds, the initiative and onus of responsibility must continue to rest with the rulers themselves. He felt that constitutional development in the States once begun could not in the nature of things be regulated and limited in the same way as administrative advance and that no policy conceived by the British Government could by itself maintain the rulers or ensure against their eventual capitulation to Congress agitation.

It was at this stage that the second World War broke out. The position then was that, owing to the unyielding attitude of the rulers, as well as of the major political parties in British India, the federal scheme was at its last gasp. The Hindu Mahasabha was the only political organization which had all along supported it. The Congress and the Muslim League were opposed to the federal scheme for different reasons. The Congress wanted radical changes to be made in the scheme of the Act. For instance, it was dissatisfied with the degree of responsible government at the centre and it urged that the States' representatives in the federal legislature should be elected and not nominated. There was a small section of Congressmen who were not unwilling to give federation a trial; but they were powerless against the majority.

The second World War had come and the Empire needed the help of the rulers in men, money and material. It was not the time to rub them the wrong way. On 11 September 1939, Lord Linlithgow announced in his address to both Houses of the Central Legislature that, while federation remained as before the objective of His Majesty's Government, 'the compulsion of the present international situation and the fact that, given the necessity for concentrating on the emergency that confronts us, we have no choice but to hold in suspense the work in connexion with preparations for federation.' This marked the close of a crucial chapter in the modern history of India. What a colossal waste of money and energy expended over a period of twelve years! But as in a Greek tragedy, events were inexorably shaping the climax.

III

THE PARTING GIFT

THE weeks following India's entry into the war were full of feverish activity. Lord Linlithgow had interviews with leaders of the various political parties in the country. On 18 October 1939 he issued a statement repeating the 'clear and positive' policy of His Majesty's Government that Dominion Status was the natural issue of India's progress. He announced that at the end of the war consultations would be held with representatives of the several communities, parties and interests in India, and with the Indian rulers, with a view to securing their aid and co-operation in the framing of such modifications in the details of the plan embodied in the Government of India Act of 1935 as might seem desirable. He also announced his intention to set up a consultative group, representative of all major political parties in British India and of the rulers, to bring about a closer association of India with the prosecution of the war. Nothing came of this declaration as both the Congress and the Muslim League rejected the Viceroy's offer. The Congress ministries in seven provinces had already resigned and the administration had been taken over by the Governors. In Assam, too, the Congress ministers resigned but an alternative ministry was formed.

The implications of the Viceroy's statement, so far as the States were concerned, were discussed with him by the Standing Committee of the Chamber of Princes on 25 January 1940. The rulers demanded that no commitment affecting their rights or interests should be made without their consent. Lord Linlithgow undertook to honour in full the treaty obligations of His Majesty's Government. Subsequently, at a meeting of the Chamber of Princes held in March 1940, the rulers declared their determination to render every possible assistance to His Majesty's Government in the prosecution of the war and their complete approval of the war aims of the Allies. At the same time, they demanded the preservation of their autonomy and the protection of their rights in any future constitution of India.

The communal situation by this time had considerably deteriorated and no understanding could be brought about between the two major communities. In January 1940, Jinnah declared that the Hindus and the Muslims formed two separate nations, and that both must share the governance of their common motherland. Three months later, at the Lahore session of the Muslim League, he declared that the Muslim nation must have a separate independent State of Pakistan. In all subsequent discussions on constitutional advance this attitude on the part of Jinnah and the Muslim League was the dominant factor.

The war entered its acute phase with the fall of France. Neville Chamberlain resigned and Winston Churchill formed a National Coalition Government in which L. S. Amery became the Secretary of State for India. On 8 August 1940, Lord Linlithgow advanced some new proposals on behalf of His Majesty's Government. He offered a certain number of seats in the Governor-General's Executive Council to representative Indians. He also proposed that a War Advisory Council should be established containing representatives of the States and of British India. Lastly, he promised that after the conclusion of the war, a body representative of the 'principal elements in India's national life' would be called upon to devise the framework of a new constitution. This offer was subject to the proviso that 'they could not contemplate transfer of their present responsibilities for the peace and welfare of India to any system of government whose authority is directly denied by large and powerful elements in India's national life.' The Congress rejected the offer; the Muslim League followed suit. Nevertheless, on 22 July 1941 the number of members of the Governor-General's Executive Council was increased from seven to twelve. The members of the Executive Council till then had been four Europeans and three Indians. In the new Council, the number of Indian members was eight, chosen from among British Indian politicians who owed no allegiance either to the Congress or the Muslim League. The same day, a National Defence Council consisting of twenty-two members from British India and nine representatives of the States was set up, but it attracted little or no attention.

After the rejection of the 'August Offer', the British Government for over eighteen months made no further overtures to the political parties. But towards the close of 1941, the war situation had changed for the worse. Germany was knocking at the gates of Stalingrad. On 7 December Japan entered the field of war and within the incredibly short period of twelve weeks won remarkable success against what the Japanese propagandists called the A.B.C.D. Powers — America, Britain, China and the Dutch. Singapore surrendered on 15 February 1942. By then Japanese naval units were already harassing British shipping in the Bay of Bengal. On 7 March Rangoon fell to the Japanese and with their troops fanning across Burma, India was brought direct into the zone of war.

On 11 March 1942 Churchill declared in the House of Commons that 'the crisis in the affairs of India arising out of the Japanese advance has made Britain wish to rally all the forces of Indian life to guard their land from the menace of this invader.' He announced that the War Cabinet was sending out Sir Stafford Cripps, then Lord Privy Seal, to India with a set of proposals approved by the Cabinet in order to remove the doubts and apprehensions in the minds of the Indian parties and to convince their leaders how those proposals constituted a far-reaching advance towards satisfying Indian aspirations. Churchill made it clear however that the proposals which Sir Stafford Cripps was bringing were 'to be accepted as a whole or rejected as a whole.'

Sir Stafford Cripps arrived in India on 22 March and on 29 March revealed his proposals at a press conference. The Cripps offer consisted of two parts. The long-term plan postulated that immediately after the cessation of hostilities a constitution-making body would be set up to frame the constitution of a new Indian Union which would have the full status of a Dominion with the power to secede, if it chose, from the British Commonwealth. This body would be elected by an electoral college consisting of the members of the lower houses of the provincial legislatures for which fresh elections would be held. The British Government undertook to accept and implement forthwith the constitution framed by this body on two conditions. Firstly, any province or provinces which were not prepared to accept the new constitution would be entitled to frame by a similar process a constitution of their own giving them the same full status as the Indian Union. The second condition was that a treaty should be negotiated between the British Government and the constitution-making body to cover all matters arising out of the transfer of responsibility, particularly the protection of racial and religious minorities.

Until the new constitution was framed the British Government 'desire and invite the immediate and effective participation of the leaders of the principal sections of the Indian people in the councils of their country, of the Commonwealth and of the United Nations.'

So far as the States were concerned, the Cripps declaration was very brief. It stated 'whether or not an individual State elects to adhere to the constitution, it will be necessary to negotiate a revision of its treaty arrangements so far as this may be required in the new situation.' The States were to appoint representatives to the constitution-making body in the same proportion to their total population as in the case of representatives of British India as a whole and with the same powers as British Indian members. The States would be free to adhere or not to the new constitution.

The rulers were not associated with the Cripps discussions in the same way as the representatives of British India. The immediate object of Sir Stafford Cripps was to make possible the formation of a war-time government at the centre consisting of representatives of British Indian parties. The rulers, though interested, were not directly affected; but the scheme for making a new constitution after the war applied to all-India and with that they were deeply concerned.

The rulers met Sir Stafford Cripps on 2 April 1942. The Jam Saheb of Nawanagar, then Chancellor of the Chamber of Princes, the late Maharajah Sir Sadul Singh of Bikaner and Maharajah Sir Yadavindra Singh of Patiala represented the rulers and the Nawab of Chhatari represented the Nizam. The rulers raised several points for elucidation.

The first point raised was whether in the event of a number of States not finding it feasible to adhere to the Union, such States or groups of States would have the right to form a Union of their own with full sovereign status. Regarding this Sir Stafford said that personally he did not see any fundamental difficulty in the suggestion but as that situation had not been considered in connexion with the present scheme he was not able to give a definite reply. Some searching questions were then asked regarding the implications of adherence to the Union, such as whether the people of the State would become subjects of the Union; whether the Union would acquire paramountcy over the States; and whether it would be possible for a State to join the Union while reserving the dynastic and personal

7

affairs of the ruler to the exclusive jurisdiction of the Crown. The replies given were to the effect that everything would depend upon the nature of the arrangements actually made. In any case, it was definite that the British Government did not contemplate transferring the paramountcy of the Crown to any other party. The adherence of a State to the Union would have the effect of automatically dissolving the Crown's obligations to it. On the other hand, paramountcy would continue to be in force in the case of States which did not join the Union.

Another point raised was whether in the case of non-adhering States the Crown would continue to retain its obligations towards them and would enforce them through the usual sanctions. Sir Stafford Cripps replied that this was so; the British Government would provide for everything necessary to implement their treaty obligations to those States which did not join the Union. This would include the use of force in the last resort, although he was not willing to commit himself about the conditions under which such sanctions would be operated.

Some of the rulers were not clear why it was said that whether a State joined the Union or not, its entire treaties with the British Government would have to be revised. Sir Stafford Cripps explained that the intention was to revise the treaties only so far as might be required in the new situation. The provision was primarily intended to deal with those economic matters of common concern to British India and the States which were likely to be affected by the transfer of power to British India. Treaties affecting paramountcy and protection of the States would not be revised without the consent of the States concerned. Sir Stafford proposed to make this clear in a letter to the Chancellor. The question was then asked whether the proposed Union would be limited to geographically contiguous units. The reply given was that ordinarily it should be so, unless some practical arrangement was made with the intervening Union or unit; the British Government could not, however, be expected to coerce any party into such arrangements although their good offices would be available to resolve differences.

Replying to another question Sir Stafford Cripps said that it was the intention to give full freedom to all provincial units and the States to come into the new Union or to stay out. The British Government did not desire to stay in India unless the Indian peoples wanted them in their interest to stay and except to the extent that it might be unavoidable for the fulfilment of the British Government's treaty obligations to the non-adhering States.

One of the rulers asked whether in view of the impending developments the Indian Princes should make contact with the major political parties in British India. Sir Stafford replied that this was a matter for the Viceroy, but he himself thought that the Princes would be well advised to make such contacts. He had discussed the matter informally with the Viceroy, who was sympathetic to that view.

Sir Stafford emphasized that if the Indian peoples were sufficiently reasonable and broadminded it should be possible for them all to come into a single Union. Otherwise they could have separate Unions and suffer the inconvenience involved. He suggested that the first step for the smaller States should be to get into groups or into federal relations amongst themselves and that, for this purpose, the spirit of the scheme for co-operative grouping should be extended to wider units, particularly in matters of common industrial and economic interests, so that the States were not left behind British India and might pull their full weight in the development of India as a whole. This was a matter which the rulers would be well advised to discuss with the Viceroy.

Subsequently, in a letter written on 3 April, the Nawab of Chhatari raised some important issues on behalf of the Nizam. To these, Sir Stafford Cripps replied on 5 April as follows:

I have received your letter of the 3rd April in which you are kind enough to convey to me the views of His Exalted Highness in regard to the proposals which I have been discussing with the leaders of Indian opinion. I fear, however, that there are some points on which there appears to have been some misunderstanding at our interview. It is the case that His Exalted Highness will be free to decide whether Hyderabad should adhere or not adhere to any Indian Union which might be set up under these proposals if they are given effect. If, however, His Exalted Highness decided that Hyderabad should not adhere, the relations at present subsisting between the Crown and His Exalted Highness would remain unchanged and His Exalted Highness would not be free, as suggested in your letter, to cease to maintain them. Any revision of the existing treaty arrangements which might be required as a result of the creation of a new Indian Union would be by negotiation between the paramount power and His Exalted Highness and clearly might involve modification of particular treaty rights in the light of the new situation. The question whether any particular point which might be difficult to resolve by negotiation should be submitted to arbitration would be for the paramount power to decide and I can give no assurances at this stage in regard to it.

The rulers were watching the reactions of the British Indian parties to the Cripps offer. By 9 April it was generally known that both the Congress and the League were about to reject it. The rulers did not want to embarrass His Majesty's Government. The Indian States' delegation met on 10 April and adopted the following resolution which was conveyed to Sir Stafford Cripps:

The Indian States will be glad as always, in the interest of their motherland, to make their contribution in every reasonable manner compatible with the sovereignty and integrity of the States, towards the framing of a constitution for India. The States should be assured, however, that in the event of a number of States not finding it feasible to adhere, the non-adhering States or groups of States, so desiring, would have the right to form a union of their own, with full sovereign status in accordance with a suitable and agreed procedure devised for the purpose.

The Cripps offer was rejected by both the Congress Working Committee and by the Muslim League on 10 April. On 12 April Sir Stafford Cripps left for London, his mission a failure. The rulers heaved an almost audible sigh of relief. The Prime Minister of a major State wrote to Sir Henry Craik, then Political Adviser: 'I see a lot of expressions of deep sorrow in the press on the failure of the mission which has been described as a great tragedy. Personally I feel that we escaped one very narrowly.'

The Cripps mission brought home to the rulers the discomforting realization that if the interests of British India and the States came into conflict His Majesty's Government would almost certainly let down the States. Also, at about this time Jawaharlal Nehru declared, in the course of a speech, that treaties with the States must be scrapped and he dubbed those who talked of them as 'lunatics, knaves or fools.' The rulers therefore started devising ways to protect their own position and to get a positive assurance from His Majesty's Government that they would not be sacrificed on the altar of British Indian interests. The Chancellor of the Chamber of Princes wrote to the Political Adviser on 1 June 1942 raising this and other important points concerning the position of rulers in the future constitutional set-up.

This letter was the subject of prolonged discussion between the Viceroy and the Secretary of State. A reply was sent by the Political Department in January 1943. The Chancellor had requested His

Majesty's Government for an authoritative statement that they stood true to and firmly by their treaty obligations to the States and would continue to protect them according to their solemn obligations. In their reply, the Political Department pointed out that the literal interpretation of treaties had long been affected by usage and sufferance and must become increasingly related to the manner in which the States adapted themselves to the necessities of the changing times, more particularly in the matter of pooling of powers and resources for the purpose of raising the quality and stability of their public services. Subject to this consideration the rulers were assured that the fulfilment of the fundamental obligations[1] arising out of their treaties and *sanads* remained an integral part of the policy of His Majesty's Government.

The second point raised by the Chancellor in his letter related to the suggestion of Sir Stafford Cripps that an effective machinery should be established in the States for ventilating the legitimate wants and grievances of the people. The Chancellor had pointed out that the suggestion of Sir Stafford Cripps was in direct conflict with the unequivocal declaration on this subject made on behalf of His Majesty's Government by the Viceroy, at the session of the Chamber of Princes held in 1939, that the decision as to the constitution best suited to the needs of his people and his State rested with the ruler himself and that no pressure would be brought to bear on him in this respect by the paramount power. The rulers wanted to be reassured that the suggestion of Sir Stafford Cripps did not in any way affect this solemn assurance made on behalf of His Majesty's Government. The Political Department replied that His Majesty's Government endorsed Sir Stafford Cripps' suggestion not so much in their own interests as in the interests of the rulers themselves. But it was for the latter to devise the precise form of machinery best suited to achieve that object.

The Chancellor had pointed out that, according to the Cripps declaration, provinces were given the option to form a Union of their own, but that the States were not accorded the same privilege. The reply emphasized that the reason for it was to be found in the fact that the direct responsibility exercised by His Majesty's Government in regard to the administration of British India found no parallel

[1] The Crown's undertaking to the States covered broadly (a) protection of their territories against external aggression; (b) protection of their dynasties against internal disruption and (c) protection of certain rights of a primarily economic character in respect e.g. of salt, posts and telegraphs, customs, currency.

within the territories of the rulers. The suggestion presented considerable practical difficulties; the recognition of any such Union would fundamentally affect the nature of the present relationship of individual States with the Crown.

The reply concluded with the observation that the Cripps declaration, which was in very general terms, had, for reasons with which the rulers were familiar, proved abortive; and that though the main principles of that offer stood, the form and nature of their application was a matter for the future.

Lord Linlithgow had always taken a consistent attitude towards the rulers. He was against doing anything that would alarm or dishearten them. The rulers, in his opinion, were the only solid and dependable element so far as the British relationship with India was concerned. He gravely questioned the wisdom of antagonizing for no good purpose the only element in which the British Government could feel any substantial confidence, particularly when they were under binding obligations to that element.

Much adverse criticism had appeared at the time in a section of the Indian press about the demand of the rulers that the non-acceding States should be allowed to form a Union of their own. It was alleged that the rulers had been instigated to make this demand by the Political Department with the connivance of the Viceroy. When the matter came up for consideration, the Secretary of State felt at first blush that the question was one which must be faced, however reluctantly, and that the rulers' suggestion deserved sympathetic consideration. H. V. Hodson, my predecessor as Reforms Commissioner, and later I myself, opposed the proposal. Lord Linlithgow accepted our advice and told the Secretary of State that a separate Union of States was just not practical politics and that it was not worth wasting time considering it. He was emphatic that it would be disingenuous to encourage the States to go on thinking along those lines.

Before we take leave of Lord Linlithgow, I should mention one particularly important matter, namely the problem of the small States. Apart from the Western and the Central India Agencies, the problem was most acute in the Eastern States Agency and to a somewhat less degree in the Deccan States Agency and the Punjab Hill States. These States were all lumped together in Division XVII of the Table appended to the First Schedule to the Government of India Act of 1935. The federal offer which the Crown Representative sent to the bigger States was not sent to the rulers of these States. The objective at the time was to establish an all-India federation with provinces and viable States first, and to deal with the small States subsequently.

The Secretary of State thought that there were three obstacles to the inclusion of these States in a federation as separate units. In the first place, their economic resources were insufficient to meet the cost of an administration attuned to the standard which the inhabitants would expect from comparison with that obtaining in British India or in the larger States. Secondly, their officials (who were poorly paid and inadequately trained) would be incapable of administering federal law. Lastly, it was in the interest of important political elements in British India to associate with the people of the States in the constitutional struggle and to procure for them a decisive voice in their own State's administration as well as direct representation at the Centre. In the bigger States, such as Hyderabad and Mysore, it might be possible to control such agitation and keep it within constitutional limits, but in the smaller States, particularly where the people were primitive (as in the Orissa States included in the Eastern States Agency), violence was apt to call for repressive measures which were beyond the unaided resources of the State administration and would necessitate the intervention of the paramount power. Such intervention would inevitably be misrepresented in British India as an attempt to buttress oppression.

The solution proposed by the Secretary of State, in brief, was that, where smaller States could not be merged in bigger States (a process to which there were obvious limitations), the separate jurisdiction of individual rulers should be replaced by the single administration of the Viceroy. He suggested that the Orissa States should be selected for this experiment in the first instance.

The Secretary of State thought that it was unnecessary to consider what would be the ultimate political status of any such newly formed units. It was conceivable that they might continue for some time to be administered by the Viceroy and it did not seem unlikely that their ultimate destiny would be merger with British India.

Lord Linlithgow felt that even if the scheme was free from objections, he would still hesitate, in war conditions and at a time when the larger constitutional questions were postponed by common consent till after the conclusion of hostilities, to embark upon far-reaching changes in the relations of the Crown with the rulers of the small States involving large-scale reactions throughout the entire princely order and in British India. In Lord Linlithgow's view, the best plan for the solution of the problem was to continue to carry out the policy that he was pursuing. The two methods he had been adopting were (a) the administrative absorption of a small entity in a large neighbouring State; (b) the combination of smaller units for administrative purposes. The first of these two solutions was particularly suitable for insignificant entities, largely non-jurisdictional or semi-jurisdictional, such as those which existed in large numbers in the Western India States Agency and the Gujarat States Agency where the Viceroy was doing all he could to bring this process of absorption into effect. The same expedient was being pursued in the case of a very few small States in Rajputana and Central India. The second method furnished the only possible solution for such States as the majority of the Eastern and the Deccan States and certain small States in the Central India and the Punjab Agencies which, though small and unimportant, were definitely of a much higher calibre than the minute entities of Kathiawar.

The ultimate result of all these discussions was the Attachment Scheme of 1943, under which certain semi-jurisdictional States in Kathiawar and Gujarat were attached to the neighbouring States. Collectively the area covered about 7,000 square miles, with a population of 8 lakhs and an annual revenue of about Rs 70 lakhs.

In the meantime, on 8 August 1942, the Congress had passed the 'Quit India' resolution and been outlawed in consequence. On 24 October 1943, Lord Linlithgow retired and Lord Wavell came in his place.

By the end of 1944 events had taken a different shape. The epic defence of Stalingrad had halted Hitler, and his armies were thrown on the defensive. Japan had been effectively checked. It looked as though victory was only a question of time. There was intense frustration in the country and a complete lull in political activity. About this time the Nawab of Bhopal was elected Chancellor of the Chamber of Princes. He infused new life into the Chamber and forged that body into an effective instrument for developing the rulers into a 'Third Force' in Indian politics. He was an advocate of a loose centre with residuary powers in the States. With such a centre and with the Congress and the Muslim League pitted against each other, the States would occupy a key position and hold the balance.

The Nawab of Bhopal now started taking vigorous steps with the Political Department to safeguard the position of the States in any future constitutional changes. At a meeting of the Standing Committee held on 18 September 1944, the Chancellor gave notice of his intention to move the following resolution at the session of the Chamber to be held early in December:

The Chamber of Princes considers it necessary to reiterate in the most unequivocal and emphatic terms that the Crown's relationship with the States and the Crown's power in respect of the States cannot and should not be transferred to any third party or other authority without the consent of the States concerned. The Chamber requests His Excellency the Crown Representative to be pleased to convey to His Majesty's Government the grave misgivings and apprehensions aroused in the States, by the recent tendency to alter the States' relationship with the Crown and to qualify the observance of the Crown's obligations, by unilateral action without the consent of the States, notwithstanding the solemn Royal pronouncements that these Treaty Rights shall be maintained unimpaired and the recent assurance conveyed to the Indian Princes by His Majesty's Government that the fulfilment of the fundamental obligations arising out of their treaties and sanads remains an integral part of His Majesty's Government's policy.

On 26 November 1944 Lord Wavell, as the President of the Chamber, disallowed this resolution on the ground that it would be undesirable at any time to ventilate in public the subject matter of the resolution with the very delicate issues which arose out of it, more so at a time when the matter had already come under discussion between the rulers and the Viceroy. This, coupled with the replies which the Chancellor had received from the Political Department with regard to some other points which he had raised, gave dissatisfaction to the Standing Committee. Early in December, they resigned in a body as a protest against the 'gradual deterioration of the position of the States and the disregard of their legitimate interests.' On 4 December, eighty rulers met informally at Delhi under the chairmanship of the Maharajah of Gwalior and endorsed the stand taken by the Standing Committee. Lord Wavell, who was anxious to placate the rulers, met the Chancellor and had long discussions with him. Finally, on 25 June 1945, Lord Wavell gave an assurance that there would be no future transference of relationship of the States with the Crown to any other authority without their consent, provided the rulers on their part gave the assurance that their consent to any changes which emerged as a result of negotiations would

8

not be unreasonably withheld. The Chancellor had no hesitation in declaring that the rulers had no intention of withholding their consent to any adjustment which might be required under the future constitutional arrangements in India and which 'we consider reasonable in the wider interests of India.' The Standing Committee thereupon decided to withdraw their resignation.

In March 1945 Lord Wavell flew to London for consultations with the British Cabinet. He returned at the end of May. In the meantime, history had taken a flying leap and a series of explosive events had rocked the world. On 1 May, the Hamburg Radio announced the death of Adolf Hitler and within a week General Jodl signed the unconditional surrender of Germany. On the eve of Lord Wavell's departure from England, the Secretary of State informed the House of Commons that the British Government had empowered Lord Wavell to make new proposals on the composition of an interim government. In a broadcast on 15 June Lord Wavell disclosed a fresh plan designed to 'ease the present political situation and to advance India towards her goal of self-government.' He added that the measures proposed were provisional and were intended to mobilize the forces of India against Japan and to draft a new constitution. Meanwhile the Cripps offer, it was stated, remained in the field. Simultaneously with the announcement of his plan, Lord Wavell invited the leaders of the Congress and of the Muslim League, as well as others to Simla for further discussions. The members of the Congress Working Committee who were then in detention were released so that the Congress could take part in the talks. The Conference met on 30 June but failed to reach agreement. The negotiations broke down finally on 14 July.

The Labour Party withdrew from the Coalition Government in Britain after V. E. day, thus forcing an early general election, in which the Conservatives were defeated. On 26 July 1945 the Labour Party was invited to form a new government. Attlee became Prime Minister and Lord Pethick-Lawrence assumed the duties of Secretary of State for India. In September of the same year, Lord Wavell went again to England and on his return announced his second plan. The announcement reaffirmed the Government's determination to do their utmost in conjunction with the leaders of Indian opinion to promote the early realization of full self-government for India; and expressed the hope that political leaders would assume ministerial responsibility in all the provinces after the elections which had already been announced. It declared that His Majesty's Government intended to convene as soon as possible a constitution-making body to draft the future constitution of India but, as a preliminary step, the Viceroy had been authorized to consult the representatives of the provincial assemblies as to whether the concrete proposals in the Cripps declaration required any modification. 'Discussions will be undertaken with the representatives of the Indian States with a view to ascertain in what way they can best take their part in the constitution-making body.' The question arose as to who should represent the States. The Congress insisted that only popular representatives who had been elected on a wide franchise could represent them, while an important ruler went to the length of asserting: 'We fought and sacrificed our blood to win power and we mean to hold it. If Congress wants to rob us, if the British should let us down, we will fight.'

It was against this background that the annual session of the Chamber of Princes was held on 17 January 1946. Lord Wavell presided over this meeting. In his address, the Viceroy assured them that no changes in their relationship with the Crown or the rights guaranteed to them by treaties and engagements would be initiated without their consent. At the same time, he expressed his confidence that the States would take their full part in the constitutional dis-cussions, which were to be held later in the year, as well as in the proposed constitution-making body. He impressed upon them the necessity of placing their administration on modern lines for the wel-fare of their subjects, which could be done only by ensuring that all States fulfilled the three fundamental criteria of good govern-ment: political stability, adequate financial resources, and effective association of the people with the administration. In the case of the smaller States, Lord Wavell urged them to pool their resour-ces and form political entities of a sufficient size. For its part, the Chamber of Princes affirmed that the States fully shared the general desire of the country for the immediate attainment of its political stature and their intention to make every possible contribution towards the settlement of the constitutional problem. The Chancel-lor declared that it was the policy of the Chamber that the funda-mental principles of sound administration should be followed in every State and that there should be popular institutions with elected majorities to ensure close and effective association of the people with the governance of the States.

The Labour Government had now been in power for eight months and so had ample time to take stock of the Indian situation. It also had the benefit of the views of a British Parliamentary delegation which had recently toured the country. On 19 February 1946, Attlee announced the decision of the British Cabinet to send three cabinet ministers to India to settle with the Indian leaders, in association with the Viceroy, the procedure of framing a new constitution for the country. Speaking in Parliament on 15 March, he said, referring to the States:

I hope that the statesmen of British India and of Princely India will be able to work out a solution of the problem of bringing together, in one great policy, these disparate constituent parts. There again, we must see that the Indian States find their due place; there can be no positive veto on advance and I do not believe for a moment that the Indian Princes would desire to be a bar to the forward march of India. But, as in the case of many other problems, this is a matter that Indians will settle themselves.

The Mission, consisting of Lord Pethick-Lawrence, Sir Stafford Cripps and A. V. Alexander, arrived in New Delhi on 24 March 1946. Lord Pethick-Lawrence, at a press conference held the next day, said that they had come in the hope of enabling Indians to produce, or set up machinery for producing, a constitutional structure for India as a whole. On being asked whether the representatives of the States would be representatives of the rulers or of the people, Lord Pethick-Lawrence declared that the Mission would take the position as it was. 'We cannot create new structures. We have to take the position as we find it.' To a question whether the co-operation of the States was essential or mandatory, he replied: 'What we plan is to invite Indian States to take part in discussions for the setting up of machinery for framing the further constitutional structure. If I invite you to dinner, it is not obligatory for you to come.'

It was decided that the Mission should interview (1) the Chancellor, (2) the rulers of Patiala, Bikaner and Nawanagar jointly as representing the middle-sized States, (3) the rulers of Dungarpur and Bilaspur jointly as representing the smaller States and (4) the Nawab of Chhatari (Hyderabad), Sir C. P. Ramaswami Aiyar (Travancore) and Sir Mirza Ismail (Jaipur) individually. A suggestion that the Mission should interview the representatives of the States' subjects was not acceptable either to the Political Department or to the Chancellor of the Chamber of Princes. Nor did the Mission itself pursue the question.

On 2 April, at his interview with the Cabinet Mission and the Viceroy, the Nawab of Bhopal made it clear that the Indian States wished to continue their existence with the maximum degree of sovereignty. They desired no interference in their internal affairs by British India. He suggested the formation of a Privy Council of the States and British India on the lines contemplated in the Simon Report. The Nawab said that the general view of the rulers was that if there were to be two States in India, there was no reason why a third India composed of the States should not be recognized. He was definite that none of the rulers wanted a constitutional set-up of the kind contemplated in the Government of India Act of 1935. On the other hand, he was in favour of a 'loose federation' at the Centre. Lastly, he pleaded that paramountcy should not be transferred to an Indian government.

That same afternoon, the Mission met the representatives of the Standing Committee of the Chamber of Princes, which comprised the rulers of Bhopal, Patiala, Gwalior, Bikaner and Nawanagar. Answering the points raised that morning by the Nawab of Bhopal, Lord Pethick-Lawrence said that if British India became independent, paramountcy would come to an end; that the British Government did not contemplate keeping any troops in India for the maintenance of internal order; and that, therefore, as the Crown would become unable to carry out its part of the treaty obligations, the States would naturally in their turn be released from their obligations under those treaties. The Mission felt it necessary to make this position clear to the rulers but they did not propose to emphasize, or, unless it became necessary, even to mention this matter to the representatives of British India because it seemed to them that the position of the States in any conversations with the British Indian representatives might be somewhat weakened by a positive statement to that effect. The people of Great Britain would naturally wish, if possible, to retain their friendly relations with the Indian States which had subsisted so long, but any such relationship must depend on the States' position in the new India. If the States surrendered any of their sovereignty to a federation, there could not be direct relations with those States except through that federation.

Lord Pethick-Lawrence, on the question of a confederation of States, said that this was a new idea as far as the Mission was concerned and that they had not been able to consider it in detail. It seemed to him an interesting and apparently feasible suggestion and he did not wish to rule out the idea. Sir Stafford Cripps thought that there might be geographical difficulties.

The Nawab of Bhopal enquired whether the existing treaties would continue during the interim period. The Secretary of State said that they would; but his conception was that treaties and arrangements in the financial and economic fields as well as in communications might continue for an additional standstill period pending revision. The Nawab of Bhopal said that there were no separate agreements on such matters and that the treaties could not be divided up. Sir Stafford emphasized that, whatever the technical position, there must clearly be some arrangement to prevent a sudden disruption of existing economic arrangements on the day when authority was handed over to the new Indian government. Such a disruption would be damaging both to the States and to British India and might be used as a lever against the States. The interview terminated after the Mission had consented to the request of the Jam Saheb that the States' representatives should be consulted again when the future set-up of British India had been settled.

The rulers of Dungarpur and Bilaspur, as representatives of the smaller States, were interviewed on 4 April. The Maharajah of Dungarpur read out a memorandum in the course of which he said that only about half a dozen States could stand comparison with the provinces of British India and that it was therefore necessary for the smaller ones to group themselves into larger units by pooling sovereignty on a regional and linguistic basis. The smaller States feared that the larger States were attempting to absorb them; they wanted satisfactory guarantees. It was wrong to suggest that the smaller States had no future; they were prepared to make greater sacrifices than the larger ones. He suggested that with the exception of Hyderabad, Kashmir and Mysore, the rest of the States should be grouped into nine regional units.

The Rajah of Bilaspur did not agree with this idea of grouping. He said that each State must be allowed to regain its former independence and be left to itself to do as it wanted. He recognized that this was not a view which had wide support, but he considered that the States had just as much right to independence as had British India. Bilaspur would, if need be, fight to protect itself.

Incidentally, this State was less than 500 square miles in area and had a total population of a little more than a lakh!

Sir C. P. Ramaswami Aiyar, who was interviewed on 9 April, did not regard the treaties as of any particular value to the States and was not disposed to lay too much emphasis on them. But on the issue of paramountcy, he was of the unequivocal opinion that it could not be transferred to a successor government. During the interim period, paramountcy would have to be preserved, but the machinery of the Political Department would have to be revised if there was to be no undue friction. He suggested the appointment of an Adviser to the Viceroy chosen by the States and working in conjunction with a committee or advisory council selected in consultation with the States. He felt that it was impossible to conceive of 601 States being effective factors in the future unless they grouped themselves. He thought that the smaller States should be told that, if they did not group themselves, they would be left to their fate, in which case they would acquiesce.

The Nawab of Chhatari, representing Hyderabad, reiterated a demand that Hyderabad had made at the time of the Cripps negotiations, for retrocession of the territories ceded to the East India Company, and added a new claim for a free outlet to the sea. Lord Wavell asked him what port Hyderabad had in view. Chhatari said that they had thought of Goa. He added that they would not require a corridor of territory but only an 'easement' to enable them to import by rail across British Indian territory goods received at their own port. Sir Stafford Cripps said that this was a matter for subsequent discussion with British India. Sir Walter Monckton, Constitutional Adviser to the Nizam, who had accompanied the Nawab of Chhatari, said that the Nizam wanted the assistance of the British Government in these negotiations. The Nawab of Chhatari suggested that, for the interim period, the Viceroy in his capacity as Crown Representative should be assisted by an Advisory Council of States' representatives capable of voicing the opinion of the States on any proposition put forward by British India affecting the States. He made it clear that in the event of the partition of the country, it would be impossible for Hyderabad, for geographical reasons, to join Pakistan or, for ideological reasons, to join India. Hyderabad would therefore remain an independent State. If, on the other hand, there were a united India and the central government were limited to foreign affairs and defence and

if there were communal parity in the central government, it would
be easier for Hyderabad to join. The Nawab raised the question
of Berar. Sir Stafford Cripps replied that there was a *de facto* as well
as a *de jure* position to be taken into account and that the matter
would have to be deferred for later consideration.

Sir Mirza Ismail devoted the greater part of his interview with
the Cabinet Mission to his views on how the differences between the
Congress and the League could be resolved. As regards the States,
he suggested that in the interim central executive, there should be
two representatives of the States, a Muslim and a Hindu. He said
that the problem of the States was the problem of preserving their
ruling dynasties. He was in favour of doing everything to maintain
the position of the ruling families as he considered that they embodied
a valuable tradition of Indian culture and civilization. Sir Mirza
concluded by emphasizing that it would not be right for the British
to leave India with all her problems undecided.

Broadly, the position taken up by the State representatives was
that paramountcy should not be transferred to a successor government, but that it should lapse; that the States should not be forced
to join any Union or Unions; that there should be *prima facie* no
objection to the formation of a confederation of States if the rulers
so desired; and that there should be no interference in their internal
affairs by British India.

In the meantime, the Cabinet Mission had also met the leaders
of Indian political parties and communal groups. The opinions
expressed by them made a veritable cacophony. In consequence,
the Mission and the Viceroy decided on 27 April to hold a tripartite conference, with four delegates respectively of the Congress
and the Muslim League, at Simla; whereupon the scene of activities
shifted to the bracing climate of that hill-station.

The Nawab of Bhopal was invited on 9 May for further discussions with the Cabinet Mission and the Viceroy on 'suggested
points of agreement' between the representatives of the Congress
and the League. He expressed disappointment and dissatisfaction at
the fact that, while the other parties concerned had been invited for
consultation, the States had not been so consulted with regard to
the suggested points. The Nawab asked for clarification on a number
of points and the Mission cleared his doubts.

On 16 May, the Cabinet Mission and the Viceroy in consultation with His Majesty's Government, issued a statement embodying

their own suggestions and recommendations towards a solution of the Indian problem. The announcement began with a survey of facts and concluded with recommendations for the 'best arrangement to ensure the speedy setting up of a new constitution for India.' This was subsequently known as the 'Cabinet Mission Plan.' Referring to the States, the Mission said that it was quite clear that with the attainment of independence by British India, whether within or without the British Commonwealth, the relationship which had hitherto existed between the States and the British Crown would no longer be possible. Paramountcy could neither be retained by the British nor transferred to the new government. The statement went on to say that the rulers had assured the Mission that they were ready and willing to co-operate in the new development of India. But the precise form which that co-operation would take must be a matter for negotiation during the building up of the new constitutional structure and it by no means followed that it would be identical for all the States.

Under the proposed plan the States were to retain all subjects and powers other than those ceded to the Union, namely foreign affairs, defence and communications. In the preliminary stage, they were to be represented in the Constituent Assembly by a negotiating committee. In the final Constituent Assembly they were to have appropriate representation not exceeding 93 seats. The method of selection was to be determined by consultation between the parties concerned. After the provincial and group constitutions had been drawn up by the three sections of the Constituent Assembly, the representatives of the sections and of the Indian States would reassemble for the purpose of settling the Union constitution.

In their broadcasts on 16 May both the Secretary of State and Sir Stafford Cripps made only casual references to the States. They asserted that paramountcy could not be handed over to anyone and must cease; they left the future relationship between the States and British India to negotiations.

Lord Pethick-Lawrence, addressing a press conference the next day, admitted that His Majesty's Government's relations with the States were quite different from their relations with the provinces. He refused to go beyond what had been laid down in the plan. He said that the Mission did not think it would be in the interests either of the people in the States or the people in the provinces to make any rigid proposals with regard to the States. He was satisfied that

9

the rather vague and loose way in which they proposed to deal with them was at the moment the method which was most likely to bring in the results which they all desired. Asked about the status of the States in the interim period, he said that it would remain as it was. He evaded questions as to whether the States' representatives would reflect the communal strength in the States; whether the interim government which was proposed to be set up at the centre would help the rulers to put down agitation by their subjects for responsible government; whether the Political Department would sabotage the plan, and so on.

On 22 May the Cabinet Mission published a 'Memorandum on States' Treaties and Paramountcy.' This had been handed over to the Chancellor of the Chamber of Princes on 12 May; so that it came to be known as the 'Memorandum of 12 May 1946,' though it was actually released to the press only on 22 May. The memorandum affirmed that when a new fully self-governing or independent government or governments came into being in British India, His Majesty's Government's influence with these governments would not be such as to enable them to carry out the obligations of paramountcy; nor did they contemplate the retention of British troops in India for that purpose. Thus, as a logical sequence, and in view of the desire expressed to them on behalf of the States, His Majesty's Government would cease to exercise the powers of paramountcy. This meant that the rights of the States which flowed from their relationship to the Crown would no longer exist, and that all the rights surrendered by the States to the paramount power would return to them. Political arrangements between the States on the one side and the British Crown and British India on the other would thus be brought to an end. The void would have to be filled by the States entering into a federal relationship with the successor government or governments in British India, or by entering into particular political arrangements. The memorandum also referred to the desirability of the States, in suitable cases, forming or joining administrative units large enough to enable them to be fitted into the constitutional structure, as also of conducting negotiations with British India in regard to the future regulation of matters of common concern especially in the economic and financial fields.

On 17 May the Nawab of Bhopal wrote to Lord Wavell asking for further clarification of certain points in the Cabinet Mission plan. He wished to be sure that the authority of the proposed Union

Government and legislature in respect of defence would not in any way affect the right of the States to maintain their own armed forces. The finances of the Union, he demanded, should be limited to specific and agreed sources of revenue and there should be no power by implication to raise taxation by any other means. The existing rights of the States in respect of communications should not be affected. The method and manner of representation of the States in the Union legislature should rest with the government of the States or groups of States concerned. Any question raising a major issue in the Union legislature specifically affecting the States should be dealt with on the same basis as a major communal issue[1] requiring a majority of States' representatives present and voting in its favour. Furthermore, he asked to be assured that the States so desiring would be free to form a group or groups amongst themselves on such terms and for such purposes as might be mutually agreed upon. The States should have the right to call for a reconsideration of the constitution of the Union after an initial period of ten years and at ten-yearly intervals thereafter. The constitution-making body should not discuss or make any recommendations in respect of the form of government in the States or the reigning dynasties. The decisions or recommendations of the constitution-making body should not apply to any State without ratification. He was definite that the representatives of the States to the Constituent Assembly should be nominated by the State governments and entered a *caveat* against the clause in the Cabinet Mission plan that the method of selection 'will have to be determined by consultation.'

On 29 May, Lord Wavell sent a non-committal reply in which he said that most of the questions raised by the Nawab were matters for negotiation between the States and the British Indian members of the Constituent Assembly. He admitted that the arguments adduced by the Nawab of Bhopal to show that the method of selection of States' representatives must lie in the unfettered discretion of the States' governments carried weight. But he felt that any categorical pronouncement by the Cabinet Mission in the sense desired would render not easier, but more difficult, that free association between the States and British India which it had been the object of the

---

[1] Any question raising a major communal issue in the legislature should require for its decision a majority of the representatives present and voting of each of the two major communities as well as a majority of all the members present and voting.

Mission to promote. Lord Wavell concluded that the settlement of most of the matters raised by the Nawab of Bhopal did not rest with him or the Cabinet Mission since they related to the terms which the States were free to negotiate for their own association with the new constitutional structure.

The Nawab of Bhopal found Lord Wavell's letter 'disappointing'. He wrote again to the Viceroy on 2 June asserting that the States were entitled to claim that the Crown should not leave them at the mercy of British India and that, at least, they should not be placed in a worse position in the Constituent Assembly or the Union legislature than that accorded to the major communities. He specifically wanted that any question raising a major issue particularly affecting the States in the Union Constituent Assembly should be dealt with on the same basis as a major communal issue, and that the final decision in regard to the method of selection of States' representatives to that body must rest with the States themselves. The Nawab expressed the belief that it could never have been the desire of His Majesty's Government to leave the States as 'a sort of no man's child' without any effort on the part of the Crown to protect their legitimate and reasonable demands and their established and accepted rights as sovereign bodies. He concluded by appealing to the Viceroy not to be party to such a deal in the case of friends who had been faithful to their word and their promises both in fair weather and foul. This plea was followed by yet another the following day. In his reply of 4 June the Viceroy stated that he appreciated the anxieties the Nawab had expressed on behalf of the rulers; but he thought the Nawab might take a different view after he had talked over the background with Sir Conrad Corfield, the Political Adviser. Lord Wavell suggested that the Nawab of Bhopal should do this before the Standing Committee met in Bombay.

I do not know what passed between Sir Conrad Corfield and the Nawab of Bhopal. But when Sir Conrad addressed the Constitutional Advisory Committee of the Chamber of Princes on 8 June in Bombay, the Committee of State Ministers on the 9th and the Standing Committee of the Chamber of Princes on the 10th, he stated that the decision regarding the lapse of paramountcy at the end of the interim period placed the States in the best bargaining position possible for the purpose of fitting themselves into the future constitutional structure. He advised the States to set up a Negotiating Committee to settle the terms on which they would be prepared to participate in the discussions of the Constituent Assembly. His idea was that such a Negotiating Committee should be given a detailed brief, which should include instructions in regard to certain conditions such as the method of selection of States' representatives; exclusion of dynastic questions and discussion as to forms of government; final ratification by individual States, and Union finance by contribution rather than by direct levy. He appealed to the rulers to develop the local patriotism of their subjects. He promised that during the interim period the Political Department would assist the States in arranging and pursuing negotiations and in the making of practical plans for grouping and affiliation; that it would continue to protect the States, pursue the revision of existing agreements of individual States mainly in the economic sphere, and discuss arrangements for minority administrations after the lapse of paramountcy. He finally suggested that if the rulers would maintain continuous personal touch with their subjects, a considerable degree of internal support would be forthcoming and that the emergence of real constitutional monarchies in units of suitable size might be of the greatest value to the future development of India.

The points made by Sir Conrad Corfield provided material for the resolution adopted by the Standing Committee of the Chamber of Princes on 10 June 1946. The resolution expressed the view that the Cabinet Mission plan provided the necessary machinery for the attainment by India of independence, as well as a fair basis for further negotiations. It welcomed the declaration of the Cabinet Mission in regard to paramountcy, but pointed out that certain adjustments for the interim period would be necessary; that there were a number of points in the plan which still required elucidation; and that there were also several matters of fundamental importance which had been left over for negotiation and settlement.

The Standing Committee set up a Negotiating Committee and authorized the Chancellor to arrange discussions with the corresponding body of the British Indian Constituent Assembly as contemplated by the Cabinet Mission.

IV

PRELUDE TO CHAOS

THE Cabinet Mission plan of 16 May 1946, though expressed in the form of a recommendation, was really in the nature of an award, as the Mission had been unable to bring about a general agreement between the Congress and the Muslim League. The Congress agreed to participate in the Constituent Assembly to be convened under the plan for the framing of a new constitution. The Muslim League at first accepted the plan while reiterating that the attainment of a sovereign Pakistan still remained its unalterable objective; but after a somewhat acrimonious controversy between the Congress and the League over the interpretation of the plan, the Council of the Muslim League revoked its acceptance.

On 12 August, the Viceroy invited Nehru (who had become Congress President) to form an interim government which he did on 2 September. Subsequently, on 15 October, the League representatives also joined the Government.

In the meantime, elections to the Constituent Assembly were held in accordance with the procedure laid down in the plan. The Muslim Leaguers who were elected to that body refused to join it. However, the Constituent Assembly with all the other members met, for the first time, on 9 December. It elected Dr Rajendra Prasad as the President and appointed various committees to draft the different sections of the Constitution.

On 21 December the Constituent Assembly passed a resolution appointing a Negotiating Committee to negotiate with a similar body which had already been appointed by the Chamber of Princes to deal with the representation of the States in the Constituent Assembly. Nehru, speaking on the resolution said: 'I regret, I say frankly, that we have to meet the rulers' Negotiating Committee. I think that, on the part of the States, there should have been on the

Negotiating Committee representatives of the people of the States. I think even now that the Negotiating Committee, if it wants to do the right thing, should include some such representatives; but I feel that we cannot insist upon this at this stage.' This was a rather inauspicious start.

The rulers, in the meantime, had been giving careful attention to the Cabinet Mission plan in so far as it affected their position and rights. The Standing Committee of the Chamber of Princes held many meetings, and also sought the advice of the Political Department on various points. Ultimately, the Committee drew up a lengthy resolution which was adopted at a Conference of Rulers in Bombay on 29 January 1947. This emphasized certain fundamental propositions, which formed the basis of the States' acceptance of the plan. The entry of the States into the Union, the resolution stated, should be on no other basis than that of negotiation and the final decision should rest with each State. Their participation in the constitutional discussions in the meantime would imply no commitments in regard to their ultimate decision, which could only be taken after consideration of the complete picture of the constitution. The States would retain all subjects and powers other than those ceded by them to the Union. The lapse of paramountcy was stressed. The constitution of each State, its territorial integrity and the succession of its reigning dynasty should not be interfered with by the Union, nor should the existing boundaries of a State be altered except by its free consent. The Constituent Assembly was not to deal with questions affecting the internal administration or constitutions of the States. The resolution reiterated that the States' Negotiating Committee was the only authoritative body competent under the plan to conduct preliminary negotiations on behalf of the States and the Committee was authorized to confer with the corresponding body of the British India portion of the Constituent Assembly in order to negotiate the terms of the States' participation in the Constituent Assembly and in regard to their ultimate position in an all-India Union. As a further safeguard, it was provided that the results of these negotiations would be subject to the approval of the Constitutional Advisory Committee and ratification by the States.

The publication of this resolution provoked a good deal of controversy. Public opinion was considerably agitated over the statement made by some rulers that if the fundamental propositions were not accepted by the Congress, they would boycott the Constituent

Assembly. Among the rulers there was a small group which did not see eye to eye with the resolution passed at Bombay. Sir B. L. Mitter, Dewan of Baroda, under instructions from his ruler, announced on 8 February that he was negotiating direct with the Negotiating Committee of the Constituent Assembly and that he was not bound by the resolution. Accordingly, Baroda decided to join the Constituent Assembly. As early as 30 July 1946, the Maharajah of Cochin had announced his intention of participating in the Constituent Assembly and sending to it only popular representatives elected by the Legislative Council of the State.

The majority of the States still stood by the Negotiating Committee of the Chamber of Princes. This body met the British Indian counterpart for the first time on 8 February. Material differences with respect to the scope of the discussions manifested themselves at the outset. Nehru and Vallabhbhai Patel[1] suggested that, though there was no specific agenda, the question for the joint meeting to consider and decide was the manner in which the representatives of the States could enter and participate in the work of the Constituent Assembly; that the meeting should leave aside other matters which were largely academic and in respect of which there might be differences of opinion. The States' representatives, however, did not accept this position. The Chancellor, the Nawab of Bhopal, said that the Chamber of Princes by its resolution of 29 January had laid down certain fundamental propositions on which they wanted satisfactory assurances before they could enter the Constituent Assembly. Each side adhered to its own point of view and the first joint meeting ended without producing any result.

The proceedings of the second sitting on 9 February were opened by the Nawab of Bhopal, who repeated his previous day's stand that his Committee was bound under its instructions to secure a satisfactory settlement of the fundamentals. He was prepared to discuss these points either formally or informally with somebody competent to do so; and in the meanwhile proposed a postponement of the discussions. When things were again heading towards a deadlock, Sir Yadavindra Singh, the Maharajah of Patiala, intervened and asked for a clarification of the position as it had emerged from the previous day's meeting. On behalf of the Congress, Nehru made a persuasive approach to the rulers. He said that the meeting was proceeding,

[1] Vallabhbhai Patel was affectionately known as 'Sardar'. That is how I used to address him and that is how I propose to refer to him hereafter.

as it must, on the basis of the Cabinet Mission plan which had been accepted by the Congress in full with all its implications. He went on to say that the issue of a monarchical form of government in the States did not arise out of the plan; but it had been made clear by the British Indian representatives that they did not wish to come in the way of this form of government. The Congress had no idea of changing the States' boundaries. Such change must have the consent of the parties and would not be forced on them. He added that the scheme under the plan was a voluntary one and there would be no compulsion at any stage. After this conciliatory statement, the atmosphere became more friendly and the meeting went on to consider the question of filling the 93 seats allotted to the States. It was decided that a scheme of distribution should be worked out jointly by the Secretaries of the Constituent Assembly and of the Chamber of Princes and the meeting adjourned till 1 March.

In the meantime, open dissension between the Congress and the Muslim League blocs in the interim Government had come to a head. The Government of India was a house divided against itself. This was the situation when, on 20 February 1947, Prime Minister Attlee made a declaration in the House of Commons in the course of which he set a date not later than June 1948 by which Britain would transfer power to responsible Indian hands. It was also announced that Viscount Mountbatten of Burma would replace Lord Wavell as Viceroy. With regard to the States, the declaration stated:

As was explicitly stated by the Cabinet Mission, His Majesty's Government do not intend to hand over their powers and obligations under paramountcy to any government of British India. It is not intended to bring paramountcy, as a system, to a conclusion earlier than the date of the final transfer of power, but it is contemplated that for the intervening period the relations of the Crown with individual States may be adjusted by agreement.

This announcement had a considerable influence on the two Negotiating Committees at their joint meeting on 1 March. Nehru contended that the British Government's declaration had introduced an additional element of urgency and it would be greatly to the advantage of the States, no less than of the British Indian representatives in the Constituent Assembly, if the States' representatives could join the Assembly during the April session. The Chancellor replied that he appreciated that the time factor was the essence of the matter, but pointed out that discussions among the States had revealed certain differences in regard to the secretariat proposals for distribution of seats among the States. After some discussion, the meeting approved the distribution proposed by the two secretariats subject to minor adjustments which might be made subsequently. The meeting then turned to the method of selecting representatives. A sub-committee consisting of Dr Pattabhi Sitaramayya, Sir N. Gopalaswami Aiyangar, Sir V. T. Krishnamachari, Sir Sultan Ahmed, Sir B. N. Rau, Mir Maqbool Mahmood and H. V. R. Iengar, I.C.S., was appointed to consider the question. The sub-committee presented its proposals the next day. The general proposition was accepted that fifty per cent of the States' representatives should be elected and that endeavours would be made to increase the elected quota as much as possible.

Nehru invited the States' representatives to function forthwith on some of the committees set up by the Constituent Assembly, particularly the Union Powers Committee and the Fundamental Rights Committee; but the Chancellor again took up the attitude that he could not reach any decision on this point without consulting the general conference of rulers, which he promised to convene at an early date.

Lord Mountbatten, the new Viceroy, arrived in India on 22 March and took charge two days later. In the course of his first speech, he said that his was not a normal viceroyalty. The British Government were resolved to transfer power by June 1948 and a solution had to be found in a few months' time. His earnest determination to carry out the decision of His Majesty's Government to transfer power to Indian hands smoothly and speedily created a deep impression.

The general conference of rulers was summoned for the first week of April. The Chancellor's secretariat had circulated a memorandum for the meetings of the Standing Committee and the general conference. The approach in this memorandum was not acceptable to an influential section of the rulers, and the Maharajah of Bikaner, the late Sir Sadul Singh, declared his opposition to the policy recommended by the Chancellor. He questioned the advisability and wisdom of an attitude of 'wait-and-see'. In a very ably worded statement which he circulated to the rulers, the Maharajah argued:

The Cabinet Mission plan had been originally accepted by the Congress, the Muslim League and the States and even though the Muslim League subsequently decided not to co-operate, it is felt that, if the States also took up such an attitude, it would give an impression that the States were playing into the hands of certain political parties in British India.

Even if the Muslim League ultimately decided not to participate in constitution-making, it is beyond question, in the interests of the States as a whole, interspersed as they are with territories in British India, that, by June 1948, a strong central government should be created which can take over power. The only safe policy for the States, therefore, is to work fully with the stabilizing elements in British India to create a centre at least for as large a section of India as possible to start with, leaving it open for any other part to come in at a later time, which would safeguard both the States and British India in the vacuum that would be created by the withdrawal of the British Government.

The united front that is required to be put up by the States is, therefore, not by adopting a policy of 'wait-and-see' but by fully co-operating with the Constituent Assembly with all the benefits that will accrue on such a step.

It is a fact which brooks no argument that it is essential for the States to carry their own people with them and nothing must be done which would impair their loyalty and support. It is, therefore, most strongly felt that a decisive step taken with a broad vision and in the larger interests of India is not only in the interests of the States themselves but becomes imperative. Neither can the Princes afford to lose the support of their people, nor can they ignore the resultant adverse repercussions in British India. British India is keenly watching the attitude of the States but it is perhaps not sufficiently appreciated, or I fear some quarters deliberately choose to ignore the fact, that the people of the States are equally keenly watching the attitude of the Princes.

The interests of the people of the States obviously lie in joining hands with British India in establishing a strong centre. And they are keenly alive to that necessity. If the Princes were to help in attaining that object, then the interests of the people and the Princes would continue to remain identical. But, if for any reason, the Princes were to decide otherwise, they would be putting themselves in opposition to the very strong wishes and interests of their people.

There seems to be a school of thought among the States which holds that they need not take part in the Constituent Assembly at all, but can reach political agreements with the Union or central government when it is established. If they do not enter the Constituent Assembly and later on enter into political agreements with the central party, the position of those States will substantially be the same as at present in regard to the existing Government of India.

The Maharajah of Bikaner's lead was followed by the Maharajah of Patiala, who also issued a public statement deprecating the policy of 'sitting on the fence'.

The Maharajah of Bikaner saw no point in taking part in the deliberations of the general conference or of the Standing Committee. His repeated advocacy in favour of the States' entering the Constituent Assembly and its committees did not, however, affect the general opinion of the majority of the rulers. As all attempts on his part to persuade the Chancellor and the other rulers to participate in the Constituent Assembly proved ineffective, he had no alternative but to say clearly on behalf of the Bikaner State that it dissociated itself from the majority view. As his group had decided to join the Constituent Assembly and its committees, the Maharajah considered it unnecessary to attend either the meeting of the Standing Committee on 1 April or the general conference following it. He showed up at the meeting of the Standing Committee in order only to approve a letter that was to be issued to Nehru and walked out after this had been done.

Public attention was now focussed on the firm stand taken by the Bikaner-Patiala group and this had its effect on the general conference of rulers and States' ministers which met on 2 April 1947. As a result, the original draft resolution was watered down and another adopted in its stead. By this resolution, the conference reiterated the willingness of the States to render the fullest possible co-operation in framing an agreed constitution and towards facilitating the transfer of power on an agreed basis. It re-defined the general understanding reached between the two Negotiating Committees and demanded that ratification of that understanding by the Constituent Assembly should precede the participation in the work of the Constituent Assembly of the representatives of such States as might desire to do so at the appropriate stage. The resolution noted that Attlee's statement of 20 February 1947 further confirmed that paramountcy would cease at the close of the interim period and that the States would be in a position as independent units to negotiate freely in regard to their future relationship with others concerned. In view of the element of urgency introduced by Attlee's statement, the conference authorized the Chancellor and the Standing Committee to conduct negotiations with the Crown Representative in regard to matters relating to the lapse of paramountcy and arising out of the transfer of power. The States' Negotiating Committee was authorized to negotiate with the interim

Government and the competent British Indian authorities, provided that these negotiations would be conducted in accordance with the resolutions adopted by the general conference of rulers on 29 January 1947, and that the results of the negotiations would be subject to the approval of the Constitutional Advisory Committee of the Chamber of Princes and final ratification by the States.

The compromise served as a formal face-saving device and post-poned an open split, although group alignments had now become crystallized. The Nawab of Bhopal insisted that the Constituent Assembly should 'ratify' the understanding reached between the two Negotiating Committees *before* the States could enter the Consti-tuent Assembly. Nehru, when approached, took the stand that a formal ratification by the Constituent Assembly was unnecessary and all that was required of his Committee was to report the results of its negotiations to the Assembly. In view of Nehru's attitude, the Chancellor advised the States not to join the Constituent Assembly or its committees. The Maharajah of Patiala declared that Nehru's view that his committee was required only to report results to the Constituent Assembly was borne out by the proceed-ings. In any case, he thought that it was for Nehru and his colleagues to place joint decisions before the Constituent Assembly in such manner as they deemed fit. He therefore urged that the States should join the Assembly and nominate representatives to the various committees without further loss of time.

The Nawab of Bhopal made one final effort to dissuade the rulers from entering the Constituent Assembly by addressing a personal appeal to them to adhere to the decisions of the general conference. He suggested to the Maharajah of Patiala, for instance, that rulers who held offices in the Chamber should implement its recommenda-tions on such vital matters notwithstanding any personal differences of opinion. The Maharajah of Patiala promptly replied that the fact that he happened to hold the office of Pro-Chancellor imposed no special obligations on his Government, nor did it detract from his discretion to adopt such policy about vital matters as he considered necessary in the interests of his State. The Maharajah pointed out that there were no precedents indicating that any resolutions had ever been treated as particularly binding on the States whose rulers held any office in the Chamber. He told the Chancellor that he was sending his representatives to the Constituent Assembly, because he felt that the stage for the States' participation in the

Constitution-making processes had definitely come, and that any
delay in doing so would be prejudicial not only to his own interests
but also to the wider interests of the country. The Maharajah of
Bikaner, and other rulers who followed his lead, fully supported the
stand taken by the Maharajah of Patiala and decided to send
representatives to the Constituent Assembly.

On 18 April, addressing the annual session of the All-India
States People's Conference, Nehru declared that any State which
did not come into the Constituent Assembly would be treated by
the country as a hostile State. Such a State, he added, would have
to bear the consequences of being so treated. This speech provoked
a prompt rejoinder from Liaqat Ali Khan, the leader of the Muslim
League Party in the Central Legislature and the Cabinet, who in
a press statement declared that the Congress had no right to coerce
the States; and that, according to the Cabinet Mission plan and
the clarifications issued by His Majesty's Government from time to
time, the States were perfectly within their rights in refusing to have
anything to do with the Constituent Assembly. Liaqat Ali Khan
appealed to the States to 'disregard the idle threat'.

On 28 April 1947, the representatives of the States of Baroda,
Bikaner, Cochin, Jaipur, Jodhpur, Patiala and Rewa took their
seats in the Constituent Assembly. This was the beginning of the
end of the united front put up by the Chamber of Princes. Thereafter, representatives from other States started trickling one after
another into the Constituent Assembly.

We must here notice another development. The rulers and their
advisers had for some time been thinking of regional federations of
States. The Jam Saheb of Nawanagar and the Maharajah of Dhrangadhra took considerable interest in the formation of a union of the
Kathiawar States. Some of the rulers of Central India had appointed
a special committee to frame a draft constitution for their region.
In regard to the Punjab States two draft schemes prepared respectively by the rulers of Bahawalpur and Mandi were discussed. The Rajah
of Baghat had drawn up a scheme for a Punjab Hill States Union.
The rulers as well as the ministers of some of the States in Rajasthan
had proposed a scheme for the union of all the Rajput States. Some
of the rulers of the Deccan States had agreed to form a single union.
The rulers of the Orissa and Chattisgarh States were discussing
the idea of an Eastern States Union.

The attitude of the Congress towards the idea of the States

grouping themselves into unions was not favourable. Gandhiji personally was averse to the suggestion, for he had a suspicion that the proposal had been instigated by the Political Department. When the rulers of the Deccan States approached him, he advised them to consult Nehru. The latter was not opposed to the idea of their grouping themselves into a Union, but he said that the first step was for each ruler to grant responsible government to his people.

Later, in a speech at the All-India States People's Conference, Nehru said that States which could not possibly form economic units should be absorbed into the neighbouring provinces and not with other States.

However, except for the short-lived Unions of the Deccan States, the Simla Hill States and the Eastern States, none of these schemes ever came into being.

Meanwhile the Political Department was busy devising measures for its own liquidation. As a first step, a conference of Residents and Political Officers was held in the second week of April 1947 to consider steps for the contraction of paramountcy and its eventual lapse. The Secretary of State had given the Viceroy maximum discretion in carrying out the policy of relaxation of paramountcy with a view to the greatest possible devolution by the end of 1947, subject to the avoidance of any step which might prejudice the future unity of India in regard to defence and communications. The object, as explained by the Political Adviser to the conference, was to enable the States to stand on their own feet, to encourage them to hold together and at the same time to co-operate fully with British India. The programme was to withdraw Political Agents by the autumn and Residents by the end of 1947, while the main duties of the Political Department were to be wound up by the end of March 1948.

It is interesting to note that one of the steps proposed by the Political Department at this conference was to hand over the Crown Representative's forces to the various States, e.g, the Malwa Bhil Corps to Indore. The Crown Representative's Police force[1] was maintained by the Political Department from the revenues of the Government of India. The intention was not that this force should

---

[1] When I took over the States Ministry we stopped the disintegration of this force and changed its name from the Crown Representative's Police to the Central Reserve Police. It was one battalion in strength at that time. We increased it to two battalions. This was the only effective force which the States Ministry had at its disposal. It was very well trained and but for the discipline, efficiency and devotion to duty of its officers and men, we would not have been able to maintain order, particularly in the small States and in the border areas, during the crucial period following the transfer of power.

be handed over to the successor Government but that it should
be distributed piecemeal among various States or groups of States.

The conference did not come to any definite conclusions with
respect to agreement in the economic and financial fields between
the States and British India in such matters as customs, salt, opium,
excise, posts, telegraphs and so on.

It was about this time that Lord Mountbatten announced the
plan of 3 June 1947, according to which His Majesty's Government would be prepared to relinquish power to two Governments,
India and Pakistan, on the basis of Dominion Status, and this relin-
quishment of power would take place much earlier than June 1948.
In regard to the States, the plan laid down that the policy of His
Majesty's Government towards the Indian States contained in the
Cabinet Mission memorandum of 12 May 1946 remained unchanged. This announcement introduced a maximum degree of
urgency into the situation.

On the 3rd evening Lord Mountbatten met the members of the
States' Negotiating Committee and explained the plan to them.
Sir Conrad Corfield, Political Adviser, was present at the meeting,
along with Lord Ismay and Sir Eric Mieville. Lord Mountbatten
gave an account of the negotiations leading to the decision to partition the country. He explained that the main consequences to the
States of the new plan would be twofold. First, it was improbable
that the two new Dominions would have such loose centres as had
originally been contemplated. Secondly, the fact that two separate
Dominions would be voluntarily accepted into the Commonwealth
would, he hoped, represent a measure of compensation to the States,
who were the old allies and friends of Britain.

Copies of the plan were then distributed and there was a general
discussion. Sir C. P. Ramaswami Aiyar (Travancore) appealed to
the Viceroy for paramountcy to be loosened or allowed to lapse
in advance of the date of the transfer of power. Such a course would
enable the States to negotiate on equal terms with the prospective
Governments of the two Dominions. He felt that there might be
States which were not likely to join up with either Dominion and it
was even more essential for the bargaining powers of these to be
improved.

Lord Mountbatten replied that, in his opinion, the fact that
paramountcy was about to lapse rendered it possible even at that
time for negotiations by the States to be made on a basis of complete

freedom. His instructions were that paramountcy should lapse on the transfer of power. He would, however, consider the premature lapse of paramountcy in special cases if it could be proved to him that its continuation constituted a handicap to negotiation.

Sir Conrad Corfield gave it as his opinion that a number of States would be glad to see paramountcy continue to function until the transfer of power. The Nawab of Bhopal confirmed this view, subject to any opinion that might be expressed by the Standing Committee of the Chamber. Sir Conrad Corfield pointed out that paramountcy was already in process of retraction.

Sir B. L. Mitter (Baroda) asked what would happen to economic and commercial agreements when paramountcy lapsed. Lord Mountbatten said that, in order that there might be no administrative vacuum, interim arrangements would be required for the period between the lapse of paramountcy and the conclusion of fresh or modified agreements. These interim arrangements could best be made on a standstill basis with such modifications as were necessitated by the reversion to the States of the rights surrendered by them to the Crown. In negotiating these interim arrangements, the Viceroy and the Political Department would give all the assistance they could during the short remaining period.

The Nawab of Bhopal pointed out that, apart from negotiations in regard to agreements, there were also certain claims which would have to be settled in advance of the lapse of paramountcy. He suggested that an *ad hoc* organization should be set up to deal with these.

Sir A. Ramaswami Mudaliar (Mysore) stressed that the need for agreement on all these matters was as essential from the point of view of the two new Dominions as from that of the States.

Sir Conrad Corfield gave some examples of the manner in which interim arrangements on a standstill basis could be made. He said that, when the central Government decided to abolish the salt duty, they had also decided to continue to observe the terms of existing agreements and to make payments due under those agreements until such time as new ones were entered into. That was one example of a standstill interim arrangement. He next quoted the example of posts and telegraphs. When paramountcy lapsed, the States would, for instance, be free to imprison the postmaster of an imperial post office! If they did so, however, they would run the risk of cutting themselves off from all-India communications. Presumably, therefore, they

11

would agree to treat post offices with sufficient consideration to ensure their continued functioning. Another example was railways and cantonments in those States where the Crown Representative still had jurisdiction. These would revert to the States on the lapse of paramountcy. But efforts were being made to persuade the interim Government to negotiate arrangements whereby the reversion of jurisdiction would not affect the working of the railways and the accommodation of the Indian army pending the conclusion of fresh agreements. Sir Conrad said that he was not clear to what claims the Nawab of Bhopal was referring. Claims arising out of the lapse of paramountcy would be a matter for negotiation, and any decisions by the Viceroy in such matters would have no sanction behind them after the lapse of paramountcy.

Sir C. P. Ramaswami Aiyar pointed out that there were a certain number of agreements into which the States had entered to which the Viceroy was not a party. He suggested that it would be necessary for some machinery to be set up to deal with them. Sir Conrad said that efforts had been made to establish an all-India consultative committee for such purposes, but that the interim Government had not agreed to this. He stated that existing contractual agreements would be a matter for discussion with the opposite party. There had already been a number of conferences with the relevant departments of the central government regarding 'paramountcy' agreements; and he had explained to these departments that the jurisdiction was about to revert to the States and had suggested that they should make interim arrangements based on that assumption.

Sir V. T. Krishnamachari (Jaipur) advocated the necessity for setting up machinery for joint consultation in regard to existing agreements. Sir Conrad said that efforts had been made to find a formula which would embody a general standstill agreement. If these were successful, joint consultation for fresh agreements could be arranged either within each Constituent Assembly or by *ad hoc* negotiating committees.

The Rajah of Bilaspur asked whether the entry of States into either Dominion Constituent Assembly was a matter of free choice. Lord Mountbatten confirmed that it was. The Rajah then asked whether constitutions were likely to be drafted by the respective Constituent Assemblies before or after the lapse of paramountcy. Lord Mountbatten replied that the broad outlines of the constitution drafted by the existing Constituent Assembly for India were likely to be ready before the date fixed for the lapse of paramountcy. In the case of the Pakistan Constituent Assembly, he believed that Jinnah had been working on ' heads of a constitution ', but these would probably only be a guide and nothing concrete would have appeared before the lapse of paramountcy. In any case, paramountcy would lapse as soon as the new self-governing Dominions came into being: these would be set up under the Government of India Act of 1935 (amended for that purpose).

The Rajah of Bilaspur then asked what was likely to happen to States which decided to join neither Constituent Assembly. Did His Majesty's Government envisage further relations with them? Lord Mountbatten stated that until it was known what shape the two Dominions would take, this was a hypothetical question which he was not prepared, at that stage, to refer to His Majesty's Government; but it was clear that the first step should be for these States to enter into negotiations for administrative arrangements with one or other, or perhaps both, of the successor Governments in British India. Whether a State actually joined either Dominion or not, it was obvious for geographical and economic reasons that such arrangements would be essential.

Lord Mountbatten suggested that the States' Negotiating Committee should continue for the next two or three months to consider the various broad principles of the problems which were bound to arise.

Sir C. P. Ramaswami Aiyar said that there was a practical difficulty in this suggestion. Such a committee had been suggested to the interim Government, but the objection had been raised that the present States' Negotiating Committee was unrepresentative as the States' people were not represented on it. While all the members present at the meeting were ready and willing to place their experience at the disposal of the Viceroy, the reactions of the authorities of the two Dominions which it was proposed to set up should first be ascertained.

Lord Mountbatten pointed out that the greater demand would be for a committee of the representatives of the States which were likely to adhere to the Indian Constituent Assembly. Perhaps two committees might be set up to negotiate with the two Constituent Assemblies. With this view there was general agreement, provided the interim Government agreed to such a proposal. The Nawab of Bhopal said that he would put up the suggestion before the Standing Committee of the Chamber of Princes and inform the Viceroy of their opinion.

Finally, Lord Mountbatten said that, whereas he did not wish to give any official advice on what steps should be taken by those States which were doubtful whether or not to join either Constituent Assembly, he would be willing to give personal advice to anybody who came and asked for it. He had however one suggestion to make now. In coming to their decisions, the representatives of the States should cast their minds forward ten years and consider what the situation in the country, and in the world as a whole, was likely to be at that time.

Lord Mountbatten elucidated the plan next day at a press conference. No fresh ground was covered so far as the States were concerned. But to a question whether it was the intention of His Majesty's Government to confer dominion status on any State which declared itself independent, he replied emphatically in the negative. It was at this conference that he gave the first public indication that the date of 'the transfer of power could be about 15 August 1947.'

With the announcement of the plan, the Nawab of Bhopal resigned his Chancellorship of the Chamber of Princes. In his letter of resignation he stated:

Now that Your Excellency has indicated to us the policy of His Majesty's Government in regard to the future of the Indian States, and Bhopal State would, *as soon as paramountcy is withdrawn, be assuming an independent status,* I consider it desirable that I should tender my resignation of the office of Chancellor of the Chamber of Princes with effect from today. Another reason for my resignation is that the Chamber, as now constituted, formed part of a constitutional machinery which, in my opinion, will now become *functus officio.*

In another letter to the Viceroy, he stated that:

The State of Bhopal does not wish to remain associated in any manner whatsoever with the Chamber of Princes or any of its subordinate organizations. It cannot therefore be represented by the Standing Committee of that body and will negotiate direct with the successor Governments of British India in regard to its interests, and its future political relationship with Pakistan and Hindustan.

On the resignation of the Nawab of Bhopal as Chancellor, the Maharajah of Patiala, then Pro-Chancellor, took over the Chancellorship. As a matter of fact, the organization was in chaos. The

Standing Committee later adopted a resolution to the effect that, with the lapse of paramountcy, the Chamber of Princes would cease to exist. There was however a section of rulers who still felt that there was need for a strong and effective organization of the States to replace the Chamber.

The States entitled to separate representation on the Constituent Assembly, known as viable States, were now reassured that there was no threat to their separate existence. This development aroused among them consciousness of a community of interests; and joint consultations by this group, with the exception of States like Hyderabad and Bhopal, now became a feature of the princely parleys. The smaller States, on the other hand, became apprehensive regarding the attitude of the major States. This conflict of interests stood in the way of the establishment of an organization to succeed the Chamber of Princes and, with the crystallization of group alignments, the chances of any concerted action on the part of the rulers as a body receded.

The viable States then thought of having an organization of their own. A constitution was drawn up, but there was some delay in bringing the organization into existence mainly because personal adjustments amongst the rulers had a way of taking their own time. In the meantime, events were moving faster than had been generally anticipated.

The Congress in accepting the lapse of paramountcy did not foresee all the consequences that would follow. A brief experience of office soon showed the Congress leaders what a state of confusion and anarchy the country was heading for as a result of it. Reports had reached Nehru and Sardar that the Political Department was destroying all records, winding up residencies and handing over cantonment areas and the Crown forces to various States.

On 11 June, the Standing Committee of the All-India States People's Conference passed a lengthy resolution in the course of which they demanded that the Political Department and its agencies should be handed over to the new Government of India or, in the alternative, that a new central department should be created immediately to discharge the functions of the Political Department.

Nehru raised this question at a meeting of party leaders called by Lord Mountbatten on 13 June. The Congress was represented by Nehru, Sardar and J. B. Kripalani (then Congress President); the League by Jinnah, Liaqat Ali Khan and Abdur Rab Nishtar, and the Sikhs by Sardar Baldev Singh. Sir Conrad Corfield, the Political Adviser, was also present. Lord Mountbatten inaugurated the proceedings by stating that his instructions were that paramountcy should lapse not later than the date on which the transfer of power took place. The lapse of paramountcy would automatically involve the closing down of the Political Department.

Nehru said that, as he understood it, all other functions of the Political Department except paramountcy had continued, despite the 1935 Act, to be exercised by the Governor-General-in-Council. Sir Conrad Corfield said that all functions connected with the States were exercised by the Crown Representative. Nehru said that, whereas he accepted the position with regard to the lapse of paramountcy at present, surely all the other matters with which the Crown Representative and the Political Department had to deal were Government of India matters and would continue to be dealt with by them.

Sir Conrad stated that no such clear division could be made. The purpose behind the Crown Representative's functions was that neither should the States by their own action prejudice all-India interests, nor the Government of India by their action prejudice the interests of the States.

Nehru said that he had consulted many eminent lawyers and that the issue was a highly controversial one. In any case, he felt that a stage was now being reached at which very serious consequences threatened the country. He pointed out that His Majesty's Government's statement of 3 June referred back to the memorandum of the Cabinet Mission of 12 May 1946. He said that he accepted these documents as they were, but in his opinion the policy of the Political Department had been contrary to them.

Sir Conrad denied the allegation. He said that there had been full and continuous consultation with the departments of the Government of India and that full details had been supplied to them at inter-departmental conferences.

Nehru said that it was one thing to deal with a department on a specific matter but that the wider policy was quite another thing. There were many rights and obligations apart from paramountcy. To deal with each department separately concerning these would produce administrative chaos. He went on to say that he fully admitted the principle that any State could, if it so wished, join the Pakistan Constituent Assembly; but there was no trace in the

Cabinet Mission's memorandum of any State being allowed to claim independence.

Sir Conrad referred Nehru to the following passage in the memorandum on States' Treaties and Paramountcy:

The void will have to be filled, either by the States entering into a federal relationship with the successor Government or Governments in British India or failing this, entering into particular political arrangements with it or them.

Nehru said that in his opinion this did not signify the possibility of States becoming independent. Sir Conrad said that in his opinion the term 'particular political arrangements' implied relations with autonomous units.

Jinnah said that in his view the States were fully entitled to say that they would join neither Constituent Assembly. Every Indian State was a sovereign State. Nehru disagreed with the proposition.

Jinnah reiterated that in his opinion Indian States were sovereign States for every purpose except in so far as they had entered into treaties with the Crown. British India could do nothing to them. The Crown was under certain obligations to them and they to it, according to the terms of treaties and agreements which had been entered into. To say that the Governor-General or the British Parliament could lay down that every Indian State was bound to enter one Constituent Assembly or the other was not according to the law or the constitution. If the States liked to come in, they could do so by agreement, but there was no way of forcing them in.

Nehru asked what were the tests of sovereignty? One was the capacity for international relations. The States had no such capacity. Another was the capacity for declaring war. The States had no such capacity. There were 562 States. Of this number there might perhaps be a few, but only a few, which could claim semi-sovereignty. Nehru then read out several extracts from the Cabinet Mission's memorandum. He said that in his opinion the whole background of this memorandum was that the States should enter the structure of one or the other government.

Jinnah reiterated his view that the Cabinet Mission had never laid down that every State was bound to come into one or the other Constituent Assembly. They were free to decide for themselves, but there were many matters which would require adjustments. These could only be made through the Crown Representative so long as he continued. It was in the interests of both the Muslim

League and the Congress that these adjustments should be made.

Nehru said that he entirely agreed with this. He was not intending to lay down that every State must join one or the other Constituent Assembly, but that if they did not come in, they would have to come to some other arrangement. Such other arrangements could not and should not be preceded by declarations of independence.

Lord Mountbatten referred to the note which had been circulated for consideration regarding the machinery for dealing with questions of common concern between the States and the successor Governments in British India. This note proposed two alternatives — that the States should be given the option of (*a*) dealing with local representatives of the successor Governments, or (*b*) appointing representatives of the States at the headquarters of the successor Governments. Lord Mountbatten said that he felt that the alternatives should be put before the States. He had discussed in London the question of the Government of India taking over the residencies in the various States. His instructions had been that this was only to be done if the States agreed. Moreover, it was going to be very difficult to convince the States that agents of the Government of India, located in the States' territories, would not continue to represent a paramount power. In his opinion, the alternative that each State or group of States should appoint a representative, or representatives, to be located at the headquarters of the appropriate Government, would be the best arrangement. He had discussed this with the States' Negotiating Committee, the members of which had agreed with him. He emphasized the fact that he was not entitled to force a State to continue to accept an agent of the central Government in its territory.

Sir Conrad stated that he had discussed this question with a number of States' Ministers. It seemed to him that it would be a mistake to set up an organization with which the States were not likely to co-operate.

Nehru said that he considered that these suggestions proceeded from a wrong basis. He insisted that the present arrangements should continue. To have representatives of the States at Delhi would lead to very considerable delays. He did not understand how His Majesty's Government could give a ruling on which the Government of India had not even been consulted. This ruling did not flow from the memorandum of 12 May. The agents of the Government of India should continue in operation until they were withdrawn. The lapse of paramountcy should not lead to independence. Only certain functions would cease to be exercised; others would remain. It was essential to have a department to continue to deal with the States. He suggested that the Political Department and the Residents should continue to function. The political and administrative aspects should continue in operation. The choice of what machinery should be set up lay with the Government of India. If any State took up a line of opposition to the policy of the central Government, that would be considered as an unfriendly act and all the privileges which such a State enjoyed would cease.

Lord Mountbatten said that he recognized the rights of each of the two new Governments to set up a new department to deal with States' matters, but he suggested that this should not be called 'the Political Department'. A more acceptable name would be 'the States Department'. It should be set up forthwith and be divided into two sections, ready for the partition of the country. The existing Political Department would give all possible assistance and advice in the formation of this new department. Lord Mountbatten stated that, on the other hand, he was convinced that it was for the States to decide whether to send representatives to either Delhi or Karachi or to receive representatives from the successor Governments.

A second note covering a draft formula for standstill arrangements was then considered. Nehru said that he had not yet had time to study the draft. He had discussed it in the early hours of that morning with lawyers, who had raised many points of difficulty. He doubted whether the description that it covered only 'administrative' arrangements was correct. Jinnah gave it as his view that it was so.

Lord Mountbatten suggested that both parties would wish for a longer time to look into this note in detail. He considered that the States should send representatives to negotiate and sign the agreement proposed. Negotiation could be initiated through the States' Negotiating Committee, but all States would have to send fully accredited representatives for the purpose of signature.

The other question discussed was the disposal of the Crown Representative's records. The meeting considered the steps which were being taken to weed and sort out these documents and to destroy those no longer of interest.

Nehru said he thought that there could be no doubt that the

12

major portion of the records was of concern to the Government of India. He considered that there should be a committee of historians and others to look into the whole question. He could see no reason for rushing ahead with the destruction. Jinnah said that he agreed with this. He was opposed to the idea that the present Political Department should be the judge of what should be destroyed.

Sir Conrad pointed out that the present processes were being carried out in consultation with the Imperial Records Department, which was a highly skilled body. He was ready to guarantee that nothing of value would be destroyed. Amongst the documents being sorted out, there might be some which should not be handed over to the Government of India. He explained that nearly all the important documents were in the Political Department, although the residencies might also have some.

I have given a rather full account of this conference because it raised issues of far-reaching importance. The main conclusions reached were as follows:—It was decided to set up a new department, possibly called 'the States Department', to deal with matters of common concern, divided into two sections ready for the partition of the country. It was agreed that there should be a meeting between the Indian leaders and representatives of the States (possibly the States' Negotiating Committee) to consider the draft standstill formula and any other matters of common concern on a date to be decided, probably in July. It was further agreed that the Residents should go on with the destruction of ephemeral records and documents, but that the Political Adviser should apply to the Member for Education in the interim Government for the services of experts to assist in the weeding and sorting out of the Crown Representative's records. Those records which contained information regarding the private lives of the rulers and the internal affairs of States should be handed over, on the transfer of power, to the United Kingdom's High Commissioner.

On 11 June, Sir C. P. Ramaswami Aiyar announced that Travancore had decided to set itself up as an independent sovereign State. A similar announcement was made the next day on behalf of the Nizam of Hyderabad. These events gave rise to apprehension lest other States should adopt a similar attitude and India be split into fragments. Strong speeches were made at the All-India Congress Committee which met at Delhi on 14 June protesting against the 'Balkanization' of the country. A strongly-worded resolution was passed declaring that the Congress did not agree with the theory of paramountcy as enunciated and interpreted by the British Government. It affirmed that the privileges and obligations as well as the rights subsisting as between the States and the Government of India could not be adversely affected by the lapse of paramountcy. Nor would the relationship between the Government of India and the States be exhausted by it. The lapse of paramountcy did not lead to the independence of the States. The Committee refused to admit the right of any State to declare its independence and to live in isolation from the rest of India. That would be a denial of the course of Indian history and the objectives of the Indian people.

Jinnah, on the other hand, contested the Congress thesis. In a statement issued on 18 June, he unequivocally declared that, constitutionally and legally, the States would be independent sovereign States on the termination of paramountcy and that they would be free to adopt any course they liked. He was clearly of the opinion that the Cabinet Mission's memorandum did not in any way limit their choice to the extent that they had no option except to join one or the other Constituent Assembly. In his opinion they were free to remain independent if they so desired. Neither the British Government, nor the British Parliament, nor any other power or body could compel the States to do anything contrary to their free will and accord, nor had they any power or sanction of any kind to do so.

The Dewan of Travancore went to the extent of announcing his intention to appoint a Trade Agent in Pakistan.

The general tendency among the rulers was to make the best of the bargaining position in which the lapse of paramountcy placed them. The fact that during the second World War many of the major States had strengthened their armed forces could not be ignored. The decision therefore that, with the withdrawal of the British, the Indian States comprising two-fifths of the land must return to a state of complete political isolation was fraught with the gravest danger to the integrity of the country. And so the prophets of gloom predicted that the ship of Indian freedom would founder on the rock of the States.

V

STOPPING THE GAP

IN the last chapter, we have seen how a decision was taken at a
meeting of Lord Mountbatten with the leaders of the Congress
and the Muslim League to set up the new States Department. This
decision was followed by an important communication from Nehru
to Lord Mountbatten setting out his views with regard to the functions of the proposed new organization. The communication was
the subject of discussion at a meeting of the Viceroy's advisers, as a
result of which I was charged with the task of preparing, in consultation with the Political Adviser, a note which should present definite
proposals. Accordingly, I produced a memorandum in which I
suggested that the proposed department should function as a single
organization with two ministers, one from the Congress and the other
from the Muslim League, and having two secretaries in charge, so
that it could be divided into two on the partition of the country.
This memorandum was approved by Lord Mountbatten and duly
circulated among the members of the Cabinet. Nehru, on behalf
of the Congress, included the name of Sardar (who was Member for
Home and Information and Broadcasting in the interim Cabinet)
as Minister, while Jinnah on behalf of the Muslim League suggested
the name of Abdur Rab Nishtar.

A few days later, Sardar sent for me and offered me the Sec-
retaryship of the States Department. I told Sardar that it was my
intention to take all the leave I had earned and to retire from
Government service after 15 August. Ever since 1917, I had
been dealing with constitutional reforms. I had never expected
that I would see freedom for India in my lifetime. Since that had
materialized, my life's ambition was achieved. Further, I had been
overworked and was feeling the strain. I had not taken a rest for
many years. Sardar told me that because of the abnormal situation

in the country, people like myself should not think in terms of rest or retirement. He added that I had taken a prominent part in the transfer of power and that I should consider it my bounden duty to work for the consolidation of freedom. I naturally agreed with him that the country's interests, and not my personal predilections, should be the guiding factor.

Since I was the Constitutional Adviser to Lord Mountbatten and since the appointment was to take effect immediately, I was obliged to mention the matter to him. Lord Mountbatten told me that he was proposing my appointment as Governor of one of the more important provinces. I said that from my conversations with Sardar, I understood that he felt it to be in the interests of the country that I should remain for some time at least with the Government of India. Lord Mountbatten advised me to accept Sardar's offer and later on confirmed our conversation in a charming letter.

Next day I called on Sardar, showed him Lord Mountbatten's letter and intimated my acceptance of his offer. I then had a long and frank conversation with him. I reminded him that ever since I had met him, for the first time on 21 August 1946, I had made it my purpose to consult him as far as possible on important developments in the constitutional field, and I particularly added that it had been his powerful support that had made possible the transfer of power. We had indeed got on well together, resolving occasional differences of opinion by mutual and amicable discussion. The position at that time was that though I consulted Sardar, the final responsibility for whatever advice I gave to the Governor-General was mine. Now that we were to work as Minister and Secretary, I was not quite sure how far we should hit it off together. Sardar replied that the question did not arise at all and that I should not think along those lines. When I said that there was a feeling that Congress leaders distrusted the permanent Services he replied that my fears were groundless. He added that, whatever might have been the attitude of politicians to the Services in the past, he was confident that in future everyone would play the game. For his own part, he would do everything possible to bring about a most cordial atmosphere between the Cabinet and the Services. And he kept his word.

We then discussed the general situation in the country as a result of partition and the problem of the States in particular. I told Sardar that, under the Cabinet Mission plan, the States need not join either of the Constituent Assemblies, but that they could have particular arrangements with the Government of the Dominion to which they were geographically contiguous. After the announcement of the partition, the rulers on our side of the border realized that they should strengthen the Indian Union and so were gradually coming into the Constituent Assembly. They were, however, very jealous about their sovereignty and I felt strongly that they should not be rubbed the wrong way. At the same time, the attitude of some of the rulers of the big States was disconcerting and Pakistan was playing with the idea of getting some of the border States to cast in their lot with her. Sardar told me that the situation held dangerous potentialities and that if we did not handle it promptly and effectively, our hard-earned freedom might disappear through the States' door.

Sardar next referred to the consequences of the lapse of paramountcy. I remarked that it was the greatest disservice the British had done us as well as the rulers. During the course of a century, the provinces and the States had been welded together. The edifice of central authority had rested on two pillars, one with foundations in the provinces and the other in the States. In all-India matters, co-operation and uniformity of policy so far as the States were concerned had been enforced through the residencies. Important cantonments and military installations were located in the States. The Indian railway system spanned the territories of the States as well as the provinces and, in the interests of the safety and convenience of the travelling public, arrangements had been extended to the States whereby civil and criminal jurisdiction over railway lands had been handed over to the Crown Representative. One of the provincial capitals was situated in a minor State. In posts and telegraphs, control of arms and ammunition, extradition and surrender of fugitives, control of opium and other narcotics, in the overall food policy, to mention only a few matters affecting all-India security and welfare, the machinery of the Political Department and the residencies had acted as a co-ordinating agency. The Cabinet Mission had announced the lapse of paramountcy in their memorandum of 12 May 1946. I told Sardar that, though I was Constitutional Adviser to the Governor-General, I had never been consulted on this issue, and that I was unhappy about the decision. At the same time I could appreciate the point of view of the Cabinet Mission. The British public had ever been sensitive about treaties and agreements and the Labour Party might have had the fear that, if it transferred to the successor Government the rights under the treaties entered into by the Crown with the rulers, neither the Conservatives nor the British public would have stood it. Under the Cabinet Mission plan, paramountcy would have lapsed only after the constitution had been set up and power transferred to the successor Governments. Under the June 3rd plan the transfer was to take place on 15 August, and paramountcy was to lapse on that day. There were hardly two months left, and to negotiate agreements with such a large number of States during that time was obviously out of the question. The position of the States themselves was one of great anxiety. The paramount power had protected them from all internal trouble. There were only a few States which were organized to deal with such a threat; the others were without the necessary resources. Furthermore, the communal situation in British India was already causing concern, and were it to deteriorate it would spread to the States as well. The Government of India lacked the means of controlling the situation, if this happened. The army was being partitioned and it would be some time before it would again be an effective force for maintaining internal security. The situation did, in fact, appear to be charged with immense potentialities of danger.

At the same time, I suggested to Sardar that the British Government's decision to extinguish paramountcy might prove a not unmixed evil and that it was possible that good might yet come of it. The biggest advantage was that we would be writing on a clean slate, unhampered by treaties. I reminded him how the federal negotiations with the rulers had foundered on the rock of treaty rights.

I then told Sardar that I was without any ready-made plan for the solution of the States' problems. In the meantime, we should be clear in our minds with regard at any rate to the procedure by which they should be tackled. The problems were altogether peculiar and in the unsettled state of things would sometimes demand quick decisions. It seemed necessary therefore that the Prime Minister and the Cabinet should give a free hand to Sardar in dealing with them.

At its meeting held on 25 June the interim Cabinet accepted the proposal for the creation of the States Department and on 27 June a press *communiqué* was issued allotting the Department to Sardar. I was named as the Secretary.

I was more than ever convinced that in view of the disposition of some of the rulers to cast in their lot with Pakistan, of a few others to assert their independence, and the keen desire of all to safeguard their sovereignty, some sort of organic bond should be forged between the Government of India and the States if the integrity of the country was to be preserved. The States which were geographically contiguous to India must be made to feel legally and morally that they were part of it. Some time back, in December 1942, I had drawn up a scheme for Lord Linlithgow in which I had suggested an interim federal government as a solution of the current political deadlock. I had made it clear that the federal scheme, as set out in the Government of India Act of 1935, was not a practical proposition during the war emergency. Its procedure for accession, which entailed protracted negotiations for the adjustment of treaty and fiscal rights, and the creation of the new legislature, which again involved difficult administrative arrangements, were far too complicated to be embarked upon at such a time. I had suggested that we should ask the States to accede only on 'defence' and 'external affairs,' without any other commitments. Since both the subjects were handled by the paramount power and not by the States, the rulers would not be losing any of the rights enjoyed by them. The existing Central Legislative Assembly and the Council of State could be enlarged to provide for the States' nominees, who would be appointed by the Governor-General from a panel of names suggested by the rulers. It was my contention that once this scheme (which would facilitate the unification of India's war effort) was implemented, a responsible government for the whole of India could be established at the centre and as such would attract all the principal political elements. The unity thus forged might heal India's internal dissensions sufficiently to provide her leaders with a new outlook for the future constitution. Lord Linlithgow did not take any action on this suggestion. When the partition of the country was decided upon, I could not rid myself of the regretful doubt whether this vivisection would have been necessary had my scheme of December 1942 been implemented.

I felt that an analogous scheme should be tried now with regard to the States. To the two subjects of 'defence' and 'external affairs' we could add 'communications'. The Cabinet Mission had suggested that these three subjects could be ceded to the Union Government by the States.

When I next approached Sardar, I started by giving a brief

outline of the plan which I had submitted to Lord Linlithgow. I pointed out the advantages if the States were to accede on three subjects. The basic unity of India would be achieved and, when the new constitution was framed, we could thrash out the necessary details concerning the relations between the centre and the States at our leisure. I explained to Sardar how the rulers could be brought in. 'Defence' was obviously a matter which no State could conduct by itself: 'external affairs' was a subject inextricably linked with 'defence' and, as the States had never handled it before, even the largest State could not hope to do so effectively: 'communications' was a means of maintaining the very life-lines of the country and without our co-operation, the States could do nothing in this matter. I also pointed out that the communal flare-up in north India had made the non-Muslim rulers turn away from Pakistan and I suggested that we should use this development to our advantage. Provided that we did not demand any financial or other commitments, the rulers would not be unwilling to consider our proposal. However, the time at our disposal was extremely short and if we planned for accession we should get it implemented before 15 August. My most important consideration was the overall security of the country. If the rulers acceded on 'defence', the Government of India obtained right of entry into any State where internal stability was threatened. 'Defence' covered not only external aggression but internal security as well. Sardar was inclined to agree with my proposal. I requested him to put it before Nehru and get his approval. To put down anything in writing at that stage was inadvisable as there was likelihood of leakage, and premature publicity would have been harmful to the plan.

Next day Sardar told me that Nehru was in agreement with the proposal 'if we could see it through.' It seemed to me from Sardar's remark that Nehru was probably sceptical about the success of the plan. Nor was Sardar himself over-optimistic. For one thing, he was doubtful whether we could get the accession policy implemented in the few weeks before 15 August; but, as I suggested to Sardar, the very shortness of time might work to our advantage.

Incidentally, I proposed that the active co-operation of Lord Mountbatten should be secured. Apart from his position, his grace and his gifts, his relationship to the Royal Family was bound to influence the rulers. Sardar whole-heartedly agreed and asked me to approach him without delay.

13

A day or two later, I met Lord Mountbatten and mentioned to him my talk with Sardar and our tentative plan. I asked for his help in getting the States to accede on three subjects. I pointed out that they would not be losing anything in the result and suggested that it would be a great act of statesmanship on his part if he could bring it about. I felt that he was deeply touched by my remark that the wounds of partition might to some extent be healed by the States entering into relationship with the Government of India and that he would be earning the gratitude of generations of Indians if he could assist in achieving the basic unity of the country. He told me that he would think the matter over. I confess that I was seized moment-arily by the fear that Lord Mountbatten might be adversely in-fluenced by some of his advisers. But to my relief and joy, he accepted the plan. Lord Mountbatten discussed the matter with Sardar. This frank talk enabled them to explain and understand each other's point of view. I should add that Nehru, with the approval of the Cabinet, readily entrusted Lord Mountbatten with the task of negotiating with the rulers on the question of accession and also with the task of dealing with Hyderabad.

Though the main policy was thus settled, I had not yet taken over charge of the States Department. I was fully occupied at the time with the Indian Independence Bill, the adaptation of the Govern-ment of India Act of 1935 for India and Pakistan and the adminis-trative details connected with partition. We had on an average as many as seven or eight meetings a day, besides our own work in the Department, and later when the two-way exodus of populations started, the burden grew heavier. Meanwhile, Sir Conrad Corfield, the Political Adviser, had been pressing me to set up the States De-partment and was asking repeatedly for the agenda and other details of the forthcoming meeting of the rulers. Sardar and I finally held a meeting with him. His Department had circulated a preliminary draft of a Standstill Agreement between individual States and the two successor Governments. The draft provided for the discontinuance of the payments of cash contributions and of the continuance of existing administrative arrangements in respect of such matters of common concern as were specified in the schedule. The schedule dealt mainly with matters in the economic field; it did not include even 'external affairs'. When I told Sir Conrad Corfield that the Government of India had decided on the policy of accession, he literally threw up his hands in surprise. He considered the policy of accession far too ambitious and recalled the tortuous and infructuous negotiations with the rulers between 1934 and 1939. I pointed out that those negotiations had been conducted in other circumstances by the Political Department but that now in the changed conditions we hoped to succeed. It was made clear to him that, while we would welcome every assistance from the Political Department, the ultimate responsibility of negotiating with the rulers would rest with the new States Department.

I assumed charge of the States Department on 5 July. On 3 July, I had met Sardar and suggested that the first thing to do when the States Department came into being was to allay any possible suspicions on the part of the rulers and that this could be done by means of a statement defining the attitude and policy of the Government of India towards the States. Sardar agreed that such a statement was necessary and he asked me to prepare one. This I gave on 4 July 1947. I might mention that the inspiration for some of the passages in it came from Lincoln's first Inaugural Address.

Sardar was well pleased with the statement. He was satisfied that it was concise and conciliatory in tone. With its issue by Sardar the next day, the States Department was formally inaugurated. The statement appealed to the rulers to accede on three subjects. It pointed out: 'The States have already accepted the basic principle that for defence, foreign affairs and communications they would come into the Indian Union. We ask no more of them than accession on these three subjects in which the common interests of the country are involved.' The statement went on: 'This country with its institutions is the proud heritage of the people who inhabit it. It is an accident that some live in the States and some in British India, but all alike partake of its culture and character. We are all knit together by bonds of blood and feeling no less than of self-interest. None can segregate us into segments; no impassable barriers can be set up between us. I suggest that it is therefore better for us to make laws sitting together as friends than to make treaties as aliens. I invite my friends the rulers of States and their people to the councils of the Constituent Assembly in this spirit of friendliness and co-operation in a joint endeavour, inspired by common allegiance to our motherland for the common good of us all.' The statement stressed that the Congress 'are no enemies of the Princely Order, but, on the other hand, wish them and their people under their aegis all prosperity, contentment and happiness. Nor would it be my policy to conduct the relations of the new department with the States in any manner which savours of the domination of one over the other; if there would be any domination, it would be that of our mutual interests and welfare.' The statement ended with the appeal: 'We are at a momentous stage in the history of India. By common endeavour we can raise the country to a new greatness while lack of unity will expose us to fresh calamities. I hope the Indian States will bear in mind that the alternative to co-operation in the general interest is anarchy and chaos which will overwhelm great and small in a common ruin if we are unable to act together in the minimum of common tasks.'

The statement had a good press both in India and abroad. A number of foreign correspondents told me that it was a statesman-like document and at a staff meeting Lord Mountbatten congratulated me on it, saying that he considered it quite excellent.

On the morning of 5 July I took over charge of the States Department in addition to my work as Constitutional Adviser to the Governor-General. The Indian Political Service had been the close and jealously guarded preserve of the British, into which Indian officers only strayed occasionally. The entire staff of the Political Service, with a few exceptions, had either applied for pension or had opted for service in Pakistan, so that both at the centre as well as the regional headquarters we were without officers. The first task was to constitute the States Ministry. To start with, C. C. Desai, a senior officer of the I.C.S., was appointed as Additional Secretary with two junior officers to assist him. We had, of course, inherited the nucleus of the subordinate staff from the Political Department.

On 5 July I addressed a press conference in order to explain the provisions of the Indian Independence Bill which was then on the parliamentary anvil. Sardar presided. Several questions were asked relating to the States. All I could say with respect to the legal position was that the Indian States on 15 August would be neither in Pakistan nor in India and that their actual position would be difficult to define. Answering a question on agreements between the States and the Government of India on matters of common concern, Sardar said: 'Whoever denounces such agreements takes the responsibility for the consequences.'

The clause in the Indian Independence Bill mainly concerned with the Indian States was clause 7, the first draft of which was in the following form:

As from the appointed day—

(*a*) His Majesty's Government in the United Kingdom shall have no responsibility as respects the peace and good government of any of the territories which immediately before that day were included in India;

(*b*) the suzerainty of His Majesty over the Indian States shall cease and the functions theretofore exercisable by him with respect to the Indian States and any powers, authority or jurisdiction theretofore exercisable by him in the Indian States, being functions, powers, authority or jurisdiction incident to or flowing from that suzerainty, shall cease to be exercisable; and

(*c*) any powers, authority or jurisdiction which, at the date of the passing of this Act, have become exercisable by His Majesty in the tribal areas by grant, usage, sufferance or otherwise shall lapse.

This was considered at a meeting of the Viceroy's Advisers. I, as Reforms Commissioner, was opposed to the inclusion of sub-clause (b) and argued that, since the exercise of paramountcy was not based on any legislation by Parliament, its withdrawal need not be by means of parliamentary legislation. Sir Conrad Corfield, the Political Adviser, thought that two divergent views had been expressed on the matter. There were those who contended that paramountcy would automatically lapse on 15 August; but a number of eminent jurists had expressed their disagreement with this view. He therefore considered that in order to place the matter beyond doubt the sub-clause should be left in.

The next question was, whether even if paramountcy lapsed, all agreements of a commercial, economic or financial character between the States on the one hand and the British Government, the Secretary of State, and the Governor-General on the other, would cease to be legally effective. I pointed out that there were several important agreements which had been entered into for the common benefit of the States and British India where paramountcy did not enter, such as the agreement of 1920 with Bahawalpur and Bikaner regarding the Sutlej Valley canals project, and the Government of India agreement on salt with Jaipur and Jodhpur. The mutual rights and obligations of parties under such agreements could not be regarded as lapsing on the withdrawal of paramountcy. On the commencement of the Government of India Act of 1935, the Crown's rights and obligations had become for all practical and constitutional purposes the rights and obligations of the central Government and were secured as such by the provisions of the Act. The financial commitments of the central Government under agreements of this type were considerable. I therefore took the view that it would be best that these agreements should continue to be binding both on the States and on the successor Governments.

Sir Conrad Corfield, on behalf of the Political Department, contested my point of view. He referred to a meeting between himself and Lord Pethick-Lawrence at which it had been agreed that the abolition of the Crown Representative would automatically cause paramountcy to become void, together with any subsisting agreements between the Crown and the States. Sir Conrad did not agree with the view that paramountcy did not enter into the Sutlej Valley Canals Agreement of 1920 and the Jaipur and Jodhpur Salt Agreements. The first of these had been entered into on behalf of Bahawalpur by a Council of Regency controlled by the paramount power while the ruler was a minor. The Jaipur and Jodhpur Salt Agreements were typical of those which States had been required to conclude with the paramount power during the latter half of the nineteenth century in the interests of the central revenues. The Political Adviser was unable to entertain the view that the agreements should be continued after the lapse of paramountcy.

Lord Mountbatten did not take sides in this conflict of opinion. He merely forwarded both my view as well as that of the Political Department to the India Office.

It was about this time that the Secretary of State intimated that the Indian Independence Bill should include a specific denunciation of the treaties with the Indian States. Normally speaking, treaties were terminated by 'acts of State', but there was no reason why, on an occasion of this importance and in the peculiar circumstances, this should not be done by an Act of Parliament which would emphasize the legal position whereby paramountcy did not pass to the new Indian Dominions. This was considered by the Viceroy's advisers; they deprecated any such formal denunciation of treaties.

Meanwhile the Secretary of State's opinion in regard to the continuance of existing agreements was received. He stated that His Majesty's Government fully appreciated the importance attached by the Reforms Commissioner to the avoidance if possible of complete severance of relations with the States and the necessity for negotiations between parties over the whole field. But he considered that the views of the Political Department must prevail, as they were in line with His Majesty's Government's policy as stated in the Cabinet Mission memorandum. It was impossible to distinguish between agreements freely negotiated and those imposed. In any case, all had been made under the authority of the Crown and not of the executive Governments — central or provincial — of British India. It might perhaps have been possible at one time to proceed in some such manner as suggested by the Reforms Commissioner and to have assumed that the provisions of treaties and agreements remained in force until denounced or replaced by fresh agreements, the only essential initial denouncement being the termination of all rights and obligations exercised by the Crown Representative on behalf of His Majesty's Government. This would have left the States and the provinces and the two new central Governments as inheritors of all rights and obligations not falling strictly within the field of paramountcy and control over the States, thus preserving the *status quo* until changed by financial and economic agreements without, of course, impeding their future liberties of action. The Secretary of State, however, considered that it was too late to consider the merits or demerits of such a course, since a different attitude had been taken in the Cabinet Mission memorandum which definitely stated that political arrangements between the States on the one side and the British Crown and British India on the other would be brought to an end. It was thought impossible to interpret 'political' in so narrow a sense as to exclude financial or economic arrangements. The Secretary of State was satisfied that he must abide by this pronouncement of policy and he thought it inevitable that he must clarify the position in some more formal way than by a Government statement. In any case, Parliament would require this.

Formal individual denouncement, State by State, seemed to the Secretary of State much too elaborate a process and it would involve the difficult question of how to deal with those with whom there were no written treaties. One single instrument of denunciation by His Majesty's Government might be possible but would be politically undesirable. He considered it necessary therefore that both the lapse of paramountcy, as well as the denunciation of treaties, should be specifically included in the Bill. He admitted that there were certain objections, but he thought that any other course would lead to greater difficulties.

Accordingly, the Secretary of State suggested that sub-clauses (b) and (c) to clause 7 should be revised as follows:

(b) The suzerainty of His Majesty over the Indian States lapses, and with it, all treaties and agreements in force at the date of the passing of this Act between His Majesty and the rulers of Indian States, all functions exercisable by His Majesty at that date with respect to Indian States, all obligations of His Majesty existing at that date towards Indian States or the rulers thereof, and all powers, rights, authority or jurisdiction exercisable by His Majesty at that date in or in relation to Indian States by treaty, grant, usage, sufferance or otherwise; and

(c) there lapse also any treaties or agreements in force at the date of the passing of this Act between His Majesty and any persons having authority in the tribal areas, any obligations of His Majesty existing at that date to any such persons or with respect to the tribal areas, and all powers, rights, authority or jurisdiction exercisable at that date by His Majesty in or in relation to tribal areas by treaty, grant, usage, sufferance or otherwise.

In the meantime Lord Mountbatten had got the permission of the Secretary of State to show the draft Bill to the leaders of the Congress and the Muslim League in order to elicit their views. The Congress leaders considered that there was no specific provision in the Bill for the accession of the States and they wanted clause 2 to contain a specific provision to that effect.[1] With regard to clause 7, they expressed themselves very strongly that a complete abrogation of the treaties and agreements with the States would produce administrative chaos of the gravest kind. Agreements relating to railways, customs, harbours, irrigation, and the like would all disappear, and the very existence of States like Banaras and Mysore, which rested on Instruments of Transfer from the Crown, would be without any legal basis. Even the Cabinet Mission's memorandum contemplated in paragraph 4 that, pending the conclusion of new agreements, existing arrangements in all matters of common concern should continue. Paragraph 5 of the same memorandum, after referring to the lapse of paramountcy and the consequent cessation of all rights and obligations flowing therefrom, went on to state that the void so created must be filled by the States entering either into a federal relationship, or into new political arrangements with the successor Governments. But the advancement of the date of the lapse of paramountcy from June 1948 to August 1947 made it more difficult to conclude agreements. Individual negotiations of new agreements, some of them multi-partite, with a large number of States would necessarily be a long and laborious task. Consequently,

---

[1] It was assumed that this could be done by an adaptation of the Government of India Act of 1935 and that there was no necessity for a specific provision in the Indian Independence Bill for the accession of States.

they suggested that a Standstill clause to the following effect should be included in the Bill itself. 'Until new arrangements are completed, the existing relations and arrangements between His Majesty's Government and any Indian ruler in all matters of common concern shall continue as between the two Dominion Governments and the State concerned.'

The Muslim League had no comments to offer on clause 7.

Lord Mountbatten duly forwarded the views of the Congress to the Secretary of State. The Secretary of State contended that the proposed new clause amounted to continuance by parliamentary legislation for some period of the effects of agreements negotiated under paramountcy by substituting successor Governments for the Crown Representative. To this proposal, there were insuperable objections. Firstly, the States were not British territory and were not subject to parliamentary legislation placing obligations on them without their consent. Such consent could not be presumed, since enforcement of such legislation would pass from His Majesty's Government to the successor authorities with effect from 15 August. The Secretary of State could not contemplate one date for the transfer of power in British India and another for the termination of paramountcy in the States. Moreover, the States in accepting the Cabinet Mission's memorandum had made it crystal clear that they accepted the general principle of the plan on the basis of the declaration regarding the termination of paramountcy to which the British Government's adherence had been announced in the 3 June Plan. The Secretary of State, in fact, held that the Congress proposal would be tantamount to the repudiation of that undertaking.

The Viceroy, returning to the charge, pointed out that the unconditional lapse of treaties and agreements would hit the States equally hard. This was a crucial issue and he felt that something should be done, if necessary by fixing a time limit, say 31 March 1948, for the operation of the proviso. He also contended that clause 2, as drafted, left the position of the acceding States *vis-à-vis* the new Dominions entirely in the air. He suggested that the definitions of both Dominions should be modified so as to cover the States which become hereafter part of the particular Dominion by accession.

The Secretary of State accepted the recommendations for a specific provision covering the accession of the States. A new subclause was accordingly inserted at the end of clause 2:

14

Without prejudice to the generality of the provisions of sub-section (3) of this section, nothing in this section shall be construed as preventing the accession of Indian States to either of the new Dominions.

Regarding clause 7, the Secretary of State agreed to insert the following proviso at the end of that clause:

Provided that, notwithstanding anything in paragraph (*b*) or paragraph (*c*) of this sub-section, effect shall, as nearly as may be continued to be given to the provisions of any such agreement as is therein referred to which relate to customs, transit and communications, posts and telegraphs, or other like matters, until the provisions in question are denounced by the Ruler of the Indian State or person having authority in the tribal areas on the one hand, or by the Dominion or Province or other part thereof concerned on the other hand, or are superseded by subsequent agreements.

This proviso did not satisfy the Congress leaders.

The late Sir B. N. Rau, Constitutional Adviser to the Constituent Assembly, who saw Lord Mountbatten on 7 July, pointed out that it was unthinkable that 327 rulers of petty States, whose average area was about 20 square miles, average population about 3,000 and average annual revenue about Rs. 22,000; who had hitherto exercised only petty judicial powers, such as trying criminal cases involving sentence of not more than three months' imprisonment or Rs 200 fine, should almost overnight acquire the powers of life and death. He suggested that a proviso should be included that the criminal, revenue and civil jurisdiction, hitherto exercised by, or under, the authority of the Crown Representative in regard to these small States should hereafter be exercisable by, or under the authority of, the Dominion Government concerned. Lord Mountbatten supported this view and forwarded it to the Secretary of State, but to no purpose.

While the Indian Independence Bill was on the parliamentary anvil, I suggested to Sardar that since we had decided on the policy of accession we should go ahead and contact the rulers. As the time at our disposal was extremely limited, protracted negotiations were obviously out of the question and I requested Sardar to meet some of the leading rulers and States' ministers. To this he agreed. It was in this connexion that I myself met the Maharajah of Patiala for the first time; he was then acting as Chancellor of the Chamber of Princes. I complained to him that even though the Political Department was in the process of liquidation the rulers continued to be guided by the officers of that Department. The Political

Department did not see eye to eye with us on the question of accession and I suggested to the Maharajah that, by conferring with its officers, the rulers were only misleading themselves as to the policy of the Government of India. I asked for his co-operation in implementing the policy of accession and I told him frankly that 'independent of us, you cannot exist.' Our cordial talks revealed a measure of community of outlook and we parted as friends, assuring each other of mutual goodwill and co-operation.

On 10 July, a number of rulers and States' ministers met at Sardar's residence. The Maharajahs of Patiala and Gwalior, and Sir B. L. Mitter (Baroda), K. M. Panikkar (Bikaner) and Hari Sharma (Patiala) were present. Sardar urged that the States which had joined the Constituent Assembly should forthwith accede to India on three subjects, and pointed out that such a course would enable them to have a direct voice in shaping the policies of the central Government. The States' delegation appreciated the logic of the suggestion, but emphasized that the matter required careful consideration and a cautious approach. It was decided to hold a series of informal discussions with the rulers and their advisers. Various suggestions were made relating to the functions of the States Department. It was suggested, among other things, that the Department should deal only with matters of policy; that so far as the States acceding to the Union were concerned, the Department should cease to function as soon as the Union constitution became operative and that in the meanwhile it should function in consultation with an advisory committee of Ministers from the States. It was this conference which at last broke the ice, clearing away a mass of vague suspicions which the rulers had entertained about the new States Department.

The next day we issued the agenda for the conference of the rulers to be held on 25 July. It included: (1) Accession of the States on 'defence', 'external affairs' and 'communications'; (2) Standstill Agreement; (3) Advisory Council for the States Department; (4) Channels of correspondence and representation of central Government in the States.

As soon as the policy of accession had been decided upon, I communicated the decision to Akhtar Hussain, I.C.S., who was working in the Pakistan wing of the States Ministry. I asked him to inform Abdur Rab Nishtar, the League Minister for States, of our plan. Subsequently I circulated a note on this subject to both

Sardar and Nishtar. Nishtar had no comments to offer on the note.

Jinnah, of course, objected to the policy of accession. He told Lord Mountbatten that it was utterly wrong and he publicly announced that he would guarantee the independence of the States in Pakistan.

On 24 July Sardar and I met another delegation of rulers and States' ministers which included the rulers of Patiala, Gwalior, Bikaner and Nawanagar. Among the ministers were Sir B. L. Mitter (Baroda), Sir A. Ramaswami Mudaliar (Mysore), C. S. Venkatachar, I.C.S. (Jodhpur) and K. M. Panikkar (Bikaner). This meeting was a crucial one for it showed that we were making headway with our plan. It was evident that quite a number of rulers had broken away from the leadership of the Nawab of Bhopal and were prepared to come in with us.

By this time we had produced a draft Instrument of Accession, and revised the original draft of the Standstill Agreement prepared by the Political Department. These two drafts were circulated to the rulers at the special session of the Chamber of Princes on 25 July, when Lord Mountbatten addressed that Chamber for the first and last time in his capacity as Crown Representative. The speech was made *ex tempore* and without any notes and was the apogee of persuasion. He advised the rulers to accede to the appropriate Dominion in regard to the three subjects of 'defence', 'external affairs', and 'communications'. He pointed out that 'defence' was a matter which a State could not conduct for itself; 'external affairs' was something that no State had dealt with before. The continuity of communications necessitated their accession on this subject also. Lord Mountbatten said that accession on these three subjects left the rulers with all the practical independence that they could possibly use and made them free of those subjects which they could not possibly manage on their own. He assured them that their accession on these subjects would involve no financial liability and that in other matters there would be no encroachment on their sovereignty. He made it clear that though the rulers were technically at liberty to link with either of the Dominions, there were certain geographical compulsions which could not be evaded. 'Out of something like 565 States, the vast majority are irretrievably linked geographically with the Dominion of India.' He stressed the urgency of the situation and said: 'If you are prepared to come, you must come before 15 August.' He concluded with the cogent appeal: 'You cannot run away from the Dominion Government which is your neighbour any more than you can run away from the subjects for whose welfare you are responsible.' Lord Mountbatten then announced the personnel of the Negotiating Committee, consisting of ten rulers and twelve ministers, to consider in detail the items on the agenda. A number of questions were put to him by the rulers and ministers. His lucid replies helped to allay princely apprehensions and bring about an atmosphere of cordiality.

The Negotiating Committee was split into two sub-committees, one to deal with the Instrument of Accession and the other with the Standstill Agreement. These sub-committees held separate meetings daily at Bikaner House in Delhi and I had to move constantly from one sub-committee to the other to discuss debatable points. The deliberations were most businesslike. After six days and nights of hectic work, on 31 July the drafts were finalized.

By the Instrument of Accession, the States acceded to the Dominion of India on the three subjects of defence, external affairs and communications, their content being as defined in List 1 of Schedule VII to the Government of India Act of 1935, reproduced in a Schedule[1] annexed to the Instrument. Accession did not imply any financial liability on the part of the acceding States. This Instrument was intended only for the rulers of fully empowered States, which numbered 140.

[1] The matters with respect to which the Dominion Legislature may make laws for this State...

A. DEFENCE
 1. The naval, military and air forces of the Dominion and any other armed force raised or maintained by the Dominion; any armed forces, including forces raised or maintained by an Acceding State, which are attached to, or operating with, any of the armed forces of the Dominion.
 2. Naval, military and air force works, administration of cantonment areas.
 3. Arms; fire-arms ; ammunition.
 4. Explosives.

B. EXTERNAL AFFAIRS
 1. External affairs; the implementing of treaties and agreements with other countries; extradition, including the surrender of criminals and accused persons to parts of His Majesty's dominions outside India.
 2. Admission into, and emigration and expulsion from, India, including in relation thereto the regulation of the movements in India of persons who are not British subjects domiciled in India or subjects of any acceding State; pilgrimages to places beyond India.
 3. Naturalization.

C. COMMUNICATIONS
 1. Posts and telegraphs, including telephones, wireless, broadcasting, and other like forms of communication.
 2. Federal railways; the regulation of all railways other than minor railways in respect of safety, maximum and minimum rates and fares, station and service terminal charges,

Besides these 140 States, there were *estates* and *talukas*, where the Crown exercised certain powers and jurisdiction, that were also counted as 'States'. These, numbering over 300, were situated in Kathiawar and Gujarat. Under the Attachment Scheme of 1943 some of these *estates* and *talukas* were tagged on to adjoining bigger States. But with the lapse of paramountcy, the Attachment Scheme came to an end. In any case, the rulers of these *estates* and *talukas* desired that they should be reverted to their former position and that the Government of India should administer their *estates* as was done by the Political Department before 1943. Another Instrument of Accession, suitable for their status and requirements, was prepared for these *estates* and *talukas*. This document, while preserving the form of accession, vested all the residuary powers and jurisdiction in the Central Government. Subsequently an ordinance termed the 'Extra Provincial Jurisdiction Ordinance' was promulgated for the exercise of the powers and jurisdiction acquired by the Government of India in these areas.

There were a number of intermediate rulers, higher in status than the *talukdars* and *estate-holders* of Kathiawar and Gujarat, who exercised wide but not quite full powers. These States, numbering over 70, were in Kathiawar, Central India and the Simla Hills. We devised still another Instrument of Accession for these States, the object of which was to ensure that the rulers did not exercise higher powers than they had prior to 15 August 1947. The rulers

inter-change of traffic and the responsibility of railway administrations as carriers of goods and passengers; the regulation of minor railways in respect of safety and the responsibility of the administrations of such railways as carriers of goods and passengers.

3. Maritime shipping and navigation, including shipping and navigation on tidal waters; Admiralty jurisdiction.

4. Port quarantine.

5. Major ports, that is to say, the declaration and delimitation of such ports, and the constitution and powers of Port Authorities therein.

6. Aircraft and air navigation; the provision of aerodromes; regulation and organization of air traffic and of aerodromes.

7. Lighthouses, including lightships, beacons and other provisions for the safety of shipping and aircraft.

8. Carriage of passengers and goods by sea or by air.

9. Extension of the powers and jurisdiction of members of the police force belonging to any unit to railway area outside that unit.

D. ANCILLARY

1. Elections to the Dominion Legislature, subject to the provisions of the Act and of any Order made thereunder.

2. Offences against laws with respect to any of the aforesaid matters.

3. Inquiries and statistics for the purposes of any of the aforesaid matters.

4. Jurisdiction and powers of all courts with respect to any of the aforesaid matters but, except with the consent of the Ruler of the Acceding State, not so as to confer any jurisdiction or powers upon any courts other than courts ordinarily exercising jurisdiction in or in relation to that State.

recognized that it was a fair condition that they could not expect to rise in status suddenly because of the lapse of paramountcy.

In all three cases, the Standstill Agreement was common. It laid down that all agreements and administrative arrangements as to matters of common concern specified in the schedule then existing between the Crown and the States should continue 'until new arrangements in this behalf' were made.

A meeting of the full Negotiating Committee was held at Bikaner House on 31 July. Twenty-five rulers and representatives of the States were present. The drafts of the Instrument of Accession and the Standstill Agreement as passed by the two sub-committees were approved. It was at this meeting that the question of setting up an Advisory Council was discussed. In his statement of 5 July Sardar had said that he would explore the possibilities of associating with the administration of the new Department a Standing Committee representing both the States and British India. The ministers of the major States were anxious that a body of this kind should be brought into existence. Some of the rulers, like Maharajah Sir Sadul Singh of Bikaner and the Jam Saheb of Nawanagar, were not in favour of the idea. Finding that the rulers were not unanimous, we dropped the proposal.

While the Negotiating Committee was busy with its labours, the *Hindustan Times* managed to get hold of a copy of the draft Instrument of Accession and to publish it. When I met Sardar that morning, he said: 'Menon, now that the *Hindustan Times* has published the Instrument of Accession, can I see a copy of it?' As I was reporting to him twice daily on what was happening in the sub-committees appointed to finalize the Instrument of Accession and the Standstill Agreement, I was rather puzzled. But Sardar smiled and said he was only joking. Sardar had that saving sense of humour which is so great an attribute especially in a man of his position and responsibility.

There were not wanting people who criticized the idea of accession on three subjects only without any further commitments on the part of the States. They regarded such a relationship as too nebulous to be of any value. The absence of financial commitments was criticized by them in the strongest terms. They said that the entire proposition was not one over which anyone could enthuse. Such criticism was based on complete ignorance of the facts of the situation. No thought had been given to what would be the position of the States on 15 August if there were no accession; the States would be independent and the border States would be at liberty to ally themselves with Pakistan. Further, what would have happened in those troublous days if law and order in any State broke down ? These critics did not realize that, by the accession of the States on 'defence', the Government of India secured the right of entry into a State whenever internal security was threatened. Moreover, without an Instrument of Accession the Government of India could not exercise civil and criminal jurisdiction in the semi-jurisdictional and non-jurisdictional *estates* and *talukas*—a lacuna to which Sir B. N. Rau had drawn pointed attention when the Indian Independence Bill was on the anvil. The critics also overlooked the prevailing suspicion in the minds of the rulers. It was not practical politics to flaunt in the face of the States the supremacy of the Union Government when the 3 June Plan had assured them the lapse of paramountcy. The critics were completely silenced when Junagadh acceded to Pakistan; they realized then the possibilities of disintegration if the policy of accession had not been implemented.

I invariably saw Sardar at least twice a day, once in the morning and again in the evening when he would be having his dinner. This was my routine as long as both of us were in Delhi, from the time Sardar became States Minister until his death. On his part, Sardar followed the daily routine of an early morning walk when he would meet and listen to all classes of people; he would give interviews at his residence, and he would make it a point also of perusing all leading newspapers, both English and vernacular. Thus would he bring to bear on our discussions such important aspects of public opinion as might affect the problems on which we in the Ministry were engaged. My meetings with Sardar in the morning were devoted to the discussion of important matters of policy on which I would ascertain his views and obtain his decisions. In the evening, my task was to apprise him of the manner in which those decisions had been implemented, or of any fresh points which might have arisen in the course of that day. As if this were not sufficient, he would ring me up between 9.30 and 10 every night. I had to give him a sort of 'all quiet on the States front' and only then could he get to sleep. This night telephoning was continued as a never-failing practice, whether he was at the headquarters or on tour, and to my wife's chagrin it frequently happened that the telephone call came too while I was having my dinner!

Leadership is of two kinds. A leader like Napoleon, who was master of both policy and detail, wanted merely the instruments to carry out his orders. Sardar's leadership was of the second category. Having selected his men, he trusted them entirely to implement his policy. Sardar never assumed that he knew everything and he never adopted a policy without full and frank consultation. Whenever we entered into any discussion, we did so as personal friends rather than as Minister and Secretary.

On 28 July Lord Mountbatten gave a colourful reception at the Viceroy's House in honour of over fifty rulers and a hundred States' representatives. Pakistan representatives were also present. This reception was in the nature of a last-minute canvassing of voters near the polling booth. Those of the rulers who had not yet signified their intention of acceding were taken by the A.D.Cs. one by one for a friendly talk with Lord Mountbatten. When he had finished with them, he passed them on to me in the full view of the company and I, in my turn, conducted them across the room to Sardar. This had a good psychological effect on the rulers who were present.

There were, however, many rulers who did not attend this reception, and who were either hostile to the plan of accession or were sitting on the fence. As mentioned before, Hyderabad and Travancore had already announced their intention of declaring their independence and their lead was followed by several others, whose attitude was naturally causing the Government of India some anxiety.

Meanwhile, the Muslim League leaders were by no means idle. Meetings between them and some of the rulers had become almost a daily occurrence. Tempting concessions were being offered to the rulers to inveigle them into joining Pakistan. The League leaders were concentrating in particular on some of the border States.

As if the intransigence of some of the rulers and the inveigling tactics of the League leaders were not enough, it seemed that the Political Department was adding to our worries. That Department had encouraged the Nawab of Bhopal in his efforts to evolve a 'Third Force' out of the States and reports were being brought to me by some of the rulers that they were being instigated not to accede to India. This naturally upset me. I acquainted Lord Mountbatten with what I had heard. I felt that if both Sir Conrad Corfield and myself operated in the same field, it was like trying to walk simultaneously in two opposite directions. Soon after, Sir Conrad Corfield went on leave to England and retired from service.

15

On 1 August, Lord Mountbatten gave a luncheon to several of the leading rulers. The A.D.Cs. had helped to form virtual 'Aye' and 'No' lobbies of the rulers in accordance with their attitude to accession. The Maharajahs of Patiala and of Bikaner created a diversion by passing through the 'No' lobby and then roaring with laughter. The 'No' lobby consisted of 'last-ditchers' who were inclined to execute Standstill Agreements and to mark time so far as the Instrument of Accession was concerned. To deal with them it was announced at a conference of rulers and States' ministers at Bikaner House on 1 August that the Government of India had decided that Standstill Agreements would be entered into only with those rulers who executed the Instrument of Accession.

The process of getting Instruments of Accession signed involved considerable persuasion, strain and anxiety. It was easy enough to get the signatures of those rulers who had been the first to send their representatives to the Constituent Assembly; but a series of negotiations now began with those rulers who opposed the policy of accession.

I have already mentioned that soon after the announcement of the 3 June Plan, Sir C. P. Ramaswami Aiyar (Sir C. P. for short) had declared that Travancore would assert its independence with the transfer of power. In view particularly of his position in the public life of the country, this statement had deleterious repercussions and encouraged the rulers who were not favourably disposed towards the Indian Dominion. When we issued invitations for the meeting of rulers and States' representatives to be held on 25 July, the Government of Travancore replied that there was no point in their representatives attending this meeting, as the State had decided not to accede to India. It should be pointed out that at about this time the Travancore State Congress had threatened a campaign of direct action to begin from 1 August. The Congress press in India had been extremely caustic in its comments on Sir C. P. In fact there had been a sharp exchange of words between the Congress leaders and Sir C. P. in the newspapers. This was certainly not helpful.

Lord Mountbatten therefore invited Sir C. P. to New Delhi. On 20 July I had an exploratory talk with him. I explained to him the advantages which would accrue to Travancore as a result of accession. All we asked was executive and legislative authority in regard to defence, external affairs and communications. Sir C. P.

referred to the proposal of the Union Consultative Committee of the Constituent Assembly to divert to the Centre the revenues from customs, import and export duties. He pointed out that Travancore was a maritime State deriving nearly half its total revenue from these heads; and if it were to accede on these conditions, it would be reduced to a fifth-rate State. I assured him that the present accession plan had nothing to do with the new constitution and that what we were asking for was accession on three subjects under the Government of India Act of 1935 without any financial or other commitments. Sir C.P. admitted that he had not been aware of this approach. I pointed out that on 15 August the States would literally be released from the centre and would thereafter have no contact either with the centre or among themselves. This was too dangerous a position and if the transitional period was not safe-guarded, the result might be complete chaos. Transitions were always risky. In India especially, there was real danger of unsocial elements rearing their heads. One aspect of the question which was causing particular concern was the communist menace. The only remedy against this was to build up an integrated economic and political system strong enough to withstand their ideology. I then brought down the discussion to the personal plane, assuring him of my high regard both for his realistic attitude to affairs and for the part he had played in the past. It ought not be said of him that at India's critical hour he had not made his contribution towards building a united India when he had it in his power to do so. I begged him not to take any precipitate action. Whatever might be his grievances against the Congress, the utterances of its leaders ought not to deflect him from what he considered to be in the best interests, not only of Travancore, but of India as a whole. Sir C.P. replied that he could not give an answer immediately but he assured me that, 'coming from a sincere well-wisher of the States and of myself in particular, your comments will have my closest atten-tion.'

Sir C.P. met Lord Mountbatten on 21 July, when the latter tried to pin him down on the question of accession. Lord Mount-batten said that all other questions could be adjusted by negotiation and agreement later on. He added that here was a golden oppor-tunity for Travancore to play its part. The accession of Travancore would be hailed throughout India as a great act of statesmanship, nor would it entail any financial loss to the State. On the other hand, in the shaping of the future destinies of India, Travancore could play a very important part since its representatives would be sitting in the Dominion Legislature. Sir C.P. stated that he would not agree to 'accession' but to some 'agreement' on three subjects.

In a subsequent talk with Sir C.P. I made it clear that an 'agreement' on three subjects would not be acceptable, as other States would want to follow his example. A signature on the Instrument of Accession was absolutely necessary. At first he was adamant, but after a further interview with Lord Mountbatten, he agreed that accession was inevitable. As he had to be back in Trivandrum on 25 July in connexion with the death centenary of a former Maharajah of Travancore, a great composer and patron of music, he took with him the draft Instrument of Accession and a personal letter to the Maharajah from Lord Mountbatten, promising to return on 27 July. Before he could do so, a personal attack was made on him and he was wounded. But the Maharajah telegraphed to Lord Mountbatten his acceptance of the Instrument of Accession and Standstill Agreement. This announcement had a distinct effect on other rulers who were still wavering. In the meantime, Sardar appealed to the Travancore State Congress to suspend their campaign of direct action.

The late Maharajah Hanwant Singh of Jodhpur continued to be intractable. Jinnah and the Muslim League leaders had a series of meetings with him. At the last of these interviews, Maharajah Hanwant Singh had taken the then Maharajkumar of Jaisalmer with him, because the Maharajah of Bikaner would not accompany him and he shrank from going alone. Theirs were the three States geographically contiguous to Pakistan. Jinnah, I was told, signed a blank sheet of paper and gave it to Maharajah Hanwant Singh along with his own fountain pen, saying 'You can fill in all your conditions.' A discussion followed. The Maharajah was prepared to line up with Pakistan. He then turned to the Maharajkumar of Jaisalmer and asked him whether he would follow suit. The Maharajkumar said he would do so on one condition: If there was any trouble between the Hindus and Muslims, he would not side with the Muslims against the Hindus. This was a bombshell and took Maharajah Hanwant Singh completely by surprise. Sir Mohammad Zafrullah however made light of the whole affair and pressed Maharajah Hanwant Singh to sign the instrument. But the Maharajah now felt unable to take a decision. He suggested to Jinnah that he would go to Jodhpur and return the next day. The Maharajah remained at Jodhpur for three days. The atmosphere in the State was hostile to the idea that Jodhpur should cast its lot with Pakistan; the *Jagirdars* and nobles were decidedly opposed to it. The Maharajah began to waver. When he returned to Delhi after three days I was informed that, unless I handled the Maharajah quickly, the chances were that he might accede to Pakistan. I went to the Hotel Imperial and told the Maharajah that Lord Mountbatten wanted to see him. We then drove to Government House and I kept the Maharajah in the visitors' room while I went in and explained the situation to Lord Mountbatten. The Maharajah was then called in. Lord Mountbatten made it clear that from a purely legal standpoint there was no objection to the ruler of Jodhpur acceding to Pakistan; but the Maharajah should, he stressed, consider seriously the consequences of his doing so, having regard to the fact that he himself was a Hindu; that his State was populated predominantly by Hindus and that the same applied to the States surrounding Jodhpur. In the light of these considerations, if the Maharajah were to accede to Pakistan, his action would surely be in conflict with the principle underlying the partition of India on the basis of Muslim and non-Muslim majority areas; and serious communal trouble inside the State would be the inevitable consequence of such affiliation. The Maharajah started at once to ask for impossible concessions. I told him plainly: 'If you want to sign on false hopes, I will agree to your demands,' adding that most of the demands could not be conceded. He then told us that Jinnah had given him a blank paper in which he could put down all the concessions he wanted. I urged him not to be swayed by false promises. After a great deal of discussion, I gave him a letter conceding some of his demands. Thereafter he signed the Instrument of Accession.

After a few minutes, Lord Mountbatten went out of the room and the Maharajah whipped out a revolver, levelled it at me and said: 'I refuse to accept your dictation.' I told him that he was making a very serious mistake if he thought that by killing me, or threatening to kill me, he could get the accession abrogated. 'Don't indulge in juvenile theatricals,' I admonished him. Shortly after, Lord Mountbatten returned and I told him what had happened. He made light of the episode and turned it to jest.

Presently the Maharajah returned to normal and we departed in company. After leaving him at his residence, I returned to office. The whole episode became a standing joke between us later on.[1]

The Nawab of Bhopal did not attend the meeting of rulers and States' representatives on 25 July. He felt, as he put it, that they were being 'invited like the Oysters to attend the tea party with the Walrus and the Carpenter.' He, along with the Maharajah of Indore, headed a group of rulers who strenuously opposed accession. The Nawab was firmly of opinion that it would be impossible for Bhopal to 'become an organic part of either Dominion.' He suggested that he should enter into treaty relations with both the Dominions. He was handled throughout by Lord Mountbatten. I was present at most of their meetings. Lord Mountbatten's long-standing personal friendship with the Nawab played its part in the latter's decision to accede. By the first week of August the Nawab had realized that the vast majority of the rulers had opted for accession and that, if he did not come in, Bhopal would be left in an anomalous and difficult position. He wanted to know whether he could sign a Standstill Agreement without acceding. We told him that Standstill Agreements would not be signed with rulers who refused to accede. He then sent his Constitutional Adviser, Sir Mohammad Zafrullah Khan, for clarification of the terms of the Instrument of Accession. We had a long discussion. I made it clear to Sir Mohammad that it would be impossible to make any alterations in the Instrument of Accession and that Bhopal would have to join on the same terms as all other States. At last the Nawab signed, but with the stipulation that his signature should be kept secret for ten days after the transfer of power. There was no difficulty in complying with this request.

Writing to Sardar announcing his decision to accede, the Nawab said:

I do not disguise the fact that while the struggle was on, I used every means in my power to preserve the independence and neutrality of my State. Now that I have conceded defeat, I hope that you will find that I

---

[1] Here was a prince, head-strong and emotional, with considerable organizing capacity. His premature death is a matter of deep regret. During the general elections of 1952, Maharajah Hanwant Singh sent a special messenger to me in Bangalore where I had settled down after retirement. He wanted me to stand for election to the House of the People from the Jodhpur constituency, and assured me that the seat was quite safe. If I was agreeable, I was to go to Jodhpur at once. Though I obviously could not accept the offer, I was moved by his letter and sent him an affectionate reply. A few weeks later he died in a plane crash.

can be as staunch a friend as I have been an inveterate opponent. I harbour no ill feelings towards anyone, for throughout I have been treated with consideration and have received understanding and courtesy from your side. I now wish to tell you that so long as you maintain your present firm stand against the disruptive forces in the country and continue to be a friend of the States as you have shown you are, you will find in me a loyal and faithful ally.

In reply Sardar wrote:

Quite candidly, I do not look upon the accession of your State to the Indian Dominion as either a victory for us or defeat for you. It is only right and propriety which have triumphed in the end and, in that triumph, you and I have played our respective roles. You deserve full credit for having recognised the soundness of the position and for the courage, the honesty and the boldness of having given up your earlier stand which according to us was entirely antagonistic to the interests as much of India as of your own State. I have noted with particular pleasure your assurance of support to the Dominion Government in combating disloyal elements irrespective of caste, creed or religion and your offer of loyal and faithful friendship. During the last few months, it had been a great disappointment and regret to me that your undoubted talents and abilities were not at the country's disposal in the critical times through which we were passing and I therefore particularly value this assurance of co-operation and friendship.

The Maharajah of Indore not only refrained from attending the meeting of the rulers and States' representatives on 25 July, though he had already returned to India from abroad; he did not even reply to the invitation. Lord Mountbatten had an idea at one time of summoning him in order to induce him to accede but I advised him not to take any such step. With the knowledge of the States Ministry a delegation of Mahratta princes had been to the Maharajah to impress on him the desirability and wisdom of acceding to India; but he would not even talk to them. Sir Pratap Singh, Gaekwar of Baroda, later told me that they were all of them waiting in the Maharajah's drawing room, when he came in and went past them on his way upstairs as though they did not exist.

Subsequently, however, the Maharajah of Indore and the Nawab of Bhopal had an interview with Lord Mountbatten. As the Maharajah did not, during this interview, commit himself either way with regard to accession, we were not a little surprised when one morning we received in an ordinary postal envelope both the Instrument of Accession and the Standstill Agreement signed by him; just that with no covering letter. However, from that time on, he gave full co-operation to the Government of India.

Even last-ditchers like the rulers of Dholpur, Bharatpur, Bilaspur and Nabha ultimately signed. There were prolonged discussions with some of them; they no doubt sensed that the Instrument of Accession in the present form might not be available to them after 15 August and that they would then have to negotiate with the Government of India for terms which would probably be less favourable.

Some rulers signed the Instrument of Accession and forwarded it with covering letters which laid down conditions subject to which the accession had been signed. They were told that the execution of the Instrument of Accession must be unconditional and they subsequently complied.

In view of the special position and peculiar problems of Hyderabad, both Nehru and Sardar felt that Lord Mountbatten should continue to negotiate with the Nizam even after 15 August. Accordingly, on 12 August Lord Mountbatten informed the Nizam that the offer of accession would remain open in the case of Hyderabad for a further period of two months.

The rulers of all the States geographically contiguous to India, with the exception of Junagadh and two small States under Muslim rulers in Kathiawar, had signed the Instrument of Accession and the Standstill Agreement by 15 August. With regard to Kashmir, the States Ministry had made no approach to the ruler at all, though Lord Mountbatten took the trouble to visit Kashmir personally at the beginning of July to try and induce the Maharajah, who was a very old friend of his, to make up his mind to accede to either India or Pakistan.

On 14 August the States Ministry took control of all the residencies from the Political Department. At one place, the Resident refused to allow the Indian flag to be hoisted at the Residency on the morning of 15 August 1947. An ugly situation threatened. The officer realized his error in time and allowed the flag to be hoisted. But for this one incident there was no trouble anywhere.

By the policy of accession we had ensured the fundamental unity of the country. India had become one federation, with the provinces and the States as integral parts. The Standstill Agreement had provided the basis for retaining intact the many agreements and administrative arrangements which had been built up over nearly a century for ensuring that all-India interests were safeguarded and which, with the termination of paramountcy, had threatened to disappear and in the process throw the whole country into a state of confusion. All this was done in an atmosphere of cordiality and goodwill. We realized the strength of the rulers' antagonism towards anything which smacked of 'paramountcy' and our object was, as set out in the Statement of 5 July, to 'make laws sitting together as friends.' Our efforts in this direction were crowned with success. There remained only the question of the creation of an organization to fill the vacuum created by the disappearance of the Political Department and its local agencies in the States or groups of States. These officials had served not only to exercise paramountcy functions, but to do a considerable amount of routine administrative work, such as operating the various controls, issuing passports and arms licences and performing other similar duties. In order to continue this administrative work, especially in relation to the smaller States, we appointed Regional Commissioners in Rajkot, Kolhapur, Rajputana, Central India, the Simla Hill States, the Bundelkhand and Baghelkhand States and the Eastern States. Thus the gap which had threatened to balkanize the country was effectively stopped.

In his address to the Constituent Assembly on the morning of 15 August, Lord Mountbatten referred to the success of the accession policy and paid a tribute to Sardar as a far-sighted statesman. He said:

It is a great triumph for the realism and sense of responsibility of the rulers and the governments of the States as well as for the Government of India that it was possible to produce an instrument of accession which was equally acceptable to both sides; and one, moreover, so simple and so straightforward that within less than three weeks practically all the States concerned had signed the Instrument of Accession and the Standstill Agreement. There is thus established a unified political structure.

My feeling was one of profound thankfulness to God. The threatened fragmentation had been averted and the whole country had come under one political umbrella. The prophets of gloom who predicted disruption had been belied. We had obtained a breathing space during which we could evolve a permanent relationship between the Government of India and the States.

The masterly handling of the rulers by Sardar was the foremost factor in the success of the accession policy. The rulers soon came to

16

recognize him as a stable force in Indian politics and as one who would give them a fair deal. Added to this, his unfailing politeness to the rulers, viewed against his reputation as the 'Iron Man of India,' endeared him to them and created such confidence that all accepted his advice without demur.

Another factor which went a long way in winning over the rulers was of course the infectious charm and inborn tact of Lord Mountbatten. It was because of his abundant love for India, and not merely because he was obliged to do so, that he had taken upon himself the task of negotiating with the rulers on the question of accession. And once he undertook any task he invariably put the whole weight of his personality into what he was doing and spared himself no effort. Half-hearted methods and half-hearted measures are alien to him. India can never forget the magnificent service he rendered at a critical juncture in her history.

Nor can one forget the rulers, but for whose willing and patriotic co-operation the policy of accession could not have been implemented. They gave ample evidence of imagination, foresight and patriotism and, as Sardar himself remarked, they might well claim to be co-architects of a free and united India. It is not possible to name all the many rulers who co-operated with us. Sir Pratap Singh, Gaekwar of Baroda, was the first ruler actually to sign the Instrument of Accession, though I think the first announcement of accession was made by the Dewan of Gwalior, M. A. Srinivasan, on behalf of the Maharajah, Sir Jivaji Rao Scindia of Gwalior. The latter had been of great help during the negotiations and had undoubtedly exercised a healthy influence on several rulers. But the greatest share of the credit for giving a patriotic lead to the rulers and convincing them that it was in their own interest to accede to India must go to the late Maharajah Sir Sadul Singh of Bikaner and Maharajah Sir Yadavindra Singh of Patiala. The former's valuable help was acknowledged in several letters which Sardar addressed to him. Lord Mountbatten publicly referred to it in his speech at Bikaner while investing the Maharajah with the G.C.S.I. By the untimely death of Sir Sadul Singh, the country lost a patriotic ruler who had made the utmost sacrifices without bitterness. For myself, I lost a very great personal friend. Maharajah Sir Yadavindra Singh of Patiala had co-operated with us ever since my first meeting with him at the Hotel Imperial. This young ruler, who was only thirty-four years of age at that time, showed remarkably robust patriotism and his contribution cannot be lightly forgotten. The Jam Saheb too, was a tower of strength in those days of hectic negotiations. He always brought a practical mind to bear upon our problems and many an otherwise trying hour was enlivened by his sparkling humour.

VI

JUNAGADH

THE accession of the rulers was only the prelude to a final solution of the States problem. Before we could think of the next step, a threatening cloud appeared over the western horizon. This was the Nawab of Junagadh's accession to Pakistan.

Junagadh was the premier State in the group of Kathiawar States. It lay in the south-west of Kathiawar. It was bounded almost entirely by other Indian States, except for the south and south-west where lies the Arabian Sea. The State had no contiguity with Pakistan by land and its distance by sea, from Port Veraval to Karachi, was about 300 miles. The area of the State was 3,337 square miles and the population (according to the Census of 1941) numbered 6,70,719 of whom over 80 per cent were Hindus. There were several islands of Junagadh territory in the States of Gondal, Bhavnagar and Nawanagar. Similarly, parts of States which had acceded to the Indian Dominion were interspersed with Junagadh territory. Access to these as well as to certain areas belonging to Baroda State was only possible through Junagadh. Within its borders were Hindu and Jain religious shrines which have attracted pilgrims from all over India. Its railways and posts and telegraphs were an integral part of the Indian system. The railway police, telegraphs and telephones were administered by the Government of India.

Junagadh was a Rajput State under the Chudasama dynasty until 1472-73, when it was conquered by Sultan Muhammad Bedga of Ahmedabad. In the reign of Emperor Akbar it became a dependency of the Court of Delhi under the immediate authority of the *subah* of Ahmedabad. About 1735, when the Moghul Government had fallen into decay, Sherkhan Babi, a soldier of fortune and an officer under the *subah*, expelled the Moghul Governor and established his rule in Junagadh. The last Nawab of Junagadh was a descendant of Sherkhan Babi.

The Nawab, Sir Mahabatkhan Rasulkhanji, was an eccentric of rare vintage. His chief preoccupation in life was dogs, of which he owned hundreds. I was told, indeed, that he carried his love for dogs to such lengths that he once organized a wedding of two of his pets, over which he spent a huge sum of money and in honour of which he proclaimed a State holiday!

The Nawab had all along been paying lip-service to the ideal of a united Kathiawar. On 11 April 1947, in reply to some speculations in the Gujarati press regarding the State's attitude towards the future constitutional set-up of India, the Government of Junagadh issued a press note which contained the following paragraph:

What Junagadh pre-eminently stands for is the solidarity of Kathiawar and would welcome the formation of a self-contained group of Kathiawar States. Such a group while providing for the autonomy and entity of individual States and their subjects would be a suitable basis for co-operation in matters of common concern generally and co-ordination where necessary.

This clear statement had set all doubts at rest. On 22 April the Junagadh Government Gazette reproduced a speech of the Dewan, Khan Bahadur Abdul Kadir Mohammed Hussain, in the course of which he categorically repudiated allegations in the vernacular press that Junagadh was thinking of joining Pakistan; that Baluchis and Hurs had been imported into the State forces, and that the local Bahauddin College was to be affiliated with the Sind University.

At the meeting of rulers on 25 July which was addressed by Lord Mountbatten, Junagadh was represented by Nabi Baksh, the Constitutional Adviser to the Nawab and brother of the Dewan. He put several questions to Lord Mountbatten which were answered fully and frankly. Nabi Baksh told Lord Mountbatten, whom he met privately afterwards, that his intention was to advise the Nawab that Junagadh should accede to India. He gave the same impression to the Jam Saheb of Nawanagar and to Sardar whom he met during his stay in Delhi.

Early in 1947 the Dewan, Abdul Kadir Mohammed Hussain, had invited Sir Shah Nawaz Bhutto, a Muslim League politician of Karachi, to come to Junagadh and join the State Council of Ministers. In May 1947 Abdul Kadir went abroad for medical treatment. Sir Shah Nawaz took over as Dewan. Subsequently the State Government got rid of Nabi Baksh. The Nawab soon came under the influence of the Muslim League. Both the Jam Saheb of Nawanagar and the Maharajah of Dhrangadhra warned me that with Sir Shah Nawaz in the saddle there was a possibility of Junagadh going over to Pakistan.

The Instrument of Accession was sent to the Nawab for signature; when we received no reply up to 12 August 1947, I sent telegrams to the Nawab and the Dewan reminding them that the last date for the receipt of intimation of signing of the Instrument of Accession was 14 August, and requesting an immediate reply. On 13 August, Sir Shah Nawaz Bhutto, replied that the matter was under consideration.

To carry the deception further, Sir Shah Nawaz called a conference of leading citizens the same day. On behalf of the Hindu citizens a memorandum for submission to the Nawab was presented to the Dewan. The memorandum analysed the dangers that would accrue to the State if it decided to accede to Pakistan. Apart from its geographical position and the fact that the overwhelming majority of the people were Hindus, the premier status of Junagadh in Kathiawar would be lost; the trade routes would be circumscribed; commerce and industry would be crippled and there would be an immense loss of revenue to the State. It was also pointed out that the Nawab was receiving from a large number of Chiefs of Kathiawar a tribute called 'Zortalbi' and this would be affected. The memorandum urged that Junagadh should therefore accede to India. One of the Muslims who had been invited to the conference, on being asked by the Dewan for his views, gave it as his opinion that the people could have no voice in the matter and that it was the prerogative of the ruler to accede to any Dominion he liked.

Having thus staged a make-believe of consulting public opinion over the issue of accession, the Government of Junagadh on 15 August announced their accession to Pakistan in the following *communiqué*:

The Government of Junagadh has during the past few weeks been faced with the problem of making its choice between accession to the Dominion of India and accession to the Dominion of Pakistan. It has had to take into very careful consideration every aspect of this problem. Its main pre-occupation has been to adopt a course that would, in the long run, make the largest contribution towards the permanent welfare and prosperity of the people of Junagadh and help to preserve the integrity of the State and to safeguard its independence and autonomy over the largest possible field. After anxious consideration and the careful balancing of all factors the Government of the State has decided to accede to Pakistan and hereby announces its decision to that effect. The State is confident that its decision will be welcomed by all loyal subjects of the State who have its real welfare and prosperity at heart.

The decision was not communicated to the Government of India. The first intimation we had of it was a report appearing in the newspapers of 17 August. I wired immediately to the Dewan for confirmation and the next day he telegraphed to me that Junagadh had acceded to Pakistan.

This came as a surprise to the Government of India. Junagadh was an economic and administrative unit embedded in and deriving its sustenance from Kathiawar. Its detachment would turn it into a hothouse plant with no powers of survival. What worried me most was the immediate potentialities for turmoil when stability was the crying need of the hour. The Nawab's action would have undesirable effects on law and order in Kathiawar as a whole. It would extend the communal trouble to areas where at present there was peace. There was also the fear that it would encourage the intractable elements in Hyderabad.[1]

On 21 August I was instructed to address a letter to the High Commissioner of Pakistan in India pointing out the considerations of Junagadh's geographical contiguity, the composition of its population, and the need for consulting the views of the people with regard to accession. As Pakistan had not as yet accepted the accession of Junagadh, I asked for an indication of the policy of the Government of Pakistan. We waited for over a fortnight but no reply was forthcoming. A reminder was sent on 6 September but even that brought no response.

On 12 September Nehru suggested that a telegram be sent to Liaqat Ali Khan, Prime Minister of Pakistan, indicating the Government of India's willingness to accept and abide by the verdict of the people of Junagadh in respect of the accession of the State to either of the Dominions. As Lord Ismay, Chief of the Governor-General's staff at this time, was going by plane to Karachi, the telegram was sent through him instead of being telegraphed. On

---

[1] Kasim Razvi, the Razakar leader of Hyderabad, in one of his bellicose speeches said: 'Why is Sardar thundering about Hyderabad when he cannot control even little Junagadh?'

Lord Mountbatten's suggestion, a brief was given to Lord Ismay with regard to Junagadh State and the consequences of its accession to Pakistan. Lord Mountbatten directed Lord Ismay to convey to the Government of Pakistan that if they accepted the accession of Junagadh, it would lead to a dispute between the two Dominions. If Jinnah wanted any State to accede to Pakistan, he could not have chosen a worse State. Lord Mountbatten asked Lord Ismay to tell Jinnah that in his view, if this course was persisted in, it would be very difficult for any impartial observer to support the attitude of the Government of Pakistan.

Lord Listowel, the Secretary of State for Commonwealth Relations, who was then in Delhi, was also leaving for Karachi and, at the instance of Lord Mountbatten, I saw him and explained the implications of Junagadh's accession to Pakistan. He appeared to be convinced that it was quite wrong for the Pakistan Government to accept the accession of the State and promised to speak to Jinnah.

The Government of Pakistan refused to take any notice of the telegram carried by Lord Ismay on the grounds that it did not bear any number or certificate showing that its issue had been authorized, and that it had been gathered from Lord Ismay that the Minister concerned (Nehru) had refused to sign the telegram! Lord Ismay totally denied having said anything of the sort. There was a 'storm in a teacup' over this attempt on the part of Pakistan to impugn the honour of Lord Ismay and several strongly worded telegrams were exchanged between the two Dominions. Be that as it may, the Government of Pakistan telegraphed to us on 13 September that they had accepted Junagadh's accession and had also signed a Standstill Agreement.

That the accession of Junagadh to Pakistan was the result of secret negotiations was clear from a number of letters which fell into our hands after both the Nawab and the Dewan fled from the State. In one of these Sir Shah Nawaz Bhutto had written to Jinnah about the interview granted to him by the latter on 16 July, in which Jinnah had advised the Nawab to 'keep out under any circumstances until 15 August' and referred to Jinnah's assurances that he would not allow Junagadh to starve as 'Veraval is not far from Karachi.' The Dewan went on to say that Junagadh was considered by Hindus as the most sacred place after Kashi (Banaras), for it was there that Sri Krishna shuffled off his mortal coil and

Somnath had been destroyed by Mahmud Ghazni. He proceeded:

Junagadh stands all alone surrounded by Hindu rulers' territories and British Indian Congress provinces. We are of course connected by sea with Pakistan. If geographical position by land was fairly considered, Kutch, Jamnagar and other territories adjoining Junagadh geographically should be considered connected with Pakistan as they once in the past actually formed part of Sind. Though the Muslim population of Junagadh is nearly 20 per cent and non-Muslims form 80 per cent, 7 lakhs Muslims of Kathiawar survived because of Junagadh. I consider that no sacrifice is too great to preserve the prestige, honour and rule of His Highness and to protect Islam and the Muslims of Kathiawar.

A letter from the Nawab to Jinnah dated 24 August 1947, read as follows:

The reports in the Press must have given you an idea that Junagadh is showered with criticism all over. Thanks to Almighty, we are firm. We expect an early announcement of the Pakistan Government regarding Junagadh's accession to it. I am sending Mr. A. K. Y. Abrahani, Revenue Member of my State Council, to settle the terms of the Standstill Agreement. I authorize him to sign the Agreement on behalf of my State Government.

The rulers of the other States in Kathiawar condemned the accession of Junagadh to Pakistan with one voice. The Jam Saheb of Nawanagar issued a number of statements condemning the accession and stressing the integrity of Kathiawar. The rulers of Bhavnagar, Morvi, Gondal, Porbander and Wankaner also made spirited protests. The Maharajah of Dhrangadhra wrote a personal letter to the Nawab of Junagadh asking him to reconsider the decision on the ground that, apart from its leading to the disruption of Kathiawar, the step was opposed to geographical compulsions no less than to the wishes of the people. The Nawab replied after a few days:

The Indian Independence Act did not and does not require a ruler to consult his people before deciding on Accession. I think we are making an unnecessary fetish of the argument of geographical contiguity. Even then, this is sufficiently provided by Junagadh's sea coast with several ports which can keep connection with Pakistan.

The Jam Saheb of Nawanagar came to Delhi and made it quite clear to the States Ministry that the rulers and people of Kathiawar were greatly agitated over this attempt on the part of Pakistan to encroach into Indian territory. He brought many stories of harassment of the Hindu population of Junagadh and he said how difficult

17

it was to restrain the people of Kathiawar from retaliation. The States in Kathiawar had so far been able to maintain peace and order but their patience was already overstrained. The Jam Saheb pointed out that, unless the Government of India took immediate and effective steps to assure continued protection to the Kathiawar States, they would lose faith in the will and ability of the Indian Dominion to carry out all the obligations arising from their accession to India. Moreover, rumours were abroad that Pakistan was contemplating the grant of a loan for the development of Junagadh's port and there was a reported offer of military assistance.

Lord Ismay, who returned from Karachi after talks with Jinnah, asked us to discount these rumours; he suggested that the reported offer[1] of military assistance was too fantastic, and that Junagadh was such a liability politically and economically to Pakistan, that the whole thing had the appearance of a trap. The Government of Pakistan were deliberately provoking the Government of India into taking precipitate and aggressive action. We came to the conclusion that this was the real motive underlying Pakistan's action and that it was a propagandist move, part of a wider campaign in which Pakistan was posing as an innocent small nation, the victim of the aggressive designs of its big neighbour.

Lord Mountbatten had further talks with Nehru, Sardar and myself. On 17 September the Cabinet decided that, with a view to ensuring the security of the country and to maintaining law and order in Kathiawar, Indian troops and troops of acceding States should be suitably dispersed around Junagadh, but should not occupy Junagadh territory. It was also decided that I should visit Junagadh and make a final attempt to persuade the Nawab to see reason.

I left Delhi by air the next morning accompanied by the Jam Saheb and the late N. M. Buch, I.C.S., who was to take over as Regional Commissioner at Rajkot. We reached Rajkot the same evening and went to the residency. It was the first time that I had ever visited or stayed in a residency. The imposing building and luxurious surroundings impressed me so much that I no longer wondered why even British civilian officers had always considered their brethren in the Political Department the pampered pets of the Government.

---

[1] Correspondence between the Governments of Pakistan and Junagadh which subsequently fell into our hands showed that seven companies of Pakistan Reserve Police had in fact been offered to Junagadh.

After informing the Nawab, I started by car for Junagadh on 19 September, accompanied by Buch. As we proceeded on our way, I could feel the interlacing of jurisdiction which made Kathiawar such a veritable jig-saw puzzle. For a few miles, because we were in the territory of some progressive ruler like Gondal, who kept his State roads in good condition, it would be a comfortable ride, but then the car would plough through bumpy stretches and one gathered at once that this must be the territory of some other ruler who had neglected his roads. Every few miles I would see carters, who were carrying goods to the ports, paying tolls and customs duties and who were being harassed by State officials all along the route. Though my mind was fully occupied with my forthcoming interview with the Nawab, I could not help asking myself during the motor journey whether there was no way to unify Kathiawar. I realized that to keep these States as separate entities would involve too great a burden on the common man.

We were received by the Junagadh Inspector General of Police at the State border and escorted to the State guest-house where after a little while the Dewan, Sir Shah Nawaz Bhutto, came to see me. I told him that I had an important personal message for the Nawab from the Indian Cabinet. The Dewan said that the Nawab had been in bed for the past ten days and was not fit to see anyone, and that even he himself had been unable to meet him for the last four days. I again emphasized that the message was most important and was meant to be delivered personally to the Nawab and that even if he was indisposed I would like to see him for a few minutes. Sir Shah Nawaz replied that the Nawab's condition was such that it was absolutely impossible for me to see him. This did not come as a surprise to me, as I had been warned at Rajkot that the Nawab would avoid meeting me. As the next best thing, I tried to see the heir-apparent, but Sir Shah Nawaz said that even this was not possible, because the Prince was very busy with a cricket match!

All that I could do in the circumstances was to talk matters over with the Dewan himself. I pointed out to him the geographical position of Junagadh; its economic dependence on Kathiawar; the fact that the overwhelming majority of its population was non-Muslim and desirous of joining the Indian Union; the existence within the Junagadh territory of pockets of States which had acceded to India, and of pockets of Junagadh territories which were in our areas. I emphasized that Junagadh had never made any attempt to negotiate with the Indian Dominion and that till the very last day the Nawab had proclaimed his belief in the solidarity and integrity of Kathiawar.

Sir Shah Nawaz said that the State's Constitutional Adviser Nabi Baksh, who attended the meeting of the Chamber of Princes on 25 July had advised the Nawab that the interests of the State lay in acceding to Pakistan; similar advice had been given by Sir Mohammad Zafrullah Khan who had also been consulted by the Nawab. The Council of Ministers of the State which, according to Sir Shah Nawaz, consisted of members of all communities had come to the unanimous decision that the State should join Pakistan. The Council of Ministers apprehended that the Congress Government in India would soon find themselves unable to resist the inroads of extreme communist views; they also felt that Junagadh had of late not been treated properly.

I pointed out that neither of these statements could bear scrutiny. If communism were to pervade the neighbouring territories, neither Junagadh nor even Pakistan could escape its influence, particularly when Junagadh was situated in the midst of States which had acceded to India. Apart from the fact that the fears entertained were in themselves groundless, accession to one Dominion or another could not make any difference in this respect. In reply to Sir Shah Nawaz's statement that Junagadh's representative had not been given a hearing at the Delhi conference, I pointed out that, far from this being the case, Nabi Baksh had asked a number of questions which had been fully answered by Lord Mountbatten. I myself had interviewed Nabi Baksh separately and he gave me to understand that he would advise the Nawab to accede to India. I asked whether Nabi Baksh was in at Junagadh and suggested that if he was available I could prove my statement. The Dewan said that Nabi Baksh was no longer in the service of Junagadh State.

Sir Shah Nawaz agreed that he had made a mistake in not making a further approach to the Government of India before finally announcing the accession of Junagadh to Pakistan. He admitted that there was no doubt that the vast majority of the people of the State were for joining the Indian Dominion, although, he added, their opinion had been greatly influenced by the virulent writings in the Gujarati press. He agreed that the economic interests of Junagadh were bound up with the rest of the peninsula and stated that he personally was in favour of the issue being decided by means of a referendum. He suggested that a discussion should be held between India and Pakistan to which he should be invited. He would be quite prepared to repeat before such a conference the views he had expressed to me. He added, however, that if his private opinion became known outside, his position in Junagadh would become untenable and he might not be able to be of any help.

I asked him plainly, whether, if the Government of Pakistan took the stand that Junagadh must abide by its accession to Pakistan and that no referendum should be held, he would nevertheless be prepared to hold a referendum. Sir Shah Nawaz answered that, in spite of the fact that he knew Jinnah to be an obstinate man, he himself would, in such circumstances, be willing to hold a referendum, though he could not of course commit the Government of Junagadh in this matter. I felt that it was useless to continue the conversation further and that I was merely wasting my time. I told Sir Shah Nawaz that the people of Kathiawar were restive and that if they decided to take the law into their own hands it would mean the end of the Nawab's dynasty. Upon this note of warning, I closed the interview and returned to Rajkot.

Back at Rajkot I had discussions with the Jam Saheb of Nawanagar and a number of rulers and *talukdars*. At 8 p.m. I held a press conference. I began by saying that I had gone to Junagadh to see the Nawab under instructions from the Government of India. I had been unable to see him on account of his indisposition but I had been cordially received by the Dewan with whom I had had discussions. I said that the Government of India were fully alive to the needs of the situation. The Dewan had assured me that the Nawab was determined to protect and look after his Hindu subjects and that they should not feel panicky. I would duly submit my report to the Government of India, but in the meantime I could give an assurance to the rulers and people of Kathiawar that the Government of India were fully determined to protect the States which had acceded to the Indian Union.

There was an important matter which clamoured for immediate attention, and that was the doubtful attitude of the Khan of Manavadar and the Sheikh of Mangrol, neither of whom had as yet acceded to India. Manavadar, a tiny State with an area of about 100 square miles and with a vast majority of Hindus, was surrounded on three sides by Junagadh territory and on the north by the State of Gondal.

Mangrol, situated between Porbander and Junagadh, was also a very tiny State and here again the Hindus formed the overwhelming majority of the population. On the day I arrived at Rajkot, I had sent telegrams to both of them asking them to see me on the 18th at 5 p.m. The Dewan of Manavadar came instead of the Khan who was said to be suffering from boils. I told him that I wished to see the Khan himself. Accordingly, the Khan came to see me. I asked him for a clarification of his attitude. He replied that he had already entered into a Standstill Agreement with Pakistan and had asked that Manavadar should be allowed to accede to that Dominion. I explained to him that from the point of view of the Government of India it was intolerable that pockets of Pakistan should be created inside Indian territory. I found him completely bewildered. I was told afterwards that, before he came to see me, he had a telephone conversation with Karachi and that he had been advised to stand firm. I asked that his final decision should be communicated to me next morning. He promised to think over the whole matter and to come and see me again the next morning. He did not keep his promise.

Mangrol State had a special constitutional position. At the investiture of every ruler, a representative of the Junagadh State had to be present. In respect of the major portion of the State, the Sheikh was independent of Junagadh, but in respect of 21 villages, the civil and criminal jurisdiction was exercised by Junagadh, subject to a guarantee by the British Government that this power would not be misused. The Political Department had often in the past interfered with the orders of Junagadh. It was the aim of the Sheikh to assert his independence of Junagadh and on 15 August he had done so. But Junagadh refused to recognize it and was still maintaining that Mangrol was its vassal.

On the day I had left Delhi for Rajkot, the Sheikh of Mangrol had sent his Constitutional Adviser to Delhi to see the Prime Minister. In reply to my telegram, the Sheikh sent an emissary to see me but I told him that I wanted to see the Sheikh himself. He replied that the Sheikh would not be allowed to travel by car through Junagadh territory and, although he was very anxious to meet me, his car would be stopped by the Junagadh authorities. I accordingly arranged to send a car with a Nawanagar red number plate to fetch him. The Sheikh came bringing with him a telegram from his Constitutional Adviser in Delhi strongly advising him to accede to India. The only condition which he made was that we should recognize his independence *vis-à-vis* Junagadh. I saw no difficulty in acceding to his request. Firstly, with the lapse of paramountcy, Mangrol might be deemed to have obtained its independence. Secondly, we were writing on a clean slate and I saw no reason why we should not allow Mangrol to throw off the overlordship of Junagadh. The Sheikh then dictated a letter and signed both the Instrument of Accession and the Standstill Agreement.

I left for Bombay with the Jam Saheb on the 20th evening. A number of press representatives were waiting for us there. I told them that I had nothing to add to what I had told the pressmen in Rajkot; but the Jam Saheb gave a talk explaining the point of view of the Kathiawar States. This was widely reported in the Bombay press.

After dinner, I met the leaders of the Congress and the States' People's organizations in Kathiawar at the Taj Mahal Hotel. Among those present were U. N. Dhebar, Balwantrai Mehta, Samaldas Gandhi and Rasiklal Parikh. They were all of them emphatic that we had not done enough to secure a sense of safety in Kathiawar. They stressed that the Junagadh issue was a most vital one on which, if we gave way, the whole prestige of the Government would suffer badly. I explained to them how matters stood. Dhebar told me that the situation in Kathiawar was highly explosive and that none of the leaders were in a position to hold the people in leash for long. Samaldas Gandhi said that the people were prepared to take the law into their own hands and that they would organize themselves and march on Junagadh. I explained to them the difficulties of the Government of India and how any action on their part would affect Indo-Pakistan relations. Though Dhebar appreciated the difficulties of the Government of India, he could not guarantee that he would be able to control the situation. Samaldas Gandhi was determined to set up a parallel government for the State and to organize an intensive agitation throughout Kathiawar. All I could do in the circumstances was to counsel restraint on the leaders, and to warn Buch, the Regional Commissioner, to keep a watch over developments and report to me, if necessary, daily.

On the 21st morning I met Morarji Desai, Home Minister of Bombay. He told me he would be able to maintain law and order in Bombay and Ahmedabad, provided the arms and ammunition for the police which the provincial Government had asked for were supplied immediately. Morarji Desai also informed me that both the Government and the people of Bombay were anxious that we should take a firm line on the Junagadh issue. The position of the Bombay Ministry itself would depend to a great extent on our attitude. He asked me to mention this to Nehru and Sardar with all the emphasis at my command.

I returned to Delhi on the 21st evening and apprised Sardar of what had happened in Junagadh, laying stress on the explosive situation in Kathiawar. Sardar approved of such measures as had been taken, but he was not happy about the decision of the Kathiawar leaders to form a parallel government. He felt that it might lead to complications later on. The Government of India however were not in a position to take any effective action. All we could do was to counsel patience and restraint.

On my return to Delhi, Buch telephoned from Rajkot that the Sheikh of Mangrol had delivered a letter to him addressed to the Government of India, retracting his accession. This was done under pressure from Junagadh. No action was, however, taken on the Sheikh's letter, as the Governor-General had already accepted the accession.

Junagadh followed up by sending troops into Babariawad. This is a group of fifty-one villages held by *Mulgirasias*[1]. The Nawab of Junagadh claimed it as part of his State. But the *Mulgirasias* asserted that their attachment with Junagadh was made by the Political Department and that with the lapse of paramountcy they were not bound by that arrangement. Accordingly they asserted their right to accede directly to India and the Government of India accepted their accession.

These developments were considered at a meeting on 22 September at which Lord Mountbatten, Nehru, Sardar, the Commanders-in-Chief of the Army and the Navy, Lord Ismay and myself were present. I made a report on my visit to Junagadh. It was resolved that I should draft, for Nehru's approval, a telegram to the Dewan of Junagadh pointing out the constitutional position of Babariawad and Mangrol and demanding that Junagadh troops should be withdrawn forthwith from Babariawad. The telegram was sent the same day. The Commanders-in-Chief were asked to prepare appreciations of an operation designed to occupy Babariawad, including

[1] 'Mul' means original and 'girasias' landholders.

preparations to go to the assistance of Mangrol and if, but only if, Junagadh took other offensive action, to be prepared to occupy Junagadh itself.

After this meeting, Lord Mountbatten held an informal consultation with a leading British constitutional lawyer who happened to be in Delhi at that time and who was fully conversant with the position of Mangrol. The latter was of the opinion that the Sheikh could not be held to have signed the Instrument of Accession under duress. He had known that he was going to Rajkot to sign this Instrument; he had considered it for nearly three hours; and he had brought his advisers with him. On the other hand, it could well be held that duress had been applied to the Sheikh on his way back to his State and the retraction of his signature could therefore be challenged. This lawyer also gave it as his view that there could be no objection to Indian troops being sent to Mangrol.

On 24 September, the Government of India decided that a brigade, consisting of troops of the Indian Army and the forces of acceding States, should be suitably disposed in Kathiawar for the protection of States which had acceded to the Indian Union. It was also decided that an adequate force should be sent to Mangrol and Babariawad.

The States Ministry issued a press *communiqué* the next day tracing in brief the background to the *impasse*. A reference was made to my visit to Junagadh during which the Dewan had suggested a tripartite conference between Pakistan, India and Junagadh. This suggestion had not been followed up by either Pakistan or Junagadh. The Government of India, determined to find a solution to this problem, had suggested a referendum; and still adhered to the suggestion. The *communiqué* ended with an assurance that the Government of India would fully and faithfully discharge their responsibility to protect the interests of those States within and around Junagadh which had acceded to the Indian Dominion.

On 25 September, a telegram was received from the Prime Minister of Pakistan re-asserting that the Nawab of Junagadh had every right to accede to Pakistan regardless of the State's territorial location. Regarding a plebiscite, the telegram said it was a matter between the Nawab of Junagadh and his subjects.

Simultaneously a telegram was received from the Dewan of Junagadh in which he asserted that Babariawad and Mangrol were integral parts of Junagadh territory and that their accession to the Indian

18

Union was invalid. The Dewan refused to withdraw the Junagadh forces from Babariawad.

Sardar's view of the matter was that Junagadh's action in sending troops to Babariawad and refusing to withdraw them was no less than an act of aggression which must be met by a show of strength, with readiness in the last resort to use it. He pressed this point with great emphasis at a meeting on 27 September at which he, Lord Mountbatten, Nehru, Mohanlal Saxena and N. Gopalaswami Aiyangar were present. Lord Mountbatten suggested that the question might be referred to the United Nations Organization, but Sardar was opposed to the idea. He contended that there was a grave disadvantage in being the plaintiff in such cases. Both Nehru and Gopalaswami Aiyangar were also opposed to referring the issue to the United Nations Organization; so the suggestion was dropped.

Lord Mountbatten emphasized the danger of any precipitate action which might lead to war between India and Pakistan. Such a war might be the end of Pakistan altogether, but it would also be the end of India for at least a generation to come. He was anxious that India should not lose her great international position by taking incorrect action. It was finally decided that the military movements to the borders but within Indian territory then being planned should not be delayed; that Nehru should address a telegram to the Prime Minister of Pakistan giving a full exposition of the legal position of Babariawad and Mangrol and demanding that Junagadh troops should be withdrawn from Babariawad; and that the matter should be discussed at the next meeting between the Prime Ministers of India and Pakistan. At its meeting on 28 September, the Cabinet discussed the general situation in Kathiawar and directed that a telegram be sent to the Prime Minister of Pakistan. This was done next day.

The situation in Junagadh had worsened by now. More than a hundred thousand Hindus had already fled from the State. The late Maharajah of Gondal summed up the situation correctly when he said that the peace and tranquillity of the whole of Kathiawar was in danger.

Meanwhile, in accordance with the Cabinet's decision of 17 September, the disposition of troops in Kathiawar was going on apace. Brigadier Gurdial Singh was in command of the force, which was known as the Kathiawar Defence Force (or K.D.F.). The States of Nawanagar, Bhavnagar and Porbander had agreed to our request to place their State forces under the command of Gurdial Singh. All these forces were suitably deployed, their movements and manoeuvres creating a steadying effect all over Kathiawar. The Army Commander had strict orders not to violate Junagadh territory in any way.

The Kathiawar Congress leaders were going ahead with their plans. A provisional Government (*Arzi Hukumat*) of Junagadh was announced at a mammoth public meeting at Bombay on 25 September. An ably written proclamation was issued on behalf of the people of Junagadh explaining how the Nawab had forfeited his claim to the allegiance of his subjects. It announced the constitution of a Provisional Government of six members with Samaldas Gandhi as President, 'with all power, authority and jurisdiction heretofore vested in and exercised by the Nawab of Junagadh prior to 15 September 1947.' Samaldas Gandhi and his colleagues made a triumphal journey from Bombay to Rajkot, with large crowds felicitating him at wayside railway stations. He set up his headquarters at Rajkot and collected a number of volunteers.

In the meantime the States Ministry turned its attention to the estates of Sardargarh and Bantwa, which under the Attachment Scheme of 1943 had been attached to Junagadh. The Attachment Scheme had come to an end with the lapse of paramountcy. In deference to the generally expressed desire of the *talukdars* and the people of these attached *estates*, the Government of India had assumed the same residuary jurisdiction as had been exercised by the Crown Representative in the pre-attachment period. This had been made clear to the Dewan of Junagadh by a telegram on 25 August in answer to his enquiries regarding the future of the *estates* and *talukas*. In accordance with this decision, the Regional Commissioner was asked to take over the management of Sardargarh and Bantwa, which he did on 1 October.

On 1 October, at a meeting of the Joint Defence Council of India and Pakistan held at Delhi, Nehru took the opportunity to suggest to Liaqat Ali Khan that Junagadh troops should be withdrawn from Babariawad. Just then a telegram was received that Junagadh troops had entered Mangrol as well. The claim of the Nawab of Junagadh for suzerainty over 21 villages in Mangrol was itself doubtful after the lapse of paramountcy; but there was not even a semblance of justification for the Nawab's action in occupying the entire State of Mangrol. Even so, Nehru undertook not to allow Indian troops to enter either Babariawad or Mangrol until the legal position of both had been definitely established, provided Junagadh troops were immediately withdrawn. Liaqat Ali Khan would not give a definite reply on this point; but he was adamant when it came to the question of Pakistan's right to accept Junagadh's accession. He argued that a ruler had the absolute right to accede without reference to the moral or ethnic aspects of accession.

Subsequently, in a telegram to Liaqat Ali Khan, Nehru reiterated his request that Junagadh troops should be withdrawn from Babariawad and Mangrol.

On 4 October the Government of India considered the Junagadh situation. The Chiefs of Staff were directed to instruct the Commander of the Kathiawar Defence Force to prepare a plan for the occupation of Babariawad and Mangrol, in case this should be ordered, with the object of reducing to a minimum any exchange of shots with Junagadh forces in these territories. It was decided to inform the Prime Minister of Pakistan that the only basis on which friendly negotiations could start and be fruitful was the reversion of Junagadh, Babariawad and Mangrol to the *status quo* preceding the accession of Junagadh to Pakistan and that the alternative to negotiations was a plebiscite. A telegram to this effect was sent to the Prime Minister of Pakistan the next day.

A press *communiqué* was also issued by the States Ministry detailing the circumstances which compelled the Government of India to send a detachment of troops to Kathiawar. It emphasized that the troops had been given explicit instructions not to enter Junagadh or to seek passage through Junagadh territory even to reach those States which had acceded to India. The *communiqué* reiterated the Government of India's willingness to abide by a plebiscite as a method at once democratic, peaceful and just.

On 5 October, a telegram was received from Liaqat Ali Khan in which he suggested that the question whether Babariawad and Mangrol were free to accede to either Dominion, notwithstanding Junagadh's claim to suzerainty over them, should be referred for independent legal opinion to a counsel whose name might be agreed upon between the two Dominions. If this was acceptable to India, the Pakistan Prime Minister promised to issue instructions to Junagadh to withdraw troops from Babariawad and Mangrol.

To this Nehru replied that the main question of Junagadh had not been touched on at all and that it was essential to reach a settlement on that fundamental issue first.

On 16 October Lord Mountbatten was in Lahore and had a talk with Liaqat Ali Khan. On his return, he told Nehru that Liaqat Ali Khan was agreeable to a plebiscite in Junagadh subject to details being settled between the two Dominions. Liaqat Ali Khan was indisposed at the time and so it was a few days later, on 21 October, that Nehru wired to him proposing to send me to meet him at Lahore to discuss these matters. Liaqat Ali Khan promptly replied that the suggestion in regard to a plebiscite appeared to have been due to a misunderstanding. He suggested that I should go to Karachi for a preliminary discussion at Secretariat level, which would be followed, if necessary, by a Cabinet decision.

It was obvious that Pakistan was simply marking time. On 21 October, the Government of India decided that Mangrol and Babariawad would have to be occupied. Two days later a plan was drawn up. It was finally approved on 25 October. Lord Mountbatten was anxious that the occupation should be entrusted to the Central Reserve Police, but Sardar felt that this would be taking unnecessary risks; he was firm that the operation should be handled by the Indian army.

Meanwhile, news from Manavadar continued to be disquieting. It was reported to the Government of India that the Khan of Manavadar was arresting local leaders and harassing the people and that if swift action was not taken, there was danger of a flare-up in the State which was bound to spread to the neighbouring State of Gondal, in which at the time all was peace and quiet. Sardar discussed the situation with Nehru. It was ultimately decided to send a Deputy Inspector-General of Police with a small police force into Manavadar to take over the administration of the State. This was done on 22 October and subsequently a manager was appointed to carry on the administration.

On 1 November the Government of India sent a civil administrator accompanied by a small force to take over the administration of Babariawad. On the same day the administration of Mangrol[1] was also taken over by the Government of India.

In the unsettled conditions then prevailing traders refused to risk any business with Junagadh. The food situation had deteriorated

[1] Both the Sheikh of Mangrol and the Khan of Manavadar subsequently went away to Pakistan.

considerably in spite of some help given by Pakistan. The revenues of the State had also substantially decreased.

The Nawab realized that events were not going as he had anticipated; and he decided on flight. Towards the end of October, he left for Karachi with most of the members of his family, some of his dogs and much of the family jewelry. As the party was about to enter the plane, it was found that one of the Begums had forgotten to bring her child but the Nawab refused to wait; the plane took off, leaving the Begum behind to find her way later to the Portuguese settlement of Diu. The Nawab took with him the entire cash balances of the State and all the shares and securities in the treasury.

The Nawab's flight encouraged the forces of the *Arzi Hukumat,* who began to occupy various parts of the State. On 2 November the town of Nawagadh was taken over by the Provisional Government, whose volunteers had also planned to take over Kutyana, an important town in the main block of the Junagadh territory. There they met with a good deal of opposition and in their turn indulged in some looting and arson. The conduct of the volunteers in Kutyana was the only blot on the otherwise good behaviour and discipline of the *Arzi Hukumat.*

On 27 October, Sir Shah Nawaz Bhutto wrote a letter to Jinnah, in which he described the disastrous consequences which had followed in the wake of Junagadh's accession to Pakistan. He wrote:

Our principal sources of revenue, railways and customs, have gone to the bottom. Food situation is terribly embarrassing though Pakistan has come to our rescue with a generous allotment of foodgrains. There has been a harsh treatment of Muslims travelling on Kathiawar railway lines who have been subjected to several kinds of hardships and humiliations. Added to this, His Highness and the royal family have had to leave because our secret service gave us information in advance of serious consequences to their presence and safety. Though immediately after accession, His Highness and myself received hundreds of messages chiefly from Muslims congratulating us on the decision, today our brethren are indifferent and cold. Muslims of Kathiawar seem to have lost all enthusiasm for Pakistan.

Sir Shah Nawaz then went on to speak of the panic amongst officials of all ranks and continued:

No doubt Your Excellency's Government offered us seven companies of Crown Police but we felt that if they were to come and be confronted by the vast enemy forces arrayed against us it would be sheer wastage of human material and equipment. The situation has therefore so worsened that responsible Muslims and others have come to press me to seek a solution of the impasse. I do not wish to say much more. My Senior Member of Council, Capt. Harvey Jones, must have apprised you of the serious state of things. The question is delicate but I feel it must be settled honourably to the satisfaction of all. It is impossible for me to court any further bloodshed, hardship and persecution of loyal people. Myself I do not mind what suffering is imposed on me but I do not wish to take the responsibility any further if it can be avoided for thousands of His Highness' subjects. I should therefore suggest that you immediately arrange for a conference of the representatives of the two Dominions to decide the Junagadh issue.

On 31 October Sir Shah Nawaz wrote a letter to Ikramullah, Secretary, Ministry of Foreign Affairs and Commonwealth Relations, Pakistan, in which he admitted that the people were completely disheartened. Meanwhile the Nawab sent a telegram from Karachi to Sir Shah Nawaz asking him to use his 'judicious discrimination as the situation demanded.' On 5 November the Junagadh State Council held a meeting and it was decided that 'the position arising out of the economic blockade, inter-statal complications, external agitation and internal administrative difficulties make it necessary to have a complete reorientation of the State policy and a readjustment of relations with the two Dominions even if it involves a reversal of the earlier decision to accede to Pakistan.' The Dewan was authorized 'to negotiate with the proper authorities.'

Sir Shah Nawaz opened negotiations with Samaldas Gandhi on 7 November through Captain Harvey Jones, Senior Member of the Junagadh State Council, requesting Samaldas Gandhi to take over the reins of Government and to restore law and order in the State. But the Muslim Jamiat of Junagadh brought pressure on Sir Shah Nawaz to hand over the administration direct to the Government of India through the Regional Commissioner, and not through the *Arzi Hukumat*. Accordingly, on 8 November, Sir Shah Nawaz wrote the following letter to Buch, Regional Commissioner, Western India and Gujarat States:

After discussion with Samaldas Gandhi at Rajkot on 7 November, Captain Harvey Jones, Senior Member of the Junagadh State Council, brought certain proposals for the consideration of the Council. The Council is prepared to accept them under protest but before a final decision could be communicated to Samaldas Gandhi it was thought necessary to ascertain the opinion of the leading members of the public. A meeting was therefore held this evening and the views of the leaders were unanimously expressed that instead of handing over the administration to the

Indian Union through the so-called Provisional Government it should be directly given over to the Indian Union through the Regional Commissioner at Rajkot, particularly with a view to preserving law and order which is threatened by aggressive elements from outside. This arrangement is sought pending an honourable settlement of the several issues involved in the Junagadh accession. The Junagadh Government, therefore, have requested that in order to avoid bloodshed, hardship, loss of life and property and to preserve the dynasty, you should be approached to give your assistance to the administration. We have already wired to His Excellency Lord Mountbatten, Mahatma Gandhi, Prime Minister and Deputy Prime Minister of India, Hon'ble A. K. Azad and the Governor-General and the Prime Minister of Pakistan. I hope you will kindly respond to this request.

Buch rang me up immediately. I was in the Prime Minister's house. It was past midnight. Buch read out the letter he had received from Sir Shah Nawaz and told me that he had already contacted Dhebar and Samaldas Gandhi who were in favour of accepting the offer.

I passed on the news immediately to the Prime Minister. We drafted a reply to Buch and a telegram to the Prime Minister of Pakistan. The telegram to Pakistan stressed that the Government of India were acceding to the request of Dewan Sir Shah Nawaz with a view to avoiding disorder and resulting chaos. But the Government of India had no desire to continue this arrangement and wished to find a speedy solution in accordance with the wishes of the people of Junagadh. The telegram concluded by expressing the desire of the Government of India to discuss this question and other allied matters affecting Junagadh with representatives of Pakistan at the earliest possible moment.

I then went to Sardar's residence, woke him up and showed him the drafts we had prepared. He was strongly of the opinion that an offer of a plebiscite should not be made. He pointed out that the Nawab had already fled, that the administration had broken down, and that as the Dewan had been unable to carry on, he had voluntarily offered to hand the State over to the Government of India. The vast majority of the people in the State were non-Muslims. In these circumstances, to commit ourselves to a plebiscite in regard to accession was unnecessary and uncalled for. However, after a good deal of further discussion, Sardar finally agreed to the issue of the telegram.

Instructions were issued to Buch to go to Junagadh on 9 November to take over the administration. Buch had asked Captain Harvey Jones to go on to Junagadh in advance in order to ensure that there would be no opposition. Later, Captain Harvey Jones acted as pilot of the convoy, followed by Brigadier Gurdial Singh and Buch. The administration was handed over peacefully by Captain Harvey Jones and the Chief Secretary at 6 p.m. on 9 November. The Dewan, Sir Shah Nawaz Bhutto, had left for Karachi the previous day — a day before Buch entered Junagadh and took over the administration.

During that night and in the course of the next day, the State infantry and cavalry were disarmed and the treasury, the *tosha-khana* and other valuable stores sealed. Civil officers, accompanied by detachments of police or troops, went to important places in the State and took over control peacefully. There was not a single untoward incident.

When Brigadier Gurdial Singh was asked to take over charge of the K.D.F., Lord Mountbatten had advised him in my presence to 'hold the scales even' between the communities. I had not felt too happy over this homily. Brigadier Gurdial Singh was an evacuee from West Punjab. He had lost his entire family and property in the communal holocaust. During the Junagadh crisis, however, he not only displayed cool judgment and great resourcefulness, but above all he behaved in a manner singularly free from communal rancour or bitterness. A deputation of Junagadh Muslims assured me later that they had nothing to complain of either during or after the occupation. The credit for this must go to Brigadier Gurdial Singh, Samaldas Gandhi and Buch.

An emergent meeting of the Cabinet was held on 10 November to consider the dramatic developments in Junagadh. The Government of India, it was decided, could not agree to a joint Pakistan-India plebiscite in Junagadh, though they would have no objection to one held under the auspices of the United Nations Organization. In any case it was desirable to go ahead with the plebiscite in Junagadh as expeditiously as possible.

On 11 November, Liaqat Ali Khan replied to Nehru's telegram of the 9th. He contended that since Junagadh had duly acceded to Pakistan, neither the Dewan nor for that matter the ruler himself could negotiate either a temporary or a permanent settlement with India. He held that India's action in taking over the State administration and sending Indian troops to Junagadh without any

19

authorization from Pakistan and indeed without their knowledge was a clear violation of Pakistan territory and a breach of international law. With regard to the suggestion for a conference between representatives of the two Dominions, he declared that the only conditions under which Pakistan could attend the discussions would be the immediate withdrawal of Indian troops, reinstatement of the Nawab's administration and the restoration of normal conditions in and around the borders of Junagadh, including the stoppage of the activities of the Provisional Government. He considered the Government of India's action in taking charge of the Junagadh administration and in sending Indian troops to occupy the State to be a direct act of hostility against Pakistan. He demanded therefore that the Government of India should immediately withdraw their forces, relinquish charge of the administration to the rightful ruler and stop the people of the Indian Union from invading Junagadh and committing acts of violence.

Nehru in reply pointed out that, on the admission of Sir Shah Nawaz Bhutto and his colleagues themselves, the administration in Junagadh had broken down. Indeed, if the Government of India had not intervened, Junagadh would have been in a complete state of chaos, with consequent repercussions in the whole of Kathiawar. Further, it was certain that the *Arzi Hukumat* would have taken charge of the State in the conditions of chaos that prevailed there; this would undoubtedly have involved bloodshed. In these circumstances, the Government of India had to make up their mind quickly; they had no alternative but to accede to the request of the Dewan and the Junagadh State Council and take over the administration of the State. The administration was taken over without any incident and without any dissentient voice. Nehru pointed out that it was not correct to say that Pakistan had no knowledge of what was happening in Junagadh. Captain Harvey Jones, Senior Member of the Junagadh Council, had been to Karachi and Lahore where he must have held consultations with the Nawab and the Pakistan authorities. On his return, he negotiated with Samaldas Gandhi to hand over the administration to the Provisional Government. Sir Shah Nawaz Bhutto, in his letter of 8 November to the Regional Commissioner, had stated that he had already telegraphed to the Governor-General and the Prime Minister of Pakistan intimating the Junagadh Government's decision to ask the Government of India to take over the administration of the State. The Nawab himself was in Karachi and Sir Shah Nawaz was acting under his orders as the Prime Minister of the State. Furthermore, Sir Shah Nawaz took this decision with the unanimous approval of not only the State Council but also leaders of public opinion in the State. Sir Shah Nawaz had reached Karachi on 8 November and was certain to have acquainted the Government of Pakistan with the situation on that day. The Regional Commissioner, on the other hand, did not take over the administration till the evening of 9 November. Nehru regretted that the Government of India could not withdraw the Indian troops. If that were done, it would leave the way open for the Provisional Government to take charge of the entire administration and, if any attempts were made at that juncture to restore the Nawab, it would inevitably lead to conflict and result in bloodshed and anarchy which neither Pakistan nor India could view with equanimity. Nehru pointed out that the Government of India had not recognized the Provisional Government but the fact could not be ignored that the Provisional Government consisted of Junagadh subjects, who not only had a very large stake in the State but commanded considerable public support, and who had occupied a large portion of Junagadh territory of which they were in administrative charge. The Government of India could not be expected to promote a situation in which they would come into conflict with the people of the State who were fighting for their elementary rights. In conclusion, Nehru emphasized that the essence of the Government of India's policy was swift stabilization of the situation and for that purpose they wished to settle the issue with the least possible delay by means of a plebiscite.

Pakistan refused to be convinced by this statement of facts and more telegrams were exchanged. To this day Pakistan has continued to claim Junagadh as part of its territory.

On 13 November Sardar visited Junagadh. He was given a rousing reception at a mammoth gathering which he addressed in the grounds of the Bahauddin College. In the course of his speech, Sardar said that the Government of India would abide by the wishes of the people and, by way of oratorical flourish, asked the audience to indicate whether they wished the State to accede to India or Pakistan. Over ten thousand hands were immediately raised in favour of accession to India.

Sardar then visited the famous Somnath temple at Prabhas Patan. He was visibly moved to find the temple which had once been the glory of India looking so dilapidated, neglected and forlorn. It was proposed then and there to reconstruct it so as to return it to its original splendour. The Jam Saheb donated a lakh of rupees and, on behalf of the *Arzi Hukumat*, Samaldas Gandhi announced a donation of Rs 51,000 for the purpose. The proposal as well as the donations were clearly spontaneous. This was my first visit to Somnath. As a schoolboy, the story of the sack of Somnath by Mahmud Ghazni had made a profound impression on me. I never even dreamt that I should one day visit this temple. The decision to reconstruct Somnath was an act of historic justice that warmed my heart.

About this time, the Nawab of Junagadh made overtures to Sri Prakasa, the High Commissioner for India in Pakistan. He stated that if he were allowed to return to Junagadh he would be prepared to accede to India and declare a fully democratic State on any model which Sardar might draft. He offered to appoint Sir Mirza Ismail as his Dewan regardless of the amount of his salary. Sri Prakasa was however instructed not to commit the Government of India in any manner.

The task of recognizing the administration of Junagadh was taken in hand immediately. An officer of the I.C.S., S. W. Shiveshwarkar, was appointed Administrator of the State under the control of the Regional Commissioner. The administrative machinery had broken down, the financial position of the State was precarious, lawlessness was rampant and a number of imported outsiders were running the administration on a communal basis. The administration had to be balanced at all levels and particularly in the police force. This was done by fresh recruitment and by borrowing personnel from Bombay and other States. Steps were taken to dispose of the dogs which the Nawab had left behind; their maintenance alone was costing Rs 16,000 a month! An Ordinance was issued by the Governor-General authorizing the Reserve Bank of India to issue duplicates of Government Promissory Notes to the extent of Rs 1,29,34,700 as the originals had been 'lost', that is to say, been taken away by the Nawab on his flight to Karachi. Altogether, a bold policy was pursued. Apart from the reorganization of the administration, important steps were taken for the advancement of education, the promotion of public health, the construction of roads and the removal of a number of monopolies and outmoded taxes and restrictions.

As soon as normal conditions were restored, the Government of India decided to hold a referendum to ascertain the unfettered choice of the people in regard to accession. A senior judicial officer of the I.C.S., C.B.Nagarkar, who, incidentally, was neither Hindu nor Muslim, was asked to supervise it. The polling took place on 20 February 1948 and out of the total of 2,01,457 registered voters, 1,90,870 exercised their franchise. Of this number only 91 cast their votes in favour of accession to Pakistan. A referendum was held at the same time in Mangrol and Manavadar, as well as in Babariawad, Bantwa and Sardargarh. Out of 31,434 votes cast in these areas, only 39 were for accession to Pakistan. Jossleyn Hennessy of the *Sunday Times* and Douglas Brown of the *Daily Telegraph*, who were in Junagadh at that time, declared that they could find little fault with the manner in which the referendum was conducted.

Once the plebiscite had been concluded, we turned our attention to the democratization of the administration. A ministry responsible to a local legislature was not considered feasible; there were valid arguments against it. First of all, we needed time in which to reorganize the administration and to bring it to a condition of efficiency; the Muslims were certain to prefer that the Government of India should be in control of Junagadh till the situation returned completely to normal. Secondly, though the rulers of Kathiawar had signed a Covenant to amalgamate their States into the Saurashtra Union, the Union had not yet been formed and we could not visualize Junagadh's future except as a component part of that Union. Accordingly, we decided to constitute an executive council of popular representatives to assist the administrator. The Executive Council, of which Samaldas Gandhi, Dayashankar Dave and Mrs Pushpavati Mehta were members, was set up on 1 June 1948. Much good work was done by this Council; and I must pay my meed of tribute to them. During the next few months, I visited Junagadh several times; and every time I went there I found recognizable improvement in the administration and in the satisfaction of the minorities. When I went there for the final handing over of the administration to the Saurashtra Union, Junagadh had attained a degree of efficiency which could compare not unfavourably with the neighbouring province of Bombay. Samaldas Gandhi is no more. He had proved beyond doubt that he was an able administrator. A powerful speaker and trenchant writer, he had always impressed me as a dynamic personality; nor did his later political vicissitudes lessen my first opinion of him.

By the time the Saurashtra Union came into existence, Junagadh had, under a special Act passed by the State administration, elected seven representatives on a wide franchise to the Constituent Assembly of the Union. These seven members met and decided that Junagadh should be integrated with Saurashtra. The administration of the State, as also that of Mangrol, Manavadar and the erstwhile feudatories of Junagadh, was handed over to the Saurashtra Government on 20 February 1949 at a simple ceremony, in which the Chief Secretary of Saurashtra took over from the Administrator of Junagadh.

VII

THE ORISSA AND CHATTISGARH STATES

THE accession of the rulers on three subjects and the participation of their representatives in the Constituent Assembly should, as was hoped, have given the States Ministry some breathing time to evolve a scheme of permanent relationship between the States and the Government of India. But after the transfer of power, one crisis after another in quick succession supervened and engrossed the attention of the Government of India. Firstly, we had to tackle the situation in Kathiawar created by the action of the Nawab of Junagadh in acceding to Pakistan. Then, there was the two-way exodus of refugees, which threatened to engulf both Dominions in one big calamity. There followed the tribal invasion of Kashmir. Lastly, the situation in South India resulting from the non-accession of Hyderabad was causing us no little anxiety.

Amidst these preoccupations, we had perforce to take note as well of the condition of affairs in some of the smaller States. Our attention initially was drawn to the States in Orissa and in the Central Provinces (now Madhya Pradesh), known respectively as the Orissa and Chattisgarh States. There was trouble in some of these States and insistent demands were being made by the provincial Governments concerned, particularly the Government of Orissa, for the intervention of the Government of India. We were unable to give instant heed to these demands. As a first step towards developing contacts with these States, we appointed a Liaison Officer at Sambalpur, his status being raised later to that of a Regional Commissioner. A Deputy Regional Commissioner was also posted at Raipur to look after the Chattisgarh States. But other more adequate and urgent measures were needed to meet the situation; and eventually, the States Ministry had to turn its full attention to the problem of the Orissa and Chattisgarh States.

The Orissa States were 26 in number — eleven 'A' class, twelve 'B' and three 'C' class — exercising varying degrees of jurisdiction. The biggest, Mayurbhanj, had an area of 4,000 square miles and a population of about 10 lakhs. The smallest was Tigiria with an area of 46 square miles and a population of a little more than 20,000.

The Chattisgarh States numbered 15. The largest was Bastar with an area of 13,000 square miles and a population of well over half a million, whilst the smallest was Sakti with an area of 138 square miles and a population of about one lakh.

These States, particularly in Orissa, constituted one of the greatest forest areas in the country, forest revenue being for some of them the largest item of their income. An irregular mass of forest-covered hills broken by river valleys, with here and there a wide rice-growing plain, and covered for the most part with dense jungle, they were probably in the wildest and least accessible area. None the less, these States, particularly the northern ones, were situated on perhaps the most industrialized belt of country in India. Jamshedpur, the centre of the Indian iron industry, is on the borders of Seraikela. Quantities of manganese, copper, iron, coal, limestone, mica etc., abound all over this region. Excellent iron ore is available in Mayurbhanj, as well as in Bastar; a vast coalfield underlies much of Surguja and Korea; Talcher also is an outlying coalfield.

The origin of these States is obscure. Some of the rulers were descended from Rajput pilgrims who, having come on pilgrimage to Puri, stopped on their way back and carved out principalities for themselves; while others were descended from petty aboriginal chiefs. Most of them were under the suzerainty of the Moghuls and later under the Mahratta Bhonslas of Nagpur. When they came under the suzerainty of the British Government, doubts cropped up as to their rightful status. Their recognition as rulers was eventually conceded to them, in the case of the Chattisgarh States in 1863, and in the case of the Orissa States in 1888. The provincial Governments were nevertheless inclined to treat them as mere zemindars and none of them exercised the same measure of internal sovereignty as the rulers of the older and more firmly established States.

In most of these States there had been prolonged periods of minority administration, when an officer responsible to the Political Agent was in charge. Even otherwise, there were Agency officials in charge of important departments. If external control were removed, there was always the danger that many of these States would relapse into their previous backward condition.

Ever since the announcement of the Cabinet Mission proposals, some of the rulers of the Orissa and Chattisgarh States had been thinking in terms of a union. These rulers met at the Rajkumar College at Raipur and formed the Eastern States Union which started functioning from 1 August 1947. The biggest States, Mayurbhanj and Bastar, as well as some of the smaller States had kept out of the Union. The Union had an elaborate constitution. The head of the Union was the Rajah of Korea. The Union had a Premier. It also had a Chief Secretary, a joint police organization under an Inspector-General of Police and an appellate court. The Union had no legislature. It was financed by contributions from the constituent States. The joint police organization was headed by an Englishman and the police force contained a large number of Pathans and Punjabi Muslims. One could imagine the effect upon public opinion of the employment of such a force against the background of the communal situation in the country in the latter part of 1947.

Though the Union had been formed, this did not stop the agitation for responsible government in the various States. There was trouble, for instance, in Dhenkanal and Nilgiri. The ruler of Dhenkanal had, a few years previously, been asked by the Political Department to stay outside his State. Before the advent of independence, he had been allowed to return to his State. But the local *Prajamandal*, in its zeal for responsible government, occupied all Government buildings and surrounded the palace. I was told that it was only the presence of a tame leopard in the *zenana* of the palace that saved the inmates from molestation.

In Nilgiri, the agitation for responsible government led to serious trouble. The ruler of this State had, from 1942 to 1946, been deprived of his powers by the Political Department and compelled to live outside his State. This was a tiny 'B' class State with an area of 284 square miles and a population of 73,109. About 15 per cent of the population were aboriginals. There was a dispute between the local *Prajamandal* and the ruler on the issue of responsible government. Ultimately, the *Prajamandal* decided to force the pace; its idea being to form a parallel government, to occupy the villages and take over Government offices and property. In a desperate effort to maintain his position, the ruler formed a loyalist party, recruited a force of

20

Gurkhas and obtained assistance from the Rajah of Dhenkanal.

It was not, however, until the aborigines entered the arena that the situation became really grave. Towards the end of October 1947 they began to occupy the cultivated fields of the peasants and to harvest the grain. They affixed blue flags to the property they seized; anyone opposing them received short shrift. Later they started attacking villages and looting property. It was alleged that the Rajah of Nilgiri had deliberately set them against the Prajamandal, the State police having made no attempt to check their depredations. On the other hand, it was contended on behalf of the Rajah that the aborigines did not need any instigation from him; that their grievances were economic. The position became more complicated when it became evident that the communists were also taking a hand.

Whatever might be the truth as to the origin of the disturbances, what caused the greatest concern to the Government of India was the possibility that outbreaks among the aborigines might spread to those neighbouring areas in which they formed a considerable proportion of the population. The aborigines are easily excited and, being accustomed to the use of bows and arrows, are difficult for the unarmed plainsmen to withstand. Trouble with the aborigines had often broken out in the past and had cost considerable effort and expense to put down. From all points of view, it appeared that the time had come to take firm and immediate action if chaos was to be prevented. When, therefore, the Government of Orissa reported that the situation in Nilgiri was tense and that the trouble was spreading, the Government of India authorized them to send the Collector of the nearest District (which was Balasore) to Nilgiri to take over the administration of the State. This was accomplished on 14 November 1947. The Rajah of Nilgiri issued a valedictory proclamation in which he admitted that with his resources he was unable to provide the State with a modern administration.

That some of the Orissa rulers were fishing in the troubled waters of local politics was also clear. The agitation sponsored and sustained by the rulers against the Hirakud Dam project[1] was a case in point. There could be no two opinions as to the utility of the

[1] This has an interesting history. In 1945 there was a dispute between the Madras and Orissa Governments over the waterfall at Machkund. Both Madras and Orissa claimed that it was in their territory. Under the Orissa Order in Council framed under the Government of India Act of 1935, the final decision in regard to any boundary dispute rested with the Governor-General. Before he gave a decision, Lord Wavell accepted my suggestion that

project from the point of view of the States concerned and the province of Orissa as a whole. The execution of this project necessarily involved the immersion of large tracts of land. The Government of Orissa started acquiring these lands on terms very favourable to the tenants. Land acquisition has a way of creating resentment among the peasantry and the rulers of Orissa now began to exploit the situation. An anti-Hirakud agitation was started and sustained at a high pitch. The Government of Orissa charged the Maharajah of Patna with having inspired this agitation. Even Gandhiji's appeal to the rulers not to support such an obviously anti-national movement fell on deaf ears.

Bastar was also giving us cause for concern. This State had prolonged spells of minority administration, from 1891 to 1908, from 1921 to 1928 and from 1936 to 1947. In August 1946 a suggestion had been made by the Resident at Hyderabad to the Political Department that Bastar should form a political unit with Hyderabad. Immediately before the transfer of power reports were rife that the rich mineral resources of this State were about to be mortgaged to Hyderabad by means of a long lease, which, if true, would have been very much to the prejudice of India. Enquiries were made of the Political Department and after considerable trouble the relevant papers were put up to Sardar. There was clear evidence

Sir B. N. Rau should be deputed to study the dispute on the spot and make his recommendations. According to the files of the Government of India, Machkund was certainly a part of Orissa and Sir B. N. Rau in his report confirmed this view.

From then on, the Government of Madras naturally became indifferent. There was no doubt that this waterfall could generate the much needed electric power. Madras had the resources and its territory was contiguous to the waterfall. The finances of Orissa, on the other hand, were depleted and the places to be served by this electric station were so distant that the transmission charges would have been prohibitive. I went to Cuttack to bring the two Governments to a mutual understanding in regard to the working of the scheme. Orissa was then under an Adviser's regime with Sir Hawthorne Lewis as Governor and B. G. Gokhale, I.C.S., as Adviser. We had protracted discussions and ultimately both the Governments agreed to a compromise.

During these discussions I chanced to come across a report of Colonel (later Sir) Arthur Cotton in regard to flood control in Orissa. In his report, which was submitted to the Government of Bengal as early as 1858, he had recommended that, unless the Mahanadi river was thoroughly controlled, poverty, suffering and destruction of property would continue year after year in the Cuttack and Puri districts. He suggested that a dam should be constructed at Sambalpur to control the river. This suggestion of the great engineer and statesman was merely pigeon-holed. We were now taking up the threads almost a hundred years later. In my talks with the Governor of Orissa and his Adviser, I had promised that I would take up this matter as soon as I returned to Delhi. Accordingly I submitted my proposals to Lord Wavell who was extremely sympathetic. At his instance a conference was called at which Sir Archibald Rowlands, Finance Member, Dr B. R. Ambedkar, Member for Public Works and myself were present. The Government of India agreed to finance the project subject to an examination of technical details. Sir Hawthorne Lewis laid the foundation stone at Hirakud in March 1946.

that the Political Department was anxious to complete the deal in a hurry. Sardar and I had a discussion on the subject with Sir Conrad Corfield, who took the stand that his Department was the guardian of the minor ruler and that it was at liberty to enter into the contract in his interests. Sardar told him that he would not allow the interests of the people to be bartered away in this manner.

Shortly before the transfer of power, the Maharajah, Pravir Chandra Deo, had been invested with full ruling powers. We were informed that Hyderabad agents were trying to get at him with a view to obtaining the lease. Sardar invited the ruler to Delhi. I was surprised that full ruling powers should have been conferred on so young and inexperienced a boy. Sardar told him that the Government of India would take a very serious view of the matter if he were to barter away the mineral resources of his State. Our apprehensions and suspicions of the attitude of Hyderabad were subsequently confirmed by the forebodings of a senior British Political Officer who had opportunities of studying events at close quarters. This officer had written to the Government of India:

From the Hyderabad border to Bailadila iron ore areas, it is hardly 100 miles with a good fair weather road. The country is sparsely populated and the local Marias can be easily tempted by plenty of drink and tobacco. Hyderabad's negotiations with the Indian Dominion seem to have come to a deadlock and in the difficult times ahead, it is not inconceivable that Hyderabad may do some propaganda and encourage infiltration with a view ultimately to carve a slice out of Bastar if the difficulties and preoccupations of the Government of India serve them as an opportunity. I sincerely hope that my forebodings may not prove correct but in any case, I submit we cannot afford to remain complacent, and should henceforth regard Hyderabad as a potential danger, particularly in a terrain sparsely but predominantly inhabited by plastic aboriginals and administered by rulers and their officers whose loyalty to the Indian Government is yet to be tested.

Soon after the States Ministry was set up, Harekrushna Mahtab, then Premier of Orissa, had submitted a memorandum to Sardar in which he enumerated various administrative difficulties created by the territories of the Orissa States being interlaced with the province. The most important related to law and order; smuggling across the borders; the administration of controls, especially in regard to food, and the development of communications and river valley projects. Mahtab suggested that, on the analogy of the solution applied in

Burma where the Shan States had created a similar problem, some machinery should be set up for the common administration of certain subjects in both the Orissa States and the province. The States Ministry could not take any action on Mahtab's memorandum as our hands were full with more pressing matters.

On the other hand, the crisis in Nilgiri State made us realize that unless we retained the initiative, we should be overwhelmed by events. Accordingly, on 20 November 1947, a meeting was held in my office in Delhi, at which Harekrushna Mahtab and the Regional Commissioner of Sambalpur were present. Three tentative conclusions were reached at the meeting: first, that the Eastern States Union should not be recognized by the Government of India; secondly, that the 'B' and 'C' class States should be asked to agree to common administration of certain subjects by the provincial Government; and thirdly, that the States Ministry should call a meeting of the rulers of 'B' and 'C' class States at Cuttack some time in December.

The next day I acquainted Sardar with the tentative conclusions which had been reached at the meeting with Harekrushna Mahtab. We proceeded to discuss at great length the problems generally that confronted us in the smaller States. The supreme need was the maintenance of law and order. We could not risk chaos in any part of the country. The communal holocaust and the consequent exodus of refugees had created a critical situation in northern India. The attitude of the Nizam and his advisers towards accession and the activities of the Razakars and the communists held potentialities of danger to peace in the south. The army had not yet been reorganized; we had sent a considerable portion of it to Kashmir. Hence, if any serious trouble broke out in any part of the country, we had no sufficient means at our disposal to put it down. We had therefore to act on the first warning. In the case of the Orissa States, lawlessness was spreading and every party, including the Congress, was fishing in troubled waters.

We had to take note of the fact that, with the transfer of power, there was increasing agitation in the Orissa States for responsible government. The people were politically very backward; there was a substantial element of aborigines in the population. There was hardly any political organization worth mentioning. The area of most of the States was small and the resources inadequate for any modern administration. In some, the grant of responsible government by the rulers had led to strange results. In one of the States the ruler and the ministers agreed to divide the revenues of the State equally between them, without any provision for the administration! In another, responsible government was followed by the closure of all public offices!

The first problem to tackle was the future of the Eastern States Union. The Union was not homogeneous, nor could it be justified on any consideration — linguistic, ethnical or geographical. The people of the Orissa States spoke Oriya and their affinities were with Orissa proper. The Chattisgarh States, on the other hand, were inhabited by Hindi-speaking people; so their future obviously lay with the Central Provinces. Two of the most important States, as well as some smaller ones, had kept out of this Union, which had no assured source of income (it was financed by contributions from the various constituent States which were in arrears); which totally ignored the people of the States, and which, in fact, was little more than a rulers' trade union. In these circumstances it was clearly impossible for the Government of India to recognize this Union.

If it were decided to dissolve the Eastern States Union, a possible alternative would be to form one Union of the Orissa States and another of the Chattisgarh States. But neither of these Unions would have the requisite resources to maintain a reasonable standard of administration. Moreover, the Orissa States had cut the province of Orissa into three bits and their formation into a Union would perpetuate that anomaly; while the Chattisgarh States were scattered all over the Central Provinces.

With this alternative ruled out, the choice before us was either (1) to bring about a sort of administrative co-operation between the province and the States as suggested by Harekrushna Mahtab, or (2) to merge the Orissa States with the Orissa province and the Chattisgarh States with the Central Provinces.

Although at first blush I was inclined to accept Harekrushna Mahtab's suggestion, it was found on examination to bristle with difficulties. His suggestion, if implemented, would be bound to create constant friction between the State authorities and the provincial government, so that the Government of India would have their hands full with arbitrating between these two authorities. The points in dispute being mainly administrative, no judicial tribunal would be in a position to arbitrate. The selection of subjects for common administration was bound to prove difficult, if not impossible. Equally thorny was the problem of fixing the basis of financial contribution to be made by the States for the subjects taken over by the provincial government. And, having made such contributions, would the States have enough resources left to run the administration of the residuary subjects?

I mentioned to Sardar the view of the Orissa Sub-Committee set up by the Simon Commission in 1929 and presided over by C. R. Attlee. This Committee had suggested that, if Orissa were to be made into a separate entity, some arrangements should be made with the Orissa feudatory States for mutual relationship in administration. Sir Hawthorne Lewis, who possessed unrivalled knowledge and experience of Orissa and who later became the Governor of that province, had stated that the province of Orissa and the Orissa feudatory States could not be kept in water-tight compartments and both should have to be brought into some mutual relationship in administration. As late as 1940, the Secretary of State for India had himself envisaged that the Orissa States should ultimately have to become an integral part of the province of Orissa.

Sardar was quite definite that the Eastern States Union should not be recognized. He felt that a Union which was unrepresentative even in relation to the rulers and which paid no heed to the rights of the people had no justification to exist. He was opposed to the creation of two separate Unions of the Orissa States on the one hand and the Chattisgarh States on the other.

As for Harekrushna Mahtab's proposals, it could only result in friction and bad government; it certainly did not contribute to the solution of the problem of the smaller States. Sardar was prepared to go all out to secure the merger of all three classes of Orissa States with the province of Orissa. He told me, however, that we should first tackle the 'B' and 'C' class States, and deal later with the 'A' class States. He asked me to invite all the rulers of the Orissa States to Cuttack for a discussion and to go there myself in the second week of December.

At the end of our discussion I pointed out to Sardar that the proposed merger of the States was contrary to the assurances held out in his own statement of 5 July and in Lord Mountbatten's address to the Chamber of Princes on 25 July 1947. It was true that, at that time, we were anxious by the policy of accession on three subjects to preserve the integrity of the country, thus preventing the States from becoming so many 'Ulsters' in the body politic. Nevertheless, a guarantee once given could not be lightly set aside, unless it could be proved that there were overwhelming consider-ations which were demonstrably in the interests of the country. The fact of the matter was that we did not realize that the weakness in the States' structure was the smaller States. While admitting the force of my arguments, Sardar felt he could not be a party to an attempt to perpetuate something that was inherently incapable of survival. The ultimate test of fitness for the survival of any State was its capacity to secure the well-being of its subjects. He was quite sure that the Orissa States' rulers could not do this. Further, the compul-sion of events had brought about altered circumstances and, by im-plementing their policy of merger, the Government of India would only be saving the rulers from the fury of their subjects newly awakened to a consciousness of their rights.

The States Ministry now concentrated on the problems likely to arise in the event of our being able to persuade the rulers of the Orissa States to merge their States with the province of Orissa. The first problem related to the privy purse of the rulers. Since they were surrendering their States for all time, it was but elemen-tary justice that some form of *quid pro quo* should be conceded to them. We had before us the precedent set by the British Govern-ment who, in the process of establishing their empire, gave liberal pensions to those rulers who were deprived of their States. The Government of India have continued since to discharge some of these obligations. We considered that, in equity, these rulers should be given allowances (styled as Privy Purses) for their maintenance and that such allowances should not be terminated with the present rulers but should be continued to their successors.

As regards the basis on which the privy purse was to be fixed, we had two precedents to guide us. The first was the formula evolved by the Political Department in 1945 in consultation with a Sub-committee of the Chamber of Princes. This formula gave the rulers a privy purse on the basis of a percentage of the average revenues of the State for the previous five years. The percentages suggested were 25 per cent for all revenues up to Rs 5 lakhs; 20 per cent for Rs 5 lakhs to 10 lakhs; 15 per cent for Rs 10 lakhs to 25 lakhs; 10 per cent for Rs 25 lakhs to one crore; 7 per cent for the second crore; 5 per cent for the third crore; 3 per cent for the fourth crore and an overall maximum of Rs 25 lakhs for revenues above Rs 4 crores.

The second precedent before us was the award of a Congress Sub-committee consisting of Dr Rajendra Prasad, Dr Pattabhi Sita-ramayya and Shankarrao Deo in connexion with the formation of the Deccan States Union. This was known as the 'Deccan States Formula'. Under this formula, the rulers were to get privy purses at the rate of 15 per cent on the first Rs 5 lakhs of the average annual revenue; 10 per cent on the next five lakhs and 7½ per cent on revenue above Rs 10 lakhs. The Deccan States formula did not fix a ceiling, but it provided a minimum of Rs 50,000 per annum.

The Political Department's formula, we thought, was on too gene-rous a scale, while the Deccan States formula, though not so hand-some, also erred on the liberal side. We felt that there should be a maximum privy purse; we were against fixing any minimum. In the formula that we devised (subsequently known as the Eastern States Formula) the rulers were to get 15 per cent on the first lakh of the annual revenue; 10 per cent on the next Rs 4 lakhs, and 7½ per cent on all revenues above Rs 5 lakhs, subject to a maximum of Rs 10 lakhs. The financial year 1945-46 was taken as the basic year for the calculation of the privy purse.

The rulers were already immune from taxation in their own States; unless, therefore, we made their allowances tax-free, we should be taking away with our left hand what we gave with the right. It was accordingly decided that the privy purse would be free of all taxes.

We further conceded certain private properties, including palaces, and guaranteed the personal privileges of the ruler, his wife, his mother, the heir-apparent and his wife. Succession to the *gaddi* was also guaranteed. The basic idea was that the Government of India should not create, as an aftermath of merger, any social or economic problems for the rulers or for their numerous dependents.

Another problem was whether the cessation of the rulers' authority, jurisdiction and power should be in favour of the provincial govern-ment, or of the Government of India. There was a clear advantage in the Centre taking over the States and then employing the agency of the provincial governments for their administration; for then, at any rate until the new constitution was framed, the Government of India could retain control over the provincial governments in respect of the administration of those areas. It was obvious that, since the States and the districts in the province had to be welded into one

21

unit, the help and guidance of the Central Government would be necessary. The Law Ministry produced a merger agreement embodying all our points in five articles, which served as a model for all such agreements made subsequently.

Sardar accepted the proposals and asked me to inform our Finance Minister as well as the Premier of Orissa about the basis and quantum of the privy purse. Both accepted the rates suggested as reasonable.

In the meantime, it was reported to us that cracks were developing in the Eastern States Union. We were told that, at a meeting of the Council of Rulers, the Rajah of Khairagarh had presented a note favouring full and unconditional co-operation with the neighbouring provinces, including, if necessary, the merger of the States. The rulers of Korea and Patna were wholly opposed to the suggestion. Many of the rulers of the smaller States held the view that each should decide for himself, take his own course, and scrap the Eastern States Union. As a last minute endeavour to save the Union and to obtain recognition from the States Ministry, the rulers of Korea and Patna came to Delhi on 1 December bringing with them the ruler of Khairagarh. They met Sardar the same day. He pointed out to them that the fate of the 'B' and 'C' class States was inextricably bound up with the adjoining provinces and that they could not stand on their own feet. The Oriya-speaking States must be integrated with Orissa and the Hindi-speaking States with the Central Provinces. Sardar was emphatic that the Eastern States Union should be dissolved. He said that suitable machinery should be evolved for joint administration of certain subjects between 'A' class States and the province. As the rulers were to meet at Cuttack quite soon, this question could be discussed then.

After this meeting, Sardar and I again reviewed the position. I pointed out that joint administration on certain subjects between 'A' class States and the province was fraught with innumerable administrative difficulties. It was for this reason that we had rejected a similar proposal by Harekrushna Mahtab with regard to 'B' and 'C' class States. I could not conceive a half-way house between the *status quo* and a complete merger of the 'A' class States with the province.

A few days before I was to leave for Cuttack, Sardar told me that he would also be coming. This change in the original programme caused me some misgiving; for I had thought that if I failed to bring about the merger, whether partial or complete, Sardar could then have tried his hand as the higher authority, but that if the two of us went together and failed to accomplish anything, the entire plan would collapse. Our success or failure at Cuttack was bound to have a great psychological effect on rulers all over India; and we could not therefore risk a failure. A former official of the Political Department had warned me not to deal with Orissa first as the rulers were supposed to be intractable. But the situation in Orissa was clamouring for immediate attention and we had no alternative but to tackle it. Sardar had made up his mind and there was no use my arguing this matter with him. Accordingly, on 13 December we went to Cuttack.

On reaching Cuttack, we had a meeting with the provincial ministers as well as the Governor. I explained to them the tentative plan we had in mind. There was some discussion. In the end it was decided not only that the 'B' and 'C' class States should be amalgamated with the province of Orissa, but that the 'A' class States also should be tackled in the same way.

We took the rulers in two batches. The conference of 'B' and 'C' class States' rulers took place at 10 a.m. on 14 December 1947. The rulers of Athgarh, Baramba, Daspala, Hindol, Khandpara, Kharsawan, Narsinghpur, Nilgiri, Pal-Lahara, Rairakhol, Ranpur and Talcher were present, as well as the Rajmata of Ranpur. On our side, there were Sardar, Harekrushna Mahtab, K. V. K. Sundaram, I.C.S., of the Law Ministry, the Regional Commissioner for the Eastern States, V. Shankar, I.C.S., Sardar's Private Secretary, and myself, besides the Revenue Commissioner and the Chief Secretary of Orissa.

Sardar inaugurated the proceedings with a most persuasive speech. He said that the safety of the rulers as well as of the people was in danger in Orissa, and that the situation demanded immediate solution. He had come to Cuttack to tender friendly advice to the rulers, not as a representative of the old paramountcy or of any foreign power, but as a member of a family trying to solve a family problem. Orissa as a federal unit could only thrive and progress if it was a compact whole and was not torn asunder by multifarious jurisdictions and authorities which ruined its compactness. These States had no resources, no man power, and nothing on which any stable government could be built up; obviously therefore they could not work responsible government. There had been a parrot cry of late in India for responsible government in the States; and some rulers had used one section of the population against another to maintain their position. Responsible government in petty States had no meaning. He advised the rulers to cease exposing themselves as targets in these troublous times and to divest themselves of all power and authority. The Government of India would, in their turn, guarantee the privileges, honour and dignity of such rulers. The growing discontent among the people cried out for an immediate remedy. He concluded that if his advice were not listened to, the rulers, after being ousted by their people, would have in the end to come to Delhi, by which time things might have gone so far that he would no longer be in a position to help them.

We gave the rulers copies of our draft agreement for merger. There was some desultory discussion, during which the young Rajah of Ranpur said that he had already granted responsible government. But Sardar pooh-poohed the idea of responsible government in such petty States. The Rajah then enquired whether he could stand for election to the Orissa Legislative Assembly. Sardar replied in the affirmative and added, in characteristic fashion, that instead of diving in a narrow well, the ruler would be entitled to swim in an ocean. The main part of the discussions turned on the privy purses. I explained how these amounts were fixed. There was a strong demand that they should be increased. Sardar was firm and said that if the privy purses were to be settled in perpetuity, he did not wish them to be fixed so high as to become a target of attack. The rulers asked for some time to consider the agreement. But it was only a formal request. They realized that their continued existence depended on the goodwill of their people and the support of the Government of India, both of which they lacked and that if, owing to agitation, the administration of their States were ultimately taken over by the Government of India they might not even get the privy purse which was now being guaranteed to them. That same evening I met the rulers again. Sardar was not present at this discussion. Ultimately the twelve rulers agreed to the merger and signed the agreement. It was decided to ask the rulers of the remaining three States who had been prevented from attending by illness, or for other reasons, to sign later.

After lunch on 14 December, we met the rulers of the 'A' class States of Bamra, Baudh, Dhenkanal, Gangpur, Kalahandi, Keonjhar, Mayurbhanj, Nayagarh, Patna, Seraikela and Sonepur. Sardar explained the position to them on the same lines as he had done to the rulers of the 'B' and 'C' class States. He told them that the Orissa States were like ulcers on the body of the province and that they must either be cured or eliminated. If they listened to his advice they could be cured; otherwise they might find themselves uprooted by the people.

The Maharajah of Mayurbhanj said that he had already granted responsible government in his State and that a ministry was functioning. Hence he could not make any commitment without consulting his ministers. In view of this and having regard to the area, population and revenue of the State, he was left out of the discussions.

The Maharajah of Patna (who was the spokesman for the rest of the rulers) said that while accepting the need for collaboration with the provincial government, the rulers did not agree with the suggestion in the draft agreement circulated to them that the transfer of all powers to the province was the right solution. Assurances were then asked from us on such points as the maintenance of the territorial integrity of the States, representation of the people and the rulers in the legislatures, private properties, palace guards, security of permanent services, privileges and exemptions and so on. We were extremely accommodating in our attitude, except on the question of privy purses. Here we firmly refused to depart from the principle adopted in the case of the 'B' and 'C' class States.

As the discussions proceeded, it became clear that the rulers of the 'A' class States were not agreeable to the proposal for merger. The Maharajah of Patna wanted time for further consideration. Sardar almost lost his patience at this and said that if the friendly advice which he tendered was not acceptable and the problem remained as before, he could not answer for the consequences. I then suggested that the rulers should consider the agreement for a few hours and that we might meet again at ten that night. They agreed and the conference was adjourned.

Sardar was very much disappointed with the attitude of the rulers. As we were leaving the Conference room someone remarked that it would not be difficult to foment unrest and make the position of the rulers intolerable. I observed that were we to sow the wind of unrest the country would reap the whirlwind of chaos. I went on to say that if the choice before us was peace with the *status quo* or chaos with merger, I would unhesitatingly vote for the former. The need of the hour was peace. Sardar agreed with me.

At ten o'clock that night, the rulers of eight 'A' class States met me. Sardar was not present, nor was Harekrushna Mahtab. At the outset, the Maharajah of Patna pointed out that the merger agreement did not tally with the talks he had had with Sardar in Delhi. I replied that the mere collaboration on five or six subjects between the States and the provincial government, which was all that had been discussed in Delhi, did not by any means solve the problem. I repeated the arguments against this sort of arrangement and emphasized that the integration of all Orissa States with the province was essential for the peace and progress both of the States and of the province. The Maharajah of Patna then made the suggestion that there should be a federation of the States with the province on certain specified subjects, and that for the rest the States should be treated as autonomous units. I pointed out the practical difficulties that were inherent in the proposition and the friction it would create between the provincial legislature and government on the one hand and the federal and State authorities on the other. I enquired in what way such a cumbrous arrangement would benefit the people of the States. I told the Maharajah that, even under his scheme, the subjects which were left to the States would still have to be administered in responsibility to a legislature. If that was the position, it would be in the interests of both the rulers and the people to agree to the proposal of the Government of India. The Maharajah then explained that, as the rulers were signatories to the Eastern States Union Constitution, it was obviously necessary for them to examine the legal position as to how best they could withdraw from it before signing the merger agreement. He asked for time and the meeting was adjourned.

It was now midnight and Sardar was leaving the next morning for Nagpur. If no agreement were reached with the rulers of the 'A' class States before he left, there was every likelihood that their attitude later would stiffen. And failure with these rulers would affect disastrously our negotiations with the Chattisgarh rulers whom we were to meet the next day. Indeed, all our plans would go awry unless something was done to bring round these rulers.

I took the Rajah of Dhenkanal into my confidence. He was an important 'A' class ruler; but in view of the Prajamandal agitation for responsible government he could not maintain his position inside his State without the support of the Government of India. He readily agreed to the merger of his State when I promised him that, in that event, all his demands, such as were considered reasonable, would be conceded. I then requested him to go and inform the Maharajah of Patna and others of his decision to merge his State with Orissa, adding that if they did not follow his example the Government of India would be compelled, in the conditions prevailing in Orissa, to take over the administration of their States.

The Rajah of Dhenkanal must have conveyed the message, for the Maharajah of Patna came to me in the very early hours of the morning. We had a frank talk. I pointed out to him that law and order had practically broken down in Dhenkanal and that other States were on the brink of trouble. While admitting that his State was at the time free from it, I told the Maharajah that it would not be long before the agitation spread to his State. In the general unrest I was certain that unsocial elements would take a hand. The situation in northern India could not be unknown to him. If the rulers would not realize their responsibilities the Government of India could not forget theirs. Rather than allow the peace of the province to be endangered, the Government of India would go to the length of even taking over the administration of the States. The crying need of the hour was peace. The Maharajah asked me whether the Government of India were really serious about taking over the administration of the States and whether I would put this down in writing. I told him that, in the circumstances explained by me, the Government of India would have no option but to do so and that I would certainly record as much in writing.

After this discussion, the Maharajah of Patna brought in the other rulers. We then began consideration of the agreement clause by clause. The rulers of Patna, Seraikela, Gangpur and Sonepur gave me a memorandum containing a list of their demands. These were: (1) that the Orissa Legislature should be bicameral and that in the Upper House the rulers of the twenty-six Orissa States or their successors should be permanent members; (2) that the terms of succession of the rulers should continue to be the same as in the Instrument of Accession signed by them in August 1947; (3) that the privy purse of the rulers should be fixed in perpetuity and guaranteed on the same uniform basis and principle as would be the case with other larger States, and (4) that the personal rights and prerogatives of the rulers as heretofore enjoyed should continue. I retained the memorandum but told the rulers that it would be difficult for the Government of India to accede to all their demands.

The rulers then raised points regarding their private properties and personal privileges, and security from victimization of State servants on account of their past loyalty. I accepted several amendments to the merger agreement in as conciliatory a spirit as possible. Some of the proposals I deferred until the views of the Government of Orissa could be obtained. In the hearing of all those present, I dictated a letter to the Chief Secretary of Orissa asking for the views of the provincial government and emphasizing that the Government of India desired the proposals of the rulers of 'A' class States on these points to be met as far as possible. After this, there was no further difficulty and the rulers of Baudh, Dhenkanal, Gangpur, Kalahandi, Patna, Seraikela and Sonepur put their signatures to the merger agreement. The original copies which had been signed by the rulers were so full of corrections and amendments that they looked like galley proofs after correction by the proof reader. We had no time to get the agreement retyped.

After the rulers had signed the agreement, I gave the following letter to the Maharajah of Patna as promised:

I am glad that you have signed the agreement. I mentioned to you the peculiar position which your State occupies among the Orissa States. The Government of India are most anxious to maintain law and order. We cannot allow your State to create problems for the Government of Orissa and if you had not signed the agreement, we would have been compelled to take over the administration of your State.

The rulers of Baudh and Kalahandi asked me for similar letters, which I gave them.

The rulers and I had been in almost continuous session from ten o'clock of the previous night to about nine in the morning of the 15th. Sardar and his party had gone to the railway station and were waiting for me, but it was more than two hours before I was able to join them. Sardar was very pleased when I handed him the merger agreement signed by the rulers of the 'A' class States. Harekrushna Mahtab even presented me with a silver filigree cigarette case as a memento of the occasion. I told Sardar about the letter I had given to some of the rulers which I felt might occasion some criticism, but Sardar assured me that there was no need to worry.

We then left for Bhubaneshwar and from there flew to Nagpur. We met the rulers of the Chattisgarh States at 4.30 p.m. on 15 December. Mangaldas Pakvasa, Governor of the Central Provinces, R. S. Shukla, the Premier and D. P. Mishra, the Home Minister were also present. The rulers of ten States, besides the Regent Rani of Nandgaon, the heir-apparent of Surguja and the Dewans of Jashpur and Changbhakar attended the meeting. Sardar inaugurated the proceedings with a brief account of what had happened at Cuttack and made an appeal to the rulers to sign the merger agreement, thereby handing over their burden of woes and worries to the provincial government. The ruler of Kawardha requested Sardar to protect the States as they had been protected by the British in the past and added that he was prepared to accept the paramountcy of the Dominion Government. Sardar replied that protection from internal disorders could not be extended to the State unless it had specifically acceded to the Dominion Government in internal affairs as well. As for reviving paramountcy, there could be no justification for doing so because in free India all were alike and no Indian could be paramount over another.

A number of points were raised relating to the privy purse, the principles governing the classification of private property, and the constitutional position of the ruler and his rights and privileges. Several questions were asked and explanations given. The rulers still wanted some time to study the merger agreement. Sardar replied that the agreement was a very simple proposition and more a matter for the rulers themselves to decide than for lawyers to advise upon. I suggested that the rulers might be given a couple of hours in which to study the agreement and the meeting was adjourned till 10 p.m.

When the rulers met again, I had the feeling that they were apprehensive mainly about their privy purses. The ruler of Korea asked that the privy purse should be fixed in perpetuity so that it could not be altered on account of any change in the Government, and that it should be incorporated in the Constitution Act so as to make it enforceable by recourse to the Federal Court. Sardar assured him that the agreement which the rulers were signing embodied a guarantee given by the Government of India and that the intention was to incorporate it in the new Constitution.

After this categorical assurance, the ten rulers present signed the merger agreement. The Regent Rani of Nandgaon signed on behalf of the minor Rajah; and the heir-apparent of Surguja and the Dewans of Jashpur and Changbhakar agreed to get the signatures of the rulers of their respective States. Sardar thereafter left the meeting. Those of the rulers who had already granted responsible

22

government were anxious to have something to show to their people with regard to the merger agreement. I explained that the Chief Secretary of the Central Provinces would be writing a letter to all the rulers explaining that responsible government was neither feasible nor advantageous to the people of small States; that Sardar felt that it would be much more in the interests of the people to share responsible government with a larger unit like the Central Provinces.

The inevitable consequence of the merger of the Orissa and Chattisgarh States was the dissolution of the Eastern States Union. Telegraphic orders were issued for the transfer of their police force to the control of the Governments of Orissa and of the Central Provinces respectively.

On 16 December 1947, after reaching Delhi, Sardar issued a statement explaining the background and the policy underlying the merger of the Eastern States. The statement laid stress on the fact that democracy and democratic institutions could function efficiently only where the unit to which these were applied could subsist in a fairly autonomous existence. Integration was clearly and unmistakably indicated where, on account of its smallness of size; its isolation; its inseparable link with a neighbouring autonomous territory in practically all matters of everyday life; its inadequacy of resources to open up its economic potentialities; the backwardness of its people, and its sheer incapacity to shoulder a self-contained administration, a State was unable to afford a modern system of government. It went on to say that in many of the Eastern States, large-scale unrest had already gripped the people; while in others, the rumblings of the storm were clearly to be heard. In such circumstances and after careful and anxious thought, Sardar had come to the conclusion that for smaller States there was no alternative to integration. He paid a tribute to the rulers, who had shown commendable appreciation of the realities of the situation and a benevolent regard for the public good. 'The Princes have by their act of abnegation purchased in perpetuity their right to claim the devotion of their people.' The statement concluded by drawing attention to 'the stakes involved': 'some 56,000 square miles of territory with a population of about 8 million, a gross revenue of about Rs 2 crores and immense potentialities for the future.'

By this time, the newspapers were full of what had taken place at Cuttack; and my letter to the rulers which had found its way into print was the subject of criticism. Telegrams had been sent to

Gandhiji and Nehru. So Sardar asked me to meet Gandhiji and Nehru and explain matters. Accordingly, I went to Gandhiji and gave a detailed account of what had happened. I explained that the situation in Orissa was explosive. I referred to the part the communists were playing and how inflammable the aborigines were. I pointed out that the opposition of the rulers to the Hirakud Dam project had not abated in spite of his intervention and that there would be considerable heart-burning in the country if, because of the opposition of the rulers, that scheme were put into cold storage. The question that faced us in Orissa was: which was paramount, the interests of the people or the interests of the rulers of the Orissa States? I laid stress on the fact that the Orissa States, with the exception of a few like Patna, were badly administered; and that with the new awakening among the States subjects, there was no doubt that most of the rulers would be driven out. This would lead to chaos and anarchy in Orissa, which could not but have repercussions in other parts of the country. It was only the realization that the Government of India would take over the administration of the States that brought round the rulers of the 'A' class States.

Gandhiji listened patiently and professed himself entirely satisfied. In his characteristic way, he told me that the merger of the States was like giving castor oil to children. It was for the ultimate good of the rulers. He also told me that I was at liberty to quote his approval.

I next met Nehru, explained to him the circumstances in which the letter was given to the rulers, and told him that the States Ministry would submit a detailed summary for the consideration of the Cabinet. I communicated the gist of my conversations with Gandhiji and Nehru to Sardar. In due course the Cabinet approved the agreements relating to the merger of the Orissa and Chattisgarh States.

On 23 December 1947, in exercise of the powers conferred by sub-section 2 of section 3 of the Extra Provincial Jurisdiction Act, 1947 (No. XLVII of 1947), the Government of India delegated to the Government of Orissa the power to administer the Orissa States in the same manner as the districts in that province. The Central functions were reserved for the Government of India. It was however provided that the exercise of the power thus delegated would be subject to the control of the Central Government and that the delegation would not preclude the Central Government from exercising the power thereby delegated. A similar notification was issued delegating the governance of the Chattisgarh States to the Government of the Central Provinces.

It was but natural that this merger should provoke criticism from princely circles. The question was raised by them when they had a conference with Lord Mountbatten on 7 January 1948. The conference was attended by the rulers of Jodhpur, Bikaner, Bhopal, Rewa, Kotah and Alwar, as well as the Dewans of Kashmir, Indore, Kolhapur, Udaipur, Bikaner, Jaipur, Kotah, Alwar and Rewa, and representatives of Travancore, Cochin, Patiala and Jodhpur. In his inimitable way, Lord Mountbatten defended the merger of the Orissa and Chattisgarh States. He explained the system of mediatization introduced by Napoleon in 1806 and added that his own family came from the Grand Duchy of Hesse which had absorbed about a dozen small principalities. The ruling families of the States thus merged were able to avoid the impact of the German Revolution of 1918. He was personally very much in favour of the system of mediatization or merger.

Lord Mountbatten emphasized that there was no intention of applying the merger system to the larger States. Indeed the rulers of the larger States should welcome the principle of merger being applied to the smaller ones because the whole Indian States system would stand condemned by the example of its worst participants.

I said that the principle of merger would not be applied to those States which had individual representation in the Constituent Assembly and which obviously had a future and possibilities of development. I pointed out that Mayurbhanj had been left out of the merger scheme. In the course of further discussions, it was mentioned that there was an impression among the rulers that the intention of the Government of India was to absorb all the States in the provinces and none in the neighbouring bigger States. I said that while the Government of India believed in, and would proceed with, the policy of the merger of smaller States, they believed equally in the policy of building up bigger units of States which, with the grant of full responsible government, would have the same status as the provinces. The principle of merger would be applied whether the unit with which a State was merged was a province or a State. The determining factors were geographical contiguity and linguistic, administrative, cultural and economic affiliations.

1. Lord Mountbatten addressing the Chamber of Princes for the first and last time as Crown Representative.

2. Sardar discussing the communal situation and the refugee problem with the premiers of the Punjab and the U.P. and rulers of border States.

3. The author conferring with the rulers of A class States in Orissa.

4. Sardar and the author being received by the Governor and Chief Minister of the Central Provinces at Nagpur.

5. Sardar inaugurating the Saurashtra Union by swearing-in the Jam Saheb of Nawanagar as Rajpramukh.

6. Council of rulers and ministers of Saurashtra Union. Third and fourth from right are the Rajpramukh and U.N. Dhebar, then Chief Minister, now President of the Congress.

7. Prime Minister Nehru inaugurating the Madhya Bharat Union
by swearing-in the Maharajah of Gwalior as Rajpramukh.
Seated on right is the Maharajah of Indore.

Bihar had desired to be represented at the Cuttack conference, as the province had territorial claims on some of the Orissa States. But their representatives were delayed by floods and could not arrive in time. The Rajah of Kharsawan had pointed out that his State was surrounded by the Singbhum district of Bihar and that the Adibasis were anxious that the State should merge into that province. I suggested that he should first agree to merge with Orissa and that the wishes of the people regarding the ultimate merger of that State with Bihar or Orissa could be ascertained later through a plebiscite. The Rajah agreed. Soon after the merger an agitation was set afoot in Seraikela and Kharsawan for their merger with Bihar, on the ground that the majority of the population were Adibasis and that geographically the two States were part of the Singbhum district of Bihar. This formed a bone of contention between the two neighbouring provinces. Orissa was anxious to retain these States; Bihar wanted to draw them into its fold. It was the first case in which regional rivalry and territorial ambitions overcame the common allegiance to the Congress of two provincial Congress administrations. The Rajahs also took part in the agitation, which brought about a certain degree of chaos, so that for some time the administration in both these erstwhile States could only be carried on with the help of the military police. We could not allow such a situation to continue. A conference was called in New Delhi of the representatives of the Governments of Bihar and Orissa, who agreed to abide by my arbitration. After hearing both sides of the case and after ascertaining the views of Sardar, I decided that Seraikela and Kharsawan, being two islands in the district of Singbhum, should go to Bihar. They were handed over to Bihar on 18 May 1948.

The Maharajah of Mayurbhanj had kept aloof from the merger on the ground that he had granted responsible government and so could not move without consulting his ministers. But in the course of a year, the so-called popular ministers had run through the major part of the savings of the State, the administration was almost at a standstill and there was considerable unrest among the people. The Maharajah came to me and confessed that it was a mistake on his part not to have merged his State along with the other Orissa States. He told me frankly that if something was not done immediately, the State would go bankrupt. He was loath to see the savings of the State, which he had built up with great difficulty, recklessly squandered away. He pleaded that the State should be taken over by the Government of India at once. I discussed the matter with the Premier of Mayurbhanj, who agreed. On 17 October 1948 the Maharajah signed an Instrument of Merger. The State was taken over by the Government of India on 9 November and a Chief Commissioner was appointed to administer it.

Later, however, we decided that Mayurbhanj should go to Orissa, as it was linguistically and culturally linked with that province. When this decision became known, there was an intense agitation by the Adibasis who wanted the State to be merged with Bihar. It seemed to me that the agitation was not spontaneous, but it looked as though the Adibasis would get out of control. I went again to Baripada the capital of Mayurbhanj. On the day of my arrival I saw streams of Adibasis pouring on to the *maidan* facing the bungalow where I was staying and, by the evening, some thousands of them had collected. The Adibasis' way of conducting public meetings was rather peculiar in that they kept up a continuous session of eating, dancing and speech-making, with occasional intervals for sleep. Sometimes these meetings would last for two or three days at a stretch. I felt that it was imperative that I should point out to the Adibasi leaders the error of their ways. Accordingly I sent for their leader, one Sonnaram, who brought along a few of his colleagues. I explained to them that there was not a single valid reason why Mayurbhanj should merge with Bihar. If contiguity were the only criterion, the State could as well be amalgamated with West Bengal. Culturally and economically, its affinity was with Orissa and I pleaded with them to call off the agitation. Sonnaram, however, did not appear to be convinced by my arguments. I then decided to address the Adibasis direct. I spoke to them that afternoon and my speech was translated into their dialect by the Superintendent of Police. I could see that they had no interest whatever in this agitation, that the whole demonstration was artificial and that these simple and unsophisticated people were being incited by interested agitators. The agitation continued even after the merger of Mayurbhanj with Orissa; but eventually it fizzled out.

On 1 January 1949, Mayurbhanj was merged with Orissa. This completed the merger of all the States in that province.

VIII

SAURASHTRA

AFTER settling the problem of the Orissa and Chattisgarh States, we turned our attention to Kathiawar. This peninsula, situated at the northern end of the country's western seaboard, has earned a niche for itself in Indian annals. Many are the heroes of mythology and history who have hailed from Kathiawar. Dwaraka, where Sri Krishna reigned, has been identified as Kathiawar. Sri Krishna left his mortal body at Dehotsarga. Sudama, whose friendship with Sri Krishna has been immortalized, came from Porbandar, or Sudamapuri as it was called. Junagadh gave us the famous devotional poet, Narsinh Mehta, whose hymn *Vaishnava Janato* used to be recited daily at Gandhiji's prayer meetings. Kathiawar was also the birthplace of Dayananda Saraswati, the founder of the Arya Samaj. Somnath is the first of the twelve *Jyotirlingas*. The edicts of Asoka are inscribed on a rock in the gorge between Junagadh and the Girnar Hills. Shatrunjaya Hill, near Palitana, is the holy place of the Jains and is as much revered by them as is Kashi (Banaras) by the Hindus. The Gir forests are the only abode of lions in the world outside Africa. To cricket, Kathiawar has given players of the calibre of Ranji in the past and Duleep, Amar Singh and Vinoo Mankad in recent years. Above all, Porbandar in Kathiawar was the birthplace of Gandhiji.

At the earliest date of which we have any historical knowledge, Kathiawar was governed by the lieutenants of the Maurya kings. It also formed part of the Gupta empire, whose viceroys governed from Wanthali. Later on, Senapatis became kings of Kathiawar and established themselves at Vallabhinagar (modern Vala). When the Guptas were ousted, the Vallabhi dynasty extended its sway over Kutch and Lat Desha (between Gujarat and Rajputana). In the eleventh century Kathiawar came under Muslim authority.

The sack of Somnath by Mahmud Ghazni in 1024 and the capture of Anhilwad by the Muslims in 1194 were the prelude to the conquest of Kathiawar by the Khaljis and Tughlaks. In 1573 Gujarat was conquered by Akbar, and his viceroys at Ahmedabad exacted periodical tribute from Kathiawar through troops sent there from time to time. In the latter half of the eighteenth century the Mahrattas supplanted the Moghuls and every year Kathiawar was visited by Mahratta forces for the collection of tribute. In 1803, some of the *talukdars* of Kathiawar applied to the British Resident at Baroda for protection. Colonel Walker, who was the Resident, wrote to the Governor-General:

With the reservation of their acknowledged tributary payments, Kathiawar States are independent and at liberty to form connections with other powers. They are under no obligations of service, and neither the Peshwa nor the Gaekwar intend to exercise an authority in Kathiawar beyond the demand of their respective contributions.

In 1807, the forces of the East India Company and of the Gaekwar, under Colonel Walker, advanced into Kathiawar 'with the object of relieving the province of the double scourge of periodical invasions and internecine conflicts.' The rulers and *talukdars* of Kathiawar were guaranteed security from the visitation of Mahratta forces, in return for which they bound themselves to pay voluntarily a fixed and settled tribute to the East India Company, to keep the peace amongst themselves and to maintain order within their own limits. In 1817 the Peshwa ceded to the Company his share of the Kathiawar tribute and, in 1820, the Gaekwar agreed to the collection and payment of his share by the Company. Whatever other changes might have taken place in Kathiawar, the main framework of Colonel Walker's settlement remained practically undisturbed till the transfer of power in 1947.

The States in Kathiawar comprised the fourteen salute States of Junagadh, Nawanagar, Bhavnagar, Dhrangadhra, Porbandar, Morvi, Gondal, Jafrabad, Wankaner, Palitana, Dhrol, Limbdi, Rajkot and Wadhwan; seventeen non-salute States; and 191 other small States exercising varying degrees of jurisdiction. The area was a little over 22,000 square miles with a population of nearly four million. The following extract from an article which appeared in the *Tribune* in July 1939 gives a graphic picture of the problem of the smaller States in Kathiawar:

As many as 46 States in this Agency have an area of two or less than two square miles each. Eight of them, namely, Bodanoness, Gandhol, Morchopra, Panchabda, Samadhiala, Chabbadia, Sanala, Satanoness and Vangadhra are just over half a mile each in area. Yet none of these is the smallest State in Kathiawar! That distinction goes to Vejanoness which has an area of 0.29 square mile, a population of 206 souls and an income of Rs. 500/- a year. There is nothing in the annals of the Indian States — Gujarat States excepted — which can beat this record. This is not all. Even these tiny principalities do not seem to be indivisible units. Some of them are claimed by more than one 'sovereign' officially described as shareholder. Thus Dahida, with an area of two square miles, has six shareholders and Godhula and Khijadia Dosaji, being one square mile each in extent, have two shareholders each; while Sanala, 0.51 in area, is put against two shareholders. Such instances can be easily multiplied up to thirty to forty.

The administration of the Kathiawar States was further complicated by the fact that many of them had scattered islands of territory outside their individual boundaries. Nawanagar, Gondal and Junagadh, for instance, had respectively nine, eighteen and twenty-four separate areas of territory. Thus the map of Kathiawar was divided into about 860 different jurisdictions. Communications were in a primitive condition. Internal trade was rendered difficult by the export and import duties which the various units levied at different rates; and this encouraged extensive smuggling and black market operations. Since an offender in one State could escape apprehension easily by going into another, administration of justice and maintenance of law and order were greatly handicapped. In fact, all the worst effects of political fragmentation were to be seen in Kathiawar.

Four years before the transfer of power, the Political Department had, under their Attachment Scheme, joined some of the smaller units to the neighbouring big States. The scheme covered an area of 7,000 square miles with a population of 8,00,000. It provoked bitter opposition from the rulers of the smaller States. After the transfer of power the position of these attached units became a problem by itself. Their rulers asserted that since paramountcy had lapsed they were no longer bound by the Attachment Scheme and this had deleterious results in many parts of Kathiawar.

Soon after the announcement of the June 3rd Plan, the Political Department retroceded the jurisdiction enjoyed by the Crown Representative in the Civil Stations at Rajkot and Wadhwan and over railway lands, and handed over nearly all buildings, whether belonging to the Central Government or the Consolidated Local Fund, either to the States or to the Joint Central Organization, a body which had been created to perform common functions relating to the issue of passports, arms licences, and interstatal extradition. Important records in the Residency were either destroyed or removed. A few rulers who were still minors were invested with ruling powers.

As soon as the States Ministry came into existence, we saw that we had no alternative but to take over the residuary jurisdiction in semi-jurisdictional and non-jurisdictional States. The Instrument of Accession, which had been evolved after discussion with these rulers, laid down that in these areas the Government of India would exercise all such powers, authorities and jurisdiction in respect of civil and criminal justice as had formerly been exercised by the Crown Representative. To begin with, we appointed an officer on special duty at Rajkot. Soon after, we appointed a full-fledged Regional Commissioner for Kathiawar with headquarters at Rajkot. The first incumbent was N. M. Buch, I.C.S.[1]

These measures were only in the nature of stop-gap arrangements to fill the vacuum created by the lapse of paramountcy, for they could not even touch the fringe of the problem of the Kathiawar States. The people here were politically more conscious. The local Congress organization, the Kathiawar *Rajakeeya Parishad,* had the benefit of the advice and guidance of Gandhiji and Sardar, so that it was better organized and more disciplined than its counterparts elsewhere and had its roots among the people. As to the rulers of the salute States, the size of the State was no indication at all of their wealth. Many of them acquired their wealth from business outside their States. For instance, in Gondal and probably also in Morvi, a considerable proportion of the State's income came from investments; direct taxation was very light. Some of these States possessed all modern amenities and were well administered. At the other end of the scale were the rulers of the semi-jurisdictional and non-jurisdictional States who had no resources of any kind; the financial burden of their administration had always to be borne by the Government of India.

Following the transfer of power, there was a wave of agitation all

---

[1] The untimely demise of this brilliant administrator in March 1954 at the early age of 46 was not only a grievous personal blow to me but a serious loss to the Government and the country.

over Kathiawar for responsible government. This had unhealthy repercussions on the maintenance of law and order. We badly needed some time to think and hammer out a plan. But events were marching ahead of us. Junagadh had further aggravated the situation. With the influx of refugees from Sind, the communal situation seemed likely to deteriorate and extremist opinions of all kinds appeared to be gaining strength.

Backed by the Kathiawar *Rajakeeya Parishad,* the agitation for responsible government was gathering momentum. In the past, the rulers particularly of the smaller States had depended on the British Government for help. Now the States' subjects were able not only to muster their own strength, but to obtain overwhelming support from the rest of the country. The result was that many rulers found themselves unable to maintain order. For instance, in Muli, a tiny State, the agitators took forcible possession of the courts, government buildings and the jail. The Regional Commissioner had to send a small police force and the local Congress leaders were ultimately persuaded to call off the agitation. The ruler appointed a Dewan selected by the Regional Commissioner and gave him full powers. But the rulers of some other States thought it safer to negotiate direct with the Parishad workers, rather than through the Regional Commissioner, an unsatisfactory development from the point of view of the Government of India.

Even in Dhrangadhra, which had a progressive ruler (C. Rajagopalachari, who succeeded Lord Mountbatten as Governor-General, remarked that he had never seen a ruler possessed at so young an age of such poise and dignity), there was danger of a major clash, for the agitators had announced their intention of marching on the palace. In all their activities the agitators had freely invoked the name of Sardar and it was found necessary to issue a contradiction. The States Ministry sent a telegram to the Peasants' Conference held at Dhrangadhra clarifying its position and asking that the widest publicity be given to the fact that Sardar strongly deprecated any violent or unconstitutional action.

Bhavnagar was the first of the bigger States to feel the pressure of the demand for responsible government. The Maharajah went to Gandhiji for guidance. Gandhiji directed him to Sardar, who advised him to yield to the people's wishes. It was agreed that Balwantrai Mehta should be the Premier of Bhavnagar. The Maharajah agreed to accept any privy purse that might be settled by

Gandhiji. It was decided that responsible government in Bhavnagar should be inaugurated by Sardar. This decision had a far-reaching effect on the rulers of the salute States in Kathiawar.

The Government of India could not encourage the idea of responsible government in the smaller States. Even Bhavnagar, with the largest revenue among the Kathiawar States, was without the resources necessary for a modern democratic administration. If therefore the prosperity and future welfare of Kathiawar was to be assured the first step should be to consolidate these fragmented areas. How this problem should be tackled was our next consideration.

The States Ministry thought of various schemes. We toyed with the idea of reviving the Attachment Scheme in another form. One suggestion was that the whole of Kathiawar should be divided into four groups built round Bhavnagar, Nawanagar, Junagadh and Dhrangadhra. I mentioned this idea to the Jam Saheb but we did not discuss it. Subsequently it was held that any scheme of attachment was inherently defective, in as much as it would not solve the main problem. The smaller States would feel that under the scheme they had to make the sacrifices while the bigger ones merely stood to profit by it. Then again, if Kathiawar were divided into four units, these separate units would still not have the requisite resources to run a modern administration.

Yet another scheme which was considered was the amalgamation with the province of Bombay of the semi-jurisdictional and non-jurisdictional States, the salute and non-salute States being left for later consideration. But these semi-jurisdictional and non-jurisdictional States did not by themselves form a compact and homogeneous area; and in any case, such a plan furnished no final solution of the problem. At last, we reached the irresistible conclusion that the only satisfactory solution was the unification of all the States in Kathiawar. The entire area was made up of States with no Indian territory in its midst; such being the case, the idea of the whole of Kathiawar as a separate State possessed considerable merit.

I discussed with Sardar the various schemes we had considered. Sardar agreed that, in order to ensure the future prosperity of Kathiawar, we could not do otherwise than amalgamate all the States into one unit.

Sardar was conscious of the tremendous difficulties involved. He told me that, if we could secure the unification of these States, it would be a splendid achievement; but he added that I should also keep in mind the possibility of their merger with the province of Bombay. I expressed the belief that, while the rulers might agree to the proposal for unification under certain conditions, they would certainly oppose any move for merger with the Bombay province.

I then had discussions with U.N. Dhebar and other Congress leaders of Kathiawar. In fact, it was in Dhebar's presence that I dictated the outlines of a scheme for the unification of Kathiawar based on my discussion with Sardar. As Dhebar was going to see Gandhiji, I asked him to show the scheme to him. He did so and told me later that Gandhiji had agreed to and blessed the scheme. I showed it to Sardar and he too gave his approval.

The scheme envisaged the amalgamation of all the Kathiawar States, big and small, into one unit to be known as the United State of Kathiawar. A Constituent Assembly was to be elected on the basis of one member for every two lakhs of the population. This Constituent Assembly would frame a constitution for the new State based on full responsible government, with a single legislature, executive and judiciary for the whole State. In the event of the formation of a linguistic province comprising the Gujarati-speaking areas, Kathiawar would automatically merge in it. Meanwhile, a Joint Council of Ministers of Kathiawar and Bombay would be set up to discuss matters of common concern, and the appellate jurisdiction of the Bombay High Court would be extended to Kathiawar. Instead of there being a single head of the Government, the headship of the new State would vest in a board of three comprising the rulers of Nawanagar, Bhavnagar and a third to be elected by the rulers of the remaining salute States.

It was settled that I should meet the rulers of Kathiawar and discuss the scheme with them after the inauguration of responsible government in Bhavnagar, which was timed to take place on 15 January 1948. A draft covenant incorporating the principles of the scheme was prepared for my discussion with the rulers. Provision was made in the draft for a privy purse on the basis of the Eastern States formula.

The Prime Minister was very busy at the time and I was unable before leaving Delhi, to acquaint him with the outlines of the proposed integration; but I explained the scheme to his Private Secretary, who promised to acquaint him of the facts as soon as possible. Sardar suggested that, between my discussion with the rulers and the finalization of the scheme, it would be advisable to get the approval of the

Cabinet; but the difficulty was that if the conferences with the rulers proceeded satisfactorily, they would have to be pinned down to an immediate agreement before they had time to change their minds; for, if the matter was not clinched at the psychological moment, there was a danger that the whole scheme might fall through. Sardar was satisfied that there could be no difference of opinion with regard to the proposed unification of Kathiawar, especially as it had Gandhiji's blessing.

Responsible government was inaugurated by Sardar at Bhavnagar on 15 January 1948. It was an epoch-making function. From Bhavnagar we flew with Dhebar and Balwantrai Mehta to Rajkot, where Sardar addressed a mammoth meeting. This was the first time I heard Sardar speaking in Gujarati. I never thought that it was possible to make such a powerful and virile speech in Gujarati. Though I could not follow the speech in its entirety, I was able to catch its meaning here and there. Another thing that impressed me was the perfect discipline of the vast crowd. In the course of his speech, Sardar dropped a hint as to the coming event. He said that little pools of water tend to become stagnant and useless, but that if they are joined together to form a big lake, the atmosphere is cooled and there is universal benefit. The significance of the parable was not lost on the audience. After wishing me all success in my forthcoming negotiations with the rulers, Sardar left for Ahmedabad.

The night of the 15th and the whole of the 16th were spent in informal discussions with the popular leaders of Kathiawar as well as with the rulers of the salute States.

At 10.30 in the morning of 17 January I met the rulers of the salute States at the Rajkot Residency. K. V. K. Sundaram of the Law Ministry and N. M. Buch were also present. In the course of my address, I emphasized the *raison d'être* for a unified Kathiawar State. As the speech underlined the factors behind the new policy, I may perhaps be permitted to quote it here in full:

I am grateful to Your Highnesses for responding to my invitation today. The question which I propose to raise is of the greatest possible importance not only to Your Highnesses but to your subjects. As Your Highnesses will have seen in the newspapers, His Highness the Maharajah of Bhavnagar has granted full responsible government to his people and similar reforms on a lesser scale are expected to be granted in the bigger and smaller States in Kathiawar. This rapid progress of the States towards responsible government, not only in Kathiawar but elsewhere in India, has created a new situation for both the Central Government and the States.

It is necessary to recall the history of events that led to the present political situation in the Indian States. In order to keep the country together after the lapse of paramountcy, the rulers of the States patriotically accepted accession to the Dominion of India on the three essential subjects of defence, foreign affairs and communications. This in itself was not a final solution from the point of view either of the States or of the Dominion. But it helped to secure in some measure that integrity of India which had in the past been accomplished by paramountcy. Paramountcy had meant the internal as well as the external security of the States, so that the Princes had been shielded, so to say, from the political aspirations and ambitions of their people. They were now brought face to face for the first time with their people, and many of them were not prepared for the change. It has also to be remembered that the new Government which has taken over at the Centre is a people's Government and one could expect the Government of India to have a predisposition in favour of the people's rights, just as under the old system the paramount power might have had a bias in favour of the rights of the ruler when they conflicted with the interests of the people. The present Government are the champions of the people's rights. When I say that, I do not mean that it is the policy of the Congress Government to do anything inimical to the existence of the rulers. What the Government of India would like is a peaceful transfer of power to the people without any kind of violence to the princely order.

When the people's demand grew in intensity, the rulers, big and small, took the line of least resistance and became ready to grant responsible government. But responsible government, however desirable, is not an end in itself. It is to be desired and demanded as an indispensable preliminary to securing the final object, which is the welfare of the people. It follows that a State should possess the minimum resources to make it a viable unit of administration, for if this is not the case, the system of responsible government will itself break down. The people of the States are bound to measure their condition by the conditions in neighbouring provinces; and the greater the disparity between them, the greater will be their discontent. Such a situation has explosive possibilities which may result in entirely unexpected consequences. The Government of India have not gone back on any of the promises made to the rulers before they acceded to the Dominion. They are only anxious that the question should be tackled in good time and that a fair and equitable solution should be arrived at as the result of a deliberate policy. If this is not done, it is possible that events may get out of hand. This is now the problem before us.

I may frankly confess that, although we were in touch with the currents of opinion in the States, the march of events took us by surprise. The first warning we had was from the Eastern States, where the people started conflicts with the rulers who could not stand on their own resources. Some of them started terrorizing the Prajamandals, others came to the Government of India for help. We then felt that unless we had a deliberate policy, not only would the future of the States and their rulers be in danger but law and order would break down. Accordingly, Sardar Patel went to Orissa, where he had a conference with the rulers. There were three alternatives. The first was to continue as under the old regime, keeping the States distinct and separate. There were about forty States, the majority of which being very small could not work any system of responsible government. To go on as before was therefore clearly out of the question. The second was to combine them into one unit. This was not practicable. These States were scattered and the Orissa States differed linguistically from the Chattisgarh States. Therefore the third alternative of absorbing them into the neighbouring provinces had to be adopted; and to this the rulers ultimately agreed.

In Kathiawar, except that some of the States are bigger, the problem is more or less similar and does not brook delay. Here also we have three possible courses. All the States could join the Bombay Province; or by a variant of the Attachment Scheme, the smaller States could be absorbed in the bigger States and a small number of fair-sized units could be produced. Another solution would be for all the States to join together and form a bigger and viable unit. There is also the alternative of keeping the present state of affairs unchanged which, of course, Your Highnesses would agree is impracticable.

Your Highnesses should realize that there is no escape from one fundamental proposition, and that is, that all the States have to follow a uniform policy. If one ruler grants responsible government others would be compelled to follow suit. Similarly, if any particular concession in any matter, say land revenue, is granted in one State, Your Highnesses cannot resist similar demands in other States.. This means that throughout Kathiawar it is essential that a uniform policy should be followed in all important matters.

So far as the practical solution in Kathiawar is concerned, we are convinced that it does not lie in the attachment of smaller units to the larger States. The difficulty about the Attachment Scheme and the creation of a smaller number of major States is that even this will not produce viable units from the point of view of modern administrative standards. Besides, the rulers of smaller States which are absorbed are likely to look upon such treatment as invidious but this difficulty will not arise if all the States, big and small, are treated alike. Then there is the alternative of complete merger in the Bombay Province. From the point of view of forming a greater Gujarat, as a linguistic unit of the Dominion, there is much to be said for such a merger. For the present, however, the formation of a United Kathiawar State will probably commend itself more to the sentiment of Your Highnesses as well as to that of the people of Kathiawar. In population, area and revenue, Kathiawar as a whole is of sufficient size and importance to form a unit with possibilities of development.

We have also to consider what is best in your own interests. The grant of complete responsible government, I can assure you, is quite inescapable in all the States. Under such a system, the ruler will be no more than the constitutional head, and whatever privileges are guaranteed to him will be guaranteed by the State Constitution. If, on the other hand, the States were to join together to form a new unit, it may be possible to obtain guarantees for the rulers from the Central Government with regard to their position, privy purse, privileges and so on. This, I feel, will be a much safer position for them. In this fast moving world one cannot predict the exact course of events with any certainty, but one can make a reasonable appraisement of the future and then decide what is best for those concerned. The solution which the Government of India are anxious to see adopted is one in which the best interests both of the rulers and of the people are secured. I am convinced that the suggestion for the formation of a United Kathiawar State by the amalgamation of the existing States, *estates* and *talukas* in this region is such a solution; and if Your Highnesses are prepared to accept this in principle, it will not be difficult to work out the details.

One great advantage of the proposal is that it will enable the problems affecting Kathiawar to be treated on uniform lines. Another advantage is that the problem of the future administration of Junagadh will be automatically solved.

His Highness the Maharajah of Bhavnagar has already declared himself in favour of a United Kathiawar State. I may also remind you of the metaphor aptly employed by Sardar Patel on this subject, of how a large lake cools the whole atmosphere while small pools become stagnant and do no good to anyone. I hope Your Highnesses will therefore be able to accept the scheme which, while it secures your own essential interests, will also promote a patriotic purpose.

The logic of facts has to be recognized. It is not possible for the 222 States of Kathiawar to continue their separate existence under modern conditions for very much longer. The extinction of the separate existence of the States may not be palatable, but unless something is done in good time to stabilise the situation in Kathiawar, the march of events may bring about still more unpalatable results. Whether you should recognise this truth which is obvious to any outside observer or whether

24

you should continue as now and accept the risks which the future may have in store for you is for Your Highnesses alone to decide. The Government of India will gladly accept a scheme for the unification of Kathiawar if it commends itself to you, and I have reason to believe that such a scheme will also have the blessing of Mahatma Gandhi.

The rulers asked for time to consider the proposal and wished to send a deputation to Delhi to discuss it with the Government of India. I told them that stabilization of the situation was urgently necessary and that if they thought the integration of States was in the interests of Kathiawar and India, there was no point in taking time. Nor, if they thought otherwise, was there any purpose in their coming to Delhi. They then wished to consider the question in private. I agreed and left the meeting. From time to time they called me in for clarification of doubts.

I could now sense the general attitude of the rulers. The Maharajah of Bhavnagar, having granted responsible government, was not averse to integration and the Maharajah of Dhrangadhra openly supported the scheme. All now depended on the attitude of the Jam Saheb; the other rulers were not likely to take a different line from the one adopted by these three rulers. I had a private talk with the Jam Saheb. I hinted to him for the first time that if the efforts to form a Union of all the Kathiawar States proved unsuccessful, the Government of India might have to merge Junagadh and the semi-jurisdictional and non-jurisdictional States with the province of Bombay, in spite of the fact that such a step might have certain administrative difficulties. He himself could not do otherwise than concede responsible government in his State, as the Maharajah of Bhavnagar had done, and thereafter the initiative would pass from his hands to the popular ministry. If thereafter the popular ministry should decide to amalgamate his State with Kathiawar, he would have to acquiesce in such a decision and the credit would go to the popular ministry rather than to the ruler. The Jam Saheb was in favour of preserving the entity of Kathiawar and for perpetuating rulership in some form but the logic of events was not lost on him. He told me that he would abide by whatever advice I might give in the interests of the country.

When I returned to the conference I told the rulers that the integration or disintegration of Kathiawar was entirely in their hands. The choice was theirs. By uniting among themselves they could have a unified Kathiawar. The rulers realized, as the Jam Saheb had already told them, that the alternative to a unified Kathiawar was

the disintegration of the States. If the proposal was not acceptable
to them the Government of India might merge Junagadh and the
semi-jurisdictional and non-jurisdictional States with the province
of Bombay. The Government of Bombay and the Gujarati-speaking
population would welcome such a move. The Maharajah of Bhavnagar had already granted responsible government and, if the popular
ministry decided to go along with these States to Bombay, the Maharajah could not prevent it. In that contingency, the remaining eleven
salute States would be unable to hold out for long and would ultimately have to merge with Bombay. The rulers again had discussions
among themselves and in the evening they communicated to me their
unanimous decision to agree to the principle of a unified Kathiawar.
I drafted a *communiqué* embodying this decision and read it to the
rulers, who approved of it. Immediately after, it was released to the
press. This was a landmark in the history of Kathiawar.

Later, I had discussions with the rulers about the headship of the
new Union. My original idea had been that it should vest in a board
of three rulers; I now dropped that idea and reverted to that of a
single head. The rulers wanted to have a voice in the selection of the
head of the Union, but they were not unanimous among themselves
in regard to the procedure. In the end, a formula was devised which
was accepted by all the rulers. It prescribed that there should be a
Council of Rulers consisting of all the covenanting salute States; that
there should be a presidium of five, of which the rulers of Nawanagar
and Bhavnagar should be permanent members; that one member of
the presidium should be elected by the non-salute States from among
themselves, while the other two should be elected from among themselves by the Council of Rulers other than the rulers of Nawanagar
and Bhavnagar; and the Council of Rulers should elect one member
of the presidium as the President and another as the Vice-President.
Thereafter, the rulers met separately and elected the Jam Saheb and
the Maharajah of Bhavnagar as the President and Vice-President
respectively of the presidium.

After this meeting I went with Sundaram and Buch to Junagadh,
returning to Rajkot on the 19th. It was during this journey that we
revised the draft covenant we had brought from Delhi, in the light
of our discussions with the rulers. One question that arose was the
designation of the head of the State. The title of 'Governor' would
have been suitable if we intended to treat the Union in the same way
as the provinces; but since the Maharajah of a State was to be its

head, that term was hardly appropriate. In the course of our discussion, our attention was drawn to the covenant of the United Deccan State, which provided for a Council of Rulers called the Rajmandal with a President to be styled the Rajpramukha, the office being filled by yearly rotation from amongst the members of the Rajmandal. There was also to be a Vice-President to be known as the Uprajpramukha. We considered these designations as appropriate to the members of the princely order. Accordingly the head of the Union was named the Rajpramukh. The draft covenant was amended also in other important respects.

The draft covenant as revised was placed before the rulers when I met them on 20 January. They asked for time to consider the document, so I adjourned the meeting till the next day. In the afternoon I met the rulers of the non-salute States and, after informing them that the rulers of the salute States had already accepted the principle of a United Kathiawar, suggested that they should do likewise. They agreed and I told them that the draft Covenant would be placed before them for consideration next day.

The following morning the Covenant was discussed with the rulers of the non-salute States; they agreed to the main principles. In the afternoon, I went into the draft, clause by clause, with the rulers of the salute States. They accepted our proposal with regard to the designation of the head of the State as Rajpramukh.

The discussion then turned to the principle on which the privy purse should be fixed. The rulers of the salute States insisted upon clearing up this point before proceeding to consider other clauses of the Covenant. As they were giving up all they regarded as sacrosanct, they asked for generous treatment. The original proposal was on the basis of the Eastern States formula. But the rulers stood out stubbornly against this, and asked for 20 per cent of the gross revenues of their States, and in addition, provision for ceremonies such as the marriages of their children and so forth. In support of their claims, they said that the conditions in Kathiawar were entirely different from those in the Eastern States, both in respect of the cost and standard of living and of their own prestige and obligations. They added that they had been giving allowances to poor relations, and charities to deserving causes, none of which could suddenly be cut off. Altogether, it was a plea for easing the transition.

I argued that it was to their interest that the privy purse, whatever the amount, should be fixed in perpetuity and that this could only be if it was reasonable; that by making extravagant demands they would alienate public sympathy. I insisted that the amount, whatever it was, should cover all charges, and that the new Union could not undertake any further obligations. At this, the rulers said that they were discussing this question on the understanding that a settlement on the basis of consent and goodwill was desired; but that if the Government of India were determined to impose their own terms, they had nothing further to say. I then talked separately with the Maharajahs of Nawanagar, Dhrangadhra and Porbandar and pleaded with them not to allow their personal interests to stand in the way of the success of a project manifestly advantageous to the country. Finding that there was no prospect of an agreement on the basis of the Eastern States formula, I had no alternative but to fall back upon the Deccan States formula. This meant that the rulers would get 15 per cent on the first Rs 5 lakhs of actual annual revenue, 10 per cent on the next Rs 5 lakhs and $7\frac{1}{2}$ per cent on revenues above Rs 10 lakhs. I insisted that under no circumstances could we go above a maximum of Rs 10 lakhs.

The fixation of the actual figures presented considerable difficulty. In the first place, there was no reliable data regarding the revenues of the different States. The figures available with the Regional Commissioner did not in all cases tally with the figures presented by the rulers. Secondly, owing mainly to the high level of prices, the land revenue figures in recent years had become inflated. As against this, there must be set the consideration that, in the case of the maritime States, owing to war-time restrictions the figures of customs revenues were abnormally low. A quick decision was so important that it was considered best, in the case of the rulers of salute States, to fix the amount of the privy purse on the basis of the available figures without further investigation, an average of three years being taken in every case.

The Covenant exempted the privy purse from taxation either by the new Union or by the Dominion of India. This was the undertaking we had given to the rulers of the Orissa and Chattisgarh States and there was no reason why we should depart from it in the case of the Kathiawar rulers.

The provision in the original proposals for merging the State of Kathiawar in a Gujarat province when formed met with strong opposition from the rulers, who feared that in such an event the presidium would disappear and they themselves would lose the position

guaranteed to them in the Covenant. While they had no objection
in principle to Kathiawar forming part of the Gujarat province,
they maintained that this was a proposition which should be considered on its merits when the time came; they declined to commit
themselves in advance. On this issue the Jam Saheb said that while
he had no objection to taking the fences as they came, it was too
much to expect the rulers in their present frame of mind to take
two at a time. The most therefore that I could get the rulers to agree
to was a formula in negative terms, by which the inclusion of Kathiawar in a Gujarat province was not precluded under certain conditions. I did not think I should risk the failure of the entire scheme
by insisting upon our original proposal, especially as it did not
affect our first objective which was the consolidation of Kathiawar,
nor prejudice our ultimate one, which was the inclusion of this area
in a Gujarati-speaking province.

It was suggested in the original scheme that the jurisdiction of the
Bombay High Court should extend to the new State of Kathiawar.
This proposal was not acceptable to the rulers. Local patriotism
also was averse to Kathiawar being subordinated to Bombay.
Kathiawar, it was claimed, should be treated on the same lines as a
province and should have its own High Court. There would be no
objection however to appeals going to the Federal Court in appropriate cases. The rulers feared that judicial subordination to
Bombay would not only be the first step towards the absorption
of Kathiawar in the Bombay province but also the liquidation of
the rulers as such. I pointed out to them that if the Kathiawar
Constituent Assembly decided to confer appellate jurisdiction on
the Bombay High Court, the Government of India were bound to
accept the recommendation. I told them on further consideration
that this question should more appropriately be decided by the
Kathiawar Constituent Assembly than by a provision inserted in the
Covenant; the provision was accordingly omitted. The rulers accepted a Joint Advisory Council representing Bombay and Kathiawar to
investigate and discuss subjects of common concern and to make
recommendations to their respective Governments.

The rulers wanted the provisions of the Covenant to be guaranteed
by the Government of India. They argued that the transaction was
essentially a reciprocal one. The rulers surrendered their sovereign
powers and rights in consideration of certain terms including a fixed
privy purse. The other party to the transaction, namely, the United

State of Kathiawar, had not yet come into existence. It was therefore urged that the terms should be guaranteed by the Government of India. I could not deny the force of this argument. On behalf of the areas under our administration, we were a direct party to the Covenant. I felt that, having initiated the negotiations and brought them to a conclusion, we were in honour bound to guarantee the performance of the contract. There were several other points, which I need not dwell upon which were settled after considerable discussion.

After obtaining the concurrence of the rulers of the salute States to the Covenant, I met the rulers of the non-salute States. There was difficulty in settling their privy purses, because some of them till 15 August 1947 had been attached to major States and no reliable figures were readily available. The rulers preferred that, as in the case of salute States, a settlement as to the amount of their privy purses should be arrived at immediately. It was ultimately agreed that, where a State had a popular representative Assembly and ministers and the latter certified the revenues to be correct, the figures already accepted or certified in this manner should be taken as final. In other cases, where the figures appeared to be reasonable, no further scrutiny would be undertaken; where, on the other hand, the figures *prima facie* appeared unreasonable, a financial officer would be deputed to go into them. This procedure was accepted also by the remaining categories of rulers. Their privy purses were fixed later.

It must be mentioned that the scale of privy purses given to the Kathiawar rulers was not given to any other rulers in India. In fixing the privy purses of rulers elsewhere, we adhered to the Eastern States formula, though I was hard put to it to explain this differentiation.

The Covenant was to be signed only by the rulers of salute and non-salute States. The rulers of the semi-jurisdictional and the non-jurisdictional *estates* and *talukas* were requested to sign an agreement, by which they agreed to the merger of their *estates* and *talukas* with the United State of Kathiawar and authorized the Regional Commissioner, who was administering them, to hand them over to the Rajpramukh.

On the night of the 21st the draft Covenant, with its eighteen Articles and two Schedules, was finalized. Since this served as a model for all subsequent Unions of States, the salient features of the document may here be summarized.

Article I was devoted to the definition of certain terms used in the Covenant.

In Article II the covenanting States agreed to integrate their territories into one State, with a common executive, legislature and judiciary, to be known by the name of the United State of Kathiawar. (This name was later changed to Saurashtra. In fact, the Kathiawar peninsula had been known as Saurashtra since puranic times and had been described as such in the *stotra* relating to the twelve *Jyotir-lingas*. Even the crest of the Nawab of Junagadh had the word 'Saurashtra' inscribed on it.)

Article III provided for a Council of Rulers, a Presidium, and the method of election of the President and Vice-President. The President so elected was to be the head of the State with the designation of Rajpramukh.

Article IV dealt with the salary and allowances of the Rajpramukh and provided that in the event of his absence or illness, the Vice-President should perform his duties.

Article V brought into being a Council of Ministers. For the purpose of choosing the first team, the Rajpramukh was to convene a meeting of the members of the electoral college of Kathiawar which had been formed for electing representatives to the Constituent Assembly of India.

Article VI provided for the taking over of the administration of the various covenanting States by the Government of the new Union.

Article VII enabled the new Government to take over the military forces of the covenanting States.

Article VIII vested the executive authority of the new State in the Rajpramukh.

Article IX dealt with the formation of a Constituent Assembly for the purpose of framing a constitution for the United State of Kathiawar within the framework of the Covenant and the Constitution of India.

Articles X, XI, XII and XIII guaranteed the privy purses, private properties, privileges and succession to the *gaddi* of the rulers.

Article XIV protected the rulers from proceedings in any court of law for acts done or omitted to be done by them, or under their authority, during the period of their administration.

Article XV dealt with the setting up of a Joint Advisory Council for the discussion of matters of common concern between the new Government and the Government of Bombay.

Article XVI guaranteed the continuance in service, or compensation in lieu, to the members of the permanent services taken over from the covenanting States, as well as their pensions and salaries.

Article XVII provided that, except with the previous sanction of the Rajpramukh, no proceedings, civil or criminal, should be instituted against any person in respect of any act done, or purporting to be done, in the execution of his duty as the servant of any covenanting State before integration.

Article XVIII declared that the Government of Kathiawar were not precluded from negotiating a Union with other Gujarati-speaking areas on such terms and conditions as might be agreed to by the Council of Rulers as well as the ministry.

The first schedule listed the amount of privy purse payable to the rulers; and the second related to the composition of and method of election to the Kathiawar Constituent Assembly.

The date fixed for the signing of the Covenant was 22 January. Even at this stage the rulers asked for more time but I impressed upon them that, having worked at such a hectic pace night and day for the past four days, they should not think of any postponement. Moreover, since the acceptance of the Union had already been announced, it would only create misunderstanding among the people if the Covenant was not signed at once. The Jam Saheb, as the Rajpramukh-designate, had to sign first. He took the Covenant to Jamnagar promising to send it back the next day. He did so, whereafter I got the signatures of all the rulers present at Rajkot. Buch was entrusted with the task of getting the signatures of the remaining rulers.

There are two things which I should mention here. The first is the poignant spectacle of the rulers parting with their proud heritage. No ruler had thought even a month previously that he would have so soon to part with his State and rulership. Something which had been in their families for generations and which they had regarded as sacrosanct had disappeared as it were in the twinkling of an eye. Though all of them put up a bold front, the mental anguish they were going through was writ large on their faces. Neither at Cuttack nor at Nagpur had I seen anything to compare with what I witnessed at Rajkot. The scene here was to the last degree moving and will ever linger in my memory. The old Maharajah of Morvi came to me and asked whether the Government of India would allow him to abdicate and permit his son, who would succeed him, to sign the Covenant.

Realizing the Maharajah's sentiments, I readily acceded to his request. Incidentally, I must mention here that Morvi State was well governed and that the Maharajah left the largest cash balance in relation to the size of the State, which was only 820 square miles in area.

The other thing was a telephone call from Sardar at Ahmedabad. Because of the terrific pressure at which I had been working I had been unable to keep him informed of the hour-to-hour developments. There was many an occasion when it was a question of touch and go whether I should succeed or fail. On the evening when the Covenant was finalized, he rang me up and told me that he had heard that the privy purse was fixed at rather a high figure. I do not know who communicated this news to him. Owing to the strain of the past four days I had actually lost my voice and so could not explain to him on the phone the basis and background on which I had fixed the figures. But the incident depressed me very much. That evening I went to bed with high fever. I was taken to Jamnagar next day for treatment and was laid up there for three or four days. As soon as I was better I returned to Delhi.

On my return I was asked by Lord Mountbatten to meet Kingsley Martin, Editor of the *New Statesman and Nation* who was then on a visit to Delhi. He discussed the Kashmir issue with me. I told him of the various considerations governing the situation but, as far as I can remember, did not commit myself to any definite views. (This talk was to crop up during my discussion with Gandhiji later on the same day.) Then I went to Sardar. I was still much upset and wanted to tell him what I had felt about his remark over the telephone regarding the scale of the privy purse. But before I could open my mouth he told me to go and see Gandhiji.

I went to Birla House and stayed with Gandhiji for over an hour while he was having his evening meal. Gandhiji began by referring to my interview with Kingsley Martin. I told him that I thought he had sent for me to discuss the Kathiawar integration and I enquired of him whether he also thought that the privy purse fixed for the rulers was too generous. Gandhiji said that he had heard it was so. I then explained to him the provisions of the Covenant and the whole background. Compared with the rulers of Orissa, the privy purses fixed for the Kathiawar rulers were higher, and I anticipated that we might have to spend about Rs 80 lakhs on them annually. But the advantages of integration could not be measured in terms of money alone. Even were we to consider the issue from the purely financial point of view, we should take into account the annual expenditure of Rs 25 to Rs 30 lakhs we were incurring on the administration of the semi-jurisdictional and non-jurisdictional States in Kathiawar. The integration of Kathiawar would enable us to remove that anomalous and detested Viramgam customs cordon which was costing several lakhs for its maintenance. As the Nawab of Junagadh had left for Pakistan we would not have to pay him the privy purse of Rs 10 lakhs. Some of the rulers had been spending large amounts on themselves and their relations; for instance, in Junagadh the Nawab spent between Rs 30 and Rs 40 lakhs annually for his personal expenses. These would now stop. Since some of these States were rich, they would leave cash balances which might amount in aggregate to between Rs 10 and Rs 12 crores. I also told Gandhiji that during the federal negotiations in 1936 and 1937 the Government of India were prepared to pay one and a half crores of rupees for acquiring customs rights over one of the ports in Kathiawar. If all these things were taken on the credit side and juxtaposed with privy purses on the debit side, the pecuniary consideration involved would be very insignificant. The advantages accruing to the people from the formation of a consolidated Kathiawar could not be measured in terms of money. Some of the States in Kathiawar had a fairly high standard of administration and if they had held out, the integration of Kathiawar would not have materialized. Gandhiji appeared quite satisfied with my explanation.

He mentioned the privy purse of Rs 10 lakhs included in the Covenant for the Maharajah of Bhavnagar who, while granting responsible government, had agreed to abide by Gandhiji's decision in the matter of his privy purse. I told Gandhiji that the Maharajah had actually left the meeting while we were discussing the privy purse and that we ourselves thought that we could not in justice treat Bhavnagar any differently from the rest of the rulers. Gandhiji nodded his head but said nothing.

The formation of the Saurashtra Union and the merger of the Eastern States had, in fact, given Gandhiji great satisfaction, but he was able to foresee the shape of things to come. Being a robust realist, he exclaimed prophetically 'How are we to manage these States? Where are the political leaders to run them and the man-power?' After a pause he continued, 'Well, we have to leave it to Sardar to cope with the situation.'

Gandhiji brought the conversation back to my interview with Kingsley Martin and said that he was against any sort of division of Kashmir, which was to him a testing ground for the Hindu minority as was Hyderabad for the Muslim minority. He gave an account of his own conversation with Kingsley Martin and told me: 'You can come to me whenever you like. Either you convince me that Kashmir should be divided or I will argue the matter with you and convince you to the contrary.' His readiness to listen to the other point of view and to convert people by argument and persuasion was one of the qualities that made one almost adore Gandhiji. I could not take my eyes away from his face which was lit up by animation as he spoke. It was past five and it was time for the prayer meeting; but before I left, he mentioned how happy he was about the Kathiawar unification and complimented me on the part I had played in bringing it about.

I was extremely happy after this interview with Gandhiji. But this was the last time I was to talk with him. Three days later while going to his daily prayer meeting and even as Dhebar, Rasiklal Parikh and Buch (who had an appointment with him after the meeting) were waiting to see him, he fell a victim to the assassin's bullet. It is some consolation that the Kathiawar integration was completed while Gandhiji was still alive and that he lived to know about it and to bless its fruition.

I went back to Sardar and told him of my interview with Gandhiji and of his reactions. The Covenant, with a summary of the discussions leading to the signing of it, was duly submitted to the Cabinet, who approved of it in its entirety. Though as a constitutional Governor-General, Lord Mountbatten did not attend Cabinet meetings, copies of all the relevant papers used to be sent to him as a matter of course. When he saw my note to the Cabinet on the Saurashtra integration, he wrote: 'I have read with the greatest interest your note on the unification of Kathiawar. I am lost in admiration of the masterly way in which you handled this matter and I cannot refrain from sending you this short brief note to congratulate you most heartily on all that you have achieved. This is another wonderful feather in your cap.'

The inauguration of the United State of Kathiawar was performed by Sardar at Jamnagar on 15 February 1948. The oaths of office were administered to the Jam Saheb as Rajpramukh, to the members of the presidium and to the ministers. That same morning a meeting of the electoral college for the Constituent Assembly had been called and, on the proposal of Balwantrai Mehta, U. N. Dhebar was elected leader. He thus automatically became the Premier of the new Kathiawar ministry.

In an inspiring message to the Jam Saheb of Nawanagar, Nehru sending his hearty congratulations said:

The consolidation into one administrative unit of the vast number of States with varying degrees of sovereignty in the Kathiawar peninsula is in itself a great step forward. The fact that a system of responsible government should have been simultaneously agreed upon makes this event one of the most notable in contemporary Indian history. I have every hope that this far-sighted act of statesmanship will be fully justified in the growing economic prosperity and happiness of the people of Kathiawar.

The Jam Saheb's speech on this occasion was equally inspiring. In the course of it he said:

The point that I wish to make on behalf of my Order in Kathiawar is this: it is not as if we were tired monarchs who were fanned to rest. It is not as if we have been bullied into submission. We have by our own free volition pooled our sovereignties and covenanted to create this new State so that the United State of Kathiawar and the unity of India may be more fully achieved and so that our people may have that form of government which is today most acceptable to them and which I hope and pray will prove beneficial to them.

The new State did not possess any territory on 15 February. The administration of the States was to be handed over only by 15 April. Bhavnagar, Chuda and Bajana were among the first States to hand over their administration. Until all the States were taken over, there was a certain amount of bitterness in the air, as some of the rulers were eager to utilize the interval in rewarding their relations, friends and officers as well as in helping themselves. The new government was, of course, anxious that the resources of the States should not be frittered away. There were accusations and counter-accusations. I sent a general letter of advice to all the rulers. I must mention here that the Maharajah of Porbandar, who is in every respect an accomplished and cultured man, handed over his State with everything intact. He even went to the length of surrendering the silver vessels in his palace.

With regard to the capital of the new State, there was competition between Jamnagar and Rajkot. A committee was appointed to look into the question, but its recommendations were never published.

For all practical purposes, the capital continues to be in Rajkot, while the Rajpramukh continues to live in Jamnagar.

Subsequent to the formation of the Union three supplementary covenants were negotiated with and executed by the rulers. The first, which was signed by the rulers in November 1948, provided that the Jam Saheb of Nawanagar should hold office as Rajpramukh for life and not for five years as had been provided in the original covenant. By then we had created other Unions and, owing to the exigencies of the circumstances, had accepted it as inevitable that the various Rajpramukhs would hold office for life. There was no reason why the Jam Saheb should be treated differently. Moreover, the holding of the office was for life only in the case of the first incumbent. Thereafter the Government of India could review the position and make such arrangements as they thought necessary. It was in this supplementary covenant that the United State of Kathiawar was renamed the 'United State of Saurashtra'.

The second supplementary covenant, executed in January 1949, provided for the integration with Saurashtra of the administration of Junagadh, Manavadar, Mangrol, Bantwa, Babariawad and Sardargarh and the participation of the elected representatives of these States in the Saurashtra Constituent Asssembly.

The third supplementary covenant, executed in January 1950, provided that the Constitution adopted by the Constituent Assembly of India should be the Constitution for the Saurashtra Union. It also provided that the Constituent Assembly of Saurashtra should form, together with the Rajpramukh, the interim legislature of the State.

A United State of Saurashtra thus came into being after centuries of political fragmentation, no longer a number of separate stagnant pools, but one vast expanse of fresh and limpid water.

IX

THE DECCAN AND GUJARAT STATES

THE States in Bombay, on account of their geographical position, were divided into two groups—Baroda and the Gujarat States in the north, and the Deccan States in the south.

We will deal first with the Deccan States. They were, besides Kolhapur, seventeen in number. The rulers of Akalkot, Jath, Mudhol, Phaltan and Sawantwadi were Marathas, whose ancestors had carved out these kingdoms in the wake of the general confusion consequent on the decline of the Peshwas. The rulers of Aundh and Bhor were Brahmins; their States had originally been granted to their ancestors by the Maratha kings of Satara. Sangli, Wadi, Ramdurg, Jamkhandi, Miraj Senior, Miraj Junior, Kurundwad Senior and Kurundwad Junior were known as the Patwardhan States. Their rulers were also Brahmins, though of a different sect; they claimed descent from a common ancestor, Haribhatt, who had been in the service of the Peshwas. Janjira and Savanur were Muslim rulers; the former was descended from the Habshis who came from East Africa in the military service of the Brahmani rulers, while the latter belonged to the Miyana tribe of Pathans.

These States formed scattered islands in the politically-conscious province of Bombay and the populations of most of them were not unaffected by that proximity. Some of the rulers had both education as well as a progressive outlook. The ruler of Aundh, for instance, had granted responsible government as early as 1939. The Rajah of Phaltan, after the merger of his State, became a minister of the Bombay Government and continues to be so at the time of writing.

On 28 July 1946 the rulers of some of the Deccan States met Gandhiji at Poona and requested his blessing to a scheme for the union of their States. Gandhiji did not encourage the idea but told them to lay the proposal before Nehru. Accordingly, the Rajah of

Phaltan communicated with Nehru, who was not averse to the idea of a Union, but advised that the first step was for the rulers concerned to grant responsible government. Kamalnayan Bajaj was the mediator between the rulers and the Congress. It was probably due to him that the Congress did not sustain its earlier objections to the formation of this Union. K. M. Munshi (a leading Congressman, who had been Home Minister in Bombay's first Congress ministry) was entrusted with the task of drafting a covenant, which he did in great detail. The covenant provided for the formation of a United Deccan State. There was to be a Rajmandal or Council of Rulers, of all the covenanting States. This Council was to elect as President by yearly rotation one of its members who would be known as the Rajpramukh and who would be the head of the State, and another member as Vice-President with the title of Uprajpramukh. The covenant provided for a High Court, a Judicial Commission, a Constituent Assembly and an interim government of the United Deccan State.

The Congress set up a sub-committee consisting of Dr Rajendra Prasad, Dr B. Pattabhi Sitaramayya and Shankarrao Deo to settle the privy purses of the rulers of the Union. The final covenant including provision for the privy purse at the rate fixed by the sub-committee was ratified on 17 October 1947 by the rulers of Aundh, Bhor, Kurundwad Junior, Miraj Senior, Miraj Junior, Phaltan, Ramdurg and Sangli. The Rajah of Aundh was elected the first Rajpramukh and the Rajah of Bhor the first Uprajpramukh. A Constituent Assembly of twenty-five elected members was set up to draft the final constitution for the Union. The 20th December was the day fixed for the inauguration of the Constituent Assembly and the formation of the interim ministry.

This Union was obviously not founded on a firm basis. The Deccan States belonged to two linguistic areas — Maharashtra and Karnataka. They were not contiguous and the intervening territories all belonged to the Bombay province. The small State of Bhor for instance, with an area of 910 square miles, was split up into three different portions, and there were several islands of Indian territory inside the State itself. Moreover, out of a total of seventeen States, only eight had come into the Union. At about this time the Rajah of Jamkhandi announced that he was prepared to merge his State with the Bombay province if his people so desired; the local Prajamandal also passed a resolution favouring this course. The rulers of Jath and Akalkot were inclined to follow suit. The Rajmandal had run into difficulties with regard to the constitution of an interim ministry. Some of the rulers were in favour of a cabinet of five, while others felt that each of the eight States should be represented by a minister. In spite of their best efforts no compromise was achieved.

A delegation from the Rajmandal came to see me at New Delhi on 10 December 1947 to find out the Government of India's attitude towards the Union. There was agitation in some of the States for merger with Bombay. I did not commit myself to any definite view. Sardar and I were about to leave at that time for Cuttack to meet the rulers of Orissa. We did not even know whether we would succeed in merging the Orissa and Chattisgarh States with their respective provinces.

When the rulers met Sardar the next day, he told them that, if a ruler and his people were agreed about the need for merger with the Bombay province, he would accept the proposition. He saw no objection to the Deccan States Union functioning even if some of the covenanting States seceded and merged with the Bombay province. He thought that the wishes of the people could, if necessary, be ascertained by a plebiscite.

When next I had an opportunity of seeing Sardar, I suggested that it would be unwise to commit ourselves at that juncture; that we ought not to touch the Deccan States before evolving a policy, and that no policy could be evolved until after our return from Cuttack. Dealing with the problem piecemeal would create confusion, if not actual trouble. Furthermore, if the principle of merger was to be decided by a vote of the people we would be creating serious complications for ourselves. So far as I was concerned, I preferred to proceed on the assumption that the Government of India, as representing the people of the country as a whole, had enough popular sanction behind them. Sardar's view however was that once two or three States had merged with Bombay, others were bound to follow suit, that ultimately all the States would merge and that the Union would automatically cease to exist.

The rulers of Orissa agreed to the merger of their States on 15 December. Their decision reacted on the Deccan rulers who felt that they should also definitely declare themselves for merger. On 21 December the Rajmandal passed the following resolution:

In view of the trend of public opinion and current events and the general feeling among the people of the United Deccan State, the Rajmandal

26

resolve that if the people of the State and the constitution-making body desire that instead of proceeding with the framing of the constitution, steps may be taken to merge the State into the Bombay Province, the Rajmandal will not stand in their way.

The resolution was duly communicated to the States Ministry. In accordance with Sardar's directions, Kamalnayan Bajaj had told the rulers that the appropriate course was for them to consult the prajamandals of the various States and that the Constituent Assembly of the Union should then pass a resolution accepting the merger. In Aundh, the ruler proposed to refer the question of merger to a plebiscite. Such a step in one State would set up demands for a similar proceeding in others. Aundh being a very small State and divided moreover into detached areas, could not remain separate. We therefore advised the ruler, who finally agreed, to drop the idea.

But in all the other States, the prajamandals gave an unequivocal verdict in favour of merger with Bombay. At its very first meeting on 26 January 1948, the Constituent Assembly of the United Deccan State resolved that 'it is of the opinion that it is in the interest of the State and its people that all the States forming units of the United Deccan State do merge with the province of Bombay of the Indian Union.' Kamalnayan Bajaj was authorized to negotiate the terms of merger with the rulers and the Government of India.

Bajaj started negotiating with the rulers, who took the stand that, as the Union had already come into existence, it should merge in Bombay as a body and that the provisions in the covenant relating to private property, the privy purse and so forth should apply. They were particularly anxious to retain the privy purse which had been fixed by the Congress sub-committee, which was much more liberal than the privy purse which we had given to the rulers of the Orissa and Chattisgarh States. On 19 January, Sardar was in Bombay and the rulers of the Deccan States met him and put forward their point of view. Sardar told them that since the Union had not been recognized by the Government of India, its covenant had no validity and that the States would therefore have to merge individually. We had just decided to form the Kathiawar States into a separate Union. This left the Deccan rulers with no alternative but to agree to merge their States individually.

In fact, the law and order situation precipitated the merger of these States before Bajaj could conclude his negotiations with the rulers. The trouble started in Ramdurg, where there was not much love lost between the ruler, a Deccani Brahmin, and his people who were mostly Lingayats. In 1939 a serious outbreak of rioting had occurred in the State and several of the leaders had been sentenced to long terms of imprisonment. An agitation was now whipped up to secure the release of these convicted persons. Administration more or less broke down and the Rajah requested our Regional Commissioner at Kolhapur to arrange for the immediate transfer of the administration to Bombay. This he did.

After the assassination of Gandhiji, riots broke out in some of the other States. Exploiting the fact that the assassin was a Maharashtrian Brahmin, a section of the Marathas (the leading non-Brahmin community) launched a campaign of assault, murder, loot and arson, aimed at the Brahmin and Bania communities. The effects were general all over Maharashtra and were particularly felt in certain of the States, notably Kolhapur. The smaller States could not cope with the situation, so that the rulers were obliged to ask us to accept the merger of their States with Bombay in advance of their signing the agreements.

A meeting of the rulers of the Deccan States was called at Bombay on 19 February 1948. It was presided over by B. G. Kher, then Premier of Bombay. C. C. Desai, I.C.S., represented the States Ministry. Kher complimented the rulers both on their political sagacity and on the spirit of renunciation implicit in their agreement to merge. He assured them that the Government of Bombay would honour that agreement in letter and in spirit. The Government, impressed by their spirit of sacrifice, were fully resolved to be generous in their dealings with the rulers. The discussion centred mainly on the privy purse. C. C. Desai explained the slab system of fixing the privy purse on the Eastern States formula and resisted all attempts to liberalize it on the model of the original Deccan States formula. The privy purse was calculated accordingly in each case and entered in the agreement. All the fourteen rulers present then signed the merger agreements. The Rajah of Akalkot was not present, but his brother took the agreement for his signature. The ruler of Wadi also signed the merger agreement. His was a nonjurisdictional State, but the ruler preferred to accept a privy purse rather than become the landlord of his former State. Some of the rulers expressed the hope that since they had been deprived of their ruling powers and had thereby become, in a sense, unemployed, the Government of India would give sympathetic consideration to the

possibility of their employment in suitable spheres of public administration. Some of them had had military training and were anxious
to enlist in the Indian Armed Forces; others would be happy to join
the Foreign Service. In consultation with other ministries, the
Ministry of States subsequently prepared a scheme for utilizing the
services of some of these rulers.

Only two States declined to send any representatives to the Bombay
meeting. One, Sawantwadi, had a young Maratha ruler who was
related to the rulers of Baroda and Kolhapur and desired to merge
his State with Kolhapur. Disturbances had broken out in the State.
When the Regional Commissioner visited it, he found that a parallel
government had been formed and that it had arrested all the State
functionaries. In these circumstances the Rajah made haste to sign
the instrument of merger and the Government of Bombay took over
the administration.

The other State which stood out was Janjira, a small maritime
State under a Muslim ruler. The administration of law and order
in this State was already vested in the Government of Bombay. We
now informed the ruler that he must sign the merger agreement
and that the Government of Bombay would take over the entire
administration of his State. The Nawab consented.

The merger of the Deccan States became effective on 8 March
1948. The total area thus merged was 7,815 square miles with a population of 16,93,103 and an annual revenue of Rs 1,42,15,599.

At this stage I must digress a little to deal with the Dangs. This
territory, which lay between the Surat and Nasik districts of Bombay,
was parcelled among fourteen chiefs. Of these, thirteen were Bhils
while one was a Kokani. The chiefs' revenue consisted mainly of
the following items: an annual subsidy for their forest and *abkari*
rights; land revenue at Rs 6-8-0 per plough; a fee of annas eight per
head on all cattle that entered the Dangs and on cattle of non-Dangi
residents; and lastly, various *Giras* allowances from the surrounding States and British territory. The population, numbering less
than half a lakh, consisted chiefly of Kokanis, Bhils and Warlis. This
area of about 650 square miles lay under the administrative charge
of a Deputy Political Agent having his Headquarters at Ahwa. We
felt that the future of this small territory lay with Bombay, and on
19 January 1948 the Governor-General, under section 290 of the
Government of India Act of 1935, issued an order merging the Dangs
with Bombay. The Government of India however did not wish this

area, with its aboriginal population, to be pitchforked straightaway into a province like Bombay without some safeguard. The order of merger therefore stipulated that the Dangs should form a separate district and be administered by a Collector.

Later on, the Gujarat Provincial Congress Committee agitated for the Dangs to be pegged on to the contiguous Gujarati district of Surat, while a counter-agitation was raised by the Maharashtra Provincial Congress Committee for its merger with the Marathi district of Nasik. Neither side was in the least concerned with the future of these primitive people, who were merely the bone of contention between two linguistic areas competing for some sort of aggrandizement.

We now come to the Gujarat States. There were seventeen full jurisdictional States and 127 semi-jurisdictional and non-jurisdictional units (which when subdivided according to the number of shareholders came to 271). Many of the rulers of the jurisdictional States were Rajputs belonging to the Solanki, Chohan, Waghela, Sisodia, Parmar and Gohel clans. The rulers of Balasinor, Cambay, Sachin and Radhanpur were Muslims. Most of the rulers of the semi-jurisdictional and non-jurisdictional units were Kolis, Bhils, Molesalams or Barias. The full jurisdictional States covered an area of 11,917 square miles and had a population slightly exceeding 21 lakhs but the total annual revenue was less than a crore and a half. The northernmost of these States, namely, Palanpur and Radhanpur, were close to the Pakistan border.

None of these States was large enough or had the resources to maintain an administration suitable to modern needs. Their territories were interlocked and interspersed with territories of the Baroda State and the Ahmedabad and Kaira districts of Bombay. The existence of 127 non-jurisdictional and semi-jurisdictional units, which were under the direct administrative control of the Government of India, still further complicated the problem.

The future of these States was the subject of discussion with the leaders of local Congress organizations when they came to see me at Delhi. The Maharana of Lunawada also met me at Delhi on behalf of the rulers. The formation of Saurashtra had roused hopes in the rulers of the Gujarat States that if they formed a union with Baroda their separate existence would be maintained. This was stressed by the Maharana. I made it clear to him that the only possible arrangement for the Gujarat States was merger with the province of Bombay.

I told him that if there was any justification for the merger of the Eastern and of the Deccan States, it was ten times stronger in the case of the Gujarat States. I added that I would be visiting Bombay soon and would discuss the matter with the rulers.

I went to Bombay on 17 March 1948. I had an informal meeting with the rulers. The first thing I did was to announce that the formal meetings with the rulers of the full jurisdictional States would be held not in the Bombay Secretariat, but at the residence of the Maharajah of Rajpipla. This had a good effect. We met continuously for three days, the discussions generally extending into the late hours of the night. The rulers urged that their States should not be merged with Bombay, but that they should rather be formed into a Union. They suggested that if this were not possible, a joint Union of the Gujarat States with Baroda should be formed. I explained to them at length that a Union of the Gujarat States by themselves could not be regarded as a practical proposition and that union with Baroda was dependent on the attitude of its Maharajah. The rulers asked for an opportunity of discussing the matter with the Maharajah of Baroda who was in Bombay at the time. I agreed to their request and postponed the discussions till the evening of the 18th.

The rulers approached the Maharajah of Baroda but he definitely rejected their proposal for the formation of a Union of the Gujarat States with Baroda. He was obviously opposed to the obliteration of Baroda's identity in the new Union. Later on I met the Maharajah and he told me that the rulers had approached him and that he had returned a negative reply. When I saw the rulers on the 18th evening they, too, told me of their interview. I informed them that in the circumstances they had no alternative but to agree to a merger with Bombay. They still showed a great deal of hesitancy and asked for time to draw up an alternative scheme to send on to me in Delhi. I explained that any such idea was futile. At the same time I assured them that sympathetic consideration would be given to any claims which they might put forward regarding their privy purse, personal privileges and so on. The rulers still asked for time to consider the position and I adjourned the meeting till the 19th.

We met again on the evening of the 19th. The rulers complained that they were being rushed. They said that the time given to them was extremely short and that they wanted some breathing space before actually handing over the administration of their States to the

Government of Bombay. I felt that some concession was called for. After considerable discussion, I agreed that, while they should sign the merger agreement immediately, the date of transfer of the administration of their States would be put off till 5 June. Thus they would have about eleven weeks to adjust their affairs and to ease the process of transfer. They were satisfied with this arrangement.

The rulers then raised various issues which they considered vital from their point of view. The first was their privy purse. I told them that this would be calculated on the basis of the Eastern States formula. They asked for a Council of Rulers to be set up to settle disputed successions. Their idea was that when any dispute about succession occurred among the Gujarat rulers, it should be referred to such a council, which would in its turn invite the opinion of the High Court of Bombay and return a verdict in line with the views of the High Court. The concession was not new, for we had granted it in the case of Saurashtra. When I found that it would meet the sentiment of the rulers, I agreed to the proposal. It was incorporated in a collateral letter addressed to them, but the provisions of the new Constitution in regard to succession referred to in Chapter XXIV made this concession a dead letter.

The rulers then asked for an assurance that the cash balances and other assets of their States as on the day of transfer of their administration would, as far as possible, be spent for the benefit of the people of the States. I readily agreed to this. Several other minor concessions for which they pleaded were exactly the same as those granted to the rulers of the States forming the Saurashtra Union. I agreed to give an assurance on these points in a collateral letter.

After these discussions, the late Maharajah of Rajpipla expressed on behalf of the rulers their desire to integrate their States with the province of Bombay and made the following statement:

We have the pleasure to inform you that, as rulers of Gujarat States, we believe our Mother Country and particularly Gujarat looks up to us to make all sacrifices in the wider interests of India as a whole. We, therefore, have cheerfully responded to the call of duty and decided to take the first step in forming the province of Maha Gujarat by integrating our States with the province of Bombay. We invoke God's blessings on our decision.

I thanked the rulers on behalf of the Government of India and commended them for their sacrifice and public spirit. The merger agreements were then signed by the rulers. The total area affected by this merger was a little over 27,000 square miles with a population of 26,24,000 and an annual revenue of Rs 1,65,00,000.

I had kept B. G. Kher and Morarji Desai (the Premier and the Home Minister, respectively, of Bombay) fully informed of these events. After the agreements were signed, I suggested that they should make arrangements to take over the administration of all the full jurisdictional States by 5 June 1948. With regard to the semi-jurisdictional and non-jurisdictional units, the rulers at my request signed a covenant integrating their territories with Bombay; and the Regional Commissioner handed over the administration of these units, on behalf of the Government of India, to the Government of Bombay. The administration of the full jurisdictional States was actually assumed on 10 June 1948.

There remained one more Gujarat State. This was Danta, which was no more than 347 square miles in area and had a population of a little over 31,000. Nevertheless, the ruling family had an importance of its own, as it claimed to be the head of the Parmar clan of Rajputs and to be descended from the celebrated Emperor Vikramaditya of Ujjain. After the merger of the Gujarat States, repeated efforts were made to get into contact with the Maharana of Danta. He was a deeply religious man and was in the custom of spending several hours a day in performing religious rites and ceremonies. He used, in fact, to be so immersed from eight in the evening till nine the next morning throughout the period from June to September every year. Eighty per cent of the population of his State consisted of Bhils. This aboriginal population presented a most difficult problem of law and order to Bombay. We were anxious to avoid taking over the State against the wishes of the Maharana. On 7 October 1948 the Maharana wrote to me that owing to his religious bent of mind and his dwindling interest in mundane affairs, it was not possible for him to attend to State work. He begged to be allowed to abdicate and requested that his son and heir-apparent be recognized as the ruler. The Government of India accepted the proposal. The new ruler signed the merger agreement on 16 October 1948 and the State was taken over by the Bombay Government on 6 November.

Kolhapur was now the only State (excepting Baroda) left in Bombay; and though its turn came roughly a year later, this is the place to treat of it. The Kolhapur dynasty was founded by Tarabai, the heroic wife of Rajaram, son of Shivaji the Great. Kolhapur claimed high rank among the Mahratta States and the ruler bore

the distinctive and honorific title of *Chhatrapati Maharaj*. The State
had an area of 3,219 square miles, a population of nearly 11 lakhs
and an annual revenue of Rs 128 lakhs. The last Maharajah, Sir
Rajaram Chhatrapati, died on 26 November 1940 leaving no male
heir. A six-weeks old boy was recognized as his successor, and a
Council of Regency was set up with the Dowager Maharani as its
President. Shortly after, the child died and the Political Department,
on 31 March 1947, recognized the adoption of Vikramasinha Rao
Maharaj, the Maharajah of Dewas Senior, as Shahaji Chhatrapati
II. The Dowager Maharani was never reconciled to this succession;
and the new Maharajah had to start under the initial handicap
of being considered, at least by a section of the people, as an
outsider.

At the time of the merger of the Deccan States we had left Kolhapur alone as we felt that the time was not ripe. Any hasty step might
have alienated the feelings of the Mahrattas, who looked to the ruler
of Kolhapur as their head. But in January 1948 the assassination of
Gandhiji led to serious rioting in the State. The situation arising out
of the disturbances was discussed between the ruler and the States
Ministry and, as a result, the ruler agreed to the appointment of an
administrator nominated by the Government of India.

The financial position of the State was found to be unsatisfactory
and an officer was deputed to enquire into it. On his recommendation a loan was granted by the Government of India to the State.
Meanwhile, constant pressure was exerted on us from one quarter
or another for its merger and it was even suggested that we
should hold a plebiscite. The unique position of Kolhapur and the
possibility that any precipitate action would give rise to a regional
controversy decided us against the idea of a plebiscite. We felt also
that without the free consent of the Maharajah no merger could
take place.

The Maharajah was eventually invited to Delhi for discussion.
The conversations proceeded in a friendly spirit and in February
1949 the Maharajah signed an agreement merging his State with
Bombay. His privy purse was fixed at Rs 10 lakhs. Sometime back
we had received a petition requesting the Government of India to
appoint a Commission to enquire into the validity of the adoption of the ruler. The Maharajah was aware of this, and the fear
that his title to the *gaddi* might be questioned may have hastened
his decision. I should add here that, with but one exception, the

27

Government of India refused to upset any decisions relating to succession taken by the Political Department before the transfer of power, irrespective of the merits. We felt that if we started interfering, it would have a most unsettling effect.

The administration of Kolhapur State was taken over on 1 March 1949 at a big public function at which B. G. Kher, the Premier of Bombay, presided. On behalf of the Government of India, I handed over the administration to the Government of Bombay.

The merger of Kolhapur, the most important State in the Deccan, thus took place, much to Sardar's relief, smoothly and with no untoward incident.

X

VINDHYA PRADESH

BOUNDED on three sides by the United Provinces and on the south by the Central Provinces, there lies a tract of lowland comprised of two distinct territorial divisions, Bundelkhand and Baghelkhand. Lack of road and railway communications and, indeed, the very nature of the country had made this area practically inaccessible to outsiders. It possessed, however, great potentialities of development in agricultural and forest wealth.

Bundelkhand was originally held by the Chandelas who were ousted by the Bundelas, a clan of Rajputs, at the beginning of the thirteenth century. The Bundelas held high positions under the Moghul emperors; they reached the pinnacle of their glory in the time of Chhatrasal, a contemporary of Shivaji. The Bundelkhand States were carved out of the domains of Chhatrasal by his descendants and others.

Baghelkhand comprised, besides the important State of Rewa, a few other smaller States. The ruling family of Rewa belonged to the Baghela clan of Rajputs which was descended from the Gujarat family that ruled at Anhilwara Patan in the thirteenth century. A member of this family migrated to central India and obtained possession of Bandhogarh, which remained the capital of the Baghelas until it was captured by Akbar in 1597, when Rewa became the chief town. But Akbar made over his conquests to the Baghela ruler, from whom the present ruling family is descended.

The area of the Bundelkhand States was about 12,000 square miles, with a population of a little over 17 lakhs and a revenue of about a crore. Rewa State was almost equal in size, population and revenue to all the Bundelkhand States put together.

Bundelkhand and Baghelkhand consisted of thirty-five States. They were for the most part backward and could boast of very little local talent. The Bundelkhand Rajput was traditionally averse to any kind of work or discipline. Historically, Baghelkhand and Bundelkhand had always led a separate political existence and there was traditional hostility between these two Rajput clans. The Baghelas considered themselves to be of purer Rajput origin and did not normally intermarry with the Bundelas.

There was hardly a State of this group against the ruler of which the Political Department had not at some time or other taken action. Some rulers had been deposed; a few had been asked to keep out of their States, and the powers of others had been curtailed either temporarily or permanently.

The future of these States now engrossed the attention of the States Ministry. In particular, we were worried about the Bundelkhand States, most of which were very small. At least fifteen of them had an area of less than 50 square miles, whilst two of them had an area of less than 10 square miles. Orchha had the largest revenue of a little over Rs 20 lakhs, while a dozen small States had an income of less than Rs 50,000.

We examined various alternatives with regard to the future of these small States. We considered their merger with the United Provinces and with the Central Provinces. There were several valid arguments against any such course. The United Provinces was already very large. Districts in the United Provinces which were originally part of Bundelkhand, such as Jalaun, Banda and Hamirpur, were the least developed districts of the province and it was held that further additions to these three districts, or the creation of new districts contiguous to them, would not result in good administration. The Central Provinces had only recently received a considerable enlargement of territory in the form of the Chattisgarh States. The province had not yet fully digested these new acquisitions; to add further undeveloped and backward tracts would not be in the interests of the people.

The creation of a separate union of States other than Rewa was also considered and rejected, since such a Union would not possess the requisite resources, the total revenue of all these States being only a little over Rs 1 crore.

The only feasible proposition was to create a Union of all the States including Rewa. There was, however, one objection to this course. Rewa had been declared a viable State, since it had individual representation in the Constituent Assembly. Immediately after the merger of the Orissa and Chattisgarh States I had assured a conference of rulers presided over by Lord Mountbatten that the principle of merger would not be applied to viable States. It was therefore incumbent on us to leave Rewa alone.

It was in the first week of March that a delegation from Rewa met me at Delhi. They assured me that Rewa would be prepared to enter a Union provided certain concessions were offered.

Subsequently, I had a discussion with Sardar. I suggested to him that, if the Maharajah of Rewa was himself willing to consider the proposed union of all the Baghelkhand and Bundelkhand States, we might seriously take up the proposition. He agreed that I should visit Rewa and discuss the proposal with the rulers concerned. He added that, if the Maharajah of Rewa was himself a willing party, we need not be bound by the undertaking already given. I also inform- ed Sardar of the various demands which had been made on behalf of the Maharajah of Rewa by the delegation which met me at Delhi. He agreed that some of the demands were difficult to accept and suggested that I should study the situation on the spot and act according to my own judgement.

I went to Rewa on 11 March 1948. The town of Rewa lacked even the most elementary amenities of civilized human existence. The plight of the people was appalling. The Maharajah, whom I saw first, told me that if the local leaders so advised, he would have no objection to enter into a Union. He was too young and inexperienced. My negotiations had therefore to be with the local leaders, while the Maharajah remained an interested but silent spectator. The main concern of these popular leaders seemed to be to guard the Maharajah's interests. Added to this, whenever they asked for some concession, they backed it by the plea that if it was not granted the henchmen of the ex-Maharajah, Gulab Singh, who was the father of the present Maharajah, would create trouble for them. Gulab Singh had been deposed by the Political Department and forbidden to enter Rewa State. When he left the State he had taken with him several crores of rupees, yet paradoxically enough he led a most beggarly existence. At the time of my visit to Rewa he was at Allahabad. I was told that he was against Rewa losing its identity and was prepared to spend any amount of money to prevent it.

The first demand of the leaders was that the Maharajah of Rewa should be made the permanent Rajpramukh of the proposed Union. I opposed it on the ground that it was undemocratic and that it might give rise to difficulties in the formation of other Unions. I agreed, however, to give Rewa a weightage in the election of the Rajpramukh and the Uprajpramukh, commensurate with the State's importance.

The next demand put forward was that the Constituent Assembly of the proposed Union should have the option to frame a constitution of either a unitary or a federal type. I realized that the inspiration for this came from a similar provision in the covenant of the Saurash-tra Union. But, in the case of Saurashtra, the provision was made in order to placate the sentiments of the rulers of the bigger States; we were certainly aware of the constitutional anomalies and the practical difficulties involved. I was loath to concede a similar demand in this case; but since the constitution was to be drawn up within the frame-work of the Constitution of India, I decided to agree to the demand. Such a provision does not appear in the covenants of Unions formed subsequently.

Now I was confronted by the leaders with another demand. This was that Rewa should have the right to opt out of the new Union if a majority of the State's representatives in the Constituent Assembly so desired; otherwise, the question as to whether or not Rewa should join the proposed Union should be postponed until after the elections to the Constituent Assembly so as to give the leaders an oppor-tunity to gauge popular feeling on the subject. I felt that, if I acceded to this request for postponement, the Union might be put off indefi-nitely. On the other hand, if the first demand was accepted, Rewa could be induced to join the Union immediately. The leaders assured me that there was not the slightest chance of Rewa exercising the option to get out of the Union; but if such an option were not provided in the covenant, the ruler as well as the leaders would put them-selves entirely in the wrong in the eyes of the public and this would give a handle to the ex-Maharajah and his henchmen to create trouble. After prolonged discussion I found that it would be impossible to get Rewa into the Union if I did not concede the point. I therefore agreed to insert an article in the covenant to the effect that, if three-fourths of the representatives of Rewa in the Constituent Assembly of the proposed Union voted within one month from the date of the first meeting of the Constituent Assembly in favour of opting out of the Union, the covenant in so far as it affected Rewa would not be operative. This was undoubtedly a very large concession to the separatist tendencies of the Rewa leaders. But I had no doubt that, once the Union was formed, the States Ministry would be able to control the future policy and see to it that Rewa did not opt out of the Union.

Yet another demand was that, until the Constituent Assembly met, Rewa and Bundelkhand should have two separate ministries, one at Rewa and the other at Nowgong, with the Maharajah of Rewa as the common Rajpramukh. These two ministries would make room for a common ministry drawn from among the members of the Constituent Assembly after the Assembly met. Here again, the plea was put forward that if the popular leaders agreed to a joint executive for both the regions to begin with, the anti-merger party sponsored by ex-Maharajah Gulab Singh would make capital out of it. In order to bring the Union into being, I agreed to this suggestion and promised to send a letter to the Maharajah before I returned to Delhi.

Thereafter, a great deal of time was taken in discussing the privy purse of the Maharajah. Here, instead of putting a curb on the Maharajah's demands, the popular leaders were making a specious plea for him. In 1945-46 Rewa had a total revenue of Rs 1,14,22,125. On the basis of the Eastern States formula, the privy purse of the Maharajah of Rewa would be Rs 9,72,500. Mainly because of the insistence of the local leaders that the privy purse should be fixed at Rs 10 lakhs, I agreed to round off the figure to that sum.

After these discussions with the representatives of Rewa, I proceeded on the 12th afternoon to Nowgong. Here there was a lovely house, which had been the residence of the Political Agent before the transfer of power. The flowers in the garden and the green lawns were a great relief after the arid atmosphere of Rewa. The climate, too, was more agreeable. I met the rulers, as well as the Prajamandal representatives of the Bundelkhand States, and gave them the gist of my discussions with the Maharajah of Rewa and the local leaders there. A general discussion followed.

The majority of the rulers desired that the proposed Union should be named Vindhya Pradesh, a view which was endorsed by the Prajamandal leaders. I thought the suggestion an excellent one and accepted it.

There were a few States and portions of States which either formed islands in the United Provinces or were geographically contiguous to it and it was my idea to merge them with the United Provinces. I also wanted to include one of the States (Datia), which was an island inside Gwalior, in the proposed Madhya Bharat Union. But the rulers pointed out that the exclusion of these States would render the position of Rewa in the proposed Union absolutely preponderant and weight the scales against the permanence of the Union. This argument had considerable force, and in view of the pronounced local patriotism which I had found in Rewa, I considered it desirable to strengthen the other elements. Therefore, I included all these States in the proposed Union for the time being, leaving the matter of adjustment of territories for future negotiation.

In the proposed Union there would be thirty-six seats in the Constituent Assembly of which eighteen would go to Rewa and the remaining eighteen to other States. I hoped that this would curb the separatist tendencies of Rewa.

A strong demand was put forward by the rulers both of salute and non-salute States that there should be no differentiation between them in the formation of the Council of Rulers. I could not agree to this proposal as its acceptance would make the Council too unwieldy. Besides, I felt that having too many rulers of the smaller States in the Council would result in the formation of cliques. My solution was to include, besides the rulers of all the 13 salute States, the rulers of the four most important non-salute States of Alipura, Kothi, Sarila and Sohawal and to allow the rest of the rulers of non-salute States to elect two members from among themselves. The Council would thus consist of nineteen members; but while all the other members would have one vote each, the Maharajah of Rewa would have fifteen votes in the election of the Rajpramukh and the Uprajpramukh and so would be able to ensure his election as Rajpramukh if he could secure only two of the remaining votes. This was generally accepted by the rulers.

The other important matter was the settlement of the privy purse. The 1945-46 revenue was taken as the basis and the Eastern States formula was applied. Some of the non-salute States in this region were extremely small, and I was asked to make a slight concession in favour of their rulers. I agreed to round off the privy purse for the rulers of two States, namely Banka Pahari and Bijna, to Rs 3,000 per annum and for the rulers of Dhurwai, Kamta Rajaula and Naigawan Rebai, to Rs 5,000 per annum.

In the light of these discussions, the covenant was finalized and signed by the Bundelkhand rulers on 13 March. I then returned to Rewa and after some discussion the Maharajah also appended his signature to the document. I addressed a letter to the Maharajah in which I requested him to form two broad-based ministries of popular leaders, one for Rewa and the other for Bundelkhand, with himself as the common Rajpramukh.

When I returned to Delhi I apprised Sardar of what had happened in Rewa and Nowgong. I told him that I had been most reluctant to include some of the provisions in the covenant, such as freedom to the Constituent Assembly to frame either a unitary or a federal constitution; the right to Rewa to opt out if a majority of the State representatives so desired; and the provision for two separate ministries till the Constituent Assembly met. It was true that we had given the Saurashtra Constituent Assembly freedom to frame either a federal or a unitary constitution, but in that Union the Congress party was in a predominant position and it would not be difficult for Sardar to control developments there. Here there was no political party or organization, so that it was somewhat risky to have conceded the demand. I told Sardar that all these were concessions to Rewa's separatist tendencies, but my over-riding purpose had been to form a Union at any cost; once it was formed and came under our control, we could adjust the future policy on the right lines. Sardar thought that lack of political material and deficient financial resources might affect the permanence of the new Union, and he asked me to keep a very close watch on developments in this region.

The new Union was inaugurated in April 1948 by N. V. Gadgil, then Minister for Works, Mines and Power. This Union had an area of 24,598 square miles, a population of 35,69,455 and an annual revenue of Rs 2,43,30,734.

The experiment of two ministries proved an utter failure; in July, the States Ministry succeeded in persuading them to fuse into a composite ministry for the whole area. It was hoped that a common Government representative of the people of all the integrated States would operate as a unifying force and eliminate disruptive local affiliations. But the performance of the new ministry, which did not last even for a year, proved disappointing. Widespread corruption and nepotism and continued dissensions and mutual recriminations among the ministers resulted in a most distressing situation, which reached its climax when one of the ministers was caught red-handed in Delhi accepting an illegal gratification from the representative of a mining concern. Later a prosecution was launched against another minister, though this was withdrawn. In view of the various allegations made against them, Sardar called the ministers to a meeting

28

in Delhi. In the course of the discussions, the Ministers made charges and counter-charges and accused each other of various acts of omission and commission which reflected gravely on their integrity, efficiency and administrative capacity. Sardar advised the ministers to resign; which they did on 14 April 1949. N. B. Bonarji, I.C.S., Regional Commissioner, took charge as Chief Minister on the following day.

Even so, it was found that owing to lack of experienced officials, political dissensions and intrigues, and above all the want of adequate financial resources, very little progress could be made in the development of this area. The finances of the Union came under close scrutiny during the discussions connected with the Federal Financial Integration when it was held that with its poor resources the Union could not hope to stand by itself.

In September 1949 N. M. Buch, I.C.S., was deputed to investigate and report on the administrative and political situation in Vindhya Pradesh. His report revealed an alarming state of affairs. During its few months of office the popular ministry had thrown the administration into utter confusion. The finances were in a deplorable state and the Union was on the verge of bankruptcy. There was no abatement of the regional rivalry between Bundelkhand and Baghelkhand. Further, some of the officers whom we had borrowed from the Central Provinces to run the administration were alleged to have been carrying on an open propaganda for the disintegration of the Union and its merger with the Central Provinces and this had created widespread popular resentment.

Sardar was most anxious to find a solution with regard to the future of this Union, which he was convinced could not stand by itself. We had a long discussion on the subject. There were three possible choices: (1) to continue the present system of administration with an official Chief Minister; (2) to convert the Union into a centrally administered area; and (3) to disintegrate the Union and distribute the territories between the United Provinces and the Central Provinces. In view of the prevailing situation, the selection of another ministry was out of the question, because of the lack of suitable political material. Sardar's view, in fact, was that the Union should be parcelled between the United Provinces and the Central Provinces.

I was not happy about this. I explained to him the undesirable consequences of making further additions to either the United Provinces or the Central Provinces. Moreover, the disintegration of one

Union was likely to unsettle the rest. If the British had managed with over five hundred States for more than a century, surely we could manage with six Unions for at least ten years. From the merely political point of view, the parties could not have much objection to a Ministry-cum-Adviser regime. My own opinion was that Vindhya Pradesh for its own good should continue to be a separate unit so that the Government of India would be better able to look after its finances and development. Such an arrangement would give us a breathing space after the recent major territorial and political changes.

Sardar, however, was convinced that Vindhya Pradesh could not exist as a separate unit. Nor did he think that the Union was likely to throw up any leaders of ability in the near or even distant future. On financial grounds the Union was a weak one. In the circumstances, he asked me to take steps for its dissolution and for the distribution of its territory between the United Provinces and the Central Provinces.

It was an embarrassing duty that Sardar had entrusted to me. The ink was scarcely dry on the original covenant forming the Vindhya Pradesh Union, and here were we about to ask the rulers to abrogate that covenant and agree to the disintegration of the Union. The rulers would certainly be reluctant to do so. Nor would the local politicians view it with favour.

The first thing was to invite the rulers of Rewa and Panna (an influential ruler in Bundelkhand) to Delhi for a discussion. I felt that if they agreed to the proposal, others could be persuaded to take the same line. Both these rulers came to Delhi on 20 November and I had several discussions with them. I told them that the plan was to divide the Union between the United Provinces and the Central Provinces, but that some of the territory might also have to go to Madhya Bharat. The Maharajahs did not commit themselves.

We drafted an agreement. This draft abrogated the original covenant. It also laid down in its Article III that 'the ruler of each of the States ... hereby cedes to the Government of India, with effect from the aforesaid day (26 December 1949) full and exclusive authority, jurisdiction and powers for, and in relation to, the governance of that State; and thereafter the Government of India shall be competent to exercise the said powers, authority and jurisdiction in such manner and through such agency as it may think fit.' This agreement had to be signed and the territorial distribution effected at an early date, for the new Constitution of India was to come into force on 26 January 1950. After that date, any distribution of territories would require the sanction of the local legislature and Parliament. When the plan for the disintegration of Vindya Pradesh became known, the Vindhya Pradesh Congress Committee passed a resolution against the proposal. Some of the rulers were in close sympathy with the Congress attitude.

I convened a conference of the rulers at Nowgong on 17 December. The Maharajah of Rewa had wired to me that he was too ill to attend; nevertheless, I went to Nowgong on the 17th. I was informed that for various personal reasons the Maharajah of Rewa was opposed to the proposal. He was unwilling that the Rewa State should be split up, and was anxious that the allowances he was getting as Rajpramukh should be added to the privy purse. Further, the popular ministry had sanctioned the payment of Rs 35 lakhs to the Maharajah by way of compensation for certain buildings which belonged to the Maharajah and which were being utilized as government offices; but the States Ministry had considered this payment unjustifiable and had asked the Maharajah to refund the amount. He now desired that order to be rescinded. However I decided to go ahead and confer with the other rulers. I wrote to the Maharajah of Rewa that I would go to Rewa the next day and requested him to come to a final decision by that time in regard to the new agreement.

The rulers' conference began in the Agency House at Nowgong at 3 p.m. I explained to them the history of the formation of Vindhya Pradesh and the situation leading to the collapse of the popular ministry. I said that the question whether the Union could stand by itself as an independent Union had been fully examined and that the Government of India had come to the conclusion that, for financial and administrative reasons, Vindhya Pradesh was nothing but a liability. I went on to say that Sardar had studied this matter very closely; that he had come to the conclusion that merger with the neighbouring provinces was in the best interests of the people as a whole, and that it was his wish that the rulers should accept his advice and sign the agreement. I also said that I had heard from various quarters that it was the wish of some of the rulers that the people should be consulted. But my own advice was that this matter should be left to Sardar, who was the trusted leader of the people and was in the best possible position to judge what was good for the country. Finally, I pointed out that it was in the rulers' interest to co-operate with the Government of India and sign the document, rather than to leave the matter to be decided by the legislature after 26 January 1950.

A discussion followed and the meeting adjourned to meet again at 7 p.m. when after further discussion the rulers of Orchha, Ajaigarh, Maihar and Khaniadhana signed the agreement. The other rulers said that they would sign after the Maharajah of Rewa had signed and that they would go with me to Rewa. I told the rulers that the Maharajah of Rewa was holding out not so much on the ground of principle as for certain personal and financial advantages. The rulers had therefore to consider whether it was wiser to make their signatures dependent on Rewa's rather than to sign first. This suggestion had very little effect on them and when I left next day for Rewa I took with me the rulers of Panna, Chhatarpur, Nagod, Kothi, Sarila and Alipura.

At Rewa, I went to the residence of S. N. Mehta, I.C.S., who had succeeded Bonarji as official Chief Minister. The rulers who accompanied me suggested that they should call on the Maharajah of Rewa first and acquaint him with the discussions held at Nowgong. Accordingly, they went to the palace. Later, the Maharajah of Rewa sent me a message that he would see me at two that afternoon.

Chaturvedi, an official minister and White, the Chief Secretary, accompanied me to the palace. The route to the palace was chosen by Chaturvedi. When we drew near, we found that a crowd of about two thousand had assembled at the gates and would not allow us to proceed. Every attempt on our part to move forward was resisted by the mob, some members of which began to pull at the doors of the car and to shower us with pamphlets. The Chief Secretary expostulated with the crowd, but they would not listen to him. I told them in my imperfect Hindi that I was there by the orders of Sardar to get the agreement signed by the rulers and that if they had anything to say they should send their representatives to Delhi. The mob however was in no mood to listen. Those in front shouted that Vindhya Pradesh should be kept intact; that the people should be consulted regarding its future. They would not let the car through to the palace and wanted me to go back. All efforts to persuade the mob to see reason having failed, I had no choice but to return. No police were present at the palace gates or anywhere along the route.

The Chief Minister and the Inspector-General of Police were awaiting my return. I told the former what had happened and expressed the view that the demonstration could not have been held, or even organized, without the Maharajah's knowledge. It had taken place within a stone's throw of the palace and within his hearing and it was his business to have sent word to me not to come by that gate. I decided therefore not to go to the palace again and directed Mehta, the Chief Minister, to take the document to the Maharajah who should either sign it, or state in writing that he was not prepared to do so. I asked him to bring back the answer at once as I was leaving for Delhi that evening.

When Mehta went to the palace with my message, the other rulers who were present were so perturbed at the turn of events that they said they would sign the agreement whatever the Maharajah of Rewa might decide to do. The Maharajah of Rewa himself had grown nervous and ultimately signed the agreement.

It was the first time I had ever faced a hostile mob. The situation had ugly possibilities. But the absence of police arrangements proved beneficial. If the police had been present and had resorted to force, it is difficult to say what might have happened.

On my return to Delhi, I found that Sardar had already been given a garbled version of the events at Rewa. At first he was very angry with the Maharajah as well as with the local leaders and officials. I myself was angry enough with the local officials for their incompetence; but in the end we made light of the whole episode.

Soon after this, Sardar invited the Premiers of both the United Provinces and the Central Provinces for a discussion regarding the distribution of Vindhya Pradesh between those two provinces. The discussion revealed a wide divergence of opinion between the two Premiers. Sardar wanted them to come to a mutual agreement and was unwilling to force a settlement on them. But agreement was not reached and the Government of India had no alternative but to take over Vindhya Pradesh as a centrally administered area. This was done on 1 January 1950. This arrangement had, its advantages, for one thing, if ever these two divergent areas of Bundelkhand and Baghelkhand were to be fused into one compact whole and be properly developed, it was the direct administration of the Government of India that could best achieve that task.

Vindhya Pradesh was placed under a Lieutenant-Governor, instead of a Chief Commissioner, under the Government of Part C States Act of 1951. It now has a legislature and a ministry responsible to it, though with restricted powers.

XI

MADHYA BHARAT

THE Madhya Bharat Union comprising 25 States[1], with an area of 47,000 square miles, sprawls across the central region of India. Its irregular boundary meets the Bombay Province in the south and south-west, Rajasthan in the west, the United Provinces in the north and north-east, and Bhopal and the Central Provinces in the east. The whole of this region, except for a small portion, lies in the plateau of Malwa.

Malwa, by its geographical position, has been exposed to cultural impacts from the north as well as from the south. It underwent a change of masters more often than many other parts of India and was invariably an appanage to the domains of every monarch who became the master of the Gangetic Plain. Both during the time of the Moghuls and of the Mahrattas, Malwa was used as the highway to the south.

Malwa formed part of the empires of the Mauryas, the Guptas and Harsha. When the Rajputs established their sway over the greater part of northern India, Malwa also came under their control and Rajput kingdoms flourished there. These kingdoms later succumbed to the might of the Moghul empire. Under the Moghuls Malwa was a compact unit and formed a *subah*. After the death of Aurangzeb, the Mahrattas made a bid for the conquest of northern India and in the latter part of the eighteenth century Malwa came to be divided between the Mahratta rulers of Gwalior and Indore belonging, respectively, to the Scindia and Holkar families.

Gwalior and Indore were perpetually at war. Their ruling houses fought a series of battles, of which some of the fiercest took place when they were nominally at peace. If, in the beginning of the nineteenth

[1] The number includes erstwhile salute and non-salute States, together with a few minor estates which were subsequently integrated.

century, the rulers of these two States had presented a united front against the British, how different might have been the history of India! It was the Third Anglo-Mahratta War of 1817-18 that finally broke the power of the Mahrattas. Sir John Malcolm was entrusted with the task of settling this region. His masterly handling of the situation is one of the finest achievements of any British administrator. Under his settlement, the map of Malwa was redrawn. The two Mahratta States of Gwalior and Indore were enclosed within carefully demarcated limits. Fifteen Rajput and a few Muslim States which had been under the suzerainty of either Gwalior or Indore were made independent of them and brought under British protection. In Lee Warner's picturesque description, Malwa after Malcolm's settlement 'presented the appearance of a sea suddenly petrified while in a condition of stormy unrest and disquietude.' Malcolm's settlement remained more or less intact until the transfer of power in August 1947.

The most important of the Mahratta States was Gwalior. This State was founded by Ranuji Maharaj. He rose rapidly, in the service of the Peshwa, to the front rank of Mahratta chiefs, acquired possessions in Malwa, and died in 1750. But the Scindias reached the meridian of their glory in the time of Madhoji Scindia who, though nominally a servant of the Peshwa, possessed a formidable army organized by French officers and made himself the virtual ruler of northern India. It was he who made the titular Moghul Emperor, Shah Alam II (already helpless amidst violence, confusion and anarchy) his puppet and utilized the fiction of Moghul sovereignty to establish Mahratta supremacy throughout the north. By 1792, Madhoji Scindia had established his ascendancy over the Rajputs and the Jats and his power and splendour in northern India were absolute. Grant Duff referred to the death of Madhoji Scindia in 1794 as 'an event of great political significance both as it affected the Mahratta Empire and the other States of India.'

The reign of his grand-nephew and successor, Daulat Rao Scindia, brought a series of disasters to Gwalior, culminating in a treaty of subsidiary alliance in November 1817. Sir John Malcolm observed that the Scindia was 'forced to abandon his cherished prospects and to become, at the very moment he was recognized as its most powerful chief, the marked deserter of the cause of his nation.' In 1818 an adjustment of boundaries was effected, the British Government receiving Ajmer and other districts and ceding lands of equal value.

During the great revolt of 1857 the British Indian contingent in Gwalior mutinied and the Maharajah sought refuge at Agra. Gwalior was retaken by the British in June 1858 and the Maharajah was reinstated, but the historic fort of Gwalior continued to be occupied by the British till 1886, when it was restored to the Maharajah.

The rulers of Gwalior have not as a rule been prone to extravagance. Successive rulers had, in fact, exercised the greatest economy in their administration. When the Government of India integrated Gwalior, apart from cash balances amounting to Rs 3.09 crores we inherited two funds amounting to about Rs 17 crores which the Scindias had built up; one was the Gwalior Investment Fund and the other was the Gangajali Fund. The latter has an interesting history. It was started by the Scindias originally as a reserve to fall back upon in case they were defeated in battle and had to flee the country. Whenever new ornaments were made, the old ones were put into a jar along with any spare money which remained. Thus was the nucleus of the fund built up. When the country had become settled, it was treated as a reserve to be utilized in times of natural calamity such as famine. Considerable sums of money were put into this Fund from time to time. Moreover, the Scindias had increased the revenues of the State by shrewd investments in industrial concerns. If the cash balance and the amounts of the Gangajali Fund and the Gwalior Investment Fund were to be invested at a reasonable rate of interest, the income would more than meet the total privy purses fixed for the rulers of all the twenty-five States which constitute the Madhya Bharat Union.

The present Maharajah, Sir George Jivaji Rao Scindia[1], succeeded his father in June 1925 at the age of nine. He was invested with full ruling powers in November 1936. He is a young man with a progressive outlook and extremely pleasant manners, cautious by nature and deferential to his elders. He has always moved with the times. He had announced his intention to grant responsible government as early as December 1946, and in May 1947 he readily gave his support to an interim government of popular representatives as well as a constitution-making body. He was the first among the rulers of the five

[1] The Maharajah has an imposing array of titles. His full name with all his titles reads: Lt.-General Mukhtar-ul-Mulk, Azim ul-Iqtidar, Rafi-ush-Shan, Wala Shikoh, Mohta-Sham-i-Dauran, Umdat-ul-Umara, Maharajadhiraja Alijah Hisam-us-Saltanat Sir George Jivaji Rao Scindia Bahadur, Shrinath Mansur-i-Zaman, Fidwi-i-Hazrat-i-Malik-i-Muazzam-i-Rafi-ud-Darjat-i-Inglistan.

21-gun salute States to agree to integration, a step which was moti-
vated by no other reason than the good of the country.

Indore, the other important State, was founded by Malhar Rao
Holkar. He was born in 1694. His soldierly qualities brought him
into prominence under the Peshwa. The territories acquired by
Malhar Rao at one time stretched from the Deccan to the Ganges.
He was succeeded by his grandson, Male Rao, who had no issue, and
when he died his mother Ahalyabai came to the throne. She
was reputed to be not only an exemplary ruler but also a model of
Hindu piety. Her temple occupies a commanding position on the
crags of Maheswar overlooking the Narmada river. She was
succeeded by Tukoji Rao Holkar. His son, Jaswant Rao, in 1805,
concluded a treaty of peace and amity with the British Government.
But further disturbances ensued and in 1818 Malhar Rao II entered
into another treaty, called the Treaty of Mandsaur, which till the
transfer of power continued to define the relations of the State with
the British Government. There had been long spells of minority
administration under British officials by which the State had
greatly benefited.

The present Maharajah, Sir Yeshwant Rao Holkar, started very
well indeed and was noted for his progressive views. I recall his
having written a letter to the President of the United States during
the second World War stressing the imperative need of satisfying
nationalist demands in India. This got him into trouble with the
Political Department and he retired into his shell. Later he went
to the other extreme and joined the group which tried to evolve
a 'Third Force' out of the States. During our negotiations for accession on three subjects, the Maharajah was certainly not helpful, but
he did ultimately accede and thereafter fully played his part. He is
the only ruler, other than the Nizam, who had the foresight to create
a trust of all his properties. After the integration of the State, he
requested the States Ministry to recognize his only daughter, Usha-
devi, as his heir. In view of his uniformly good relations with the
Government of India after his accession to the Indian Union, and in
accordance with the precedent of a former ruler Ahalyabai, the
President (on the advice of Sardar and the Prime Minister) recognized the daughter as heir-apparent.

Next in importance to Gwalior and Indore were the States of Dhar
and Dewas. In the eighteenth century these two States, together
with Gwalior and Indore, controlled the whole of central India;

but subsequently they declined in importance. The ruling families of both Dhar and Dewas were Puars and claimed descent from the Parmara Rajputs. But the Puars of Dewas, by intermarriage with the Mahrattas, lost their status as Rajputs. The Dewas State was divided between two brothers which meant that there were two States — Dewas Senior and Dewas Junior.

The other States were Ratlam, Alirajpur, Barwani, Jhabua, Khilchipur, Narsingarh, Sailana, Sitamau, Jobat, Kathiwara, Mathwar, Rajgarh, Nimkhera, Jamnia and Piploda. These were all Rajput States founded in the fourteenth and fifteenth centuries. On the Mahratta conquest of Malwa in the eighteenth century, these States had been reduced to the position of tributaries of the Scindia or the Holkar, but they were later restored by Sir John Malcolm.

There were also four Muslim States, Jaora, Kurwai, Muhammadgarh and Pathari. The Nawab of Jaora was descended from Gafoor Khan who was the brother-in-law of the predatory leader Amir Khan, founder of the Tonk State. Kurwai was founded by an Afghan named Muhammed Diler Khan who was in the service of the Hindu Rajah of Kurwai and on whose death he seized the State. Muhammadgarh was orginally part of Kurwai until it was bequeathed to a younger son of the chief in 1753. The rulers of Pathari were descended from Dost Muhammed, the founder of the Bhopal family.

These States comprised an area of approximately 47,000 square miles and all of them consisted of blocks of territories separated by intervening portions of other States. This had produced an extraordinary interlacing of jurisdictions in which boundaries crossed and re-crossed each other, a veritable jumble not unlike the States in Kathiawar. Linguistically, culturally and economically Malwa formed one compact unit. The prevailing language was Hindi and throughout history Malwa had always been a homogeneous tract, till the advent of the Mahrattas.

In the chapter on the Integration of the Orissa States, I have referred to the meeting that Lord Mountbatten had with various rulers in January 1948. The merger of the Orissa States had already been completed by then and Lord Mountbatten told the rulers that the mediatization of the small States was inevitable. Soon after this, several of the rulers of the smaller States in Central India came to Delhi to see me in order to find out the probable future of their States. I told them that we were quite prepared for mediatization and were anxious to have as large an administrative unit in Central India as possible. I was also approached from time to time by representatives of the Congress organizations in Central India. It must however be said here that these organizations were far from strong and, excepting in Gwalior and Indore, existed only in name. Anyhow, I advised them to work in support of unification, rather than agitate for responsible government in States which by themselves could have no future.

A glance at the map of Central India before integration reveals how difficult it was, because of the scattered nature of the smaller States, to form a Union of these States without touching Gwalior or Indore or both. On the other hand, we had given a definite assurance that the Government of India would not touch the viable States. The problem, therefore, was how to bring the two viable States of Gwalior and Indore into the scheme of a new Union. The first thing to do, I thought, was to sound the Maharajah of Gwalior and to find out how he would react to the idea of a Union of all the States in Central India, including Gwalior.

I met the Maharajah in February 1948 and broached the subject to him. He was, at the start, shocked by my suggestion. But I pointed out that the Government of India could not very well leave the smaller States alone. If they had been contiguous to a province, we could have merged them with it. A Union of these States by themselves was out of the question because they did not form a compact area and, even if they did, they would not constitute a viable administrative unit. Owing to the fertility of its soil, Malwa could play a great part in India's economy. If we could integrate all the States of this region into one Union, it would go a long way to promote the agricultural development of the country.

The ideal solution therefore seemed to be to create a Union of all the States in this region including Gwalior and Indore. If Gwalior chose to stand out of such a Union, the Government of India would have no alternative but to create a Union round Indore. Though I had not discussed the matter with either the Maharajah of Indore or his advisers, I had reason to believe that the Maharajah would not be averse to such a step. The constitution of such a Union would render the position of the Gwalior possessions in Malwa extremely vulnerable. I reminded the Maharajah that his State was split into several bits, the main part being in the north and the richer portions being in the heart of Malwa. I added that if he kept out of the Union, it would not be long before the Malwa portions of his State would express a desire to join the Malwa Union, and, if that blessed word 'self-determination' was applied, the chances were that they would be allowed to do so. In that case Gwalior would lose the best part of its territories and the State would cease to be viable. My arguments appealed to the Maharajah and left him less unfavourably disposed to the idea of a Union than he had been at first.

In the meantime, one of the ministers of Indore came to Delhi and I held discussions with him as well. He was anxious not only that the interests of his ruler should be safeguarded, but also that the capital of the new Union should be located at Indore. He gave me to understand that subject to these conditions the Maharajah of Indore would be in favour of joining the Union. But as I had not had any talk with the Maharajah himself, I felt it a matter of importance to ascertain his attitude. I therefore arranged a joint meeting with the Maharajahs of Gwalior and Indore at Bombay. This was, I believe, the first time after many years that the rulers of these two States met and discussed matters of mutual interest.

Towards the middle of March I went to Bombay and met the Maharajahs of Gwalior, Indore and Dewas Junior, as well as representatives of the Prajamandals of Gwalior and Indore, at the residence of the Maharajah of Gwalior. The formation of a Union of Gwalior and Indore and the other Central India States was discussed at length. Ultimately the proposed Union was accepted in principle, subject to certain provisions safeguarding the interests of the two viable States. It was further agreed that I should prepare a covenant covering the points raised, and take it to Gwalior by the end of the month for further discussion with the two Maharajahs and their ministers.

I went to Gwalior on 30 March and held continuous discussions over the next two days jointly and individually with the Maharajahs of Gwalior, Indore and Dewas Junior. I also discussed the problem with the representatives of the local Bar, Prajamandals, Chamber of Commerce, local industries and others. At Bombay, the Maharajah of Gwalior had expressed his willingness to join the Union on certain conditions. But I found that since then he had resiled from this position; nevertheless, he still seemed willing to abide by the advice of Sardar and myself. He pointed out that there was a strong feeling against the Gwalior State losing its identity in the proposed Union and said that he was finding it difficult to withstand it. He showed me a number of telegrams of protest which he had received from people all over the State. I also found that the Maharani was opposed to the Gwalior State altogether losing its identity. It was pointed out to me that Gwalior was a viable unit by itself. I was also told that a belief was prevalent that the Mahratta States were being singled out for obliteration, while the Rajput States like Jodhpur, Bikaner and Jaipur were being left alone.

I proceeded to Indore on 2 April. The discussions I had with the Maharajah of Indore showed that he, too, was averse to his State's identity being completely lost in the Union. He was strongly in favour of two Unions, as were also the popular representatives and the local ministry. Their idea was that two Unions should be formed, one round Gwalior and the other round Indore. They argued with a great deal of force that while the unification of all the States in this region into one Union must be regarded as the ultimate aim, the formation of two viable units out of these States should be regarded as a satisfactory half-way house. The suggestion was put forward that all the smaller States in the region should surrender their sovereignty to the Government of India, which would in turn transfer this sovereignty to Gwalior or Indore according to the geographical contiguity or propinquity of the State or part of the State concerned; that this arrangement should be reviewed after a period of ten years, and that the question of amalgamating these two States should then be decided by a plebiscite.

It was clear that the strained relations between the ruling families of Gwalior and Indore in the past and their anxiety each to lead a separate existence would not conduce to the smooth working of a Union of both States, at any rate in the initial stage. The traditional hostility between the two ruling families had seeped through to their subjects as well. Moreover, some experienced administrators, whose opinion I held in great esteem, had advised me against obliterating the indentity of viable States, which numbered only 15 or 16. If we touched Gwalior we could scarcely leave the other viable States alone. Furthermore, such a step would be a fundamental departure from the declared policy of the Government of India. If the two rulers were unwilling to join the Union, we could not compel them to do so. Besides, a strong body of local opinion supported their attitude. There existed a genuine loyalty to the *gaddi* in both Gwalior and Indore and the administrative systems of both States were fairly efficient. Taking all these factors into account, it seemed wise to go

slow with the formation of a single Union in this area. Our purpose
would be served if we formed two Unions to begin with. At the same
time, I could not help feeling that if we failed to take advantage
of the fluid situation then prevailing to integrate all the States, such
an opportunity might never come again. I resolved to place all
these facts, together with my reactions, before Sardar.

I returned to Delhi and discussed the problem with Sardar. The
discussion centred round two main issues—whether we should touch
the viable States; and, if so, whether Gwalior and Indore should be
integrated into two Unions or one. With regard to the first, Sardar
agreed generally that once Gwalior and Indore were integrated into
one Union, we should have to adopt the same policy in regard to
all the States in the country, but his personal view was that,
with the exception of Hyderabad and Mysore, which could not but
stand by themselves, all the other States should be grouped into
Unions. He told me that integration was really to the advantage of
the rulers themselves. In that event, the Government of India would
look after the privy purse and private properties of the rulers. If the
viable States were allowed to exist as separate units, the rights and
privileges of the rulers would be at the mercy of the local legislatures;
and he was not altogether confident that the local leaders would
give the rulers a square deal.

On the second issue, Sardar pointed out that if two Unions were
formed, one round Gwalior and the other round Indore as a sort
of halfway house, agitation would still continue for their fusion.
There would consequently be unrest and discontent; and in such an
atmosphere the two new Unions would find it difficult to flourish.
From the point of view of administrative efficiency, one Union
was certainly better than two and he repeated more or less the same
arguments that I had adduced in this connexion before the Maharajah of Gwalior. Furthermore, the creation of two Unions would
amount virtually to the enlargement of the territories of Gwalior and
Indore, both of which would swallow up the smaller States near
their territories: the two Unions would therefore merely be Gwalior
and Indore with their domains enlarged. Sardar said that this position was likely to be exploited by other States for their own aggrandizement at the expense of smaller States. Why should not Patiala,
for instance, incorporate with itself Nalagarh and Kalsia, or other
Phulkian States? Why should not Bikaner swallow Jaisalmer?
Why should not Udaipur expand itself by absorbing smaller States

round its borders? Sardar felt that for this reason, if for no other, the scheme of one Union was likely to be more acceptable to the rulers of the smaller States than a scheme of two. He contended further that once responsible government had taken deep root in the proposed two Unions, it would be impossible to persuade the popular leaders to give up what they would by then have acquired. He therefore asked me to get into touch with the rulers with the definite object of forming one Union.

I invited the rulers of the States to a conference in Delhi, but in the meantime I saw the representatives of the Gwalior and Indore ministries. I communicated to them Sardar's arguments in favour of one Union, and asked them to discuss the matter among themselves with a view to arriving at a solution. After a joint meeting lasting for two days, the two ministries informed me on 18 April that they had found it impossible to arrive at an agreed solution and that they still regarded the formation of two Unions as essential. I felt there was no use my arguing with them any further; in order to save time and energy I took them to Sardar. There was not much argument after that; they accepted Sardar's advice and agreed to the principle of one Union!

As the Maharajah of Gwalior was still hesitant, I had several informal talks with him. I told him that if he still persisted in the view that two Unions should be formed we could both go to Sardar and I would help him to argue his case. I also had an opportunity of discussing the matter with the Maharani whose progressive outlook enabled her to appreciate my arguments. I met the Maharajah again and told him that he was not the only ruler of a viable State who was being called upon to make some sacrifice, and that it was Sardar's view that ultimately only Hyderabad and Mysore should remain as separate entities. Moreover, the Maharajah had already granted responsible government, so that in any case he could only be the constitutional head of the State; while if he accepted the formation of one Union, he would be the constitutional head of the whole of Central India. I told him that eventually the rulers of Hyderabad and Mysore would occupy the same position as was being offered to him. But the important thing was that, if he agreed to the formation of one Union, his privy purse and private properties would be guaranteed by the Centre and would not be at the mercy of the local leaders. I asked him to make up his mind taking these factors into consideration. By this time he was so thoroughly perplexed that he turned to me and said: 'Tell me honestly whether the integration of my State is in the interests of my people and myself. Tell me as a friend and not as States Secretary.' I told him that, considering all the circumstances and future possibilities, I had no doubt that joining the Union would be the best course of action for him. Between the guarantee of the privy purse by the local legislature and by the Government of India, the choice was easy enough. He could certainly trust the Government of India. The Maharajah then agreed.

Meanwhile, I had discussions with the Maharajah of Indore, who was prepared to be guided by the advice of the States Ministry and of his Premier.

A conference of all the rulers was held in the States Ministry's office on 20 April and went on for three days, during which the draft covenant which I had prepared was discussed to the last detail.

In my draft I had put down 'Madhya Bharat' as the name of the new Union; but it was urged that the name should be reminiscent of Gwalior as well as Indore and finally, as a compromise, I accepted the suggestion that the Union should be called the United State of Gwalior, Indore and Malwa (Madhya Bharat). Though this cumbrous title was put into the final covenant, the Union has always been known as 'Madhya Bharat'.

A prolonged discussion ensued regarding the constitution of the Council of Rulers and the election of the Rajpramukh and Uprajpramukh. It was decided that in the Council of Rulers every member should be entitled to that number of votes which was equal to the number of lakhs of population in his State. The Maharajah of Indore and his advisers were afraid that the weightage which Gwalior would thus obtain would enable the Maharajah of Gwalior not only to ensure for himself the Rajpramukhship in perpetuity, but also to use his votes to prevent the Maharajah of Indore from becoming the senior Uprajpramukh. In order to allay such fears, it was suggested by way of compromise that the present Maharajahs of Gwalior and Indore should be the Rajpramukh and senior Uprajpramukh respectively of the new Union and that they should hold office for life. It was agreed that in the election of the two junior Uprajpramukhs neither the Maharajah of Gwalior nor of Indore would exercise a vote. This seemed to me in the circumstances a reasonable solution of a difficult problem. The necessary changes were made in the covenant.

Much time was taken in discussing the privy purse. It was found

30

quite impossible to find a solution on the basis of the maximum figure of Rs 10 lakhs so far as the two major States of Gwalior and Indore were concerned. The Maharajah of Gwalior was then taking Rs 32 lakhs as his privy purse and the Maharajah of Indore Rs 18 lakhs, both these amounts having been already agreed to by the legislatures of the States concerned. The two Maharajahs put forward their claims that, since they were merging their viable States voluntarily, they should not be treated less favourably in the matter of their privy purse than States of similar status which were standing out, and whose privy purses had been fixed by popular legislatures. The rulers put forward the plea that their privy purses should not be cut down merely because they were joining the Union. After a great deal of discussion the privy purse of the Maharajah of Gwalior was fixed at Rs 25 lakhs and that of the Maharajah of Indore at Rs 15 lakhs. In agreeing to these amounts, I had in mind the fact that the Maharajah of Baroda at any rate was drawing much more than Rs 25 lakhs at the time. These decisions were finally accepted by the Maharajahs as well as by their respective ministers who had all along been giving them considerable backing.

In view of the fact that the privy purses had been fixed at a figure higher than the basic maximum, I insisted that the allowances for the Rajpramukh and the senior Uprajpramukh should be fixed at a lower figure. After some discussion they agreed that the Rajpramukh and the senior Uprajpramukh should each receive a consolidated allowance of Rs 2½ lakhs per annum. I made it clear that the higher privy purses would be applicable only to the present Maharajahs and not to their successors, in whose case the Government of India would not guarantee a privy purse of more than Rs 10 lakhs each per annum.

In regard to the other rulers, the Eastern States formula was accepted, so that there was not much difficulty in calculating and fixing their privy purses. The total privy purse of all the rulers of the Union came finally to Rs 59,67,750.

Having settled the privy purses and the relative positions of the Maharajahs of Gwalior and Indore, I turned to other problems. In some of the States there were areas where the population was predominantly Bhil. The Bhils are an aboriginal race and extremely backward. They are very excitable and it would be risky to entrust them to the care of an inexperienced democratic government. It was therefore decided to treat the regions where more than fifty per cent of the population were Bhils as scheduled areas, and to

confer the authority to make laws for the peace and good government of these areas on the Rajpramukh, subject to the control of the
Government of India. These areas were specified in Schedule II
of the covenant.

The peculiar feature of Gwalior, as of almost all the Central India
and Rajasthan States as well as Hyderabad, was the existence of a
feudal system known as the *jagirdari* system, a legacy of the past.
Under this system, the land revenue of a territory was assigned to a
chief or a noble, known as the *jagirdar*, to support troops, police and for
specified service. Ownership of these lands was hereditary subject
to recognition by the ruler. These *jagirdars* exercised considerable
revenue, police and judicial powers. They were virtually States
within the State.

In March 1921 the Government of India had restored to the Gwalior Durbar suzerain rights over certain landholders and *tankadars* to
whom the British Government in the earlier part of the nineteenth
century had guaranteed in perpetuity certain estates and allowances. This restoration affected forty-three estates. As a result of this
settlement the Gwalior Durbar granted new perpetual *sanads* to these
forty-three holders. At the time of the integration, the right to resume
jagirs or to recognize succession to them was being exercised by
the Maharajah of Gwalior. Other rulers of Central India exercised
similar powers wherever there were *jagirs*. It was agreed that this
right should be vested in the Rajpramukh until other provision
was made by an Act of the legislature of the new Union. Such an
interim arrangement would make the transition easier.

The Maharajah of Gwalior was most anxious that provision should
be made in the covenant for the administration of the Gangajali
Fund. He considered it undesirable to place the entire corpus of the
Fund at the disposal of the new government of the Union without
some safeguard. The Maharajah was also anxious that provision
should be made in the covenant for the control of the investments of
the Gwalior State outside Gwalior by a Board of Trustees or
Directors under the guidance of the Governor of the Reserve Bank
of India. The necessary provisions were duly incorporated in the
covenant.

As mentioned earlier, immediately before the transfer of power
the Government of India had accepted from States, big and small,
accession on three subjects without any financial commitments. Since
then much water had flowed under the bridge. We had merged

the Orissa and Chattisgarh and the Deccan States with the provinces. We had taken over the Punjab Hill States and constituted them into a Chief Commissioner's province under the control of the Government of India. We had formed the Saurashtra, Matsya, Vindhya Pradesh and the first and second Rajasthan Unions. The position of these Unions *vis-à-vis* the Government of India was the same as that of the various covenanting States before integration. The relationship of these Unions with the Centre was still confined to three subjects.

We were now about to create the biggest of the Unions so far. Once the separate identity of the several States was obliterated and a new Union was created, the special position we had promised to the States would no longer apply. Whatever might have been the policy before integration, there was no reason why we should treat these Unions any differently from the provinces. The obligations of the Government of India to these Unions could not be less.

The main purpose behind the formation of these Unions was that the conditions obtaining in them should be equated as early as possible to those prevailing in the neighbouring provinces. It naturally followed that the Unions should be in a position analogous to that of the provinces in such vital matters as development of industries, factory legislation, labour welfare, regulation of mines, banking and insurance. As things stood, the States were very far behind and had a lot of leeway to make up. If this was to be done efficiently and speedily there was no alternative but that these Unions should concede to the Dominion Legislature the same power of legislation which it exercised *vis-à-vis* the provinces in regard to all federal and concurrent subjects.

I may mention that when we formed the Second Rajasthan Union (described in Chapter XIV), a permissive provision to this effect was included in the covenant. A permissive provision in regard to such a vital matter was not enough. Once the local ministries and legislatures acquired these powers, they would be loath to surrender them. Instead of the permissive provision adopted in the case of Rajasthan, a mandatory provision was introduced in the covenant of the Madhya Bharat Union to the effect that:

The Rajpramukh shall, as soon as practicable, and in any event not later than the fifteenth day of June 1948 execute on behalf of the United State an Instrument of Accession in accordance with the provisions of Section 6 of the Government of India Act, 1935, and in place of the

Instruments of Accession of the several covenanting States; and he shall by such Instrument accept as matters with respect to which the Dominion Legislature may make laws for the United State all the matters mentioned in List I and List III of the Seventh Schedule to the said Act, except the entries in List I relating to any tax or duty.

The rulers readily agreed, as they felt it would help to create a strong Central Government. There was some hesitation on the part of the ministers, but after some discussion they also agreed. I myself felt that this provision would ultimately knock the bottom out of the demand for separate constitutions for each Union.

The representatives of the States pleaded that, at the initial stage when the Union started to function, any big change in the financial position would throw the whole machinery out of gear. These Unions for the most part would need not only all their existing financial resources but also help from the Centre. Moreover, a provision had been included in the draft Constitution, under which the powers of the Centre in regard to the levy of taxes would be regulated by agreement having effect for a period of ten years from the commencement of the new Constitution. The draft Constitution had also provided for the appointment of a Finance Commission to enquire into and report upon the financial relations between the Centre and the units. It was therefore urged by the popular leaders that the Central Government would be prejudging the whole issue if they were to ask for the accession of the Union on matters relating to taxation. The arguments appeared to be cogent. The taxation powers were accordingly kept with the new Union.

As events in regard to the States were moving rather fast, this far-reaching provision in the Madhya Bharat covenant did not attract much public notice. But as soon as the news appeared in the papers, the late N. Gopalaswami Aiyangar (then Minister for Transport) rang me up to say that this provision revolutionized the entire concept of the relationship between the Centre and the States, and was as important as the formation of the Union itself. This Article was subsequently applied to other Unions by supplementary covenants.

There was another peculiar provision, necessitated by the rivalry between the two States, which I was obliged to include in the covenant. Both the Maharajah of Indore and his ministers were of the opinion that if the Maharajah of Gwalior became the Rajpramukh and if there was no provision in the covenant for consultation between the two Maharajahs, the interests of Indore were likely to suffer. I argued that such a provision was unnecessary, because the States Ministry would be there to see that the interests of every component part of the new Union were fully safeguarded. They pressed, however, for a specific provision. An addition was made in the covenant that 'the Rajpramukh may from time to time consult the senior Vice-President in important matters connected with the administration of the United State.'

The setting up of a Constituent Assembly which would also be the interim legislature did not involve much trouble. It was agreed that the Constituent Assembly should consist of 75 members, of whom 40 would be elected by the members of the Gwalior legislature, 15 by the members of the Indore legislature, and 20 by an electoral college representative of the other States to be constituted by the Rajpramukh in consultation with the Government of India.

As an interim arrangement, the Rajpramukh was empowered to promulgate ordinances for the peace and good government of the Union or any part thereof, which would have the like force of law as an Act passed by the interim legislative assembly.

It was strongly urged on behalf of the Maharajahs of Gwalior and Indore that they should be allowed to exercise their personal powers of suspension, remission, or commutation of death sentences, in respect of any person who might have been, or should hereafter be, sentenced to death for a capital offence committed within the territories of Gwalior or Indore. This was a small concession to the personal sentiments of these two Maharajahs and one which would not in any way militate against the complete integration of their States. The proposal was agreed to.

The future relations between Gwalior and Indore depended largely on the choice of the capital. The Maharajah of Gwalior, backed by his ministers, pressed the claims of Gwalior. The Maharajah of Indore along with his ministers insisted on Indore. In the end we decided that the summer capital should be at Indore and the winter capital at Gwalior. The controversy over the question of the capital is not yet settled; but for the time being at any rate, both parties have accepted Nehru's award that the capital shall be at Gwalior for six-and-a-half months and at Indore for five-and-a-half months.

The covenant was signed by practically all the rulers on 22 April 1948. There remained only a few estates and these were subsequently integrated by means of agreements between the Chiefs concerned and the Rajpramukh.

The Madhya Bharat Union, the largest we had formed up to that time, comprising an area of nearly 47,000 square miles, with a population of over 70 lakhs and a revenue of about Rs 8 crores, was inaugurated by Nehru on 28 May 1948.

XII

PATIALA AND THE EAST PUNJAB STATES UNION

THE States in East Punjab were six in number. Four of them, namely Patiala, Nabha, Jind and Faridkot were Sikh States. The first three were known as Phulkian States by virtue of a common ancestor, Phul. Phul was descended from Baryam, to whom Emperor Babur in 1526 had granted the *chaudrayat* (office of revenue collector) of the waste country to the south-west of Delhi. Phul received a *firman* from Emperor Shah Jahan continuing to him this office. From his eldest son descended the families of Nabha and Jind and from his second the Patiala family. The Faridkot family, which was founded in the middle of the sixteenth century sprang from the same stock as the Phulkian chiefs. These four Sikh States were under the suzerainty of Maharajah Ranjit Singh, but by the Treaty of Amritsar of 1809 they came under British protection.

The remaining two States were Kapurthala and Malerkotla. The Kapurthala rulers belonged to the Ahluwalia family. The real founder of the family was Rajah Jessa Singh, a contemporary of Nadir Shah. The Malerkotla rulers were Sherwani Afghans who traced their descent from Sheikh Sadruddin, who had received a gift of sixty-eight villages near Ludhiana in East Punjab when he married the daughter of Sultan Bahlol Lodi.

These States lay in three separate blocks. The main block comprising the territories of Patiala, Nabha, Jind, Malerkotla and Faridkot was in the centre of East Punjab and was fairly compact. Kapurthala State, composed of two enclaves in the Jullunder district, was in the north of East Punjab. The outlying districts of Narnaul, Dadri and Bawal, which formed parts of Patiala, Jind and Nabha States respectively, lay within the geographical orbit of the southern districts of

East Punjab. There were also islands of Patiala State in what is now Himachal Pradesh.

Before partition the Sikhs constituted the majority community in Faridkot; the Muslims in Kapurthala, and the Hindus in Jind. In Patiala the Sikhs formed, according to the census of 1941, 47.3 per cent of the total population. The partition and the consequent two-way migration materially affected the population ratio in these States. In Patiala especially there was a rise in the ratio of Sikhs because of the large influx into the State of refugees belonging to that community.

The first reaction of the Sikhs to the announcement of partition was one of bewilderment. Though their leaders had accepted the June 3rd Plan, they never realized that they would be driven away from the canal colonies in West Punjab to the development of which their labour had so greatly contributed. Nor could they have imagined the magnitude of the suffering and privations which the partition would entail. The Sikhs are a compact community, whose interests were mainly concentrated in what had been the united Punjab. Most of their important shrines are in the territories which now form part of Pakistan. Although numerically a minority, they had virtually held the balance in the politics of undivided Punjab. Now that their homeland was partitioned and they felt they had lost everything, they set about planning for their future. When some of the Sikh leaders — mainly those having pro-Akali sympathies — saw that States could be merged with neighbouring provinces, they sponsored a plan for merging the Punjab States with East Punjab. The chief exponent of this idea was Giani Kartar Singh.

On the other hand, Nationalist Sikh opinion (which was not how-ever very vocal) was in favour of a separate Union of all the Punjab States. Its leader was Jathedar Udham Singh Nagoke, who was particularly opposed to the merger of these States in East Punjab. The Rajah of Faridkot, supported by some Akali Sikh leaders, was toying with the idea of a Union of Faridkot, Jind, Kapurthala and Nabha — excluding Patiala, in the hope that he would be enabled to play a decisive part in Sikh politics. But Jathedar Udham Singh Nagoke was definitely against the formation of any Union which did not include Patiala. What he favoured was a separate Union of *all* the Punjab States. Such a Union, he thought, would operate as a stabilizing factor in Sikh politics, which had at the time became vitiated by a variety of personal factors.

31

While informal discussions were taking place in regard to the future of the Punjab States, trouble arose between the Rajah of Farid-kot and the States People's Conference, the President of which was Sheikh Abdullah. The Rajah's alleged ill-treatment of political prisoners and of Muslim evacuees induced the States Ministry to intervene. I discussed the situation with Sardar and, with his appro-val, approached Lord Mountbatten. Lord Mountbatten suggested that, before we took any action against the Rajah of Faridkot, it would be better to consult a few of the leading rulers. Accordingly, a meeting of the Maharajahs of Gwalior, Bikaner and Patiala and the Jam Saheb of Nawanagar was held, at which Lord Mountbatten presided. The consensus of opinion among the rulers was that the administration of the State should be taken over by the Government of India. In the conditions prevailing in the country at the time, the Rajah of Faridkot had no choice but to agree. The administration was taken over the next day.

There was an interesting interlude to this episode. We had asked the Maharajah of Gwalior at short notice to come to Delhi to attend the rulers' meeting and, since he had no transport available at the time, we sent a plane for him to Gwalior. It appears that he grew nervous at this sudden and abrupt summons. Stories of the compli-city of certain rulers in the assassination of Gandhiji were very much in the air; the Maharajah of Alwar had already been served with notice not to leave the confines of Delhi. The Maharajah of Gwalior told us that he had bidden sad good-bye to his wife and friends before getting into the plane. All of us had a hearty laugh over this; but it goes to show the state of tension in the country at the time.

As regards other Punjab State rulers, the Maharajah of Jind had no interest in political affairs. At the time of the integration, the Maharajah of Kapurthala was a very old man indeed; he died a year or so after the formation of the new Union. The Maharajah of Nabha had always been dominated by people around him and was mainly concerned with *shikar* and similar pursuits. The Nawab of Maler-kotla was a man of undoubtedly pleasant manners; all the same, I could not dispel the feeling that he was one of those whose attitude towards life was governed largely by self-interest.

The Maharajah of Patiala was of course the most important of the rulers in this area. The house of Patiala enjoyed the distinction of having been blessed by the tenth Sikh Guru as his own. The area, population and revenue of Patiala State exceeded those of all the rest of the East Punjab States put together. The Maharajah had rendered great service to the nation by standing solidly against the manoeuvres of the group of rulers who were anxious to evolve a 'Third Force' out of the States.

We were watching the Sikh political situation both in East Punjab and in the Punjab States. The demand for the amalgamation of the Punjab States and the new State of Himachal Pradesh with East Punjab was gathering momentum among the Sikhs. It was time, I felt, that the Government of India stepped in. I went to Sardar to discuss the situation. He was then convalescing at Dehra Dun after his heart attack. He was, of course, fully acquainted with the seesaw game of Sikh politics. There were four alternatives before us. Firstly, we could amalgamate Himachal Pradesh and the East Punjab States with East Punjab, leaving out Patiala which had been declared a viable unit. Secondly, we could amalgamate Patiala together with Himachal Pradesh and the East Punjab States with the province. Thirdly, we could leave Himachal Pradesh and Patiala alone and amalgamate the States of Kapurthala, Nabha, Jind, Malerkotla and Faridkot into a single Union. Fourthly, we could integrate all the Punjab States, including Patiala, into one Union. So far as the first two alternatives were concerned, we had to take note of the fact that, when we formed Himachal Pradesh, we had turned down the demand of the rulers and of some of the Prajamandal leaders of that area that the Punjab Hill States should be constituted into a Union on the Saurashtra model. This we did on the ground that such a Union lacked the resources to develop into a self-reliant unit. At the same time, we agreed to keep it as a separate centrally-administered unit until it could be given greater autonomy. The people of this hill area had expressed lively concern at the prospect of throwing in their lot with the people of the plains. We should therefore have to leave Himachal Pradesh alone. The merger of the main block of the Punjab States with the province of East Punjab was not a practical proposition at the time. The two-way migration had imposed on the province a strain which had reached breaking point; the administrative machinery was hard pressed between the maintenance of law and order and the problem of refugees; until the stress of partition on the political as well as administrative set-up of the province eased, it seemed best not to amalgamate any territories with East Punjab. The province must be given time to reorganize and stabilize its own administration and politics. Sardar agreed that in the circumstances we should keep East Punjab, Himachal Pradesh and the East Punjab States as three separate administrative units.

If the East Punjab States had to be kept as a separate unit, how were we to set about the business? The formation of a Union of these States without Patiala was not feasible. They had an area of 3,693 square miles, a population of about fourteen lakhs and an annual revenue of a little less than Rs 2 crores. The revenue figure was based on the inflated income of the war years and there was no doubt that it would fall considerably in normal times. From the point of view of resources, such a Union could not survive for long. Moreover, these States were separated from one another by intervening portions of East Punjab and Patiala.

In dealing with these States we had to take two more important factors into account. The States were so near the border that from the point of view of defence it was imperative that they should be capable of producing a strong combination, administratively efficient and financially stable. Besides, Sikh politics were in so fluid a state that we felt that, until they became crystallized, there was immediate need for a Union of all the Punjab States under the control of the Government of India.

My task was to convince the Maharajah of Patiala where his interests lay. I put all the facts before him. I told him that unless he joined the Union, our choice would be between accepting the Union of the other States or merging them all with East Punjab. In either event, it would be difficult for Patiala to continue in isolation for very long. The Maharajah's original plan had been to draw the smaller States closer to his own by making arrangements with them on a basis of affiliation. But we were not prepared to entertain any proposal which would perpetuate the separate existence of the smaller States. Somewhat earlier, a scheme had been presented to the States Ministry, on his behalf, suggesting the amalgamation of the Punjab States, other than Patiala, into one State and a union of this State and the State of Patiala on a federal basis for certain essential purposes. I explained the difficulties involved in this arrangement *vis-à-vis* the two States and their relationship with the Central Government. In the end, this impracticable scheme was dropped.

By this time we had formed Vindhya Pradesh and Madhya Bharat, and the Maharajahs of viable States like Gwalior, Indore and Rewa had agreed to pool their sovereignties with those of their

8. Lord Mountbatten in conversation with Sardar during his illness.

9. Sardar having discussions with Sheikh Abdullah and Bakshi Ghulam Mahommed during his visit to Kashmir early in November 1947.

10. The rulers of Patiala and the East Punjab States with author.

11. The author signing the Patiala and East Punjab States Union covenant.

12. Sardar inaugurating the Patiala and East Punjab States Union by swearing-in the Maharajah of Patiala as Rajpramukh.

13. Sardar leaving the Durbar Hall after inaugurating the Rajasthan Union.
On the right is the Maharajah of Jaipur, on the left the Maharajah of Kotah.

neighbours. I advised the Maharajah of Patiala to emulate their example.

In the course of our talks, the Maharajah more than once expressed to me the desirability of properly canalizing Sikh politics. I suggested to him that a separate Union of the Punjab States would satisfy the legitimate aspirations of reasonable elements in the Sikh community and also afford them an opportunity to mobilize their activities on constructive and non-communal lines. It seemed to me that, once the Congress-Nationalist Sikh coalition was well established in the Union of the Punjab States, it was bound ultimately to affect the politics of East Punjab. The Maharajah finally shared my view and accepted the principle of a Union of the Punjab States including Patiala.

I then went to Dehra Dun and gave Sardar the gist of my talk with the Maharajah. Sardar was delighted with the idea of a Union of the East Punjab States and told me to discuss the details with the rulers and their advisers. I met first the Maharajah of Patiala. His advisers were anxious that the Maharajah should not only be made the Raj-pramukh for life but that this position should be guaranteed to his successors. I assured them that the Government of India were fully cognizant of the importance of the position of Patiala among the East Punjab States and that there could be no question of denying the Maharajah his legitimate place. But it was not possible to confer an hereditary Rajpramukhship on the house of Patiala. The Maha-rajah thereupon asked that a provision should be made in the cove-nant that, for the purpose of the election of the Rajpramukh, the rulers should have votes proportionate to the population of their States. He contended that such a provision had been made in the covenant for the formation of Madhya Bharat, in spite of the fact that in the Maharajah of Indore the Maharajah of Gwalior had a close second. There was no one amongst the rulers of the East Pun-jab States to challenge his position and he thought therefore that there was no reason why he should be treated differently in this respect from the Maharajah of Gwalior. I promised to discuss the position with the other rulers.

Another demand put forward by the Maharajah was that, in order to satisfy the local patriotism of the people of Patiala, the Union of the East Punjab States should be named 'the Patiala Union'. I told him that this suggestion would probably not find favour with the majority of the other rulers, but I agreed to lay this proposal also before them.

Further points urged on his behalf included the continuance of his prerogative to suspend, remit or commute death sentences in respect of capital offences committed in the territories of Patiala, as had been conceded to the Maharajahs of Gwalior and Indore in the covenant of Madhya Bharat, and the vesting of powers in the Rajpramukh corresponding to those assigned to the Rajpramukh of that Union.

With regard to the privy purse, too, the Maharajah wished to be treated in the same way as the Maharajahs of Gwalior and Indore. I promised sympathetic consideration. At the time of the signing of the covenant, his privy purse had not been fixed; so it was provided that should the sum fixed be higher than Rs 10 lakhs, such sum would be payable only to the present ruler. The amount was subsequently fixed at Rs 17 lakhs.

On 2 May there was a meeting with the remaining rulers. There was considerable opposition to the proposals that the Union should be called the Patiala Union, and that the Maharajah of Patiala should be given voting strength according to the population of his State. After prolonged discussion, certain adjustments were made. It was agreed that, for the purpose of election of the Rajpramukh, the rulers of the Union should each have votes equal in number to the lakhs of population in their States. The Maharajahs of Patiala and Kapurthala were to be the first Rajpramukh and Uprajpramukh respectively and were to hold office for life. The Maharajah of Patiala would not exercise his votes in the election of the Uprajpramukh.

The Union was tentatively to be called the Patiala and East Punjab States Union (PEPSU for short) till such time as the Constituent Assembly of the Union should adopt a more suitable title.

In addition to the six major States of Patiala, Jind, Nabha, Faridkot, Malerkotla and Kapurthala, there were two non-salute States, Kalsia and Nalagarh, and a demand was put forward that they also should be allowed to join the Union. Kalsia State, though formerly included in the Punjab Hill States Agency, had nothing in common with the Hill States. Much of its territory was contiguous to Patiala and the Ambala district of the Punjab. Moreover, the Maharajah of Patiala had been appointed Regent for the minor ruler by the Crown Representative and as such he urged that Kalsia should be integrated with the new Union and not be merged with East Punjab. The State was allowed to join the Union. The case of Nalagarh was almost analogous. It had been affiliated with Patiala for administrative purposes and this arrangement had been operative for the previous two years. Nalagarh was also allowed to join the new Union.

On 5 May the covenant was signed by the rulers of all the eight States, the Maharajah of Patiala signing also on behalf of the minor ruler of Kalsia.

Before the covenant was actually signed, Giani Kartar Singh had come to me to advocate the merger of these States with East Punjab. This was a view also shared by Sardar Baldev Singh, who was Defence Minister at the time. I explained the policy of the States Ministry in detail to Giani Kartar Singh. I pointed out to him, firstly, that in view of the stress and strain to which East Punjab was subject at the time it would be most undesirable to burden that province with additional territory. It would take some time for the administration and politics of East Punjab to become stabilized. Further, the Government of India felt a special responsibility to ensure that these States, particularly as they were border States, should be organized on proper and efficient lines. The politics of East Punjab, as well as of these States, were in a state of flux. While the communities concerned had every right to safeguard their own particular interests, this should not be to the detriment of the country as a whole. Until, therefore, a firm and lasting position was established in which there was a clear understanding and amity between the important sections, it would be safer to keep the Punjab States as a separate entity. Giani Kartar Singh was apparently satisfied with this explanation. When the covenant was signed, the decision was applauded by the Nationalist Sikhs, as well as by Akali leaders including Master Tara Singh and Giani Kartar Singh.

The inauguration of the Union was fixed to take place at Patiala on 15 July 1948. Sardar and I reached Patiala on the 14th and I immediately started negotiations for the formation of a ministry. The talks went on without interruption till the next morning. The problem presented serious difficulties. The Prajamandal in these States represented the counterpart of the Congress organization in the provinces and was no stronger than its counterparts in other States. In most of the Indian States these orgnizations had not struck deep roots. The main difficulty in this Union was that the Prajamandal was up against the Akali Dal, a communal body which claimed to represent the majority of the Sikh community. The principal drawback of the Prajamandal was that the Sikh representatives in its fold had no adequate political stature and influence. In addition, there had come into existence, a little before the formation of the Union, a third organization called the Lok Sewa Sabha, which had the blessing of Jathedar Udham Singh Nagoke.

The leaders of the Prajamandal believed that once democracy was ushered into PEPSU no one but the head of their organization could be called upon to form the cabinet. Now, such a course would only have led to communal tension. The tendency of the Sikhs had been to regard the Prajamandal as a Hindu organization. They also cherished a strong sentiment that, as PEPSU was the only Sikh majority unit, it should have a Sikh Premier. As a consequence, we felt that our endeavour should be to form a composite ministry representative of the Congress, the Lok Sewa Sabha and the Akali Dal. The formula which I offered to the three parties to start with was four seats for the Congress, two for the Lok Sewa Sabha and two for the Akalis, with a neutral Sikh nominated by Sardar as Premier. The first of the parties to decline to join the government was the Akali Dal which, apart from the question of its relative representation, declined to give an undertaking that its representatives would eschew communal politics if they were invited to join the government. This was a clear repudiation of its earlier assurance that its representatives would be prepared to act on non-communal lines.

An effort was then made to form a government out of the Congress and the Lok Sewa Sabha, the former being now offered four seats in a cabinet of seven which was to include a neutral Premier. Because of the withdrawal of the Akali Dal, the Lok Sewa Sabha asked for increased representation, but this was not agreed to. The principal hurdle proved to be the selection of the Premier. Out of several names that were considered, the Lok Sewa Sabha supported that of Sardar Gyan Singh Rarewala, who was at that time in the service of Patiala State. The Congress representatives also considered him suitable; but after having agreed, they subsequently declined to accept him because he happened to be an official—a fact which was known to them before. The Congress representatives overplayed their hand. They felt that if they stuck to their guns they would get what they demanded, which was that the formation of the ministry should be entrusted solely to the leader of the local Prajamandal. This led to the breakdown of the negotiations.

Early next morning I reported to Sardar the failure of my efforts.

The only course left was to inaugurate the Union by swearing in the Rajpramukh. This was done formally by Sardar that day.

Another effort to form a ministry was made in August 1948. As this also failed, an official caretaker government was set up with Sardar Gyan Singh Rarewala as the Premier. This was only a stop-gap arrangement. Formal consultations with the parties continued. Ultimately, early in 1949, a ministry was set up consisting of seven members representative of the various parties. Sardar Gyan Singh Rarewala continued to be the Premier.

Patiala and the East Punjab States Union comprises an area of 10,099 square miles, with a population of 34,24,060 and an annual revenue of a little over Rs 5 crores.

XIII

RAJASTHAN

THE RAJPUTS have contributed a glorious and memorable chapter to the early history of India. Before the Muslim invasion, the whole of northern and central India was parcelled among various Rajput clans. Against the Muslim invaders the Rajputs put up a heroic resistance. Their race has become synonymous in the Indian mind with chivalry.

Akbar led a series of campaigns against the Rajput rulers. He was able ultimately to subdue most of them, Udaipur (or Mewar) being the only kingdom which resisted Moghul domination. Akbar realized however that without the co-operation of the Hindus, especially the Rajputs, he could not build up an enduring empire in India. By a policy of religious toleration and respect for their pride and sentiment he won over the Rajputs. During his time and that of his two successors the Rajputs in fact played a big part in the consolidation of the Moghul Empire. Akbar's wise policy was not followed by Aurangzeb — which was one of the reasons for the final disintegration of the Moghul Empire.

In the wake of the decline of the Moghul Empire, the Mahrattas appeared on the scene. The Rajput rulers were compelled to become tributary either to the Scindia or to the Holkar. By the end of the eighteenth century, ravaged by the Mahrattas, the Pindaris and the Pathans, the Rajput States were reduced to abject helplessness. The Mahrattas had failed to utilize the Rajputs in the consolidation of their empire; but Lord Hastings realized the immense strategic and political advantages which would accrue from their alliance. After the defeat of the Mahrattas in the Third Mahratta War, the British Government freed the Rajput States from the suzerainty of the Scindia and the Holkar and took them under their protection. Colonel Tod was appointed to settle the problems of Rajasthan.

Tod has a great place in British Indian history. If Sir John Malcolm was responsible for the settlement of Central India, Tod did an equally fine job in Rajasthan. Incidentally, Tod has left behind a history of Rajasthan which will ever remain a classic.

The Rajputana States (the present Rajasthan) comprised 19 salute States and 3 non-salute States. Except for the tiny island of British Indian territory, Ajmer Merwara, the States formed one solid block of territory. The integration of these States was done in five stages. The first was the formation of the Matsya Union, which embraced the four States of Alwar, Bharatpur, Dholpur and Karauli. The second was the formation of the first Rajasthan Union with Banswara, Bundi, Dungarpur, Jhalawar, Kishengarh, Kotah, Partabgarh, Shahpura and Tonk. The third was the inclusion of Udaipur in the first Rajasthan Union. The fourth was the creation of Greater Rajasthan by the inclusion of the remaining Rajput States of Jaipur, Jodhpur, Bikaner and Jaisalmer; and the fifth stage was the incorporation of the Matsya Union with Greater Rajasthan.

We will deal first with the Matsya Union, which embraced the four States of Alwar, Bharatpur, Dholpur and Karauli.

Alwar was founded by Rao Pratap Singh of Macheri, a descendant of Raja Udai Karan, who ruled Jaipur in the fourteenth century. The ruling family comes from Kachwaha Rajputs of the Naruka sub-clan. In 1803 the Maharao Raja accepted the protection of the British Government, with whom he concluded a treaty of offensive and defensive alliance.

In 1937 Maharajah Sir Jeysinhji was asked by the Viceroy to stay out of the State; he died in Paris later in the year, leaving no issue. The present Maharajah Sir Tej Sinhji Bahadur was adopted in 1937.

The rulers of Bharatpur claim originally to have been Yadav Rajputs, the descendants of Sri Krishna. Sue, a Yadav Rajput, is said to have migrated from Bayana to the Dig jungles and to have founded the village of Sinsini, named after Sinsina the tutelary deity. The story is that Balchand, a descendant of Sue, having no issue by his wife took unto himself a Jat woman and by her had sons who, not being recognized by the Rajputs as Rajputs, took the name of Sinsinwar from their paternal village; and that from them sprang the famous Sinsinwar Jats. The first Jat of this stock of any historical importance was Brij, a noted freebooter during the latter half of the seventeenth century. Rajaram, a nephew of Brij, was the first to establish himself at Jatoli Thun where he made himself master of forty villages. Subsequently Chauraman, the son of Brij, carved out a State for himself which was the beginning of the Bharatpur State. It was in the reign of Maharajah Surajmal (1755-63) that Bharatpur reached the zenith of its glory. Surajmal left behind a prosperous State and a formidable army. Bharatpur is noted for its famous fort which once withstood a siege by General Lake. The British first fought Bharatpur in 1805, but it was only in 1826 that the State finally came under their control. The present Maharajah Brijendra Singh succeeded to the *gaddi* in March 1929 at the age of eleven and was invested with ruling powers in October 1939.

The ruling family of Dholpur belongs to the Deswali tribe of Jats who in the eleventh century acquired lands south of Alwar. They rose to honour under the Tonwar dynasty of Delhi and settled at Bamrali, from which place they took their family name. After an occupation of nearly two hundred years, they were driven from Bamrali by the Subedar of Agra. They migrated first to Gwalior and then to Gohad, which was assigned to them in 1449 by Raja Man Singh of Gwalior. The head of the house, Surjan Deo, then assumed the title of Rana. In 1805, after various vicissitudes, the Rana was finally rescued by the British Government, who assigned to him the parganas of Dholpur, Bari and Rajakhera which constituted the State of Dholpur. The Maharajah at the time of integration was Sir Udai Bhan Sinjhi who had ascended the *gaddi* in 1911. He belonged to the old school and was a staunch advocate of the divine right of kings. He died in 1954 leaving no successor.

Karauli was a very small State, the ruling family of which belonged to the Jadon Rajput clan. It is said to have been established in 995. It had the usual ups and downs which had been the fate of every State in this area. In 1817 Karauli entered into subsidiary alliance with the British.

The aftermath of the partition and the subsequent communal holocaust had their reactions in both Alwar and Bharatpur. A troublesome Muslim sect, the Meos, had been a source of perpetual worry to the Government of Alwar. Shortly before the transfer of power the Meos became particularly active and there were communal disturbances which spread to the State of Bharatpur. The Premier of Alwar at the time was Dr N. B. Khare, at one time Congress Premier of the Central Provinces, subsequently a member of the Viceroy's Executive Council and later President of the Hindu

Mahasabha. Exaggerated accounts of his activities were reported to us. It was alleged that the Meos were being hounded out of the State, that mosques were being demolished and that Muslim burial grounds were being desecrated. A section of the press played up these allegations.

The communal situation in some of the border States was also causing anxiety. In October 1947 Sardar called a meeting of the representatives of the provincial and the State governments concerned. The Maharajahs of Alwar and Bharatpur and Dr Khare were also invited. At the meeting Sardar emphasized the paramount need for maintaining communal peace. Those who fanned the flames of communalism, he said, were the greatest enemies of the country. The representatives of the provinces and the States assured Sardar of their full support and co-operation. Dr Khare's attitude at the meeting, however, bore an air of resentment at the interference of the Government of India in the internal administration of Alwar.

The complaints against Alwar, as well as Bharatpur, subsequently increased. Some English friends of mine, who visited these two States told me that the Muslims were not safe and that they would be either exterminated or driven out of the States if the Government of India did not take immediate measures to protect them. I visited Alwar without the knowledge of the State authorities. Some of the reports given to me were certainly exaggerated; nevertheless, the communal situation in Alwar had very ugly possibilities and whatever action the State Government might take was likely to be misunderstood and misinterpreted. My personal view was that, in order to stabilize the position, Dr Khare should be replaced by a Premier of our own choice. I reported my impressions to Sardar.

The assassination of Gandhiji about this time led to a panic, in the midst of which any rumour was good enough to implicate anybody. It was alleged that Alwar had been an important training and propaganda centre for the R.S.S.[1] and that some of the conspirators responsible for the murder had been sheltered in the State. In view of Dr Khare's pronounced pro-Hindu bias, the allegations gained some credence. Sardar and I discussed the Alwar situation once more. In view of the communal tension in Alwar and of the allegations of complicity of the Alwar Government in Gandhiji's assassination, it was decided that the administration of the State should be taken

[1] Rashtriya Swayam Sevak Sangh, a well-organized and disciplined organization to propagate militant Hindu views.

over forthwith and that both the Maharajah and Dr Khare should be asked to stay in Delhi until an inquiry into the allegations was completed.

On 7 February 1948, I served the order on the Maharajah of Alwar. He was completely taken aback by the allegations and agreed to dispense with the services of Dr Khare. The latter was also ordered to remain in Delhi.

Mention has already been made about the alleged ill-treatment of Muslims in Bharatpur. There were also a few instances of looting of trains in the State territory. While we were considering what action should be taken, the Maharajah of Bharatpur accompanied by the Maharajah of Gwalior (who has been his friend since childhood) came to see me. The latter told me that the Maharajah of Bharatpur was completely at a loss to know what to do in the conditions prevailing in his State and wanted my advice. I suggested that, in the general state of panic, it was impossible for the Maharajah of Bharatpur—or for that matter anybody situated as he was, however much he might try—to keep his head above water. I advised that the best thing he could do was to hand over the administration of the State to the Government of India. The Maharajah of Bharatpur agreed and accordingly the administration of the State was taken over by the Government of India.

The result of the enquiry into the allegations against the Maharajah of Alwar and Dr Khare was that both were exonerated. An enquiry into similar allegations against the Maharajah of Bharatpur produced the same result; the Maharajah was completely exonerated. It may appear in retrospect that the action taken by the Government of India was unduly drastic; but it is certainly the case that our taking over the administration of Alwar and Bharatpur had a very steadying effect on the communal situation.

As regards the future, Sardar and I both felt that since Dholpur and Karauli were contiguous and had natural, racial and economic affinities with Alwar and Bharatpur, the four States should be integrated into a Union.

I invited the four rulers to Delhi on 27 February 1948 and put the proposal before them. They agreed. I made it clear in the course of the discussion that it might be necessary later on for this Union to join either Rajasthan or the United Provinces, as the Union by itself would not be financially self-supporting.

When I told K. M. Munshi of the prospect of forming a Union of these four States, he suggested that it should be called the Matsya Union, as this was the old name of this region to be found in the ancient books and in the *Mahabharata*. The rulers accepted this suggestion.

From the point of view of the relative importance of these States, the Maharajah of Alwar, or failing him the Maharajah of Bharatpur, should have been Rajpramukh. But because an enquiry was pending against the Maharajah of Alwar as well as the Maharajah of Bharatpur, I requested them both to stand down in favour of the Maharajah of Dholpur who was in any case the oldest of the four rulers. The Maharajah of Bharatpur readily agreed; but the Maharajah of Alwar acquiesced only after a good deal of argument and reluctance.

There was nothing special in the covenant of this Union; it followed generally the Saurashtra model. It was signed by the rulers on 28 February 1948. The Union was inaugurated on 18 March by N. V. Gadgil, then Minister for Works, Mines and Power. The new Union had an area of 7,589 square miles, a population of 18,37,994 and a revenue of Rs 183 lakhs.

Even at the time of the formation of the Matsya Union, informal talks were going on with some of the rulers of the smaller States in Rajputana with regard to their future. The States concerned were Banswara, Bundi, Dungarpur, Jhalawar, Kishengarh, Kotah, Partabgarh, Shahpura and Tonk.

The ruling families of Kotah and Bundi belong to the Hara clan of Rajputs and these two States, together with Jhalawar, constitute the tract called Haraoti. Kotah is an offshoot of Bundi and its divergence from the parent stem dates back to the early part of the seventeenth century when Madho Singh, second son of the then ruler of Bundi, acquired it by a direct and independent grant from Emperor Jehangir.

Jhalawar was created in 1838 out of a portion of the territories then belonging to Kotah.

The rulers of Dungarpur are Sisodia Rajputs and are an elder branch of the ruling family of Udaipur. One of the noted rulers of this family was Maharawal Dungar Singh, who founded the town of Dungarpur and made it his capital.

The rulers of Banswara belong to the Dungarpur family. In 1528 on the death of the ruler, his two sons broke apart, the elder succeeding to Dungarpur and the younger to Banswara.

The rulers of Partabgarh are also descended from the Udaipur ruling family. The town of Partabgarh was founded by Maharawat Partab Singh at the beginning of the eighteenth century.

In 1629, Emperor Shah Jahan granted the pargana of Phulia from the crown lands of Ajmer to Sujan Singh, a cadet of the Udaipur ruling family. This was the beginning of Shahpura State.

Tonk, the only Muslim State, was formed about the beginning of the nineteenth century by the famous Pathan predatory leader Amir Khan, the companion-in-arms of Jaswant Rao Holkar, who played so conspicuous a part in all the distractions which preceded the British settlement of Malwa. Amir Khan came into alliance with the British Government in 1817, when all his estates within the territories of the Holkar were permanently guaranteed to him by the Government.

The initiative for the formation of a Union of these States came from the rulers of Kotah, Dungarpur and Jhalawar. In fact, as early as 1946, after the Cabinet Mission plan had been announced, the Maharao of Kotah had convened a conference of ministers of some of the neighbouring States with a view to exploring the possibility of a Union. The conference of ministers came to the conclusion that their States were vulnerable at many points, that they had no kind of future and that only by pooling their sovereignties could they survive. The Maharao of Kotah espoused this scheme energetically and it was by no means his fault that some of the other rulers did not at the time fall into line.

Equally progressive was the Maharaj Rana of Jhalawar. Realizing that his small State of 813 square miles had no future at all, he was anxious to hand it over to the Government of India and seek a career for himself. After handing over his State he joined the Indian Foreign Service.

The views of these two rulers were shared by the Maharajah of Dungarpur.

The three rulers met me at Delhi on 3 March and we had a preliminary discussion. They were anxious that their States should be integrated to form a Union and welcomed my suggestion that Udaipur should also be invited to join.

The alternatives were either to unite these States with the States in Central India and Malwa and so to form a big Union, or to unite them with the south-east Rajputana States and to form a United State of Rajasthan. On both these alternatives the rulers as well as the representatives of the Congress organizations in these States were consulted. They stressed that the natural affinity of the States was more with Rajputana than with Malwa. With the exception of Banswara, Dungarpur and Partabgarh, where the populations were predominantly Bhil and the language of the majority of the people was Bhili, the language in the rest was generally Rajasthani, Malvi or Western Hindi. The rulers were all Rajputs and as such were strongly disinclined to merge their States with Malwa, where the Mahratta element was preponderant.

If Udaipur could be induced to join this Union, it would be a very satisfactory solution. I discussed the idea with S. V. Ramamurthy, then Dewan of Udaipur. Ramamurthy promptly suggested that all the States should merge in Udaipur. This suggestion was obviously unacceptable to the rulers as well as to the States Ministry. We could not countenance the idea of any single State swallowing up its smaller neighbours. It was decided therefore to go ahead with the proposal to form a Union of the States concerned and to leave Udaipur to come in later if it wished to do so. Even without Udaipur, these States had an area of 17,000 square miles, a population of nearly 24 lakhs and a total revenue of approximately Rs 2 crores.

On 4 March I again met the rulers of Bundi, Dungarpur, Jhalawar and Kotah and took up the draft covenant for discussion. The States to be included in the proposed Union did not of themselves form one compact bloc. Two of them, Kishengarh and Shahpura, were sandwiched between portions of Ajmer Merwara. My proposal was that these two States should be merged with that province. But the rulers and the local Congress representatives were so strongly opposed to the idea and so much in favour of joining the Union that I agreed to this. Tonk was another State that was cut up into two or three bits, one of which was in Malwa. It was agreed that while Tonk would join the new Union, the outlying areas of that State in Malwa should become part of the Madhya Bharat Union when that was formed.

It was decided that the Constituent Assembly of the new Union should have 24 elected representatives on the basis of one seat for every lakh of the population. It was argued that special interests, such as *jagirdars*, should have representation in this Assembly. I agreed that the Rajpramukh should be allowed to nominate four persons to represent such interests.

It was also decided that the rulers of Kotah, Bundi and Dungarpur should be deemed to have been elected by the Council of Rulers as the first Rajpramukh, Senior Uprajpramukh and Junior Uprajpramukh respectively and this decision was incorporated in the covenant.

The rulers present then signed the covenant; the other rulers did so in due course. I visited Kotah on 10 March and again on the 14th. After discussions with the Maharao of Kotah, it was decided that the Union should be inaugurated on 25 March and that the rulers of the covenanting States should make over their administration to the Rajpramukh before 15 April.

On 23 March I was informed that the Maharana of Udaipur was willing to come into the Union and I was requested to have the inauguration of the proposed Rajasthan Union postponed, pending the settlement of the terms regarding Udaipur's entry. I immediately got into touch with the Maharao of Kotah, who told me that all the arrangements for the inauguration ceremony on 25 March were complete, and that it would be extremely awkward if the function were postponed. It was therefore decided to go ahead with the inauguration of the Union, which was performed by N. V. Gadgil on 25 March 1948.

Three days after the inauguration ceremony I received official intimation that the Maharana of Udaipur had decided to join the Union.

The Udaipur ruling family is first in rank and dignity among the Rajput princes of India. According to tradition, the line was founded by Kanaka Sen, one of the descendants of Sri Rama, the hero of the *Ramayana*. No State in India put up a more heroic or prolonged resistance against the Muslims than Udaipur and it is the boast of the family that it never gave a daughter in marriage to any of the Muslim emperors. The family belongs to the Sisodia sect of the great Gehlot clan. The foundation of the Gehlot dynasty in Rajputana was laid by Bapa Rawal (ancestor of the present Maharana) who, being driven out of Idar by the Bhils and after wandering for some years over the wild country to the north of Udaipur, eventually established himself in Chitor and Mewar in 734. Since that time, with brief interruptions occasioned by the fortunes of war, Mewar continued in the possession of the present house.

Chitor was besieged and captured by the Muslims after great slaughter on no less than three occasions, by Ala-ud-din Khalji in 1303, by Bahadur Shah of Gujarat in 1534 and by Akbar in 1567; but each time the Udaipur house succeeded in regaining possession.

In the reign of Rana Udai Singh, when Chitor was sacked for the third time, the Maharana retired to the valley of the Girwa in the Aravali Hills, where he founded the city of Udaipur. Udai Singh survived the loss of Chitor by only four years. He was succeeded in 1572 by his famous son, Pratap, who disdained to submit to the conqueror. After repeated defeats, Pratap was about to fly into the desert towards Sind when fortune suddenly turned in his favour. With financial aid supplied by his minister, he was able to collect his adherents, and he surprised and annihilated the imperial Moghul forces at Dawair. He followed up his success with such energy and speed that, after a short campaign, he recovered nearly all Mewar, of which he remained in undisputed possession until his death. The State enjoyed tranquillity for some years thereafter; but in 1806 Udaipur again sustained severe reverses and was laid waste by the armies of the Scindia, the Holkar and Amir Khan and by many hordes of Pindari plunderers. To such distress was the Maharana reduced that he was dependent for his maintenance on the bounty of Zalim Singh, the famous Regent of Kotah, who gave him an allowance of Rs 1,000 a month. It was in this abject state that Maharana Bhim Singh was found in 1818, when the British Government rescued and rehabilitated him and extended their protection to the State. The administration and finances of the State were subsequently reorganized by the British. The present ruler,[1] Maharajadhiraja Maharana Sir Bhupal Singhji Bahadur, succeeded to the *gaddi* on 24 May 1930. The Maharana has no issue and has adopted a son.

On 28 March I began discussions with S. V. Ramamurthy regarding the entry of Udaipur into the Rajasthan Union. Ramamurthy desired that the Maharana should be the permanent hereditary Rajpramukh. I pointed out that I could not agree to the proposal but that I would consent to his being Rajpramukh for life. Ramamurthy then raised the question of the privy purse and asked that the Maharana should continue to receive the Rs 20 lakhs which he was taking at the time. I replied that I could not agree to fix the privy purse at a figure higher than Rs 10 lakhs but observed that a separate provision could be made with regard to the expenditure which the Maharana was in the habit of incurring for traditional, charitable and religious purposes. His allowances as Rajpramukh could also be fixed at a suitable figure.

[1] Since deceased.

Ramamurthy suggested that the name of the Union should be reminiscent of Mewar. I expressed my willingness to agree to any name that was acceptable to all the rulers. Ramamurthy also wanted the capital of the Union to be at Udaipur. I pointed out that the final decision must rest with the Constituent Assembly of the new Union. In the meanwhile, it was possible to arrive at an interim arrangement which would satisfy both Udaipur and Kotah, the two big States in the Union.

The discussions with Ramamurthy were continued next day when the rulers of Kotah, Dungarpur and Jhalawar were also present. It was agreed that the Rajasthan Union should be reconstituted by the inclusion of Udaipur and that the existing covenant should be superseded by a fresh one. It was also decided that the rulers should elect the Maharana of Udaipur as Rajpramukh for life but that this privilege would not be extended to his successors.

In view of the sacrifice the Maharao of Kotah had made in relinquishing his position as Rajpramukh, the rulers agreed to elect him as the Senior Uprajpramukh. The rulers of Bundi and Dungarpur were to continue as Junior Uprajpramukhs of the reconstituted Union.

There was considerable discussion with regard to the location of the capital. The Maharao of Kotah stressed that if Udaipur was selected as the capital, Kotah should not be relegated to an unimportant position. I felt the force of the argument. Kotah was the next biggest town to Udaipur and whatever the quality of their internal administration, the States invariably kept their capitals equipped with all modern amenities. The States Ministry were anxious that these amenities should be improved, rather than lessened. If by choosing Udaipur as the capital the importance of Kotah was affected, it would naturally cause heart-burning among the people. Finally we came to an arrangement whereby the capital of the new Government would be at Udaipur, but the legislature would hold at least one session every year at Kotah. The units of the Kotah State Forces would continue to remain in Kotah. The Forest School, the Police Training College and the Aeronautical College, as well as any other institutions which could conveniently be at Kotah, should be located there. It was also decided that in drawing up the administrative divisions of the new Union, one Commissioner's division should have its headquarters at Kotah.

The privy purse of the Maharana of Udaipur was fixed at Rs 10 lakhs. In addition, he would receive a sum of Rs 5 lakhs as his consolidated annual allowance as Rajpramukh, as well as a further sum of Rs 5 lakhs per annum for traditional, charitable and religious purposes.

S. V. Ramamurthy went back to Udaipur and acquainted the Maharana with the results of the discussions held at Delhi. On 1 April Sardar received the following letter from the Maharana:

My Prime Minister has reported to me the results of the discussions held in Delhi on the 28th and the 29th of March with Mr. V. P. Menon, Secretary of the States Ministry and the rulers of some of the States of Rajasthan. I agree to participate in the formation of the Rajasthan State on the lines reached during the discussions in Delhi. I have been prepared to take a lead in the unification of Rajputana. I am glad that with your support this is to be achieved in considerable measure.

After the Maharana of Udaipur had officially communicated his consent to join the Union, I invited all the other rulers concerned to Delhi on 10 April for a discussion of the draft covenant. The rulers of Kotah, Bundi, Dungarpur, Jhalawar, Partabgarh and Tonk were present. S. V. Ramamurthy represented Udaipur and Gokul Lal Asawa, the Premier of the existing Rajasthan Union, was also present. The draft covenant was discussed for two days. This covenant differed from the covenants of Saurashtra, Matsya and Vindhya Pradesh Unions in one important respect. In the Unions hitherto formed, the Rajpramukhs were asked as a measure of extra caution to execute a fresh Instrument acceding on the three subjects of defence, external affairs and communications. I thought that I would take the opportunity of including in the covenant of Rajasthan a permissive provision enabling the Rajpramukh to surrender other subjects from the federal and concurrent legislative lists for legislation by the Dominion Legislature. The rulers agreed to this provision. I may add that later, in the covenant of Madhya Bharat, a provision was included which made it obligatory on the Rajpramukh to accept all the subjects in both the federal and concurrent lists for legislation by the Dominion Legislature, excluding the entries relating to taxation and duties.

The covenant was finally approved on 11 April and signed by all the rulers present. In view of its political importance, the Union was inaugurated by Nehru on 18 April 1948. The Union had an area of 29,977 square miles, a population of 42,60,918 and an annual revenue of Rs 316 lakhs.

With the formation of the second Rajasthan Union only four Rajput States remained unintegrated, namely, Jaipur, Jodhpur, Bikaner, and Jaisalmer. The Maharajah of Jaipur was the head of the Kachwaha clan of Rajputs who claimed descent from Kush, a son of Sri Rama. The family flourished for eight hundred and fifty years at Narwar near Gwalior, but early in the twelfth century one Tej Karan carved out a small State near the present Jaipur and moved his capital thither. The State remained comparatively unimportant until the time of Mirza Raja Jai Singh, who was a famous general under the Moghuls. The present capital was founded by Maharajah Sawai Jai Singh in 1728 and is named after him. Jaipur suffered much from the Mahrattas, but further molestation ceased on the conclusion of a treaty with the British Government in 1818. The present Maharajah Sir Sawai Man Singhji Bahadur ascended the *gaddi* by adoption in 1922 at the early age of eleven years.

Jodhpur (or Marwar) is one of the three principal States of Rajputana. The Maharajah is the head of the Rathor clan of Rajputs. Offshoots of Jodhpur are the States of Bikaner and Kishengarh in Rajputana, Idar (now merged with Bombay) and Ratlam, Jhabua, Sitamau and Sailana now forming part of Madhya Bharat. Jodhpur State may be said to have been founded in 1459 when the seat of the government was transferred to the present capital; but a foothold was acquired in the thirteenth century when Mallani and the neighbouring tract was conquered by Siahji, a grandson of Jai Chand the last king of Kanauj, who planted the standard of the Rathors amidst the sand-hills of the Luni in 1212. Like other Rajput States, Jodhpur entered into subsidiary alliance with the British in 1818. At the time of the merger the Maharajah was Sir Hanwant Sinhji. He died in a plane accident in 1952.

The rulers of Bikaner are Rathor Rajputs. The State was founded in 1465 by Rao Bikaji, a son of Rao Jodhaji of Marwar, the founder of Jodhpur. On 9 March 1818 a treaty was concluded with the British Government. The State owes much of its prosperity to Maharajah Sir Ganga Singhji, who during his long reign of fifty-six years initiated and carried out many development projects. The Maharajah at the time of the merger was Sir Sadul Singhji, who had succeeded to the *gaddi* in 1942. He died in 1950 and was succeeded by his son Maharajah Karni Singh.

The ruling family of Jaisalmer are Jadon Bhati Rajputs and claim descent from the Yadav kings. The founder of the Jaisalmer family was one Deoraj, who was born about the middle of the tenth century and was the first Rawal. Jaisalmer, the present capital, was built in 1156 by Rawal Jaisal. The British Government concluded a subsidiary alliance with Jaisalmer in 1818.

The territories of these four States were compact blocks. Except for Jaisalmer, all of them were viable units according to the standards laid down by the Government of India. The rulers of Jaipur, Jodhpur and Bikaner were keen to preserve the identity of their States; but bigger States than theirs had been either merged with provinces or formed into Unions and it was difficult to leave them alone. We delayed taking action because we could not quite decide whether to merge these States with Rajasthan, or to integrate the border States of Jodhpur, Bikaner and Jaisalmer into a centrally administered area under a Chief Commissioner. These States had an extensive frontier with Pakistan and the boundary was, in sections, both unnatural and arbitrary. Considerable expense would be required to guard it and if these States were merged with Rajasthan, it would be a great strain on the latter's resources. Large areas of these three States were under-developed, and the communications were poor. Therefore it was obvious that the Government of India would have to help the States in their development projects. Both from the point of view of frontier security, and for the efficient tackling of the economic problems of the area, there was a strong case for the constitution of these States into a Chief Commissioner's province. We could then include Kutch in this province and thus practically the whole frontier with Pakistan would be under the direct control of the Government of India. This scheme however had more enemies than friends and ultimately, not without great regret, I had to give up the idea.

The alternative then was to integrate these four States into the Rajasthan Union. This was what Sardar favoured. He was expecting to visit Udaipur on 14 January 1949 and he wanted to take that opportunity of announcing the formation of the Greater Rajasthan Union. He asked me to get into touch with the rulers. On 11 January I went to Jaipur and discussed the question with the Maharajah and Sir V. T. Krishnamachari, the Dewan. The Maharajah said in the course of discussion that he was quite agreeable to the formation of the Union, provided it could be guaranteed that Jaipur would be the capital of the Union and that he would be the permanent hereditary Rajpramukh. I replied that these matters could be discussed when we came to details. My immediate purpose was to reach agreement with the rulers on the principle of integration of their States with Rajasthan. This would enable Sardar to make the announcement. I prepared a draft which was accepted by both the Maharajah and Sir V. T. Krishnamachari and the text was thereafter wired to the Maharajahs of Bikaner and Jodhpur. That same evening, the Maharajah of Jodhpur informed me of his acceptance of the announcement. I also received a telegram from the Maharajah of Bikaner agreeing in substance with the draft. On 12 January I left for Udaipur and had a discussion with the Maharana who also agreed in principle to the proposal.

On 14 January Sardar announced at a public meeting in Udaipur that the rulers of the four States of Jaipur, Jodhpur, Bikaner and Jaisalmer had agreed in principle to integrate their States with the Rajasthan Union. Thus, he said, Greater Rajasthan would soon be a reality, though the details had still to be worked out. This announcement was well received throughout the country.

We now started working on the details of the proposed Union and the provisions to be included in the covenant. Three sets of parties were concerned: the first being the Maharajahs of Jaipur, Jodhpur, Bikaner and Jaisalmer and their respective advisers; the second, the rulers of the existing Rajasthan Union; and the third, the popular leaders of Rajasthan particularly, Hiralal Sastri, Jai Narayan Vyas, Maniklal Varma and Gokulbhai Bhat. I had discussions with all of them, separately and jointly.

The first question raised was, who should be the head of the new Union? The popular leaders endorsed the selection of the Maharajah of Jaipur as Rajpramukh. The city of Jaipur was the obvious choice for the capital.

The Maharana of Udaipur was the seniormost ruler in the whole of Rajasthan and his position *vis-à-vis* the other rulers in Rajasthan was outstanding. The Maharana had pressed his claim to be selected as the Rajpramukh of the new Union, but he was not in good health and was unable to move about freely. On sentimental grounds, the rulers and the popular leaders suggested that he should be given a distinctive position which should not, however, prejudice the general administrative set-up of the Union. At first, it was suggested that he should be given the title of 'Maharajah Siromani,' but the Maharana did not consider this suitable and preferred that he should be called the Maharajpramukh. We saw no objection to this title. It was accordingly decided that he should be the Maharajpramukh for life but that this position and the allowances would cease with him. The Maharana was also assured that he would be included in the category of rulers entitled to a salute of 21 guns and that, on all ceremonial occasions, the Maharajah of Jaipur would voluntarily agree to yield precedence to him.

It was agreed that the rulers of Jodhpur and Kotah should be the Senior Uprajpramukhs and that the rulers of Bundi and Dungarpur should be the Junior Uprajpramukhs in the new Union; but they would hold office only for five years, whereas the Maharajah of Jaipur would be the Rajpramukh for life.

With regard to the privy purses of the rulers, it was suggested by the popular leaders that as the major States of Jaipur, Jodhpur and Bikaner were more or less on a par with Indore, whose Maharajah had been given a privy purse of Rs 15 lakhs plus an allowance of Rs 2½ lakhs as Uprajpramukh, they should be fixed at Rs 17½ lakhs per annum. It was further suggested that an allowance of Rs 5½ lakhs should be given to the Maharajah of Jaipur as Rajpramukh. Ultimately, the privy purse for Bikaner was fixed at Rs 17 lakhs, that of Jodhpur at Rs 17½ lakhs and that of Jaipur at Rs 18 lakhs. The Rajpramukh was to receive an allowance of Rs 5½ lakhs per annum.

Having settled the position and the privy purses of the Maharajahs, we turned our attention to the question of control by the Government of India over the Governments of the various Unions. As these Unions were being formed on the initiative of the Government of India, the latter felt naturally responsible for their good government. At the same time, the Government of India had no legal status to interfere if things went wrong in any of these Unions. Whatever control had been exercised hitherto was through the Congress party machine and the personality of Sardar; but this was obviously not a very satisfactory arrangement.

The task that confronted us in the Unions was stupendous. The type of administration in many of the erstwhile States had been both personal and primitive and the administrative personnel inherited from them was not equipped to undertake the responsibilities that now faced the Unions. The political organizations were in a formative state; there were not enough leaders of experience and ability. Sectarian considerations and local loyalties could not be wiped out overnight. With inexperienced politicians and with the public far from politically conscious, it would be dangerous to leave the

34

administration without some expert guidance. The Central Government had moreover to ensure that the process of integration and democratization was completed with the utmost speed and efficiency. In these circumstances, control by the Government of India over the administration of the Unions, at any rate for some time, was inescapable.

Accordingly, I suggested that a provision should be included in the Rajasthan covenant that, until the constitution framed by the local Constituent Assembly came into operation, the Rajpramukh and the Council of Ministers should be under the general control of, and comply with such particular directions as might from time to time be given by, the Government of India. The rulers readily accepted the proposal. The popular leaders resisted it but in the end, after a good deal of argument, they also agreed. The same provision was subsequently incorporated in the covenants of other Unions.

The Rajasthan covenant also included a mandatory provision, as in the case of Madhya Bharat, whereby the Rajpramukh had to execute a fresh Instrument of Accession, accepting all the subjects in both the federal and concurrent lists for legislation by the Dominion Legislature, except the entries relating to taxation and duties.

In the covenant of the second Rajasthan Union, the rulers of the convenanting States had been given one vote each in the election of the Rajpramukh and Uprajpramukhs. It seemed only fair that the bigger States of Jaipur, Jodhpur and Bikaner who were joining the Union should have some weightage. It was therefore decided that each member of the Council of Rulers should have a number of votes equal to the number of lakhs of population in their States.

In the midst of the Rajasthan States, there is a tiny island—Ajmer Merwara—which, for strategic reasons, had been kept by the British Government as a Chief Commissioner's province. Once we had formed a Union of all the Rajasthan States there seemed to be no reason why this province should continue as a separate unit. I tried, though in vain, to include it in the new Union. But in case this should become possible later on, I inserted a provision in the covenant that the Government of Rajasthan could take over the administration of the whole or any part of any area included in the provinces of India on such terms and conditions as might be agreed upon by the Government of Rajasthan and the Government of India. On the basis of these discussions and decisions the covenant was finalized and signed by the rulers.

It was decided that the Union should be inaugurated by Sardar on 30 March 1949. I flew to Jaipur in the afternoon of the 29th to supervise the arrangements for his reception. Sardar was to follow me in another plane in an hour's time. His plane failed to arrive at the scheduled time. We waited for another hour; still there was no sign of it. Growing anxious, we rang up the Delhi aerodrome. They were unable to trace the plane. It was getting dark and our fears mounted.

It was in a moment of mental agony that I remembered a plane accident which had occurred when the negotiations for the integration of the four States with Rajasthan were going on. There had been a meeting of the Maharajahs of Bikaner, Jaipur and Jodhpur and myself at Bikaner. It lasted for a whole day; and it was decided that we should have another conference at Delhi. The Maharajahs of Jaipur and Jodhpur then left for their respective capitals. The Maharajah of Bikaner asked me to stay back in order to discuss various points with him and also to meet the leading *jagirdars* and popular leaders of his State. My arrangement with the Maharajah of Jaipur was that I should pick him up the next morning on my way to Delhi. Over a hundred and fifty leaders had assembled at Bikaner and they asked for the elucidation of many points regarding the integration of the State. When the meeting with the leaders was over, I had a further interview with the Maharajah of Bikaner, which took a considerable time. Consequently, I left for Jaipur much later than I had anticipated. When my plane was over the Jaipur aerodrome, I noticed another plane in flames near the airfield and on landing I learned to my horror that the Maharajah of Jaipur was involved in the accident. I rushed to the spot in time to see him being removed to the hospital. It appeared that the Maharajah had been waiting for me, when a representative from some firm went to him and tried to sell him a plane. At first the Maharajah waved him away, but since my plane was late he consented to a trial flight. The accident may have been due to some stunt flying. The Maharajah was in a serious condition. I wonder if there is any man, at any rate in India, who has been involved in more accidents than the Maharajah of Jaipur. He recovered from his injuries, but it was many days before he could take further part in our discussions.

In that hour of suspense while waiting for Sardar's plane, I was weak enough to imagine that there was some fatality dogging the new Union. I rang up Nehru who told me to return to Delhi immediately. When I reached Delhi, Nehru told me that Sardar had already reached Jaipur. I wanted to return at once to Jaipur, but Nehru told me not to risk a night flight. Sardar's plane had developed engine trouble and had force-landed on the bed of a river a few miles from Jaipur. Only the presence of mind and skill of the pilot had averted what might have been a great tragedy. Early next morning I flew to Jaipur and when I met Sardar, he asked me: 'Why did you fly to Delhi? Don't you know that nothing will happen to me?' He then embraced me. I could not have been more overcome with emotion.

Sardar inaugurated the Greater Rajasthan Union on 30 March 1949 by swearing in the Rajpramukh and the Premier. There was rough weather ahead in the forming of a ministry; for I found that the local Congress was a house divided against itself.

I have mentioned earlier how, at the time of the formation of the Matsya Union, I told the rulers that in the event of the formation of the Rajasthan Union, the Matsya Union would have to be merged with it. In fact, at the time of the negotiations for the formation of the Rajasthan Union, we were also considering the future of the Matsya Union. Matsya at that time had a popular ministry. I invited the rulers of Dholpur, Bharatpur, Alwar and Karauli to Delhi and we had discussions on 13 February. Later during the day I also met the ministers of the Matsya Union. These discussions revealed that in the territories of the former Alwar and Karauli States opinion was unanimous that they should be merged with Rajasthan. In the two States of Bharatpur and Dholpur, however, there was no such unanimity. While some favoured integration with the Rajasthan Union, others, for reasons of affinity of language, wished to be merged with the United Provinces.

I had still further discussions with the rulers on 23 March. The ruler of Bharatpur said that the majority of his people were in favour of integration with the Rajasthan Union. The Maharajah of Dholpur favoured the same course for his State with the proviso that it should subsequently be merged with the United Provinces if it was found that the majority of the people so desired.

The matter was put before Sardar who decided that a committee should be appointed to ascertain whether public opinion in the two States was in favour of merger with the United Provinces or integration with Rajasthan. A Committee consisting of Shanker Rao Deo, R. K. Sidhwa and Prabhu Dayal Himmat Singka—members of

Parliament—was appointed on 4 April 1949 with instructions to report before the end of the month. The Committee toured the two States and heard as many shades of opinion as time allowed. In its report, the Committee expressed the view 'that the present majority opinion such as it is in both the States, ascertained by the methods we had to adopt, is for integration with Rajasthan rather than for merger with the United Provinces.' But they suggested that, after a lapse of time, the people should be given an opportunity to express their views by means of a regular plebiscite or some similar procedure. The Government of India accepted the recommendations of the Committee for the merger of these States with Rajasthan and a press *communiqué* to that effect was issued on 1 May 1949.

On 10 May a further conference of the four rulers was held at Delhi to which the Rajpramukh and the Premier of Rajasthan were also invited. The draft covenant for the integration of the Matsya Union with Rajasthan was discussed and finalized. By this covenant the four rulers abrogated the earlier covenant entered into by them and agreed that the Matsya Union should be integrated with and become part of Rajasthan. The Maharajah of Bharatpur enquired whether, in the event of Bharatpur and Dholpur choosing to opt out at a later stage, the rulers would be treated differently from those of the other covenanting States. I replied in the negative and assured them that all rulers, irrespective of whether their States were merged with provinces or formed into Unions, would have the same rights and privileges. The four rulers signed the agreement, as did the Rajpramukh of Rajasthan on behalf of the Rajasthan Union.

A provision was included in this covenant that when the Government of India were satisfied that conditions favourable to the expression of a considered opinion by the general public were established in Bharatpur and Dholpur, suitable steps would be taken to ascertain whether public opinion was in favour of continuing with Rajasthan or of merging with the United Provinces.

The administration of the Matsya Union was transferred to Rajasthan on 15 May 1949.

There was one other State the future of which remained to be settled. This was Sirohi, the ruling family of which claimed descent from Prithviraj, the Chauhan King of Delhi. The capital, Sirohi, was built in 1425. About that time the Rana of Chitor is said to have taken refuge at Mount Abu from the army of Kutb-ud-din of Gujarat and, when the force retired, refused to leave the place, having learnt how strong it was. He was, however, driven out by the Sirohi ruler's son. No other ruling prince was allowed on the hill till 1836, when the prohibition was withdrawn. Sirohi concluded a treaty of subsidiary alliance with the British in 1823 and in 1845 the ruler made over to the British Government, under certain conditions, lands on Mount Abu for the establishment of a sanatorium. These lands, together with the surrounding portion amounting to about six square miles, were made over to the British Government in October 1917 on permanent lease.

Towards the end of November 1947, a suggestion was made to Sardar that some of the States under the Rajputana Agency should be transferred to the Western India and Gujarat States Agency, because the majority of the population in those States was said to be Gujarati-speaking. The States concerned were Sirohi, Palanpur, Danta, Idar, Vijaynagar, Dungarpur, Banswara, and Jhabua. This question was discussed with the local leaders as well as with our Regional Commissioner for Rajputana. It was decided that Palanpur, Danta, Idar and Vijaynagar should be transferred to the Western India and Gujarat States Agency. The transfer was effected on 1 February 1948. Jhabua, Banswara and Dungarpur were parts of Mewar and were offshoots of Udaipur State. They were therefore allowed to continue in the Rajputana States Agency. Subsequently Sirohi was also transferred to the Western India and Gujarat States Agency.

On 19 March 1948 the rulers of the Gujarat States agreed to merge their States with the province of Bombay. At that time we had excluded Sirohi from our discussions. Our reasons for doing so were that the ruler was a minor and that the administration was carried on by a Regency Council with the Dowager Maharani as its President; more important still, there was a dispute about the succession But, once all the other States in the Western India and Gujarat States Agency were merged with Bombay we could not leave Sirohi alone. The choice was either to merge the State with Bombay or in the Rajasthan Union. I discussed the issue with Gokulbhai Bhatt, who was not only the adviser to the Dowager Maharani but also the President of the Rajasthan Provincial Congress Committee. He felt that a decision one way or the other was inopportune and suggested that Sirohi should be taken over as a centrally administered area for the time being. This was done under an agreement signed by the Maharani Regent on 8 November 1948. Two months later, on 5 January 1949, the State was handed over to the Government of Bombay for administration on behalf of the Government of India.

As mentioned above, there was a dispute over the succession to the Sirohi *gaddi*. The last Maharao Saropa Ram Singh died on 23 January 1946, leaving no son. His first Maharani was the daughter of the late Maharao of Kutch and his eldest daughter is the present Maharani of Nawanagar. He had however, contracted three other marriages. There had been two claimants to the *gaddi*; one was Tej Singh who belonged to the senior sub-branch of the Mandar branch of the ruling family; the other was Abhai Singhji, grandson of the direct brother of Maharao Umedsingh who ruled the State till 1876. In May 1946, the Crown Representative recognized Tej Singh as Maharao of Sirohi, in succession to the deceased Maharao. There had also been a third claimant, one Lakhpat Ram Singh who claimed to be a son of Maharao Saropa Ram Singh by a Rajput lady whom the ruler was said to have married by a *kanda* (sword) marriage in 1916. In December 1939, the latter submitted a memorial to the Crown Representative praying for a declaration that he was the legitimate heir-apparent to the Sirohi *gaddi*; his prayer was rejected in April 1945. Soon after the States Ministry was set up, both Abhai Singhji and Lakhpat Ram Singh asked for a reversal of the decision about succession and their request was supported by a strong body of public opinion in Sirohi.

On 10 March 1949, the Government of India appointed a Committee consisting of Sir H. V. Divatia, Chief Justice of Saurashtra, and the Maharajahs of Jaipur and Kotah to enquire into and report on the rights of the two claimants, Abhai Singhji and Lakhpat Ram Singh, to the Sirohi *gaddi* and the validity of the succession of the present Maharao. After hearing detailed arguments from the counsel of all three parties and considering the oral and documentary evidence tendered by them, the Committee came to the conclusion that Abhai Singhji belonged to the ruling family and was the rightful heir to the Sirohi *gaddi* after Maharao Saropa Ram Singh's death. The Government of India accepted the recommendations of the Divatia Committee and recognized Abhai Singhji as the Maharao.

There was a difference of opinion as to the future of the State. The Gujaratis demanded that the entire State should be merged with Bombay, while the leaders of Rajasthan were anxious that it should be merged with Rajasthan. There was some agitation in the press upon this issue which had its repercussions in Parliament. Sardar asked me to go to Sirohi and study the situation on the spot. The Gujaratis' case was that Mount Abu had been traditionally and historically associated with Gujarati culture. The well-known Jain temples of Dilawara with their beautiful carvings are situated in Mount Abu and are visited every year by the Jain population of Gujarat and Kathiawar. The ruling family also had connexions with Kathiawar and Kutch. The State was more closely connected with Gujarat than with Rajasthan. The Rajasthan case was that the State had been part of Rajputana for very many years; that the majority of the population of the State was certainly not Gujarati-speaking, and that a number of Rajput rulers had their summer residences in Mount Abu. Moreover, Rajasthan was without a single hill station.

In this controversy, neither the leaders of Gujarat nor those of Rajasthan bothered to consider the wishes of the people of the State. The popular leaders of Sirohi were themselves divided in opinion. A closer study of the situation on the spot convinced me that it would not be right to merge the whole of Sirohi with Bombay.

I returned to Delhi and discussed the matter with Sardar, who thought that a division of the State was probably the only solution in the circumstances and he asked me to get in touch with the leaders of Sirohi. I invited Gokulbhai Bhatt and other leaders of Sirohi to Delhi. I acquainted them with our tentative conclusions. The leaders were not enthusiastic about the division of the State; but they accepted it as inevitable. I also discussed the demarcation of the boundaries with them. It was decided that the Abu Road and Dilawara tehsils of Sirohi should be merged with Bombay and the rest of the State with Rajasthan. The decision was given effect to by an order under Section 290-A of the Government of India Act of 1935.

I was personally not very happy with the solution, for I felt that a division of the State would create administrative and economic difficulties. On the other hand, till 15 August 1947 Mount Abu had been administered by the Political Department separately from the State; and if those two authorities could work harmoniously together, there was surely no reason why the popular Congress Governments of Bombay and Rajasthan could not do so.

Neither in the discussions in the Constituent Assembly in November 1949, nor subsequently when this order was issued, nor yet for some period thereafter, was there any agitation against the division of the State. Today, it is a matter of regret that it should be the bone of contention between Rajasthan and Bombay.

Of all the Unions formed Rajasthan is the biggest. It has an area of 1,28,424 square miles, a population of nearly 153 lakhs and an annual revenue of over Rs 18 crores.

XIV

TRAVANCORE-COCHIN

TRAVANCORE AND COCHIN, the southernmost Indian States, occupy the south-west portion of the Indian peninsula. Few parts of India have been more richly endowed by nature. The natural beauty of the country induced Lord Curzon, during his visit to Travancore, to declare:

Since I have been in India I have had a great desire to visit the State of Travancore. I have for many years heard so much of its exuberant natural beauties, its old-world simplicity, and its arcadian charm. Who would not be fascinated by such a spectacle? Here Nature has spent upon the land her richest bounties; the sun fails not by day, the rain falls in due season, drought is practically unknown, and an eternal summer gilds the scene. Where the land is capable of culture, there is no denser population; where it is occupied by jungle, or backwater, or lagoon, there is no more fairy landscape. Planted amid these idyllic scenes is a community that has retained longer than any other equally civilised part of the Indian continent its archaic mould; that embraces a larger Christian population than any other Native State; and that is ruled by a line of indigenous princes who are one in origin and sentiment with the people whom they govern. Well may a Viceroy of India find pleasure in turning hither his wandering footsteps; good reason has he for complimenting such a ruler and such a State.

These two States, together with Malabar, have evolved a distinctive custom and culture of their own. The area is divided from the rest of India by the Western Ghats; and if a visitor were to cross the Ghats and enter Malabar, he could not fail to be struck by the change in scenery as well as in the life and customs of the people.

The ruling family of Travancore traces its descent from the ancient Chera kings of South India. In later historic times, Travancore was split up into a number of petty principalities. The consolidation of these into a single State was the achievement of Rajah Marthanda

Varma, who ruled in the first half of the eighteenth century. He brought the whole of Travancore under his sway, established order and settled the country. In January 1750, he formally and solemnly dedicated the State to Sri Padmanabha, the tutelary deity of his family; and he and his successors have ever since ruled as 'Dasas', or servants of that deity. The present ruler, Sir Bala Rama Varma,[1] succeeded to the *gaddi* in 1924 at the age of twelve and was invested with full ruling powers in November 1931. During his rule the revenues of the State were nearly quadrupled from a little over Rs 2½ crores to over Rs 9½ crores.

The present Maharajah of Cochin, Sir Kerala Varma, is, on the other hand, well advanced in age. In fact, for over a century, the Maharajahs of Cochin had all been fairly old when they succeeded to the *gaddi*. The ruling family of Cochin claims to be directly descended from Cheraman Perumal, who once ruled Kerala. Hyder Ali and later Tippu Sultan overran the territories of Cochin in the latter half of the eighteenth century, and this brought about an alliance with the English East India Company when, in 1791, the Maharajah agreed to become their tributary.

The ruling families in both the States follow the *Marumakkathayam* law, or the law of inheritance through the female line. The Maharajah, assuming that he has no brother, is succeeded by his sister's eldest son. This is generally the law followed by the majority of the Malayalam-speaking Hindus in both States.

Travancore and Cochin have always been in the forefront among the States for progressive administration. Taxation has been regulated for a very long time. The taxpayers' obligations were defined and known and collection was made on an established system. The judiciary in Travancore had an uninterrupted history of more than a century. Cochin was the first State in India to separate the judiciary from the executive. Both States were outstanding in the encouragement of education, and in point of literacy they stood first in India. Nearly one quarter of the total revenues in both States was spent on education. Women's education in particular made great strides. Travancore had a separate University. The State forged ahead in industrialization and had several industries—cement, fertilizers, chemicals, ceramics, paper, etc.

---

[1] His titles are: Major-General, Sir Padmanabha Dasa, Vanchipala, Sir Bala Rama Varma, Kulasekhara Kiritapati, Manney Sultan, Maharaja Raja Rama Raja Bahadur, Shamsher Jang.

As early as 1925 Cochin had a Legislative Council with an elected majority. It was the first of the States to send, in 1946, elected representatives to the Constituent Assembly. Soon after this, the Maharajah granted full responsible government, a step which was applauded throughout the country. Both Gandhiji and Nehru commended him highly for his statesmanship. Cochin was among the first States to accede to the Dominion of India.

Travancore, too, had a Legislature, though with limited powers. I have already referred to the initial trouble we had with Travancore in the matter of accession when Sir C. P. Ramaswami Aiyar was Dewan of the State. After he left the State in July 1947, the Maharajah introduced full responsible government and a popular ministry was installed.

The Congress had considerable strength in both States. It was well organized, with its ramifications in every part of the States and its roots among the people.

The people of the two States are of the same stock, speak the same language and have a common culture and tradition. But old animosities and narrow provincialism militated against the common handling of mutual problems. Several areas of Cochin State, including the capital, formed islands within Travancore territory. Ernakulam, the seat of the Cochin Government, gets its water supply from Travancore. Many rivers flow through and irrigate both States, but because of regional rivalry, no satisfactory agreement could be reached in respect of schemes of irrigation, the development of hydro-electric power and water supply. Diversity of jurisdiction hampered co-ordinated measures for dealing with anti-social elements. The industrial areas of Alwaye and the commercial centre of Alleppey are not far from Cochin Harbour, but customs barriers hampered trade between the two States.

I paid a visit to Trivandrum on 5 March 1949. I met T. K. Narayana Pillai, the Premier of Travancore first and the other ministers later. I told them that I had come to ascertain the wishes of the people of Travancore and Cochin in regard to the future of the two States. There were three alternatives: to form an *Aikya Kerala* (or a linguistic province of the entire Malayalam-speaking areas of Travancore, Cochin and Malabar): to form a union of Travancore and Cochin; or to leave the two States as they were for the time being. The first was not practicable unless and until the policy in regard to the formation of linguistic provinces was settled by the

14. Sardar with the Maharajah of Mysore during his visit to the State.

15. The Maharajah of Cochin on arrival at Trivandrum with the Maharajah of Travancore, the Premiers of the two States and the author.

16. Sardar and the author with the Maharajah of Cochin during Sardar's last visit to Travancore-Cochin.

17. The author with the Maharajah of Travancore inaugurating the Travancore-Cochin Union.

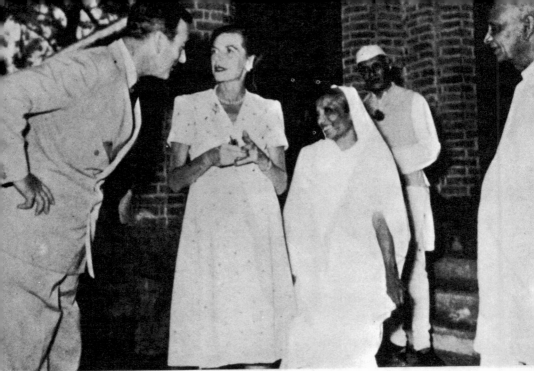

18. **Lord and Lady Mountbatten taking leave of Sardar and his daughter at Mussoorie. In the rear is Prime Minister Nehru.**

19. Lord Mountbatten signing the Standstill Agreement with Hyderabad. On his right are Nawab Moin Nawaz Jung and other Hyderabad delegates.

three-man committee (consisting of Nehru, Sardar and Pattabhi Sitaramayya) which had been appointed after the Jaipur session of the Congress in 1948. It had been the policy of the States Ministry to form Unions of States wherever possible. States more important than Travancore and Cochin, if not merged with provinces, had been dealt with in this way. I personally felt that the integration of the two States would be the right step. The Premier pointed out that they were confronted with the problem of reconciling the Tamil section of the population in the southern districts of Travancore, but I had no doubt that the problem could be tackled satisfactorily.

The next day the Premier (E. Ikkanda Warrier) and other ministers of Cochin arrived from Ernakulam and I had a general discussion with them. Later, there was a joint discussion between the Travancore and Cochin ministers in which I participated. Eventually, the ministers of both States declared their unanimous acceptance of the proposal to amalgamate Travancore and Cochin into one Union.

Subsequently, I had a meeting with the local Congress leaders. They were also of the view that the integration of the two States was the best course. At the same time, they thought that the people should be given some indication that this step was a preliminary to the formation of *Aikya Kerala*. I reminded them that the question of linguistic provinces was under consideration by a Committee. I also warned them that if, at that stage, too much emphasis was laid on the linguistic question, they would only be antagonizing the Tamil-speaking people of Travancore.

I next received a deputation of the Travancore Tamil Nad Congress. The attitude of this organization was one of hostility to the local ministry and to what they spoke of as 'the tyranny of the brute majority.' They emphasized the fact that the affinities of the Tamil community which predominated in certain taluks of the State were with those of the Tamil districts of the Madras Province. They represented to me that, should the integration of Travancore and Cochin take place, their position as a minority would become even weaker. Accordingly they wished that, if steps were going to be taken in this direction, the taluks of Travancore in which Tamilians were in a majority should be merged with the neighbouring Tamil districts of Madras. I pointed out that the question of a Kerala province, including Malabar, was outside my mission and that I was concerned only with the question of the integration of the two States. I could therefore only advise them to wait for an announcement of the final decision on linguistic provinces. I told them that they were wrong to press the linguistic argument forgetting the economic and historic ties which bound them to Travancore. It might be true that their percentage in the total population would be reduced by an amalgamation of Cochin with Travancore, but their position could be safeguarded by weightage. Other difficulties could be settled by mutual agreement. They then suggested that Travancore and Cochin should be merged with the Madras Province. I told them that this was quite impracticable.

The local Bar Association favoured the merger of Cochin and Travancore with Madras and they put forward economic and other reasons for this step. I explained to them that this would not be acceptable to the States Ministry; nevertheless, I agreed to convey their point of view to Sardar.

Finally, I had a meeting with the Maharajah of Travancore. He told me that he would prefer things left as they were for the time being. I replied that all the States in the country having been integrated, to leave Travancore and Cochin as they were would certainly lead to criticism and possibly even agitation. If the two States were forced to integrate as a result of agitation, his own position was sure to be most adversely affected. On the other hand, if the problem was tackled at once it would put him on an altogether safer basis. The Maharajah then told me that his position *vis-à-vis* the Cochin ruler would be difficult of adjustment. He added that he governed the State on behalf and as a servant of Sri Padmanabha and that he attached great importance to this position being maintained; that if no satisfactory solution on these points was possible, and if the Government of India still insisted on the integration of the two States he would rather abdicate than act against his convictions. I told him not to take a pessimistic view of the position; that there were few problems which human ingenuity could not solve. The discussions were inconclusive.

On 10 March, I visited Ernakulam, the capital of Cochin State. Here I had an important conference with the *Aikya Kerala* Committee, which had been appointed by a Convention recently held at Alwaye with the object of forming a United Kerala Province. The *Aikya Kerala* Committee were greatly disappointed when I told them that it was not the purpose of my visit to create a linguistic Kerala province, but only to find out whether the States of Travancore and Cochin could be amalgamated into one Union. One or two members of the Committee suggested that the two States should be merged with the Madras Province. I explained that the policy of the States Ministry was to form Unions of States that were contiguous. They then gave me the text of a resolution recommending that Travancore and Cochin should be integrated as a first step towards the attainment of *Aikya Kerala*. I promised to place their point of view before Sardar.

On 10 March I wrote to the Premiers of the two States asking them to let me have in writing their definite recommendations regarding the future of their States. On 12 March I received their replies. Both the Premiers after consulting their colleagues expressed themselves in favour of the early integration of the two States into a Union. Before making these recommendations, they had consulted the members of the Congress Party in the legislative assemblies of both Travancore and Cochin and the latter had endorsed the views of their respective Premiers. Both the Premiers were definitely opposed to the alternative proposal of merger with the Madras Province.

On 12 March, I had an interview with the Maharajah of Cochin and apprised him of the discussions that had taken place in Trivandrum and Ernakulam. I promised to keep him fully in touch with future developments.

I returned to Delhi and reported to Sardar that public opinion was predominantly in favour of the integration of these two States. With regard to the Tamilians in Travancore, I suggested that, as they were already in a minority in the State, they could scarcely be aggrieved at an arrangement which did no more and no less than maintain that position. In every respect other than language, their interests were identical with those of the rest of the population. Sardar agreed.

On 1 April 1949 a deputation, consisting of the ministers of the two States and representatives of the local Congress organizations, came to Delhi. The Congress leaders again raised the issue of a Malayalam-speaking province, but it was not pressed. Subsequently they and the ministers met Sardar and apprised him of their desire to integrate the two States into one Union, and on 2 April the Government of India issued a press *communiqué* accepting the proposal.

Two days later a committee was appointed consisting of V. O. Markose, a Minister of Travancore, and Panampilli Govinda Menon, a Minister of Cochin, with an official Chairman (N. M. Buch, I.C.S.), to examine and report on the various problems connected with the integration of the two States.

Soon after this, the Maharajah of Travancore visited Delhi and had discussions with both Sardar and myself. He raised some important questions. He desired that, in view of the importance of his State, he should be the permanent head of the new Union. He also preferred the title of 'Perumal', head of the ancient confederation of Kerala chieftains to that of Rajpramukh. Lastly, he felt that on account of the dedication of the State to Sri Padmanabha and the special loyalty and devotion which the rulers of Travancore owed to that deity, it would not be possible for him to take the usual oath of office as Rajpramukh. The Government of India could not accept the suggestions of the Maharajah without further discussion with the ministers and popular leaders of Travancore. The Maharajah returned to Trivandrum.

Sardar thought that I should visit Trivandrum again for further discussions. Meanwhile, a rumour had gained currency in Delhi that the Maharajah of Travancore would rather abdicate than agree to the integration of his State. C. Rajagopalachari, the Governor-General, told me that if the proposed Union involved the abdication of the Maharajah, he would advise dropping the proposal. He added that having so far secured the integration of the States with the willing consent of the rulers and the people, our objective should be to stabilize the new position and to avoid anything likely to cause bitterness. In the conditions prevailing in Travancore and Cochin, it was essential that the Maharajah's position should be safeguarded, otherwise the task of administration would be rendered difficult. I assured the Governor-General that we would endeavour our utmost to bring about a settlement acceptable to all concerned.

I reached Trivandrum on 21 May and had several meetings with the Maharajah. I told him that, with goodwill on both sides, there was no reason why we should not come to an agreement. The first hurdle was the Maharajah's inability to take the oath of office as head of the State. The devotion of the present Maharajah to Sri Padmanabha borders on fanaticism; he rules the State not as its head but as a servant of the tutelary deity. All the same, it was important that the Government of India should have some sort of assurance from the Maharajah that he would be faithful to the Constitution of India and to the new Union. In the end I suggested a solution.

The Maharajah should address a letter[1] to me, the text of which should be as follows:

On assuming the position of Rajpramukh of the United State of Travancore and Cochin, I give my solemn assurance to the Government of India that to the best of my ability, I shall preserve, protect and defend the Constitution of India and that of the United State of Travancore and Cochin and devote myself to the service of the people of India.

This letter was to be read by the Chief Justice in the presence of the Maharajah at the time of the inauguration of the new Union.

The second problem was the Maharajah's proposal that he should be Rajpramukh for life. The Maharajahs of Gwalior, Patiala and Jaipur had already been made Rajpramukhs for life and it was impossible to resist a similar demand on the part of the Maharajah of Travancore. From the point of view of both revenue and population, Travancore occupied a more important position than Cochin. But the Maharajah also proposed that there should be no Uprajpramukh and that in the case of his temporary absence, the Chief Justice of the United State of Travancore and Cochin should officiate for him. This proposal was certainly unfair to the Maharajah of Cochin, who was entitled to be the Uprajpramukh and to officiate as Rajpramukh according to precedents created in the other Unions. At the same time, there was no doubt that, in view of his age, his religious predilections and other considerations, it would be highly inconvenient for the Maharajah of Cochin to stay for any length of time in Trivandrum, which was obviously to be the capital of the new Union. The Maharajah of Travancore made it a condition that if he found his new position irksome in any way, he should be allowed to resign. I agreed to this.

As regards the Maharajah's request that he should be styled Perumal and not Rajpramukh, I told him that this could not be. Under the new Constitution of India, all heads of provinces would be called Governors and heads of Unions Rajpramukhs. Any innovation such as the one he suggested would introduce complications.

I felt that the next thing to do was to bring about a meeting of the two Maharajahs, as this would not only eliminate any feeling that they had not been fully consulted, but would also have a good effect on the people of the two States. The relations between the two rulers had been anything but cordial. For many decades the rulers of these

---

[1] The wording of the letter followed the provisions of clause 159 of the Constitution Bill in regard to the oath of office of Governors.

two neighbouring States had not been on visiting terms. As the Maharajah of Cochin was very much older than the Maharajah of Travancore, I suggested to the latter that he first should pay a visit to Cochin and that the Maharajah of Cochin could later pay a return visit. Probably because his State was the bigger of the two in area, revenue and status, the Maharajah of Travancore was reluctant to accept my suggestion; nor did I press him to do so.

On 22 May, accompanied by the Premiers of both States, I flew to Ernakulam to see the Maharajah of Cochin. I told him that I was anxious that he and the Maharajah of Travancore should meet, for that would make a good beginning. He readily accepted my suggestion that he should go over to Trivandrum for the purpose, whereupon a formal invitation was issued by the Maharajah of Travancore, who also sent his private plane and made all arrangements for the reception of his distinguished neighbour. It was the Cochin Maharajah's first aeroplane trip and he thoroughly enjoyed it. The Maharajah of Travancore received him with due pomp and ceremony and escorted him to the palace which had been specially arranged for him. The local papers were full of the meeting. It did strike the popular imagination.

I had separate and joint discussions with the Maharajahs. The Maharajah of Cochin, whom I apprised of all that took place at my talks with the Maharajah of Travancore, readily agreed to the proposal that the latter should be Rajpramukh for life, but raised the question of the position of the Cochin ruler in the future. I told him that future appointments of Rajpramukhs would be left to the Governor-General and there was no reason to believe that the interests of Cochin would be overlooked.

The Cochin Maharajah made practically no demands at all. A typical request of his was that free copies should continue to be supplied to him of the *Panjangam*, or Almanac, which was published by the Cochin Government annually and was priced at a few annas! He was prepared to efface himself completely in order that his people might enjoy a larger life. This spirit of full and ready co-operation was commended by the Governor-General in his message at the inauguration of the new Union, when he expressed his 'deep gratitude and appreciation of the prompt and generous manner in which the people and the ruler of Cochin State have helped to achieve this Union and integration involving a degree of self-effacement.'

A problem peculiar to Travancore-Cochin related to the

properties attached to temples, called *Devaswoms*. It is necessary to give some explanation of the history of the *Devaswoms* in each of these States.

Travancore had been ruled by an unbroken line of Hindu kings from the earliest times and had retained throughout the centuries its essential character of a Hindu State. The most important temple in this State has always been, and still is, the Sri Padmanabha temple, richly endowed and possessing very extensive landed properties. These were originally managed by a *Yogam* (or Synod) of eight hereditary trustees and the ruler, but at the beginning of the eighteenth century the *Yogam* was ousted and the administration of the temple together with its properties was taken over entirely by the ruler. Thereafter the temple properties became intermixed with the properties of the State. The State continued however to contribute to the maintenance of the temple and the religious ceremonies. This state of affairs continued until the time of the integration of the two States.

Apart from this temple, there were a large number of *Devaswoms* in the State founded and endowed by the people and managed by *ooralars*, or trustees. From ancient times, the Maharajah had *Melkoima* rights (the right of superior authority or overlordship) over the trustees. Before 1811, the State had no direct concern in the management of these temples; in that year Colonel Munro, the then British Resident for Travancore and Cochin, assumed the Dewanship and, in exercise of the *Melkoima* rights of the Maharajah, took over the management of the *Devaswoms* in Travancore. Three hundred and forty-eight major and 1,123 minor *Devaswoms* with all their properties, were thus taken over for management. Even then their income was considerable. In course of time, the management of yet more was assumed.

A good deal of agitation was excited on the ground that the Government of the State were spending less on the maintenance of the temples and on the religious ceremonies than the amount of revenue which accrued from the *Devaswom* properties and that they were appropriating the balance of the income to themselves. In the end, the legal position was put beyond doubt by the issue of a proclamation by the Maharajah whereby the Government of the State accepted the obligation of maintaining the temples in an efficient condition, and all lawsuits against them were barred. In 1946 the Maharajah issued another proclamation which fixed the amount payable every year to the temples at a figure of not less than Rs 25 lakhs and reserved the right of making further contributions if necessary from the State revenue. Finally, in 1948, immediately before the grant of responsible government, a proclamation was issued by which a yearly sum of Rs 50 lakhs was fixed for the maintenance of all the temples in the State, other than the Sri Padmanabha temple which was to receive Rs 1 lakh annually.

Hindu opinion in the State was unanimous in holding not only that the continued payment of the existing allotments should be guaranteed, but also that adequate compensation should be given in respect of the properties taken over by the Government and the profits derived from them. The annual contribution thus claimed ranged from Rs 1 crore to Rs 2 crores. Obviously this plea could not be accepted; at the same time it was impossible to decline the obligation of maintaining these temples, the State having taken over all their properties.

I discussed the question with the ministers, as well as with the Maharajah of Travancore. Eventually we came to an agreement by which the annual payment of Rs 51 lakhs made to the temples by the Travancore Government would be continued and out of this amount a sum of Rs 6 lakhs would be contributed annually for the maintenance of the Sri Padmanabha temple.

The most difficult issue related to the administration of this grant. After prolonged discussion it was agreed that the administration of the Sri Padmanabha temple should be conducted under the control and supervision of the Maharajah through an executive officer to be appointed by him. It was decided that there should be a committee of three Hindu members nominated by the Maharajah to advise him; and that one of the three should be nominated on the advice of the Hindu members of the Council of Ministers. With regard to the other temples in Travancore, a body to be called the Travancore Devaswom Board would be set up. This Board would consist of three Hindu members, one of whom would be nominated by the Maharajah, one elected by the Hindus among the Council of Ministers and one by the Hindu members of the Legislative Assembly of the Union.

In Cochin, unlike Travancore, the properties of the temples were administered separately as a 'reserved subject' by the Maharajah; but after the grant of responsible government, he appointed the Premier of the State to act in his personal capacity as the chief executive authority for *Devaswoms*. The Poornathrayeesa temple at

Trippunithura is the temple of the ruling family and the Maharajah asked for the control of the rituals and ceremonies in this temple, as well as for those in the Pazhayannur temple. I agreed to this request. It was decided to set up a Devaswom Board in Cochin on the same lines as in Travancore. As the *Devaswom* properties had remained separate, there was no necessity to make any special grant from State revenues. The landed properties of the temples, I should add, are subject to the land revenue and tenancy laws of the State just like any other landed properties.

These decisions were subsequently incorporated in the covenant. Later on, when the Constitution of India was being finalized, a provision was included to safeguard the payment to the temples in Travancore by making it charged and non-votable by the Legislature of the Union.

It must be emphasized here that this provision in the covenant relating to *Devaswoms* brought about a far-reaching social reform in both States. These two States had been the seat of an orthodoxy not found in any other part of India except Malabar. The Temple-entry reform in Travancore recognized to a certain extent the place of *Harijans* in the Hindu society; but under the covenant, the *Harijans* would gain a measure of control of the temples through their representatives in the Legislature and in the ministry and would also be able to hold posts in the Devaswom Department which had hitherto been denied to them.

The press had been kept fully informed of the progress of the discussions and during one of my press conferences, there were some criticisms regarding the provision for maintenance of the temples in Travancore. I pointed out to the critics that the properties of the temples taken over by the Travancore State Government had increased many times in value and yielded an income greater than the amount of contribution provided in the covenant. If the contribution was considered undesirable or excessive, the State would have no option but to return the properties to the temple. The State could not have it both ways, by refusing to return the properties while at the same time refusing to maintain the *Devaswoms*.

The Maharajah of Cochin left Trivandrum on 16 May. I promised that the question of his privy purse and private properties would be settled with him later.

I next turned my attention to the settlement of the privy purse of the Maharajah of Travancore. The total amount drawn by him annually came up to nearly Rs 27 lakhs. But as I pointed out to him, he was actually drawing only Rs 15 lakhs as his privy purse, the remaining amount being by way of amenities. After some discussion it was agreed that his privy purse should be fixed at Rs 18 lakhs. I suggested to him that a sum of Rs 10 lakhs should be provided in the covenant for his successors, because we had not agreed to a higher figure in any other case. He preferred not to have any figure mentioned, presumably in the hope that he might be able to persuade the Government of India at a later date to sanction a higher figure. I left him in no doubt that the amount could not in any event be more than Rs 10 lakhs. Ultimately, however, a provision was included in the covenant that his successors would be paid such amounts as the Government of India might decide.

The allowance payable to the Maharajah of Travancore as Rajpramukh was fixed later, with the concurrence of the ministers, at Rs 3 lakhs per annum, while a sum of Rs 66,000 per annum was also to be paid to him for the expenses of his establishment.

While we were having these discussions, the Premier of the State told me that there was considerable feeling against the retention by the Maharajah of the *Kandukrishi* lands which comprised nearly 60,000 acres and had an annual revenue of Rs 5 lakhs. In the course of our talks I broached the subject to the Maharajah and told him that his ministry and the people would greatly appreciate it if he would voluntarily surrender these lands to the State. The Maharajah agreed to do so and a proclamation surrendering these lands to the United State was signed by him simultaneously with the signing of the covenant.

I then raised with the two Premiers three points which I had reserved for discussion to the last. A provision had already been included in the Madhya Bharat covenant making it obligatory for the Rajpramukh to execute an Instrument of Accession by which the Dominion Legislature could make laws for the State in regard to all the matters mentioned in the federal and concurrent legislative lists of the Government of India Act of 1935, except the entries in the federal list relating to taxation or duties. I told the ministers that not only should an identical provision be included in the covenant but that we should go further and include a permissive provision empowering the Rajpramukh to execute a fresh Instrument of Accession on entries relating to taxation and duties. Owing to the fact that Travancore was deficient in food, the State was experiencing considerable financial difficulties. The Government of India had to go to their help and we had no option but to continue our subsidy till the State's food problem was solved. The Government of India were thus incurring a heavy liability for an unlimited period. I therefore thought it wise to include a permissive provision with regard to taxation entries.

Travancore-Cochin was the last Union to be formed. Our experience of the working of the other Unions indicated the necessity for some provision in the covenant empowering the Rajpramukh to take over the administration in an emergency and to exercise all the powers under the control of the Government of India, except in regard to the judiciary. I told the two Premiers how the situation in some of the Unions had deteriorated owing to lack of experience on the part of political leaders, lack of trained personnel and the unsettlement caused by integration. In the event of the situation worsening and an emergency arising, the Government of India had no power to take over the administration in the Unions as they had in the case of a province under Section 93 of the Government of India Act of 1935. I therefore suggested the inclusion of a provision to that effect in the covenant.

I also wanted a provision to be included that, until the constitution framed or adopted by the Constituent Assembly came into operation, both the Rajpramukh and the Council of Ministers should be subject to the powers of superintendence and control by the Government of India. Such a provision had been introduced in the covenant of the third Rajasthan Union.

At first, the Premiers were reluctant to accept these provisions on the plea that they would be a target of attack by the advocates of provincial and State autonomy. But I told them that the Government of India had a direct responsibility for the peace and good government of these States which they could not relinquish. These provisions, I said, were not intended for Travancore and Cochin alone but would be applicable to all the other Unions. In the end the Premiers agreed to their incorporation in the covenant as being in the best interests of the country.

The covenant was then drafted and finalized after further discussions with the two Premiers. By this covenant the United State of Travancore and Cochin acceded to the Indian Union on all the subjects in the federal and concurrent legislative lists of the Government of India Act of 1935. A permissive provision enabling the

Rajpramukh to accede on taxation entries also had been included. The Rajpramukh and the Council of Ministers were made subject to the control of the Government of India. In the event of a breakdown the Government of India could take over the administration of the Union. It was a strange coincidence that the first Union to come into almost identical relationship with the Centre as the provinces, should have been Travancore-Cochin, for Travancore had started with the idea of asserting its independence when the transfer of power was announced.

I also kept in touch with the local Congress leaders during these discussions. Some of them suggested that the new Union should be called the Kerala Union. I pointed out that this would raise a controversy as to linguistic affiliations; nor was it likely to be acceptable to the Maharajah of Travancore or to the Tamil-speaking people of the Union. The new Union was named the United State of Travancore and Cochin.

On 27 May I took the finalized covenant to the Maharajah of Travancore, who signed it in the presence of his Premier. I then took the other Ministers to the palace where the Premier, on behalf of himself and his colleagues, assured the Maharajah of their fullest co-operation and also of their purpose to do everything to maintain the dignity of the Maharajah and the ruling family. In reply, the Maharajah told his Ministers that they could always count on his whole-hearted support.

On the evening of 27 May I went to Ernakulam to settle the privy purse of the Maharajah of Cochin. He was at that time drawing an annual amount of Rs 1,74,000 plus other amenities such as repairs to palaces, supply and maintenance of cars and so on. Taking everything into consideration, the privy purse was fixed at Rs 2,35,000, which worked out to 0·56 per cent of the total revenues of the State. The Cochin ruling family consisted at that time of 223 princes and 231 princesses, all of whom were getting allowances from the State. There was also a separate fund for their marriage and other ceremonies, and for their education and maintenance. I met some of these princes and princesses. As I talked with them I was reminded of an aviary in a certain State which possessed a rare collection of birds. When that State was integrated the popular ministry, apparently on the principle of *ahimsa*, let the birds loose! The poor creatures were very soon devoured by other birds and beasts of prey. The princesses, at any rate, had all along led a sheltered existence;

and most of their husbands, instead of supporting them, had themselves to be maintained by the State. I felt that it would be inhuman to expose the princesses to a competitive world without making some sort of provision for them. The Government of India subsequently decided to continue the allowances to those members of the ruling family who were living on the day the covenant was signed. No responsibility was accepted in respect of any further additions to the ruling family.

On 29 May I went to the palace with the Premier to obtain the Maharajah's signature to the covenant. As I placed it before him, he opened the cap of his fountain pen; but just before signing, he replaced the cap, put down the pen and continued to sit motionless. A while later, when I reminded the Maharajah about his signature, I realized that he was saying a prayer. I felt considerably embarrassed and waited till he finished. He then signed. I assured him that the Government of India would see that his dignity and prestige were fully maintained and that he would have no cause to regret the decision he had taken. The Maharajah then met the ministers and told them that in future it would be for them to look after the ruling family and the people of Cochin. The Premier assured the Maharajah that he would carry out his wishes to the best of his ability.

One of the problems that demanded immediate attention was the capital of the United State. Ernakulam, the capital of Cochin, was obviously unsuitable mainly on account of its lack of accommodation. Trivandrum, the capital of Travancore, had plenty of accommodation, but was situated so far south that it would cause considerable inconvenience to the people of Cochin. A new capital in a central place would involve an expenditure which the State could not well afford. A compromise was therefore reached by which it was decided to have the capital at Trivandrum and the High Court and the Law College at Ernakulam. This decision had the concurrence of the ministers of both States.

The report of the Buch Committee, which had gone into the administrative and other problems connected with the integration, helped greatly in settling some of the more pressing problems on the spot.

In the course of my discussions at Trivandrum, a suggestion was put forward that it would be of immense help to trade and to the people of the two States if there were a railway link between

37

UNION IS STRENGTH!

Shankar's conception of the integration of Travancore and Cochin.

By courtesy of *Shankar's Weekly.*

Ernakulam and Quilon. I could do nothing about this at the time; but after the Union had been inaugurated, I discussed the matter with N. Gopalaswami Aiyangar, then Minister for Transport. I urged that the construction of this railway would have the effect of cementing the Union and would catch popular imagination. Gopalaswami Aiyengar agreed and authorized me to make an announcement to the effect that a survey would be undertaken as soon as possible. The announcement was made by Nehru when he visited Travancore-Cochin. When the survey was completed and the scheme finally sanctioned by the Government of India, it was Nehru who turned the first sod.

Neither Nehru nor Sardar could spare the time to go to Trivandrum to inaugurate the new Union. Sardar asked me to go instead. The Union was inaugurated on 1 July 1949.

The Union has an area of 9,155 square miles, a population of 75 lakhs and a revenue of nearly Rs $13\frac{1}{2}$ crores. In the course of my inaugural speech, I pointed out that the formation of this Union marked the end of the first phase of the work of the States Ministry and that we were entering the second phase, which was the consolidation of the work already accomplished. I appealed to the people to remember that there was only one State now and to forget past alignments and prejudices.

Personally I was more than sanguine about the success of the Union, the last in the series set up by the States Ministry. Though it was the smallest in area it had very great potentialities for future industrial development. Large quantities of ilmenite mixed with uranium as well as thorium-bearing monazite are found on the sea coast in South Travancore. Tea, coffee, cocoanut and spices bring in a substantial amount of foreign exchange. The Union ranks second in population and in revenue among the Unions. The people are politically conscious; literacy is very high; the people of both States are ethnically, culturally and linguistically one. There are of course certain difficulties ahead of the new State. The density of population, for instance, is the highest in India, being 1,015 to the square mile as against India's average of 281; the large number of educated people might well prove a threat to law and order if their energies are not utilized for the good of the State; lastly, the State is deficient in food. However, with statesmanship and patriotism on the part of the people and their leaders, these problems should not be difficult to tackle.

XV

MYSORE

HYDERABAD and Mysore are the only two States which, because of their size, population, financial resources and geographical position, remained as separate entities. In both these States the ruler became the constitutional head. Hyderabad is dealt with in subsequent chapters. We deal here with Mysore.

The present ruling family of Mysore has, but for two short breaks, been ruling the State ever since its foundation in 1399. In 1765, Hyder Ali usurped the throne but in 1799, on the fall of his son and successor, Tippu Sultan, the Hindu dynasty was restored. In 1831 the people rose in rebellion, and the British Government in consequence assumed direct management of the State. In March 1881 it was handed back to the ruling family and Maharajah Chamarajendra Wadiyar was installed. His son and successor Maharajah Sir Sri Krishnaraja Wadiyar, who ruled for forty-six years, was the most distinguished ruler Mysore ever had; the State made remarkable progress under his guidance. The present Maharajah, Sri Jayachamarajendra Wadiyar, succeeded his uncle in August 1940 at the age of twenty-one.

Mysore has earned the reputation of being one of the best administered States in the country. During the fifty years of direct management by the British the foundation was laid of a sound administrative system. Since then Mysore has had the good fortune to be managed by distinguished administrators like Sir K. Seshadri Aiyar, Sir M. Visveswaraya and Sir Mirza Ismail, all of whom left a permanent mark on the administration.

Mysore, more than any other State, led the way in industrialization. The most important industrial development in the State has been gold-mining. Several other industries, such as iron and steel, porcelain, silk, oil and soaps, sugar and electrical equipment have also been developed. Mysore was a pioneer in the field of hydro-electric projects. As early as 1900, Sir K. Seshadri Aiyar initiated the scheme (subsequently extended) by which the Cauvery Falls at Sivasamudram were harnessed for the generation of electrical power for transmission to the Kolar Gold Fields, a distance of about ninety-three miles.

It was during the administration of Sir M. Visveswaraya that the Bhadravati Iron and Steel Works and the Jog (Gersoppa) hydro-electric scheme were initiated. There is an interesting history with regard to this hydro-electric scheme. Lord Curzon was opposed to it when it was mooted for the first time; his note on the subject shows how the nature-lover got the better of the statesman:

I do not in the least agree and as long as I am in India I will be no party to ruining, in the interests of Messrs. Ritchie, Stewart & Co., or of anybody else—what is one of the greatest natural beauties in the world. No one who has visited the Gersoppa (Jog) Falls can fail to recognise that any diversion of the water power, by whatever pledges or conditions it was hedged round, must not only diminish but absolutely destroy the natural features of the place — so small is the total volume of water flowing in the river-bed and falling over into the chasm during the greater part of the year. I was myself at Gersoppa early in November when the falls — though considerably reduced below their volume in the rains — are thought to be at their best, and I do not think that at any place in the river above the falls was there more than six to eight inches of water and in most places much less. I should regard it as a wicked thing in the interests of some company or other who may want to make money to sacrifice the lovely spot. Already the Falls at Gokak, also in the Bombay Presidency have, I was told, been ruined by some mills which were erected in close proximity to them and which are worked by water power. There is no analogy between the Gersoppa Falls and those of the Cauvery at Sivasamudram which supply the electric power to Kolar for the volume of water in the Cauvery is infinitely greater and the Falls though neither so beautiful nor so lofty as those at Gersoppa are on a much larger scale. Even so, I believe that their beauty has been appreciably diminished by the amount of water taken off. In the present case, however, we are told nothing more of the object in view than that it is identical with 'large industrial purposes for developing the country', whatever that may mean. I suggest that we inform the Bombay Government and the Mysore Durbar also that it seems unnecessary to discuss the question of the boundary because it is the earnest hope and desire of the Government of India that no scheme of any kind will be admitted on whatever pretext for drawing up the water of the Sheravati River, on the bank above the Gersoppa Falls. The Government of India are quite ready to agree to a self-denying ordinance in this respect if the Mysore Durbar will reciprocate by doing the same. It cannot be doubted by any one who has seen the Falls, as the Viceroy has done, that any diversion of the water — already scanty enough at every period of the year except during or immediately after the rains — must ruin the natural beauties of the locality whatever conditions might have been imposed or accepted in advance; and the Government of India would think any industrial or economic advantage (as to the possibilities of which they have been given no information) dearly purchased at the permanent sacrifice of one of the greatest wonders of the Eastern World. I may add that the country below and all around the Falls is dense tropical jungle — so what the industrial purposes could be I cannot imagine — probably some abominable factory. If this question is brought up again — as in an age of rampant utilitarianism it is, I suppose, certain to be — I implore any successor of mine to pause before he gives his sanction to so great an outrage and if he remains in doubt then not to decide until he has paid a visit to the Falls himself. I can promise him one of the great sensations of his life — and the industrial development of the locality will once again be beneficently postponed.

The dam constructed above the waterfall conserves the waters of the river and there is an agreement with the Government of Bombay that a certain amount of water should be allowed to flow continuously. The power house is much below the waterfall and it has not affected the natural scenery in any way. I am sure that if Lord Curzon were alive and were to visit the Jog Falls today he would at least be less vehement in his objections. The electric power generated at present is 1,10,000 kilowatts with potentialities for further development.

Mysore was also the first State to establish a Representative Assembly in 1881. The functions of this Assembly were enlarged in 1923 when it was placed on a statutory basis. An Upper House was instituted in 1907, and in 1913 an elected majority was introduced and its powers enlarged. The Congress organization in the State was effective and strong. At the time of the transfer of power, Mysore had a ministry responsible to the legislature, except in respect of certain 'reserved subjects' which were entrusted to the Dewan. Shortly afterwards, these 'reserved subjects' were also handed over to the ministry and from 1949 onwards Mysore enjoyed full responsible government. The first Chief Minister was K. C. Reddy.

The process of transition by which Mysore became an integral part of the Indian Union was smooth and easy. In August 1947 the

Maharajah executed both the Instrument of Accession and the Standstill Agreement. In June 1949 he executed a revised Instrument of Accession giving the Central legislature power to legislate on all matters in the federal and concurrent legislative lists, except those relating to duties and taxation. Subsequently, Mysore also accepted the scheme of Federal Financial Integration, which came into operation on 1 April 1950.

By a proclamation of 29 October 1947, the Maharajah had set up a Constituent Assembly to frame a constitution for the State; this Constituent Assembly passed a resolution recommending that the constitution framed by the Constituent Assembly of the Indian Union should be adopted by Mysore. Effect was given to this by a proclamation issued by the Maharajah on 25 November 1949. The Constituent Assembly of Mysore became the interim legislature of the State until new elections could be held under the new Constitution.

So, gradually, the State came into complete constitutional relationship with the Centre. The only question we still had to settle was with regard to the privy purse and private properties of the Maharajah. This was decided in somewhat unusual circumstances. One morning, at an unusually early hour, Sardar's daughter Maniben rang me up and asked me to go to Sardar's house as soon as possible. As Sardar was not well, I attributed the sudden summons to a deterioration in his condition. When I arrived there, however, Sardar told me that the privy purse of the Maharajah of Mysore was still undecided and that the matter was worrying him. I did not ask him why, with all his other and more important preoccupations, he should be so anxious on this score, but I promised to go to Mysore almost at once. Soon after, I went to Mysore and had a three days' discussion with the Maharajah and his ministers, in the course of which we settled the Maharajah's privy purse, the matter of his private properties, his allowances as Rajpramukh and other details. The decisions reached were given effect to subsequently by an agreement between the Maharajah and the Government of India.

In Mysore, the demarcation between the State and the Maharajah's personal properties did not present any difficulty. This had been settled many years ago. When, in 1799, on the defeat and death of Tippu, the ruling family was restored, they were practically destitute and the long period of direct administration of the State by the British from 1831 to 1881 did not help them by any means to build up some sort of private fortune. Whatever wealth they now may have was built up by the present Maharajah and his predecessor; and it must be said to their credit that they have always contributed considerable sums towards charities, by way of donations and in a remarkable degree for the beautification of Mysore and Bangalore.

XVI

A MISCELLANY OF STATES

IN the preceding chapters I have described how regional groups of States were either formed into Unions or merged with the provinces in which they were situated. In this process a few of the States were left out and it is with them that I deal in this chapter. The States concerned are (*a*) the Punjab Hill States, Bilaspur, Kutch, Tripura, Manipur and Bhopal, which were taken over as centrally administered areas under Chief Commissioners and (*b*) isolated States which were merged with the provinces of Madras, East Punjab, the United Provinces, West Bengal and Assam.

I

There were some States over which, for administrative reasons or strategic necessity, or on some other special ground, it was necessary that the Government of India should exercise direct control; such States were taken over as Chief Commissioner's provinces. There were six of them, besides Vindhya Pradesh which was formed in the first place into a Union and later converted into a Chief Commissioner's province.

THE PUNJAB HILL STATES situated in the Himalayan region were the first group of States included in this scheme. They were twenty-one in number, with nine feudatory States. They were small in size and undeveloped. Their total area was about 11,000 square miles and their population a little over a million. The rulers claimed Rajput descent; they appeared to have obtained their territories mostly by conquest in very early times. These States underwent many vicissitudes. At the beginning of the nineteenth century, a major portion of them fell into the hands of the Gurkhas. After the expulsion of the Gurkhas, the old rulers were for the most part reinstated and brought under the British Government's protection.

The Punjab Hill States typified the problem of the Indian States in its most extreme form. There were five salute States, the largest of which had an area of about 3,500 square miles of mountainous terrain; but thirteen States were less than 100 square miles and three less than 10 square miles in area. The people were abysmally poor and backward and in most of the States even the elementary amenities were lacking.

After the transfer of power, there was an agitation in some of the States for more amenities and for the grant of responsible government. The rulers were not in a position either to control the agitation or to work out any planned programme for the future. When the trouble started, the rulers of Suket and Balsan handed over the administration of their States to the Government of India. In Chamba, one of the bigger States, the Government of India had to render police and military assistance to the ruler and subsequently to depute an officer as Dewan.

There was a demand for the merger of these States with East Punjab; but it met with vehement opposition from the rulers as well as the people. The rulers argued, and their contention was valid, that the people of these hilly areas were quite different in point of stock, manners, customs and language from the people of the plains of the Punjab. Our own view was that East Punjab was already facing many problems as a consequence of partition and that it would not therefore be wise to add further territories to it. The main problems confronting these States were the provision of primary amenities for the people, the opening of communications and the exploitation of the forest wealth. All these things would require so much planning and expenditure that the States concerned would be a liability to any province.

I invited the rulers to a conference at Delhi on 2 March 1948. They had already discussed among themselves and had prepared and given me a provisional plan for the integration of their States into a Union on the model of Saurashtra. Their proposal had the support of certain popular leaders in their States. I argued that a Union of these States had no survival value at all. The main task was to make up the leeway of centuries and to provide the people with the necessities of life. For this, manpower and finances would be required on a scale which only the Government of India would be able to furnish. I therefore suggested that these States should be integrated into a single unit and administered by the Government of India through a Chief Commissioner or a Lieutenant-Governor.

The rulers accepted my suggestion. The Rajah of Mandi, their spokesman, pressed that they should be given some voice in the administration of the new province. I agreed to an advisory council of three rulers. The new province would be named Himachal Pradesh. An agreement along these lines was drawn up and signed by the rulers on 8 March 1948. Under the Government of India Act of 1935 we could not immediately establish a Lieutenant-Governor's province. These States were therefore taken over as a Chief Commissioner's province on 15 April 1948. Its status was subsequently raised to that of a Lieutenant-Governor's province with a legislature and ministry.

BILASPUR was a tiny State among the Punjab Hill States, with an area of 453 square miles and a population of about a lakh. Geographically it was a part of Himachal Pradesh and should have been included in it but for one consideration: this was the gigantic multipurpose Bhakra Dam Project over the Sutlej. The main dam site was in Bilaspur and a substantial area of the State, including the capital and the palace, would be submerged when the dam was constructed. The project was conceived about 1919 but became a practical proposition only after the conclusion of the second World War. About the time of partition, the Government of the Punjab were negotiating with the Rajah of Bilaspur for the construction of the dam and had nearly come to an agreement with him. If the Government of the Punjab had undertaken the project, the distribution of the water would have been at their discretion. This would have been unfair to PEPSU and Rajasthan which were beneficiaries under the scheme equally with the Punjab. Under the Act of 1935, the Government of India had no power to control multi-purpose river-valley schemes. The Centre obtained this power only under the new Constitution. If, therefore, the Government of India were to intervene — and it was necessary that they should in this case — the only alternative was to take over Bilaspur as a Chief Commissioner's province. By so doing, the Government of India would inherit the jurisdiction and powers of the Rajah of Bilaspur and would have the final say. We could have achieved the same purpose if we had amalgamated Bilaspur with Himachal Pradesh, which was already a Chief Commissioner's province. But Bilaspur had problems of its own. Till such time as the Bhakra Dam was completed, displaced persons rehabilitated, and compensation paid to those dispossessed of their lands, it was essential in the interests of both the State and its people that Bilaspur should be under the care of the Centre. I had also another idea, namely that when the Bhakra dam scheme was completed, its management should be entrusted to a Board which should take over what was left of the State after submersion and develop it as part of the scheme.

I had several discussions with the Rajah both in Delhi and in Bilaspur. He was rather difficult to deal with; but ultimately, on 15 August 1948, he signed the merger agreement. As a special concession and as a temporary arrangement, the Rajah was appointed (on 12 October) as the first Chief Commissioner, with a Deputy selected by the Government of India to assist him. This arrangement was subsequently terminated and an official Chief Commissioner appointed. (Bilaspur has since, in 1954, been amalgamated with Himachal Pradesh).

KUTCH was taken over as a Chief Commissioner's province on 1 June 1948. It was a very important State in Western India; its ruler enjoyed a status superior to that of any other ruler in Kathiawar. Its area was 8,461 square miles; it had a population of a little over five lakhs and its total revenue was nearly Rs 80 lakhs.

The history of the ruling family may be said to date from the fourteenth century, when Kutch was conquered by the Samma Rajputs, who first came to the State as refugees and who stayed on to become its rulers. The British came on the scene in the early years of the nineteenth century, after the prolonged period of disorder which followed the invasion of the State by the Muslim rulers of Sind. The State had led an isolated existence; administration was in a very backward state, even though the Kutchees themselves are a very enterprising people with wide overseas trading interests.

After the transfer of power, the local Praja Parishad started an agitation for responsible government and towards the middle of March 1948, while I was in Bombay, the Maharao approached me for mediation. I had discussions with him and his advisers, as well as with the leaders of the Praja Parishad. Actually the Maharao was anxious for a peaceful solution and was prepared to grant responsible government, but I had to point out that it would be difficult to work a system of responsible government satisfactorily in a small area like Kutch. I told the Maharao that the solution was either to amalgamate the State with the neighbouring Union of Saurashtra or for the Centre to take it over as a Chief Commissioner's province.

I promised to discuss the matter with Sardar and let him know the result.

On my return to Delhi I acquainted Sardar with the discussions I had at Bombay with the Maharao and his advisers. I suggested that though Kutch was linguistically and culturally a part of Kathiawar, there were good reasons why we should keep this State directly under our control for some time to come, particularly as, with partition, Kutch had become a frontier State with Pakistan. In October 1947, when the Junagadh issue was in the forefront, we had received reports of Pakistan troop movements in the districts of Sind which bordered on Kutch. The Rann of Kutch, which separates the mainland of Kutch from Sind, dries up for some months of the year and this area is inhabited by nomadic Muslim tribes whose loyalty to the Indian Union was, to say the least, doubtful. In fact, we had found it necessary, in addition to measures taken by the Army, to send some units of the Central Reserve Police to Kutch for the protection of the area. As a result of partition we had lost the big harbour of Karachi and we were proposing to improve the Khandla Port in Kutch. This was a huge undertaking, involving an expenditure of several crores; for we had to build railway lines, construct oil installations and other major works. We also had to create a township to settle the refugees from Sind. Kutch is subject to periodical famine conditions of the utmost severity and the Central Government alone could render the financial help necessary for famine relief.

Sardar agreed that the Government of India should take over the administration of Kutch as a Chief Commissioner's province. The Maharao of Kutch was then invited to Delhi for further discussions. These lasted for three days; on 4 May 1948 the merger agreement was signed.

TRIPURA, situated on the border of Assam and East Pakistan, presented many problems. This State was of great antiquity. The traditions and history of the ruling family are preserved in the *Raj-mala,* a Bengali epic, said to be the oldest composition in that language now extant. The State comprised an area covering plains as well as hill tracts. The military prestige of the Tripura Rajahs was at its height during the sixteenth century. In the eighteenth century the State was reduced by the Nawab of Murshidabad and remained thereafter under Muslim control. The Muslims, though dominating the whole State, actually occupied only the plains areas, which were

parcelled among the nobles of their community. On assuming
control of this area in 1765, the British allowed the State to hold its
territories in the hill areas while recognizing the Rajah's title to the
zamindari in the plains. Thus, the Tripura Maharajah was both a
British Indian *zamindar* and a ruling prince. His *zamindari*, which
was largely in what is now East Pakistan, comprised an area of 600
square miles. The total area of the State was 4,116 square miles,
and its population at the time of the merger was over half a million.
The most fertile and thickly-populated part of the State is the strip of
low land along the northern, western and southern portion abutting
on Pakistan.

With the partition, Tripura was virtually isolated from India.
The capital, Agartala, as well as other important places in the State,
lay in the narrow belt of land adjoining Pakistan. Road and rail
communications between these places ran through Pakistan territory;
there were practically no communications within the State itself. The border with Pakistan was about 700 miles. Though the
State possessed a common boundary with Assam, it had no road
communications at all with Assam.

The first task was to build a road from Tripura to Assam, and
another within Assam itself to provide a connecting link with the rest
of India. The Tripura Access Road, as it was called, was an undertaking involving an expenditure of over Rs 1 crore. Till the road
was built essential supplies had to be air-lifted from time to time from
Calcutta.

When the exodus of non-Muslims from East Bengal began, Tripura
was faced with the additional task of looking after the refugees. In
all these circumstances, there was no choice but to take over Tripura
as a Chief Commissioner's province. The ruler was a minor and his
mother, the daughter of the Maharajah of Panna, was then the
Regent. She came to Delhi with her father and I had discussions
with them. The merger agreement was signed by her, on behalf of
the minor Maharajah, on 9 September and the administration of the
State was taken over on 15 October 1949.

MANIPUR had an area of 8,638 square miles, of which 700 square
miles were in the valley and the remainder in the hills. The population was a little over 5 lakhs.

The early history of the State is obscure. During the closing years
of the eighteenth century and at the beginning of the nineteenth,
the country was constantly overrun by the Burmese, who carried off

many captives and drove the rest of the inhabitants into Cachar and the hills adjoining the Manipur Valley. In 1823 when the first Burmese War broke out and the Burmese invaded Cachar, the East India Company made an alliance with the Rajah (Gambhir Singh) and a Manipuri contingent was taken into British pay. It was this contingent which, under the command of a British officer, drove the Burmese not only out of Manipur but out of the Kabaw valley as far as Kale. Subsequent negotiations with the King of Burma ended, however, in the return of the Kabaw valley to the Burmese, an annual payment of Rs 5,720 being made to Manipur by way of compensation. In 1891 there was serious trouble in the State; some British officers were murdered whereupon the State was declared forfeit to the British Government, but as an act of mercy it was subsequently re-granted to the father of the present Maharajah.

Manipur is bounded on the north by the Naga district of Assam; on the east by Burma; on the south by Burma and the Lushai Hills, and on the west by the district of Cachar. The hill tribes fall into two main sections, Kukis and Nagas, the former name being the generic term applied to tribes whose home is in certain defined mountain tracts. The hills immediately surrounding the valley are inhabited by various tribes of Nagas of whom the Tankuls are the best known.

In view of its position as a border State and its undeveloped character, it was decided to take over Manipur as a Chief Commissioner's province. The merger agreement was signed by the Maharajah on 21 September and the State was taken over by the Government of India on 15 October 1948. The details of the privy purse and private properties of the Maharajah were settled by Sri Prakasa, then Governor of Assam, in consultation with the States Ministry.

BHOPAL was the principal Muslim State in Central India. It was founded by Dost Muhammad, an Afghan adventurer who came to Delhi during the first years of the Moghul emperor Bahadur Shah's reign (1708) in search of employment. In 1709 he obtained a lease of the Berasia pargana in Malwa. He thereafter took advantage of the disorders which followed the death of the emperor to establish his independent authority in Bhopal and the neighbouring country. The State of Bhopal was not unaffected by the vicissitudes which overtook Malwa during the end of the eighteenth century and the beginning of the nineteenth. At the outbreak of the Pindari war in 1817, the British Government formed an alliance with Bhopal and a formal treaty was concluded in 1818, by which the East India Company guaranteed the integrity of the State. From 1844 to 1926 the State was ruled by three Begums. The present Nawab, Sir Hamidullah Khan, succeeded his mother (who had voluntarily abdicated in his favour) on 17 May 1926.

Sir Hamidullah Khan was a prominent member of the Chamber of Princes and was the Chancellor of that body from 1931 to 1932 and from 1944 to 1947. The Nawab's position and prestige were in fact out of all proportion to the size and revenue of his State.

After the accession of Bhopal to the Indian Union, we left the Nawab and his State alone, but he could not escape the agitation for responsible government which was then sweeping over all the States. In April 1948 the Nawab entered into an agreement with the State Prajamandal and constituted a ministry with popular leaders. But this did not solve the problem; there was also an agitation to merge the State with Madhya Bharat. The Nawab was obviously in difficulties. He wrote to Sardar on 7 January 1949 asking for his advice. There ensued some correspondence between Sardar and the Nawab as a result of which I went to Bhopal. I arrived there on 24 January and had a series of conferences for three days with the Nawab, the ministers and other popular leaders.

In my conversation with the Nawab I made it quite clear that, in my own opinion, Bhopal could not continue to exist as a separate State and that, as it had geographically, ethnically, and culturally an affinity to Malwa, it was only right that it should merge with Madhya Bharat. As an immediate step, I suggested to him that the ministry should resign and that, pending a decision as to the future of Bhopal, he should take over the administration himself. The Nawab maintained that he had done all that could be expected of him and disclaimed any responsibility for the trouble, which had been created by what he called irresponsible cliques. At one stage he even contemplated abdication, leaving it to his successor to face the music. I persuaded him to put such thoughts out of his mind. We arrived at certain tentative conclusions which I promised to place before Sardar before we resumed further discussions.

I had conversations also with the ministers of Bhopal, who urged that a local plebiscite should be taken on the question of merger. I said that it was absolutely unnecessary; that even in the case of such large States as Gwalior and Indore, we had not held plebiscites. I added that I could not believe it to be their intention to deny the representative character of Nehru, Sardar and the Central Cabinet whose policy I personally had no doubt the people would endorse. The ministers ultimately agreed to accept Sardar's decision.

Before I returned to Delhi, the Nawab and I agreed, subject to Sardar's approval, to issue a press *communiqué* stating that a satisfactory solution in regard to Bhopal was in sight and that all agitation for or against merger should be suspended. After the issue of the *communiqué*, the Nawab would take over and carry on the administration himself until the future of the State was decided. The Nawab was most anxious however that no announcement on the question of merger should be made until the future of Baroda, Kolhapur, Travancore and Cochin had been settled and announced.

Sardar agreed with the tentative conclusions reached between the Nawab and myself, whereupon a *communiqué* was issued, the Bhopal ministry resigned, and the Nawab took over the administration. We then started negotiations regarding the future of the State. The negotiations were very prolonged and involved my having to make many trips to Bhopal. It became a joke with Sardar whenever I went to Bhopal to describe the visit as a 'pilgrimage'. The Nawab had an extraordinary passion for detail; every tentative conclusion had to be written down and initialled. It would be tedious and unnecessary to describe the various stages of the negotiations. We eventually decided that the question of Bhopal's amalgamation with Madhya Bharat should be temporarily postponed and that, purely as a transitional arrangement, the State should be taken over as a Chief Commissioner's province.

The majority of the Muslims in the State were concentrated in Bhopal town; they needed to be reassured, particularly in the initial period until conditions settled down. The Bhopal State Forces were manned predominantly by Muslims drawn from Pakistan; their disbandment would require delicate handling. The Services in Bhopal, especially the Police, were overwhelmingly Muslim; the position called for readjustment. These were some of the considerations which prompted the Government of India to take over Bhopal as a Chief Commissioner's province.

Negotiations were conducted in a most cordial atmosphere. On one or two occasions the Nawab called upon M. R. Jayakar or Sir Joseph Bhore to advise him, but for the most part he argued his own case with ability and skill. We had fixed the final meeting for the signing of the agreement as 30 April 1949, but I arrived on that day to find the Nawab running a high temperature, in excruciating pain, with a specialist from Bombay in attendance. When I last visited the State, I had told the Nawab that the next time I came, I should expect the agreement to be signed by him and he had promised that this would be so. We still had some points to discuss and settle but, as things were, it seemed to me unreasonable and unkind to bother him. The Nawab however was firm. He told me that in all probability he would have to undergo an operation, but that he would sign the agreement first; and he requested me to proceed with the discussions. I was much impressed by his gesture. We settled the privy purse at Rs 11 lakhs, of which Rs 1 lakh was for the heir-apparent who happened to be his eldest daughter. The second point raised by the Nawab was that any differences arising out of the merger agreement should be subject to judicial determination by the Federal Court. I objected on the grounds that we had not included such a provision in other merger agreements and that we could not allow political matters, on which none but the government of the day should be the final authority, to be adjudicated by a court of law. There were other points, however, such as his share in the Bhopal State Railway and the succession, which were amicably settled.

After this I came out of the Nawab's room and acquainted Buch, Joint Secretary of the States Ministry, with the points we had discussed and the decisions taken. Buch reminded me that one further important point remained to be settled before the merger agreement could be signed by the Nawab. This related to the *jagirs* granted to him by his mother for his maintenance while he was the third prince. The point had completely escaped my mind and I had no choice but to trouble the Nawab again. I went back to his bedroom and suggested that he should hand over these *jagirs* to the State. This rather upset him. He told me that if that was my final view, he would abide by it and sign the agreement, but that he wanted an opportunity to appeal to Sardar. We eventually came to an understanding that he would himself pass the necessary orders for the resumption of these *jagirs* by the State before handing over the State to the Government of India; but that, before he did so, he would send an appeal to Sardar in the matter and abide by his decision. Thereafter he signed the merger agreement. The State was taken over as a Chief Commissioner's province on 1 June 1949. Bhopal now has an elected legislature and a ministry.

II

We now turn to the States which were merged with the provinces of Madras, East Punjab, the United Provinces, West Bengal and Assam.

The States merged with Madras were three, namely, Pudukkottai, Banganapalle and Sandur.

PUDUKKOTTAI was of these the most important. This State had an area of 1,170 square miles and a population of less than half a million. It is said to have been founded in 1686 by Raghunatha Raya Tondaiman. In the eighteenth century the Tondaimans rendered useful service to the British in their fight with the French round Trichinopoly, in their wars with Hyder Ali and Tippu Sultan and in the Poligar wars. In 1806 the State came formally under the East India Company. The present Rajah, Rajagopala Tondaiman Bahadur, was nominated as successor to the *gaddi* in November 1928 at the age of six, on the death of the previous ruler. The State had been well administered. It was fortunate to have had outstanding administrators like Sir A. Seshiah Sastry during the early years and Sir Alexander Loftus Tottenham during the present ruler's minority. The Nattukottai Chettiars, hereditary bankers and money-lenders of South India, had in no small measure contributed to the prosperity of the State.

I met the Rajah only once, when he was invited to Delhi to discuss the future of his State. He was just twenty-six at the time and seemed completely overwhelmed when the proposal to merge his State with Madras was put to him. Neither he nor his adviser had anything to say. The agreement was signed on 29 February 1948. The privy purse and private properties were settled subsequently in accordance with the recommendations of the Government of Madras. After the State was taken over (on 3 March 1948), there came complaints from the leaders of the people of Pudukkottai that the State was being neglected by the Government of Madras. I went to Madras and had a meeting with the Premier (Omandur P. Ramaswami Reddiar) who promised that everything possible would be done to remove the legitimate grievances of the people of Pudukkottai. Unfortunately, a good deal of dissatisfaction still persists among them.

BANGANAPALLE was a small Muslim State with an area of 275 square miles and a population of about 40,000. It was originally a *jagir* granted by the King of Bijapur. The Nawab, Fazl-i-Ali Khan Bahadur, signed a merger agreement on 18 February 1948. The administration was taken over by the Madras Government on 23 February 1948.

SANDUR was a still smaller State with an area of 169 square miles and a population of 16,000. The ruling family belonged to the Ghorpade family. According to the family legend one of their ancestors in the time of the Bahmini dynasty acquired the surname of Ghorpade from having scaled an impregnable fort in the Konkan with the aid of an iguana, known in Marathi as 'ghorpad'. I invited the ruler to Delhi. He was very difficult to deal with at first; but eventually, on 1 April 1949, he signed the agreement to merge his State with Madras. (When the Andhra Province was subsequently formed Sandur was transferred to Mysore.)

DUJANA, LOHARU and PATAUDI were three tiny Muslim States in East Punjab. Dujana had an area of 100 square miles and a population of less than 30,000; Loharu an area of 226 square miles and a population of about 28,000 and Pataudi an area of 53 square miles and a population of 20,000. These three States were created by Lord Lake as rewards for the services rendered by the founders of the ruling families in his campaigns against the Scindia and the Holkar. The grants originally were in the nature of *jagirs*, which the Government of India subsequently recognized as independent States. During the communal holocaust that followed the partition, the Nawab of Dujana went to Pakistan with whatever movable properties he could lay his hands on. The Government of India had no option but to merge the State with East Punjab. Later the Nawab appears to have regretted his action; a claim was made on his behalf for the payment of his privy purse in Pakistan, but he was told that the Government of India could not agree to pay him any privy purse so long as he was not an Indian subject.

During the communal trouble, the Nawab of Loharu was obliged to leave his State. Subsequently, I discussed the future of the State with the Nawab and he agreed to its merger with East Punjab. He signed the merger agreement on 17 February 1948 and the State was taken over by the East Punjab Government.

The Nawab of Pataudi was a well-known sportsman and cricketer. It is a matter of great regret that he should have died at a very early age. I remember him for his sane views in politics. He preached and practised tolerance and when India was in the grip of communal frenzy he was one of the few Muslims who did not allow themselves to be swept off their feet. He came to Delhi and voluntarily offered to merge his State with East Punjab. The merger agreement was signed on 18 March 1948 and the administration was subsequently taken over by the East Punjab Government. The Nawab continued to live in Delhi until his death.

COOCH BEHAR had an area of 1,318 square miles and a population of about 6½ lakhs. It was founded over three centuries ago and in 1773 entered into a subsidiary alliance with the East India Company. The present ruler succeeded his father in 1922 at the age of seven. The State had common boundaries with East Pakistan, West Bengal and Assam. It was decided that until conditions in the border area became stabilized, the State should be administered as a Chief Commissioner's province. The ruler signed the agreement on 30 August 1949 and the State was taken over by the Government of India as a Chief Commissioner's province on 12 September 1949. But in December of the same year, Sardar, after consulting the Premier of West Bengal, decided that Cooch Behar should be merged with that province. This decision took effect from 1 January 1950 by an order issued under section 290A of the Government of India Act of 1935.

Three States were merged with the United Provinces, namely Rampur, Banaras and Tehri-Garhwal.

RAMPUR was the most important of these, the only surviving representative of what was once the Rohilla power. It had an area of nearly 900 square miles and a population of nearly half a million. It was well-known for its enlightened administration. During the time of the present ruler, Sir Saiyid Raza Ali Khan Bahadur, it had made considerable industrial progress, its revenues having increased to Rs 110 lakhs per annum. After partition, the position of the Nawab became very difficult. Strong pressure was brought to bear on him not to accede to the Indian Union; but he never wavered in his loyalty to the Government of India. He was the first Muslim ruler of importance openly to accept accession. He had no communal prejudices. In order to create confidence in the Muslim minority the Nawab suggested that, for some time at any rate, the State should be taken over as a Chief Commissioner's province. His suggestion was accepted. He signed the agreement on 15 May and the State was taken over on 1 July 1949. Five months later, the State was merged in the United Provinces. It may be mentioned here that there is an Oriental Library in Rampur, containing over twelve thousand rare manuscripts and an immense collection of Moghul miniature paintings, which attracts scholars from all over the world. This library has been handed over to the Government of India to be looked after by a Trust.

BANARAS had an area of 875 square miles and a population of nearly four lakhs. It was an ancient principality and it had been absorbed by the British and constituted as a State only in 1911. The last Maharajah died in 1939 without issue, the present ruler being an adoptive heir. I had several long and tedious discussions with the Maharajah. Ultimately, on 5 September 1949, he signed the merger agreement. The administration was taken over by the Government of the United Provinces some weeks later, on 15 October.

TEHRI-GARHWAL was a hill State territorially contiguous to both Himachal Pradesh and the United Provinces. For administrative reasons it was decided to merge this State with the United Provinces. The State was founded in A.D. 688 by Rajah Kanak Pal; the present ruler claimed to be his 59th direct descendant in the male line. It had an area of 4,500 square miles and a population of nearly 4 lakhs. In 1948, following an agitation in the State for responsible government, the ruler set up a popular ministry which, however, proved an utter failure. I invited the Maharajah and his ministers to Delhi for discussions. The Maharajah is the most silent prince I have ever met. On 18 May 1949 he signed the merger agreement and on 1 August the administration was taken over by the Government of the United Provinces.

THE KHASI HILL STATES, a tribal area in Assam, were twenty-five in number. The chiefs of these States, known as Siems, were generally elected by the people: a number of them were Christians. Before the transfer of power, the Crown Representative's relations with these States were conducted through the Governor of Assam. These States did not accede to India on 15 August 1947. The old practice continued, by which the Governor of Assam administered these areas on behalf of the Government of India under the Indian (Foreign Jurisdiction) Order in Council. Later in the year these States, which had meanwhile formed a federation of their own, executed an Agreement continuing in force,with certain exceptions, existing administrative arrangements with the Dominion of India and the province of Assam. Thereafter, the rulers individually and

NEVER MISS A MEAL !

Rampur is the latest State to be merged with U.P.

By courtesy of Shankar's Weekly

collectively acceded to the Indian Union. The Instrument of Accession, subject to the provisions of the Agreement, empowered the Dominion Legislature to make laws for the Khasi Hill States in respect of any matter.

The future of these States under the new Constitution was the subject of prolonged discussion between the States Ministry and the Siems and their advisers, the Reverend Nichols-Roy being their chief spokesman. The people in the States wished to preserve their traditions and customs as far as possible; they were anxious to maintain their autonomy, and were opposed to the idea of outright merger with Assam. The Government of India ultimately decided that the district councils in the tribal areas should be given a large measure of autonomy. Detailed and specific provisions for the governance of the Khasi Hill States and other tribal areas of Assam were included in the Sixth Schedule to the Indian Constitution.

III

The amalgamation of two or more States, or groups of States, into a Union did not signify that the States so amalgamated in all cases formed one compact block of territory. For instance, when the Bundelkhand and Baghelkhand States were integrated to form the Union of Vindhya Pradesh, some of the smaller States belonging to these two groups were still left as islands in the United Provinces, in the Central Provinces and in Madhya Bharat, while islands of territory belonging to the United Provinces and the Central Provinces went along with these States into the new Union of Vindhya Pradesh. Again, there was no clear-cut boundary between the Unions of Madhya Bharat and Rajasthan, there being enclaves of one in the other. So also was the position in PEPSU, East Punjab and Himachal Pradesh. Saurashtra had enclaves in Bombay and vice versa. There were islands of Hyderabad territory in the Central Provinces, in Bombay and in Madras; as also enclaves of these provinces within the State. Travancore-Cochin and Madras had enclaves within each other.

Apart from administrative inconvenience, trade and commerce were also affected by these different jurisdictions. In one State where there was this interlacing of jurisdiction we experienced much trouble in dealing with Communists who, by hopping from one jurisdiction to another, were able for some time to foil our efforts to apprehend them.

A rationalization of boundaries, we felt, was essential. The procedure for exchange of enclaves was less complicated under the Government of India Act of 1935 than under the new Constitution. We decided therefore to tackle the problem before 26 January 1950 when the new Constitution would come into force. Besides, if we did not act while the situation was still fluid there was a possibility of the matter being postponed indefinitely, and some of the benefits of the great political and administrative change brought about by the integration of the States would be lost.

We asked the different provincial and Union Governments to prepare maps of the enclaves with which each of them was concerned. On receipt of the material from the provincial and Union Governments we held a series of meetings with their representatives. I was struck, at our meetings, by the tenacity with which some of the provincial Governments clung to the territories belonging to them. For instance, there were three bits of territory of the former Baroda State inside Saurashtra; but the Government of Bombay were not willing to transfer them to Saurashtra. Nor were the Government of Madras prepared to part with certain pockets of territory belonging to them in Travancore-Cochin. Where an enclave was large in area or population and its transfer would materially affect the revenues of the province or Union of which it formed a part, we did not press for an exchange; but there were very many small islands, some of them only a few acres in extent, whose existence as such did no good to anybody. In the end and after considerable discussion, we came to agreed settlements in regard to the majority of the enclaves. Exchange of territories, where agreed to, was effected by orders of the Governor-General or by agreements between the Rajpramukhs concerned. The main provisions of these orders were that the territories concerned would form part of the absorbing units; the laws of the surrendering units would be replaced by those of the absorbing units; and the properties and assets as well as rights, obligations and liabilities in respect of them would pass on to the Government of the absorbing unit. Exchange of territories often entails much heart-burning and political bitterness. It is a matter of satisfaction that we were able to accomplish this large-scale adjustment of boundaries without leaving any unpleasantness in its wake.

40

XVII

HYDERABAD

I

THE State of Hyderabad was founded by Mir Qamruddin Chin Qilich Khan. He was the son of Aurangzeb's general, Ghazi-ud-din Khan Feroz Jang, who traced his ancestry to Abu Bakr, the first Khalifa. In 1713, six years after Aurangzeb's death, emperor Farrukhsiyar made Mir Qamruddin Viceroy of the Deccan, with the title of Nizam-ul-Mulk Feroz Jung. Later, emperor Muhammad Shah conferred on him the title of Asaf Jah, by which title the dynasty is still known. By 1724, Mir Qamruddin had made himself virtually independent of Delhi, although he and his successors continued to profess a nominal allegiance to the Moghul emperor right up to 1858, when the British Crown assumed the governance of India. On Mir Qamruddin's death in 1748, there ensued a war of succession in which the English and the French in turn espoused the cause of rival claimants. Eventually in 1751 Salabat Jang, the third son, with the help of the French, emerged successful. The new Nizam threw in his lot with the French and, in return for their protection from the Mahrattas, ceded to them the four Northern Circar districts (now part of the new Andhra province). In 1759, however, the Circars were wrested from the French by a British force.

In 1761 Salabat Jang was deposed by his younger brother Nizam Ali Khan, who ordered an invasion of the Carnatic. The Hyderabad forces were repulsed by the British and when peace was concluded by the Treaty of 1766, the Nizam placed himself under British protection. In 1767, in quest of independence, the Nizam broke his treaty with the British and allied himself with Hyder Ali of Mysore. The joint forces of Hyder Ali and the Nizam were defeated and, by the Treaty of Masulipatam of 1768, the British again reimposed their military protection upon the Nizam. From 1778 onwards, a British Resident and a subsidiary force were installed in Hyderabad.

In 1795 Nizam Ali Khan made an unsuccessful attack on the Mahratta Confederacy at Kurdla and was compelled to submit to a humiliating peace by which he lost large territories, including most of Berar; in addition he was called upon to pay a heavy indemnity as well as arrears of *chauth*.

The Nizam turned again to the French, but British influence prevailed. The Marquess of Wellesley was able to persuade him to get rid of his French troops and to accept an increase in the British subsidiary force at Hyderabad.

In 1799 the Nizam aided the East India Company in the war with Tippu Sultan and after the latter's defeat and death the British gave a part of his territories to the Nizam. In the following year the Nizam was obliged to cede a portion of it back to the British in order to meet the cost of the increased subsidiary force.

The death of Nizam Ali Khan and the succession of his eldest surviving son, Sikander Jah, occurred on 7 August 1803, three days after the outbreak of the second Mahratta War. Before the end of the year, the war was concluded and the Treaty of Deogaon signed. Under this treaty the Nizam, for the help rendered by him to the British, obtained the whole of Berar west of Wardha, except the hill forts (which were acquired in 1822) and all the districts to the south of the Ajanta Hills held by the Scindia.

As a result of the third Mahratta War, the Nizam received a quittance of all demands on account of *chauth* and acquired, by exchange of territory, a well-defined frontier.

Sikander Jah died on 21 May 1829, and was succeeded by his eldest surviving son, Nasir-ud-Daula. By 1852 the pay of the contingent had fallen heavily into arrears. The officers and men were reduced to such straits that the only way to relieve them was by making direct payments to them from the Company's treasury. The Governor-General demanded territorial security from the Nizam in return for these payments. By the Treaty of 1853, the province of Berar, along with certain districts in the Raichur Doab and on the western frontier of Hyderabad, were assigned for this purpose, their administration being taken over by British officers under the control of the Resident at Hyderabad.

Nasir-ud-Daula died on 11 March 1857 and was succeeded by his eldest son, Afzal-ud-Daula. Due to the influence of his minister,

Sir Salar Jang, the Nizam gave the British little cause for anxiety during the Mutiny of 1857, after which the Treaty of 1853 was considerably modified to his advantage. By the Treaty of 1860, except for Berar, all the other districts assigned in 1853 were restored; the confiscated territory of the rebellious Raja of Shorapur was ceded to the Nizam, and a debt of Rs 50 lakhs due to the Government of India was cancelled.

Mir Mahbub Ali Khan was a minor when he succeeded his father Afzal-ud-Daula on 26 February 1869. He was invested with full powers of administration fifteen years later. His reign was long but uneventful. On 5 November 1902, a fresh arrangement was concluded, which reaffirmed the Nizam's sovereignty over Berar but under which the Nizam leased the province in perpetuity to the Government of India in return for an annual rent of Rs 25 lakhs. The Government of India were at the same time empowered to make such arrangements as might seem to them desirable for its administration. (Berar has since been attached to the Central Provinces). The Hyderabad contingent, with the exception of the artillery which was disbanded, was delocalized and incorporated in the Indian army, the Government of India engaging to make due provision for the protection of the Nizam's dominion. The settlement of 1902 was one of the outstanding achievements of Lord Curzon.

The present Nizam Mir Usman Ali Khan Bahadur is the seventh in the line. He succeeded to the *gaddi* on 29 August 1911. In 1918 the title of 'His Exalted Highness' was conferred on him as a hereditary distinction. Shortly thereafter, by an autograph letter from the King, he was granted the title of 'Faithful Ally of the British Government.'

Geographically, Hyderabad occupies a pivotal position in the heart of the country. The State was surrounded by the Central Provinces in the north, Bombay in the west, and Madras on the east and south. In population, revenue and importance it was the premier State in the country. The population was nearly sixteen million and the annual revenue Rs 26 crores. Its area was over 82,000 square miles. Hyderabad had its own coinage, paper currency and stamps.

Despite its position as the premier State, Hyderabad was treated by the British no differently from other Indian States. The right of intervention in internal affairs was repeatedly asserted and exercised. In October 1911, a few months after his accession, the Nizam was warned by Lord Hardinge that he was 'on his trial for two years; at the end of which it would be just as easy for the Government of India to appoint a Council of Regency as now.' In 1919, the Nizam was twice warned by Lord Chelmsford, the first time in a letter and the second in a personal interview, that the Government of India claimed the right to intervene in case of misrule.

In 1925 the Nizam, in a letter to the Viceroy, raised the question of the retrocession of Berar and asserted the claim that 'save and except matters relating to foreign powers and policies, the Nizams of Hyderabad have been independent in the internal affairs of their State just as much as the British Government in British India.' In an oft-quoted letter, Lord Reading, then Viceroy, repudiated the position taken up by the Nizam and asserted that the sovereignty of the British Crown was supreme in India and that this supremacy was not based only upon treaties and engagements, but that it existed independently of them. The Viceroy pointed out that it was the right of the British Government to intervene in the internal affairs of Indian States. He emphatically repudiated the Nizam's claim that there was an equality between the Governments of Hyderabad and Great Britain; and he added that the Nizam did not stand in a category separate from that of the rulers of the other Indian States.

The population of Hyderabad was over 85 per cent Hindu. But the civil services, the police and the army were the close preserve of the Muslims. Even in the Legislative Assembly, which the Nizam set up in 1946, the Muslims had a majority of 10 over the Hindus in a House of 132.

Soon after the announcement of His Majesty's Government's plan of 3 June 1947, the Nizam issued a *firman* declaring his intention not to send representatives to the Constituent Assembly of either Pakistan or India, and making it clear that on 15 August he would be entitled to resume the status of an independent sovereign. It had been his ambition to secure Dominion Status for his State, on the withdrawal of the British and treatment thenceforth as a member of the British Commonwealth of Nations. When he saw that clause 7 of the Indian Independence Bill did not permit the grant of Dominion Status to an Indian State, he protested against 'the way in which my State is being abandoned by its old ally, the British Government, and the ties which have bound me in loyal devotion to the King Emperor are being severed.'

On 11 July the Nizam sent a delegation to Delhi headed by the Nawab of Chhatari, President of his Executive Council, to meet

Lord Mountbatten. The other members were Nawab Ali Yawar Jung, Sir Walter Monckton, K.C., Abdur Rahim and Pingle Venkatarama Reddy. The Political Department was represented by Sir Conrad Corfield and L. C. L. Griffin; and I represented the States Department. The discussions proceeded mainly upon three points: the retrocession of Berar to the Nizam; the grant of Dominion Status to Hyderabad, and the accession of the State to the Indian Union. With regard to the first of these, Lord Mountbatten pointed out that the Indian Independence Bill had recognized the Nizam's sovereignty over Berar, but Berar was now so firmly a physical part of the Central Provinces that nothing short of war, or voluntary rendition, could give it back to him. Moreover, in 1936 His Majesty's Government had committed themselves to a promise that no change in the existing arrangement would be considered without consulting the people. Lord Mountbatten thought that if a referendum were held in Berar the likelihood was that the people would vote for the existing arrangement to continue; he was not disposed therefore to disturb the *status quo* for the time being.

Sir Conrad Corfield made the suggestion that a standstill agreement on Berar should be concluded for a period of three years and that it should include acceptance by the Congress of the stipulation that at the end of that period Berar would be handed over to the Nizam without a plebiscite. I was against this idea. I stressed that the Government of India were anxious to preserve the overall unity of the country and that if the Nizam helped in maintaining that unity, the Government of India would not mind meeting some of his demands. Finally, Lord Mountbatten suggested that a standstill agreement with regard to Berar should extend for an indefinite period, but that it should be liable to cancellation by either party at twelve months' notice. This denunciation should not however be unilateral, but should be preceded by meetings, and the period of notice should be employed in negotiations. The delegation agreed to put this suggestion to the Nizam.

On the question of Dominion Status for Hyderabad, Lord Mountbatten was quite firm and told the delegation that His Majesty's Government would not agree to Hyderabad becoming a member of the British Commonwealth of Nations except through either of the two new Dominions. Nawab Ali Yawar Jung asked what would happen if the Dominion to which Hyderabad adhered decided, after some time, to go out of the Commonwealth. Lord Mountbatten replied that he could not prophesy what line His Majesty's Government would take in such circumstances. In any case, if Hyderabad adhered on three central subjects, their representatives in the Dominion Legislature would have an important voice in the decision.

The discussion then turned to the accession of Hyderabad to the Indian Union. Both Lord Mountbatten and I impressed on the delegation that it would be to the mutual advantage of Hyderabad and India if the State acceded to the Indian Union on three subjects without any financial commitments. But the general feeling of the delegation was that the Nizam would have the greatest difficulty in taking such a course, as it would compromise his sovereignty. The delegation went even further to say that if we pressed the Nizam too hard, he might consider joining Pakistan.

Lord Mountbatten replied that there was no doubt that the Nizam was legally entitled to do so, but that the mechanical difficulty presented by the facts of geography was very real. The present chance would probably be the last, and if it were not seized on at once it might be lost for ever. Without implying any kind of threat, he foresaw disastrous results to the State in five or ten years if his advice were not taken.

In subsequent meetings with me, the Hyderabad delegation pressed for permission to negotiate a standstill agreement without executing an instrument of accession. I told them that the Government of India did not contemplate entertaining standstill agreements with any State which did not accede. Nawab Ali Yawar Jung wrote to me that in view of this decision, it would seem useless to arrange for further discussion. I replied that, because of shortness of time, it would be impossible to discuss the standstill agreement with individual States. Moreover, the problems involved were common and therefore Hyderabad should discuss the standstill agreement along with other States; accordingly the Nawab of Chhatari was being included in the Negotiating Committee which it was proposed to set up after the meeting of the Chamber of Princes on 25 July 1947.

Subsequently the Nawab of Chhatari wrote that he would not take part in the Negotiating Committee since it would be discussing the question of accession in which Hyderabad was not interested. Lord Mountbatten tried to persuade him that the course of action he was pursuing was not in the interests of Hyderabad, but on 31 July the Nawab wrote again to say that he adhered to his **original** decision and suggested the appointment of a second Negotiating Committee, consisting only of such States as had decided to stand out of the Indian Constituent Assembly. He was anxious, too, that the negotiations should be with representatives of both India and Pakistan and that the agreement should be a tripartite one.

These proposals were unacceptable and the delegation returned to Hyderabad. Lord Mountbatten knew that it would be impossible to persuade Hyderabad to accede by 15 August; at the same time he did not wish to break off negotiations with the Nizam. He therefore asked the Government of India to grant an extension of two months to Hyderabad. The Cabinet agreed and requested Lord Mountbatten to continue the negotiations.

Lord Mountbatten was hopeful that Hyderabad would ultimately accede to India. He explained to me that the main reason why the Nizam had not acceded was because, although the Muslims in the State represented only 15 per cent of the population, they filled almost all the important government posts including those in the army and the police. It was therefore a revolt on their part against which the Nizam had to guard rather than any kind of uprising by the non-Muslims, although the latter represented the vast majority of the State's population. He pleaded that some time should be given to the Nizam to educate this all-powerful minority. I must say that I did not share Lord Mountbatten's optimism.

On 8 August the Nizam wrote to Lord Mountbatten that he could not contemplate bringing Hyderabad into organic union with either Pakistan or India. He was prepared however to enter into a treaty with India. Under such a treaty, he would conform to all-India standards so far as railway communications were concerned, and would also assure through communications and mutual interchange facilities. Hyderabad would contribute an agreed number of troops for the defence of India and would be prepared to conduct the external affairs of the State in general conformity with the foreign policy of India. These were qualified by three conditions: the first was that in the event of a war between India and Pakistan, Hyderabad would remain neutral; the second that Hyderabad should have the right to appoint Agents-General wherever it thought fit; and lastly, that there must be a provision in the treaty that, if India seceded from the British Commonwealth, Hyderabad would be free to review the situation *de novo*.

This letter was acknowledged by Lord Mountbatten on 12 August.

Except for re-emphasizing the advantages of accession, the letter broke no new ground.

In his address before the Constituent Assembly on 15 August, Lord Mountbatten referred to the fact that almost all the States in India had acceded to the Dominion and that the important exception was Hyderabad. Characteristically, he struck an optimistic note saying that negotiations would be continued with the Nizam and that he was hopeful of reaching a solution satisfactory to everyone. But in the country in general and among the Hindus of Hyderabad in particular, there was considerable uneasiness. The press drew pointed attention to the fact that, with its geographical position in the very heart of the country, Hyderabad could become a threat to national stability.

On 17 August 1947 the Nawab of Chhatari wrote to Lord Mountbatten expressing his wish to resume negotiations. Lord Mountbatten agreed. The delegation was expected to arrive on 25 August. On the same day Sir Walter Monckton telegraphed to Lord Mountbatten to say that he had been compelled to resign his position as Constitutional Adviser to the Nizam, although he still had the Nizam's confidence.

Almost immediately a telegram came from the Nizam asking Lord Mountbatten to persuade Sir Walter Monckton to stay on in his service. Lord Mountbatten sent a telegram to Sir Walter Monckton, inviting him to come to Delhi. Sir Walter arrived the same day and explained that he had resigned because of a most violent attack upon him in the Hyderabad press, which had been organized by the Ittehad-ul-Muslimeen[1]; that the Nawab of Chhatari and Nawab Ali Yawar Jung had also handed in their resignations for the same reason, but that the Nizam had refused to accept that of the Nawab of Chhatari; and that he (Sir Walter Monckton) was prepared to withdraw his resignation only if the Nizam publicly dissociated himself from the Ittehad attack. Ultimately the Nizam issued a strongly worded *firman* condemning the attacks on the delegation made in the press as damaging to the interests of the State and followed this up with two letters to Lord Mountbatten confirming his confidence in Sir Walter Monckton. Thus blew over this particular 'storm in a teacup'.

[1] The Ittehad-ul-Muslimeen was a Muslim communal organization. Its leader was one Kasim Razvi who combined fanaticism with charlatanry. He had organized a shock brigade called the Razakars. The organization aimed at creating a theocratic and totalitarian State. Militarist demonstrations were part of their routine.

41

Lord Mountbatten and I discussed the latest position in Hyderabad with Sir Walter Monckton. He said that he had brought the Nizam to the point of offering a treaty which would cover the three subjects of defence, external affairs and communications and was confident that he could persuade him to accept the equivalent of accession, provided the term 'Instrument of Accession' was given some such sugar-coating as 'Articles of Association'.

This was precisely the point on which Sardar was adamant. He wrote to Lord Mountbatten saying that he saw no alternative but to insist on the Nizam's accession to the Dominion of India. He said that the slightest variation in the Instruments of Accession or in the arrangements regarding the State's association with the Dominion in regard to the three subjects would expose the Government of India to the charge of breach of faith with the States that had already joined the Dominion. Moreover, it would create the impression that advantage lay in holding out rather than coming in and that, while no special merit attached to accession, a beneficial position could be secured by keeping out. This was bound to have most unfortunate consequences. Sardar was firm on the point that the Nizam must agree to submit the issue to the judgment of his people and that he must abide by their decision. The Government of India would be content to accept whatever might be the result of such a referendum and would be prepared to include Berar in any such plan.

Accordingly Lord Mountbatten wrote to the Nizam on 27 August making the offer of a referendum under the supervision of British officers. The Nizam rejected the offer next day in a brief communication in which he said, 'the problem and constitutional position of Hyderabad are such that the question of referendum does not arise.'

On 8 September the Nawab of Chhatari came to Delhi. Lord Mountbatten, Sir Walter Monckton, the Nawab and myself met in informal conference. Lord Mountbatten told the Nawab that it was his considered opinion that all the Indian States had been offered such excellent terms in the Instrument of Accession and the standstill agreement that it was not possible to imagine a more advantageous arrangement. He said that it would be a positive disadvantage to Hyderabad to try to deal with these three subjects on its own initiative. The Nawab recognized the force of Lord Mountbatten's arguments, but said that the Nizam still wanted a treaty. At that, Lord Mountbatten told him that Sardar had written to him saying that he would only agree to an Instrument of Accession. Sir Walter

Monckton then expressed the view that he could probably bring the Nizam round to the point of offering an agreement the terms of which would be far more like the Instrument of Accession than the original offer of a treaty. I said that I could not make any commitment without seeing the document. It was finally agreed that the Nawab of Chhatari and Sir Walter Monckton should go back to Hyderabad and attempt to obtain such a document from the Nizam.

Lord Mountbatten then questioned the Nawab of Chhatari with regard to the order for arms and ammunition, worth three million pounds sterling, which had been placed with Czechoslovakia by the Hyderabad State. The Nawab replied that this had been done without his knowledge by the 'Minister of War' and that it required his sanction which he had no intention of giving. He agreed that the order should not be proceeded with, but pointed out that the Government of India had stopped the normal supply of arms to Hyderabad. Lord Mountbatten explained that this was due to a temporary difficulty and that it applied to all the States; but that he was sure the position would be eased very soon and Hyderabad would be able to obtain the arms it required.

The delegation then returned to Hyderabad. On 18 September the Nizam wrote that, short of accession, Hyderabad was ready and willing to make such a treaty of association with India as would not only secure friendly relations, but would lead to the fullest co-operation. He was afraid that accession would lead to disturbance and bloodshed in Hyderabad.

Simultaneously with this approach to us the Nizam got into contact with Jinnah with a view to securing the services of Sir Zafrullah Khan as the President of his Executive Council. In this he was unsuccessful, as Sir Zafrullah Khan had been deputed to lead the Pakistan delegation to the U.N.O.

The Hyderabad delegation, with the addition of Sir Sultan Ahmed, came to Delhi again for further discussions; Lord Mountbatten and I had a meeting with them on 22 September. The same old arguments and the same old replies in regard to accession were repeated *ad nauseam*. The delegation pointed out on behalf of the Nizam that the difference between accession and a treaty of association was one to which he attached the very greatest importance, and that the accession of Hyderabad to India would lead to bloodshed and communal trouble. They stressed that a large proportion of the Hindus in Hyderabad were loyal to the Nizam. Nawab Ali

Yawar Jung made the astounding statement that if Hyderabad
acceded, the Muslims who made up half the population of Hyderabad city would not tolerate it and that the trouble they would raise
would be uncontrollable and would spread to the districts.

Lord Mountbatten said that similar fears had been expressed concerning Rampur and Bhopal before they acceded, but they had proved groundless. He pertinently enquired of the delegation whether,
in the event of the Hindu population in Hyderabad being butchered,
they expected the Government of India to sit back and watch events.

At this stage Sir Walter Monckton intervened and said that the
Nizam feared that his signature on the Instrument of Accession would
merge the identity of the State with the Dominion of India. Lord
Mountbatten countered this by saying that the signing of the Instrument of Accession would in fact prevent such obliteration. He
added that he was willing to ask the Government of India what in-
ducements they were prepared to offer Hyderabad if the Nizam
signed the Instrument of Accession. At the same time, he wanted
the delegation to make an equally honest effort to bridge the gulf.

After the conference Sir Walter Monckton had a long talk with
me. The next morning he sent me a revised draft 'Heads of Agreement,' stating that 'the gap between us is honestly narrow.' He said
it would be worth while to consider a temporary compromise whereby an agreement of association was granted to Hyderabad (without
any of the attendant advantages which would go with accession)
for say, six months. 'First of all they would get confidence in the
Dominion and secondly (and this is the big point) they would constantly face the reality of the advantages they would gain by acceding,
while the points of pride and face would fade away.' The delegation
left for Hyderabad.

I found the draft Heads of Agreement on examination to be most
unsatisfactory. I had a meeting with Lord Mountbatten and apprised
him of the views of the States Ministry. On 24 September Lord
Mountbatten wrote to the Nizam that the Government of India were
of the opinion that the Heads of Agreement did not afford a satisfactory solution, in that they gave no legislative power to the Dominion on the three subjects. Moreover, in external affairs, Hyderabad, while disclaiming any immediate intention of pursuing
an independent foreign policy, demanded the right to enter into
direct political relations with any foreign power — a right which it
had never exercised in the past. Lord Mountbatten stressed the fact

that if Hyderabad acceded, there would be no difficulty in securing the continuance of all existing rights; nor need the Nizam apprehend any interference in his internal sovereignty.

After reaching Hyderabad Sir Walter Monckton reported to Lord Mountbatten that during his absence the Nizam's attitude had stiffened. There was now no likelihood of his reconsidering the question of accession. Indeed, it looked as though he would prefer that the negotiations should break down rather than that the uncertainty which now existed should continue. Sir Walter added that it was plain that Pakistan influences were at the root of the change in the Nizam's attitude, and that the latter wanted him to go to Karachi on 1 October to seek an interview with Jinnah.

On 26 September the Nizam wrote again to Lord Mountbatten. This letter was only a rehash of his previous letters, but he re-emphasized two aspects. He stressed the unique position of Hyderabad, whose sovereignty and right to independence as a result of the lapse of paramountcy should be recognized. The other was his persistence in the belief that Hyderabad's accession to India would result in vast bloodshed in South India as a whole.

Even before the transfer of power the Nizam had pressed the Government of India to withdraw their troops from Hyderabad and to vacate and hand back all the cantonments in the State. Once or twice during the negotiations this point had been pressed by the Hyderabad delegation, but I had given a non-committal reply. The issue was again raised by the Nizam, but the Government of India decided to take no action pending the outcome of the negotiations.

When the delegation was in Delhi in September, they had suggested that I should visit Hyderabad early in October for further discussions. Lord Mountbatten thought that I should take advantage of this invitation and Sardar agreed with him. Accordingly I informed the Nawab of Chhatari that I would be arriving in Hyderabad on Wednesday, 8 October. On the 6th, however, I was surprised to receive a letter from the Nawab asking me not to go to Hyderabad, as the Government of Hyderabad had reason to think that my visit would excite demonstrations and counter-demonstrations. He suggested that it would be better for the delegation to come to Delhi. When I received this letter I felt sure that the Government of Hyderabad were unable to stand up to the Ittehad-ul-Muslimeen, who must have pressed for the cancellation of my visit. I telegraphed immediately to the Nawab:

I deeply regret that the law and order situation in Hyderabad should have so gone beyond the Government's control as to compel you to ask me at the last moment to abandon my visit which was arranged at the instance of your representatives and in consultation with your Government. If you still think that continuance of negotiations in such circumstances would yield any useful results, we have no objection to your delegation coming here on Thursday.

It was in this somewhat strained atmosphere that Lord Mountbatten resumed negotiations with the Hyderabad delegation on 10 October. He first of all referred to the letter sent by the Nawab of Chhatari requesting me to cancel my visit. The Nawab was most apologetic and gave several explanations, which did not however carry much conviction with me.

On the main question, Sir Sultan Ahmed enquired of me what were the concrete and substantial advantages that Hyderabad would gain by accession. I told him that, although I could not commit the Government of India, I could instance several advantages that would accrue to Hyderabad, the most notable of which would be the position of Berar; priority in the construction of railways; help in the economic development of the State, and an outlet to the sea.

After protracted discussion, both Sir Sultan Ahmed and Sir Walter Monckton enquired whether, if full accession was not acceptable to the Nizam, it would be possible to achieve the same object by any other method. Lord Mountbatten replied in the negative, adding that it would be extremely difficult to treat Hyderabad any differently from other States which had acceded to India.

It was clear that we had reached a stalemate in our negotiations which had been going on now for three months. There was no advance in the respective positions of the Government of India and the Nizam. Nor could we, in view of the situation existing at the time, afford to break off the negotiations. After a careful weighing of the pros and cons, I came to the conclusion that if we could get from Hyderabad the substance of accession by an agreement, we should compromise to that extent. This would involve some loss of face for the Government of India *vis-à-vis* other States, but that would be offset by Hyderabad being committed not to accede to Pakistan. With this idea in my mind I went to Sardar. I expressed my personal belief that, in view of the existing political and communal situation in the country, as well as the commitments of the Army, it was necessary at any price to purchase peace in the south. With the threat of the Razakars the position of the Hindus in Hyderabad was extremely precarious. I suggested therefore that if we could get from Hyderabad the substance of accession by an agreement, this would at least give us some breathing-time. Sardar agreed that in politics one sometimes had to accept the second best, but he withheld his final decision till he had seen the relevant documents.

Thereafter I told Lord Mountbatten and Sir Walter Monckton that I hoped to be able to persuade Nehru and Sardar to accept a Standstill Agreement if the Nizam would be prepared to concede in it the substance of accession. The Hyderabad delegation went back on 11 October. They returned on the 16th and gave me a draft agreement as well as the draft of a collateral letter from the Nizam. We had several meetings to discuss these documents. On 17 October, I told them that the Government of India were unable to accept either the draft agreement or the letter. The delegation agreed to revise the drafts in the light of my criticisms. On the morning of the 18th we met again, but the revised drafts were still unacceptable. At our next meeting that same afternoon, I told them that the Government of India were prepared to consider a much shorter Standstill Agreement, but not the elaborate one which they had prepared. In any case, since we were making no progress, I suggested that we should confer with Lord Mountbatten. We did so on Sunday, the 19th. I explained to Lord Mountbatten what had taken place between the Hyderabad delegation and myself, adding that if the delegation stood by their drafts it would not be possible for me to proceed further without consulting Sardar. Lord Mountbatten asked me to ascertain Sardar's reactions and proposed that we should meet that evening.

Sardar was emphatically of the view that rather than accept the agreement as drafted by Hyderabad we should break off negotiations. I then saw Sir Walter Monckton and told him that unless our position regarding defence and external affairs was fully met, there was no use for further discussion. But when I communicated Sardar's view to Lord Mountbatten, he said that it would be a great pity if the negotiations were to break down. Later in the evening, he met Sir Walter Monckton and myself and suggested that I should produce a draft agreement and a collateral letter which in my opinion would be acceptable to the Government of India.

Accordingly I prepared these revised drafts, which I discussed

informally with Sir Walter Monckton. He suggested some minor
changes which I accepted, and subsequently the agreement and the
collateral letter were sent to me formally by the delegation as the
proposals of the Government of Hyderabad. I submitted these drafts
first of all to Sardar and then to Nehru, along with a draft reply
from Lord Mountbatten to the Nizam's collateral letter. These documents were approved by Sardar, Nehru and Lord Mountbatten.
The Hyderabad delegation took the drafts away with them, when
they left on 22 October, to obtain the Nizam's approval, promising
to be back by Sunday the 26th.

Immediately on arrival in Hyderabad, the delegation submitted
the documents to the Nizam, who decided to refer the matter to his
Executive Council for advice. The Council sat on three consecutive
days, 23, 24 and 25 October, the members of the delegation being
present throughout these meetings. Eventually, it was decided by
six votes to three that the Council should advise the Nizam to
accept the agreement.

On the 25th evening the delegation went to the Nizam and reported
the decision of the Executive Council. The formal report of the
President of the Council was also sent to him. The Nizam formally
approved the decision of the Executive Council that same night,
but strangely enough postponed signing the agreement till the next
day. When on the evening of the 26th the delegation went to him
for his signature, he once more postponed signing until the next
morning, which was the date on which the delegation was to
leave for Delhi.

A melodrama was now enacted in Hyderabad by the Ittehad-ul-
Muslimeen. At about 3 o'clock on the morning of 27 October, a
crowd estimated at about twenty-five to thirty thousand surrounded
the houses of Sir Walter Monckton, the Nawab of Chhatari and Sir
Sultan Ahmed, which were all adjacent. Loudspeakers entreated
the crowd to remain orderly and to create no disturbance — beyond
preventing the delegation from leaving for Delhi. No Hyderabad
police were present.

At about 5 a.m. the Nawab of Chhatari managed with great
difficulty to make contact with the State army authorities, who
evacuated the delegates and Lady Monckton to the house of a
British officer of the Hyderabad State Forces. After a few hours the
Nizam sent a message to the delegates that they should not leave for
Delhi for a few days. Simultaneously he informed Lord Mountbatten

by telegram that, owing to 'unforeseen circumstances' the delegation were unable to return forthwith and that he trusted the Governor-General would not mind if they came on 30 or 31 October at the latest. Lord Mountbatten had no choice but to agree.

In the afternoon of 27 October the Nizam met his delegation. He wanted them to stay on while he took final stock of the situation. He was full of righteous indignation against the Ittehad-ul-Muslimeen and against Kasim Razvi in particular. He said with some show of anger that he would force Razvi to accept the decision taken by the Executive Council.

The next morning he had another interview with the delegation and without consulting those present (amongst whom, of course, was the President of the Executive Council), he suddenly called Razvi to the meeting. Razvi spoke of the agreement as leading to the extinction of Hyderabad and pleaded for a chance to reopen negotiations with the Government of India by a fresh delegation. He asserted that he would get the Government of India to accept the original agreement which had been rejected by them. When pressed to state the reasons which led him to believe that he could succeed where the delegation and notably Sir Walter Monckton had failed, Kasim Razvi said: 'As the hands of the Indian Union are fully occupied with their troubles elsewhere they will be in no position to do anything to us or to refuse our demands if we insist.' It may here be mentioned that the tribal invasion of Kashmir had started on 23 October and that Indian troops had been flown there on the 26th.

Sir Walter Monckton, the Nawab of Chhatari and Sir Sultan Ahmed all explained to the Nizam that the course of action which had been suggested by Razvi was wholly illusory and disastrous. But when they saw that the Nizam was inclined to listen to Kasim Razvi, all of them tendered their resignations. On 30 October the Nizam had a last interview with Sir Walter Monckton and Sir Sultan Ahmed, whose advice he sought on a letter which he had drafted to Lord Mountbatten. They refused to give any opinion; but Sir Sultan Ahmed promised to deliver the letter in person.

Sir Sultan Ahmed arrived at Delhi on 31 October. The letter which he delivered from the Nizam was in the nature of a threat. The Nizam wrote to say that if the negotiations with the Government of India were to break down, he would immediately negotiate and conclude an agreement with Pakistan. Sir Sultan Ahmed told Lord Mountbatten and myself that the Nizam had sent two persons

to Karachi who had returned on 29 October. He attributed the
Nizam's volte face to some message which he must have received
from Karachi as well as to the effrontery of Kasim Razvi.

The Nizam now selected a new delegation consisting of Nawab
Moin Nawaz Jung, Abdur Rahim and Pingle Venkatarama Reddy.
The first two were among the three members of the Nizam's Executive Council who had voted against the acceptance of the Standstill
Agreement. Abdur Rahim, a communalist fanatic of little or no
ability, was a prominent member of the Ittehad. Nawab Moin
Nawaz Jung, the leader of the delegation, was at that time Hyderabad's Minister for Police and Information. There was an identity
of interests between him and Kasim Razvi and he fully subscribed
to the doctrine of independence for the State. It was he, more
than anyone else, who made an amicable settlement between India
and Hyderabad practically impossible. Pingle Venkatarama Reddy
was selected probably only because he was a respectable old Hindu;
he had no political following, nor had he any opinion of his own.

Lord Mountbatten was extremely upset at the new developments
in Hyderabad and particularly by the replacement of the old
delegation by a new one. Sardar's annoyance was even greater. He
told me that the only decent course for us was to send back the new
delegation by the very same plane by which it arrived!

The new delegation arrived in Delhi on 31 October. That same
evening Nawab Moin Nawaz Jung had an informal interview with
Lord Mountbatten who, for once, was not his usual amiable self.
I was present at this interview. The Nawab said that he intended
to leave no stone unturned to come to an amicable settlement. Lord
Mountbatten pointed out that an 'amicable settlement' had already
been reached, it was not so much a question of leaving no stone unturned, as of not upsetting the existing stones. Nawab Moin Nawaz
Jung then suggested that the discussions should proceed on the basis
of the original draft agreement which had been brought by the old
delegation, but this Lord Mountbatten refused to consider. He
pointed out that it was odd that the delegation should try to reopen
negotiations on the basis of a document which had already been
rejected by the Government of India. The Nawab then wanted to
know the background of the recent negotiations. Lord Mountbatten
replied that he had no time to indulge in recapitulation and asked
him to get all the details from Sir Sultan Ahmed, who was then
staying in Delhi.

On 2 November, the delegation had a formal interview with Lord Mountbatten and myself. Nawab Moin Nawaz Jung read out copious extracts from the correspondence between the Nizam and Lord Mountbatten in order to justify the Nizam's volte face. Lord Mountbatten explained his efforts to bring about an agreed solution between the Government of India and the Nizam. He had persuaded the Government of India to grant a two months' extension for the negotiations. The Government of India were definitely for accession, while the Nizam wanted a treaty, so that the two parties had started poles asunder. He had been trying for many weeks to bring them together. Bit by bit the differences had been ironed out. For the first time the Government of India were prepared to consider a Standstill Agreement without accession. This was an immense step forward.

Nawab Moin Nawaz Jung was anxious for some changes in the draft agreement, but Lord Mountbatten was firm. He said that both the Government of India and the Nizam had declared their intention of signing, when suddenly the Nizam repudiated his part of the bargain. The only possible explanation he could think of was that Hyderabad considered India's position to have immensely deteriorated during the last few days. That was an entirely false assumption. The Government of India were still prepared to sign the agreement; if it were repudiated by the Nizam, the responsibility for breaking off negotiations would be his alone.

The delegation met me on several subsequent occasions. Initially, I pointed out to them that we had received information with regard to the complicity of Hyderabad officials in border incidents. I warned them that these small incidents might lead to large events. I added that the Government of India could not remain unconcerned if complaints of ill-treatment came from the Hindus of Hyderabad. It was in the interests of Hyderabad itself not only that justice should be done to the majority community, but that the majority community should feel that justice was being done.

With regard to the agreement, I told the Nawab that the Government of India and Lord Mountbatten were of one view that it should either be accepted or rejected as it stood. I added that we had come down step by step from our original position in order to avoid a conflict with Hyderabad. If the Nawab's protestations that Hyderabad wanted to remain on friendly relations with India were genuine, I saw no reason why Hyderabad should not accede to the Indian Dominion. This would at once clear the air and it would put the two Governments into correct relationship with each other. If Hyderabad stood out of the Indian Dominion, the Hindus of the State would have a justifiable grievance that the Muslim minority was the arbiter of their fate, though they might not dare to express it; Indian opinion would certainly be resentful. In the interests of Hyderabad itself, it should accede, and it was in the belief that the State would ultimately do so that the Government of India had agreed to a Standstill Agreement for one year. They knew the difficulties of the Government of Hyderabad *vis-à-vis* the Ittehad-ul-Muslimeen, and, as they did not want to force the issue, they had made this compromise. They had taken that decision after very deliberate consideration and they could not now change the Agreement in any way whatsoever.

Nawab Moin Nawaz Jung said that if they went back with the Agreement without having gained any sort of concession, it would be very difficult and extremely embarrassing for the delegation. I told him that the difficulties were created not by the Government of India, but by the Nizam himself. He must make up his mind either to rule the State himself or be ruled by the Ittehad-ul-Muslimeen. In the latter event the Government of India could not help the Nizam. The Nizam as well as his Executive Council had accepted the Agreement. If he now changed his attitude because of a show of force by a truculent party, the conclusion was irresistible that he acquiesced in its tactics. In such circumstances negotiations were impossible.

Then the delegation asked whether, if no amendment of the agreement was possible, we would consider some alterations in the collateral letter. The main point which they wanted to put in the letter was that the State should be able to appoint not only trade agents but political representatives. I told him that if the Nizam wanted to appoint political agents he might do so, provided they worked in complete subordination to our High Commissioners, or ambassadors, as the case might be. The delegation was not prepared to accept this. I informed them that the Government of India could not in any case go beyond what was contained in the letter.

They then raised the question of arms and ammunition. They asked for a provision to the effect that if Hyderabad did not get the arms and ammunition it required within a reasonable time, it must be permitted to import its requirement from outside. I told them that if we agreed to such a provision, we could not resist similar claims from other States, and that therefore we could not concede the point.

Lastly, they wanted it stated in the collateral letter that the Nizam suspended the exercise of his full sovereignty on the three subjects for one year only. I replied that the position was made sufficiently clear in the Agreement itself. I explained that the collateral letter could not add to, nor subtract from, the Agreement. If the Nizam were to insist on including this point in his letter I would reply by merely drawing his attention to the last clause of the Agreement.

The next day Nawab Moin Nawaz Jung met Lord Mountbatten, who took him to task for the unstatesmanlike terms of the Nizam's letter in which he threatened to conclude a Standstill Agreement with Pakistan if he did not sign one with India. He told the Nawab frankly that the time had come when the Nizam must finally make up his mind one way or the other. His failure to sign the Standstill Agreement would be a minor inconvenience for India; for the Nizam it was likely to be a well-nigh irretrievable disaster. Lord Mountbatten emphasized the falsity of the assumption that India was in a weak position and too preoccupied with other matters to be able to give the Hyderabad problem its full attention.

The delegation left for Hyderabad on 7 November. At this time Lord Mountbatten was due to leave for England for a fortnight to attend the wedding of the present Queen, then heir to the throne, who was marrying his nephew the Duke of Edinburgh. The Nizam therefore wrote that he would like to defer negotiations till Lord Mountbatten's return. After consulting the Government of India, Lord Mountbatten agreed. At the same time he advised the Nizam that he should do everything in his power to restore the confidence of the Hindus in the State.

In the meantime the Nizam had accepted the resignation of the Nawab of Chhatari as President of his Executive Council. Pressure was being brought to bear on him by the Ittehad-ul-Muslimeen to appoint in the Nawab's place either Mir Laik Ali or Zahid Hussain. The former, a prominent businessman in Hyderabad, had been a representative of Pakistan to the United Nations; the latter was the Pakistan High Commissioner for India. The Nizam consulted Jinnah, who advised him not to appoint either of them. The Nizam had also sought Jinnah's advice on the negotiations that were going on with the Government of India; but the latter refused to commit

himself. Despite Jinnah's advice, the Nizam appointed Laik Ali as
the President of his Executive Council. This he did at the behest of
Kasim Razvi; included in the Executive Council were also other
nominees of Razvi. The Hyderabad Government thus came virtually under the control of Razvi.

It was about this time that Kasim Razvi visited Delhi. Razvi no
doubt felt that he was now the arbiter of Hyderabad's destinies. He
had an interview with Sardar and also came and saw me in my office.
I cannot say that I was impressed by his appearance, despite his
gleaming eyes and the beard which he sported beneath a fez worn
at a rakish angle. The moment he started talking I could see that his
was a fanaticism bordering on frenzy. He declared that Hyderabad
would never surrender its independence and that the Hindus were
happy under the Nizam. I told him that Hyderabad was in the
heart of India and that the Government of India were keenly
interested in the peace of the country. Either the Nizam must come
in like any other ruler and accede, or he should agree to a referendum. If, as the Nizam claimed, the Hindus were happy under his
rule, he could have no possible objection to such a course. Razvi's
reply was that if the Government of India insisted on a plebiscite,
the final arbiter could only be the sword. I told him that so irresponsible an attitude would land him and the Nizam in disaster.
He then shook hands with me and walked out.

Lord Mountbatten returned to India on 24 November. The
Hyderabad delegation arrived in New Delhi and had their meeting
with him on the 25th. It was a most tortuous proceeding; the
delegation fought step by step for verbal alterations and even punc-
tuation marks.

The delegation returned to Hyderabad without any material
change in the agreement or the collateral letter. The two documents were signed by the Nizam on 29 November 1947.

The Standstill Agreement contained only five articles. The preamble emphasized that it was the aim and policy of the Dominion
of India and of the Nizam to work together in close association and
amity for the mutual benefit of both. The first Article laid down
that, until new arrangements in this behalf were made, all the
agreements and administrative arrangements on matters of common
concern, including defence, external affairs and communications,
which had existed between the Crown Representative and the Nizam
before the transfer of power, would be continued as between the

Government of India and the Nizam; but that the Agreement did not impose any obligation or confer any right on the Dominion either to send troops to assist the Nizam in the maintenance of internal order, or to station troops in the State except in time of war. By Article II, the Government of India and the Nizam agreed to appoint their agents in Hyderabad and Delhi respectively, and to give them every facility for the discharge of their functions. Article III stressed that under the Agreement the Government of India would not exercise any paramountcy functions in their relations with Hyderabad; and that nothing in the Agreement should be deemed to create in favour of either party any right continuing after its termination, or derogate from any right which, but for the Agreement, would have been exercisable by either party after the date of its termination. Article IV laid down that any dispute arising out of the Agreement should be referred to two arbitrators, one to be appointed by each of the parties, and an umpire selected by those arbitrators. Article V stipulated that the Agreement would come into force immediately and would remain in force for a period of one year.

In the collateral letter the Nizam asserted that he was in no way permanently prejudicing his rights as an independent sovereign, but admitted that he was in some respects suspending the exercise of certain of those rights during the currency of the Agreement. He raised several issues such as the diplomatic and trade representation of Hyderabad in foreign countries; the return of residencies; the supply of arms and ammunition to the State; facilities to import 'soft' vehicles; withdrawal of Indian troops from the State; the return of cantonments; the continuance of his rights in regard to currency, coinage and postal rights, and so on.

In his reply Lord Mountbatten expressed on behalf of the Government of India the hope that the Standstill Agreement would provide a basis for a satisfactory long-term solution. He reiterated that Hyderabad's interests were inextricably bound up with those of India and hoped that before the Standstill Agreement expired it would be possible for Hyderabad to accede to India. With regard to the points raised by the Nizam, Lord Mountbatten gave his assurance that they would be sympathetically considered by the Government of India.

The Nizam also wrote a secret letter to Lord Mountbatten undertaking not to accede to Pakistan. This letter contained two other points: firstly, that if the Indian Union decided to secede from the

Commonwealth, the Nizam would regard himself as being at liberty to reconsider his position; and secondly, that in the event of a war between India and Pakistan, he would remain neutral. Both these points were noted by the Government of India.

On 29 November Sardar laid the Agreement and the letters on the table of the Constituent Assembly which was then functioning as a Parliament. He said that the Government of India fully appreciated the internal difficulties of Hyderabad and, in consistence with their policy of securing agreement, not by coercion but with the maximum degree of goodwill on both sides, and having due regard to the overall position in India, they felt that an Agreement of this nature, even for a limited period, would have considerable advantages. He hoped that the period of one year would enable Hyderabad and India to forge closer relations and to pave the way for permanent accession. He added that this settlement made it clear that Hyderabad did not propose to accede to Pakistan and finally paid a very high tribute to Lord Mountbatten for his services in this connexion.

Earlier in the day I met Nehru in the corridor of the Secretariat. Referring to the Agreement he said: 'This means we shall have peace for one year.' That, in fact, summed up the attitude all over the country.

XVIII

HYDERABAD

II

LOOKING back at the events of 1947, it is interesting to recall the divergence of approach on the part of the personalities concerned towards the Standstill Agreement with Hyderabad. Nehru felt that the Agreement would purchase communal peace in the South for at least one year. Lord Mountbatten was sanguine that it would allow heads to cool and hearts to soften and that before the expiry of the Agreement the Nizam like all the other rulers would accede to India. The Nizam and his advisers conceived the Agreement as providing breathing-space in which to secure the withdrawal of the Indian troops from Hyderabad and eventually to build up their position and strength to a stage when they would be able to assert the independence of the State. Sardar was doubtful of the bonafides of the Hyderabad Government. I assured him however that during this span of one year the Nizam had either to agree to accession or to grant responsible government to his people and that, if he refused to adopt either of these courses, the Government of India would have to reconsider the very basis of their approach to the Hyderabad problem.

In accordance with Article II of the Standstill Agreement, the Government of India appointed K. M. Munshi as their Agent-General in Hyderabad. I did not then know Munshi very well; but I had particularly been impressed by the way in which, as Home Minister in Bombay from 1937 to 1939, he had handled the communal situation there. When we informed the Government of Hyderabad of Munshi's appointment, the Nizam made certain conditions. First of all he wanted Munshi to be no more than a Trade Agent. I replied to Laik Ali drawing his attention to Article II of the

Agreement, under which the functions of the Agent-General were certainly not confined to trade.

Next, the Nizam's Government raised the question of the ceremonials to be observed on the occasion of the assumption of charge by the Agents-General. It was obvious that their purpose was to treat the Government of India as on an equal footing with themselves and to regard the exchange of Agents-General in the same manner as an exchange of ambassadors between two independent countries. The States Ministry was definitely against this. In point of fact, no ceremonies were observed, nor was there any presentation of credentials when the respective Agents-General assumed office.

A trivial but none the less significant dispute arose over the question of the accommodation that was to be provided in Hyderabad for Munshi, the Nizam refusing to give him even temporarily, till he found accommodation elsewhere, either the Bolarum or Chanderghat residency. Ultimately two of the buildings belonging to the Indian Army were placed at the disposal of Munshi and his staff.

The Nizam's Government started pressing for the speedy withdrawal of the Indian troops and for the supply of arms and ammunition for the Hyderabad army and police. A delegation of Hyderabad officials met the representatives of the Government of India on 24 December 1947. We agreed to the supply of arms and equipment. The position with regard to the Indian troops was that most of them had already been withdrawn from Hyderabad State. There were some troops left in Secunderabad and Jalna. Those in Jalna belonged to the Indian Pioneer Corps, which was in process of disbandment. We told the delegation that it was not possible to shift the centre while disbandment was going on. The Government of Hyderabad agreed to give us time till the end of April to complete the disbandment. We on our part agreed to expedite the evacuation of troops from Secunderabad.

Till Munshi went to Hyderabad we did not realize, nor did anyone bring to our notice, that there were large quantities of army stores lying in Hyderabad. These stores were being guarded only by chowkidars. The Government of India issued orders that the withdrawal of stores and the withdrawal of the remainder of the Army from Hyderabad should be co-ordinated in such a way as to leave no stores behind without adequate protection.

Almost before the ink was dry on the Standstill Agreement, the Nizam's Government issued two ordinances in quick succession.

The first imposed restrictions on the export of all precious metals from Hyderabad to India. The second declared Indian currency to be not legal tender in the State.

I wrote to the Government of Hyderabad on 25 December 1947 pointing out that these two ordinances were violations of the Standstill Agreement. The Government of India should have been consulted and I asked why the Government of Hyderabad had omitted to do so. We received a lengthy but evasive reply.

On top of this, the Government of India received information that the Government of Hyderabad had advanced a loan of Rs 20 crores to Pakistan in the form of Government of India securities of equivalent value. We later found out that the loan was negotiated by Nawab Moin Nawaz Jung, the Hyderabad Minister (who was incidentally the brother-in-law of Laik Ali), while actually conducting negotiations with the Government of India on the Standstill Agreement.

This was not all. The Government of Hyderabad informed us officially that it was their intention to appoint agents in several foreign countries. They had already appointed a Public Relations Officer in Karachi without any reference to the Government of India.

It was against this background that, on 30 January 1948, a Hyderabad delegation headed by Nawab Moin Nawaz Jung came to Delhi and met me and other officials of the Government of India. In his preliminary observations, the Nawab made pointed reference to what he spoke of as the constant adverse propaganda in the Indian press against the Government of Hyderabad. He said that the demand for independence in Hyderabad was the inevitable reaction of the demand for accession on the part of India. Referring to the currency ordinance, he said that it had been promulgated with a view to popularizing Hyderabad's own currency; that it did not in any way affect the economy of India; and that it involved no constitutional breach. With regard to the restriction on the export of metals, the Nawab said that this did not constitute a ban. It only meant that permission was required from the Ministry of Finance of the Government of Hyderabad for such export. Referring to the loan to Pakistan, Nawab Moin Nawaz Jung said that this had been sanctioned by the Nizam before the present Hyderabad Ministry took office and before they had entered into the Standstill Agreement with India. He emphasized that the transaction was purely economic, that it

had no political significance whatever and was merely in the nature
of an investment. With regard to the appointment of a Publicity
Officer in Karachi he said that the publicity policy of Hyderabad
had been laid down two years ago; that there was nothing new in it,
and that its purpose was simply to make the activities of the Government of Hyderabad understood in other places with a view to promot-
ing better understanding. By way of countercharge, Nawab Moin
Nawaz Jung then listed a series of complaints against the Government of India which included the serious bottleneck in imports to
Hyderabad from abroad and the non-supply of arms and ammunition as promised in the collateral letter.

In reply I pointed out that the Government of India would never
have entered into a Standstill Agreement with Hyderabad except on
the basis that the State would eventually accede to India. Prior to
the transfer of power the Government of Hyderabad could not have
passed any legislation banning the export of precious metals, or
declaring Indian currency not legal tender, without the express
approval of the Political Department. That position was continued
for one year under the Standstill Agreement. The Government of
Hyderabad had violated the Standstill Agreement by passing these
ordinances without consulting the Government of India. Under
the preamble, the Standstill Agreement was for the mutual benefit
of Hyderabad and India and surely it could not be contended that
the currency ordinance or the ban on the export of metals benefited
India; on the contrary, it had just the opposite effect. With regard
to the loan to Pakistan, the Government of Hyderabad could not
have granted a loan to any foreign country before 15 August 1947,
for they then had no foreign relations except through the paramount
power. Therefore the loan was yet another breach of the Standstill
Agreement. Above all, why had not the Government of Hyderabad
informed the Governor-General or the Government of India of this
loan during the negotiation of the Standstill Agreement? I finally
told the delegation that we had taken expert legal opinion on the
matter and that there was no doubt whatsoever that all these
measures constituted a unilateral infraction of the Standstill
Agreement.

There followed some discussion. I stressed that the Government
of Hyderabad should repeal the two ordinances in question and
ask the Government of Pakistan to return the loan of Rs 20 crores.

Referring to the activities of the Razakars, I said that the

Government of India took a grave view of the situation created by them in Hyderabad. It appeared to the Government of India that every encouragement had been given by the Hyderabad Government to this reactionary and communal organization. Disquieting reports had been received from Government of Madras of the activities of the Razakars on their border.

Laik Ali, the President of the Nizam's Executive Council, had meanwhile come to Delhi and had seen Sardar. Sardar told him quite firmly that an internal settlement in the State was the first requisite for a satisfactory understanding between India and Hyderabad and requested him to work to that end. The discussions could not be continued because of Gandhiji's assassination on the evening of 30 January. Laik Ali and the Hyderabad delegation subsequently returned to Hyderabad.

The activities of the Razakars had meanwhile increased in intensity. Razvi had thrown all restraint to the winds and was indulging in most objectionable speeches, calculated to inflame communal passions both inside and outside Hyderabad. In one of his speeches he alleged that the Government of India were supplying arms and materials illicitly to the Hindus of Hyderabad; in another he declared that the Razakars were the liberators of the Muslims of India. Munshi had several discussions with Laik Ali with a view to curbing the activities of the Razakars. Their agreed conclusion was that as a first step there should be simultaneous action by both Governments. Hyderabad should prohibit the Razakars from assisting the police in maintaining law and order, while the Government of India should take action against the Communists on their side of the border. This matter was to have been discussed with Sardar when Laik Ali and Munshi came to Delhi, but for the reason already stated this was not possible.

About this time the Government of Madras asked for military assistance in border areas to ward off the incursions of the Razakars and Hyderabad troops into Indian territory. A conference of the Premiers of Madras, Bombay and the Central Provinces was held in the States Ministry on 21 February to discuss the question. The Home Ministers of Bombay and Madras as well as K. M. Munshi were also present. Sardar presided and gave a brief review of the situation. He said that the differential treatment meted out to Hyderabad in the matter of the Standstill Agreement was because of the unique position of the State. The idea was not only to give the Nizam time to consider the problem but to gain a little respite ourselves. He had assented to the Agreement in the hope that if it was properly worked it would open the way for a permanent settlement. Since he could see no reciprocity of this sentiment on the part of Hyderabad, he agreed that the Government of India should be ready for all eventualities. He then referred to the activities of the Razakars and the way in which they were terrorizing the Hindu population of the State. He mentioned the currency ordinance and the loan to Pakistan, which were clear breaches of the Standstill Agreement, and he told the conference of the talks he had had with Laik Ali. Finally, he made it clear that he was not anxious about the accession of Hyderabad to India, but that he would not compromise on the issue of responsible government.

There followed a general discussion regarding the border incidents. Munshi mentioned that he had entered into a pact with Laik Ali for their prevention but he was not certain that the Government of Hyderabad would implement it. The Premier of Bombay stated that some Socialists and Congressmen operating from the Bombay side of the border were using fire-arms. It was decided that whoever was using fire-arms on our side should be disarmed. The Premier of Madras described the difficulties created in his province by Communists who had entrenched themselves in the border districts of Andhra and Hyderabad and were indulging in hit-and-run tactics. In fact in these border areas the people went to the extent of saying that the Razakars ruled by day, while the Communists ruled by night. The Government of Madras wanted military aid, but the Government of India could spare no troops at the moment. The provincial governments were asked to strengthen their borders with military police. Several minor administrative decisions were also taken.

By this time, the Nizam had recalled Sir Walter Monckton from London and he, together with Laik Ali and Nawab Moin Nawaz Jung, came to Delhi and on 2 March had an interview with Lord Mountbatten. I was present at the interview. Laik Ali mentioned that he was going to Karachi the next day and that he would try 'to bring about better understanding between India and Pakistan.' Lord Mountbatten referred to the loan of Rs 20 crores to Pakistan. He pointed out that negotiations for this loan had been going on at the same time as the final negotiations on the Standstill Agreement and that he was astounded that not a word about the loan had been mentioned to him at that time. Nawab Moin Nawaz Jung replied that the Government of Hyderabad had thought themselves free to invest funds and securities within the Commonwealth as they pleased. Since he had not been sure what effect it would have on the negotiations for the Standstill Agreement, he had not informed the Governor-General about it. I refuted as irrelevant Nawab Moin Nawaz Jung's argument that the loan was to a member of the British Commonwealth. I told him that under the Standstill Agreement Hyderabad could not enter into relations with any foreign country, not even with a Commonwealth country, except through the Government of India. The Government of India could never agree to this loan.

Lord Mountbatten suggested that in any future dealings that he might have with the Hyderabad delegation, they should come clean and not hold back from him anything germane to the issue. He considered that the greatest service Laik Ali could do on his visit to Karachi was to arrange that the loan, which consisted of Government of India securities, should not be realized during the term of the present Standstill Agreement. I suggested that to agree that the loan would not be realized only during the term of the Standstill Agreement was no less open to objection. Sir Walter Monckton gave it as his opinion that it would be very difficult to give a guarantee extending beyond that period. Lord Mountbatten thought that the point would resolve itself in the course of the formulation of the long-term agreement.

Lord Mountbatten then referred to the Currency Ordinance, which the Government of India regarded as a hostile move and which had gone a long way to embitter relations. The importance lay not in the legal but in the practical aspect of the matter. He considered that it was in Hyderabad's own interests to put it right. Laik Ali undertook to see how the ordinance could be modified to the satisfaction of both parties.

I said that I had received reports that new airfields were being built in Hyderabad and inquired of Laik Ali if it was true. He replied that only one airfield was being extended so that it could take Dakota aircraft. (We discovered later that this statement was untrue.)

Lord Mountbatten emphasized that if the Government of Hyderabad wished to resolve the differences which existed between Hyderabad and India, they would do well to examine all the steps which they intended to take from the point of view of likely repercussions on their relations with India. In both Hyderabad and India, there were certainly people who did not desire that the Standstill Agreement should work, but he could give the assurance that so far as India was concerned Nehru, Sardar Patel and the Government as a whole were not of this number. They sincerely wanted to make it work, although they could easily have said that they would not abide by it in view of the breaches that had been committed by Hyderabad. He was anxious that the same spirit should prevail among the members of the Government of Hyderabad. Laik Ali said that he too was extremely anxious to make the Standstill Agreement work.

Lord Mountbatten then referred to the activities of the Razakars and urged Laik Ali to ban the organization. Laik Ali put forward the amazing plea that 'it had precipitated itself into being because of the apprehensions of the Muslims in Hyderabad that their lives were in danger.'

Laik Ali said that he had made a note of points which he considered might, if introduced, improve the Standstill Agreement. I replied that there was no purpose in a supplementary agreement unless a friendly atmosphere between India and Hyderabad was first created. It was my view that the way to create such an atmosphere was by accession. It would be difficult to reach it so long as Hyderabad stood out, as it appeared to many, as a Pakistan island within India. I pointed out that other States with considerable Muslim minorities had acceded and that the Muslims had remained safe. I said that unless the suspicion between India and Hyderabad were removed, a permanent solution could not be found. The Government of India would not give up their objective that Hyderabad should accede; but if responsible government were set up in the State, they would leave the question of accession to be decided by the people.

Sir Walter Monckton said that it was no good talking of accession until we had got rid of all traces of suspicion and distrust.

The next day Laik Ali left for Karachi. He returned on 4 March, when Lord Mountbatten and I had a further meeting with the Hyderabad delegation. Laik Ali said that he had arranged with the Government of Pakistan not to cash the securities during the pendency of the Standstill Agreement and promised to make a public statement to that effect.

Lord Mountbatten then mentioned that Sardar Patel had just left him and had asked him to tell the delegation that the Government of India were firm on the issue of full responsible government in

Hyderabad. It was Sardar Patel's view that if such a step were taken all difficulties would be resolved and that it was out of the question for Hyderabad to remain the only authoritarian State in India.

Lord Mountbatten gave it as his personal opinion that the position of Hyderabad would be strengthened in the eyes of the world if the Nizam were to declare his intention to introduce responsible government and that all the greater then would be the prospects of the Nizam and his successors remaining constitutional rulers of the State in perpetuity. If the right opportunity was missed or if time was lost, there was a chance that the Nizam might lose his throne altogether through the sheer compulsion of events.

Laik Ali said there was danger in introducing responsible government too soon. He promised to reconstitute the Nizam's Executive Council and undertook to send me a statement which he intended to issue in this connexion, for simultaneous release in Delhi and Hyderabad.

Lord Mountbatten then raised the question of accession and entreated Laik Ali to realize the advantages which would accrue to Hyderabad from it. Laik Ali expressed the hope that satisfactory understanding could be reached without the use of the word 'accession'. He declared that Hyderabad had no intention of becoming a pocket of Pakistan or of allying itself with Pakistan in any way whatsoever. I was firm, however, that India would not be satisfied with anything less than accession.

After the meeting, a storm blew up over the issue of a joint *communiqué* about our deliberations. A draft was prepared by Sir Walter Monckton, but Sardar did not accept it. Lord Mountbatten was due to see Sardar in this connexion in the afternoon of 5 March; but during lunch, Sardar had a very bad heart attack, after which he was completely laid up and was forbidden by his doctors to do any work whatever for some days. There was no one else who could assume responsibility for reversing Sardar's decision about the wording of the draft *communiqué*. No *communiqué* was therefore issued.

On his return to Hyderabad, Laik Ali announced that he proposed to call a Round Table Conference of the party leaders in the State. Kasim Razvi promptly retorted that he would not take part in the conference. Laik Ali invited some of the leaders of the State Congress but they said that such discussions would only be fruitful if Swami Ramanand Tirth, President of the State Congress, was released. In a statement, the State Congress leaders made it quite clear that unless full responsible government was granted without any reservations and the Nizam agreed to accede to India, they would continue to be in opposition. Laik Ali thereupon decided not to release Swami Ramanand Tirth.

Laik Ali and Nawab Moin Nawaz Jung held continuous discussions with K. M. Munshi to explore the possibilities of carrying out the provisions of the Standstill Agreement. Nothing came out of these discussions, in the course of which, however, it became apparent that Laik Ali's aim was not the fulfilment of the Agreement but the enlargement of its scope.

K. M. Munshi had a very delicate and difficult role to play. While the relations of the Government of India with the Nizam's Agent-General in Delhi (Nawab Zain Yar Jung) were cordial, Munshi was treated with definite hostility by the Government of Hyderabad and his relations with them were extremely strained. Because of the suspicion with which he was viewed by the Government of Hyderabad he was virtually a prisoner in his own house.

Meanwhile, the Government of Hyderabad had not implemented a single undertaking given by them. No announcement with regard to the loan to Pakistan as promised by Laik Ali had been made; the Currency Ordinance had not been modified, while the ban on the export of precious metals and oilseeds continued to operate. No step, as promised by Laik Ali, in respect of the reconstitution of the Nizam's Executive Council had been taken. The Razakars, so far from being banned, had become an intolerable nuisance. Border raids showed no signs of abatement. Up to this time we had only tried to press our point of view informally upon the Government of Hyderabad. But now the Government of India decided that we should bring the breaches of the Standstill Agreement to their notice officially. Accordingly, on 23 March, I addressed a letter to the President of the Nizam's Executive Council which was sent to Munshi to be delivered personally to Laik Ali. Since the letter listed *in extenso* the main breaches of the Standstill Agreement by the Hyderabad Government, I give it in full:

I am directed to address you on the relations between the Government of India and H.E.H. the Nizam's Government.

The Government of India consider that a position has been reached in the discussions relating to the Standstill Agreement when definite and prompt steps have to be taken to prevent the relations between the two

Governments as well as the security of the areas on both sides of the Hyderabad border from deteriorating further.

The Government of India have given the most careful consideration to the views which have been placed before them by you and other representatives on behalf of H.E.H.'s Government at the various discussions which have taken place since January 1948. They have come to the conclusion that H.E.H.'s present Government have failed to carry out the obligations under the Standstill Agreement as hereinafter stated:—

(*A*) They have committed a breach of the existing agreements and arrangements relating to External Affairs: (a) by giving a loan of twenty crores to a foreign power, to wit, the Pakistan Government; (b) by appointing a Public Relations Officer in Pakistan (now recalled).

(*B*) They have also failed to carry out their obligations relating to Defence, that is to say: (a) by repudiating the obligations arising out of the Indian States Forces Scheme, 1939; (b) by increasing the strength of the State Forces without the approval of the Government of India; (c) by failing to forward an Annual Return in respect of the Police Forces; (d) by supporting and taking assistance from the Razakars, a private army of irregulars, functioning in collaboration with the Ministry and the Police of Hyderabad.

(*C*) They have further committed a breach of the agreements and arrangements in respect of Communications by entering into an agreement with the United Press of America for setting up a transmitting and/or receiving station at Hyderabad without the concurrence of the Government of India.

(*D*) They have further committed a breach of the agreements and arrangements as to other matters of common concern in the following respects: (a) by making the use of Indian currency for cash transactions illegal in the State; (b) by banning the export of gold, and groundnuts and other oilseeds.

We have already brought these breaches to your notice in our discussions, but regret that so far they have not been set right.

H.E.H.'s Government will appreciate that as soon as the Standstill Agreement was executed the Government of India began to perform an essential part of the Standstill Agreement by withdrawing the Indian Army stationed at Bolarum. Practically the whole of it had been withdrawn by the end of February. The Government of India are also anxious to fulfil their other obligations. H.E.H.'s Government are aware that the obligations under the Standstill Agreement are reciprocal. The Government of India therefore expect that H.E.H.'s Government will fully cooperate with them by forthwith taking action in order to fulfil their obligations under the Standstill Agreement in the following manner, that is to say: (a) by withdrawing twenty crores loan notes handed over to the Pakistan Government; (b) by agreeing to a joint commission being appointed to examine and determine the agreements and arrangements relating to matters of Defence; (c) by furnishing a Return of the strength, organisation and equipment of the Police in the form in which it used to be done prior to August 15, 1947; (d) by banning the organisation of Razakars; (e) by repealing the Ordinance making the use of Indian currency for cash transactions illegal in the State; (f) by cancelling the ban on the export of gold, groundnuts and other oilseeds; and (g) by cancelling the agreement, if any, with the United Press as regards the transmitting and/or receiving station for foreign news.

The peculiar position of the Ittehad-ul-Muslimeen in Hyderabad and of the Communists on the border causes the gravest concern to the Government of India. They consider that in the interests of peace inside the State and on both sides of the border the Ittehad-ul-Muslimeen should be banned and its organisations wound up. If the activities of the Ittehad are not immediately stopped, it is apprehended that a very grave situation will develop involving the security not only of the Hyderabad State, but also of the adjoining provinces of C.P., Bombay and Madras.

I am accordingly to request that H.E.H.'s Government will take prompt and definite steps to fulfil their obligations arising out of the Standstill Agreement and to ban the Ittehad as suggested. The Government of India will appreciate a very early reply indicating the action which H.E.H. the Nizam's Government decides to take, or has taken, in respect of the various matters set out in this letter.

The letter was presented to Laik Ali personally by Munshi on 26 March. Munshi told me later that Laik Ali at first appeared upset (though he was not unprepared for some such action on our part), but that his next reaction was to go off into heroics, declaring that the Nizam was willing to die a martyr and that he and lakhs of Muslims were willing to be killed.

Supported by the Razakars, the ruling clique in Hyderabad was now in a militant mood. The Nizam's advisers, it was reported to me, had assured him that if India resorted to any economic blockade it was not likely to be effective, as Hyderabad could easily stand on its own legs for the next few months, during which time public opinion in the world could be mobilized in its favour. India was stated to be very weak and to be incapable of military action now or at any time. All the Muslim countries were friendly to Hyderabad and would not permit any military action to be taken against it. The Hyderabad radio went to the extent of announcing that if there was a war against Hyderabad thousands of Pathans would march into India.

The Razakars continued to meet every night at different centres and their leaders made the wildest speeches. El Edroos, the Commander-in-Chief of the Hyderabad forces, called upon the people in a radio talk to be ready for any emergency.

On 5 April 1948 Laik Ali sent Nehru a very long reply, of seventeen typed pages, in which he refuted the allegations of breach of the Standstill Agreement and made certain countercharges against the Government of India. The last paragraph, which is reproduced below, summarizes the main points taken by Laik Ali:

The Nizam's Government is anxious to carry out fully its obligations under the Standstill Agreement, as they are ascertained to be. I have, in the course of this letter drawn attention to questions upon which the two Governments do not at present see eye to eye as to the extent and character of their respective obligations. Meantime, the economic blockade of Hyderabad is being tightened every day, and a propaganda war of nerves is being carried on against us at full blast. Our latest reports are that troop concentrations are taking place in the Indian Union all round Hyderabad and there have been instances of military personnel of the Union Government going about in our territory in mufti with concealed weapons. Nevertheless we want friendly settlement and I, on my part, would like to do all that is humanly possible to achieve this end, so long as it is consonant with our dignity and honour. If I have not succeeded in removing the sources of disagreement and if you do not think that further discussions would remove them, I have to draw your attention to Article IV of the Agreement which provides that any dispute arising out of the Agreement or out of agreements or arrangements thereby continued should be referred to arbitration. It seems to the Nizam's Government that arbitration, as provided for in that Article, is the proper course in the circumstances which have arisen to resolve our difficulties. I am therefore to suggest that, to ensure the smooth working of the Agreement from now onwards, both Governments should agree to submit to arbitration all outstanding points between them, which can no doubt be formulated without delay by the appropriate officers of our respective Governments.

On the very same day, the Nizam wrote to Lord Mountbatten saying that the letter of the States Ministry 'was in the nature of an ultimatum to be regarded as a prelude to an open breach of friendly relations.' He too, repeated Laik Ali's proposal for arbitration. He further complained that economic pressure had been applied with growing intensity against Hyderabad, and he threatened in the event of there being an open breach to publish the documentary evidence. He appealed to Lord Mountbatten not to be a party to the imposition of economic pressure and warned him that if the policy of attempted coercion was persisted in, the peace not only of Hyderabad but of the whole of South India would be endangered.

The Nizam's letter was brought in person by Sir Walter Monckton, who met Lord Mountbatten and myself on the night of 6 April. I could feel that Sir Walter was upset by the tone and contents of my letter to Laik Ali and was ready to do battle with me. I told him that the letter had not been in the nature of a threat at all and that I stood by every word of it. Whatever might be the legal arguments on both sides, the practical position was that we had reached a stalemate in our negotiations with Hyderabad. This stalemate was doing no good either to Hyderabad or to India and in fact was only helping the Razakars and the Communists who were getting stronger every day. Nor could effective steps to curb their activities be taken by either the Government of Hyderabad or the Government of India unless there was complete co-operation between the two Governments. I was studying the reports daily and I was by this time more worried about the activities of the Communists and the Razakars than about accession or responsible government for Hyderabad.

At the time when the States Ministry's letter to the Hyderabad Government was issued, Lord Mountbatten was not in Delhi. I thought he had an idea that the letter had been drafted and despatched by the States Ministry without it being referred to Nehru, who probably would not have agreed to its issue. Lord Mountbatten did not mention anything about this, but as I felt that Sir Walter Monckton had the same idea, I assured Lord Mountbatten that the letter had been prepared under the instructions of Sardar and Nehru and that both had approved its issue.

If my letter had upset the Nizam and Sir Walter Monckton, the Government of India were also perturbed by a singularly rabid and raucous speech delivered by Kasim Razvi on 31 March at the inauguration of the Hyderabad Weapons Week[1] which was published in most of the Indian newspapers on the morning of 7 April. In this speech Kasim Razvi indulged in a good deal of sabre-rattling and urged the Muslims of Hyderabad not to sheathe their swords until their objective of Islamic supremacy had been achieved. He exhorted them to march forward with the Koran in one hand and the sword

---

[1] The Ittehad-ul-Muslimeen observed a Hyderabad Weapons Week with the object of collecting arms and ammunition, and money with which to buy them, on the plea that the Government of India had failed to supply arms and ammunition to the Hyderabad State.

in the other to hound out the enemy. But the most sinister part of the speech was his declaration that 'the forty-five million Muslims in the Indian Union would be our fifth columnists in any showdown.'

Sir Walter Monckton saw Nehru on the evening of 7 April, but their discussion was inconclusive. The next evening there was a meeting between Sir Walter Monckton, Nehru and Lord Mountbatten. Nehru referred to Kasim Razvi's speeches and enquired who constituted the Government of Hyderabad — was it the Nizam and his Government or was it Kasim Razvi? Sir Walter Monckton promised to take up the matter with the Nizam on his return and, while making a strong issue of it, to advise him to take drastic action against Razvi.

Sir Walter then raised the question of the flow of goods into Hyderabad. Nehru said that he was not aware of any orders issued by the Government of India for the economic blockade of Hyderabad. It might be that the merchants themselves had decided not to send any goods to Hyderabad because of the uncertain political situation there, but he had impressed on all the provincial governments the desirability of letting ordinary goods go through. It was of course difficult in the circumstances to allow warlike stores to be imported by Hyderabad and there might have been a measure of confusion on the part of local officials between warlike and other stores. Any slowing-down process which had occurred had undoubtedly been due to reactions to events in Hyderabad and to rising tension. He promised to take up the matter with the provincial governments and other authorities once again.

The next subject discussed was the introduction of responsible government in Hyderabad. Nehru pointed out that in all the acceding States, the rulers had either introduced responsible government or declared their intention of doing so in the very near future; Hyderabad was the solitary exception. Lord Mountbatten said that the Nizam seemed to fear that the introduction of responsible government in his State would result in accession to India. He asked Nehru whether he would agree to Sir Walter Monckton giving the Nizam a private assurance that if accession did come about he would receive treatment and guarantees identical to those which had been given to other rulers who had acceded. Nehru said that he most certainly agreed.

Finally Nehru assured Sir Walter Monckton that the Government of India did not intend to invade Hyderabad nor to impose an economic boycott on the State. Sir Walter thanked Nehru for these assurances and said that he would go back to Hyderabad and make his report to the Nizam and would in particular recommend that the Nizam should take drastic action against Razvi and that he should move towards responsible government as soon as possible.

On 8 April Lord Mountbatten sent a reply to the Nizam's letter of 5 April which had been brought by Sir Walter Monckton, and conveyed in it some of his personal feelings and thoughts on the prevailing situation. He traced much of the mistrust and suspicion of the day to the unfortunate incident in Hyderabad in the early hours of the morning of 27 October when the Razakars prevented the original delegation from leaving for Delhi. If such methods of coercion had been checked, the story of the relations between India and Hyderabad would have been written by a very different and far happier pen. He pointed out that, with the exception of the Nizam, the ruler of every State in India had introduced or declared his intention of introducing responsible government. As an impartial observer and as a well-wisher of the State, he emphasized the imperative need for introducing a government truly representative of the desires and aspirations of the people of Hyderabad as a whole. He concluded by saying:

Let us not believe that however serious a situation may become, there is nothing that can be done to retrieve it, and that all we can do is fatalistically to await the worst. I will continue to do my best. I have told you how I think you could help.

After his return to Hyderabad, Sir Walter Monckton wired to Lord Mountbatten on 11 April advising him that the Government of Hyderabad were satisfied that the *jehad* speech of Kasim Razvi had in fact never been delivered and that the report had simply been a calculated attempt to prevent the resumption of friendly relations. But the Indian papers were able to quote from a carefully chosen list of similar utterances by Razvi. On 12 April under an authoritative Associated Press of India date line, Razvi perpetrated an even more grotesque verbal aggression. He asserted: 'The day is not far off when the waves of the Bay of Bengal will be washing the feet of our Sovereign.' He went so far as to declare that he would plant the Asaf Jahi Flag on the Red Fort in Delhi.

On 14 April Sir Walter Monckton returned to Delhi, followed the next day by Laik Ali. I was present at the interview which

Laik Ali had with Nehru on the 15th. He began by saying that the *jehad* speech of Kasim Razvi was a pure concoction. Nehru intervened and said that he had had the matter investigated and that there had undoubtedly been a rally. Whether Razvi made that particular speech or not was not really material, because he had made several other speeches which were even more objectionable. Laik Ali said that he had warned Razvi, but he added that the statements of various Indian Congress leaders had given rise to a feeling that an armed invasion of Hyderabad was imminent. Nehru said that the talk of a showdown was altogether absurd; the speeches made in India were merely the result of mounting anger against Hyderabad. He asked Laik Ali to realize that it was impossible for an independent State to have foreign territory right in its very heart. Hyderabad must accede to the Union, not by force or compulsion, but by a peaceful settlement. He said that there were two conflicts in the Hyderabad situation. The first was the conflict between the strategic needs of India, (by which no foreign power could remain inside Indian borders) and Hyderabad's desire to remain independent. The second was the conflict between the authoritarian regime of the State and the democratic urges of the people.

Laik Ali now tried to draw a red herring over the course by a reference to Munshi, complaining that Munshi spoke and regarded himself as the conqueror of Hyderabad. Nehru replied that, apart from what Munshi might have said or felt, it was quite clear to him that if one wanted to create and maintain an atmosphere of crisis, that objective was very efficiently served by the Razakars. I added that, quite apart from Munshi, the provincial governments of the Central Provinces, Bombay and Madras had been bitterly complaining of the activities of Razakars and that it was impossible to ignore those complaints which were, every one of them, detailed and specific. The Government of India could not ignore that there was great panic among the Hindus in Hyderabad, or the fact that there was an exodus from the State.

Speaking of the long-term objective, Laik Ali said that he did not think in terms of accession, but of close political accord. Nehru asked him who was going to decide the matter — the Nizam or the people? Laik Ali said that both would do so. Nehru then asked who was to be the deciding factor in the event of disagreement. Laik Ali said there would be no disagreement; Hindus came to see him frequently

45

and he knew the Hindu mind. Nehru observed that he had no doubt that various prosperous Hindus whom Laik Ali had met might have expressed this view, but he asked him to remember that the bulk of the people of Hyderabad were in a state of terrible poverty and that the only government which could solve their problems was a democratic government. Laik Ali said that he was not enamoured of slogans, but he thought that it would be reasonable if both Hindus and Muslims were to share the Hyderabad ministry on a fifty-fifty basis. Nehru replied that the Government of India could not possibly agree to an intermediate stage between an authoritarian regime and full responsible government, except if the Government of Hyderabad were to define their objective as full responsible government and the intermediate stage was of brief duration.

On 16 April, Laik Ali had an interview with Sardar at which I was present. Sardar referred to Kasim Razvi's speech — the one that both Razvi and Laik Ali had denied. The Government of India, said Sardar, had irrefutable proof that it had been delivered and they therefore could not accept the denial. He then explained the standpoint of the Government of India. He said that he could not contemplate for Hyderabad any relationship different from that of the other States and that there was no other way by which the question could be settled. If the Hyderabad question was not settled and if things went on as they were going without check, it would be impossible for the present Government of India to justify their existence. The present state of affairs would not have been tolerated for a single moment if the old Political Department had been in existence.

Warming up Sardar said:

You know as well as I do where power resides and with whom the fate of the negotiations must finally lie in Hyderabad. The gentleman [Kasim Razvi] who seems to dominate Hyderabad has given his answer. He has categorically stated that if the Indian Dominion comes to Hyderabad it will find nothing but the bones and ashes of one and a half crores of Hindus. If that is the position, then it seriously undermines the whole future of the Nizam and his dynasty. I am speaking to you plainly because I do not want you to be under any misapprehension. The Hyderabad problem will have to be settled as has been done in the case of other States. No other way is possible. We cannot agree to the continuance of an isolated spot which would destroy the very Union which we have built up with our blood and toil. At the same time, we do wish to maintain friendly relations and to seek a friendly solution. That does not mean that we shall ever agree to Hyderabad's independence. If its demand to maintain an independent status is persisted in, it is bound to fail.

In conclusion Sardar asked Laik Ali to go back to Hyderabad and, after consulting the Nizam, to take a final decision, 'so that both of us know where we stand.'

Throughout the interview Laik Ali appeared nervous. It seemed to me that he was completely taken aback by the forthright manner in which Sardar put forward his views.

While these meetings with Laik Ali were going on, there were also three days of intensive discussions between Lord Mountbatten, Nehru, Sir Walter Monckton and myself. In the end, a tentative programme was drawn up. The four points calling for the Nizam's agreement were: (1) immediate steps to bring the Razakars under control, beginning with a ban on Razakar processions, public demonstrations, meetings and speeches; (2) the release of imprisoned State Congress members, beginning at once with the leaders; (3) genuine and immediate reconstruction of the existing government to make it representative of all communities; and (4) the formation of a Constituent Assembly by the end of the year and the early introduction of responsible government. In the course of the conversations, Sir Walter Monckton told Lord Mountbatten that he proposed to advise the Nizam to confirm his acceptance of these points by changing his Prime Minister.

Laik Ali had a further interview with Sardar on 17 April. Laik Ali told Sardar of his meeting with Nehru and said that with regard to the constitutional reforms the position was very difficult, as he had to settle what was to be the proportion of the communities. Sardar replied that what Laik Ali contemplated was not responsible government in the true sense of the term but in any case that was a question of detail. What was required was an agreement on principles. If the Nizam would only implement what had been generally conceded in all the other States and what had been recognized as the natural aspirations of the people, he would not only bring peace to Hyderabad but would ensure the permanence of his own position and that of his dynasty.

Laik Ali said that his efforts would be directed towards the avoidance of bloodshed. That was his primary consideration, and it was with that point of view that he had undertaken the discussions. Sardar replied that the responsibility lay with the Nizam and his government. He then asked me to read out a report which had been received from the Government of Bombay regarding the depredations of the Razakars in two villages, one in Bijapur and the other in Sholapur. The Razakars had gone into these villages, killed a number of the inhabitants and looted property. Sardar asked how any government could be expected to tolerate such a state of things. The Government of Bombay had asked for military help and we were in honour bound to defend our own villages. With entrenched camps on both sides there was danger of conflict. Sardar then pointed out that the formula which Nehru had given represented the minimum demands. He hoped the Nizam would reflect on the terms calmly and make a wise decision.

That same evening I had a further meeting with Laik Ali at his own request. After recalling the circumstances in which the Standstill Agreement was concluded, I told him that our experience of the working of the agreement was not reassuring, for there had been many breaches on the part of Hyderabad. Laik Ali interrupted me to say that there had been no breaches. I told him that whatever might be the technical arguments, the fact was that the Hyderabad Government was following a policy which ran counter both to the spirit and to the letter of the Standstill Agreement. This, together with the background of the negotiations, led the Government of India to think that it was the object of Hyderabad not to work the Standstill Agreement, but to gain time. Referring to the activities of the Razakars, Laik Ali said that he appreciated the point of view of the Government of India, but that he was not in a position to deal with them in the way the Government of India desired. We went over the points which Nehru had handed over to him. He appeared to be under the impression that Nehru and Sardar had different views on the question of Hyderabad but I very soon corrected this impression.

I put it clearly to Laik Ali that the issue was the alternative between accession and the grant of responsible government. Once Hyderabad acceded, the question of responsible government would be a matter for the Nizam and his people. If for any reason the Nizam found it difficult to accede, the Government of India would press for the grant of responsible government. Laik Ali said that responsible government would inevitably lead to accession and that if that were so, rather than grant responsible government, he would prefer that the State should accede. Laik Ali found difficulties in the way of either course and he made the alternative suggestion that there should be an interim constitutional arrangement on the basis of parity between Muslims and Hindus, with a promise of responsible government in ten years. I replied that such a solution was not acceptable. I told him that if his object was to protect the legitimate interests of Muslims, there was a better way. He should announce the grant of responsible government at once and convene a Constituent Assembly, to be elected on the same franchise as for the Madras Legislative Assembly. The Nizam could lay down that in the constitution all legitimate interests, including the culture of the Muslim minority, would be adequately safeguarded and, if the safeguards were really confined to legitimate matters, nobody could object. Sir Walter Monckton arrived towards the end of the talk. Though he did not take part in the discussion he told Lord Mountbatten later that the solution I had put forward was unexceptionable.

The Hyderabad delegation now left Delhi and it was expected that the Nizam would implement the five-point programme without delay. On 22 April, he wrote to Lord Mountbatten that the constitutional relationship between the ruler and the people of Hyderabad should be viewed purely as an internal matter. He issued a *firman* the next day, but it was to the last degree disappointing. It contained an expression of hope that 'those political parties which are not represented in the present interim Government in Hyderabad will join and take a proper share in shouldering the responsibility of the Government.' But the psychological value of this meagre concession was thrown away in the sentence: 'I have felt apprehensive that mere imitation of a form of Government elsewhere might poison the atmosphere of our country in the same way as it is doing in other places.'

Lord Mountbatten felt that if he could only get the Nizam to Delhi, it would provide him with an opportunity of talking to him as man to man. Accordingly on 1 May he wrote to the Nizam inviting him to Delhi and assuring him of a most cordial welcome. On 9 May the Nizam replied that his visit to Delhi at that juncture was certain to give rise both inside and outside Hyderabad to just those grave misunderstandings which he wished to avoid. He therefore requested Lord Mountbatten to visit Hyderabad.

By now it was the middle of May and within a month Lord Mountbatten was to bid good-bye to India. The only problem tackled by him which had so far defied solution had been Hyderabad and he was most anxious to do something to resolve it within the short time available to him. It was out of the question for him to go to Hyderabad. He sent Alan Campbell-Johnson, his Press Attaché, to meet the Nizam and to study the situation and report to him. When Lord Mountbatten made this suggestion to me I entirely agreed. Alan Campbell-Johnson reached Hyderabad on 15 May and had an interview with the Nizam at which Laik Ali was present. He also had interviews with Nawab Moin Nawaz Jung, Kasim Razvi and El Edroos and with K. M. Munshi. His impressions were that the Nizam was the key man in the situation and that, with regard to the main issue of the relations with the Indian Union, nothing was being done without his approval. He reported further that the Nizam was in a mood of aggressive fatalism.

Meanwhile the situation on the border was going from bad to worse and it looked as though the lines of communication passing through Hyderabad were in jeopardy. On the evening of 22 May the mail train from Madras to Bombay was attacked at Gangapur Station inside the Hyderabad State. The attack, which was made by a large party of men armed with daggers, hockey-sticks and lathis, was clearly premeditated. The train was attacked from both sides and the casualties were reported to be two killed, eleven seriously injured and thirteen missing. Among the missing were at least four women and two children. Though a Hyderabad police officer armed with a gun was present on the platform he did nothing to prevent the attack. A British Field Officer in the service of the Indian Union who was in the train at the time informed us that, while the mob attacked the train, armed Razakars stood by on the platform. I addressed the Government of Hyderabad immediately, insisting that they should furnish effective guarantees that similar incidents would not recur.

On 23 May Laik Ali arrived in Delhi and saw me that same evening. He was unrealistic and vacillating as ever. He saw Nehru later that night, but no progress was made at their discussion either.

The next day I went to Mussourie to see Sardar. No negotiations took place with Laik Ali that day.

On 25 May Lord Mountbatten had a five-hour interview with Laik Ali, at only a part of which I was present. Lord Mountbatten laid stress upon the serious consequences which would ensue if a settlement between Hyderabad and India could not be reached. Laik Ali said definitely that he could not get accession through, nor could he advocate responsible government in Hyderabad, because that would without doubt lead to accession.

I had another meeting with Laik Ali at his own request on the night of 25 May which went on till the early hours of the 26th. In the course of our talk, Laik Ali gave it as his opinion that as the announcement of an intention to hold a plebiscite on the accession issue would result in a deterioration in the law and order position in Hyderabad, he was in favour of an Instrument of Association, in place of an Instrument of Accession, accompanied by the introduction of responsible government. I told him that, once he agreed to the introduction of responsible government, much of our misunderstanding would disappear and I implored him to find a way out of the present tension. He then requested me to give him a memorandum containing what in my opinion was the minimum the Government of India might consider as a basis for discussion. I agreed to do so on the definite understanding that such a document in no way committed the Government of India and that it was intended only to focus the points of discussion.

Accordingly I drew up a draft Heads of Agreement, which was divided into two parts. The main features of the first part were five in number. Firstly, the Nizam's Government would, in respect of defence, external affairs and communications, pass such legislation as the Government of India might request them to enact. Should they fail to do so, the Government of India would themselves have power to enact such laws. Secondly, the strength of the Hyderabad army would not exceed an overall figure of 20,000. The provisions of the Indian States Forces Scheme of 1939 would apply *mutatis mutandis* to these forces, while the Government of India would undertake to supply arms, ammunition and equipment on the scales and conditions laid down in the scheme, and would have the right of periodical inspection. Thirdly, the Government of Hyderabad should agree that all irregular forces or other formations of a military character would be disbanded. Fourthly, the Government of India would not station their armed forces in the Hyderabad State, except on the declaration of a state of emergency. Lastly, the Nizam's Government would have no political relations with any other country in the world. They would however be permitted to establish trade agencies for the purpose of building up commercial, fiscal and economic relations. The agencies would function under the supervision of and in closest co-operation with the diplomatic representatives of the Government of India.

The second part of the Heads of Agreement dealt with the

introduction of responsible government in Hyderabad. Immediately after the agreement was signed a new interim Government would be formed in Hyderabad. Of the total strength of the Cabinet including the Prime Minister, not less than fifty per cent would be non-Muslims. The interim Cabinet would summon a Constituent Assembly before 1 January 1949 to be elected from territorial constituencies on a broad franchise and not less than sixty per cent of the membership would be non-Muslim. As soon as the Constituent Assembly had been summoned, the existing Executive and Legislature would be dissolved and a new Executive, which would command the confidence of the Constituent Assembly, would be constituted. Not less than sixty per cent of the strength of the Cabinet would be non-Muslim. The Constituent Assembly would frame a constitution for the State. The legitimate religious and cultural interests of the Muslims would be safeguarded for a period of ten years. For a period of five years after the new constitution came into effect the relations between the Nizam's Government and the Government of India would be as set out in Part I. The communal proportion in the public services of Hyderabad including the army would be adjusted to secure proper representation of all the communities so that by 1 January 1954 not less than sixty per cent of the services would be non-Muslim.

The Heads of Agreement were discussed on the morning of Wednesday 26 May at a meeting at which Lord Mountbatten, Nehru, Laik Ali and I were present. Laik Ali specifically agreed to the principle of overriding legislation by the Government of India as contained in the draft Heads of Agreement. He also consented to the figure of 20,000 as the strength of the Hyderabad army. He was anxious, however, to get further instructions from the Nizam and so left for Hyderabad the same day.

On 30 May, Laik Ali wrote to Lord Mountbatten's Conference Secretary, Lt.-Colonel Erskine Crum, who had circulated a note of the meeting held on 26 May, saying that he wished to modify the statement that he had agreed to the principle of overriding legislation. The Conference Secretary replied that at the meeting on 26 May Laik Ali had agreed categorically, unequivocally and in the clearest possible terms to the principle of overriding legislation by the Government of India.

On the same day the Nizam wrote a letter to Lord Mountbatten stating that he had already invited Sir Walter Monckton to return from England immediately and, as Sir Walter was expected on

3 June, he asked for a little time in sending his reply. In another letter he referred to the suggestion of Lord Mountbatten and Nehru that Laik Ali should be replaced by somebody unconnected with the Razakars. The Nizam said that the nomination of the Prime Minister of Hyderabad was purely an internal matter and rested entirely with him. Laik Ali, wrote the Nizam, had been a moderating influence with all extremist sections and had controlled the situation with tact and firmness. In a third letter the Nizam invited Lord Mountbatten to pay a visit to Hyderabad before his departure from India. As his departure had been fixed a long time ago for 21 June, and as the invitation was received only at the beginning of June, there was clearly no time left for such a visit. In his reply Lord Mountbatten expressed regret and concern at the further delay which had been occasioned and hoped that when Laik Ali returned to Delhi he would be fully empowered by the Nizam to reach a final agreement.

Laik Ali returned to Delhi on 6 June accompanied by Sir Walter Monckton. They produced some new draft proposals, but these did not in my view provide a basis on which a settlement could be reached and I had no hesitation in telling Sir Walter that they would be unacceptable to the Government of India. I repeated this to Laik Ali and pointed out that, unless the Government of Hyderabad treated the question of accession and responsible government in a realistic way, there was no possibility of any agreement being reached.

The next day I went to Dehra Dun to consult Sardar, who was extremely unhappy about the latest developments in regard to Hyderabad. He was deeply disappointed that even after so much profitless discussion with so many Hyderabad delegations we should still be thinking of producing formulas for their acceptance. He referred to the Razakars who had perpetrated crime upon crime in the villages in our territory. He felt most strongly that a stage had been reached when we should tell the Nizam quite frankly that nothing short of unqualified acceptance of accession and of the introduction of undiluted responsible government would be acceptable to the Government of India. Sardar said that it was useless to waste any more time. He wanted the delegation to be presented with a brief letter calling for accession and responsible government. He was quite definite that any delay would place the Government of India in a worse position both politically and militarily. Sardar put forward these views in letters addressed to Nehru and Lord Mountbatten.

46

On 8 and 9 June I had further discussions with the Hyderabad delegation and on the second day Sir Walter Monckton produced a further revised draft of the Heads of Agreement. This document again did not meet the point of view of the Government of India. I made it clear to the delegation that the Government of India could make no compromise in respect of the issues which they regarded as fundamental. But whatever the long-term solution, it was immediately necessary to stop the state of lawlessness which now existed and to establish good neighbourly relations. The Government of India insisted on the disbandment of the Razakars and on the reconstitution of the Government of Hyderabad on a popular basis. Moreover, it was essential that the Government of India should have the overriding power to legislate on the three subjects of defence, external affairs and communications if the Nizam's Government, on the request of the Government of India, failed to do so within a reasonable period. I also made it clear that the Government of India could not agree to an overall strength of more than 20,000, including followers, for the Hyderabad army.

As a result of these discussions, the draft Heads of Agreement as well as a draft *firman* to be issued by the Nizam was prepared. Laik Ali said that as he had no authority to accept the demands that had been put forward by the Government of India, he would have to return to Hyderabad to obtain further instructions. I stressed the urgency of coming to a decision. The delegation returned to Hyderabad on 10 June.

On the 12th, Sir Walter Monckton came back to Delhi and reported that the proposals which the delegation had taken with them had been approved by the Nizam and his Executive Council with the exception of two main points, although there were still a number of subsidiary points on which they wished to have further discussions. The two main points, upon which Hyderabad was apparently prepared to break off negotiations rather than agree, were: overriding legislation by the Government of India, and the composition of the Constituent Assembly with a majority of non-Muslims.

I told Lord Mountbatten quite frankly that I for one would never agree to these amendments and even Sir Walter Monckton thought that there was little chance of Sardar accepting them. But Lord Mountbatten said that he must make one more attempt before he left India and insisted on going up in person, with Nehru and myself, to Dehra Dun on 13 June. As I had anticipated, Sardar flatly rejected the amendments and only when Lord Mountbatten appealed to him personally to give him a chance to settle the Hyderabad affair in a friendly spirit before his departure, did he give way and largely as a personal gesture to him. The proposed amendments were agreed to at a meeting of the ministers of the Government of India at Dehra Dun the same day. These amendments provided for (1) the deletion of the provision for overriding legislation and substitution of the clause, 'if the Nizam's Government fails to pass the required legislation with due despatch, the Nizam will forthwith pass the necessary ordinance under his own powers' and (2) omission from the draft *firman* of any reference to the composition of the Constituent Assembly. It was also agreed to omit any reference to parity between Hindus and Muslims in connexion with the interim Government and to substitute a phrase to the effect that the interim Government would be formed in consultation with the leaders of the major political parties of Hyderabad.

On the evening of 13 June Sir Walter Monckton rang up Hyderabad and suggested that the rest of the Hyderabad delegation return to Delhi the following day. He emphasized that the delegation should come armed with plenipotentiary powers to settle the various points still outstanding. The Hyderabad delegation arrived on the 14th and Sir Walter pointed out to Laik Ali the changes which had been made in the draft *firman*.

These changes in favour of Hyderabad were really substantial. But either their appetite grew by what it fed on, or the delegation were determined to wreck the negotiations by asking for the impossible. At the meeting with Lord Mountbatten on the night of 14 June the delegation threw a bombshell by asking for four further amendments to the draft Heads of Agreement. The first of these was that the Government of India would request Hyderabad to pass legislation on the three subjects only when that legislation was similar to the legislation in force in India; in other words, if there was a law applicable throughout India we could ask the Nizam's Government to extend only that law to Hyderabad, but we could not ask Hyderabad to enact any law exclusively applicable to Hyderabad. Secondly, Hyderabad was to be allowed to retain 8,000 irregulars in addition to 20,000 regular troops; thirdly, the Razakar organization was to be disbanded gradually, not all at once; and fourthly, the state of emergency under which India might station troops in Hyderabad was to be defined by the inclusion of the words

'under section 102 of the Government of India Act, 1935.' It might
be mentioned here that under section 102 an emergency could only
be declared when the security of India was threatened either by
war or by internal disturbance.

Laik Ali also raised the question of economic and fiscal freedom
for Hyderabad. Lord Mountbatten suggested that an undertaking
that the Government of India would examine this question might be
included in a letter from Nehru to the Prime Minister of Hyderabad.
Laik Ali did not comment on this suggestion.

A meeting of the Cabinet was held late in the night of 14 June to
consider the four amendments suggested by the Hyderabad delegation. In the interests of peace and of reaching a settlement the
Cabinet agreed to all of them.

Lord Mountbatten saw the Hyderabad delegation again on
15 June when he informed them that the Government of India had
agreed to all their four amendments. Laik Ali thereupon raised
the question of economic and fiscal freedom for Hyderabad.
Lord Mountbatten explained that it was impossible for the
Government of India to give a specific undertaking on this point
immediately, not only in view of the time that consideration of it
would take, but in particular because the Finance Minister and other
financial experts were in London in connexion with the Sterling
Balance talks. At the end of this meeting Laik Ali raised a further
point, namely, the inclusion of an arbitration provision in the new
Heads of Agreement. It was explained that, while the arbitration
provision in the Standstill Agreement would continue to apply for
all existing arrangements, the new points covered in the Heads of
Agreement were not subject to arbitration.

Later that same day Laik Ali left for Hyderabad. Lord Mountbatten made it clear to him that the Government of India had given
way on so many points that no further amendments should now be
suggested and that the Government of Hyderabad should either
totally accept or totally reject the settlement. Sir Walter Monckton
remained in Delhi.

No news was received from Hyderabad until the evening of the
following day when a telegram was received by Lord Mountbatten
from the Nizam stating that he had consulted his Executive
Council and had been advised by them not to accept the settlement
as it stood. He raised four points which if met would make the
documents acceptable to him. Firstly, he was anxious that in the

paragraph of the draft *firman* relating to the Constituent Assembly the words 'on a basis which I shall consider later' should be left in. Secondly, in the paragraph relating to the interim Government he wanted the words 'in consultation with the leaders of the major political parties' to be omitted. The Nizam alleged that these changes had been found in the final copies given to Laik Ali towards the end of his meeting with Lord Mountbatten, but Laik Ali had only discovered them on his return to Hyderabad. Thirdly, the Nizam wanted the issue of freedom for Hyderabad in trade and economic and fiscal matters to be embodied in the agreement. Fourthly, he wanted a provision for arbitration.

Even Sir Walter Monckton considered the new amendments utterly unjustifiable and ridiculous and it was decided that he should fly down to Hyderabad during the night in order to discuss them with the Nizam. Lord Mountbatten wrote a detailed letter in which he answered the four points which the Nizam had raised and this was sent through Sir Walter Monckton who promised to underline it. The following is the full text of the letter :—

I have received your telegram of the 16th June and thank you for the expressions of appreciation contained therein.

I note that your Council have advised you not to accept the draft *firman* and Heads of Agreement. It is, of course, for them to give such advice to Your Exalted Highness as they may think fit. But I must confess to being amazed, and I feel that this amazement can scarcely fail to be generally felt throughout the world, that they have chosen four such extraordinary points on which to advise rejection.

The first, and according to your telegram the most serious, point on which your Council appear to be prepared to break off negotiations, with all the human misery which such action will entail, is in connection with the addition of the words 'on a basis which I shall consider later' in sub-paragraph (i) of paragraph 2 of the *firman*. I am absolutely at a loss to understand by what mental processes your Council can have come to the decision that this is a breaking point. The fact that the basis of the Constituent Assembly is going to be decided at a later date is inherent in the omission of mention of that basis in the *firman*. The addition of the words which your Council suggest appears to me to be altogether superfluous, and to call this a 'material alteration' is nothing short of ridiculous. Also it is incorrect to say that the inclusion of these words was agreed upon. The addition of a sentence containing not only these words but also certain others was suggested by your Prime Minister on the afternoon of Monday, 14th June, but he withdrew this request after discussion, and it was thereupon agreed to leave this paragraph unaltered.

The second point raised by your Council concerns an alteration in the wording of sub-paragraph (ii) of the *firman*. So far as I can make out from your telegram your Prime Minister has informed you that this alteration was made only in the final copy of the *firman* which was handed to him during (not, as you say, at the end of) the meeting which I held with him and the other members of the Hyderabad delegation on Tuesday, 15th June. There is no doubt that the alteration was known to Sir Walter Monckton early on Monday, the 14th and that he explained the reasons for the change to your Prime Minister on the same day. I do not suppose that you will suggest that an alteration made known to Sir Walter Monckton was deliberately withheld by him or by us from your delegation or your Prime Minister. In any case I cannot believe that you seriously suggest that any such change of wording could conceivably amount to a breaking point sufficient to justify ending the negotiations between the two Governments. There can at best have been a misunderstanding. I cannot believe that you asked Sir Walter Monckton for his recollection before making this point.

With regard to the third point on which your Council have based their recommendation that you should reject the terms, namely your demand for freedom in trade, economic, and fiscal matters, your Prime Minister has perhaps failed to inform you of my efforts to persuade him of the physical impossibility of obtaining the unqualified agreement of the Government of India to this in the time available, particularly in view of the present absence in London of the Finance Minister and most of the experts in these matters. He may also have failed to explain to you that he did not disclose to me the importance which he attaches to this point right up to the morning of Tuesday, 15th June. Until then this matter had been covered in a footnote and he had never previously suggested to me any different treatment. If Your Exalted Highness finds yourself unable to trust the good faith of the Government of India in this matter I must confess to you that I can see very little hope of that mutual trust, without which no agreement can work, being obtained. I have a higher opinion of the bona-fides of the Government of India.

The fourth point which your Council have put forward as a reason for breaking off negotiations concerns the absence of a provision regarding arbitration. They appear to have rightly informed you that the arbitration provision in the Standstill Agreement will continue in force for all the existing arrangements and agreements covered in that. I am personally unable to envisage a case under the new Heads of Agreement in which arbitration might be resorted to. Furthermore, when the members of your delegation were asked to suggest one such example they were unable, even after considerable thought, to do so. To break off negotiations because an arbitration clause applies to some but not all the provisions appears to me to ignore the facts that: (a) an arbitration clause is in any event inappropriate to some of the provisions of the Agreement, as your delegation admitted; and (b) that arbitration is in general an unsatisfactory and ineffective alternative to goodwill as a means of ensuring the proper implementation of agreements of this kind.

To sum up, I cannot bring myself to believe that it is Your Exalted Highness's intention to reject this settlement, which it has taken so many hours and so much effort to reach, for the four reasons which you have quoted as having been put forward by your Council. If this is your serious intention, I cannot help thinking that the world will regard your Council's reasons as a disingenuous subterfuge to avoid honestly admitting that they are unwilling to undertake the other steps for which the agreement provides, including for instance the disbandment of the Razakars.

On the afternoon of 17 June Lord Mountbatten received a telephone message from Sir Walter Monckton with the one word 'Lost'. By the evening a reply was received from the Nizam to Lord Mountbatten's letter in which he even went back on his earlier commitment to allow Indian troops to be stationed in the State in an emergency. The following is the full text of the Nizam's telegram:

As Your Excellency knows Sir Walter Monckton flew down from Delhi during the night and has seen me this morning. He has satisfied me that the changes in the draft *firman* to which I referred in my telegram of sixteenth June were contained in drafts which he saw on Monday fourteenth June and that he thought that my Prime Minister had received copies on the afternoon of the same day. In these circumstances I am anxious to take the first opportunity of correcting the impression contained in my telegram that the changes were not made known to my representatives in Delhi until the last moment. Many drafts were being prepared upon both sides and the members of my delegation were constantly engaged in discussions with Your Excellency and various representatives of your Government so that a misunderstanding on this matter could easily arise. My telegram had to be sent when Sir Walter Monckton was in Delhi. If he had been here the mistake could not have arisen.

Although the negotiations have been protracted and we all want to reach a final agreement I am afraid it is impossible to do so within a day or two. We are now within sight of settlement on most of the important issues but there remain questions upon which agreement must be reached before the final result which we both desire can be achieved. I cannot doubt that we could reach accord on the outstanding questions of phraseology in the *firman* but my Council are also greatly troubled about the refusal of India to agree even in principle to fiscal freedom and control over Hyderabad's overseas and export trade being secured to the State. My Prime Minister drew attention to this important matter at an earlier stage in his discussions with Pandit Nehru and yourself. Later a draft giving effect to our suggestion was furnished to Mr Menon. I can understand that the subject is one which will require examination in detail but I must ask for the principle to be conceded. Further my Council cannot advise me to agree to leaving India free to station troops except in the border areas of the State whenever India chooses to declare a state of emergency. I should be found very ready to co-operate in any grave emergency. There is also the question of arbitration to which I referred in my previous telegram.

While for these reasons I cannot accept the drafts in their present form I earnestly hope that negotiations will be continued and a settlement reached in a very short time. Hyderabad will always owe much of its success in finding a happy compromise to Your Excellency's readiness to help us on our way and for this we shall always be grateful.

On the evening of 17 June Nehru held a press conference. While setting out that India would not undertake any further protracted negotiations with Hyderabad and that the Draft Agreement was the utmost limit to which the Government of India could go, Nehru said 'we will pursue an open door policy so far as these proposals are concerned and the Nizam is welcome to accept them any time he chooses.'

XIX

HYDERABAD

III

ON 21 June 1948, three days after the breakdown of negotiations with Hyderabad, Lord Mountbatten left India and was succeeded as Governor-General by C. Rajagopalachari. Lord Mountbatten was extremely disappointed at the breakdown of the negotiations. He had been sanguine that he would be able to bring about a settlement with the Nizam. Certainly the Nizam could not have had a better friend.

But it was obvious to anyone conversant with current Hyderabad politics that the Laik Ali Cabinet, under the control of the Razakars, would agree neither to accession nor to responsible government. The minority community, which was holding a virtual monopoly of all offices under the State Government, could not view with equanimity the grant of responsible government, for that would spell the end of their privileged position. The Nizam and his advisers were possessed by the notion that India was unable to take any action against Hyderabad because her hands were full with Kashmir and other problems. The anti-Indian attitude of a section of the British press, and the plea for Hyderabad's independence voiced by some British political leaders, confirmed the Nizam in his uncompromising attitude.

Tension now began to mount both in Hyderabad and India. Charges of border raids and breaches of the Standstill Agreement were made on both sides. In an atmosphere surcharged with mutual suspicion and excitement, it was only natural that many incidents should be exaggerated and that rumours should often be given credence without verification. But in the confusion three things, which clearly indicated that all was not well with Hyderabad, stood out prominently. These were the resignation of J. V. Joshi, a member of the Nizam's Executive Council; the Communist-Razakar alliance; and the gun-running by one Sidney Cotton. In his letter of resignation addressed to Laik Ali, Joshi pointed out that the law and order situation in the Jalna, Aurangabad, Parbhani and Nanded districts in the State, had completely broken down; that incidents were not lacking where the police had joined the Razakars in looting, arson, murder and rape and molestation of the womenfolk; and that, in their despair, many Hindus had sought shelter outside the State. To quote his words:

A complete reign of terror prevails in Parbhani and Nanded districts. I have seen in Loha a scene of devastation which brought tears to my eyes — Brahmins were killed and their eyes were taken out. Women had been raped, houses had been burnt down in large numbers. My heart wrung in anguish.... Under the circumstances, I cannot continue to lend my name to a Government which is powerless to prevent these heart-rending atrocities which I have seen with my own eyes.

The terrorism inside the State was not merely directed against Congressmen or Hindus: even Muslims who did not agree with the Razakars received short shrift. Over ten thousand State Congress members were in jail and the Congress organization was banned.

The most disconcerting news which reached us was that the Razakars had allied themselves with the Communists. In 1943 the Nizam had banned the Communist Party throughout the State. This ban was now lifted. Moreover, we came to know that the Communists were being supplied with arms.

In addition to this, attempts were being made to smuggle arms and ammunition into Hyderabad. An Australian by the name of Sidney Cotton was reported to be engaged in aerial gun-running, with Karachi as his base. The supplies were made by night and Bidar and Warrangal were the receiving airfields. It was difficult to check these flights, or the quantity of arms supplied, but at the time the affair was given great, and possibly exaggerated, prominence in the Indian press.

It was about this time that the Government of Pakistan began to cash a portion of the Rs 20 crores of Government of India Securities which the Government of Hyderabad had offered to them as a loan, despite the solemn promise we had been given by Laik Ali that no portion of the Securities transferred to Pakistan would be cashed during the pendency of the Standstill Agreement.

The Government of India therefore issued an ordinance declaring that any Government Securities held by, or on behalf of, the Nizam, the Government of Hyderabad and the Hyderabad State Bank, were not transferable without the approval of the Central Government. The currency chests of the Government of India in Hyderabad were also withdrawn. Further, the export to Hyderabad of gold, silver, jewellery and Indian currency was prohibited. This had become necessary because the Government of Hyderabad were using all their available resources for the purchase of arms and ammunition from abroad. The Nizam's Government protested against these measures. The Government of Pakistan also protested against the ordinance which froze the Securities, but Nehru informed Liaqat Ali Khan that the action was not directed against Pakistan at all.

These developments, coupled with border raids and frequent attacks on trains passing through the State territory, had thrown the Standstill Agreement completely into the background. The Government of Hyderabad had raised the question of arbitration on breaches of the Standstill Agreement, but infringements of the agreement had become relatively unimportant in the context of the grave and increasing deterioration of law and order in the State.

Our information at the time was that, in addition to 200,000 Razakars with small arms, the State forces numbered 42,000 regulars and irregulars, besides an unascertained number of Pathans, who had previously been imported into the State. The neighbouring provincial Governments were extremely concerned about the border raids and in May 1948 it was found necessary to station troops round Hyderabad in order to prevent these incidents and to give some measure of confidence to the people.

Opinion among the advisers of the Government of India was not unanimous on the question of what action should be taken in regard to Hyderabad. The section which favoured a policy of drift had a ready excuse in the bogey of large-scale communal disorders which would follow any positive action against Hyderabad. They apprehended that in Hyderabad the Hindus would be butchered in thousands, and that there would be a general slaughter of Muslims in India. There were others who spoke of mass Muslim uprisings in south India, particularly among the Moplahs. This fantastic suggestion was made by people who had never seen a Moplah, much less understood his mentality, and who knew nothing of the situation in

Malabar at the time. While it remains true that almost anything is possible in times of great tension and that therefore steps would undoubtedly have to be taken to guard against eventualities, I felt certain that fears of large-scale communal disorders were exaggerated, if not wholly illusory.

Another of such fears was that, if India took any action against Hyderabad, Pakistan would interfere. My own opinion was that Pakistan was surely not going to risk a war with India on the Hyderabad issue.

There was also some propaganda to the effect that Hyderabad aircraft would bomb cities like Bombay, Madras, Calcutta and even Delhi. This propaganda caused a certain amount of apprehension amongst the people of the neighbouring provinces.

Last but not least, the personality of Major-General El Edroos, Commander-in-Chief of the Hyderabad State Forces, was used as an argument against any action. A British general, when discussing the Hyderabad issue with me, said that in the hands of El Edroos, even an ill-disciplined rabble could be converted into something like the famous French Foreign Legion!

Both press and public opinion started openly accusing the Government of India of inaction in the face of flagrant and repeated violation of Indian territory. The stories brought by evacuees from Hyderabad added considerably to the public indignation. Attacks on through trains had created panic and the Government of India had been forced to guard each train with an armed escort. The attitude of the Parliament reflected the general uneasiness in the country.

But every time any action against Hyderabad was mooted, the communal bogey was put forward as an excuse for inaction. Our military authorities did not think that they woud have any difficulty in suppressing communal disorders however widespread, though they insisted — quite rightly—that their planning must take account of the possibility of such disorders in different parts of the country so that they would be prepared to cope with them swiftly and effectively. We recruited several Gurkha battalions from Nepal at a considerable cost to the Indian exchequer. Even after such precautionary measures had been taken there was still tendency to procrastinate.

Meanwhile Laik Ali was pressing that the Hyderabad issue should be taken to the United Nations Organization. On 17 August, he wrote to Nehru charging India with a series of flagrant breaches of the Standstill Agreement. He complained that there was a total economic blockade of Hyderabad, which was causing serious disruption in the life of the community, and he alleged that Indian troops had repeatedly violated Hyderabad territory. Therefore, he informed us, Hyderabad had decided to solicit the good offices of the United Nations Organization in order that the dispute between Hyderabad and India might be resolved and a peaceful and enduring settlement arrived at.

A reply was sent on 23 August to the effect that the Government of India regarded the differences between them and Hyderabad as a purely domestic issue and, considering Hyderabad's historic as well as present position in relation to India, they could not agree that Hyderabad had any right in international law to seek the intervention of the United Nations Organization or any other outside body for the settlement of the issue.

The American Chargé d'Affaires in New Delhi apprised us meanwhile of the fact that the Nizam had written to the President of the United States requesting that he should arbitrate and that the latter had refused.

On 28 August, the Nizam's Agent-General in New Delhi informed us that, as a Hyderabad delegation would be presenting their case to the United Nations, they would be glad of air transport facilities. We replied that as the Government of India regarded the Indo-Hyderabad dispute as a purely domestic one, they did not recognize the Nizam's claim to invoke the good offices of the United Nations in that connexion. Nevertheless, a Hyderabad delegation, headed by Nawab Moin Nawaz Jung, went to Karachi and from there proceeded to America and presented their case to the Security Council.

By the end of August the law and order situation inside the State and its environs had become quite intolerable. On 31 August, Rajagopalachari wrote a letter to the Nizam in which he said that it was morally impossible for the people of India to ignore the conditions prevailing in Hyderabad and requested the Nizam to do something wise and courageous to terminate the present state of alarm and insecurity. He specifically asked that the Razakar organization should be banned and that the Nizam should invite the Government of India to re-post an adequate military force at Secunderabad. If these steps were taken, there would be no fear in the public mind in Hyderabad and elsewhere regarding the security of person and property in the State and a satisfactory basis of friendship would be laid.

The Nizam replied on 5 September that 'a very wrong impression of insecurity of life, honour and property in Hyderabad prevails at your end.' He was emphatic that Indian troops could not be allowed to remain in Hyderabad; he averred that his own troops were perfectly well able to safeguard the life and property of his own subjects and were fully capable of dealing with the situation.

On 7 September I addressed a letter to Laik Ali in which I pointed out that raids into Indian territory, attacks within Hyderabad territory on non-Muslims and on Muslims who were opposed to the Razakars, and the holding-up of trains involving violence to passengers and the looting of goods had become matters of almost daily occurrence. Murder, rape, arson and pillage were gruesome and recurring features of atrocities which had created widespread anarchy within Hyderabad itself and grave anxiety in the neighbouring areas of the Indian Union. The activities of the Razakars constituted a threat to communal peace in India and the whole situation served to demonstrate the unwillingness and incapacity of the Government of Hyderabad to put an end to violence and anarchy. This being the case, the Government of India formally requested the Government of Hyderabad to take immediate steps to disband the Razakars and to facilitate the passage of Indian troops through the State, so that they could return to Secunderabad in such strength as might be deemed necessary for the prompt and effective restoration of law and order.

On 9 September, the Nizam wired to Rajagopalachari asking him to use his good offices with the Government of India to appreciate Hyderabad's point of view as communicated in the discussions of June and to create an atmosphere of better understanding. Rajagopalachari replied that the immediate question to be tackled was the restoration of public confidence and a sense of security, and repeated that the Nizam should invite the Government of India to re-post Indian troops as a guarantee of peace and as a demonstration of his determination to settle matters amicably.

On 10 September Laik Ali wrote to Nehru stating that the Razakar movement had sprung up entirely as a result of the raids which were being carried out on Hyderabad territory from bases across the borders and a state of fear arising from the constant threat from the Indian Union. With regard to the proposal that Indian troops should be stationed at Secunderabad, Laik Ali said that the Government of Hyderabad were fully competent to deal with the law and order situation in the State and that they took a very serious view of this suggestion. The Nizam's Government would regard any such action not merely as a violation of the Standstill Agreement but as a gross infringement of the territorial sovereignty and integrity of Hyderabad.

We replied to this letter the following day, asserting that the Nizam's Government appeared determined to regard facts, not as they were, but as they wished others to believe them to be; that the only law that now prevailed in the State was the law of the jungle, by which the Razakars and their allies preyed upon a large majority of the helpless citizens, or upon those who had the misfortune not to share their opinion or to participate in their activities; and that, in these circumstances, the Government of India regarded themselves as free to take such action as they considered necessary. The responsibility and the consequences, grave as they might well be, must rest on the shoulders of the Government of Hyderabad.

The Razakars did not spare even missionaries and nuns. Early in September the States Ministry received complaints that some foreign missionaries had been assaulted and some nuns molested by the Razakars.

The position that confronted the Government of India was indeed serious. Could they tolerate the growing influence of the Razakars and the Communists? Could they watch with equanimity the incursions into Indian territory and the attacks on Indian trains? Could they continue to be helpless spectators of the expulsion of Hindus from the State, or, in the case of those unlucky enough to remain inside, of their subjection to atrocious treatment? If the answer was in the affirmative, a policy of drift was justified; if not, the sooner they took action, the better would it be both for India and for the people of Hyderabad. Whatever the popular view and however grave the apprehension of the possibility of a prolonged conflict, our own military appreciation was that the Hyderabad forces would not be able to stand up to the vastly better-equipped and trained Indian Armed Forces, and that the only problem was how so to plan the campaign that resistance would collapse within the shortest possible time. We attached the greatest importance to the question of the duration of the conflict, for only by bringing it to the speediest conclusion could we ensure that reprisals would not be carried out, whether in an organized manner or by mobs, against the helpless people within the Hyderabad State, or that grave reactions would not take place outside. The military view was that the campaign could not last beyond three weeks. Actually, everything was over within less than a week. For this the greatest possible credit is due to the extremely detailed and careful planning of the Defence Ministry and the Services Headquarters.

On 9 September, after a careful evaluation of all the considerations and only when it was clear that no other alternative remained open did the Government of India take the decision to send Indian troops into Hyderabad to restore peace and tranquillity inside the State and a sense of security in the adjoining Indian territory. This decision was communicated to the Southern Command, who ordered that the Indian forces should march into Hyderabad in the early hours of Monday the 13th. It is significant (as will be seen later) that even after this date had been fixed, efforts were made to postpone it till the 15th.

The Indian forces were commanded by Major-General J.N. Chaudhuri under the direction of Lt.-General Maharaj Shri Rajendrasinhji, who was then the General Officer Commanding-in-Chief, Southern Command. This operation was given the name 'Operation Polo' by the Army Headquarters. It was a two-pronged advance, the main force moving along the Sholapur-Hyderabad road, a distance of 186 miles, and a smaller diversion moving along the Bezwada-Hyderabad road, a distance of 160 miles. There was some stiff resistance on the first and second days. After this, resistance petered out and virtually collapsed. On our side the total casualties were slight but on the other side, owing to scrappy operations and lack of discipline, the Irregulars and the Razakars suffered comparatively more casualties. The number of dead was a little over 800. It is unfortunate that so many should have died in this action, though the number is insignificant when weighed against the killings, rape and loot inflicted by the Razakars on the Hindus of the State. On the evening of 17 September, the Hyderabad army surrendered. On the 18th the Indian troops, under Major-General Chaudhuri, entered Hyderabad City. The operation had lasted barely 108 hours.

It might well be that the operation would have lasted much longer. On the very first day the advancing Indian troops captured Lieutenant T. T. Moore, an ex-British Army Commando and Special

Services Officer, who had been employed by the Hyderabad army since August 1947 and who was driving in a loaded jeep in the direction of Naldrug. It was discovered that his jeep was full of explosives, while his personal papers showed that he had been given the responsibility for arranging demolitions. He had been sent at top speed by the Hyderabad Army Headquarters to demolish the Naldrug and other bridges. He had been told that the Indian army advance would take place on 15 September. If the Indian army had marched in on the 15th and not on the 13th, they would have found all the important bridges blown up. Nature would have added to their difficulties, for with the rains setting in, the heavy army vehicles would have been bogged.

On 17 September Laik Ali and his cabinet tendered their resignations. The Nizam sent for K. M. Munshi (who had been under house arrest ever since the Police Action began) and informed him that he had given orders for his army to surrender; that he would be forming a new government; that Indian troops were free to go to Secunderabad and Bolarum, and that the Razakars would be banned. Munshi communicated this to the Government of India. In reply I conveyed to Munshi that the Military Commander would be in charge of the administration and that the question of the formation of a new cabinet did not arise. Munshi was asked not to commit the Government of India in any manner whatsoever, but to leave it to the Military Governor to deal with all further problems under the orders of the Government of India.

Major-General Chaudhuri took charge as Military Governor on 18 September. Simultaneously with the occupation of Hyderabad, Lt.-General Rajendrasinhji issued a proclamation asking the people to remain calm and not to give way to panic. The people were asked to render every assistance to the Military Governor's administration and not to obstruct it in any way, and peace and protection were guaranteed to all law-abiding citizens. The members of the Laik Ali ministry were placed under house arrest. Leading Razakars were apprehended. It was reported that Kasim Razvi was at his brother-in-law's house which was at some distance from Hyderabad City. Razvi was arrested on 19 September.

On 23 September the Nizam sent a cable to the Security Council withdrawing the Hyderabad case. Certain foreign powers continued to press for the discussion of the case, but ultimately it was dropped.

48

There was not a single communal incident in the whole length and breadth of India throughout the time of the operation.

There was universal jubilation at the swift and successful ending of the Hyderabad episode and messages of congratulation poured in to the Government of India from all parts of the country.

Ever since the breakdown of the negotiations in June there had been a demand for the deposition of the Nizam; after the Police Action this gathered volume. Some of the newspapers suggested the abolition of the Asaf Jahi dynasty and the disintegration of the Hyderabad State. Zain Yar Jung had raised this subject with me before the Police Action. I told him that I had reason to believe that the Government of India would look to the practical side of the matter and would take such decision as would be not only in the interests of Hyderabad State but of India as a whole. I added that it was my personal view that, once Hyderabad came into line with the other States, it would be in the best interests to continue with the present Nizam as head of the State.

When immediately after the Police Action I was asked to go to Hyderabad, the first question I raised with Sardar was that of the future of the Nizam. I urged that the Nizam had been ruling for over thirty-seven years; that he had a position not only in the State and among his co-religionists in the rest of the country, but also a certain prestige abroad. The abolition of his dynasty immediately in the wake of the Police Action would have a very unsettling effect on the Muslims. Personally I had no doubt that the Nizam should be allowed to continue. Once a fully democratic government was established in the State and the Nizam became the constitutional head, there would be no more trouble from that quarter. Sardar agreed with this view and told me that he would consult Nehru. He informed me on the following day that Nehru also agreed.

I left for Hyderabad accompanied by H. M. Patel (Defence Secretary) and Shavax A. Lal. The latter had been Law Secretary to the Government of India and was at the time Secretary to the Governor-General, with whose permission his valuable services were being utilized by the States Ministry. The first thing we did on arrival was to see Munshi. The strain to which he had been subjected had told on his health; he was running a high temperature, and it was, I think, on the same day that he was taken to Bombay for treatment.

I saw representatives of both Muslims and Hindus. The former informed me of a general depression among the Muslims. They said that, ever since 1947, a responsible section of the Muslims in the State had been opposed to the policy of the Nizam and his Government, a policy which had brought nothing but disaster. They hoped that the Government of India would repair the damage done especially to the financial position of the State. While deterrent punishment should be meted out to the Razakars, there were many innocent people who had got mixed up with them and to whom leniency should be shown. I replied that the Military Governor was fully aware of the position and that one of our instructions to him was to protect all legitimate interests of the minorities. We would of course look into the finances of the State later; that obviously could not be done immediately.

The attitude of the Hindus was naturally one of exultation. I warned their leaders that any untoward incident for which their followers could be held responsible would reflect on the Government of India and that the latter would be compelled to take severe action. I told them that they should lend full support to the Military Governor's administration and that the sooner they helped to bring conditions in the State back to normal, the easier would it be for the Government of India to hand over the administration to the popular leaders.

We then saw Major-General Chaudhuri with whom we had a general discussion. The civil team that was to assist him had not yet been assembled and the problem that faced the Military Governor was extremely serious. The administrative machinery had almost broken down. Many civil and police officials had deserted their posts and the finances of the State were in utter confusion. There were anti-social elements ready to take advantage of the disordered conditions. In the cities there were large concentrations of Muslims from the Indian Union and from Pakistan who had been 'invited' by the previous Government to Hyderabad and also Muslims from the villages of the State who had come in fear of retaliation by the victims of the Razakars. There were also tens of thousands of Hindus who had returned to the State from neighbouring provinces to which they had fled from the Razakar terror.

The first question we discussed was the basis of administration of Hyderabad. There were two choices before us. The first was to administer the State under martial law; the second, which was more acceptable from all points of view, was to carry on the administration with the co-operation and in the name of the Nizam. The Nizam, whom I saw that same afternoon, was ready to co-operate. Shavax Lal and I then sat together to work out a formula which without affecting the subordination of the Military Governor in service matters to the G.O.C.-in-C., Southern Command, invested him not only with full executive authority, but also with power to issue regulations having the force of law. The formula was embodied in a *firman* which was promulgated by the Nizam on the following day. This *firman* provided the basis for the authority we exercised in Hyderabad until the new Constitution came into force.

We agreed that our first task should be to round up the Razakars, to restore communal peace in the State and to return the Hindu and Muslim refugees to their homes and resettle them. Our next, not in point of importance but because everything could not be attempted simultaneously, was to contain and root out the Communists. On these tasks the Military Governor concentrated his efforts.

The sternest measures were taken against anti-social elements and the situation was soon brought to normal. Brigadier Verma, Commander of the troops, with a guide from the Hyderabad army, toured the areas where trouble was anticipated, in a van installed with loud-speakers, and addressed public meetings. The fact that the Commander was going around unescorted and unarmed, trying to revive confidence amongst the people, had an extremely good effect on the morale of the minority community.

I called on the Nizam and we had a talk lasting more than an hour. He was in an agitated state of mind and was obviously apprehensive about his future. I recalled the various attempts made by the Government of India to come to an amicable settlement with him, and showed him how short-sighted had been his attempts to assert his independence. Ever since the establishment of the Asaf Jahi dynasty in 1712, the Nizams had always been foreigners on Deccan soil. In the early days they had relied on the support either of the French or the British, and in the end it had been the British who had saved the dynasty from extinction and kept it on the throne. To continue his dynasty when the British left India, the Nizam had to have the support either of the Government of India or of his own subjects, but having neither the one nor the other, he had landed himself in this predicament. After all, he must have known that the Muslims were in a minority and that he could not ensure the continuance of his dynasty on their support alone. The Government of

20. Lord Mountbatten, N. Gopalaswami Aiyangar and the author discussing the Hyderabad question at a party on 30 May 1948.

21. A Razakar rally. Kasim Razvi
is third from left in the front row.

22. Sardar discussing the Hyderabad problem with
his advisers. Left to right : Major-General J. N.
Chaudhuri, M. K. Vellodi, I.C.S., N. M. Buch,
I.C.S., V. Shankar, I.C.S., Sardar and the author.

23. Prime Minister Nehru is greeted by the Nizam during his visit to
Hyderabad State.

24. Conference of Rajpramukhs convened by the States Ministry to discuss the future of the Indian States Forces. On the left are the Rajpramukhs of PEPSU, Madhya Bharat, Rajasthan and Saurashtra.

25. Inspecting a section of the arms seized from the Communists in Telengana. Left to right are N. Gopalaswami Aiyangar, Prime Minister Nehru, the author and N. M. Buch.

India were not vindictive and had no intention of deposing him. Once Hyderabad had fallen into line with the other States in its relationship with the Centre, and provided the Nizam discarded his past mentality, remained loyal to the Indian Union and worked in the interests of his people, the Government of India would continue him on the *gaddi*. I then referred to the huge sums of money — I think it was Rs 22 crores — which the Nizam had spent on armaments and propaganda. I enquired of him what good that had brought to his State, apart from the enrichment of a few people who were involved. The whole finances of the State were in a thoroughly disorganized state and I looked to him to rehabilitate them. I told him that all his resources should be placed at the disposal of the new Government of the State, so that he could repair the damage and earn the goodwill of his subjects. The Nizam listened to me patiently. He assured me that, in spite of all that had happened in the past, he would be loyal to the Indian Union and work in the closest collaboration with the Government of India for the benefit of his people. He asked me to communicate this both to Sardar and Nehru.

It was after my interview with the Nizam that I expressed to Major-General Chaudhuri a desire to see Kasim Razvi, who was under detention in one of the military barracks. Major-General Chaudhuri took me there. I told him that I would prefer to see Razvi alone. Surprise was writ large on Razvi's face when he saw me. When I greeted him he told me that he never expected that I would shake hands with him. I said to him: 'Did I not tell you when you met me in Delhi that you would land yourself in this predicament?' Shorn of his bombast, Kasim Razvi looked woebegone. He told me that he had great plans for communal peace in south India, but I replied that I had seen enough of the results of those plans, though I had been in Hyderabad State for only a short time. I asked him whether he was well looked after and whether he wanted any particular facilities which could be given to him. He assured me that he was being well looked after and that he did not want anything.

After my return from Hyderabad D. S. Bakhle, I.C.S., took charge as Civil Administrator to assist the Military Governor. Some of the key posts in the districts and in the headquarters were entrusted to Indian officers borrowed from the neighbouring provinces, and those Hyderabad officers who had run away in the wake of the Police Action were asked to come back and report for duty before 30 October.

Later, I went again to Hyderabad accompanied by H. M. Patel, the Defence Secretary. Lt.-General Rajendrasinhji, General Officer Commanding-in-Chief, Southern Command, was also there. The object of our visit was to discuss with the Military Governor and Bakhle the problems facing Hyderabad and to work out a plan for its future governance. The administration of the State would have to be handed over to the popular leaders as soon as possible. Immediate transfer of power to them was, however, beset with several practical difficulties. Hyderabad had passed through a revolution and many settled things had become unsettled. The law and order situation was still fluid, the Razakars had not yet been brought under control and the Communists were still a menace. The financial position of the State was chaotic and until we brought order out of chaos and were able to lay the foundations of a structure which would command the confidence of the people, it would be unwise to hand over the State to a popular ministry. The services, especially the police, were in a completely disorganized state. They were the close preserve of the Muslim minority. In the police, nearly 95 per cent were Muslims and many of them were pro-Razakar. The army was completely Muslim. There was only a sprinkling of Hindus at the Headquarters; the position was more or less the same in other services. The continuance of Muslims in this privileged position could only act as an irritant to the Hindus. At the same time, any change would have to be brought about gradually.

Taking all factors into account, we drew up a plan which was approved by the Cabinet and which formed generally the basis of the administration of Hyderabad till it was handed over to a popular ministry.

The administration headed by Major-General Chaudhuri continued till December 1949, when an administration with M. K. Vellodi, I.C.S., as Chief Minister was installed. In 1950, for the first time, four representatives of the Hyderabad State Congress were taken into the administration as ministers. After the general elections, in March 1952, a Congress ministry under B. Ramakrishna Rao was set up. Vellodi became Adviser to the new Government.

The administration was thus virtually under the control of the Government of India for a little over three years. This was all too short a period in which to accomplish many desirable reforms. Nevertheless, thanks to the wise and efficient administration of the Military Governor and his Civil Administrator as well as of the

Vellodi Ministry, the Government of India were able to hand over the administration with the foundations of an efficient government well laid.

We were able to restore complete confidence among the Muslims. The Razakars were disbanded and many of them were detained under the Public Safety Regulations. After October 1948 the Military Governor's administration reviewed the cases of such Razakars as had not been involved in any serious crime and released the bulk of the detenus. Those accused of serious crimes, including Razvi, were brought to open trial. Razvi was found guilty and sentenced to a term of imprisonment.

I have already mentioned that the finances of the State were in a completely disorganized state. At the instance of the States Ministry, the Government of Hyderabad in 1950 appointed a Committee with A. D. Gorwala (a retired I.C.S. officer with great administrative experience) as chairman to make recommendations for reorganizing the administration and effecting economies. The Committee submitted its report on 1 October of the same year. It made far-reaching recommendations intended to modernize the administration and to bring the administrative machinery on a par with that of the neighbouring Governors' provinces. It estimated that if its recommendations were implemented the Government of Hyderabad would be saving Rs 350 lakhs per annum. The Government of Hyderabad generally accepted the recommendations of the Committee, though some of them could not be implemented due to the peculiar circumstances then prevailing in the State. For example, in regard to the reduction of police expenditure, the Government of Hyderabad could not effect the saving of Rs 115 lakhs recommended by the Committee in view of the Communist menace in the Telengana and Warrangal districts. By the implementation of the recommendations of the Gorwala Committee and by other measures taken by the Government of Hyderabad, Vellodi's Ministry was able by 1952 to balance the budget of the State.

One of the pressing problems which the Government of India had to deal with was the serious situation caused by the activities of the Communists. Owing to Communist trouble in the State the Nizam's Government in 1943 had banned the party. The Communists went underground and in the initial stages they offered some resistance to the Razakars. Subsequently they allied themselves with the Razakars who, for a time, had become the virtual masters of Hyderabad. Indeed, shortly after the Laik Ali Ministry came into power, the ban on the Communist party was lifted. The Razakars and the Communists were truly an ill-assorted pair, for whereas the former wanted to establish a Muslim oligarchy in the State, the latter's purpose was to exploit the turmoil and confusion so that they could take possession of the State and ultimately spread their tentacles to the rest of India. Each wanted to use the other for its own ends. The Police Action however had practically eradicated the Razakars; only the Communists remained.

The Communists had entrenched themselves in Nalgunda and Warrangal districts which were extremely backward and neglected. In Nalgunda for instance, the district headquarters were without railway and telegraphic communications. The feudal system under which the landholders exacted labour and tribute from the peasantry provided fertile soil for Communist activities.

In the beginning the Communists under the direction of their leaders divided the State into district, taluka and village organizations, and militant bodies were set up for guerilla warfare which included even women and children. The villagers were terrified of them and were afraid to give information about their movements and hide-outs. I toured some of the villages of Warrangal and, to recount only one instance of how the villagers were terrorized by the Communists: in a village consisting of several huts the Patwari's house had been burnt down and looted and his wife been murdered. This happened twenty yards away from the villagers' huts, but when I asked their owners whether they had seen the burning of the Patwari's house they feigned complete ignorance. I was told that for fear of the Communists the villagers invariably behaved like that.

After the Police Action, no house-to-house search was conducted in Hyderabad City for confiscation of arms; the Military Government accepted the arms voluntarily surrendered in response to its appeal. But a considerable number of arms had found their way to the Communists through the Razakars. The terrain also, with its outlying forests and lack of communications, was ideally suited for guerilla warfare. The Communists exploited this to great advantage.

The first desideratum was to banish all fear of the Communists from the mind of the masses by demonstrating to them that the Government of India were strong enough to protect them. The banning of the Communist party, together with the disposition of the army and the special police, gradually revived the confidence of the rural population. Vigorous steps were taken to put an end to the terrorizing of the masses by the Communists. All available resources were thrown into this all-out drive. Armed police were borrowed from Madras, the Central Provinces and Bombay. We were able to bring the menace under control only after three years of ceaseless effort. One might well imagine what would have happened had the Communists been allowed an undisturbed lease of life.

Early in 1951, the question was raised of removing the ban on the Communist party in the State, but the States Ministry held that there could be no question of removing the ban unless the Communists eschewed violence and surrendered all the arms in their possession. Propagation of an ideology could not in a democracy be prohibited so long as it was peaceful; but when it was supported not by argument but by force, it could not be tolerated. Later, however, on the eve of the general elections, the Government of India removed the ban and permitted the Communists to participate in the elections.

Simultaneously with the suppression of the violent activities of the Communists, a positive policy had to be followed. We had to assure the people both by propaganda and by action that the Government of India were out to better their economic condition. The first step was to abolish the *jagirdari* system (briefly described in Chapter XI) which existed in a most acute form in Hyderabad. This coupled with the appointment of an Agrarian Committee largely neutralized whatever appeal communism might have had for the masses.

The first *jagirs* to be taken over were the Nizam's own, which were known as the *Sarf-e-Khas*. These were yielding him a net surplus, after deducting the expenses of administration, of Rs 124 lakhs per annum. The Nizam agreed to surrender all his rights over these lands and in return the Government of India gave him a compensatory allowance of Rs 25 lakhs per annum for his lifetime.

Apart from this, the State was dotted with tiny islands comprising villages belonging to various categories of *jagirdars*. On 15 August 1949, by the Jagir Abolition Regulation, these too were abolished. The administration of all *jagirs* was taken over by an Administrator during September 1949 and the process of their integration with the district administration was completed by the end of March 1950.

49

As an interim arrangement, an overall relief of 12½ per cent in the then land revenue assessment was granted to the tenants of these lands and greater relief was given in areas where the rates fixed by the *jagirdars* were higher. This reform was hailed with joy by the five million people living in *jagir* areas.

The *jagirdars* and their shareholders and dependents were also treated justly. For the first six months an interim allowance was paid to them ranging between 41⅔ per cent to 75 per cent of their annual income from the *jagir*, based on the size of the income of the *jagir*. Subsequently, the *jagirdars* were paid commutation sums, which were also worked on a graduated scale being most favourable to the lower income groups. The form and manner and the number of instalments for payment of the commutation amount had to be settled. For this purpose I went to Hyderabad in August 1950. I had prolonged discussions with the Government of Hyderabad as well as the representatives of the *jagirdars*. Eventually a formula based on the following principles was evolved: (a) that the payment of the commutation amount should not involve any undue strain on the State finances, (b) that the scheme of payment should be so arranged that the entire amount would be paid off within a reasonably short period, and (c) that under no circumstances should the State be saddled with the burden of a heavy debt in the shape of interest on loans to pay off the *jagirdars*, or of converting payments due to *jagirdars* as an interest-bearing loan. The resulting formula provided for payment in ten equal annual instalments to those of the *jagirdars* and their dependents whose commutation amount worked out at Rs 10,000 or less. The bigger *jagirdars* with a gross income of over Rs 25 lakhs were to be paid their commutation sum in twenty equal annual instalments. The number of instalments for the group falling between these two extremes was fixed at fifteen.

The *jagirs* in Hyderabad State yielded a revenue of about Rs 3·5 crores including land revenue, revenue from excise duty, forests etc. The total commutation sum payable by the State would work out roughly to Rs 18 crores which would be paid in instalments, causing an annual burden on the State's finances of about Rs 114·5 lakhs. In addition the State accepted the liability for the administration of the *jagirs*, providing educational, medical and other social welfare amenities in these areas, as well as payment of pensions to those of the *jagir* employees who could not be absorbed in State service.

Hyderabad thus went a step ahead of the other States in India which were still grappling with this problem. Sardar was very happy with the manner in which this complicated and controversial issue had been resolved with the willing consent of the parties and he desired that a similar settlement should be effected, by negotiation, in every other Union where the problem existed.

Immediately after the installation of the Military Governor's administration, the Nizam issued a proclamation which brought the Hyderabad State into line with the other States on accession and other matters. On 23 November 1949 he issued a *firman* accepting the Constitution framed by the Constituent Assembly of India as the Constitution of Hyderabad.

This chapter would not be complete without a reference to the criticism which was levelled against India for the Police Action in Hyderabad. Most of the British newspapers roundly condemned India. Questions were asked in the British House of Commons and even the British Foreign Secretary, Ernest Bevin, went to the extent of accusing India of developing a warlike mentality. None of those critics could in fact have been aware of the extent to which the Government of India had gone to bring about a peaceful settlement with Hyderabad.

Ever since the subsidiary alliance had been imposed on Hyderabad in 1798, the British had never treated the Nizam differently from the other rulers. Not only had the paramount power exercised full and exclusive control over all the external affairs of Hyderabad, but even in its internal affairs the sovereignty of the Nizam had from time to time been overborne and limited by the intervention of the paramount power. Geographically, culturally, economically and politically, Hyderabad had always been an integral part of India. No natural barriers separated the border areas, the population was completely homogeneous with the population of the surrounding Indian provinces, and the State had been entirely dependent upon India for its railways, its postal, telegraphic and telephonic services and its air communications. Economically, the State had never been an independent entity in any sense of the term, but had always been an integral part of India. This position, which had existed for over a century-and-a-half, could not surely be wiped out overnight by a mere declaration of the British Parliament with regard to the lapse of paramountcy.

Laik Ali had complained that the people who fought for the

independence of India were now themselves denying independence to Hyderabad, and there were not lacking Britishers who backed up Laik Ali's plea. But when they talked of independence for Hyderabad, they were thinking only in terms of the Nizam and his coterie, and not of the people of the State.

One look at the map will show that the Nizam's territories extended right across the peninsula and could, if the Nizam's designs had materialized or if the Communists had succeeded in their efforts, have practically cut off the south from the north.

It is interesting to note that in our dealings with Hyderabad we had been governed by a point of view which almost entirely coincided with that of a distinguished member of the Indian Political Service. As early as 1926, the problem of Hyderabad was pithily summed up in a memorandum by Sir William Barton, the then British Resident:

There can be no doubt that it (Hyderabad) owes its very existence to the British connection. The Asafia family had not taken strong root in the Deccan in 1800; in point of fact, it may be said that it has never ceased to be foreign. Without the British, it must have relied on the handful of Muslims domiciled in the State; a forlorn hope against Maratha resurgence. Left entirely to himself it is doubtful if the present Nizam would be able to maintain himself for any length of time.

Three strong currents of political activity converge on Hyderabad: the Maratha, the Andhra and the Kanara movements. The object of these movements is to build up again the old provinces where the various peoples predominated; and their success would mean the disappearance of Hyderabad. Already a subtle campaign of propaganda is going on from the three directions indicated. Good government is the only antidote to this poison, and it must be regretfully observed that the Nizam's attitude for the past five years leaves but a faint hope that he would, if he realised his dreams of unchecked absolutism, consider the welfare of his people in the least degree.

The limitations on internal sovereignty which paramountcy implies have been shown to exist as fully developed in the case of Hyderabad as elsewhere. The present ruler desires to revert to the position existing before, in 1798, his ancestor made over to the British the military control of his territories. Such a reversion is impossible so long as he enjoys military protection. Without such protection a Hindu insurrection would soon sweep away Muslim rule unless the British Government allowed the Nizam to recruit mercenaries and to import the latest military arms and equipment from outside. Would the co-religionists of the Hindus in the State, in Bombay, Madras and the Central Provinces stand quietly by and see their compatriots massacred? The British Government would unquestionably be involved. It is in fact impossible, treaty or no treaty, to allow an unfettered despotism to be set up in Hyderabad.

If, in August 1947, the Nizam had acceded and had introduced responsible government, he would have won the affection of his subjects, but since both these measures had to be brought about by the action of the Government of India, the people naturally feel that they owe him nothing. This is one of the factors, which, as Sir William Barton prophetically pointed out, gave momentum to the agitation among a section of the people for the disintegration of the State.

It is axiomatic that no nation can afford to be generous at the cost of its integrity, and India has no reason to be afraid of her own shadow.

XX

JAMMU AND KASHMIR STATE

JAMMU AND KASHMIR came into existence as a separate State only in 1846. Till the fourteenth century Kashmir was ruled by a series of Buddhist and Hindu dynasties, whose annals are related in the celebrated versified Sanskrit chronicle known as the *Rajatarangini*. It was during this epoch that the old remains of Kashmir at places like Anantnag, Bijbehara, Pandrattan, Sankaracharya, Pattan and Martand were constructed. A Muslim dynasty then established itself and continued to rule till 1587, when Akbar invaded Kashmir and made it an appanage of the Moghul Empire. For another two hundred years it remained the summer residence of the Moghul emperors, who have left their traces in the Hari Parbat Fort, the pleasure gardens of Shalimar, Nishat, Achabal and Verinag and, indeed, in the magnificent Chenar tree which abounds everywhere. In 1752 Kashmir passed from the then feeble control of the Moghul emperor into the powerful grasp of Ahmad Shah Abdali of Afghanistan and for the next sixty-seven years it was held for the Pathans by a series of governors who were more or less independent of their king. In 1819 it was conquered by Maharajah Ranjit Singh, the great Sikh ruler. Till 1846 it remained under the Sikhs and was administered by their governors.

In the latter half of the eighteenth century, Jammu was ruled by a Dogra chief of Rajput descent, named Ranjit Deo. He died in 1780 and there ensued a quarrel for succession. This gave the Sikhs the opportunity of turning Jammu and the neighbouring hill tracts into a dependency. Three great-grand nephews of Ranjit Deo, namely Gulab Singh, Dhyan Singh and Suchet Singh, entered the service of Maharajah Ranjit Singh. They rendered such distinguished service that the latter in 1818, conferred the principality of Jammu on Gulab Singh with the hereditary title of Rajah; Bhimber and Chibal, including Poonch on Dhyan Singh; and Ramnagar on Suchet Singh. Both Dhyan Singh and Suchet Singh were subsequently killed.

With the death of Ranjit Singh in 1839, the Sikh power — as one writer puts it — 'exploded, disappearing in fierce but fading flames.' In 1846, at the close of the first Sikh War, Gulab Singh appeared on the scene as mediator between the English and the Lahore Durbar. In the negotiations that followed, the Sikh Maharajah was called upon to pay an indemnity to the East India Company of Rs 1 crore, in addition to a large forfeit of territory in the Punjab. As the indemnity was beyond his means to pay, he ceded all his hill territories from the Beas river to the Indus including Kashmir and Jammu. But Lord Hardinge, then Governor-General, considered the occupation of the whole of this territory inadvisable on the ground that it would increase the extent of the British frontier and the military establishment for guarding it; also because it would create new and conflicting interests, while the districts in question (with the exception of the small vale of Kashmir) were for the most part unproductive. On the other hand, the ceded tract comprised the whole of the hereditary possessions of Gulab Singh, who, being eager to obtain an indefeasible title to them, came forward and offered to pay the war indemnity on condition that he was made the independent ruler of Jammu and Kashmir. A separate treaty embodying this arrangement was concluded with Gulab Singh at Amritsar on 16 March 1846. Under this treaty Gulab Singh acknowledged the supremacy of the British Government and in token of such supremacy agreed to present annually to the British Government one horse, twelve shawl goats of approved breed and three pairs of Kashmir shawls. This arrangement was later altered; the annual presentation made by the Kashmir State was confined to two Kashmir shawls and three *romals* (handkerchiefs).

The Treaty of Amritsar marks the commencement of the history of the Jammu and Kashmir State as a political entity. The treaty put Gulab Singh, as Maharajah, in possession of all the hill country between the Indus and Ravi, including Kashmir, Jammu, Ladakh and Gilgit; but excluding Lahoul, Kulu and some other areas including Chamba which, for strategical purposes, it was considered advisable to retain and for which a remission of Rs 25 lakhs was made from the crore demanded, leaving Rs 75 lakhs as the final amount to be paid by Gulab Singh. Gulab Singh had some difficulty in obtaining actual possession of the province of Kashmir. The last

Governor appointed by the Sikhs made for a time a successful resistance; and it was not until the end of 1846 that Maharajah Gulab Singh with the aid of British troops was established in Kashmir.

No subsidiary force was imposed on Gulab Singh. Political relations between the Government of India and the State commenced in the year 1849 and were conducted by the Punjab Government through the Maharajah's agent at Lahore. No representative of the Government of India was located in the State and it was not until the year 1852 that the first 'Officer on Special Duty' in the State was appointed. This officer resided in Kashmir during the summer months only. Maharajah Gulab Singh died in 1857 and was succeeded by his son Ranbir Singh. The channel of political relations with the State, however, continued as heretofore until 1877, in which year the Officer on Special Duty was placed under the immediate orders of the Government of India with instructions to correspond direct with them on all matters of political importance. In 1885, after the death of Maharajah Ranbir Singh and the accession to the *gaddi* of Maharajah Pratap Singh, the designation of the Officer on Special Duty was changed to 'Resident in Kashmir' who was permanently located in Srinagar.

Lt.-General Maharajah Sir Hari Singh, who was the ruler of Jammu and Kashmir at the time of the transfer of power, ascended the *gaddi* on 23 September 1925.

At the time of the partition, the State had important international boundaries. To the east was Tibet, to the north-east lay the Sinkiang province of China and to the north-west was Afghanistan. A tongue of Afghanistan territory, Wakhan, is north of Gilgit and is west of the main route from Gilgit to Kashgar over the Mintaka Pass. A few miles beyond lies Russian Turkestan.

Geographically, the State falls into four natural regions. In the south lies Jammu; in the centre is the Happy Valley of Kashmir which contains the summer capital, Srinagar; to the north is Gilgit; and between the Kashmir Valley and Tibet is the province of Ladakh.

Jammu and Kashmir always had a preponderance of Muslims. But the population ratio was affected to some extent after the partition, particularly in Jammu, as a result of migration to and from Pakistan. In Ladakh the majority are Buddhists.

Though the Muslims formed the largest community in the State, there were complaints that the majority of the posts both in the

Government and the Army were being held by Hindus. In 1932, the All-Jammu and Kashmir Muslim Conference, with Sheikh Abdullah as its moving spirit, was established to fight for the rights of the Muslim community. By 1939 this body shed its communal complexion and changed its name into the 'National Conference'; and it was subsequently affiliated to the All-India States Peoples' Conference. Repeated campaigns against the Maharajah were launched by the National Conference and Sheikh Abdullah was imprisoned on several occasions. In 1946 he organized the 'Quit Kashmir' campaign against the Maharajah and, as a result, was sentenced to a long term of imprisonment, but by this time he had acquired a considerable hold over the people of the State.

Before proceeding to the events of 1947, it is necessary to refer to the Gilgit Agency. Gilgit was part of the territories of Jammu and Kashmir. A Political Agent in Gilgit was first appointed in the year 1877 but he was withdrawn in 1881. The Agency was re-established under the control of the Resident in Kashmir in 1889. It comprised: (1) the Gilgit Wazarat, (2) the State of Hunza and Nagir, (3) the Punial Jagir, (4) the Governorships of Yasin, Kuh-Ghizr and Ishkoman, and (5) Chilas. In 1935 Soviet Russia had taken virtual control of Sinkiang in Chinese Turkestan, a move which made it necessary for the Government of India to take over the administration of the Gilgit Sub-Division from the Jammu and Kashmir State. They did so on a sixty-year lease and undertook sole responsibility for the administration and defence of the area. For a period of twelve years after 1935, except for the war years of 1942-46, Gilgit Sub-Division was administered under this lease by a British Assistant Political Agent of the Indian Political Service. The Gilgit Scouts, commanded by British officers who were specially chosen for a responsible and somewhat delicate task, had also been built up. When the June 3rd plan was announced, the Political Department retroceded the area to the Maharajah and the Gilgit Scouts were also handed over to him. The retrocession of Gilgit was accepted by the Maharajah with jubilation.

I have already narrated how, after the setting up of the States Ministry, we were having exploratory talks with the rulers and their representatives for the accession of the States geographically contiguous to India. Pandit Ramchandra Kak, the Prime Minister of Jammu and Kashmir, was in Delhi at the time. On the suggestion of the Maharajah of Patiala, we invited him to one such conference but he failed to attend it. He met me subsequently at the Governor-General's house. I asked him what the attitude of the Maharajah was in regard to accession to India or Pakistan, but he gave me very evasive replies. Kak also met Sardar. I could not understand the man nor fathom his game. Lord Mountbatten subsequently arranged an interview between Kak and Jinnah.

After the announcement of the June 3rd plan, when Lord Mountbatten was discussing the policy of accession of the Indian States to one Dominion or the other, he became particularly concerned about Kashmir. Here was a State with the biggest area in India, with a population predominantly Muslim, ruled over by a Hindu Maharajah. Lord Mountbatten knew Sir Hari Singh well, having been on the Prince of Wales' staff with him during His Royal Highness' tour in 1921-22. He accepted a long-standing invitation from the Maharajah to visit Kashmir again and went there in the third week of June.

Lord Mountbatten spent four days discussing the situation and arguing with the Maharajah. He told him that independence was not, in his opinion, a feasible proposition and that the State would not be recognized as a Dominion by the British Government. He assured the Maharajah that, so long as he made up his mind to accede to one Dominion or the other before 15 August, no trouble would ensue, for whichever Dominion he acceded to would take the State firmly under its protection as part of its territory. He went so far as to tell the Maharajah that, if he acceded to Pakistan, India would not take it amiss and that he had a firm assurance on this from Sardar Patel himself. Lord Mountbatten went further to say that, in view of the composition of the population, it was particularly important to ascertain the wishes of the people. The Maharajah appeared quite incapable of making up his mind and so Lord Mountbatten asked for a meeting with him and his Prime Minister on the last morning of his visit. At the last moment the Maharajah sent a message to say that he was confined to bed and begged to be excused.

Immediately after the transfer of power on 15 August, Lord Ismay went up to Srinagar. Lord Mountbatten had asked him to persuade the Maharajah to take one course or the other as soon as possible; but nothing came out of Lord Ismay's efforts.

In fairness to Maharajah Hari Singh, it must be said that, situated as he was, it was not easy for him to come to a decision. If he acceded to Pakistan, the non-Muslims of Jammu and Ladakh as well as considerable sections of Muslims led by the National Conference would definitely have resented such action. On the other hand, accession to India would have provoked adverse reactions in Gilgit and certain areas contiguous to Pakistan. Furthermore, at least at that time, the road communications were with Pakistan and the forest resources, particularly timber which constituted a considerable portion of the State's revenue, were being transported by rivers which flow into Pakistan.

But there was an obvious line of action which the Maharajah might have taken. He could have called a conference of representatives of the people of Jammu and Kashmir and discussed the question with them. But the Maharajah was in a Micawberish frame of mind, hoping for the best while continuing to do nothing. Besides he was toying with the notion of an 'Independent Jammu and Kashmir'.

Shortly before the transfer of power Pandit Kak was replaced as Prime Minister by Major-General Janak Singh. The Government of Jammu and Kashmir then announced their intention of negotiating Standstill Agreements with both India and Pakistan. Pakistan signed a Standstill Agreement. But we wanted time to examine its implications. We left the State alone. We did not ask the Maharajah to accede, though, at that time, as a result of the Radcliffe Award, the State had become connected by road with India. Owing to the composition of the population, the State had its own peculiar problems. Moreover, our hands were already full and, if truth be told, I for one had simply no time to think of Kashmir.

Even after the execution of the Standstill Agreement, the relations between Kashmir and Pakistan were far from cordial. The Government of Jammu and Kashmir complained that, in an effort to coerce the State into acceding, the Pakistan authorities had cut off the supply of food, petrol and other essential commodities, and hindered the free transit of travellers between Kashmir and Pakistan. At this time the Government of Jammu and Kashmir requested the Government of India for 5,000 gallons of petrol which Pakistan had been unable to provide. We sent only 500 gallons to meet the immediate necessity of preventing a complete breakdown of transport in Srinagar.

Military pressure was also applied by Pakistan in the form of hit-and-run border raids. This was along a 450-mile frontier, resulting in the State troops being dispersed and deployed along a wide distance with no adequate reserve, and rendering the defences too thin to resist an all-out attack.

Early in October, Major-General Janak Singh was replaced by
Mehr Chand Mahajan[1] as Prime Minister of Jammu and Kashmir.
On 15 October, the latter complained to the British Prime Minister
that the Government of Pakistan had broken the Standstill Agreement by discontinuing supplies of essential articles, and that the
railway service from Sialkot to Jammu had been stopped without
any reason. He represented that the whole of the State border from
Gurdaspur to Gilgit was threatened with invasion and that it had
already begun in Poonch. He asked that the Dominion of Pakistan
should be advised to deal fairly with Jammu and Kashmir and to
adopt a course of conduct consistent with the good name and prestige of the Commonwealth of which it claimed to be a member. No
reply was received from the British Prime Minister. On 18 October
the Jammu and Kashmir State sent a protest to the Governor-General
and the Prime Minister of Pakistan against the breaches of the Standstill Agreement and the continuous raids. To this Jinnah replied on
20 October protesting against the tone and language of the communication and ascribing the delay in the despatch of essential supplies
to the 'widespread disturbances in East Punjab and the disruption of
communications caused thereby particularly by the shortage of coal.'

The all-out invasion of Kashmir started on 22 October 1947. The
main raiders' column, which had approximately two hundred to
three hundred lorries, and which consisted of frontier tribesmen
estimated at five thousand — Afridis, Wazirs, Mahsuds, Swathis,
and soldiers of the Pakistan Army 'on leave'—led by some regular
officers who knew Kashmir well advanced from Abbottabad in the
N.W.F.P. along the Jhelum Valley Road. They captured Garhi
and Domel and arrived at the gates of Muzaffarabad. The State
battalion, consisting of Muslims and Dogras stationed at Muzaffarabad, was commanded by Lt.-Colonel Narain Singh. All the Muslims
in the battalion deserted; shot the Commanding Officer and his
adjutant; joined the raiders, and acted as advance-guard to the
raiders' column. It may be mentioned that only a few days before
Lt.-Colonel Narain Singh had been asked by the Maharajah whether
he could rely on the loyalty of the Muslim half of his battalion. He
unhesitatingly answered, 'More than on the Dogras'. He had been
in command of this battalion for some years.

---

[1] A leading lawyer who had been a judge of the undivided Punjab High Court. Subsequently he was appointed as a judge of the East Punjab High Court. He retired as
Chief Justice of the Supreme Court.

The raiders then marched towards Baramula along the road lead-ing to Srinagar, their next destination being Uri. All the Muslims in the State Forces had deserted and many had joined the raiders. When Brigadier Rajinder Singh, the Chief of Staff of the State Forces, heard of the desertion of the Muslim personnel and the advance of the raiders, he gathered together approximately 150 men and moved towards Uri. There he engaged the raiders for two days and in the rearguard action destroyed the Uri bridge. The Brigadier himself and all his men were cut to pieces in this action. But he and his colleagues will live in history like the gallant Leonidas and his 300 men who held the Persian invaders at Thermopylae. It was but appropriate that when the *Maha Vir Chakra* decoration was instituted, the first award should have been given (posthumously) to this heroic soldier.

The raiders continued to advance and on 24 October they captur-ed the Mahura Power House, which supplied electricity to Srinagar. Srinagar was plunged in darkness. The raiders had announced that they would reach Srinagar on 26 October in time for the *Id* cele-brations at the Srinagar mosque.

On the evening of 24 October the Government of India received a desperate appeal for help from the Maharajah. They also received from the Supreme Commander information regarding the raiders' advance and probable intentions.[1] On the morning of 25 October a meeting of the Defence Committee was held, presided over by Lord Mountbatten. This Committee considered the request of the Maha-rajah for arms and amunition as also for reinforcements of troops. Lord Mountbatten emphasized that no precipitate action should be taken until the Government of India had fuller information. It was agreed that I should fly to Srinagar immediately in order to study the situation on the spot and to report to the Government of India.

Accompanied by Army and Air Force officers and by the late D. N. Kachru, I flew by a B.O.A.C. plane to Srinagar. This was one of the planes which had been chartered for the evacuation of British nationals from Srinagar. When I landed at the airfield, I was

[1] On 15 August, when the country was partitioned, the Indian Army, the Royal Indian Navy and Royal Indian Air Force were summarily partitioned mainly on a religious basis between the two Dominions. (All six Commanders-in-Chief Army, Navy and Air Force of both Dominions, were British). The last Commander-in-Chief of undivided India, Field-Marshal Auchinleck, became Supreme Commander for the purpose of completing the partition of the Armed Forces. He was kept informed of all movements and in turn kept both Dominions equally informed. When he received a message from Pakistan Army Headquarters giving information regarding the raiders' advance and probable intentions he very rightly passed it on to the Government of India.

oppressed by the stillness as of a graveyard all around. Over everything hung an atmosphere of impending calamity.

From the aerodrome we went straight to the residence of the Prime
Minister of the State. The road leading from the aerodrome to Srinagar was deserted. At some of the street corners I noticed volunteers
of the National Conference with *lathis* who challenged passers-by;
but the State police were conspicuous by their absence. Mehr Chand
Mahajan apprised us of the perilous situation and pleaded for the
Government of India to come to the rescue of the State. Mahajan,
who is usually self-possessed, seemed temporarily to have lost his
equanimity. From his residence we both proceeded to the Maharajah's palace. The Maharajah was completely unnerved by the
turn of events and by his sense of lone helplessness. There were
practically no State Forces left and the raiders had almost reached the
outskirts of Baramula. At this rate they would be in Srinagar in
another day or two. It was no use harping on the past or blaming
the Maharajah for his inaction. I am certain that he had never
thought of the possibility of an invasion of his State by tribesmen nor
of the large-scale desertions of Muslims from his army and police.
By that time, Srinagar had very little contact with the mofussil areas
and it was difficult to find out the real situation. The one hopeful
fact was that Brigadier Rajinder Singh had promised to hold the
raiders as long as possible from reaching Baramula and we knew that
he would fight, if necessary, to the bitter end.

The first thing to be done was to get the Maharajah and his family
out of Srinagar. The reason for this was obvious. The raiders were
close to Baramula. The Maharajah was quite helpless and, if the
Government of India decided not to go to his rescue, there was no
doubt about the fate that would befall him and his family in Srinagar. There was also a certainty that the raiders would loot all
the valuable possessions in the palace. In these circumstances I
advised him to leave immediately for Jammu and to take with him
his family and his valuable possessions.

After assuring myself that he would leave that night and after
gathering all the information I could from people who were in a
position to give it, I went to the Guest House in the early hours of
the morning for a little rest. Just as I was going to sleep, Mahajan
rang me up to say that there were rumours that the raiders
had infiltrated into Srinagar and that it would be unsafe for us to
remain any longer in the city. I could hardly believe that the raiders

could have reached Srinagar, but I had to accept Mahajan's advice. The Maharajah had taken away all the available cars and the only transport available was an old jeep. Into this were bundled Mahajan, myself and the air crew of six or seven. When we reached the airfield, the place was filled with people, in striking contrast to its deserted appearance when I arrived there the previous evening. As I was about to get into the plane, a Hindu lady rushed up to me with her two daughters and with tears in her eyes begged me to take them in the plane to Delhi. She feared that her daughters might meet the fate of thousands of other Kashmiri women. I had no option but to agree and they got into the plane. The pilot told me that at the hotel where he and his crew had their dinner, not a single soul talked and that, but for the noise of forks and spoons, the whole hotel was hushed in silence. It was all horribly depressing and, due to the sobs of the two young girls of whom I had taken charge, I was hardly able to collect my thoughts.

We left Srinagar in the first light of the morning of 26 October and immediately on my arrival in Delhi I went straight to a meeting of the Defence Committee. I reported my impressions of the situation and pointed out the supreme necessity of saving Kashmir from the raiders. Lord Mountbatten said that it would be improper to move Indian troops into what was at the moment an independent country, as Kashmir had not yet decided to accede to either India or Pakistan. If it were true that the Maharajah was now anxious to accede to India, then Jammu and Kashmir would become part of Indian territory. This was the only basis on which Indian troops could be sent to the rescue of the State from further pillaging by the aggressors. He further expressed the strong opinion that, in view of the composition of the population, accession should be conditional on the will of the people being ascertained by a plebiscite after the raiders had been driven out of the State and law and order had been restored. This was readily agreed to by Nehru and other ministers.

Soon after the meeting of the Defence Committee, I flew to Jammu accompanied by Mahajan. On arrival at the palace I found it in a state of utter turmoil with valuable articles strewn all over the place. The Maharajah was asleep; he had left Srinagar the previous evening and had been driving all night. I woke him up and told him of what had taken place at the Defence Committee meeting. He was ready to accede at once. He then composed a letter to the Governor-General describing the pitiable plight of the State and reiterating his request for military help. He further informed the Governor-General that it was his intention to set up an interim government at once and to ask Sheikh Abdullah to carry the responsibilities in this emergency with Mehr Chand Mahajan, his Prime Minister. He concluded by saying that if the State was to be saved, immediate assistance must be available at Srinagar. He also signed the Intrument of Accession. Just as I was leaving, he told me that before he went to sleep, he had left instructions with his ADC that, if I came back from Delhi, he was not to be disturbed as it would mean that the Government of India had decided to come to his rescue and he should therefore be allowed to sleep in peace; but that if I failed to return, it meant that everything was lost and, in that case, his ADC was to shoot him in his sleep !

With the Instrument of Accession and the Maharajah's letter I flew back at once to Delhi. Sardar was waiting at the aerodrome and we both went straight to a meeting of the Defence Committee which was arranged for that evening. There was a long discussion, at the end of which it was decided that the accession of Jammu and Kashmir should be accepted, subject to the proviso that a plebiscite would be held in the State when the law and order situation allowed. It was further decided that an infantry battalion should be flown to Srinagar the next day. This decision had the fullest support of Sheikh Abdullah, who was in Delhi at that time and who had been pressing the Government of India on behalf of the All-Jammu and Kashmir National Conference for immediate help to be sent to the State to resist the tribal invasion.

Even after this decision had been reached Lord Mountbatten and the three British Chiefs of Staff of the Indian Army, Navy and Air Force pointed out the risks involved in the operation. But Nehru asserted that the only alternative to sending troops would be to allow a massacre in Srinagar, which would be followed by a major communal holocaust in India. Moreover, the British residents in Srinagar would certainly be murdered by the raiders, since neither the Pakistan Commander-in-Chief nor the Supreme Commander was in a position to safeguard their lives.

Never in the history of warfare has there been an operation like the airlift of Indian troops to Srinagar on 27 October and on subsequent days, an operation put through with no previous thought, let alone organized planning, and at such remarkably short notice. The Defence Headquarters consisting of British and Indian officers worked almost non-stop from 26 October. The lack of adequate lines of

communication and of intelligence of the enemy strength and dis-
positions made planning very difficult. In the early hours of the
morning of 27 October over a hundred civilian aircraft and R.I.A.F.
planes were mobilized to fly troops, equipment and supplies to Srinagar. The R.I.A.F. and civilian pilots and ground crews rose to the
occasion and worked heroically to make the airlift a success. The
enthusiasm with which the airforce personnel, civilian and military,
worked that morning was phenomenal. Some of the pilots did several
sorties in the course of the day. Nor should one forget to mention the
civilian airline companies but for whose wholehearted co-operation
the airlift could not have been possible.

Lord Mountbatten, who had been Chief of Combined Operations
and Supreme Allied Commander, South East Asia, said that in all
his war experience he had never heard of an airlift of this nature
being put into operation at such short notice and he complimented
all concerned on the astonishing performance. It has been suggested
in certain quarters that the fact that so many Indian troops could be
flown in to Srinagar at such short notice was proof of its having been
a pre-planned affair. I quote the following note signed by the three
British Commanders-in-Chief of the Army, Air Force and Navy as a
clear refutation of this allegation:

It has been alleged that plans were made for sending Indian forces to
Kashmir at some date before 22nd October, on which day the raid on that
State from the direction of Abbotabad began.

2. The following is a true time-table of events, as regards decisions
taken, plans made, orders given, and movements started, in this matter:

(1) On 24th October the C-in-C, Indian Army, received information
that tribesmen had seized Muzaffarabad. This was the first indication of the raid.

(2) Prior to this date, no plans of any sort for sending Indian forces
into Kashmir had been formulated or even considered.

(3) On the morning of 25th October, we were directed to examine
and prepare plans for sending troops to Kashmir by air and road,
in case this should be necessary to stop the tribal incursions. This
was the first direction which we received on this subject. No steps
had been taken, prior to the meting, to examine or prepare such
plans.

(4) On the afternoon of 25th October we sent one staff officer of each,
the Indian Army and the R.I.A.F., by air to Srinagar. There they
saw officers of the Kashmir State Forces. This was the first
contact between officers of our Headquarters and officers of the

Kashmir State Forces on the subject of sending Indian troops to Kashmir.

(5) On the afternoon of the 25th October we also issued orders to an infantry battalion to prepare itself to be flown, at short notice, to Srinagar, in the event of the Government of India deciding to accept the accession of Kashmir and send help.

(6) On the morning of 26th October the Staff Officers, mentioned in sub-paragraph (4) above, returned from Srinagar and reported on their meetings with officers of the Kashmir State Forces.

(7) On the afternoon of 26th October we finalised our plans for the despatch by air of troops to Kashmir.

(8) At first light on the morning of 27th October, with Kashmir's Instrument of Accession signed, the movement by air of Indian forces to Kashmir began.

3. No plans were made for sending these forces, nor were such plans even considered, before 25th October, three days after the tribal incursions began.

The immediately available unit was a Sikh battalion which was stationed on internal security duties in the Gurgaon District near Delhi. The Commander of this battalion was Lt.-Colonel Dewan Ranjit Rai. The tasks assigned to him were to secure the airfield in Srinagar, to render assistance to the Government of Kashmir in maintaining law and order in Srinagar and, if possible, to drive away any tribesmen who might have entered the city. As only meagre information was available as to the strength of the enemy and it was not known whether the airfield had fallen into their hands, Lt.-Colonel Rai was told to circle above it and, if there was any doubt, not to land but to fly back to Jammu. At 10-30 a.m. after tense suspense, a wireless flash from Srinagar airfield announced the safe landing of the first of our troops. We heaved a sigh of relief; the airfield was now in our hands.

Lt.-Colonel Rai found on landing that the enemy was at Baramula, the strategic bottle-neck which opens into the Srinagar Valley. Once the raiders were allowed to enter and fan out into the Srinagar plain, all would be lost. Lt.-Colonel Rai therefore decided to advance to Baramula with a view to stopping the raiders there. The transport was provided by Bakshi Ghulam Mahomed, who was Number Two in the National Conference. When Lt.-Colonel Rai contacted the so-called 'raiders' he found them to be an organized body of men armed with light and medium machine-guns and mortars, and led by commanders who knew modern tactics and the use of ground.

Sometime after the battle had been joined, Lt.-Colonel Rai discovered that the strength of the raiders was far superior to his and he therefore decided to withdraw to Pattan on the main Baramula-Srinagar road, 17 miles from Srinagar. While conducting the withdrawal, he was killed in action. By his initiative and determination, this gallant officer helped to check the advance of the raiders on Srinagar. He was posthumously awarded a *Maha Vir Chakra*.

Meanwhile, at Lahore, Jinnah was getting impatient. His private secretary, Kurshid Ahmad, was already in Srinagar but after the arrival of the Indian troops he was arrested and sent back to Pakistan. The moment Jinnah heard that India had accepted the accession of Jammu and Kashmir and that Indian troops had been air borne to Srinagar, he gave orders to General Gracey, the Acting Commander-in-Chief of the Pakistan Army, to rush troops to Kashmir. Gracey represented to Jinnah his inability to issue any instructions in this respect without the approval of the Supreme Commander. Field-Marshal Auchinleck flew to Lahore on the morning of 28 October and explained to Jinnah that, in the event of Pakistan troops entering Kashmir, which was now legally a part of India, every British officer serving in the Pakistan Army would automatically and immediately be withdrawn. Jinnah therefore cancelled his order for Pakistan troops to march into Kashmir. He then sent a message through Auchinleck to Lord Mountbatten and Nehru inviting them to Lahore for a conference to discuss the Kashmir problem.

Lord Mountbatten was eager that the invitation should be accepted and that he and Nehru should go to Lahore, but Sardar was strongly opposed to either of them making the visit. He said that, as Pakistan was the aggressor in this case, it was not right to follow a policy of appeasement by running after Jinnah. If Jinnah wanted to discuss the matter he should come to Delhi. Nehru was inclined to agree with Lord Mountbatten. He argued that we had not gone to Kashmir for territorial acquisition and if we could find a peaceful solution of the problem we should not stand on prestige.

As there was a difference of opinion between Sardar and Nehru the matter was naturally referred to Gandhiji. That night I had a telephone call from his secretary who told me that Gandhiji wanted to see me urgently. I went to Birla House and found Nehru and Sardar conferring with Gandhiji. Gandhiji asked me what my objections were to Nehru going to Lahore. I replied that when this was mooted to me by Lord Mountbatten I was entirely opposed to the idea and I gave reasons for my stand. While the discussions were going on we noticed that Nehru was looking flushed and tired. It was found that he was actually running a high temperature. His going to Lahore was therefore out of the question. A few days later Liaqat Ali Khan cast doubts on the genuineness of Nehru's illness, but the truth is as I have stated. It was then decided that Lord Mountbatten should go alone.

Just as Lord Mountbatten was getting ready for his Lahore trip the Government of Pakistan issued a statement, on 30 October, in which they characterized the Kashmir accession as being 'based on fraud and violence and as such cannot be recognized.' The statement went to the fantastic extent of asserting that the State troops had been the first to attack the Muslims in the State and the Muslim villages in the Pakistan border and that this had provoked the Pathan raiders. This was certainly not conducive to the creation of a friendly atmosphere.

In the meantime Sheikh Abdullah had been invited by the Maharajah to form an interim emergency government, which he did. By this time the strength of our troops in Srinagar had been increased. Three more battalions had reached Srinagar. We had also flown in a brigade headquarters.

Before the Jinnah-Mountbatten parleys took place, another drama had been enacted. I have already mentioned that, soon after the announcement of the transfer of power, the Gilgit Agency had been retroceded to the Maharajah. The Maharajah then appointed a Governor for that area. The Governor, accompanied by Major-General H. L. Scott, Chief of Staff of the Jammu and Kashmir Army,[1] reached Gilgit on 30 July. On arrival they found that all the officers of the British Government had opted for service in Pakistan. There was no State civil staff available to take over from these officers. The Gilgit Scouts also wanted to go over to Pakistan. In addition to the Scouts, 6 J & K Infantry battalion (half Sikhs and half Muslims) was the only State force unit available. It was commanded by Lt.-Col. Majid Khan and was stationed at Bunji, 34 miles distant from Gilgit. At midnight of 31 October the Governor's residence was surrounded by the Gilgit Scouts. The next morning the Governor was put under arrest and a provisional government was established by the rebels. The Muslim elements (including officers) in the State

---

[1] Major-General Scott was succeeded by Brigadier Rajinder Singh as Chief of Staff after 15 August 1947.

force garrison had deserted; the non-Muslim elements were largely liquidated. Those who survived escaped to the hills and then joined the State force garrison at Skardu. On 4 November Major Brown, the British Commandant of the Gilgit Scouts, ceremonially hoisted the Pakistan Flag in the Scouts' lines and in the third week of November a Political Agent from Pakistan established himself at Gilgit.

On 1 November Lord Mountbatten, accompanied by Lord Ismay, flew to Lahore and had a long conference with Jinnah. Jinnah contended that the accession of Kashmir to India had been brought about by violence. Lord Mountbatten retorted that the violence had come from the tribal invaders. He went on to say that, as the Indian troops in Srinagar were being built up, it was now remote that the tribesmen would ever be able to enter Srinagar. Jinnah then proposed that both sides withdraw at once and simultaneously. When Lord Mountbatten asked him to explain how the tribesmen could be induced to remove themselves, Jinnah's reply was: 'If you do this I will call the whole thing off.' Lord Mountbatten then suggested that a plebiscite should be held in the State. Jinnah objected and said that, with the presence of Indian troops in the State and with Sheikh Abdullah in power, the people of the State would be far too frightened to vote for Pakistan. Lord Mountbatten then suggested a plebiscite under the auspices of the United Nations Organization. But Jinnah pressed for a plebiscite to be held under the joint control and supervision of the Governors-General of India and Pakistan. Both Lord Mountbatten and Lord Ismay were at pains to explain to Jinnah that the fact that he was also President of the Muslim League gave him a special position in Pakistan which Lord Mountbatten did not enjoy in India. Jinnah might therefore be able to offer joint control, but Lord Mountbatten, being a strictly constitutional Governor-General, was in no position to accept the offer. The conversations were inconclusive. Lord Mountbatten returned to Delhi.

On 2 November, Nehru in a broadcast speech said that every step in regard to Kashmir had been taken after the fullest thought and consideration of the consequences. 'Not to have taken these steps would have been a betrayal of a trust and cowardly submission to the law of the sword with its accompaniment of arson, rape and slaughter.' He emphasized that the struggle in Kashmir was the struggle of the people of Kashmir under popular leadership against the invader. He declared his readiness, when peace and the rule of law had been established, to have a referendum held under some such international auspices as that of the United Nations.

This was followed on 4 November by a broadcast from Lahore by Liaqat Ali Khan. He laid stress on the 'immoral and illegal ownership' of Kashmir resulting from the 'infamous' Amritsar Treaty of 1846. He contended that it was a dishonest rewriting of history to present the rebellion of the enslaved people of Kashmir to the world as an invasion from outside just because some outsiders had shown active sympathy with it. He contended that it was not Kashmir but a tottering despot that the Indian Government and their camp followers were trying to save and that the accession of Kashmir to India was a fraud perpetrated on its people by its cowardly ruler with the aggressive help of the Government of India.

Sardar and Baldev Singh, the Defence Minister, visited Srinagar on 3 November. They discussed the political situation with the Kashmir ministers and the military position with Brigadier L. P. Sen, who was in command of our troops. They returned to Delhi on 4 November and gave a detailed report of the military situation to the Defence Committee. Brigadier Sen had certainly done all that could be expected with the resources available to him, but they had no doubt whatever that the army needed to be strengthened. This view was accepted. It was decided to establish a new divisional headquarters (Jammu and Kashmir Division) in Kashmir. Major-General Kalwant Singh was selected to take over command of the new division. He was instructed to concentrate all his efforts on the taking of Baramula, for that place commands the entrance to the Valley of Kashmir and it was felt that its recapture would reduce the chances of further tribal incursions.

Major-General Kalwant Singh left for Srinagar the next day. On 8 November his forces occupied Baramula. When the Indian troops entered the city they found that it had been stripped by the tribesmen of its wealth and its women. Out of a normal population of 14,000 only one thousand were left. The devastation by the raiders was indeed ghastly, reminiscent of Nadir Shah's sacking of Delhi. A number of foreign correspondents bore testimony to the arson and pillage, loot and rape which had been indulged in by the tribesmen in Baramula.

On the day Baramula was retaken, there was a meeting of the Joint Defence Council of both Dominions in Delhi. Lord Mountbatten had made vigorous attempts to induce Jinnah and Liaqat

Ali Khan to attend this meeting, but his efforts were fruitless. Pakistan was represented by Abdur Rab Nishtar and Mahommad Ali, Secretary-General to the Government of Pakistan. Nehru was present at this meeting. Later he discussed the Kashmir problem with Abdur Rab Nishtar, but with no tangible result. I fared no better with Mahommad Ali.

In the meantime, the Indian Army was going ahead with its efforts to dislodge the raiders. By 11 November, it had reached the heights of Uri; the tribesmen were in such a hurry to withdraw that they gave up Tangmarg and Gulmarg without firing a shot.

On 21 November Nehru made a statement in Parliament. After a rapid review of the events of the previous four weeks, he reiterated his promise that the people of Kashmir would be given the chance to decide their future under the supervision of an impartial tribunal such as the United Nations Organization.

In the first week of December, Liaqat Ali Khan came to Delhi to attend another meeting of the Joint Defence Council. Lord Mountbatten was anxious that Nehru should take the opportunity of discussing the Kashmir issue with him. But Nehru had just received from Liaqat Ali Khan a telegram which was most objectionable and contained very offensive references to Sheikh Abdullah. He was not therefore disposed, at first, to meet the Pakistan Prime Minister. Subsequently, however, he agreed. Lord Ismay, who was present at the meeting, was asked to try to commit to paper certain broad views which Lord Mountbatten had put forward and with which the two Prime Ministers appeared to agree. Lord Ismay later had a meeting with Mahommad Ali and myself and we produced a draft as a basis for discussion between the two Prime Ministers. The terms of the draft were that the Government of Pakistan would use all their influence to persuade the Azad Kashmir[1] forces to cease fighting and the tribesmen to withdraw from Kashmir territory as quickly as possible; that the Government of India would withdraw the bulk of their forces from Kashmir territory as soon as the fighting had ceased and the tribesmen began to withdraw, leaving only small contingents at certain points on the frontier; that simultaneously with the cessation of hostilities, an approach would be made to the U.N.O. jointly by both the Governments requesting them to hold a

---

[1] At a very early stage of the tribal invasion Radio Pakistan broadcasted a *communique'* announcing the formation of a provisional Government of Kashmir known as 'Azad Kashmir Government' somewhere in Poonch under Sardar Mohammed Ibrahim.

plebiscite in Kashmir under their auspices and to send to Kashmir a Commission which would make recommendations to the Governments of India, Pakistan and Kashmir as to the steps which should be taken to ensure a fair and unfettered plebiscite; that in order to create proper conditions, all citizens of the State who had left it on account of the tribal invasion would be welcome to return and to exercise their franchise ; outsiders who had recently entered the State would not be entitled to participate in the plebiscite; there would be no victimization; all political prisoners would be released as soon as possible; and no restrictions would be imposed on legitimate political activity. We all felt at the time that there was every possibility of an amicable settlement.

Liaqat Ali Khan returned to Karachi and a day or two later Mahommad Ali followed.

Meanwhile Sardar and Baldev Singh, who had visited Kashmir again, reported to the Defence Committee that there were large concentrations of tribesmen in certain places in West Pakistan; that no sooner had Liaqat Ali Khan returned to Karachi from Delhi than he encouraged more raiders to enter Kashmir and made speeches to the effect that Pakistan would never give up Kashmir; and that the raiders had indulged in the most ghastly atrocities including wholesale murder of non-Muslims and abduction and auctioning of Kashmiri girls. These reports corroborated certain independent reports which Nehru had already received. This naturally hardened the attitude of the Government of India. Lord Mountbatten, however, used his influence with both Prime Ministers to keep alive the spirit of negotiation. When Liaqat Ali Khan telegraphed to Nehru urging the continuance of talks, Nehru at once responded and accompanied Lord Mountbatten to the meeting of the Joint Defence Council which was held at Lahore on 8 December.

The two Prime Ministers and Lord Mountbatten discussed the Kashmir problem from three in the afternoon until almost midnight. Nehru said that the first step should be a declaration by the Government of Pakistan that they would use all their influence to persuade the raiders who had entered Kashmir from outside to withdraw and to take steps to see that no further invaders would go in. He pointed out that Pakistan had made no effort to prevent the raids taking place through and from Pakistan territory. In fact, Pakistan had become the base of operations against a State which had acceded to India and become part of Indian territory. This amounted to little less than an act of war and indeed it was being treated as such by the Pakistan newspapers which were openly talking of the Indian troops as 'the enemy'. Before there could be a plebiscite, the fighting must cease and the obvious way to stop fighting was to withdraw the raiders.

Liaqat Ali Khan said that nothing would be easier for him than to sign an appeal calling on the raiders to withdraw. But they would certainly take no notice of such an appeal. The result would be that the relations between the two Dominions would deteriorate still further. India would accuse Pakistan of not having meant the appeal. Another result of such an appeal would be that the position of Liaqat Ali Khan's Government would be seriously compromised. It was too young and too moderate a government to be strong. It was being continuously attacked in the vernacular press for its failure to support the Azad Kashmir Government and if it fell it was probable that an extremist government would take its place. Liaqat Ali Khan also pointed out that any physical measures to stop the raiders would mean that Pakistan would have in effect to go to war with them. He suggested that India should withdraw all her forces from Kashmir and set up an impartial administration before a plebiscite could take place. He wanted a neutral administrator to be appointed in place of Sheikh Abdullah.

Nehru replied that the Government of India could not withdraw all their troops from Kashmir for, if they did so, the State would be at the mercy of the armed men from Poonch and other areas, and chaos would undoubtedly ensue. Nor could they promise a neutral administration. The administration was entirely a matter for the people of Kashmir to decide. Sheikh Abdullah had been fighting for responsible government for over fifteen years and he and his followers had made considerable sacrifices to attain their objective. The National Conference was the premier political organization in the State, analogous to the Congress organization in India or the Muslim League in Pakistan. His was the first responsible ministry the State ever had. It had succeeded the autocratic rule of the Maharajah and it had knit the people together on non-communal lines. Nothing came of these discussions. And thus yet another attempt at a negotiated settlement proved fruitless. It was at this meeting that Lord Mountbatten suggested that the United Nations Organization might be called upon to fill the third-party role to mediate between India and Pakistan, but no decision was reached on this suggestion.

52

After the Lahore meeting of the two Prime Ministers, Lord Mountbatten was convinced that a negotiated settlement between the two Dominions on the question of Kashmir was practically impossible. He was also apprehensive that, if a solution were not found, the fighting in Kashmir might degenerate into open war between the two Dominions, a contingency which he was anxious to avoid at all costs. He therefore pressed both Gandhiji and Nehru to adopt his original suggestion to invoke the good offices of the United Nations Organization. Nehru ultimately accepted the suggestion, though some of his colleagues had misgivings about the wisdom of the step.

An official letter of complaint is a necessary preliminary to any such reference to the U.N.O. Therefore, on 22 December 1947 Nehru personally handed over a letter to Liaqat Ali Khan (who had come to Delhi for another meeting of the Joint Defence Council) in which he drew pointed attention to the aid which the raiders were deriving from Pakistan.

They have free transit through Pakistan territory. They are operating against Kashmir from bases in Pakistan. Their modern military equipment could only have been obtained from Pakistan sources; mortars, artillery and Mark V mines are not normally the kind of armament which tribesmen possess. Motor transport, which the raiders have been using, and the petrol required for it, could also be obtained in Pakistan only. Food and other supplies are also secured from Pakistan; indeed, we have reliable reports that the raiders get their rations from military messes in Pakistan. According to our information, large numbers of these raiders are receiving military training in Pakistan, which could only be under officers of the Pakistan Army.

Accordingly, the Government of India formally asked the Government of Pakistan to deny to the raiders: (1) all access to and use of Pakistan territory for operations against Kashmir, (2) all military and other supplies, (3) all other kinds of aid that might tend to prolong the struggle. Liaqat Ali Khan promised to send his reply.

No reply had come when, on 31 December, the Government of India formally appealed to the United Nations Organization.

That very same day, but after the application to the Security Council had been despatched, Liaqat Ali Khan's reply was received. It was a lengthy catalogue of counter-charges. It alleged that the Government of India were out to destroy Pakistan. He wanted the intervention of the U.N.O. to extend from the question of Junagadh to that of genocide.

My direct concern as Secretary, States Ministry, with the Kashmir problem ceased with the reference of the case to the United Nations Organization. Thereafter the problem in its major aspects became the concern of the External Affairs Ministry.

Major-General Kalwant Singh left Kashmir on 1 May 1948 to take up the appointment of Chief of General Staff. Before his departure, the Jammu and Kashmir Force was split into two divisional commands. Major-General K. S. Thimmayya was appointed as General Officer Commanding, Srinagar Division, and the late Major-General Atma Singh as General Officer Commanding, Jammu Division. The six months of Major-General Kalwant Singh's command were perhaps the most crucial in the history of the Kashmir operations. He had to handle an extremely difficult situation, which he did with the utmost skill and credit leaving a secure and stabilized military position for his successors both of whom later distinguished themselves in their respective commands. Major-General Thimmayya's outstanding achievement was the successful execution of his daring plan of relieving Leh and Ladakh Valley from the raiders, while to the late Major-General Atma Singh and his men is due the honour of having relieved Poonch after a year of heroic resistance by its garrison.

The Kashmir operations have been referred to as the 'Battle of the Jawans'. There were indeed many unrecorded acts of heroism performed by the common soldier, who had to fight for every inch of ground under extremely difficult and trying conditions.

The Indian Air Force had rendered yeoman service in Kashmir under the able command of Air Vice-Marshal S. Mukerji. Whenever I think of Kashmir of those days, the picture of one brave soul stands out in my mind, that of the late Air-Commodore Mehar Singh. He was perhaps the most outstanding hero of the Indian Air Force; his daring exploits will always be remembered with sincere admiration by his colleagues and friends. Though at times impatient of control, he was full of an abounding keenness and enthusiasm which he communicated to all those with whom he came into contact. It was Mehar Singh who took Major-General Thimmayya on that perilous flight, over an uncharted mountainous route more than 23,000 feet above sea level, and landed him safely at Leh on an improvised airstrip which had been constructed by a Ladakhi engineer at a height of 11,554 feet. Subsequently the Indian Air Force flew across troops and equipment.

In the last week of December 1948, the members of the United

Nations Commission for India and Pakistan visited New Delhi and
Karachi and put forward certain proposals with regard to the holding
of a plebiscite in Jammu and Kashmir after normal conditions had
been restored. Both Governments having accepted them, the Government of India saw no reason why hostilities should not cease at once,
that is without waiting for the Commission's formal announcement.
They accordingly, on their own initiative, directed their Commander-
in-Chief, Sir Roy Bucher, to inform Sir Douglas Gracey, Commander-
in-Chief of Pakistan, that the Indian troops would cease fire, provided the Commander-in-Chief of Pakistan could give an assurance
of immediate effective reciprocal action on his part — which he did.
A cease-fire was ordered by both Army commands to take effect
from midnight of 1 January 1949. By this time, let me add, the initiative was definitely in our favour along the entire front.

India's stand with regard to Kashmir will not be understood by
those who are determined not to understand it. Even among friends
and well-wishers of India, there are some who believe that India was
wrong in accepting the accession of Kashmir. They argue that since
the country was partitioned on the basis of the 'two-nations' theory,
Kashmir with its predominantly Muslim population should have
gone to Pakistan.

Whatever views Jinnah and the Muslim League might have
preached before the partition, the Congress leaders in agreeing to the
partition did not endorse the 'two-nations' theory. If the division
was on the basis of the Muslims being a nation separate from the
Hindus and the rest, the Muslims who still remain in India would
have become aliens — a proposition which is unthinkable. Further,
if the country had been partitioned on the 'two-nations' theory, what
necessity was there for holding a plebiscite in the North-West Frontier Province with its 90 per cent Muslim population, or for consulting
the legislatures in Bengal and the Punjab? The separation of predominantly Muslim areas from the rest of India was in the nature of
a political division. The arrangement was that Pakistan would retain
and look after its minorities, while India would do the same with
regard to the Muslims. Thirty-five million Muslims still continue
as citizens of India and this would not have been possible on any
other basis.

Reverting to the 'two-nations' theory, what justification was there
for Jinnah's attempt to secure the accession of the predominantly
Hindu States of Jodhpur and Jaisalmer? That he failed to secure

their accession was not through any lack of effort on his part. At least, in the case of these two States, he could have pleaded geographical contiguity, but even that was wanting in the case of Junagadh. When the Government of Pakistan accepted the accession of Junagadh, where the population was over 85 per cent Hindu, the 'two-nations' theory stood itself repudiated.

When accepting the accession of Junagadh, the Government of Pakistan emphasized that in their opinion the ruler of a State had an absolute right to accede to either of the Dominions. But when the Maharajah of Jammu and Kashmir acceded to India the Government of Pakistan denied that right to him. On the other hand, the attitude of the Government of India on the question of accession had always been consistent. They held that where there was a conflict between the ruler and the people on the issue of accession, the will of the people must ultimately prevail. That was the position taken up in Junagadh. In Kashmir, unlike Junagadh, the ruler's decision to accede to India was supported by the premier political organization in the State — the National Conference. Nevertheless, the Government of India unilaterally announced that the people of Kashmir must decide their own fate after the tribal raiders had been driven out and law and order had been restored to normal. This was an offer by India to the people of Kashmir; Pakistan did not come into the picture.

Personally, when I recommended to the Government of India the acceptance of the accession of the Maharajah of Kashmir, I had in mind one consideration and one consideration alone, viz., that the invasion of Kashmir by the raiders was a grave threat to the integrity of India. Ever since the time of Mahmud Ghazni, that is to say, for nearly eight centuries, with but a brief interval during the Moghul epoch, India had been subjected to periodical invasions from the north-west. Mahmud Ghazni had led no less than seventeen of these incursions in person. And within less than ten weeks of the establishment of the new State of Pakistan, its very first act was to let loose a tribal invasion through the north-west. Srinagar today, Delhi tomorrow. A nation that forgets its history or its geography does so at its peril.

We had no territorial ambitions in Kashmir. If the invasion by the raiders had not taken place, I can say in the face of any contradiction that the Government of India would have left Kashmir alone. Indeed, Lord Mountbatten on his return to England publicly stated that he had, on the authority of the Government of India, informed the Maharajah that he was perfectly free to accede to Pakistan if he chose to do so.

To contend that the tribal invasion of Kashmir was wholly a spontaneous affair would be too huge a strain on human credulity. That it was a pre-planned and well-arranged affair can today admit of no doubt. Despite the denials of the Pakistan Government, the Commission of the Security Council found that regular Pakistan forces were engaged in the operations. It is a fact that several top-ranking British officers serving in Pakistan did have an inkling of these preparations and plans, though I do not suggest that they took any hand in their execution.

We came to know later that, as soon as the June 3rd plan was announced, Kashmir became the subject of attention and study in certain military circles. Why was there a demand on the Survey of India for so large a number of maps of Kashmir? What was the mysterious 'Operation Gulmarg', copies of orders in respect of which fell into the hands of those who were not meant to receive them?

I must admit that Sir George Cunningham, who had relieved General Sir Robert Lockhart as Governor of the North-West Frontier Province, sent warnings of the move of these tribesmen to General Lockhart who had now become Commander-in-Chief of the Indian Army; but these warnings were vague, probably because Cunningham himself was not being kept fully in the picture by his own government. In any case, these reports failed at the time to excite any feeling of undue alarm or concern in the Government of India.

The spontaneous desertion of the entire Muslim element of the Kashmir State Forces; the appearance at the psychological time of Jinnah's private secretary at Srinagar, the presence of Jinnah himself at Lahore, cannot be ascribed entirely to coincidence.

Equally relevant was the side issue of Gilgit. Gilgit was as much a frontier agency as the Khyber or the Malakhand, and not a political agency in Indian States like Bhopal or Simla. A senior British officer of the Political Department who knew this area well had warned the Government of India in a note that Kashmir could not hold large parts of the Gilgit Agency against Swat and Chitral; that it could not possibly maintain internal peace or a reasonably efficient administration nor even supplies for its troops; that without planes or parachutists it could not send either a staff or reinforcements beyond the Valley of Kashmir for six months of the year; that it could not control or replace the rulers of the Agency or the Scouts, and that it could not bear the heavy cost of frontier administration and defence. The Political Department nevertheless retroceded the agency to the Maharajah. In view of the lapse of paramountcy, the retrocession was probably inevitable; but the fact remains that no sooner was Gilgit handed over to the Maharajah than it came under the mercy of Pakistan.

The leader of the raiders was a mysterious officer called 'General Tariq' who was later identified as none other than Major-General Akbar Khan of the Pakistan Army. He was succeeded by Major-General Sher Khan. They were ably assisted by Mahomed Zaman Kiani, Burhanuddin and other erstwhile officers of the Indian National Army.[1]

The planners of this tragic holocaust are entitled to commendation for the originality of the plan and the swiftness with which it was executed. Where they failed was in their ignorance of the fundamental characteristics of the 'raider'. They did not take into account his love of loot and licence which kept him in Baramula for days, days which to them proved fatal.

Secondly, the brains behind the maelstrom did not realize our capacity to mobilize our transport aircraft, military and civil, with such speed and skill as enabled us to land our forces in time when every second mattered.

'Men are never more the slaves of fate than when they deem themselves its masters.'

---

[1] The Indian National Army was organized in Malaya during the war by Subhas Chandra Bose with the help of Japanese military authorities and consisted of Indian prisoners of war in Japanese hands with the object of fighting the Allies and eventually securing the freedom of India.

XXI

BARODA

NO ruler in India ever succeeded to a richer heritage than Major-General Farzand-i-Khas-i-Daulat-i-Inglishia, Sir Pratap Singh Gaekwar, Sena Khas Khel, Shamsher Bahadur, Maharajah of Baroda. He inherited a rich legacy of goodwill, of ample resources and reserves and a sound administrative system. Yet, within a very few years he had squandered away this invaluable heritage and brought on his own head the drastic action which the Government of India were obliged to take against him.

The Gaekwar family first rose to prominence in 1720-21, when Shahu of Satara, Sivaji's grandson, appointed Damaji Rao Gaekwar to his army as second-in-command, with the title of *Shamsher Bahadur* or 'Illustrious Swordsman'. Equally distinguished was the latter's nephew and successor, Pilaji Rao, who was Lieutenant, or Mutalik, of the Maratha forces, with the additional title of *Sena Khas Khel* or 'Chief of the Special Troops', and who laid the foundation of the family's dominions in Gujarat, with Baroda as capital. Pilaji's son, Damaji, with the assistance of the Peshwa Balaji Rao, continued the conquest of Gujarat till, in 1755, the Moghul Government in Ahmedabad was entirely subverted. The death of Damaji in 1768 was the signal for family dissensions which were fomented by the Peshwa. The disorder brought the State into relations with the British Government, with whom, in 1772, Damaji's son, Fatehsingh Rao, concluded an offensive and defensive treaty. Fatehsingh Rao died in 1789. In 1802 and 1805 the third prince in succession from him, Anand Rao Gaekwar, entered into fresh treaties with the British Government. Among other provisions, the maintenance of a subsidiary force was agreed to, for which territories yielding Rs 11,70,000 were ceded to the British. In 1815 connexions between the Gaekwar and the Peshwa were severed. In 1817 a supplementary treaty was concluded which provided for the cession to the British Government of all the rights that the Gaekwar had acquired over the Peshwa's territories in Gujarat; the consolidation of both the British and the Gaekwar's territories by the exchange of certain districts; the co-operation of the Gaekwar's troops with the British in time of war; an increase of the subsidiary force; the maintenance of a contingent of 3,000 horse at the disposal of the British Government, and the mutual surrender of criminals.

Sir Pratap Singh's grandfather and predecessor, Sir Sayaji Rao, ruled for fifty-eight years. In 1877, he was invested by the British with the title of 'Farzand-i-Khas-i-Daulat-i-Inglishia', or 'Favoured Son of the British Empire'. His reign was one of all-round progress and prosperity for the State. With the assistance of a number of eminent Dewans, Sir Sayaji Rao modernized the administration; and Baroda earned the well-deserved reputation of being one of the most progressive States in the country. Its area was 8,236 square miles and the average annual revenue about Rs 7 crores.

Sir Pratap Singh succeeded his grandfather in 1939; and continued for some time to follow in the footsteps of his illustrious predecessor. But after three or four years, he fell under the influence of bad advisers. He contracted a second 'marriage' in circumstances which gravely reflected on his position as a ruler. He had been married in 1929 to Maharani Shanta Devi of the Ghorpade family of Kolhapur who had borne him eight children, before his 'marriage' in 1944 to Sita Devi, the daughter of a landlord in Madras province. Sita Devi had already been married in 1933 and had a son by her first husband. But in October 1943 she announced her conversion to Islam and obtained a declaration from a court that her marriage was dissolved by reason of the conversion. Between 26 and 31 December 1943, it is said, she was reconverted to Hinduism through the Arya Samaj, whereafter Sir Pratap Singh 'married' her. In an attempt to give the 'marriage' legal sanction, Sir Pratap Singh took the extraordinary step of amending the Baroda law against bigamy with retrospective effect so as to provide that nothing in it 'shall apply or shall be deemed ever to have applied to His Highness.' The 'marriage' and the circumstances in which it took place created adverse popular reactions. It was not recognized by the British Government nor by the Government of India.

In 1944, Sir Pratap Singh raised his privy purse from Rs 23 lakhs to Rs 50 lakhs a year and also, in spite of the express injunctions

left by his predecessor, he kept on advancing money to himself
from State funds.

It must be said to the credit of Sir Pratap Singh that Baroda was
the first State in 1947 to send its representatives to the Constituent
Assembly. He also gave a lead to the other rulers by agreeing, shortly
before the transfer of power, to sign the Instrument of Accession.
But much of the merit was taken away by his subsequent action in
bargaining about his own position at a time when the country was
in difficulties. In September 1947 the situation in Kathiawar was
causing concern to the Government of India by reason of the accession of the Nawab of Junagadh to Pakistan. The rulers of the Kathiawar States co-operated whole-heartedly with the Government of
India. But when we approached Sir Pratap Singh, he laid down
certain conditions which, on the face of it, were completely unacceptable. This is what he, in his own hand, wrote to Sardar on
2 September 1947:

My Dewan came and saw me yesterday and explained the situation about
Junagadh. Baroda will be ready to shoulder the responsibility of maintaining law and order as well as peace and tranquillity of the whole of Kathiawar and Gujarat on the following conditions: (1) the Indian Dominion
shall pass on to Baroda jurisdiction of all the six agencies, viz., Mahikanta,
Rewakanta, Sabarkanta, Palanpur, Western India States and the Gujarat
States along with whatever power the Dominion Government enjoy today
over them. (2) The Indian Dominion Government shall undertake to help
the State of Baroda with armed forces in times of extreme emergencies
whenever any such occasions arise. (3) The ruler of Baroda should be
declared the King of Gujarat and Kathiawar, so as to have sovereign
powers. (4) The State of Baroda undertakes to remain a Faithful Ally of
the Indian Dominion and shall carry out its obligations so far as the three
dominion subjects, viz., Defence, External Affairs and Communications
are concerned. In other words, Baroda shall continue to be an integral
part of the Indian Dominion.

Sardar gave him the only possible reply, which was that the
Government of India did not need his help. He added that he found
it difficult to believe that Sir Pratap Singh could have put forward
such a proposition in any seriousness at all and warned him at the
same time that his territorial ambitions would spell nothing but
disaster. The fact of the matter was that Sir Pratap Singh wanted
to emulate the Nizam. In those days, apart from emphasizing his
special position as Faithful Ally of the British, the Nizam was
putting forward claims to being an independent ruler. Sir Pratap

Singh's ambition was to occupy in Western India a status similar to that to which the Nizam aspired in the Deccan.

Later, when he found that his attitude had vexed the Government of India, he put the blame on his Dewan, the late Sir B. L. Mitter who, however, denied having had anything to do with it.

After India had attained independence, it became impossible for a State such as Baroda to resist the demand for responsible government. Early in January 1948, the movement began to gather momentum. It was partly stimulated by the formation of the Saurashtra Union and the installation of a popular ministry there. I went to Bombay to discuss the question of constitutional reforms in the State with Sir Pratap Singh. The Congress was represented by Darbar Gopaldas. After some discussion, Sir Pratap Singh agreed to set up a Constituent Assembly which would frame a constitution for the State. It would also serve as an interim legislature, subject to the reservation that matters relating to the ruler and his prerogatives, privy purse, summoning and dissolution of the legislature and conferring of titles would be beyond its purview. He also agreed to set up an interim popular ministry responsible to the legislature. He promised to implement these decisions without delay by a proclamation. It took him four months to issue the proclamation and when in April 1948 he eventually did so, the text was altogether different from the one which had been agreed between us.

It was at this time that Sir Pratap Singh wrote a letter to Sardar in which he complained of the lack of consideration shown him by the States Ministry. Sardar replied to him as follows:

You have referred to the part which you played in the solution of the problems of constitutional relationship of Indian States with the Indian Union. It was perhaps fortunate that at that time you happened to be outside India and the prevailing local intrigues did not affect you. But I should like to remind you that when we were in difficulties about Junagadh our approach to you met with a reply which shocked me beyond words. You bargained about your own position at a time when India was in difficulties. You said that you did so under the advice of your then Dewan Sir B. L. Mitter. The latter of course denies it. Whatever it may be, it is impossible for Your Highness to escape the responsibility for writing that letter. You have taken pride in being a popular ruler and more constitutional than any in India. But perhaps again under misguided advice, Your Highness, behind the back of Menon and Darbar Gopaldas, with whom you had come to a definite agreement, both regarding Dr. Jivraj Mehta and regarding the text of announcement, has made changes which are both changes of substance and on the face of it in the direction of whittling down what was previously granted. Moreover, some other States gave better reforms some months ago whereas in Baroda it was only the pressure of public opinion that made Your Highness to act after so much delay.

Soon after receiving this letter, Sir Pratap Singh appointed Dr Jivraj Mehta as the head of the interim ministry. After doing so he left for Europe in May 1948, without approving the names of the other ministers. He would not reply to any of Dr Mehta's communications and the result was that there was delay in selecting the rest of the ministers.

After Dr Jivraj Mehta took charge as Dewan, he discovered that Sir Pratap Singh had been making huge withdrawals of money both from the State and from the Reserve Funds and that he had been disposing of quantities of jewellery. In the beginning, these advances had been treated as loans. But on 19 April, shortly before the new ministry was to assume charge, Sir Pratap Singh issued an order to the effect that 'as the amount of *Tasalmat* (loans) standing against the name of His Highness has been utilized, it should be written off.' This amounted to Rs 220 lakhs. On 29 May he withdrew a further sum of Rs 105 lakhs from the State Treasury; sixty-five lakhs as an advance free of interest and forty lakhs for the marriage of his daughters, which, according to him, were to be celebrated quite soon.

Jivraj Mehta called a meeting of the legislature at which fifty-one out of fifty-eight members were present, and explained to them the financial position of the State. The legislature had no legal status to pass any motion directed against the ruler and therefore the members met separately and passed two resolutions. The first was passed *nem con*, only the three Government officers and the Dewan who presided remaining neutral. It questioned Sir Pratap Singh's fitness to rule, declared that he had forfeited the confidence of the people, called upon him to abdicate in favour of his eldest son, and requested the Government of India to set up a Council of Regency during the minority of the new ruler and to take such action as might be necessary to safeguard the interests of the State. By the second resolution, which was passed with only two members out of the fifty-one voting against it and one remaining neutral, the members noted with regret the dissipation of over Rs 3½ crores and requested the Government of India to appoint a committee to go into this matter and to take suitable action.

These resolutions and the popular reaction created by them had the effect of bringing Sir Pratap Singh posthaste from Europe and straight to Delhi to meet Sardar. The Dewan and the President of the Baroda Congress had also come to Delhi. In discussions with Sardar and myself, Sir Pratap Singh agreed forthwith to grant complete responsible government without any reservations. He also agreed to appoint a 'Council' consisting of Maharani Shanta Devi, the Dewan and the Minister for Law to exercise all his powers and functions during his absence from the State. He promised to reimburse the State Treasury with the amounts he had taken; and agreed to the appointment by the States Ministry of an officer to scrutinize his past financial transactions and to draw up a correct inventory of the jewellery. A *communiqué* embodying the arrangement was issued on 25 August.

The Government of India appointed a senior officer of the Indian Audit and Accounts Service to conduct these investigations. But Sir Pratap Singh did not give him any assistance. The Special Officer reported that the Maharajah's failure to produce certain accounts had been a very great handicap to him in getting at the facts. The preparation of an inventory of the jewels he found even more difficult, because several valuable pieces had been removed from the Jawaharkhana[1]; and many others had been broken up and new ornaments made. Moreover, fresh purchases to the extent of nearly Rs 1½ crores had not been entered in the Jawaharkhana account, and there had been large gifts of an irregular kind. With one or two modifications, the report of the Special Officer was accepted, on the ruler's behalf by his legal adviser, as being correct. An alarming state of affairs was revealed. Between the years 1943 and 1947, in addition to his annual privy purse of Rs 50 lakhs, Sir Pratap Singh had withdrawn from the State Investment Reserve, a sum of nearly Rs 6 crores, while several valuable jewels, including the famous seven-strand pearl necklace and the diamond necklace with the three priceless stones, 'Star of the South', 'Eugene' and 'Shahee Akbar', as well as two pearl carpets, had been removed and sent to England. According to the custom in Baroda, as also in some other States, such jewellery is only for the use of the family and must be returned to the Jawaharkhana after use.

Sir Pratap Singh's relations with the new popular ministry were

[1] Room where the jewels and other articles of value of the ruling family are kept in safe custody.

none too happy. He complained to me more than once that he was
subject to frequent pin-pricks and that he was not being consulted
by the ministry on any matter relating to the administration of the
State. On one occasion, while he was relating his woes to me, I
broached the subject of Baroda's merger with Bombay. I told him
that, having granted responsible government, he had become merely
the constitutional head of the State. His State was not a homogeneous unit but consisted of several straggling bits of territory, interspersed between Gujarat and Kathiawar. Baroda could undoubtedly be
treated as a viable unit of administration, but the fact had to be
faced that, while he himself was a Mahratta, the vast majority of his
subjects were Gujaratis. One could not be sure that linguistic rival-
ries might not flare up at any time and, if they did, his position would
be far from secure. I explained to him that the situation was full of
potential danger for him and his family and I advised him therefore
to agree to the merger of Baroda with Bombay, in which case the
Government of India would look after his privy purse, his privileges
and position. Sir Pratap Singh did not commit himself either way;
but I was pleasantly surprised later to receive from him a letter in
which he said that he would be agreeable to the merger when both
Sardar and I considered the time to be ripe.

If, at that time, Sir Pratap Singh was a source of worry to the
States Ministry, the popular administration was no less so. There
were charges and counter-charges. The situation in Baroda was,
on the whole, very unsatisfactory. In January 1949 Sardar made up
his mind to visit Baroda; but he asked me first to see Sir Pratap Singh
and get him to agree to the merger of his State with Bombay so that
he could announce it during his visit. I invited Sir Pratap Singh to
Delhi for discussion. Sardar also talked with him. Sir Pratap Singh
told me that he could come to a final decision regarding the merger
of his State only after consulting the Maharani, Shanta Devi. I went
with him to Bombay where he had a discussion with the Maharani.
She told him that she was against the merger but that Sir Pratap
Singh could take whatever decision he chose. She then went away
to Baroda.

Sir Pratap Singh, his Legal Adviser, K. K. Shah, and I then sat
down and discussed the advantages and disadvantages of the two
courses of action open to him, namely, to merge his State with
Bombay or to remain the constitutional head of the State of Baroda.
I reiterated all that I had previously told him regarding the

advantages of the proposed merger. He was visibly upset and was for a time so overcome by emotion that he was unable to make up his mind. We continued the discussions till very late in the evening, considering and reconsidering every phase of the problem. In the end, he was convinced that he would not get a fair deal from his own ministry and that his hope for the future lay in the Government of India; and he therefore agreed to merge his State with Bombay. Since we had 'no time to discuss the privy purse and the date of handing over the administration, these were left blank in the agreement which he signed. After signing, he literally broke down. I assured him that in all matters relating to his privy purse, his personal privileges and his properties, I would do my best to secure for him the best possible deal. I communicated the news to Sardar and left that evening for Delhi.

A day or two later, Sir Pratap Singh went to Baroda and met Sardar with the request that he should not, during his stay in Baroda, mention anything about the decision to merge the State with Bombay. Sardar agreed. Subsequently Sir Pratap Singh mentioned the decision to his Executive Council, which endorsed it by a resolution on 28 January 1949; and on the 31st, the Maharajah announced the decision in a press *communiqué*.

After settling the question of merger, I took up various other matters with Sir Pratap Singh, including his privy purse and private properties. We came to an amicable settlement and exchanged confirmatory letters on 14 February. It was agreed that his privy purse should be fixed at Rs 26½ lakhs. Sir Pratap Singh agreed to set apart the corpus of two State trusts[1] of Rs 1 crore each, the creation of which had been announced by his predecessor. He promised to return to the State some part at least of the moneys he had taken. He assured me that the Jawaharkhana records would be brought up to date, that separate lists of the private and State jewels would be compiled and that he would bring back the pearl and diamond necklaces and other jewels which he had taken to England. He also agreed to my suggestion that he should create a trust of all his personal property, including his jewels, buildings, cash securities and racing establishments, both in India and abroad, for the benefit of the Maharani and their children.

[1] The income from these Trusts would be available for works of public utility in the rural areas of the erstwhile Baroda State and for the advancement of education. The Baroda University would be amongst the institutions which would benefit from these Trusts.

On 21 March, the blanks in the covenant relating to the privy purse etc. were filled in. The administration of the State was taken over by the Government of Bombay on 1 May at a public function at which I was present. On the same day, Sir Pratap Singh issued a farewell message to the people of the State.

Nothing is more difficult than to try to help a person who refuses to help himself. Despite constant reminders, Sir Pratap Singh failed in every single respect to fulfil his promises. He not only did not restore to the Jawaharkhana the jewels he had taken away from it, but continued to send more to England. I met him again in November 1949 and told him that if he failed to bring the jewels back from England, the Government of India were likely to take a serious view of the matter. He then made a promise that if he were given five weeks' grace he would retrieve them. I agreed to the suggestion and, in order to prevent him from taking anything more in the meantime, had the Jawaharkhana sealed. He brought back the most important jewels in the following January, but one of the seven strands of the pearl necklace was missing. This he agreed to replace, but experienced jewellers told me that it would be almost impossible to match the missing strand, that it would take many years and immense labour to do so and would cost lakhs of rupees. The diamond necklace had been broken up, but fortunately the three famous stones were still there. The two pearl carpets were never returned.

By this time, the States Ministry was convinced that, unless a trust was formed of the jewels and other private properties, Sir Pratap Singh would fritter them all away and leave the Maharani and her children destitute. I therefore went to Baroda early in August 1950, accompanied by the Maharajahs of Gwalior and Kolhapur who, together with the Maharajahs of Baroda and Indore, were the chief Mahratta rulers in the country. Morarji Desai, then Home Minister of Bombay, was also with us. Two public trusts of Rs 1 crore each were settled, and a trust deed was drawn up and signed by Sir Pratap Singh. A few outstanding details of his private property were also settled and he agreed to create a trust of all his properties. I suggested that as the legal formalities for the creation of a trust would take some time, he should agree to appoint an interim committee which would advise him in all financial transactions as well as look after the jewellery, and that this committee might consist of himself as chairman and his eldest son and the Maharajah of Kolhapur as members. The Maharajahs of Gwalior and Kolhapur thought my suggestion was in the best interests of the family and urged Sir Pratap Singh to implement it, which he agreed to do. But after we left, Sir Pratap Singh again relapsed into procrastination and nothing was done.

In some of the States merged with provinces and in some of the Unions, administration had not been satisfactorily organized. The shortage of experienced officers and, in some cases, the inexperience of the popular ministries had brought about a certain amount of discontent among the people. This situation was exploited by some of the rulers. Sardar was lying seriously ill in Bombay and it was not expected that he would ever return to Delhi.

Sir Pratap Singh began to adopt an attitude of defiance. He dispensed with the services of such an experienced adviser as K. K. Shah, who had been a good and moderating influence even though his advice was not always acted upon. Sir Pratap Singh preferred to surround himself with advisers whose only object was to exploit him. Early in December 1950 Sir Pratap Singh addressed a memorial to the President of India in which he challenged the legality of the merger of Baroda with Bombay. Though this was addressed to the President it also found its way into the press. It was necessary to reply to the challenge publicly and without delay, for we did not want to leave Sir Pratap Singh and those who thought like him in any doubt as to the attitude of the Government of India.

On 15 December 1950 Sardar passed away in Bombay and a few days later N. Gopalaswami Aiyengar (who was then Minister for Transport) became in addition the Minister for States. On 27 December I was authorized to reply to Sir Pratap Singh's letter. As the reply is of some importance, I quote it here in full:

I am desired to acknowledge receipt of the letter dated nil addressed by Your Highness to the President of India. By his letter dated December 10, 1950 the Prime Minister has already pointed out to Your Highness the untenable and unreal nature of your contentions and the Government of India have very little to add to that letter except inviting Your Highness's attention to certain facts and circumstances which you have ignored.

The case which Your Highness has endeavoured to make out seems to rest mainly on a two-fold argument: that the merger of Baroda with Bombay was brought about without your concurrence and that the developments consequent upon the execution of the Merger Agreement were not warranted by the terms of the Agreement. The first part of the argument is completely in conflict with the facts of the case; as regards the second, nothing but its natural and intended result has followed the agreement and it is a matter of amazement to me that an attempt should

now be made to call into question the inevitable consequences of the decision embodied in the agreement, which was deliberately taken by Your
Highness after mature consideration. I do not propose to enter into a
detailed argument about the various matters discussed in your letter
and shall only touch in a broad way on the main issues you have
raised.

In sub-paragraphs (3) and (4) of the penultimate paragraph of the letter,
Your Highness has stated that the efforts to bring about a merger or integration of the Baroda State were 'one-sided' and that the merger or integration of the Baroda State was effected without Your Highness's concurrence and without consulting Your Highness's wishes. It is a matter of
surprise that Your Highness has so completely forgotten, within the short
space of less than two years, all the discussions Your Highness and your
Advisers had with me before the merger. During those discussions, all
the aspects of the proposal were fully considered. It was only after Your
Highness was satisfied about the wisdom and the advantages of adopting
that course that you came to a deliberate decision to merge the Baroda
State with the province of Bombay. However, to refresh your memory,
I reproduce below extracts from the written communications exchanged
between us on the subject: On the 19th December 1948, that is, nearly five
months before the merger, Your Highness wrote to me as follows *in your
own hand:* 'Mr K. K. Shah has reported to me the conversation he had
with you. I very much appreciate your attitude. As stated in my previous
letters I consider it a privilege to accept the advice of Sardar and yourself
in all matters. The question of merger is also left to you and Sardar. I
shall be agreeable to merger when both of you think that the time is ripe
to take that course'. On learning that Your Highness had decided to
merge Baroda State with the province of Bombay, Your Highness's Executive Council (which, in accordance with your announcement dated
11th April 1948, consisted of popular Ministers) passed the following resolution on the 28th January 1949: 'In the wider interests of India as a whole
and also looking to the needs of proper advancement of the economic,
agricultural and industrial development of the areas included in the State
and for reasons of administrative convenience, the Council agrees with
the decision of His Highness the Maharajah Saheb to merge the State of
Baroda with the province of Bombay'. On the 31st January 1949 Your
Highness issued the following press communiqué: 'In accordance with
the advice given to me by Sardar Patel I have decided to integrate my
State with the province of Bombay. This action of mine has been endorsed
by my Executive Council.'

Finally, by the Agreement dated the 21st day of March 1949, between
the Governor-General of India and Your Highness, Your Highness ceded
full and exclusive authority, jurisdiction and powers for and in relation to

the governance of the State and agreed to transfer the administration of the State to the Government of India with effect from the 1st day of May 1949. Need I draw your attention to the terms of your farewell message to the people of Baroda dated 1st May 1949? After all this, to state as Your Highness has done that the merger of Baroda State with Bombay was brought about against your wishes or without your consent is a travesty of facts. It is significant that Your Highness could not yourself escape using, in relation to your own decision, the words 'merger' and 'integration', the meaning or connotation of which is beyond dispute. It is indeed impossible for me to understand how, after having agreed to the merger of Baroda with Bombay and signed the Agreement, to which you very rightly refer as the 'Agreement of Merger', you could say that the State continues and should continue as a separate entity.

It should serve no useful purpose to engage in an academic discussion with Your Highness about the various pseudo-legal arguments set out in your letter. You have stated that the Merger Agreement 'was with the Dominion Government and not its successors.' Presumably the implication is that, with the inauguration of the Republic of India, the Agreement of Merger stood terminated and the *status quo ante* was restored. The proposition is not only patently bad in law but also so completely divorced from the realities of the situation that it would be waste of time to take it seriously and controvert it. I will merely say that it seems to me incredible that Your Highness should directly or impliedly argue that the Republic of India has not succeeded to all the rights, liabilities and obligations of the Government of the Dominion of India.

Your Highness seems to lay great emphasis on the terms of the Instrument of Accession signed by Your Highness in August 1947. The whole object of this Instrument was to establish a limited constitutional relationship between the Dominion of India and the State of Baroda on a federal basis. I wonder if Your Highness's contention is that this federal relationship continued even after the cession by Your Highness to the Government of India of full and exclusive jurisdiction and power in relation to the governance of your State. As Your Highness has yourself stated, under the terms of the Agreement of Merger, the Dominion Government became competent to exercise the ruler's powers, authority and jurisdiction in relation to the governance of the State in such manner as it thought fit. Quite obviously, with the execution of the Agreement, which transferred all powers pertaining or incidental to the governance of the State to the Government of India, the Instrument of Accession as well as the Standstill Agreement stood completely superseded. The Government of India having succeeded to Your Highness's powers and authority both sovereign and non-sovereign took such measures as they considered necessary to give effect to the merger. The stages by which the merger was completed were determined in this case, as in the case of other merged States, by the requirements of proper governance.

I believe Your Highness is aware that, in their main provisions, all the Merger Agreements, including the one signed by Your Highness, are identical in terms. It is inconceivable that it could have been the intention of the parties that all the merged States numbering about 300, some of them with areas less than 100 square miles, would continue as separate entities territorially, or in any other form or manner. Under the terms of the Merger Agreements the rulers of the merged States divested themselves of all ruling powers; no further consent was, therefore, required on their part in respect of the consequential measures adopted by the Government of India.

Article 1 of the Constitution only registers what was a necessary corollary of the merger. While this is the background of the provision contained in the Article, I wish to make it quite clear to Your Highness that the Constituent Assembly of India (on which the State of Baroda was represented) derived its authority from the sovereign people of India including the people of Baroda. Quite independently, therefore, of the terms of any agreement, the Constitution framed by this sovereign body stands supreme and is binding on every citizen of India.

Your contention that Article 1 of the Constitution is *ultra vires* is therefore patently untenable. I wonder if Your Highness has given any thought to the grave risks involved in your making such a contention. Acts done or purported to be done under the Constitution may, in proper cases, be questioned before a duly constituted Tribunal but no one is competent to impugn any of its provisions. Indeed, it would be an act of disloyalty for any Indian to question the binding character of the Constitution itself or of any of its Articles or Schedules.

Your Highness has obviously been badly advised. You have attempted to go back on your solemn declarations. You have gone even further and challenged the Constitution of India to which you now owe the generous provisions made therein for maintaining your status and dignity including such advantages as a liberal privy purse and other privileges. I must make it clear that the Government of India take a very serious view of the stand taken by you and they have to consider the question whether the continued enjoyment by Your Highness of your present status and position which depend on your recognition by the President as a ruler is consistent with your attitude, as disclosed in your letter, of what amounts to repudiation of the Constitution.

Before I conclude I wish to emphasise that such momentous political changes as the recent transformation of the Indian States are governed by the dynamic urges of the times. In democratic and free India, large scale administrative and territorial integration of Indian States was as inevitable as the liquidation of autocracy. The Princes gave evidence of foresight and statesmanship in forestalling the events instead of allowing themselves to be overtaken by them. The Government of India as well as the Indian people have shown appreciation of the ready co-operation of Princes in the unification of the country, by according them a position of privilege and honour. It is therefore to be regretted that in questioning the validity of the commendable decision Your Highness took, of your free volition, in the interests of the people of Baroda no less than in your own, you have not only seriously prejudiced your own position but also hurled a blow at the niche of honour which, by their patriotic conduct, rulers have sought to build for themselves. I have no doubt most of the Princes themselves will view Your Highness's ill-advised action with disapproval and concern, for they must realise that those amongst them who have set their eye on misplaced personal ambition, not only follow a suicidal path for themselves but also imperil the future of the entire body of Princes.

The warning contained in the letter fell on deaf ears. Sir Pratap Singh was 'got at' by some politicians who made fantastic promises and gave him false hopes with regard to his future position and status. They found here a prince of no will of his own and easily amenable to influence and, what is more, with plenty of money to squander. Encouraged by them, he was in no mood to listen to reason.

It was about this time that some of the rulers met in Bombay with a view to forming a Rulers' Union. I had warned a few of them of the consequences of this step. They listened to my advice, but others persisted in the idea and in February 1951 they formed the Union at Bombay. Sir Pratap Singh accepted the presidentship of the organization. He visited several States on the ostensible pretext of 'shikar'; but we were informed that his real intention was to work up an agitation amongst the rulers as well as the *jagirdars* and *zamindars* against the merger of the States. Reports reached us that he was financing press propaganda in furtherance of his plan.

In Baroda, Sir Pratap Singh visited various villages and organized and even addressed public meetings. The Government of Bombay took a very serious view of these activities and represented to us that Sir Pratap Singh should be stopped from visiting Baroda for purposes of propaganda. In Rajasthan, he had a powerful ally in the late Maharajah of Jodhpur. It was reported to me by one of the Maharajahs that, in the event of a war breaking out between India and Pakistan, it was the ambition of some of the rulers to get back their States!

It was evident that if these activities were not nipped in the bud,

a genuine crisis might result. It was hardly fifteen months since the
new Constitution had come into force and only four months since
Sardar's death. I knew that the rulers could not attempt any sort
of *coup d'état* much less succeed in one. I was aware that the vast
majority of the princes would remain loyal. But this small group
could, if they chose, foment local trouble. We could not afford to
show weakness or complacency.

I discussed the situation with Gopalaswami Aiyengar acquainting
him with the activities of Sir Pratap Singh and his friends. I pointed
out that in some of the Unions and merged States, the administration had not been fully organized, that there was a certain amount
of dissatisfaction among the people and that, in some of the Unions
at any rate, the governments were far from efficient. In these circumstances, we could not allow rulers to step in and take advantage
of the situation. I suggested that we should put a stop to Sir Pratap
Singh's activities and that this could only be done by de-recognizing[1]
him as the ruler of Baroda. After all, the Government of India were
paying him a handsome privy purse and this demanded from him
loyalty and good behaviour; if the privilege was abused, there was
every reason why it should be withdrawn. Gopalaswami Aiyengar
agreed that Sir Pratap Singh should be de-recognized and asked me
to prepare a note for the Prime Minister. The next day I got the
paper ready and both of us went to Nehru, who wanted some time
to think over the matter. We decided to meet again next day. Meanwhile, I went to the President, Dr Rajendra Prasad, and apprised
him of the developments. Next day, Nehru, Rajagopalachari (Home
Minister at the time), Gopalaswami Aiyengar and myself met and
considered the charges against Sir Pratap Singh. It was decided that,
under clause 22 of Article 366 of the Constitution, Sir Pratap Singh's
recognition as ruler should be withdrawn and that his son, Yuvaraja
Fatehsingh, should be recognized as the Maharajah of Baroda in his
place. In the course of the discussion it was suggested that Sir
Pratap Singh should be given an opportunity to make any submission
he might wish in regard to this order within one month. I was not
happy about this suggestion. But the important thing was to get
the order served on Sir Pratap Singh without delay. I went to the
President to obtain his concurrence in the action proposed. The
President approved. The order of de-recognition ran as follows:

[1] De-recognition implied the stoppage of the privy purse and other privileges which Sir
Pratap Singh enjoyed as the Maharajah of Baroda. His son would get Rs 10 lakhs under
the general agreement and not the Rs 26½ lakhs which was being paid to Sir Pratap Singh.

The Government of India have for some time past been considering with grave concern the activities of His Highness Maharajah Sir Pratap Singh Gaekwar of Baroda. The activities in which he has been indulging since his installation on the *gaddi* in 1939 are well-known, especially to the people of Baroda. His dissipation of crores of rupees of public funds was the subject of discussion in the Dhara Sabha of Baroda, the members of which passed resolutions calling upon His Highness to abdicate in favour of his eldest son and requesting the Government of India to institute an enquiry into the circumstances relating to the misuse and misappropriation of public funds.

His activities after the coming into force of the Constitution of India have been particularly objectionable. He challenged the Constitution of India and contended that the merger of Baroda with Bombay was brought about without his concurrence and was not warranted by the terms of his agreement with the Government of India. The Government of India pointed out to him that, in challenging the validity of the merger and the Constitution of India, he had indulged in an act of disloyalty to the country and that the Government of India would have to consider whether he could continue to enjoy his present status and position which depended on his recognition by the President under the Constitution which he sought to repudiate.

Undeterred by this warning, he has in subsequent correspondence defied the authority of the Government of India, even charging them publicly with 'malicious distortion of facts'. Furthermore, it has been brought to the notice of the Government of India, and they have every reason to believe, that His Highness is organising and financing various activities with a view to undoing the constitutional settlement arrived at with rulers of Indian States. They have also reason to believe that he has been giving support generally to the reactionary and anti-national elements in the country.

For these and other reasons, the President has regretfully come to the conclusion that the continued enjoyment by the Maharajah of his present position as the ruler of Baroda is prejudicial to the interests of the country.

Accordingly, in exercise of the powers vested in him under Article 366 (22) of the Constitution, the President hereby directs that, with effect from the date of this order, Major-General His Highness Maharajah Sir Pratap Singh Gaekwar, G.C.I.E., do cease to be recognised as the ruler of Baroda and that his eldest son Yuvaraj Fatehsingh be recognised as the ruler of Baroda.

The order was served on Sir Pratap Singh by two officers of the States Ministry on the evening of 12 April at his house in Delhi. In communicating the order, the States Ministry informed him that, should he so wish, he could make any submission to the President in regard to that order within one month.

Nehru took the earliest opportunity to apprise Parliament of the step taken. On 14 April after placing the order on the table of the House, Nehru said:

I need not remind the House that the integration of States has been brought about peacefully and with the willing co-operation of the rulers. In view of this co-operation received from the rulers, generous provision has been made in the Constitution regarding their privy purse and the maintenance of titles, privileges and dignities. This privileged position inevitably imposes corresponding obligations and standards of behaviour and loyalty to the Constitution. The rulers took a wise decision and a great majority of them, I have no doubt, still consider that their decision was a wise one. They have given no cause for complaint. A few of them, however, have not appreciated the obligations that rest upon them and their behaviour has not been satisfactory. The Maharajah of Baroda has been one of them. The Honourable Minister for States made a reference in Parliament on the 3rd of April to some of these rulers. It is with great regret and reluctance that the Government have had to take action in this particular case. But any challenge to the Constitution of India or any other unconstitutional or anti-national activities on behalf of the rulers cannot be tolerated by Government and very prompt action has to be taken so that the very privileges and resources we have placed at their disposal may not become means for subversion of the Constitution and of the peace of the land, when we have so many difficulties and dangers to face.

Morarji Desai, then Home Minister of Bombay, said in a letter to Nehru that there was little doubt that if the anti-merger agitation had been allowed to continue, it would have gathered strength and that once the movement of disgruntled persons had gained momentum it would have become exceedingly difficult for the government to deal with it. The strong action taken by the Government of India would serve as a constant reminder to erring princes.

Both in Parliament and the country the action was acclaimed as a highly desirable step and the newspapers throughout India were almost unanimous in their support of it. The foreign press generally speaking appreciated the step. The *Manchester Guardian*, for example, observed: 'The Government of India has struck back quickly. It is likely to have no more trouble from the princes. Nobody will risk his comfortable income.'

The step taken by the Government of India had indeed the desired effect. The rulers who had formed the Union were in a great hurry to scuttle the organization and nothing more was heard about undoing the merger of the States. I left the States Ministry shortly after this. I had the satisfaction at least of knowing that the edifice which we had built so laboriously would no longer be threatened, not from any princely quarter.

On 18 April Sir Pratap Singh submitted a long memorial to the President. He denied the charges levelled against him and suggested that in the event of his explanations in the memorial being considered inadequate or unsatisfactory, the question of his 'de-recognition' might be referred to the Supreme Court under Article 143 of the Constitution. The President did not consider that there was any question of fact or law for the decision of which he need seek the assistance of the Supreme Court. The withdrawal of recognition was a political act and when deciding on such an act, he had necessarily to rely on the judgment of his duly constituted advisers in political matters. Later on, Sir Pratap Singh himself withdrew this suggestion.

It is truly a tribute to Indian womanhood that, in spite of what Maharani Shanta Devi had suffered at the hands of Sir Pratap Singh, it was she, and she alone, who pleaded for him when he was in trouble. Accompanied by her husband, she came to see me. First of all, I had a talk with Sir Pratap Singh, in the course of which he told me that he had been misled by certain people whose position and status in public life had justified his reposing confidence in them and that, having been wrongly advised by these people, he had been prevailed upon to do a number of things which he had afterwards regretted and for which he now wished to apologize. He requested me to help him once again and promised that if he were given another chance he would not abuse it.

I then had a talk with the Maharani and after giving her a complete account of Sir Pratap Singh's activities, I asked her what other course she thought the Government of India could have followed than the one they had taken. Though she did not reply to my question, I could see that she was convinced by what I had said. I explained to her that in the light of Sir Pratap Singh's representation, it was open to the President to reconsider the question of his reinstatement; at the same time I made it particularly clear that, if the matter were left to me, I should not change the decision.

Thereafter, Sir Pratap Singh and the Maharani were given interviews by the President, Nehru and Gopalaswami Aiyengar. On 5 May the President gave them a further hearing, at which

55

Gopalaswami Aiyengar was also present. Throughout these interviews Sir Pratap Singh's appeal took the form of asking for what he called 'another sporting chance' and he went on to say that he would behave well in the future and would give no further cause for complaint.

The Maharani made a most spirited plea on behalf of her husband. She represented that Sir Pratap Singh had learned his lesson and should therefore be treated with leniency. She also said that she had the authority of her husband for saying that he would have no objection if, as a condition of his reinstatement, a committee were appointed to manage his private properties; that he would not leave India without the permission of the States Ministry; and that, if at any time the Government of India felt he should resign in favour of his son, he would voluntarily do so. The feelings of the Maharani in the circumstances were deeply appreciated by the President; but her request had to be viewed in the light of the disappointing story of Sir Pratap Singh's past and not the least in that of his conduct towards herself.

Sir Pratap Singh's submissions and the connected papers were carefully considered by the President who, on 20 May, decided finally to reject his appeal for reinstatement.

Thus ended the 'Baroda episode'. It is distressing that there should have been the necessity to de-recognize any ruler, much less Sir Pratap Singh Gaekwar whose illustrious predecessor will live in history as a model of Indian kingship. I have no doubt that the action taken against Sir Pratap Singh was absolutely necessary in the conditions prevailing at the time. Any hesitation on our part would have led to serious local situations. On the other hand, I have no doubt that this man, easily amenable as he was to the influence of others, was exploited by unscrupulous people for their own selfish ends.

I should add that subsequently the Government of India decided to allow Sir Pratap Singh to continue to use the title of 'His Highness' and they also conceded to him an allowance for his maintenance.

XXII

I

ADMINISTRATIVE CONSOLIDATION

IN the preceding chapters, I have described how the Indian States were affected by the policy of integration. Out of 554 States, Hyderabad and Mysore were left territorially untouched. Two hundred and sixteen States were merged in provinces in which they were situated, or to which they were contiguous. Five States were taken over individually as Chief Commissioners' provinces under the direct control of the Government of India, besides twenty-one Punjab Hill States which comprised Himachal Pradesh. Three hundred and ten States were consolidated into six Unions, of which Vindhya Pradesh was subsequently converted into a Chief Commissioner's province. Thus, as a result of integration, in the place of 554 States fourteen administrative units had emerged. This was merely a physical or geographical consolidation.

The next step was to fit these various units into a common administrative mould. The task was not an easy one. Administration in the erstwhile States was in varying stages of development and generally, barring a few exceptions, it was both personal and primitive. There were States such as Mysore, Baroda, Travancore and Cochin, in which there was a well-organized administrative machinery. Such States could stand comparison with their neighbouring provinces and in some respects were even ahead of them. At the other end were smaller States where, owing mainly to the slenderness of their resources, the rulers were not in a position to discharge even the elementary functions of government. The entire administration often consisted merely of some tax gatherers and a few policemen who were sometimes styled 'State troops'.

Between these two extremes, there were several States with

administrative systems of varying degrees of efficiency. Even a tiny State had all the paraphernalia of a big State. The casual visitor to any one of the capitals would probably come away with a highly favourable impression; but beyond the capital one would, in not a few States, find squalor and great poverty among the people.

The revenue administration was in a very elementary stage. Where the *jagirdari* system prevailed, the *jagirdar* was practically a miniature ruler who performed many of the functions of the government. He collected the revenues and maintained some sort of record, but the rate at which they were collected was left to his own discretion. In States where there was no *jagirdari* system, the ruler's whims were untrammelled even by these feudal curbs and he was truly the personification of the State. Survey and settlement were unknown over very large tracts and the administration of land records, even in settled areas, was in the poorest of poor shapes.

The judiciary in most of the States left much to be desired. The appointment of judges was frequently made and terminated at the will of the ruler, who was also the final Court of Appeal. In many States there was no system of codified law. Numerous obsolete laws cluttered up their statute books. In some of the States there existed in theory a complete separation of the executive and the judiciary; in practice this had no meaning, in that judges were removable at the pleasure of the ruler and the Dewan, who very often assumed to themselves the functions of the highest executive as well as judicial authority.

Lastly, except for one or two of the States, the system of responsible government was unknown. In some there were legislatures with elected majorities; but in others, the legislatures were composed predominantly of nominated members. In either case, it was the ruler who retained the final veto in all aspects of legislation and administration.

Though the All-India States Peoples' Conference had been in existence since 1927, it had made little headway in most of the States, as the rulers had severely curbed its activities. Nor did they allow any infiltration of politicians from British India. In their keenness to maintain their personal rule, they viewed with distaste any agitation on the part of their subjects for responsible government.

In striking contrast to conditions in the States was the position in the provinces. At the time of the transfer of power, provincial administration had reached a high standard of efficiency. There was a uniform system of law, an organized judiciary, a highly developed land revenue administration and an administrative apparatus capable of organized endeavour, an objective appraisal of situations and an impartial implementation of the government's policy. The broad framework of the structure of the public services had been built up over a century and experienced men, who had been selected on the basis of competitive examinations and trained to shoulder responsibility, were available to man the pivotal posts. There were popular ministries elected on a wide suffrage, the provinces enjoyed a large measure of provincial autonomy and political organizations had everywhere taken deep roots and thrown up popular leaders with administrative ability.

The policy of integration could have no meaning if it did not obliterate the wide disparity between the amenities enjoyed by the people of the provinces and those of the States. Integration, either in the sense of physical merger with a neighbouring province or consolidation into a separate Union of States, was more in the nature of an opportunity than a fulfilment. Positive and co-ordinated action had to be taken to establish a machinery of government through which the people could seize the opportunity to give themselves adequate administrative and social services and real scope for progress and for full development. The difficulty of the task varied in proportion to the extent to which the particular State had been affected by the policy of integration and the stage of development it had reached on the day of merger.

The problem that confronted us in States like Hyderabad and Mysore was easy enough. In Hyderabad, after the Police Action, the administration was reorganized and the Government of India assumed all central functions leaving the provincial functions to the State Government. The responsibility for audit and accounts was taken over by the Comptroller and Auditor-General of India. Similar action was taken in Mysore where, otherwise, very little change was called for.

In the case of individual States taken over as Chief Commissioners' provinces, namely Bhopal, Kutch, Manipur, Tripura and Bilaspur, the problem that confronted us was again not difficult. Their area was very small compared to an ordinary district in a province. The Chief Commissioners selected to run these administrations were generally officers with considerable administrative experience and ability. The responsibility assigned to them was to bring these new provinces into line with the administration obtaining in Delhi in the matter of the structure of the services, the judicial set-up, the revenue and financial systems and the police organization. The Chief Commissioners worked under the overall supervision of the States Ministry who also controlled their budgets. Till the new Constitution came into force, we constituted advisory councils in some of these provinces to advise the Chief Commissioner on administrative matters. These councils had a majority of non-official representatives.

In the case of States merged with provinces, simultaneously with their merger the Government of India assumed control of all central subjects leaving the provincial subjects to be administered by the provincial governments concerned. Where isolated small States were merged in big provinces like Madras and the United Provinces, the difficulties of the provincial governments were again few. On the other hand, where as in Orissa the province had doubled its size, or in the Central Provinces and Bombay where very large and important areas were merged, major difficulties had to be overcome. In the first place, the provincial governments had to absorb some of the States into old districts and constitute others into new districts. Secondly, their administrative structure and revenue and judicial systems had almost immediately to be brought into line with the system prevailing in the districts of the provinces in which they were absorbed. Outmoded and vexatious taxes and imposts had to be repealed and the provincial and central laws to be extended.

In Orissa and Bombay particularly, the accretion of a large number of State servants to the cadres of the provinces created dissatisfaction among those belonging to the merged States on the ground that they were not given their due place, as well as among the services of the provinces concerned on the ground that their service rights had been suddenly and adversely affected by the injection into their cadres of a large number of outsiders. It was possible to solve this problem only in some rough and ready sort of way.

The people of the merged States initially found the process of integration neither smooth nor particularly pleasing. The headquarters of each State, imbued with a sense of individual importance, were completely submerged in the new order of things. The sense of remoteness from the centre of power which had shifted overnight to a distant city and an impersonal administration caused them no little uneasiness. Nor were their grievances fully comprehended by governments who were in a hurry to bring the new order into effect.

In spite of all this, the process of welding these States as part and parcel of the province was, on the whole, accomplished without much disaffection among the people. This was in large measure due to the fact that the provincial governments, generally speaking, had a trained and efficient civil service as well as ministers of administrative experience.

Once the States were merged with the provinces, the people could not go without representation in the provincial legislatures. This was secured by Orders under Section 290-A of the Government of India Act of 1935. Under these Orders the States merged in the provinces were given representation in the provincial legislatures in the same proportion to their population as the strength of the provincial legislature bore to the population of the province exclusive of the States. Since the preparation of electoral rolls on the basis of the then existing provincial franchise and other steps for conducting elections would have inevitably caused considerable delay, it was decided to fill the additional seats by nomination by the Governor-General. The legislatures so expanded were those of Bombay, Madras, the Central Provinces, the United Provinces, Orissa, Bihar, Punjab and West Bengal.

We came up against a real problem when we took up the case of States formed into Unions, or groups of States constituted, like Himachal Pradesh and Vindhya Pradesh, into Chief Commissioners' provinces. The task before us was to build up a homogeneous administrative structure out of several separate and distinct administrative systems of the covenanting States. This had to be done from material which varied in quality to a remarkable degree. In effect, if these administrations were to be brought to the level of the Governors' provinces — which was our objective — we had to reorganize the administrative pyramid from its base in the village to its apex in the central secretariat. The Chief Commissioners had the advantage that they were directly under the Government of India and that they were unhampered by any local ministry or legislature. They themselves were officers of ripe experience. Once the policy was decided in consultation with the Government of India, it was not difficult for them to implement that policy.

It was in the Unions of States that the problem of administrative integration proved to be of the greatest complexity. The tasks confronting the Union Governments were many and varied. They had to divide the Union for administrative purposes into districts, *taluks* and *tahsils* etc. They had to create a central secretariat, with all its ramifications, throughout the Union. They had to find adequate and efficient personnel to run the administration from top to bottom. In this process, they had to screen the existing officers and to discharge, after payment of reasonable compensation, those who were unfit. The relative seniority of the officers had to be fixed and their pay and conditions of service to be made uniform throughout the Union. Provision had to be made to impart necessary training to the untrained and to ensure that recruitment and promotion was made strictly on the basis of merit. They had to organize a uniform police administration from the *thanas* at the base to the headquarters of the Inspector-General of Police. They had to bring the varying revenue systems of all the component States into one mould. Taxation had to be made uniform. The financial system including audit and accounts had to be reorganized. Boards of Revenue had to be constituted on the lines of those existing in the provinces. The judiciary had to be completely reorganized and High Courts on the model of provincial High Courts to be set up. Obsolete laws had to be repealed and central and provincial laws to be applied. Public Service Commissions had to be constituted. And, above all, even during this period of flux and transition, the daily tasks of administration — the maintenance of law and order, the dispensing of justice, the disbursement of salaries, and the collection of State dues — had to be carried out with greater vigour and increased efficiency.

As soon as these Unions were formed, we took up the question of providing them with new legislatures. Travancore and Cochin each had a legislature functioning on a wide franchise and the amalgamation of the two legislatures into one presented no difficulty. In the case of Saurashtra also, the question was solved without difficulty. There was a Constituent Assembly which had been set up to frame a constitution for the Union. This was converted into the legislature of the Union.

In the case of Madhya Bharat there were, at the time of integration, legislatures functioning in the two bigger States of Gwalior and Indore. These legislatures were asked to elect forty and fifteen members respectively to the legislature of the Union. The other States constituting the Union were required, through an electoral college, to return twenty members to represent them. For Rajasthan and PEPSU, we could not constitute a legislature as most of the States constituting these Unions had no legislatures. In these two Unions, it would have involved setting up a fresh legislature on the basis of a new electoral roll. We gave up the idea firstly because the administrative machinery was not geared to the task, and secondly because general elections on the basis of adult franchise had in any case to be held in both provinces and Unions in 1952 after the new Constitution came into force.

In the three Unions, namely, Travancore-Cochin, Madhya Bharat and Saurashtra, where there were legislatures, responsible ministries were set up. In the other Unions, where there was no legislature but whose position it was necessary to equate in this respect to that of Unions with a legislature, *ad hoc* non-official ministries were constituted drawn from members of the Congress organizations functioning in the Unions at the time.

Soon after the ministries were installed, experienced officers were loaned to the Unions to man the key departments. They comprised an Adviser, a Chief Secretary, a Finance Secretary and an Inspector-General of Police, and, in some cases where the revenue system had to be completely overhauled, a senior revenue official. In order to reorganize the judiciary, we selected either a judge of one of the provincial High Courts, or a retired judge, to be the first Chief Justice of each of the Union High Courts. The first Chairman of the Public Service Commission was similarly selected from outside. After these officers had taken their positions, we deputed an officer with considerable administrative experience (M. J. Desai, I.C.S.) to tour the various Unions and, in consultation with the State officials, to prepare a scheme of administrative integration. After studying the reports of M. J. Desai, we called a meeting of the various Premiers and their official Advisers for a discussion in Delhi, as a result of which the States Ministry drew up, with Sardar's approval, a set of principles governing the integration of the component States into a Union in all its aspects. In each of the Unions a Minister was made specifically responsible for the administrative integration. The official Adviser was to have the right of attending Cabinet meetings and he was also to place his expert knowledge and experience at the disposal of the Ministry, which in its turn would consult him on all matters of administration, including the policy of and procedure for integration. In the case of a difference of opinion between the official Adviser and the local ministry, the matter was to be referred to the States Ministry for final decision. We also laid down that all new legislation, budgets, and appointments to the posts of Chief Justice of the High Court, Members of Boards of Revenue and Public Service Commissions, should be subject to the approval of the Government of India. We required periodical reports from these Unions on the progress of integration. The Comptroller and Auditor-General appointed a special Deputy to deal with matters relating to the audit and accounts in these Unions.

The process of administrative integration in Rajasthan proved very difficult, because at first there had been a Union, with Kotah as the capital; then there had been another, with Udaipur as the capital; then it had become Greater Rajasthan, with Jaipur as the capital ; and later on, a whole Union, namely Matsya (which had itself been constituted from four States), had been amalgamated with it. The Rajasthan Union has an extensive frontier with Pakistan, which was at first guarded by the Indian Army and the Central Reserve Police; but in the end the Government of Rajasthan had to take over the responsibility and for this purpose we had to recruit, train and equip a military police force.

Much had to be done in a very little time, as the entire process had to be completed before the new Constitution came into force. Also, simultaneously, we were making preparations in these Unions for general elections to the new legislatures on the basis of adult franchise. This was a great additional strain on their administrations, especially as they had not yet had time to organize and settle down.

The new Unions lacked internal strength and stability. The impulse for integration came mainly from the Government of India, and the personalities of Nehru and Sardar furnished the main cohesive force. There were practically no political organizations to kindle or sustain the spirit of national patriotism. The Congress organizations composed of old Prajamandals had not taken deep roots in the soil. They were riven by factions centring on personalities and deriving sustenance, surprisingly enough, from traditional feuds. The top servants of the States lacked even the opportunity to work together for any common purpose, and the majority of them were inevitably steeped in old jealousies and intrigues. Some found it both profitable and congenial to hitch their wagons to the new political leaders from their respective regions, thus exposing the new administration at its very birth to the strain and stress of regional pulls and factious intervention. If there was one element in the new set-up which served the Unions with single-minded devotion, it was the band of officers contributed by the States Ministry who, by their zeal and labour, laid the foundations of a stable administration.

Almost the first task was to reorganize the service personnel inherited from the various States. Some of them were men of considerable ability and experience, but under the autocratic regime they lacked, through no fault of their own, those traditions of objectivity, impartiality and fairness which were associated with the public services in the provinces. By means of rules and regulations; by the organization of service cadres; by the constitution of Public Service Commissions; by precept as well as example, every effort was made to re-orientate the outlook of these State servants and thus to lay the foundations of organized public services in the new Unions. It was, however, soon realized that if the parochial outlook and regional loyalties inherited from the erstwhile States were to be exorcised from the administrative services, it could be done only by extending the senior cadre of the all-India services to the Unions.

I might mention here that after the transfer of power there was a crisis in the position of the permanent services. The revenue and district administrations in the top ranks were almost entirely controlled by the Indian Civil Service. The cadre of this service had already been very substantially reduced because there had been no intake of officers during or after the war years. At the time of the partition, almost the entire British element had retired from service and the senior Muslim officers had opted for service in Pakistan. To remedy this shortage in manpower, the Government of India organized the Indian Administrative Service and the Indian Police Service, so as to enable them to perform those functions which under the old system had been performed by the Indian Civil Service and the Indian Police Service. The Government of India also set up a Special Recruitment Board to select persons of the necessary calibre from all walks of life (including service personnel) to fill administrative posts at various stages of seniority. It was the one great merit of the all-India services that they were recruited on an all-India basis and by open competition, and because of the fact that they were interchangeable between the Centre and the provinces, they were able to develop a wider outlook. The States Ministry thought that the obvious solution of their own problems in the Unions and in Hyderabad and Mysore was to utilize the services of the Special Recruitment Board and to extend the I.A.S. and I.P.S. Scheme to them. The Union Governments, at any rate some of them, who wanted to fill all the senior appointments with officers of their own Unions, did not take kindly to this proposal. We discussed the whole matter at a meeting of the Rajpramukhs and the Premiers in Delhi in April 1949. As a result of these and subsequent discussions and after considerable persuasion, all the Unions of States, as well as Hyderabad and Mysore, accepted the scheme.

There was scant appreciation of the complexity of the problem of administrative integration. The process of integration had embraced every conceivable activity, and given rise in all directions to a basic urge towards uniformity and standardization. But this urge often manifested itself in opposite and contradictory directions. Progress in the merged States had inevitably been lopsided, for while in some States there were no welfare services to boast of, in others developments had taken place in such isolated fields as happened to attract the ruler's fancy or interest. The efforts of the new ministries to improve and extend the welfare services were often judged by their failure to extend throughout the Union the 'progress' which had been achieved by some isolated covenanting State in a particular field. Quite the opposite criterion was applied in the field of taxation. Here it was expected that uniformity would be achieved by the reduction of the taxes to the fewest collected in any of the covenanting States and to the lowest level obtaining anywhere in the Union. Similarly, while it was expected that the Union's ill-qualified employees would receive the same salary as their counterparts in the neighbouring provinces, it was claimed that their performance should be judged in the light of their own particular experience and that the standards to be prescribed should not be such as to exclude employees from the least-developed States from finding jobs under the new regime. Obviously there was a gap between resources and requirements which only strong and wise administrators could be expected to bridge.

Few of the men who were called to the helm of affairs in the new Unions had long or distinguished experience of public affairs. They had only seen autocratic regimes in actual practice, and this, too, from a distance. The ministers had administered their portfolios as if they were heads of departments. The Secretariat had had no vital or creative role to play and because the area to be administered was comparatively small, there was inadequate decentralization of power. Effective aids to co-ordination were lacking and the idea that the Premier should be the head of the Cabinet and the chief co-ordinator of policy, or that the Chief Secretary should be the king-pin in the secretariat and head of the civil services, was scarcely known.

Parochial patriotism and loyalty to the erstwhile States were so pronounced, and caste and communal claims had been sanctified by past practice to such an extent, that it was impossible to view any question of policy solely on its merits. Decisions on proposals relating to integration had to be taken by ministers and they very often found it difficult to give decisions purely on administrative or financial considerations. For instance, in some of the Unions the division into various districts and the location of the district headquarters was done, not on any administrative or financial consideration, but purely on political grounds. In others the administration had been burdened by the continuance of unsuitable and surplus personnel.

I must confess to my sense of disappointment that though we were able, before the new constitution came into force, to lay the foundations of an administrative, financial and judicial machinery in all the Unions on the same lines as that of the provinces, the States Ministry was not able to accomplish all that it had set out to do in the matter of administrative integration. We could certainly have done better if the local ministries had co-operated more with the Government of India and with the officers deputed by them. These ministries were in too much haste to equate the position of the Unions with that of the provinces, unmindful of the leeway of centuries that had to be made up before such a position could be attained.

There are still many things to be done. For instance, survey and settlement still have to be undertaken in some of the Unions. Revenue administration still awaits reorganization. Special attention has also to be paid to law and order and to the training of suitable and efficient administrative personnel. If the governments of the Unions do not tackle these and like problems with a real sense of urgency, if they fail to build up a well-knit and efficient administrative system, grave weaknesses are bound to manifest themselves in the country's body politic.

XXII

II

INCORPORATION OF THE STATES
FORCES INTO THE INDIAN ARMY

IN the first chapter, I have mentioned how, in the last decade of the eighteenth and the early years of the nineteenth century, subsidiary forces were imposed on the Indian States by Lord Wellesley and the Marquess of Hastings. These consisted of troops of the East India Company which were stationed in or near the territory of the ruler who paid for them and whose duty it was to protect the States against external enemies and, subject to certain conditions, against internal rebellion. How this benefited the Company has already been indicated. Besides these subsidiary forces, the States were called upon to maintain an auxiliary or contingent force whose primary function was to preserve internal peace, but who could be called upon in an emergency to act in co-operation with the troops of the Company. Forces of this kind were maintained in Hyderabad, Baroda, Bhopal, Gwalior, Jodhpur, Kotah and Palanpur, but in general they proved neither efficient nor reliable and after the Revolt of 1857 all of them were disbanded. The only exception was the Hyderabad contingent, which was reorganized in 1902 upon a different footing.

In 1885, when war on the north-west frontier of India seemed imminent, the rulers of the Indian States placed their entire resources at the disposal of Her Majesty's Government. Again, in the year of Queen Victoria's Jubilee, many of the rulers offered to contribute in a most liberal way to the defence of the Empire. Lord Dufferin, the then Governor-General, advised those rulers who possessed specially good fighting material, to raise armies of such efficiency as would fit them to go into action side by side with Imperial troops. Accordingly, several of the States in Rajputana, and a few in Bombay as well as Hyderabad and Mysore raised what were known as 'Imperial Service Troops'. These were organized on the basis that they should have greater efficiency, better equipment, concerted action upon a pre-arranged plan, and, above all, the willing subordination of each State to the general scheme. They belonged absolutely to the rulers concerned and were recruited from amongst their subjects. At the same time they were regularly inspected by British officers and were available to the paramount power in time of emergency. Their equipment and armament were the same as those of the British-Indian Army and in training, discipline and efficiency, they had a high standard of excellence.

In addition to this, many of the States, both big and small, maintained troops of their own for internal security and for ceremonial purposes. These forces had little military value. Since most of the States depended on them rather than on their police for the maintenance of internal order, the latter were in general not well organized.

After the conclusion of the first World War, it was considered necessary to reorganize the 'Imperial Service Troops'. Accordingly, in 1920, a Select Committee of the rulers and representatives of the States discussed proposals for reform with the Government of India and their recommendations were embodied in a scheme which later came to be known as the 'Indian States Forces Scheme of 1920'. In its actual working, however, this scheme revealed certain defects. For instance, there was no limit to the number of troops that a State could maintain, the chief consideration whenever proposals for a new unit were mooted being the capacity to finance the increased strength. One of the consequences of this was that the Government of India found themselves unable to provide the initial issue of arms and connected equipment, so that a scheme which was intended to increase efficiency led in the main to a mere increase in strength, with little emphasis on training and equipment.

For these reasons, in 1939, a new scheme was evolved, which was also known as the 'Indian States Forces Scheme'. It was voluntary in character, and was based on the understanding that in times of emergency the rulers would place a part of these forces at the disposal of the Crown Representative. Before a State could join the Indian States Forces Scheme, the Crown Representative had to be satisfied that the financial resources of the State were adequate to maintain the contemplated units. It also lay within his discretion to accept or refuse the entry of a particular State. An essential part of the scheme was that the acceptance by the Crown Representative of an offer of troops for service outside the State did not absolve the State from the responsibility of providing troops for its internal security and for the protection of its internal communications.

The units of the Indian States were classified as follows:

(*a*) *Field Service Units:* These were units which the rulers undertook to place at the disposal of the Crown in times of emergency.

(*b*) *General Service Units:* These units 'may, if the State concerned so decides, also be offered to the Crown Representative.'

(*c*) *State Service Units:* Their primary role was the maintenance of the internal security of the State.

The Field Service Units were to be complete in the sense that they were to consist of regiments of cavalry, batteries of artillery, companies of sappers and miners, battalions of infantry, etc. and were to be maintained 'on a satisfactory standard as regards officers, training, discipline, maintenance of arms, vehicles, equipment and clothing and general conditions of service, including pay, pensions, rations and accommodation.'

A General Service Unit, if offered and accepted for service under the Crown, was to conform in full to all the conditions laid down for the Field Service Units.

The Field Service Units were entitled to the free initial issue, replacement and repair of arms and connected equipment, by the Government of India. This was also given to the General Service Units, if they were accepted for service outside the State by the Crown Representative; otherwise, both the General Service and State Service Units were to get their arms and equipment from the Government of India at cost price.

At the time of partition in 1947, forty-four States were maintaining forces under the Indian States Forces Scheme. In addition, a large number of States had forces outside this scheme. These non-I.S.F. Units were of the category mainly of police and ceremonial units. This was a loophole in the scheme, lending itself to a very large unauthorized increase of troops in many of the States. In Hyderabad, for instance, the number of non-I.S.F. troops was so large as to be out of all proportion to ceremonial and other requirements. The pay and conditions of service of non-I.S.F. Units were not comparable to those of the I.S.F. Units, nor were they liable to be inspected by Indian Army Advisers.

The Indian States Forces and their predecessors, the Imperial Services Corps, have a distinguished record of military service. No less than ninety-eight Indian States Forces units were placed at the disposal of the Crown during the second World War by the rulers of Indian States and a large number of decorations were earned by the officers and men belonging to them. At the time of the partition the strength of the Indian States Forces was 75,311 all ranks.

Immediately after the partition, the Government of India were faced not only with the difficulties arising out of the large-scale movements of displaced persons, but also with the situation in Kashmir. Several units of the Indian Army were either not readily available for service, or had not reached their allotted stations. We had therefore to appeal to the States to help by placing their forces at the disposal of the Government of India; and to their eternal credit it must be said that many of the rulers were ungrudging in their readiness to do so without regard to their own difficulties. In some cases these difficulties were indeed real, because the police in the States had not been well organized and the non-I.S.F. units were unable to maintain law and order without the backing of trained troops.

In the Instruments of Accession, which the rulers signed in August 1947, the States Forces were excluded from the scope of 'defence' and therefore, except when they were attached to or operating with any of the armed forces of the Dominion, the authority over them vested exclusively in the rulers or in the State governments, as the case might be. The question of the future of the States Forces began to receive consideration soon after the general pattern of the integration of the States had been worked out. They were dealt with in four different categories, namely (1) States merged into neighbouring provinces; (2) States taken over to be administered by the Central Government as Chief Commissioners' Provinces; (3) Hyderabad and Mysore; and (4) States formed into Unions other than Travancore and Cochin.

As the States which fell into the first two categories had transferred their full powers, authority and jurisdiction to the Government of India under their Instruments of Merger, the incorporation of the States Forces in the Indian Army was not a difficult problem, although the political aspect of large-scale disbandment had always to be kept in mind. Immediate disbandment of these forces was ruled out, in spite of the fact that these forces consisted for the most part of small units and were not in very good shape. Such a step would have had a very unfortunate effect on the morale of the Indian States Forces as a whole, several of whose units were serving in various operational areas with the Indian Army.

After the Government of India had taken them over, therefore, they were allowed to remain, in the first instance, in their original locations and on the same terms and conditions of service as had obtained until then. Arrangements were gradually made for the absorption into the Indian Army of suitable persons from these forces, and such of those who could not be absorbed, either because they were unfit or were not willing to serve, were granted mustering-out concessions on rather a generous scale formulated by the Government of India.

Hyderabad had the largest number of State Forces, but after the Police Action these were progressively reduced and reorganized, and on 1 April 1950 their entire control became vested in the Indian Army.

In the cases of Mysore, Travancore and Cochin, the State Forces were not under the control of the respective rulers. The ministries concerned agreed to hand over their control to the Indian Army, and the Government of India took them over from 1 April 1950.

In the case of Unions other than Travancore-Cochin, we had provided in their covenants that the authority to raise, maintain and administer the State Forces would be vested exclusively in the Rajpramukh, subject to any directions or instructions that might from time to time be given by the Government of India. This was done in view of the past association of these forces with the rulers. The relative expenditure was to be met from the Union revenues. The problem of integrating these forces with the Indian Army presented many difficulties. It was thought desirable that the assumption by the Government of India of full control over them should be a gradual rather than a precipitate process and a provision was therefore included in the Constitution enabling Part 'B' States which had any armed forces immediately before the commencement of the Constitution to continue to maintain them after such commencement, subject to such general or special orders as the President might from time to time issue. The arrangements made for the control of the State Forces incorporated the following features:

(1) That these forces would be commanded by an officer of the Indian Army lent to the Rajpramukh for the purpose;

(2) That the strength and organization of these forces would be fixed with reference to the role which they would play in the defence of India;

(3) That in consequence there should be a reconstitution and reorganization of these forces on the pattern of the Indian Army;

(4) That officers would be selected through the same machinery and in the same manner as for the Indian Army and their promotions etc. would also be similarly regulated; and

(5) That there would be a certain amount of interchangeability of officers between the Indian Army and these forces.

As a result of financial integration, the Central Government took over the liability for paying these forces and it became necessary for the above arrangement to be terminated. As a result of further discussions with the Rajpramukhs, the States Forces were completely taken over by the Government of India and became part of the Indian Army for all purposes with effect from 1 April 1951.

XXIII

FINANCIAL INTEGRATION

PRIOR to 15 August 1947, the Indian States had each its own economic and fiscal policy, independent of British India and of one another; the Government of India and the provincial Governments, on their part, followed their own economic policies without taking into account the interests of the States.

This lack of co-ordination has been graphically described by the Joint Select Committee on Indian Constitutional Reforms (1933-34):

The existing arrangements under which economic policies, vitally affecting the interests of India as a whole, have to be formulated and carried out are being daily put to an ever-increasing strain, as the economic life of India develops. For instance, any imposition of internal indirect taxation in British India involves, with few exceptions, the conclusion of agreements with a number of States for concurrent taxation within their frontiers, or, in default of such agreement, the establishment of some system of internal customs duties—an impossible alternative, even if it were not precluded by the terms of the Crown's treaties with some States. Worse than this, India may be said even to lack a general customs system uniformly applied throughout the Sub-Continent. On the one hand, with certain exceptions, the States are free themselves to impose internal customs policies, which cannot but obstruct the flow of trade. Even at the maritime ports situated in the States, the administration of the tariffs is imperfectly co-ordinated with that of the British India ports, while the separate rights of the States in these respects are safeguarded by long-standing treaties or usage acknowledged by the Crown. On the other hand, tariff policies, in which every part of India is interested, are laid down by a Government of India and British India Legislature in which no Indian State has a voice, though the States constitute only slightly less than half the area and one-fourth of the population of India.... Moreover, a common company law for India, a common banking law, a common body of legislation on copyright and trade-marks, a common system of communications, are alike impossible. Conditions such as these which have caused trouble and uneasiness in the past, are already becoming, and must in the future increasingly become, intolerable as industrial and commercial development spreads from British India to the States.

I have already mentioned how, during the federal negotiations, the rulers insisted on the maintenance of the *status quo* in fiscal matters and refused to surrender any financial powers to the federal Government. This was the rock on which federation had foundered in 1939. The stress and strain of the second World War compelled some measure of co-ordinated action in this respect, but it was merely of a temporary nature.

It was in view of the reluctance of the rulers to part with their financial independence and also because of the shortness of time at our disposal, that we found it expedient, while inviting them to accede on defence, external affairs and communications, not to ask them for any financial commitments.

Many of the States had been getting a substantial portion of their revenues by the levy of indirect taxes, particularly excise and inter-State customs duties. The maritime States of Kathiawar had levied customs duties of their own and this had resulted in a customs cordon being set up by the Government of India at the frontiers between these States and the province of Bombay. Thus, within the country there was a large number of tariff walls.

The framers of the Constitution realized that if they wished to weld British India and the Indian States into a unified structure, they should have to tackle this problem. One of the earliest steps taken by the Constituent Assembly, therefore, was the appointment of an Expert Committee, with the late Nalini Ranjan Sarkar as Chairman, to advise on the financial provisions of the Union Constitution. This Committee was directed, among other things, to examine how the Indian States could be fitted into the general pattern of financial relationship obtaining in the rest of India between the Centre and the provinces. Its report, published in December 1947, drew attention to the difficulties in dealing with the financial problems relating to the Indian States which, as the Committee observed, arose as much from the lack of statistical data as from the complication of the problem itself; for the conditions differed widely not merely between the provinces and States, but even from State to State. The Committee endorsed the observations made earlier by the Union Powers Committee of the Constituent Assembly that it might not be possible to impose a uniform taxation throughout

the Indian Union all at once and suggested that uniformity of taxation throughout the units should, for an agreed period of years not
exceeding fifteen, be kept in abeyance; and that the incidence of the
levy, realization and apportionment of the taxes in the various State
units should be subjected to agreements between them and the
Union Government.

The Sarkar Committee recommended that it should be made
obligatory, within as short a period as possible, for each State to
arrange for the preparation and authorization of a periodical budget
and the maintenance of proper accounts and audit and to send copies
of its budgets, accounts and audit reports to the Union Government.
The Committee thought the gradual abolition of internal customs
could be achieved over a period of ten years, without payment of
compensation to the State Governments.

In the case of maritime customs, however, the Committee considered that the Central Government should take over their administration and give the States such compensation for loss of revenue as
might be fixed by a Commission appointed for the purpose. With
regard to other taxes, they recommended (1) that the Central
Government should levy Central excise in all the States, but give
grants to the States concerned on the basis of the average revenue
enjoyed by them in the preceding three years; (2) that the Indian
Income Tax Act should be applied to all the federating States and a
separate States Income Tax Pool constituted from which a share
not exceeding 75 per cent of the net proceeds attributable to each
State should be paid to them, as against 60 per cent recommended
for provinces; (3) that a suitable basis of compensation should be
worked out by a Commission for the extinction of financial privileges
and immunities enjoyed by the States; (4) that States which came
into the above arrangements should pay their contribution for defence
and Central Services through the share of the net proceeds of the
Central taxes retained by the Centre, and that States which acceded
but did not come into the above arrangements should pay a contribution to the Centre, the amount of which would be determined by
the proposed Commission.

Though the Sarkar Committee laid down certain principles on
the basis of which the problem could be tackled, they realized that
a uniform policy applicable to all the States would be difficult of
achievement in one step. Therefore they suggested that the President
should be empowered by Order to adopt any financial arrangements

he might deem expedient with each State, pending suitable legislation by the Federal Legislature after consultation with the States.

When the Sarkar Committee submitted their report they assumed that the States would retain their sovereignty and independence; they had no idea of the pattern that would emerge as a result of the integration of States. Once the States as such ceased to exist, the fiscal barriers had also to go, so that we now had to consider the problem of financial relations from an entirely new angle. In the case of States merged with the provinces, the Central Government took over the Central assets and liabilities, while the provincial assets and liabilities went to the provinces. In the case of States or groups of States taken over as Chief Commissioners' provinces, the entire administration, together with the assets and liabilities, was taken over by the Central Government.

The Unions constituted out of several States presented a special problem. The individual States had lost their separate existence and the tariff walls maintained by them disappeared at one stroke. Though the Unions could still maintain the barriers against the rest of India, actually they did not do so. For instance, the Saurashtra Ministry started negotiations with the Government of India on the question of the abolition of the customs cordon at Viramgam; as a result of these negotiations and subject to payment of compensation, the Government of India took over the customs administration of Saurashtra. Thus was solved a problem which had baffled solution for decades. Similarly, when the Travancore-Cochin Union was inaugurated, it was announced that the inter-State transit duties which existed between the two States would immediately be abolished.

The urgent need for getting down to the fundamentals of this problem was stressed at a conference of representatives of the States, Unions of States and provinces, which had been convened by the Government of India for the purpose of discussing the question of the losses incurred by the sale of imported foodgrains at concessional rates. During and after the war years the country was forced to import very considerable quantities of foodgrains at high cost. The individual consumer, or at least the poorer consumer, was not in a position to buy these foodgrains at such exorbitant cost. The Government of India were therefore compelled to sell at subsidized rates. The Government of India had in fact agreed to meet 75 per cent of losses sustained by the provinces. At this conference, held in September 1948, the representatives of the States and the Unions of

States pressed for similar assistance from the Centre to meet some portion of their losses resulting from the sale of imported foodgrains. Travancore[1] alone had been incurring a loss of some crores of rupees on this account and it was impossible for the State finances to bear the strain. The Government of India viewed this request from the broad interests of India as a whole and agreed straightaway to help the States and Unions to the extent of 50 per cent of their losses. But this arrangement, by which the States and Unions derived benefit at the expense of the central tax-payer, could not continue indefinitely. Moreover, we were bound, after the formation of the Unions, to determine their financial relationship with the Government of India. It was therefore agreed at this meeting that an expert committee should go into the whole range of the States' finances and consider the possibility of integrating them with the Centre.

The Indian States' Finances Enquiry Committee was appointed by a resolution of the Government of India (Ministry of States) on 22 October 1948, with Sir V. T. Krishnamachari as Chairman, S. K. Patil, M.P., and N. Dandekar, I.C.S. as members, and G. Swaminathan of the Indian Audit and Accounts Service as Secretary. Among other things, the Committee was asked to investigate and report on the desirability and feasibility of integrating federal finance in Indian States and Unions of States with that of the rest of the country, in order that a uniform system might be established throughout India. States merged with provinces and States taken over as Chief Commissioners' provinces were excluded from the enquiry. Subsequently, as a result of discussions with the Government of Bombay, the Committee was asked to report also on the financial problems arising from the merger of Baroda with Bombay.

As was to be expected, the Committee had to contend with several obstacles. The Governments of the States and Unions of States were anxious to retain their independence in financial matters. Some of the more advanced thought (and quite understandably) that they could make better progress by retaining for themselves the expanding revenues from income tax, central excise, etc. Some owned long stretches of railway lines in their territory and could not think of their being merged with the Indian railway system or administered by the Central Government. All were afraid that if they were to part with 'federal' assets and sources of revenue without adequate

---

[1] Travancore and Cochin had not been integrated at the time.

'compensation', their progress would be arrested and they would continue for a long time as backward members of the Indian Union.

It was a remarkable achievement of the Krishnamachari Committee that it succeeded in dispelling these fears. The Committee laid stress on the fact that if the 'Objectives' resolution of the Constituent Assembly was to be implemented, it was essential that provinces and States should be equal partners of an Indian Union in which all power and authority would be derived from the people. It was equally important that the Central Government should function in the States over the same range of subjects and that it should exercise the same powers as in the provinces. There should likewise be equality in the basis of contribution to the 'federal' finances from the constituent units, for example in regard to the levy and collection of 'federal' taxes. It was only on the basis of complete equality in these directions that provinces and States alike could share the common service rendered by the Central Government, including grants-in-aid, subsidies and other forms of financial and technical assistance.

The Committee visualized federal financial integration as involving a two-fold process—one, a 'functional' partition of the State Governments into a 'State' portion and a 'federal' portion; and the other, the merger of the 'federal' functions of the State governments with the Central Government in India. This would constitute a new Union of India which would perform 'federal' functions for both provinces and States alike. Viewed from this angle, financial integration would not mean that the rest of India would 'acquire' the rights of the Indian States in their railways and other 'federal' assets and sources of revenue by payment of 'compensation', but that there would be a pooling of all the 'federal' resources of the people of the States and the rest of India for administration by a new Union Government, whose power and authority would be derived from all the units. The Committee recommended therefore that there should be no question of payment of any 'compensation' by one part of India to another for the assets and resources of revenue which were to be pooled for administration by the Centre.

At the same time, the apprehensions of the State governments that the process of financial integration would upset their budgetary position were allayed by a transitional scheme of financial assistance, under which the Central Government would completely reimburse for a period of five years the net loss arising from the transfer of 'federal' sources of revenue, as well as 'federal' items of expenditure, to the

Centre; and the reimbursement would continue thereafter on a gradually diminishing scale for another five years. The Committee visualized that after the transitional period of ten years the scheme of grants-in-aid to cover the 'revenue-gap' would be merged in the general scheme of financial assistance for all the Unions and States of the Indian Union.

The Committee recommended that income tax should be introduced in all the Unions and States, including those where there was none, at rates which would be suited to local conditions, and that it should be brought up to the full Indian level within a maximum period of five years. The assessment and collection would be made by the Central Government's officers under the Indian Income-Tax Act. They further recommended that simultaneously with the federal financial integration, the internal customs duties should be abolished. The loss of revenue would be covered by the direct and indirect gain resulting from financial integration, together with the proceeds from the Sales tax which they recommended should be introduced in these Unions. In exceptional cases the abolition of the internal customs duties should be gradual and be achieved within a period which should not exceed five years in any State. No compensation should, however, be paid in any case. The question whether privy purses should be a federal or provincial liability was left open, but alternative schemes of financial integration were worked out (a) on the assumption that the liability would continue to be borne by the States and (b) on the basis that the liability would be taken over by the Centre.

The Committee also laid down the basis for the allocation of liabilities between the Centre and the States. The Committee was positive that the integration of the federal finances of the States with those of the Government of India should not be a gradual process. They emphasized that the integration of all federal taxes, duties and revenue, including railways, posts and telegraphs and currency and mints, should be completed in every respect from the outset.

The Committee also drew up detailed schemes by which the main principles of their recommendations were made to apply to individual States and Unions of States.

The Committee had drawn up their recommendations after detailed discussions with the governments of the States and Unions and after getting their concurrence. Their recommendations were examined by the Government of India and the States Ministry held further discussions with the representatives of the States and Unions from 26 September to 9 October 1949. As a result of these discussions we came to the conclusion that the responsibility for payment of the privy purses fixed under various covenants and agreements should be taken over by the Government of India. It was during these discussions that agreement was also reached on the principles for the computation of the grants-in-aid which were to be paid to the States and Unions in order to make up their revenue-gaps as a result of the transfer of federal sources of revenue to the Government of India. These and other conclusions reached were embodied in each case in a 'Memorandum of Agreement'.

My personal view was that in the initial period the States and the Unions should not be handicapped by lack of resources and that they should therefore be generously treated. The Government of India appreciated the point of view and it was decided that Travancore-Cochin, Mysore, Hyderabad and Saurashtra, should receive annual grants-in-aid of Rs 280 lakhs, Rs 345 lakhs, Rs 116 lakhs and Rs 275 lakhs respectively.

The scheme provided that these four States would be entitled to receive either the aforementioned grants-in-aid, or their share of divisible Union taxes and duties, as fixed from time to time, whichever was greater. As a result of this arrangement, Hyderabad is now receiving a sum of about Rs $3\frac{1}{2}$ crores per annum against the grant-in-aid of Rs 116 lakhs mentioned above; but in the case of Mysore, Travancore-Cochin and Saurashtra, their share of Central taxes being still well below the guaranteed grants-in-aid, they continue to receive the latter.

In PEPSU, Rajasthan and Madhya Bharat, where the 'federal' expenditure in the 'basic-year' (1949-50) exceeded the 'federal' revenues, the financial integration resulted in an immediate 'gain' to these Unions. It was agreed that their Governments should make a contribution of such 'gains' to meet the privy purse payments to the rulers. The amount of such contribution is being reduced annually and will be wiped out altogether, by 1955-56 in the case of Rajasthan and Madhya Bharat and by 1960-61 in the case of PEPSU.

Meanwhile the Constituent Assembly had taken up the draft Constitution of India for the second reading. By this time we had decided that the Unions and the States should be brought into the future Union of India on practically the same basis as the provinces.

Hence a few provisions were added to provide the necessary constitutional framework within which the financial integration of the States with the rest of India could be achieved. As soon as the Constitution came into force, the Memoranda of Agreements executed and ratified by the States and Unions of States, were embodied in formal agreements under the relevant articles of the Constitution.

Simultaneously with the execution of the integration agreements early in 1950, action was also initiated on innumerable points of detail — legislative, administrative, budgetary and so on. The transition in April 1950 was effected smoothly, and complete financial integration with the Centre of all the States and Unions of States, with the exception of Jammu and Kashmir, became an accomplished fact as from the commencement of the financial year 1950-51. The scheme drawn up by the Krishnamachari Committee ensured the uniform application of all federal taxes to these States and Unions of States with effect from 1950-51. Thus, in one step, a variety of fiscal laws and procedure which had obstructed the economic development of the country was effaced.

With regard to income tax, provision had to be made for the grant of a rebate of tax in certain States (Hyderabad, Mysore, Saurashtra, Rajasthan and Madhya Bharat) for a transitional period, so that the net tax collected in these States could be brought up to the full Indian level over a period not exceeding five years.

On 1 April 1950 (13 April in the case of PEPSU) the Central Government took over the direct administration of the railways, posts and telegraphs, audit and accounts, and of all departments of federal revenue and currency, coinage and mints of these States and Unions of States.

In November 1951, a Finance Commission presided over by K. C. Neogy was appointed by the President as required under article 280(1) of the Constitution. This Committee examined at length the question of the share of the States and Unions in income tax and Union excise, as also of grants-in-aid under articles 273 and 275 of the Constitution. As a result of this enquiry, it was found that, except in Mysore, Saurashtra and Travancore-Cochin, the divisible share of income tax and Union excise was greater in the Unions than the revenue-gap grant guaranteed to them under their agreements. They therefore recommended that these three States should receive annually Rs 40 lakhs, Rs 40 lakhs and Rs 45 lakhs respectively, as grants-in-aid under the substantive portion of article 275(1) of the Constitution. Moreover, they were also to receive the revenue-gap grant after allowing for the share of divisible taxes. Under the Commission's recommendations, Hyderabad would on an average get Rs 359 lakhs, Madhya Bharat Rs 146 lakhs, Mysore Rs 368 lakhs, PEPSU Rs 65 lakhs, Rajasthan Rs 289 lakhs, Saurashtra Rs 302 lakhs and Travancore-Cochin Rs 323 lakhs per annum.

Further, all these States and Unions are now participating in the National Five-Year Plan and are receiving financial and technical assistance from the Centre. The Centre has promised assistance amounting to Rs 46.5 crores to the seven Part 'B' States.

In the agreements with Saurashtra, Rajasthan, Madhya Bharat and PEPSU, there was a special clause promising financial and technical assistance from the Centre to enable them to meet their individual difficulties; these arose from the fact that the component States which made up the Unions were in various stages of development and that unless special help was rendered by the Central Government they could not be brought up to the same standard as the provinces. In the first instance, the Government of India earmarked a sum of Rs 3 crores for distribution to these Unions, to be spent on development schemes pending the carrying out of an enquiry. In 1953 an enquiry was conducted under the chairmanship of N. V. Gadgil, M. P. The Committee concluded that any special developmental needs of the Unions were a matter for the National Planning Commission, but at the same time recommended further assistance in the shape of Rs 8 crores to these four Unions.

The advantages of financial integration cannot be over-emphasized and in assessing them I cannot do better than quote the observations of the Krishnamachari Committee in this respect:

Firstly, their people and Governments will take their place in the polity of India alongside of the people and Governments in the rest of India and share in its wider life with equal rights and obligations. Secondly, administrative standards and efficiency will increase by closer contacts with the administration of the Central Government and especially by the uniform accounting and audit system which will result from the supervision of the Auditor-General of India, recruitment to the higher services on an all-India basis, a unified judicial system and access to technical advice and assistance furnished by the Central Government. Thirdly, States will have their share of such federal revenues as may be made divisible from time to time and of the grants, loans and other forms of financial assistance given by the Centre, on the same basis as Provinces; and impetus will thus be given to development programmes in these areas...

There will then emerge uniformity of law, rates, interpretation and administration of all federal fiscal measures resulting in uniform policies, principles and practice in the levy, assessment, and collection of Central taxes and duties. And tax-evasion, always a serious evil, will be more effectively checked. The abolition of internal customs duties will result in freedom of trade within the country. A co-ordinated trade and tariff policy will have a uniform impact throughout the country. Ports and other important links in the country's system of communications and transport will be free to serve their natural hinterlands. National and regional economic planning on an all-India basis will become possible. In this, as in all other respects, the States will play their part, and they will become entitled to all the benefits which accrue from the execution of such plans as require the aid of Central resources and technical assistance. India will thus have an opportunity to emerge as a well-knit unit, fully integrated in all spheres, political, constitutional and economic. Its essential fundamental unity will be reinforced.

XXIV

ORGANIC UNIFICATION

THE Cabinet Mission plan had recommended a weak federal
Centre confined to defence, external affairs and communications. Under this plan, all the residuary powers were to be
vested in the provinces. This was a compromise between the Congress
demand for a United India and the Muslim demand for a separate
State of Pakistan.

With the secession of the Muslim majority areas from the rest of
India and their constitution into a separate State under the June 3rd
plan, the motive for an attenuated Centre disappeared, so far at any
rate as the relationship of the Government of India with the provinces
was concerned.

The States had acceded on the three subjects of defence, external
affairs and communications without any other commitment, financial
or otherwise. This was undoubtedly a tenuous relationship, but there
was no other practicable course open to the Government of India
at the time.

The Constituent Assembly was sitting in Delhi and the representatives of practically all the States were participating in its deliberations.
We had thought that, as a result of the joint deliberations between
the representatives of the provinces and the States, a closer relationship on a wider range of subjects would be forged between the Centre
and the States. But no one was particularly optimistic about it.

The policy of integration, which started with the merger of the
Orissa States with the province of Orissa and the integration of the
Kathiawar States into the Saurashtra Union, was a pointer to the
ultimate solution of the States problem.

In regard to the States merged with provinces and those taken
over as Chief Commissioners' provinces, the administrative and
legislative functions were exercised by the Government of India in

virtue of the powers vested in them by the Extra Provincial Jurisdiction Act, 1947. Under this arrangement, for instance, a law passed by the Dominion Parliament did not automatically apply to the merged States, but had to be extended to them by a notification under that Act. The Government of India intended to take appropriate steps for the complete merger of these States with the rest of India well before the new Constitution of India came into force. Accordingly, the Government of India Act of 1935 was amended by inserting three new sections, viz., sections 61-A, 290-A and 290-B. By orders issued by the Governor-General, the States merged with provinces were treated as part and parcel of the provinces in all respects, while the new Chief Commissioners' provinces came under the control of the Government of India, like the Chief Commissioner's province of Delhi. These statutory amendments enabled the Government of India not only to give to the merged States representation in the provincial legislatures, but also to rationalize the boundaries of the various units by transferring the territories between the provinces, Unions and Chief Commissioners' provinces. Hereafter there was no constitutional problem so far as States merged with provinces or States taken over as Chief Commissioners' provinces were concerned.

Let us now trace the constitutional developments in the amalgamated States or Unions. The first of such Unions was Saurashtra. After its formation we considered the necessity for a fresh Instrument of Accession on the three subjects to be executed by the Rajpramukh, in supersession of the various Instruments of Accession that had been executed by the rulers of the covenanting States. We were advised that, as a measure of abundant caution, such an Instrument was necessary. Accordingly, the Rajpramukh of Saurashtra executed a fresh Instrument acceding on defence, external affairs and communications.

What we had done in Saurashtra was to create, in place of many States, a single Union with a common executive, legislature and judiciary. The rights, duties and obligations of individual States became the rights, duties and obligations of the Saurashtra Union. But in the process, the Government of India did not acquire *vis-à-vis* this Union any power other than that of legislation in respect of the three subjects which had been given to us by the various covenanting States before integration.

We provided in the covenant for the setting up of a Constituent Assembly to frame a constitution for the Union of Saurashtra 'within the framework of this covenant and the Constitution of India and providing for a government responsible to the legislature.'

Subsequently, we formed the Matsya, the first Rajasthan and the Vindya Pradesh Unions; their covenants in essence followed the Saurashtra pattern.

When the second Rajasthan Union, with Udaipur as capital, was being formed in April 1948, a permissive provision was included in the covenant to enable the Rajpramukh to surrender more subjects from the federal and concurrent lists for legislation by the Dominion legislature. There had been some opposition to this move, but it went through.

A few days later we began to negotiate the formation of the Madhya Bharat Union. In that covenant, we made it mandatory on the Rajpramukh to execute an Instrument of Accession acceding on all the federal and concurrent subjects in the Government of India Act of 1935, excepting the entries relating to any tax or duty.

When the Patiala and East Punjab States Union was formed a similar provision was included in the covenant. Shortly thereafter in May 1948 a conference of Rajpramukhs and ministers of all Unions was held at Delhi. It was decided that a revised Instrument of Accession should be executed by the Rajpramukhs acceding on all the subjects in the federal and concurrent lists, as in the case of the Madhya Bharat Union. This was considered a good opportunity to settle another important point which had been agitating the mind of the States Ministry. Under the Government of India Act of 1935 the Governor-General could, in case of any dispute in which a complaint was received from a province as to interference with water supplies, give a decision on the matter after it had been initially investigated by a commission. So far as the States were concerned, this part of the Act applied only if the ruler of a State specifically accepted its provisions in his Instrument of Accession. Once Unions of States had been formed there was no reason why they should be treated differentially from the provinces. The matter was discussed with the Rajpramukhs who agreed to a provision in the revised Instrument of Accession declaring that the provisions relating to water supplies in Part VI of the Government of India Act of 1935 would apply in relation to their respective Unions.

In June 1949, the Maharajah of Mysore, with the concurrence of his ministers, similarly executed a revised Instrument of Accession.

59

A satisfactory position was thus reached with regard to the division of authority between the Unions and the Centre in the legislative field; but there was still no provision for control over the ministries functioning in the various Unions. This further change was made at the time of the formation of the third Rajasthan Union in whose covenant a provision was included whereby, until a constitution framed by the local Constituent Assembly came into operation, the Rajpramukh and the Council of ministers would be under the control of, and comply with such particular directions as might from time to time be given by, the Government of India.

Similar provision was made in the covenant of Madhya Bharat, as also in the covenant of the Travancore-Cochin Union. Later on it was decided to include a provision to the same effect in the Constitution itself, for which reason we did not proceed with the amendment of other covenants.

The last Union to be formed was that of Travancore-Cochin. In the covenant of this Union we introduced two new provisions. The first enabled the Rajpramukh to take over the administration of the Union with the prior concurrence of the Government of India in the event of a situation arising in which the government of the Union could not be carried on in accordance with the provisions of the covenant. This was on a par with section 93 of the Government of India Act of 1935 which applied to the provinces. The second was a permissive provision enabling the Rajpramukh to accede not only on all federal and concurrent subjects, but also on the taxation entries in the federal list. In regard to the former provision, we did not amend the covenants of other Unions, because of the subsequent decision to insert a provision in this respect in the Constitution itself. Nor did we proceed further with the second provision pending the report of the Indian States' Finances Enquiry Committee.

The constitutional position thus reached was that, except in the field of finance regarding which a separate enquiry was being conducted at the time, the Unions of States had come in their relations with the Centre into exactly the same position as the provinces.

While these political and constitutional changes were taking place in quick succession, another process had been going on. Though we had provided for the setting up of constituent assemblies in all the Unions, such a body was functioning only in Saurashtra. In Mysore, Travancore and Cochin similar bodies had been set up. Later, we realized that it would be unwise and even dangerous to leave the framing of constitutions to local constituent assemblies without some guidance and co-ordination by the Government of India. The States Ministry therefore set up a committee to frame a model constitution which could be adopted by the States and Unions, the governments of which were requested meanwhile to suspend all action in this respect until its report was available. This committee was appointed in November 1948 under the chairmanship of the late Sir B. N. Rau. The committee drafted a model constitution for the Unions and States and recommended the following procedure for its adoption, namely, that the Rajpramukh or the ruler should, where necessary, by a proclamation authorize the constituent Assembly of his Union or State to take the model constitution into consideration; that the constituent assembly should consider the model draft and pass a resolution requesting the Constituent Assembly of India to incorporate it in the Constitution of India; and that the ruler or the Rajpramukh, as the case might be, should thereafter formally accede to the Indian Union set up by the Constitution of India.

Owing to a number of practical difficulties the procedure suggested by the Rau Committee could not be implemented. Constituent assemblies had not been constituted in the Unions of Rajasthan, PEPSU, Vindhya Pradesh and Madhya Bharat, where the new governments had just got into their stride. It would not have been possible therefore for the new governments to delimit the constituencies and to make arrangements for elections within a reasonable period of time.

The question had to be settled as a matter of great urgency, since the new Constitution was scheduled to come into operation on 26 January 1950. The entire subject was discussed in detail with the Chief Ministers of the various Unions and States at a conference held in Delhi on 19 May 1949. It was decided that separate constitutions for the several Unions and States were not necessary and that the Constitution, as framed by the Constituent Assembly of India, should apply to them as well. Accordingly, the States Ministry appointed an official committee to examine the draft Constitution of India and to suggest amendments to be incorporated in it with a view to approximating the position of the States and Unions to that of the provinces. This committee's recommendations were discussed with the Drafting Committee of the Constituent Assembly and the amendments were finalized.

Towards the end of September 1949, copies of the draft Constitution of India and of the lists of amendments proposed were flown to Saurashtra, Travancore-Cochin and Mysore, where constituent assemblies were functioning at the time, so that they could consider them before they were finally adopted by the Constituent Assembly of India. The Saurashtra Assembly accepted the Constitution and the proposed amendments without reservation, but the Mysore and Travancore-Cochin Assemblies took advantage of the opportunity to suggest certain amendments; whereafter delegations from both the States came to Delhi and had discussions with me. One of the points they suggested was that the provisions of article 371 of the draft Constitution regarding the control of the Government of India over the governments of the States and Unions should not apply to them. They pointed out that they had experience of democratic institutions and that they were actually working responsible government at the time. I told them that, while the Government of India could not make such modification in the constitutional provisions as would meet their demand in this respect, Sardar would be prepared to give an assurance that the Government of India would treat Mysore and Travancore-Cochin differently from the rest of the Unions. The relevant article of the draft Constitution gave discretion to the President in this respect. Subsequently, Sardar made an announcement to this effect in the Constituent Assembly.

Another objection raised by the Mysore delegates was to the use of the term 'Rajpramukh'. This title had been chosen after due deliberation and all the Unions without exception had accepted it. However, we told the Mysore delegates that they could use the title 'Maharajah' for all internal purposes.

The delegates from Travancore-Cochin desired that the payment of Rs 51 lakhs from the State's revenues to the Travancore Devaswom Board, for which we had included a provision in the covenant, should be given constitutional recognition and this we agreed to do.

The amendments affecting the States and Unions were then incorporated in the Constitution. It was decided that the acceptance of the Constitution should be by the Rajpramukh or by the ruler, as the case might be, on the basis of a resolution to be adopted by the constituent assembly where such a body existed. This was done in the case of Saurashtra, Mysore and Travancore-Cochin.

In the case of the Unions where no constituent assembly had been set up, it was decided between the States Ministry and the Union

Government concerned that the Rajpramukh would issue a proclamation accepting as the constitution of the Union the Constitution framed by the Constituent Assembly of India. In recommending this procedure to the Constituent Assembly, Sardar pointed out that legislatures were not functioning in these Unions, that it would take time to bring them into existence and that it was not desirable that the enforcement of the Constitution should be held up until such time. He added: 'The legislatures of these States when constituted under the new Constitution may propose amendments to the Constitution. I wish to assure the people of these States that any recommendations made by their first legislatures will receive our earnest consideration.'

Under the arrangements just mentioned, the provisions in the various covenants for constituent assemblies became inoperative and it became necessary to delete them. This was done by a supplementary covenant.

While the Constitution of India was being finalized, there was no legislature in Hyderabad which could be consulted by the Nizam. The Hyderabad Legislative Assembly *A'in* (that is to say, the Charter of the Legislative Assembly of the State) had been repealed by a *firman* issued by the Nizam in December 1948. It was intended to bring into existence instead a constituent assembly for the State which could be consulted about the future of the State. A regulation authorizing the preparation of electoral rolls for the purpose had been promulgated by the Military Governor on 14 December 1948, but the constituent assembly was not expected to meet before March 1950. The Nizam's *firman* accepting the Constitution of India was therefore issued without consulting any elected body, but it was made expressly subject to 'the ratification of the decision of the people of the State whose will, as expressed through the constituent assembly of the State proposed to be constituted shortly, must finally determine the nature of the relationship between the State and the Union of India, as also the constitution of the State itself.'

The Constituent Assembly of Hyderabad which was to have been convened in March 1950 did not actually meet, because changes in the electoral arrangements had become necessary in consequence of the exchange of enclaves. Meanwhile arrangements were being made to hold elections to the Hyderabad Legislative Assembly on the basis of adult suffrage under the provisions of the Constitution of India. To avoid the duplication and waste of effort which would have been caused by two such elections, first for the Constituent Assembly and then for the Legislative Assembly, it was decided that the Legislative Assembly of the State should be given an opportunity at its first session to express its opinion on the constitutional provisions affecting Hyderabad. This opportunity was not however taken advantage of and no such discussion took place in the Hyderabad Legislative Assembly, or for that matter in any other Union legislature.

In the case of Jammu and Kashmir, Yuvaraj Karan Singh, the Regent of the State, issued a proclamation that the Constitution of India in so far as it was applicable to the State would govern the constitutional relationship between that State and India.

On 26 January 1950, the new Constitution came into force and under it the component parts of India were divided into four categories. In the first category, called Part A States, were placed the nine Governor's provinces,[1] with their territories augmented by the merger of numerous States. The three large States of Hyderabad, Jammu and Kashmir and Mysore and the five Unions of Madhya Bharat, PEPSU, Rajasthan, Saurashtra and Travancore-Cochin were placed in the second category of Part B States. The three old Chief Commissioners' provinces of Ajmer, Coorg and Delhi and the seven new ones of Bhopal, Bilaspur, Himachal Pradesh, Kutch, Manipur, Tripura and Vindhya Pradesh formed the third category of Part C States. The fourth category comprised the Andaman and Nicobar Islands, which continue to be directly administered by the Centre through a Chief Commissioner and are not treated as a 'State' in the new Constitution.

This classification of the major States of India into Part A and Part B States does not connote any fundamental constitutional difference between them. A great achievement of the new Constitution is the assimilation of the position of the former Indian States and Unions with that of the former Governor's provinces. Neither in its relationship with the Central Government nor in its internal structure and powers is a Part A State essentially different from a Part B State. Such minor and unimportant differences as do exist are traceable to the fact that while, as the successors of the old Governor's provinces the Part A States had already been welded into

[1] They were Assam, Bihar, Bombay, the Central Provinces and Berar (renamed Madhya Pradesh), Madras, Orissa, Punjab (commonly known as East Punjab), the United Provinces (renamed Uttar Pradesh) and West Bengal.

a federal structure, a few further adjustments and modifications were found necessary for completing that process in the case of Part B States.

Part VI of the Constitution of India lays down the constitution for Part A States in respect of the executive, the legislature and the judiciary.

Part VII applies the whole of Part VI to Part B States with certain modifications and omissions. For 'Governors', for instance, 'Rajpramukhs' are substituted. The latter however have exactly the same powers which Governors have in Part A States.

While the salaries of the Chief Justices and other judges of the High Courts in Part A States have been fixed in the Second Schedule to the Constitution, the salaries of the Chief Justices and judges of the High Courts in Part B States are to be determined by the Rajpramukh in consultation with the President.

In Part VII of the Constitution there are two additional provisions. The first is that in Madhya Bharat there should be a minister in charge of tribal welfare who might in addition be in charge of the welfare of the Scheduled Castes and backward classes. The second relates to Travancore-Cochin, where the sum of Rs 51 lakhs payable to the Travancore Devaswom Board under the covenant is made a charged expenditure on the revenues of that State.

There are other special provisions affecting Part B States in the Constitution. The most important of these is article 371[1] which provides that:

Notwithstanding anything in this Constitution, during a period of ten years from the commencement thereof, or during such longer or shorter period as Parliament may by law provide in respect of any State, the Government of every State specified in Part B of the First Schedule shall be under the general control of, and comply with such particular directions, if any, as may from time to time be given by, the President:

Provided that the President may by order direct that the provisions of this article shall not apply to any State specified in the order.

I have explained the reason why this provision was considered necessary but it might be apt if I were to quote the relevant extract from Sardar's speech when commending the article to the Constituent Assembly:

We are ourselves most anxious that the people of these States should

---

[1] The application of this article was withdrawn, so far as Mysore was concerned, in 1952 and remains a dead letter regarding other States.

shoulder their full responsibilities; however, we cannot ignore the fact that while the administrative organisation and political institutions are to be found in most of the States in a relatively less developed state, the problems relating to integration of the States and the change over from an autocratic to a democratic order are such as to test the mettle of long established administrations and experienced leaders of people. We have therefore found it necessary that in the interest of the growth of democratic institutions in these States, no less than the requirements of administrative efficiency, the Government of India should exercise general supervision over the governments of the States till such time as may be necessary.

It is natural that a provision of this nature which treats States in Part B differently from Part A States should cause some misgivings. I wish to assure the honourable members representing these States, and through them the people of these States, that the provision involves no censure of any government. It merely provides for contingencies which, in view of the present conditions, are more likely to arise in Part B States than in the States of other categories. We do not wish to interfere with the day-to-day administration of any of the States. We are ourselves most anxious that the people of the States should learn by experience. This article is essentially in the nature of a safety valve to obviate recourse to drastic remedies such as the provisions for the breakdown of the constitutional machinery.

The other provisions relate to certain financial adjustments between the Centre and Part B States during the transitional period, in order to fill up the revenue-gap caused by federal financial integration.

Under the terms of the merger agreements and covenants, the privy purses payable to the rulers were to be paid out of the revenues of the States concerned. In the case of States merged with the provinces, their identity was completely obliterated by the Constitution. The privy purses of these rulers had therefore to be taken over by the Centre. For the same reason, as well as on the grounds that the privy purses were fixed and guaranteed by the Central Government, that they were political in nature and that similar payments are not made by the provinces, the Union Governments urged on us that the payment of privy purses in their case also should constitute a charge on the Central Government. This was accepted and article 291 accordingly provides that:

(1) Where under any covenant or agreement entered into by the ruler of any Indian State before the commencement of this Constitution, the payment of any sums, free of tax, has been guaranteed or assured by the Government of the Dominion of India to any ruler of such State as privy purse—(a) such sums shall be charged on, and paid out of, the Consolidated

Fund of India; and (b) the sums so paid to any ruler shall be exempt from all taxes on income.

(2) Where the territories of any such Indian State as aforesaid are comprised within a State specified in Part A or Part B of the First Schedule, there shall be charged on, and paid out of, the Consolidated Fund of that State such contribution, if any, in respect of the payments made by the Government of India under clause (1) and for such period as may, subject to any agreement entered into in that behalf under clause (1) of article 278, be determined by order of the President.

Article 363 specifically excludes the covenants and the merger agreements from the jurisdiction of the Courts, except in cases which may be referred to the Supreme Court by the President. This is because we did not want these political settlements to be subject to pronouncements by courts of law. At the same time the Government of India considered it necessary that constitutional recognition should be given to the guarantees to the rulers in respect of their rights, privileges and dignities. Accordingly, article 362 provides that in the exercise of their legislative and executive authority, the legislatures and executives of the States would have due regard to these guarantees.

Another important provision is article 366 (22) regarding the recognition of rulers. Though the rulers had lost their States and powers, they still continued to enjoy considerable prestige inside their erstwhile States. We had guaranteed them privy purses and other personal rights and these in turn imposed on the rulers corresponding obligations of loyalty to the Constitution of India. Generally speaking, the rulers accepted the new dispensation cheerfully and with loyalty. To provide against the possibility of stray instances of rulers abusing the special position given to them, clause (22) was inserted in article 366, the effect of which is that a 'ruler' must be recognized as such by the President. If the President either does not recognize, or withdraws his recognition of any ruler, such ruler would not be entitled to the privy purse and other privileges. It was under this article that the recognition of Sir Pratap Singh, Gaekwar of Baroda, was withdrawn. The same article provides that succession to the *gaddi* must also receive the recognition of the President.

Similarly, 'Rajpramukh' is defined in clause (20) of the same article as the person who is recognized for the time being by the President as the Rajpramukh of the State. It follows therefore that the President is competent to remove a Rajpramukh from his office by withdrawing his recognition, though occasions for the exercise of this power must be very rare.

The administration of each of the ten Part C States, which is the responsibility of the Government of India, was carried on initially through a Chief Commissioner who was appointed by the President; but the growing demand in some of these States for a local legislature and a responsible ministry led, towards the end of 1951, to the passing of the Governance of Part C States Act. Elected legislative assemblies and responsible ministries were established under this Act in six of these States; Vindhya Pradesh and Himachal Pradesh were placed under a Lieutenant-Governor instead of a Chief Commissioner. In all of them, however, the powers of the local legislature and ministry were subject to reservation. The tiny hill State of Bilaspur[1] and the frontier States of Kutch, Manipur and Tripura continued under the direct control of Chief Commissioners.

One other matter which remains to be dealt with is the position of Jammu and Kashmir State. The ruler of this State had executed an Instrument of Accession on the three subjects, in the same way as had other rulers. When the Constitution was being finalized, the choice before us was either to leave the State out of the purview of the Constitution or to include it as a Part B State. Since the legal fact of accession was beyond question, we decided to include it among Part B States; but its relations with the Government of India were confined to the terms of the Instrument of Accession, namely defence, external affairs and communications, subject to the proviso that other provisions of the Constitution could be applied in relation to Jammu and Kashmir in consultation with the Government of that State.

The new Constitution of India completed the process of the integration of the States. There is no disparity between Part A and Part B States in respect of the fundamental rights of the citizen. They have legislatures elected on adult franchise with ministries responsible to them. Their relationship with the Centre is identical with that of Part A States, except in regard to the control of the Government of India for a transitional period, as provided in article 371. The Auditor-General of India has complete control of the audit system in these States and the jurisdiction of the Supreme Court extends

---

[1] Parliament has since passed an Act for the amalgamation of this State with Himachal Pradesh.

to them. The High Courts are constituted with powers identical to those of Part A States. All the citizens of India, whether resident in Part A or Part B or Part C States, enjoy the same fundamental rights and the same legal remedies by which to enforce them. Thus, finally and for ever the artificial barriers created by the erstwhile States have been abolished and in their place has emerged, for the first time, a united and democratic India under a strong Central Government.

If one were asked to name the most important factors that have contributed to the stability of the country, there is little doubt that one would mention at once two factors: the first being the integration of the Indian States and the second a Constitution framed with the willing consent of the people.

XXV

THE COST OF INTEGRATION

I HAVE explained the implications of the lapse of paramountcy. The rulers became undisputed masters in their own States, possessing unrestricted sovereignty and completely independent of the Government of India. The June 3rd plan did not alter this position. Even if the rulers acceded on the three subjects of defence, foreign affairs and communications, their internal autonomy in other matters remained unaffected.

As late as February 1947, Nehru had assured the Negotiating Committee of the Chamber of Princes that neither the monarchical form of government, nor the integrity of the States, would be touched. Sardar had repeated this guarantee a few months later in his statement of 5 July. While asking the States to accede on three subjects, he assured the rulers that 'in other matters we would scrupulously respect their autonomous existence.' Lord Mountbatten underlined these assurances in his speech to the Chamber of Princes on 25 July 1947 that (except for defence, external affairs and communications) 'in no other matters has the Central Government any authority to encroach on the internal autonomy or the sovereignty of the States.'

It was in the background of these categorical assurances that the States Ministry embarked on the policy of integration. The alternative to a peaceful and friendly settlement of the States' problem was to allow political agitation to develop in the States and to create, especially in the smaller ones, dire confusion and turmoil. Anyone conversant with the conditions in the country after partition must be aware of the inherent dangers of such a course. The condition of the country at the time demanded stability and we had to take strong action against any agitation of which anti-social elements might take advantage.

The only course therefore was to negotiate a friendly settlement with the rulers. If we expected them to hand over their States un-conditionally and for ever, we had of course to give them something in return. It could not be 'heads I win, tails you lose.'

The grant of privy purses to the rulers was a sort of *quid pro quo* for the surrender by them of all their ruling powers and for the dissolu-tion of their States. Apart from the privy purses, we permitted them to retain certain private properties and guaranteed them the personal rights, privileges and dignities which they had hitherto been enjoy-ing. We believed that these concessions would, in due course, enable the rulers and their successors to adjust themselves to the new order of things and to fit themselves into the modern social and economic pattern. A discontented group of rulers with their numerous depen-dents would have been a serious problem to us.

In fixing their privy purses and settling the private properties of the rulers we were breaking entirely new ground. The privy purses and such other amenities as were enjoyed by the rulers varied from State to State, so that there was no uniform basis upon which to work. The only guidance we had in the fixation of the privy purses was the formula of the Political Department and that of the Congress Sub-Committee for the Deccan States; but we felt that both these erred on the generous side. We therefore evolved what came to be known as the 'Eastern States formula', under which the ruler of a State with an average annual revenue of Rs 15 lakhs would get an annual privy purse of Rs 1,30,000. Under the Deccan States for-mula he would have got Rs 1,62,500, or nearly 25 per cent more. Under the Political Department's formula, the figure would have been Rs 3,00,000. It may be mentioned here that out of 554 States, over 450 had an annual revenue of less then Rs 15 lakhs.

Saurashtra was the only instance in which we departed from the Eastern States formula and gave a higher rate of privy purse. The position before us was either to agree to the increase and thus con-solidate Saurashtra, or to postpone or perhaps give up altogether the idea of consolidation. An immediate decision was called for and taken. Anyone conversant with the conditions in Saurashtra before integration, with its fragmented sovereignties entailing financial loss and the appalling human misery which was everywhere to be seen, must have considered the additional sum involved but an insignificant price to pay for the immeasurable benefits accruing from consolidation. Gandhiji himself, as I have already mentioned, appeared to be satisfied with the settlement.

In the subsequent integrations we departed in eleven cases from the ceiling of Rs 10 lakhs and fixed the amounts of the privy purse on an ad hoc basis. They were: Gwalior (Rs 25 lakhs), Indore (Rs 15 lakhs), Patiala (Rs 17 lakhs), Baroda (Rs 26·5 lakhs), Jaipur (Rs 18 lakhs), Jodhpur (Rs 17·5 lakhs), Bikaner (Rs 17 lakhs), Travancore (Rs 18 lakhs), Bhopal (Rs 11 lakhs), Mysore (Rs 26 lakhs) and Hyderabad (Rs 50 lakhs in Hyderabad currency). In all these cases, except Hyderabad and Mysore, the rulers were drawing very much higher amounts by way of privy purse and other amenities. In some of them the amounts had been fixed by the local popular ministries. All these States were viable units; they were key States which could have made or marred the policy of integration. Barring Hyderabad, Patiala and Bhopal, the privy purses were fixed after consultation with either the responsible ministry or the popular leaders of the Union. For instance, in the case of Jaipur, Jodhpur and Bikaner the privy purses were fixed on the basis of a joint note given to me by Hiralal Sastri, Jai Narain Vyas, Maniklal Verma and Gokulbhai Bhatt, who were the top-ranking Congressmen in Rajasthan at the time.

The Nizam of Hyderabad had, ever since he came to the *gaddi*, been drawing a privy purse of Rs 50 lakhs in Hyderabad currency (which works out to Rs 43 lakhs in Indian currency). In 1947-48 this amount represented not more than two per cent of the State revenues. This privy purse was continued.

The Maharajah of Patiala had an equal status with the rulers of Jaipur, Jodhpur and Bikaner and in fairness we could not give him less than had been given to those rulers.

As far as the Nawab of Bhopal was concerned, though the privy purse was fixed at Rs 11 lakhs the actual amount was only Rs 10 lakhs, the remaining one lakh having been set aside for his heir-apparent. The Nawab's successors would receive only Rs 9 lakhs annually.

In the case of all these rulers we laid down that the increased amounts would be payable to them only for life and that, so far as their successors were concerned, the Government of India would pay such amounts as they might decide, and in any case not more than Rs 10 lakhs.

The privy purse is intended to cover all the expenses of the ruler and his family, including the expenses on account of his personal staff, his palaces and the marriages and other ceremonies in his household. The Government of India, or the government of the Union or State concerned, will not pay anything more.

The Rajpramukhs, and in some cases the Uprajpramukhs, are entitled, under Article 158 (3) read with Article 238 (4) of the Constitution, to receive such allowances as may be fixed by the President. These allowances vary from Union to Union. But the Nizam receives no allowance as Rajpramukh; in fact, the Government of Hyderabad do not spend anything for the upkeep of the head of the State.

Excluding these eleven, there are 91 rulers who draw a privy purse of Rs 1 lakh and above. Of these, 47 draw above Rs 1 lakh, but below Rs 2 lakhs; 31 draw above Rs 2 lakhs but below Rs 5 lakhs, and 13 draw between Rs 5 lakhs and Rs 10 lakhs. Fifty-six rulers draw less than Rs 1 lakh but above Rs 50,000. The remaining 396 rulers draw below Rs 50,000 per annum. For instance, there is the ruler of Katodia in Saurashtra, who draws Rs 192 per annum while the rulers of the twenty-two non-salute States of Vindhya Pradesh draw an average monthly privy purse of Rs 700. The total of the privy purses, according to the White Paper laid before Parliament, amounts to Rs 580 lakhs. Out of this, by the deaths of the Maharajahs of Bikaner and Jodhpur and the de-recognition of Sir Pratap Singh Gaekwar of Baroda, Government's commitment has already been reduced by Rs 31 lakhs annually.

It is difficult to assess with any degree of accuracy the total of the privy purses drawn by all the rulers, together with the additional amounts spent by them on themselves and their families, before integration; but a rough calculation of the total amount thus spent would be in the region of Rs 20 crores a year. This is a conservative estimate and does not include the special taxes imposed by rulers of the smaller States, in some of which whenever the ruler wished, for instance, to purchase a motor-car, a tax would be imposed on the people for the purpose! Similarly, taxes were levied to meet the expenses of marriages in the ruling families.

Apart from the privy purses, the Government of India had, in the various merger agreements and covenants, guaranteed to the rulers the full ownership, use and enjoyment of all private properties (as distinct from State properties) that belonged to them on the date of the agreement or covenant. Each ruler had to furnish an inventory of all such immovable property, securities and cash balances held by him as his private property either to the Government of India or the

Rajpramukh of the Union. Whatever was not included in the inventory went automatically to the successor government. In case of any dispute as to whether any item was the private property of the ruler or the property of the State, the matter was to be referred to the arbitration of a judicial officer, whose decision would be final and binding on both parties.

In most of these States there was no demarcation between the private property of the ruler and the property of the State; and it was impossible to evolve a uniform principle which could be applied to States like Hyderabad, Mysore, Baroda and Gwalior on the one hand, and to petty semi-jurisdictional and non-jurisdictional States in Kathiawar and Gujarat on the other. The problem bristled with difficulties. We were anxious to settle it amicably and without recourse to arbitration.

The rulers of the States constituted into Unions were asked to submit their inventories to the Rajpramukhs. The idea was that the Rajpramukhs in consultation with their ministers would settle the problem themselves and that the States Ministry would be called upon only to put its final seal on the settlement. But the Union Governments found the task difficult without some guidance from the Centre. A conference of the Rajpramukhs and Chief Ministers was accordingly called in September 1948. It was, I think, at this conference that U. N. Dhebar, Chief Minister of Saurashtra, produced a practical scheme for the settlement of the private properties of the rulers which he had evolved after discussion with the Rajpramukh of Saurashtra. This was discussed and certain broad principles were formulated. The Rajpramukhs were asked to scrutinize the inventories of the rulers using these principles as a guide.

The broad principles evolved at this conference were as follows. Immovable properties were to be allotted to the rulers on the basis of previous use, having regard to their actual needs and the needs of the administration. Farms, gardens and grazing areas were allowed to be retained by some of the rulers, but the position of the ruler in respect of these would be the same as that of a private landholder and he would be subject to the revenue laws and assessment. With regard to investments and cash balances, only those to which the State could lay no claim were to be recognized as the private property of the ruler. Though we laid no claim to the personal jewellery of the ruling family, such ancestral jewellery as was 'heirloom' was to be preserved for the ruling family; and valuable regalia would remain in the custody of the ruler for use on ceremonial occasions. The civil list reserve fund built up by the rulers for marriages etc. was allowed to be retained by them. Excepting temples situated within the palaces, other temples and properties attached to them were to be constituted into trusts and the public would have the right to worship at these temples.

Though these broad principles had been laid down, their application could not be rigid. It was a difficult and delicate task calling for detailed and patient examination of each case. All the Rajpramukhs as well as their Chief Ministers requested the Government of India as the guarantor of the covenants to assist them in the settlement of the private properties. It was urged that I should visit the headquarters of the various Unions and assist the Rajpramukhs personally to settle this problem. I first went to Jamnagar. The Rajpramukh as well as the Saurashtra ministry had already scrutinized carefully the inventories and prepared a list of the properties which could be conceded to each ruler. Each list was then finalized across the table at a conference at which the Rajpramukh, the Chief Minister and the Finance Minister, the ruler concerned and myself were present. The private properties of all the Saurashtra rulers were settled within two or three days.

The principles and procedure adopted at Saurashtra were applied to other Unions. I visited the headquarters of the various Unions and, after discussions with the rulers, finalized their private properties.

Sardar himself settled the private properties of the Rajpramukhs after consultation with the Chief Ministers of the Unions.

So far as the rulers of the States merged in provinces were concerned they were asked to send their inventories initially to the provincial governments who were expected, like the Rajpramukh in the case of the Unions, to settle the problem. The first province to do so was the Central Provinces. Pandit Ravi Shankar Shukla, the Premier, settled the inventories of the rulers of Chattisgarh States without any fuss or trouble. There was a feeling at the time that the settlement erred on the generous side. But his policy certainly paid dividends, for the rulers of those States adjusted themselves willingly to the new order. In Orissa, on the other hand, there was considerable difficulty. We had to depute an officer to scrutinize the inventories and make recommendations, on the basis of which, and with the concurrence of the Orissa ministry, the

private properties of the Orissa rulers were finalized by me. In
Bombay, thanks to the realistic attitude of Morarji Desai, then
Home and Revenue Minister, the problem did not present any great
difficulty and it was settled by me after a three days' conference with
each ruler and the representatives of the provincial Government.

With regard to stray States merged in provinces like the United
Provinces and Madras, the problem was settled on the same lines.
In the case of rulers of States taken over as Chief Commissioner's
provinces, the inventories were scrutinized directly by the States
Ministry and were settled at a conference of the rulers concerned.

The discussions were often prolonged, sometimes nerve-racking.
But this vexed question, which involved 554 States, was settled
on an equitable basis within a remarkably short period and without
recourse even in a single case to arbitration. This was due in large
measure to the accommodating spirit shown by the rulers and the
local ministries concerned.

When the administration of the States was taken over, the new
governments — both of the Unions and the provinces — inherited
cash balances and investments to the value of over Rs 77 crores.[1]
A sizable portion of this had been built up by the rulers in investments in industries in British India. During the settlement of the
private properties, the rulers had surrendered over five hundred
villages, in addition to thousands of acres of scattered areas of the
jagir lands claimed in the inventories. They also gave up their claims
to approximately Rs 4½ crores. Other properties given up included
palaces, museums, buildings, stables, garages, fleets of motor-cars,
aeroplanes etc. The value of the palaces of some of the rulers in
Delhi, which have since been taken over by the Government of
India, would alone amount to many lakhs of rupees.

The Nizam's private immovable properties were settled after I
left the States Ministry. But, as I have indicated, he had surrendered
in 1949, at the instance of the States Ministry, his personal estates
yielding an annual net revenue of Rs 124 lakhs, in return for a
compensation of Rs 25 lakhs per annum during his life-time. He
had also agreed to give an annual loan of Rs 50 lakhs for a limited
period towards the Tungabhadra project. Besides this, he has invested
over Rs 40 crores from his private resources in government securities
and shares. He has also formed a trust of his jewellery. The proceeds

---

[1] This does not include the figures for Hyderabad and Mysore, as they were continuing
States, and the cash balances etc. continued to remain with them.

of any jewellery which may be sold will also be invested mainly in Government securities. Recently the Nizam has created a trust of over Rs 5 crores known as the 'Nizam's Charitable Trust'. Charities are not confined to Hyderabad but extend without distinction of caste or creed to the whole of India. In discussions before the formation of the Trust he had invited me to become one of the Trustees.

So much for the financial aspect of integration. Neither in October 1949, when the provisions in the Constitution relating to the States were being discussed in the Constituent Assembly, nor in March 1950 when a full and comprehensive White Paper on the States with full details of the privy purses was placed before Parliament, was there any criticism whatsoever, either as regards the principles on, or the rate at which the privy purse was fixed. On the contrary, Dr Pattabhi Sitaramayya, then President of the Congress and one of the signatories to the Deccan States formula, congratulated Sardar on having negotiated and settled 'almost the minimum' privy purse. Pattom A. Thanu Pillai (ex-Chief Minister of Travancore-Cochin) expressed the view on behalf of the States that the proposed provisions in regard to the privy purse etc., should be acceptable to members coming from the States. Two other members spoke on the subject of exemption of the privy purse from income tax; and a point of view which they urged was that the concession should be extended to the rest of the members of the ruling families.

There has been a tendency recently to regard the price paid for integration in the shape of privy purses as too high. We cannot strike a balance-sheet without juxtaposing the assets against the liabilities. For this purpose, we may ignore the consummation of the great ideal of a united and integrated India, which has affected the destinies of millions of people; the federal sources of income including the railway system of about 12,000 miles which the States surrendered to the Centre without any compensation; and the abolition of internal customs as a result of integration, which has greatly benefited trade and commerce in the country. But we should certainly take into account the assets we have received from the States in the shape of immense cash balances and investments amounting to Rs 77 crores, as well as buildings and palaces. If these are weighed against the total amount of the privy purses, the latter would seem insignificant.

XXVI

RETROSPECT AND PROSPECT

WHEN the British Government decided to transfer power to India, they no doubt found it the best solution of a difficult problem to declare that the paramountcy which they exercised over the Indian States would automatically lapse. The rulers generally welcomed this decision; and, after all, the parties directly concerned were the British Government and the rulers. Thus had the edifice, which the British themselves built up laboriously for more than 150 years, been demolished overnight! There were many well-wishers, both British and American, conversant with the problem of the Indian States, who said at the time that the seriousness of the problem had not been appreciated at all outside India and that it was graver than any other that faced the country. Even in India there were very few who realized the magnitude of the threatened danger of balkanization.

It was easy enough for the British Parliament to declare the lapse of paramountcy, but could such a declaration wipe out the fundamentals on which paramountcy rested? With the departure of the British, the Government of India did not cease to be the supreme power in India. Essential defence and security requirements of the country and geographical and economic compulsions had not ceased to be operative; nor had the obligations of the Government of India to protect their territories against external aggression and to preserve peace and order throughout the country become any the less. Why else had the British Government themselves asserted time and again in their relations with the Indian States that their supremacy was not based only upon treaties and engagements, but existed independently of them?

At the same time, there is no doubt that had paramountcy been transferred to a free India with all the obligations which had been assumed by the British Government under the various treaties, engagements and *sanads*, it would scarcely have been possible for us to have solved the problem of the Indian States in the way we did. By the lapse of paramountcy we were able to write on a clean slate unhampered by any obligations.

The weakest link in the princely chain was the existence of a large number of small States. Their rulers were naturally apprehensive about their future. The rulers of the bigger States, on the other hand, welcomed the lapse of paramountcy in the hope that they would be able to preserve their territorial integrity and have enough bargaining power to forge a satisfactory relationship with the Centre. What they failed to realize at the time was that the new Government of India could not possibly uphold the idea of autocracy in the States and that for their very existence the rulers had to have either the support of their people, or the protection of the Government of India. The former the rulers generally lacked; the latter had automatically terminated with the lapse of paramountcy.

Our first task to prevent the balkanization of the country and to stop any possible inveiglement of the States by Pakistan was to bring the States into some form of organic relationship with the Centre. This we did by means of the expedient of accession on three subjects, as well as a Standstill Agreement which kept alive the relations subsisting at the time between the States and the Government of India. The rulers were at first suspicious of this move, but most of them realized that, with the partition of the country, if they did not give their full support to the Government of India there was real danger that the country would be submerged in one big deluge. The rulers of the bigger States could have stood out and could have given us as much trouble, if not more, than Hyderabad or Junagadh. They certainly had their armies intact and their forces could — in some States at any rate — stand comparison in point of organization, equipment and efficiency with the Indian Army. It was indeed highly selfless and patriotic on the part of these rulers to have placed the wider interests of the country above their own. Some of them even went to the extent of lending us all their troops at a critical period regardless of their own internal security.

Gradually the realization dawned on them that after the advent of independence they would have no choice but to grant responsible government to their people, which meant that their own future would be governed by the whims of their ministries; but that, if they agreed to integration, their interests would be better safeguarded by the Government of India. Besides, they would be earning the goodwill of the country.

Fears regarding the likely attitude of popular ministries were not entirely groundless. Take the case of Kashmir: no sooner had Sheikh Abdullah secured complete power than he insisted that the Maharajah should stay out of the State. It was on Sardar's persuasion that the Maharajah agreed to do so, though reluctantly. The Government of India negotiated a settlement in regard to his privy purse and other matters. Sheikh Abdullah refused to honour the agreement and the Government of India are still paying the privy purse from their own coffers.

No policy of a democratic government, however beneficial, can be wholly immune from criticism. The integration of the Indian States was no exception. There were some who accused the States Ministry of having 'stampeded' the rulers into the new order; there were others who were opposed to the integration of the so-called viable States, and not a few regretted the loss of the ruler's personal touch.

Normal development of political progress had been arrested in most of the States. Glaring disparity between the condition of the people and the urges of the times often results in revolutionary activities. There was a danger of local organizations of a revolutionary or communal character stepping into the breach and entrenching themselves in power. This we had to avoid at any cost if we were to establish stability and ordered government in the country. We had to act quickly while the situation was still in a fluid state.

The advocates of viable States could not have studied the geographical aspect of the problem. Even they conceded that the smaller States had to go. There were two courses open: to merge the small States in the provinces in which they were situated or to which they were contiguous; and, in cases where this was not possible, to merge them with the nearest large State. In the latter event, would we be justified in perpetuating the entity of the bigger State? This was exactly the problem which confronted us in Central India and Malwa, where a number of small States were embedded between the bigger States of Gwalior and Indore. Once we had integrated Gwalior, which was one of the five premier States in India, could we leave lesser viable States alone? Further, the viability of a State must have some relation to its revenue. There were only nineteen States which had a revenue of Rs 1 crore and above and seven had a revenue from Rs 50 lakhs to Rs 1 crore. Rewa State, for instance, with a revenue of nearly Rs 115 lakhs had been declared as viable. But after surrendering a fair size of its revenue to the Centre for the administration of defence, external affairs and communications, could it provide adequate modern amenities and perform the functions of a Welfare State?

The personal touch of the ruler was possible in the pre-independence days when the ruler was an autocrat. I am not one of those who fail to see anything good in a benevolent autocracy. I remember going to Bikaner, during the exodus of many thousands of refugees from Bahawalpur State to India, to discuss with the Maharajah and his Dewan, K. M. Panikkar, the arrangements for their reception in the Bikaner State. In a single day, the Maharajah made all the necessary arrangements, including the requisitioning of buildings, the provision of food and the allotment of money for other expenses. This is a striking example of how a benevolent autocracy can produce good and quick results. The difficulty, of course, is to find an autocrat who will also be benevolent; in the case of hereditary rulers it does not follow that the successors of a benevolent autocrat would themselves also be benevolent. But the days of autocracy — benevolent or otherwise — are gone beyond recall. With the attainment of independence, no ruler could resist the demand for responsible government; and if there was to be no friction between the ruler and his ministers, the responsible government had to be without any condition or reservation. Once complete responsible government is granted, where is the ruler's touch? An example of this is to be found today in Mysore in spite of its excellent traditions.

Yet another criticism, which is being levelled nearly four years after the inauguration of the new Constitution, is against the quantum of the privy purses fixed for the rulers. In the chapter on 'The Cost of Integration', I have indicated that, apart from other advantages, viewed solely against the assets we have received from the States, the total annual expenditure on privy purses is insignificant. I would remind those who are now attempting to reopen the question of the words of explanation and advice given by Sardar when commending to the Constituent Assembly the adoption of article 291 of the Constitution:

The privy purse settlements are therefore in the nature of consideration for the surrender by the rulers of all their ruling powers and also for the dissolution of the States as separate units. We would do well to remember that the British Government spent enormous amounts in respect of the Mahratta settlements alone. We are ourselves honouring the commitments of the British Government in respect of the pensions of those rulers who helped them to consolidate their empire. Need we cavil then at the small — I purposely use the word small — price we have paid for the bloodless revolution which has affected the destinies of millions of our people?

The capacity for mischief and trouble on the part of the rulers if the settlement with them would not have been reached on a negotiated basis was far greater than could be imagined at this stage. Let us do justice to them; let us place ourselves in their position and then assess the value of their sacrifice. The rulers have now discharged their part of the obligations by transferring all ruling powers and by agreeing to the integration of their States. The main part of our obligation under these agreements is to ensure that the guarantees given by us in respect of privy purses are fully implemented. Our failure to do so would be a breach of faith and seriously prejudice the stabilisation of the new order.

The merger agreements and covenants are bilateral documents. As Sardar very rightly remarked, the rulers discharged their part of the contract by surrendering their States and powers. They are now bereft of any bargaining power. Because a creditor is too weak or poor to enforce his rights, a debtor should not, in honour, refuse to discharge his debt. As an honourable party to an agreement, we cannot take the stand that we shall accept only that part of the settlement which confers rights on us, and repudiate or whittle down that part which defines our obligations. As a nation aspiring to give a moral lead to the world, let it not be said of us that we know the 'price of everything and the value of nothing'.

After integration, the rulers settled down and adjusted themselves to the new order of things. By reopening the question of the privy purse we are again unsettling them.

No one can normally live apart from his environment. The rulers, many of them, have inherited very large families whose maintenance has been taxing their resources. In some cases marriages of girls and other ceremonies also constitute a heavy drain on their income. It would be asking too much of human nature to expect at least the present generation of rulers completely to forget their past. They cannot throw their hundreds of dependents and followers out on the streets simply because they have ceased to be rulers. If they turned them adrift without any provision, the social, economic and political repercussions, especially in the present state of unemployment, would be serious.

Sardar's attitude was certainly very different. He was definite that we should honour all the commitments which we had made to the rulers. He regarded them as 'co-architects' and was anxious to retain their goodwill, to utilize them as partners in the work of national consolidation and reconstruction.

Another section towards whom Sardar wanted a considerate policy to be adopted was the *jagirdars*. He had no doubt that the system had to go, but he was against any sort of violent expropriation, which he always described as '*choree*' (theft), or '*daka*' (dacoity). The criterion he had in mind was, if we robbed Peter to pay Paul, what was Peter to do? He was as much concerned about the future of the *jagirdars* as about the future of the tenants. There was certainly no sadistic socialism in his make-up. He felt that, if the *jagirdars* were dispossessed without equitable compensation, their basis of livelihood would be gone and they would be ready recruits to the ranks of the anti-social elements in the country. That is why he insisted that their lands should be taken only on payment of reasonable compensation for a limited period in order that they might be able to adjust themselves. He was firmly of the opinion that the smaller *jagirdars*, who had nothing except their lands to live on, should not be dispossessed.

In August 1947, when the transfer of power took place, very few could have conceived as possible the revolutionary change that was to come over the States within such a short time. Speaking in September 1948, Nehru confessed:

Even I who have been rather intimately connected with the States People's movement for many years, if I had been asked six months ago what the course of developments would be in the next six months since then, I would have hesitated to say that such rapid changes would take place... The historian who looks back will no doubt consider this integration of the States into India as one of the dominant phases of India's history.

By the time the Constitution came into force on 26 January 1950, we had integrated geographically all the States and brought them into the same constitutional relations with the Centre as the provinces. The administrative integration in the Unions was proceeding apace. The scheme of financial integration was already worked

out and finalized and it was to come into operation within a few
months. The Indian States Forces were to be absorbed into the
Indian Army.

By the partition India had lost an area of 364,737 square miles
and a population of 81½ millions. By the integration of the States,
we brought in an area of nearly 500,000 square miles with a population of 86½ millions (not including Jammu and Kashmir).

In the words of Sardar, 'the great ideal of geographical, political
and economic unification of India, an ideal which for centuries
remained a distant dream and which appeared as remote and as
difficult of attainment as ever even after the advent of Indian independence' was consummated by the policy of integration. But
Sardar was too robust a realist to adopt an attitude of complacency.
He said:

The real task has just begun and that task is to make up for the loss of
centuries, to consolidate the gains that we have secured, and to build
in them [Part 'B' States] an administrative system at once strong and
efficient. We have to weave new fabrics into old materials; we have to
make sure that simultaneously the old and the new are integrated into a
pleasing whole — a design which would fit well into the pattern of all
India.

We had demolished the artificial barriers between the States *inter
se* and the rest of India and had indeed laid the foundations for an
integrated administrative and financial structure. But the real integration had to take place in the minds of the people. This could
not be accomplished overnight. It would take some time for the
people of the erstwhile States to outgrow their regional loyalties
and to develop a wider outlook and broader vision. In the words
of Sardar:

Almost overnight we have introduced in these States the superstructure
of a modern system of government. The inspiration and stimulus has come
from above rather than from below and unless the transplanted growth
takes a healthy root in the soil, there will be a danger of collapse and
chaos.

The task requires great vision and patience. The best governed
State is the one that possesses a sound political system and an efficient
administrative system. Each of these is indispensable if the State is
not to fall into anarchy. But in most of the Part 'B' States we have
yet to build up a stable political and administrative structure.

It was for this reason that it was decided to include a salutary provision (article 371) in the Constitution, ensuring that the governments of Part 'B' States would be under the control of, and comply with such particular directions, if any, as might from time to time be given by, the President.

The guidance of the Government of India implied that the experienced administrators whom they deputed should hold a limited number of key posts in the administration. This arrangement was to be for a limited period and was to be a co-operative enterprise in which the ministries and services of the Unions would work together with the officials deputed by the Government of India in a joint effort to promote not only the well-being of the Unions, but the wider interests of the country as a whole.

Sardar played the role of the wise parent. Unseen and almost unheard, he helped the ministers in the Part 'B' States to acquire experience and the discordant party elements to cultivate a team spirit. Whenever any trouble arose or any new difficulty had to be faced, the States Ministry was there to plead the cause of the new Unions.

Even during the time of Sardar, the ministers in the various Unions showed an impatient anxiety to be placed on an equal footing with the ministers of the Part 'A' States. They forgot the responsibility of the Government of India for the good governance of the Unions which they had created and, in some cases, the ministers at the time were not even responsible to any legislature. I remember a meeting which Sardar had with the Chief Ministers of some of the Unions, when they argued against the institution of Advisers for an entire hour. Sardar listened to them patiently and without interruption and then, in his own inimitable manner, told them that they were free to do without Advisers, as indeed they were wise and experienced persons, although he himself, being only a novice, considered it necessary to have an Adviser in myself. This was enough to silence the critics.

The power of superintendence and control vested in the Central Government by article 371 of the Constitution has suddenly fallen into disuse. Thus our plan to build up in each of these Unions a sound administrative and economic system and to lay down for them a programme for their ordered development has been made more difficult. The Government of India are now left only with the power to take over the administration when a complete breakdown of the administration occurs. The ministries in these States, bereft of the guidance of the Government of India, have now to gain experience the hard way — and often at the expense of the tax-payer!

Shortly after Sardar's death, a Bill was passed by Parliament for the regulation of the administration of Part 'C' States. Elections were held and full-fledged ministries were subsequently set up in Himachal Pradesh, Vindhya Pradesh, Bhopal, Ajmer and Delhi. It was not the policy of Sardar, so far as I know, to have in Part 'C' States ministries responsible to local legislatures, since those States had neither the resources nor the manpower to run a parliamentary government. Under the direct administration of the Government of India the Indian Parliament could have looked after the interests of their people. In the case of Delhi, we departed from the sound principle that in its capital the Central Government should be supreme. The experiment of responsible government has resulted in both friction and lowering of the standards of administration. I remember Sardar telling me that the solution for Delhi was the establishment of a corporation on the same lines as those of Bombay or Calcutta.

If the States individually or jointly taken over as Chief Commissioners' provinces had been merged initially with any neighbouring province or Union, there was every possibility of their not receiving the special attention and help, financial and otherwise, which the Government of India alone were in a position to give. After the special conditions which necessitated their being taken over as Chief Commissioners' provinces were fulfilled, it was our intention to take up the question whether they should be merged in the nearest Part 'A' or Part 'B' State.

I have already mentioned in chapter XIV how, when we were negotiating for the integration of Travancore and Cochin, there was a demand that the neighbouring district of Malabar should be tagged on to the new Union so as to form a separate linguistic province of Malayalam-speaking people. I had stated in reply that the States Ministry was not concerned with the linguistic redistribution of provinces; that the Congress had already appointed a committee consisting of Nehru, Sardar and Pattabhi Sitaramayya to go into the question, and that it was only after that committee made its report that the Government of India could take any decision on the issue. The Committee subsequently recommended that the linguistic redistribution of provinces should not be touched for ten years to come, making an exception only in the case of Andhra.

There was similarly a demand for the dismemberment of Hyderabad and also a move for the amalgamation of Saurashtra with Bombay. The dismemberment of Hyderabad was bound to raise the issue of linguistic provinces in a big way in South India, while the amalgamation of Saurashtra with Bombay would create unnecessary suspicion in the minds of Maharashtrians. Both Sardar and I had seen enough of provincial jealousies and wranglings in the course of the merger of States with provinces. These Unions and States had to make considerable leeway in the administrative and economic spheres. This was our first task and it would be hampered, if not retarded, by any premature dislocation of existing arrangements. It was possible that the process of economic development would bring in its wake other loyalties and interests. We felt that Time should be given a hand in moulding the future of these Unions and States. As a distinguished British administrator once said: 'I do not think they know so well as we old ones what a valuable gentleman Time is. How much better work is done when it does itself than when done by the best of us.'

The first elections under adult suffrage in all the States passed off without any hitch and resulted in a general victory for the Congress. This was mainly due to the remarkable hold of the organization on the people of the country and, in particular, to Nehru's personal appeal to the masses. Even then, the Congress could not secure a clear majority in Travancore-Cochin, Madras, Orissa, Rajasthan and PEPSU. Later events have indicated the need for great vigilance. In most of the Part 'B' States the Congress Party is a house divided against itself. There are constant group erosions and internecine bickerings, and the result is that the ministers have to spend a considerable portion of their time in consolidating their position *vis-à-vis* the party to the detriment of the administration.

Contemporary opinion has already anticipated the verdict of history in regard to the integration of the States. To have dissolved 554 States by integrating them into the pattern of the Republic; to have brought about order out of the nightmare of chaos whence we started, and to have democratized the administration in all the erstwhile States, should steel us on to the attainment of equal success in other spheres. For the first time India has become an integrated whole in the real sense of the term, though this is but the foundation on which to build a prosperous Welfare State. An amorphous mass of aspirations has to be integrated. Life has to be made meaningful for the millions who have led a twilight existence. New tracks must be laid for the questing spirit.

In the tasks that lie ahead, India would do well to remember the pregnant words of Sardar that 'it will be folly to ignore realities; facts take their revenge if they are not faced squarely and well.'

APPENDIX I

PRINCIPAL APPOINTMENTS IN INDIA CONNECTED WITH INDIAN STATES BEFORE THE TRANSFER OF POWER

(The name in italics is that of the Headquarters of the Officer in each Agency)

(A) APPOINTMENTS CONNECTED WITH OR UNDER THE POLITICAL DEPARTMENT

ASSAM — Governor of — *Shillong*

  KHASI STATES — Political Officer for the (Deputy Commissioner, Khasi and Jaintia Hills) — *Shillong*

  MANIPUR — Political Agent and Superintendent — *Manipur*

BARODA AND GUJARAT STATES AGENCY — Resident for Baroda and the Gujarat States — *Baroda*

  REWAKANTHA, SURGANA AND THE DANGS — Secretary to the Resident (ex-officio Political Agent) — *Baroda*

CENTRAL INDIA — Resident for — *Indore*

  BHOPAL — Political Agent in — *Bhopal*

  BUNDELKHAND — Political Agent in — *Nowgong*

  MALWA — Political Agent in — *Indore*

EASTERN STATES — Resident for the — *Calcutta*

  BENGAL STATES — Secretary to the Resident (ex-officio Political Agent)— *Calcutta*

  CHATTISGARH — Political Agent — *Raipur*

  ORISSA STATES — Political Agent — *Sambalpur*

GWALIOR, RAMPUR AND BANARAS — Resident at Gwalior and for the States of Rampur and Banaras — *Gwalior*

HYDERABAD — Resident at — *Hyderabad, Deccan*

KASHMIR — Resident in — *Srinagar*

KOLHAPUR AND DECCAN STATES AGENCY — Resident for Kolhapur and the Deccan States — *Kolhapur*

MADRAS STATES — Resident for the — *Trivandrum*

MYSORE — Resident in — *Bangalore*

PUNJAB STATES — Resident for the — *Lahore*

  PUNJAB HILL STATES — Political Agent — *Simla*

PATAUDI, LOHARU AND DUJANA — Secretary to the Resident (ex-officio Political Agent) — *Lahore*

RAJPUTANA — Resident for — *Abu*

EASTERN RAJPUTANA STATES — Political Agent — *Bharatpur*

JAIPUR — Resident at — *Jaipur*

MEWAR — Resident in; and Political Agent, Southern Rajputana States — *Udaipur*

WESTERN RAJPUTANA STATES — Resident — *Jodhpur*

WESTERN INDIA — Resident for the States of — *Rajkot*

EASTERN KATHIAWAR AGENCY — Political Agent — *Wadhwan*

SABAR KANTHA — Political Agent — *Sadra*

WESTERN KATHIAWAR AGENCY — Political Agent — *Rajkot*

(B) APPOINTMENTS CONNECTED WITH OR UNDER THE EXTERNAL AFFAIRS DEPARTMENT

BALUCHISTAN — Agent to the Governor-General, Resident and Chief Commissioner in — *Quetta*

KALAT — Political Agent, and Political Agent in charge of the Bolan Pass and of the Chagai District — *Mastung*

BHUTAN — Political Officer in Sikkim — *Gangtok*

NORTH-WEST FRONTIER PROVINCE — Governor of — *Peshawar*

DIR, SWAT AND CHITRAL — Political Agent — *Malakand*

SIKKIM — Political Officer in — *Gangtok*

APPENDIX II

MEMORANDUM ON STATES' TREATIES AND PARA-MOUNTCY presented by the Cabinet Mission to His Highness the Chancellor of the Chamber of Princes on 12 May 1946.

1. Prior to the recent statement of the British Prime Minister in the House of Commons an assurance was given to the Princes that there was no intention on the part of the Crown to initiate any change in their relationship with the Crown or the rights guaranteed by their treaties and engagements without their consent. It was at the same time stated that the Princes' consent to any changes which might emerge as a result of negotiations would not unreasonably be withheld. The Chamber of Princes has since confirmed that the Indian States fully share the general desire in the country for the immediate attainment by India of her full stature. His Majesty's Government have now declared that if the Succession Government or Governments in British India desire independence, no obstacle would be placed in their way. The effect of these announcements is that all those concerned with the future of India wish her to attain a position of independence within or without the British Commonwealth. The Delegation have come here to assist in resolving the difficulties which stand in the way of India fulfilling this wish.

2. During the interim period, which must elapse before the coming into operation of a new Constitutional structure under which British India will be independent or fully self-governing, paramountcy will remain in operation. But the British Government could not and will not in any circumstances transfer paramountcy to an Indian Government.

3. In the meanwhile, the Indian States are in a position to play an important part in the formulation of the new Constitutional structure for India, and His Majesty's Government have been informed by the Indian States that they desire, in their own interests and in the interests of India as a whole, both to make their contribution to the framing of the structure, and to take their due place in it when it is completed. In order to facilitate this they will doubtless strengthen their position by doing everything possible to ensure that their administrations conform to the highest standard. Where adequate standards cannot be achieved within the existing resources of the State they will no doubt arrange in suitable cases to form or join

63

administrative units large enough to enable them to be fitted into the constitutional structure. It will also strengthen the position of States during this formulative period if the various Governments which have not already done so take active steps to place themselves in close and constant touch with public opinion in their State by means of representative institutions.

4. During the interim period it will be necessary for the States to conduct negotiations with British India in regard to the future regulation of matters of common concern, especially in the economic and financial field. Such negotiations, which will be necessary whether the States desire to participate in the new Indian Constitutional structure or not, will occupy a considerable period of time, and since some of these negotiations may well be incomplete when the new structure comes into being, it will, in order to avoid administrative difficulties, be necessary to arrive at an understanding between the States and those likely to control the succession Government or Governments that for a period of time the then existing arrangements as to these matters of common concern should continue until the new agreements are completed. In this matter, the British Government and the Crown Representative will lend such assistance as they can should it be so desired.

5. When a new fully self-governing or independent Government or Governments come into being in British India, His Majesty's Government's influence with these Governments will not be such as to enable them to carry out the obligations of paramountcy. Moreover, they cannot contemplate that British troops would be retained in India for this purpose. Thus, as a logical sequence and in view of the desires expressed to them on behalf of the Indian States, His Majesty's Government will cease to exercise the powers of paramountcy. This means that the rights of the States which flow from their relationship to the Crown will no longer exist and that all the rights surrendered by the States to the paramount power will return to the States. Political arrangements between the States on the one side and the British Crown and British India on the other will thus be brought to an end. The void will have to be filled either by the States entering into a federal relationship with the successor Government or Governments in British India, or failing this, entering into particular political arrangements with it or them.

NOTE:—The following explanatory note was issued by the Cabinet Mission in New Delhi on the date of publication (22 May 1946):—

The Cabinet Delegation desire to make it clear that the document issued today entitled *'Memorandum on States' Treaties and Paramountcy presented by the Cabinet Delegation to His Highness the Chancellor of Princes'* was drawn up before the Mission began its discussions with party leaders and represented the substance of what they communicated to the representatives of the States at their first interviews with the Mission. This is the explanation of the use of the words 'Succession Government or Governments of British India' an expression which would not of course have been used after the issue of the Delegation's recent statement.

BOOKS AND PUBLICATIONS
CONSULTED

CAMPBELL-JOHNSON, ALAN: *Mission with Mountbatten*, 1950.

COUPLAND, REGINALD: *The Constitutional Problem in India*, 1944.

CURZON, LORD: *British Government in India*, 1925.

DUNBAR, SIR GEORGE: *A History of India*, 2 *vols*. 1949; *India and the Passing of Empire*, 1951.

GANDHI, M. K.: *The Indian States' Problem*, 1941.

GRAHAM POLE, D.: *India in Transition*, 1932.

KAYE, JOHN WILLIAM: *Life and Correspondence of Major-General Sir John Malcolm, G.C.B.*, 1856.

LEE WARNER, SIR WILLIAM: *The Native States of India*, 1910.

LINLITHGOW, THE MARQUESS OF: *Indian Speeches*, 1936-1943.

LOTHIAN, SIR ARTHUR: *Kingdoms of Yesterday*, 1951.

LUMBY, E. W. R.: *The Transfer of Power in India*, 1954.

MAJUMDAR, R. C., H. C. RAY CHAUDHURI AND KALIKINKAR DATTA: *An Advanced History of India*, 1950.

MAJUMDAR, R. C. AND DR. A. S. PUSALKAR (Ed.): *The Age of Imperial Unity*, 1951; *The Classical Age*, 1954.

MEAD, HENRY: *The Sepoy Revolt: Its Causes and Consequences*, 1857.

MELLOR, ANDREW: *India Since Partition*, 1951.

MOUNTBATTEN OF BURMA, EARL: *Speeches as Viceroy and Governor-General*, 1947-48.

NEHRU, JAWAHARLAL: *Independence and After*, 1949.

PANIKKAR, K. M.: *Indian States and the Government of India*, 1927; *The Founding of the Kashmir State*, 1953.

SHIVAPURI, S. N.: *The Grand Hypocrisy*, 1952.

SIMON, THE RT. HON. VISCOUNT: *Retrospect*, 1952.

TENDULKAR, D. G.: *Mahatma: Life of Mohandas Karamchand Gandhi* (8 vols.), 1951-1954.

THOMPSON, EDWARD: *The Making of the Indian Princes*, 1943.

TUPPER, CHARLES LEWIS: *Our Indian Protectorate*, 1893.

WOODRUFF, PHILIP: *The Men Who Ruled India — The Founders*, 1953; *The Guardians*, 1954.

Montagu-Chelmsford Report on Indian Constitutional Reforms, 1918.

All-Parties Conference, 1928: *Report of the Committee appointed by the Conference to determine the Principles of the Constitution for India,* 1928.

Report of the Indian States Committee, 1928-1929, 1929.

Report of the Indian Statutory Commission (2 vols.), 1930.

Indian Round Table Conference (Cmd. 3778).

The Government of India Act, 1935.

Memoranda on the Indian States, 1940.

India (Lord Privy Seal's Mission) Cmd. 6350, April 1942.

Constitutional Proposals of the Sapru Committee, 1945.

India (Cabinet Mission) Cmd. 6821, 6829, 6835, 6861, 6862.

White Paper on Kashmir, 1948.

White Paper on Hyderabad, 1948.

Hyderabad's Relations with the Dominion of India (in three volumes issued by the Government of Hyderabad and Berar, 1948).

India Since Partition, 1948.

Defending Kashmir, 1949.

White Paper on Indian States, 1950.

Report of the Federal Financial Integration Committee, 1950.

GLOSSARY OF INDIAN TERMS

Abkari: Excise duties.

Adivasi: Aborigines.

Ahimsa: Non-violence.

Arzi Hukumat: Provisional government.

Azad Kashmir: Independent Kashmir.

Begum: The Muslim woman ruler, or the wife of a Muslim ruler, of an Indian State.

Bhonslas: The Mahratta ruling family of Nagpur State before its annexation by Lord Dalhousie.

Chauth: Military impost levied by Shivaji and his successors on conquered territories.

Crore: Ten millions, or one hundred lakhs.

Devaswoms: Properties and money donated to temples for their maintenance in Travancore and Cochin.

Dewan: Prime Minister of an Indian State.

Dhara Sabha: Legislative Assembly in Baroda. Also used as a general term for the Legislature or Legislative Chamber of a State.

Durbar: Ruler's Court.

Firman: An edict or administrative order issued by or in the name of an oriental sovereign, associated in India with the Nizam.

Gaddi: Throne.

Gaekwar: The ruling family of Baroda State.

Harijan: The name bestowed by Gandhiji on the untouchables in the Hindu fold.

Holkar: The ruling family of Indore State.

Jagir: An assignment of the land revenue of a territory to a chief or noble for specified service.

Jagirdar: The holder of any assignment of revenue; one who holds a jagir.

Jagirdari: The system of jagirdars.

Jamiat: Association of Muslim divines.

Jawaharkhana: Room in the palace where jewellery, regalia and other valuables are kept.

Jawan: Private soldier in the Indian Army.

Jehad: War waged by Muslims for a religious cause.

Ji: An affix added to names denoting respect, e.g. Gandhiji.

Jyotirlinga: The manifestation of God Shiva as Jyoti (light).

Kanda: Sword. A *kanda* marriage means that the bride is married to the bridegroom's sword.

Kandukrishi: Personal estates of the Maharajah of Travancore corresponding to Crown Lands.

Khadi: Handspun and handwoven cloth which Congressmen are enjoined to wear.

Khan: The Muslim ruler of a small Indian State.

Lakh: One hundred thousand.

Maharajah: The Hindu ruler of an Indian State; other names are Maharana, Maharajrana, Maharao and Maharawal.

Maharani: The Hindu woman ruler, or the wife of a Hindu ruler, of an Indian State.

Marumakkathayam: Matriarchal system of inheritance prevalent amongst the Malayalam-speaking people of the west coast of India.

Melkoima: The right of superior authority.

Mulgirasias: Original landholders.

Mulkgiri: Mahratta armies sent to collect *Chauth* and *Sardeshmukhi.*

Maulana: Literally 'our master'; a term of reverence.

Nawab: The Muslim ruler of an Indian State. Also used as a title by descendants of former Muslim rulers or chieftains, and by big Muslim landlords.

Ooralars: Trustees.

Panchayat: A village council of five members; a council of village elders.

Pandit: A prefix to a name generally used to denote membership of the Brahmin caste. Sometimes also applied to Hindu teachers and scholars irrespective of caste.

Pargana: A territorial unit into which provinces were divided during the Moghul period.

Patwari: Village headman.

Prajamandal: States People's association.

Prajaparishad: States People's association.

Rajah or *Rana:* The Hindu ruler of a small Indian State. Also used as a title by big landlords.

Rajpramukh: Literally first among the rulers and is the title of the head of the new Part 'B' States.

Rajmandal: Council of Rulers.

Rajmata: Mother of the Hindu ruler of an Indian State.

Rani: Wife of the Hindu ruler of a small State.

Sabha: Assembly or conference. Also an association.

Sangh: Organization.

Sanad: Generally a title deed, a letters-patent or Charter. In the context of the relationship between the British power and the rulers of Indian States, it denoted 'a document of title embodying a clear and distinct statement or a formal expression of the terms of an agreement.'

Sardeshmukhi: Levy of 10 per cent other than

chauth, collected from conquered territories by Shivaji on the basis of his claim as the hereditary Sardeshmukh or chief headman of Maharashtra.

Shikar: Big game hunting.

Stotra: Religious hymn.

Swaraj: Self-rule. This word was used by Dadabhoy Naoroji at the Calcutta Congress of 1906.

Taluka: An estate; applied to a tract of proprietary land usually smaller than a zamindari, although sometimes including several villages and not infrequently confused with a zamindari.

Talukdar: The holder of a taluka; generally applied to a special class of landlords in Uttar Pradesh.

Talukdari: The tenure, office, or estate of a talukdar.

Thakur: The ruler of a small Indian State; or a jagirdar.

Toshakhana: Room where jewellery, regalia and valuables are kept.

Yuvaraja: Hindu heir-apparent of an Indian State. In Travancore and Cochin he is styled as *Elayaraja.*

Yuvarani: Wife of the *Yuvaraja.*

Zamindar: Big landholder.

Zenana: That part of a house in which the women of a family are secluded.

Zortalbi: A tribute which used to be paid by some of the chiefs of Kathiawar to the Nawab of Junagadh.

INDEX

WORLD AFFAIRS: National and International Viewpoints
An Arno Press Collection

Angell, Norman. **The Great Illusion, 1933.** 1933.

Benes, Eduard. **Memoirs:** From Munich to New War and New Victory. 1954.

[Carrington, Charles Edmund] (Edmonds, Charles, pseud.) **A Subaltern's War.** 1930. New preface by Charles Edmund Carrington.

Cassel, Gustav. **Money and Foreign Exchange After 1914.** 1922.

Chambers, Frank P. **The War Behind the War, 1914-1918.** 1939.

Dedijer, Vladimir. **Tito.** 1953.

Dickinson, Edwin DeWitt. **The Equality of States in International Law.** 1920.

Douhet, Giulio. **The Command of the Air.** 1942.

Edib, Halidé. **Memoirs.** 1926.

Ferrero, Guglielmo. **The Principles of Power.** 1942.

Grew, Joseph C. **Ten Years in Japan.** 1944.

Hayden, Joseph Ralston. **The Philippines.** 1942.

Hudson, Manley O. **The Permanent Court of International Justice, 1920-1942.** 1943.

Huntington, Ellsworth. **Mainsprings of Civilization.** 1945.

Jacks, G. V. and R. O. Whyte. **Vanishing Lands:** A World Survey of Soil Erosion. 1939.

Mason, Edward S. **Controlling World Trade.** 1946.

Menon, V. P. **The Story of the Integration of the Indian States.** 1956.

Moore, Wilbert E. **Economic Demography of Eastern and Southern Europe.** 1945.

[Ohlin, Bertil]. **The Course and Phases of the World Economic Depression.** 1931.

Oliveira, A. Ramos. **Politics, Economics and Men of Modern Spain, 1808-1946.** 1946.

O'Sullivan, Donal. **The Irish Free State and Its Senate.** 1940.

Peffer, Nathaniel. **The White Man's Dilemma.** 1927.

Philby, H. St. John. **Sa'udi Arabia.** 1955.

Rappard, William E. **International Relations as Viewed From Geneva.** 1925.

Rauschning, Hermann. **The Revolution of Nihilism.** 1939.

Reshetar, John S., Jr. **The Ukrainian Revolution, 1917-1920.** 1952.

Richmond, Admiral Sir Herbert. **Sea Power in the Modern World.** 1934.

Robbins, Lionel. **Economic Planning and International Order.** 1937. New preface by Lionel Robbins.

Russell, Bertrand. **Bolshevism:** Practice and Theory. 1920.

Russell, Frank M. **Theories of International Relations.** 1936.

Schwarz, Solomon M. **The Jews in the Soviet Union.** 1951.

Siegfried, André. **Canada:** An International Power. [1947].

Souvarine, Boris. **Stalin.** 1939.

Spaulding, Oliver Lyman, Jr., Hoffman Nickerson, and John Womack Wright. **Warfare.** 1925.

Storrs, Sir Ronald. **Memoirs.** 1937.

Strausz-Hupé, Robert. **Geopolitics:** The Struggle for Space and Power. 1942.

Swinton, Sir Ernest D. **Eyewitness.** 1933.

Timasheff, Nicholas S. **The Great Retreat.** 1946.

Welles, Sumner. **Naboth's Vineyard:** The Dominican Republic, 1844-1924. 1928. Two volumes in one.

Whittlesey, Derwent. **The Earth and the State.** 1939.

Wilcox, Clair. **A Charter for World Trade.** 1949.

DATE DUE

GAYLORD			PRINTED IN U.S.A.